NETWORK DYNAMICS
IN EMERGING REGIONS
OF EUROPE

NETWORK DYNAMICS IN EMERGING REGIONS OF EUROPE

David A Dyker
University of Sussex, UK

Imperial College Press

Published by

Imperial College Press
57 Shelton Street
Covent Garden
London WC2H 9HE

Distributed by

World Scientific Publishing Co. Pte. Ltd.
5 Toh Tuck Link, Singapore 596224
USA office: 27 Warren Street, Suite 401-402, Hackensack, NJ 07601
UK office: 57 Shelton Street, Covent Garden, London WC2H 9HE

Library of Congress Cataloging-in-Publication Data
Network dynamics in emerging regions of Europe / edited by David A Dyker.
   p. cm.
   ISBN-13: 978-1-84816-373-7
   ISBN-10: 1-84816-373-8
  1. Europe--Economic conditions--21st century. 2. Europe--Social conditions--21st century.
3. System theory--Social aspects. 4. Business networks--Europe. 5. Social networks--Europe.
6. Information networks--Social aspects--Europe. I. Dyker, David A.
   HC240.N445 2010
   338'.064094--dc22
                                                           2009053165

British Library Cataloguing-in-Publication Data
A catalogue record for this book is available from the British Library.

Copyright © 2010 by Imperial College Press

All rights reserved. This book, or parts thereof, may not be reproduced in any form or by any means, electronic or mechanical, including photocopying, recording or any information storage and retrieval system now known or to be invented, without written permission from the Publisher.

For photocopying of material in this volume, please pay a copying fee through the Copyright Clearance Center, Inc., 222 Rosewood Drive, Danvers, MA 01923, USA. In this case permission to photocopy is not required from the publisher.

Typeset by Stallion Press
Email: enquiries@stallionpress.com

Printed in Singapore by B & Jo Enterprise Pte Ltd

ACKNOWLEDGEMENTS

This book is based on research undertaken under the rubric of the Sixth Framework Programme project *Understanding the Relationship between Knowledge and Competitiveness in the Enlarging European Union ('U-Know')*, Contract no: cit-02 85 19. The editor and authors are grateful to the European Union and the European Commission for the financial, intellectual and moral support they have given us.

David A. Dyker
University of Sussex
July 2009

CONTENTS

Acknowledgements		v
List of Tables		xi
List of Figures		xv
List of Contributors		xix

Introduction		1
Chapter 1	Alignment, Misalignment and Dynamic Network-Based Capabilities *Nick von Tunzelmann*	3
Section 1	**Innovation Networks**	**23**
Chapter 2	The UK Innovation System, from a Misalignment Perspective *Nick von Tunzelmann*	25
Chapter 3	Still Divided by Transformation? Characteristic Features of the German Innovation System and the Barriers to Extending It to East Germany *Peter Franz*	45
Chapter 4	The Governance and Management of Technical Change in Transition Countries *David A. Dyker*	63
Chapter 5	Mutual Perception of Science and Industry in Innovation Networks — Evidence from East Germany *Jutta Günther and Cornelia Lang*	87

Chapter 6	The Slovakian Innovation System — Why Does It Not Work? *Silvester Salis*	109
Section 2	**Labour Markets, Job Matching and Social Networking**	**131**
Chapter 7	Job Matching, Human Capital Accumulation and Economic Development *David A. Dyker*	133
Chapter 8	Human Capital and Skills in Hungary — Matching Demand and Supply *Andrea Szalavetz*	143
Chapter 9	Labour Market Constraints in Romania: The Challenge of Skill Mismatch in a Transforming Economy *Dragos Pislaru*	159
Chapter 10	Horizontal and Vertical Mismatch in the Labour Market among Graduate Students with Generic or Vocational Higher Education *Pål Børing*	185
Chapter 11	Human Resources and Skills Gap in a Regional Context: The Case of Campania *Maria Del Sorbo*	207
Chapter 12	Urbanisation and Network Alignment Issues in Istanbul: Informal Networks in Housing and Labour Markets *Ozge Aktas*	233
Section 3	**Industrial Networks and International Spillovers**	**253**
Chapter 13	Knowledge Spillovers, Innovation and Firm-Level Productivity Growth in Slovenia *Jože P. Damijan, Črt Kostevc, Matija Rojec and Andreja Jaklič*	255

Chapter 14 The Impact of Technology on Skills in Estonian 277
Wood-Based Industries
Kadri Ukrainski

Chapter 15 FDI and the National Innovation System — Evidence from 303
Central and Eastern Europe
Jutta Günther, Björn Jindra and Johannes Stephan

Chapter 16 The Impact of Outward FDI on Home-Country Employment 333
in a Low-Cost Transition Economy
Jaan Masso, Urmas Varblane and Priit Vahter

Chapter 17 Network Alignment in the Automotive Clusters 361
of Turkey and Poland
Guldem Ozatagan

Index 385

LIST OF TABLES

Table 1.1	Modes of governance and their failures	9
Table 1.2	Examples of intrinsic (particular) as opposed to systemic failures of governance modes	10
Table 1.3	Channels of learning (after Malerba, 1992)	13
Table 3.1	German patent applications differentiated by 31 technological fields, 1995, 2000 and 2005	48
Table 3.2	Patent applications effective in Germany in selected fields of automotive technology, 2001–2007, from selected countries	49
Table 3.3	German patent applications and patent density by *Länder* and region, 1995, 2000 and 2005	53
Table 3.4	Selected indicators for the public-sector science and research system at the *Länder* and regional levels	55
Table 6.1	Innovation in Slovakia	114
Table 9.1	Youth unemployment rates in the EU	167
Table 9.2	Unemployment rate, ILO definition, by level of education, gender and rural/urban residence, 2006	168
Table 9.3	Romania and the Lisbon educational indicators	170
Table 10.1	Descriptive statistics for the new graduates who answered the questionnaire in the Graduate Surveys: The net sample	189
Table 10.2	Estimates of multinomial logistic regressions: The probability of being mismatched as opposed to being employed without being mismatched six months after graduation: The net sample	196
Table 11.1	Competences classification, examples	211
Table 12.1	Population of Istanbul, 1927–2000	234
Table 12.2	Housing information networks in Yesiltepe: How they heard about their current neighbourhood	240
Table 12.3	House ownership in Yesiltepe	241
Table 12.4	Employment status	247
Table 13.1	Determinants of firm-level innovation in Slovenia, 1996–2002	260
Table 13.2	The probability of a firm innovating in Slovenia, 1996–2002 (results of a probit model)	261

Table 13.3	Impact of R&D and innovation on TFP growth of Slovenian firms, 1996–2002	265
Table 13.4	Growth in VA/Emp (difference in logs) two periods after innovation $(t + 2) - t$	267
Table 13.5	Growth in VA/Emp (difference in logs) between two and four periods after innovation $(t + 4) - (t + 2)$	267
Table 13.6	Growth in VA/Emp (difference in logs) two periods after innovation $(t + 2) - t$ [Process innovation]	267
Table 13.7	Growth in VA/Emp (difference in logs) between two and four periods after innovation $(t + 4) - (t + 2)$ [Process innovation]	268
Table 13.8	Growth in VA/Emp (difference in logs) two periods after innovation $(t + 2) - t$ [Product innovation]	268
Table 13.9	Growth in VA/Emp (difference in logs) between two and four periods after innovation $(t + 4) - (t + 2)$ [Product innovation]	268
Table 13.A1	The probability of firms innovating products and processes in Slovenia, 1996–2002 (Results of a probit model)	275
Table 14.1	Examples of technological advance in the wood sector	279
Table 14.2	Increased skill requirements and underlying changes in wood technology	283
Table 14.3	Coverage of data sources by number of employees	287
Table 14.4	Differences in mean values of indicators across groups of firms by innovative activities	295
Table 14.5	Skill demand by types of skill in the Estonian wood sector	296
Table 15.1	Country composition of total population of manufacturing firms with foreign investors	311
Table 15.2	The IWH FDI micro database — country composition and response rates	311
Table 15.3	Average importance of strategic motives for investment, by host economy	313
Table 15.4	Correlation between interaction with scientific institutions and determinants of degree of embeddedness	327
Table 16.1	Number of firms by sector, and presence of inward and outward FDI, 1996–2002	335
Table 16.2	The role of the four groups of firms in the Estonian economy in 2002 (% of the sector totals)	344
Table 16.3	Annual average employment growth rate of firms with inward or outward FDI	345
Table 16.4	Change in employment after implementing outward FDI, 1995–2002	347

Table 16.5	Employment growth model parameter estimates: robust regressions	349
Table 16.6	Probit model for making new outward FDI	351
Table 16.7	Effect of OFDI on employment growth at home (ATT): propensity score matching results for the service sector	353
Table 16.8	Effect of outward FDI on employment growth at home (ATT): propensity score matching results for the manufacturing sector	353
Table 16.9	Year-by-year matching for the service sector: the first year of OFDI	354
Table 16.10	Matching results for indirect and direct investors: the service sector, 2000–2002	354
Table 16.A1	Summary statistics of regressors used in the employment growth model and probit model for new outward investments	359
Table 16.A2	Testing for balancing property by testing for differences in means: the service sector, 2000–2002	360
Table 17.1	Survey results by country	369
Table 17.2	Network alignment in Bursa and Upper Silesia	370
Table 17.3	Type of network and innovation: test of homogeneity of variances	372
Table 17.4	Type of network and innovation: robust tests of equality of means	372
Table 17.5	Results of ANOVA: variation in innovation within and between the different types of networks	373
Table 17.6	Post-hoc (LSD) test for differences in innovativeness by type of network	375
Table 17.7	Type of network and innovative behaviour: a synthesis	376

LIST OF FIGURES

Figure 1.1	(A) NIS structure of Freeman; (B) NIS structure of Nelson	6
Figure 1.2	Porter's industrial dynamics model	7
Figure 1.3	Vanichseni's industrial innovation system	8
Figure 1.4	The functions of the firm in a national system setting	14
Figure 1.5	Resource networks, from the viewpoint of the firm	16
Figure 1.6	Spatial interactions, viewed as modes of governance	16
Figure 6.1	GDP growth, unemployment rate and inflation 1998–2007 (%)	110
Figure 6.2	Gross Domestic Product per capita in PPS (EU25 = 100)	111
Figure 6.3	GERD and BERD as a percentage of GDP	113
Figure 6.4	Innovation system of Slovakia	116
Figure 9.1	Romania: Male and female employment rates (%)	162
Figure 9.2	Total employment rate, 2006 (%)	163
Figure 9.3	Part-time employment in 2006 (% of total employment)	164
Figure 9.4	Vacancy rates in the new EU member states 2005–2007 (%)	165
Figure 9.5	Percentage of firms reporting deficiencies in worker skills as an important obstacle to firm operation and growth (2005)	165
Figure 9.6	Romania: Net average earnings (Monthly, year on year % change)	166
Figure 9.7	Unemployment by education and gender, 2006 (% of total unemployment)	169
Figure 9.8	Romanians in Spain and Italy (thousands)	171
Figure 9.9	Total unemployment rate, 2006 (%, LFS)	172
Figure 9.10	Romania: Male and female unemployment rates (%, LFS)	172
Figure 9.11	Romania: Male and female unemployment rates for age group 15–24 years, 2006 (%, LFS)	173
Figure 9.12	EU: Unemployment rates for age group 15–24 years, 2006 (%)	174
Figure 9.13	Long-term unemployment (% of total unemployment)	175
Figure 9.14	GDP per person employed (EU-27 = 100, PPS)	176
Figure 9.15	Romania: Labour cost index (2000 = 100, constant prices)	176

xvi   *List of Figures*

Figure 9.16	Tax wedge on labour, 2006	177
Figure 9.17	Rigidity of employment index	178
Figure 10.1	Graduates with higher degrees and all first degree graduates in business administration from public HEIs	188
Figure 10.2	Mismatched graduates as a percentage of the labour force six months after graduation, by type of education: The net sample	194
Figure 10.3	Mismatched graduates as a percentage of the labour force six months after graduation, by gender and type of education: The net sample	202
Figure 11.1	GDP per capita in Campania and the EU, 2000–2004	208
Figure 11.2a	S&T graduates aged 20–29 years per 1,000 inhabitants, all regions, average 1998–2006	218
Figure 11.2b	S&T graduates aged 20–29 per 1,000 inhabitants, Campania, the Mezzogiorno and Italy, average 1998–2006	218
Figure 11.2c	S&T graduates aged 20–29 per 1,000 inhabitants, Campania, the Mezzogiorno and Italy, trend 1998–2006	219
Figure 11.3a	Employment in R&D per 1,000 inhabitants, all regions, average 1995–2005	220
Figure 11.3b	Employment in R&D per 1,000 inhabitants, Campania, the Mezzogiorno and Italy, average 1995–2005	220
Figure 11.3c	Employment in R&D per 1,000 inhabitants, Campania, the Mezzogiorno and Italy, trend 1995–2005	221
Figure 11.4a	Public expenditure on R&D (% of GDP), all regions, average 2000–2005	221
Figure 11.4b	Public expenditure on R&D (% of GDP), Campania, the Mezzogiorno and Italy, average 2000–2005	222
Figure 11.4c	Public expenditure on R&D (% of GDP), Campania, the Mezzogiorno and Italy, trend 2000–2005	222
Figure 11.5a	Company expenditure on R&D (% of GDP), all regions, average 2000–2005	223
Figure 11.5b	Company expenditure on R&D (% of GDP), Campania, the Mezzogiorno and Italy, average 2000–2005	223
Figure 11.5c	Company expenditure on R&D (% of GDP), trend 2000–2005	224
Figure 11.6a	Total public and private expenditure on R&D (% of GDP), all regions, average 2000–2005	224
Figure 11.6b	Total public and private expenditure on R&D (% of GDP), Campania, the Mezzogiorno and Italy, average 2000–2005	225

List of Figures xvii

Figure 11.6c Total public and private expenditure on R&D (% of GDP), 225
Campania, the Mezzogiorno and Italy, trend 2000–2005
Figure 11.7a Patents registered at the EPO per million inhabitants, 226
all regions, average 1995–2002
Figure 11.7b Patents registered at the EPO per million inhabitants, 226
Campania, the Mezzogiorno and Italy, average 1995–2002
Figure 11.7c Patents registered at the EPO per million inhabitants, 227
Campania, the Mezzogiorno and Italy, trend 1995–2002
Figure 11.8 S&T employees in Italy, 1971–2000 (thousands) 228
Figure 14.1 Trends in investment in transportation equipment 289
per employee (€, adjusted for PPP)
Figure 14.2 Trends in investment in computers and related systems 289
per employee (€, adjusted for PPP)
Figure 14.3 Relative wages (left) and productivity (based on 290
value added, right)
Figure 14.4 The distribution of employees by ISCO-88 occupational 291
groups and ISCED-97 educational levels in forestry
Figure 14.5 The distribution of employees by ISCO-88 occupational 291
groups and ISCED-97 educational levels in the
wood-processing industry
Figure 14.6 The distribution of employees by ISCO-88 occupational 292
groups and ISCED-97 educational levels in the pulp
and paper industry
Figure 14.7 The distribution of employees by ISCO-88 occupational 292
groups in the furniture industry
Figure 15.1 Share of FIEs with R&D activity across host economies (%) 315
Figure 15.2 R&D intensities of R&D-active FIEs: aggregated averages 316
over three indicators across host economies
Figure 15.3 Share of FIEs with innovative activity across countries 317
and types of innovation (%)
Figure 15.4 Innovation intensities of FIEs with product innovation 318
across host economies
Figure 15.5 Aggregated share of sales attributable to new or significantly 319
improved products across countries (%)
Figure 15.6 Average levels of autonomy from foreign investors 321
in technology-related business functions of FIEs
across countries
Figure 15.7 Importance of exploiting and augmenting strategies 322
across countries

Figure 15.8   Structure of sales across countries: averages   324
               of destinations of sales
Figure 15.9   Structure of supplies across countries: averages   325
               of origins of supplies
Figure 15.10 Intensity of cooperation with local scientific institutions   326
               across host economies

LIST OF CONTRIBUTORS

Ozge Aktas
D.Phil. Student
School of Social and Cultural Studies
University of Sussex, UK

Pål Børing
Research Fellow, NIFU STEP, Norway

Jože Damjan
Associate Professor
Faculty of Economics
University of Ljubljana, Solvenia

David A. Dyker
Honorary Professorial Fellow
SPRU — Science and Technology Policy Research
University of Sussex, UK

Peter Franz
Department of Urban Economics
IWH Halle, Germany

Jutta Günther
Head of Department of Structural Economics
IWH Halle, Germany

Andreja Jaklič
Assistant Professor
Faculty of Social Sciences
University of Ljubljana, Solvenia

Björn Jindra
Department of Structural Economics
IWH Halle, Germany

Črt Kostevc
Assistant Professor
Faculty of Economics
University of Ljubljana, Solvenia

Cornelia Lang
Department of Macroeconomics
IWH Halle, Germany

Jaan Masso
Senior Research Fellow
Faculty of Economics and Business Administration
University of Tartu, Estonia

Guldem Ozatagan
D.Phil. Student
School of Social and Cultural Studies
University of Sussex, UK

Dragos Pislaru
General Manager
GEA Strategy & Consultancy
Bucharest, Romania

Matija Rojec
Associate Professor
Faculty of Social Sciences
University of Ljubljana, Solvenia

Andrea Salavetz
Senior Research Fellow
Institute for World Economics of the Hungarian Academy of Sciences, Hungary

Silvester Salis
Research Fellow
Institute of Forecasting
Slovak Academy of Sciences, Slovakia

Maria Del Sorbo
Visiting D.Phil. Researcher
SPRU — Science and Technology Policy Research
University of Sussex, UK
PhD Researcher, University of Salerno, Italy

Johannes Stephan
Lecturer and Research Fellow
Technical University of Freiberg, Germany

Nick von Tunzelmann
Professor of the Economics of Science and Technology
SPRU — Science and Technology Policy Research
University of Sussex, UK

Kadri Ukrainski
Research Fellow
Faculty of Economics and Business Administration
University of Tartu, Estonia

Priit Vahter
Ph.D. Student
Faculty of Economics and Business Administration
University of Tartu
School of Economics, University of Birmingham, UK

Urmas Varblane
Professor of International Business
Faculty of Economics and Business Administration
University of Tartu, Estonia

INTRODUCTION

CHAPTER 1

ALIGNMENT, MISALIGNMENT AND DYNAMIC NETWORK-BASED CAPABILITIES

NICK VON TUNZELMANN

1. Introduction — The Tasks Facing Network Alignment

'Network alignment' is a term that has been found useful in comparing the relative performance of development processes, particularly in the context of catching-up or transitional changes. It is intended to be a description of overarching links (or lack of them) in production/innovation/knowledge systems at varying levels of geographical units — especially the national, regional and local, though both wider applications (e.g. to the EU) or narrower (to the micro level) are equally feasible. Its comprehensive nature is both a strength in regard to its broad-ranging, umbrella-like properties and — to date — a limitation, in being unbounded and thus very difficult to specify in any precise way.

The latter issue contrasts with the major steps taken in recent years towards quantifying 'social network analysis' (SNA), which has developed powerful tools to measure such concepts as network centrality.[1] An important objective should be bringing such techniques within the ambit of network alignment. A stumbling block at present is that SNA tends to assume the existence already of a (single) network, usually with well-defined boundaries, and so the concepts like centrality are comparatively unambiguous. An individual unit is clearly located either near the centre of 'the' network, near its outer limits (periphery), or somewhere in between; the focus is on dyadic relationships.[2] Once the network alignment situation of multiple networks with fuzzy boundaries arises, the measurement becomes far less straightforward. Even so, the challenge ought to be taken up — but this task remains ahead.[3]

Much the same issue arises in connection with 'systems' and, more specifically, 'system integration'. Again, much of the recent literature is written as if the organisation in focus has one particular system to integrate, whereas in actuality it normally

---

[1] See for instance Carrington *et al.* (2005); Hanneman and Riddle (2005). Note, however, that 'centrality' has several meanings.
[2] For example, Kenny *et al.* (2006). The focus is usually on 'homophily', i.e. the pairing of similar partners, rather than, say, complementarity. More complex formats such as triads or groups are sometimes studied.
[3] Though see Perini (2009) for some initial steps towards reconciling SNA and network alignment.

finds itself spread across many 'systems' of different types, some more 'systemic' in the way they function than others. We will come back later to the differences between systems and networks, but in the meantime they can be regarded as analogous in these respects.

The ubiquity of network alignment is easy to illustrate from the level of an individual person. Many — indeed, probably most — readers of this book as academics will be engaged repeatedly (often several times a day) in differing networks. Some of these are discipline-based networks, of colleagues in the subjects in which we were trained or have later acquired. Another grouping of networks concerns the 'production' of research, teaching and administration, in functions that relate variously to our specific research units, membership of university/institute committees, sitting on national bodies like research council committees, and so forth. A third grouping relates to 'outputs', and these include teaching links with other universities globally, and research linkages that may be equally widespread. This somewhat stylised tripartite division into suppliers of inputs (like the scientific disciplines in which we were educated), producers and users of outputs is aimed at paralleling the experience of firms, and indeed all organisations. It brings out the multiplicity of the relevant networks at each level, though needing to go further into the bidirectional connections between the levels, e.g. through expecting to learn as much from 'users' as the knowledge supplied to them. All of this is to say nothing of social networks — of family, local associations, etc.

If such complexity applies at the comparatively insignificant individual level, how are we to see the totality? Unquestionably the notion of a single network is an immense abstraction, however amenable it may be to analytical tools and quantification (which we happen to support). The same goes *a fortiori* for a more complex organisation such as a firm, or even more complex organisations such as local or national governments.

The principal task confronting network alignment is thus to assess the consistency of this heterogeneity of networks in their ability to orient their effectiveness towards attaining certain goals for the relevant system. The organisations generally studied are at or towards the most complex end of what has just been cited (governments and the like). The systemic goals will be analysed somewhat further hereafter, but in the meantime we can take them to be development-oriented. The main point to be made here has rather to do with complexity — that far from there being any tendency towards a mega-consolidation of the multitude of networks, their numbers are probably expanding at a rapid pace, hence intensifying the need for 'alignment'. Can we find in our (ill-defined) patterns of individual networks an equivalent to Adam Smith's 'invisible hand' that he established for a system of individual agents?

Section 2 of this chapter outlines some of the forebears of the network alignment approach. Section 3 looks at 'systems', by way of a background to the issues raised by alignment: specifically at spatially oriented systems (typified by 'national systems of innovation'), governance systems, and complex systems which incorporate both, together with other elements. Some of these (in particular the micro level of firms and the macro level of governments) are investigated in Section 4, cast in the more dynamic light of capabilities and learning. The tricky issue of how to measure network (mis)alignment is then taken up. Section 5 gives some brief conclusions.

2. Antecedents of Network Alignment

The network alignment approach thus tackles high-order complexity, in considering 'networks of networks', located in 'systems of systems'. The price paid for this generality is, as already implied, a blunter set of tools available for analytical purposes.

The origins of the network alignment perspective derive from at least three strands of the literatures that blossomed in the later 1980s and into the 1990s. The first of these is the 'systems of innovation' approach, resuscitated in the work of Freeman and especially in his study of Japan (1987). Freeman himself saw predecessors dating back at least as far as the political economist Friedrich List, publishing his agenda for the emerging nation state of Germany in 1844 (Germany was not actually united as a nation until 1871), though based on his observations in another young country, the USA, in the 1820s. Freeman's work was taken further in two major collected works of the early 1990s: Lundvall's book on national systems of innovation (NSIs) in 1992, which took what we shall later describe as a primarily functional approach to national systems, and that also on NSIs edited by Nelson in 1993, which took a more structural–organisational line. The focus here was primarily on spatially focused systems, most obviously national systems, though it was also soon applied to regional and local systems at one end, and what Freeman (2002) was to term continental systems — or even a global system — at the other end.

If the impetus here lay on political economy perspectives, the background of the second group of relevant authors came mostly from political science. These scholars shared for the most part a German or middle-European base (Marks *et al.*, 1996). They were concerned with 'multi-level systems of governance', such as those found in Germany with its reuniting nation, its federal system of comparatively powerful *Länder*, and its central role in the European Union. That is, they too were considering regional, national and supranational systems, but as overlapping (political) entities rather than as alternatives as in the NSI approach. The unifying element in this spatially heterogeneous context tended instead to be located in sectoral perspectives (Kim and von Tunzelmann, 1998), or what subsequently came to be known as 'sectoral systems of innovation' or SSIs (Malerba, 2004). Growth poles emerged around new technologies and sectors. It should be noted that, though SSIs were thought of as consolidating factors across the various spatial boundaries, there exists an alignment problem that lurks not far below their surface. Malerba, for instance, defines sectors as demarcated by groups of closely related products, much in line with the conventional boundaries of 'industries', whereas the Swedish approach (Bergek *et al.*, 2008) sees technological systems as being defined by areas of technology. Neither are very purist about their (contrasting) definitions in reality — Malerba for example treats biotechnology as a 'sector' whereas it is evidently not a product area but a technology, and conversely the Swedish group admits product boundaries into its technological categories. We shall see later that this matters quite a lot.

A third source for network alignment, and in fact the closest to it in spirit, is based in France, and particularly around the CEPREMAP institute in Paris (Jessop, 2001). This can be called the 'social system of accumulation' school, though it is more popularly known as the '*régulation*' school. As one of its architects, Robert Boyer, has pointed out, '*régulation*' in the French sense does not mean 'regulation' in English, and he translates it as 'tuning'. It is, in fact, very close to what we mean by 'alignment'. For the most part, the French school has emphasised the role of aggregate wages, in a rather post-Keynesian sense, and in the context of national labour markets: in particular the potential for misalignment between production (keeping labour costs down) and consumption (keeping wage-based demand high). Our use of this approach focuses instead mostly on technology and knowledge, though this can also be said of some of their work.

3. Systemic Approaches

3.1. *National systems of innovation*

National systems of innovation (NSIs), like the others that we shall be assessing, can be approached either from a functional point of view or from an agent-based one. These positions are stylised so far as they relate to national technological systems in the panels of Fig. 1.1, the left-hand panel showing a simplified representation of the perspective of Freeman (1987) in his path-breaking study of Japan, the right-hand one that implied in many of the chapters of Nelson's collected national studies of 1993.

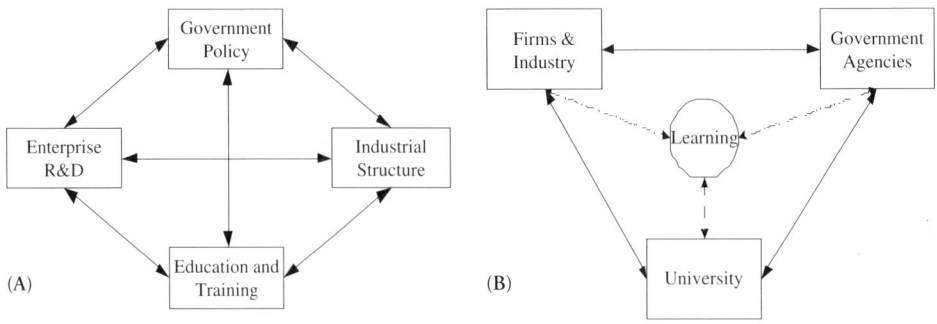

Fig. 1.1. (A) NIS structure of Freeman; (B) NIS structure of Nelson.

The diagrams exaggerate the differences of actual execution of the studies (for instance Freeman's strong emphasis on the former Japanese ministry MITI in his assessment of government policy), but serve to highlight one aspect of complexity — that there is a many-to-many relationship between the functions and the agents that provide them. Thus, for example, education and training in Fig. 1.1(A) is supplied by all three types of agents in Fig. 1.1(B), and so on. Clearly there will be issues of alignment that arise immediately, and do indeed emerge as a focal point in practice, of the intermingling of education and training provision from each source.

A very different approach emerges from the literature on industrial economics and strategic management, focusing, as in Porter's work (1990), on competitiveness as a national target. Figure 1.2 stylises the Porter 'diamond', with elaborations of the factors of 'chance' and 'government' that are concessions to reality in the model. Technology does not appear explicitly in this framework, though its influence is exerted mainly through 'factor conditions'.

A recent paper by Vanichseni (2000) aimed to bring the function-based technology perspective of Freeman *et al.* into alignment with the industrial economics viewpoint of Porter, as in Fig. 1.3. In this enlarged model, the technology component, if that is what it can be termed, appears as the left 'diamond', and the industry component as the right one. 'Firms and Industry Structure', as the common point of reference, takes on the critical role of a fulcrum between the two sub-systems. It is noteworthy that the system being discussed here is much broader than innovation, including production and even consumption (and reproduction), in line with the French school of *régulation*. The primary attention is implicitly directed at spatial proximity — generally the nation-state, though increasingly sub-national ('regional systems of innovation') and supra-national ('continental systems') as well.

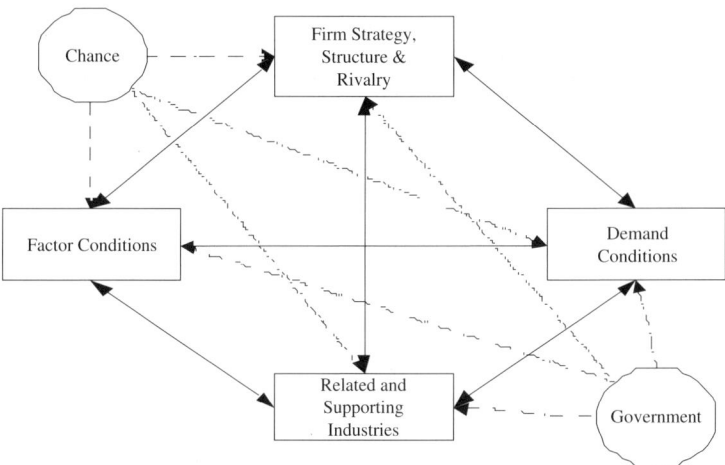

Fig. 1.2. Porter's industrial dynamics model.

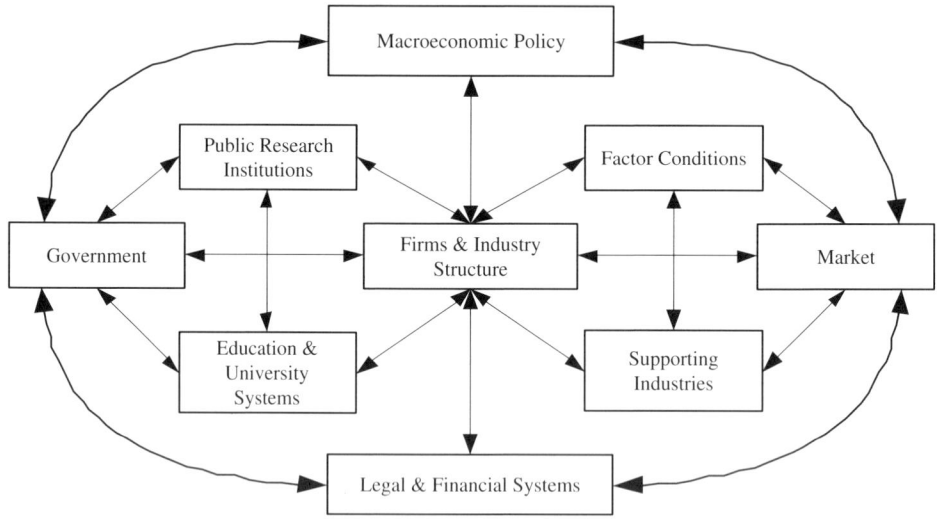

Fig. 1.3. Vanichseni's industrial innovation system.

In this version of the model, 'Macroeconomic Policy' and 'Legal and Financial Systems' are taken as broader contexts, though they too could be endogenised in an even more complex structure. The notion of firms and industries as a fulcrum will be returned to below, after we first develop the key concepts relating to network governance.

3.2. *Governance systems*

We take as a short-hand definition of 'governance' that by Prakash and Hart (1999): governance is 'organising collective action'. Here those agents undertaking such organising actions are the key actors in national and regional (etc.) systems of innovation. The concept of governance embraces: (i) structure, (ii) control and (iii) processes. The modes of governance surveyed here, as is conventional, are: (i) markets, (ii) hierarchies (both corporate and political) and (iii) networks. For our purposes, and in contrast to a lot of more precise terminology in sociology, 'networks' are defined residually, as all forms of collective action that do not primarily involve either financial exchange (markets) or the exercise of power (hierarchies). To exclude the kinds of social networks referred to earlier, such as those based on kinship (though of course some of these may lie underneath our chief focus), we will confine our attention here to collective action that involves collaboration in the development of knowledge, and in large part to those concerned with knowledge associated with production and technology. In practice, many such knowledge exchanges in the real world will at the same time involve elements of market exchange or power imbalance. However, we will suppose that in the networks that concern us these supplementary modes of governance are secondary to the main desire to interact through knowledge formation, and usually *ex post*. Thus the transactions of goods and services that come about, say, through markets, in our instances come about *after* the partners have agreed on the nature of those products, e.g. between a component supplier and an automobile manufacturer.

Each mode of governance is associated with a particular type of 'failure': market failure, corporate failure, government failure and 'network failure'. Around each of these, except the last, a substantial literature has accumulated, which we will not try to summarise beyond listing the quaint terminology of 'hands' that has developed alongside the modes of governance and their respective sources of failure. Some of these are listed in Table 1.1.

Network failures relevant to knowledge flows at the system level include the following situations (von Tunzelmann, 2004):

1. The network required to permit the interflow of knowledge does not exist;
2. The network required does exist, but is anti-developmental (e.g. based on a *nomenklatura* system);
3. The networks do exist and are pro-developmental, but function in ways that make them incompatible with achieving the development goals.

Social network analysis is mostly concerned with the first of these, particularly through Burt's notion of 'structural holes' (Burt, 1992), e.g. in 'clusters'. It is clear from an abundance of empirical evidence, including that on the CEE countries noted below, that network (mis)alignment in reality involves the consideration of targets as well as instruments. The most interesting case of the three is probably the third, and is in fact the one on which much of the study of network alignment to date has focused.

Networks and their failures should be distinguished in principle from the more widely studied areas of 'systemic failure', even though both concepts are relevant to our area of investigation. System failures are regarded as those that arise not in individual instances (here labelled 'intrinsic') — specific to the individual market, corporation, etc. — but across the systems in question (Larsen and von Tunzelmann, 2006). Table 1.2 gives some randomly chosen examples by way of illustration.

Table 1.1. Modes of governance and their failures.

Mode of governance		Mode of failure	
Markets	Invisible hand	Market failure	Trembling hand
Hierarchies (corporate)	Visible hand	Corporate failure	
Hierarchies (political)		Government failure	Grabbing hand
Networks	Greeting hand	Network failure	

Table 1.2. Examples of intrinsic (particular) as opposed to systemic failures of governance modes.

Governance mode	Examples of intrinsic failure	Examples of systemic failure
Markets	Under/over-supply of good	Shortage economy
Corporate hierarchy	Bankruptcy of firm	Antiquated organisational systems across a nation
Political hierarchy	Corrupt ministers	Central planning problems
Networks	Too few/many members	Network misalignment

Networks and their failures constitute a row of the matrix whereas system failures constitute a column, cutting across all modes of governance failures. A parallel could perhaps be drawn with the concepts of partial disequilibrium and general disequilibrium in economics.

3.3. Complex systems

A major reason accounting for both the growing importance of networks and for their failures, both intrinsic and (especially) systemic, in modern times is the growth of 'complexity'. As we have charted elsewhere, the sources of this rising complexity can be traced both in breadth ('relational complexity') and depth ('cognitive complexity') (Wang and von Tunzelmann, 2000). The former concerns the range of constituents involved and the latter the degree of difficulty associated with the constituents, i.e. sophistication. Many of the problems confronting the agents in national and other systems of innovation in recent decades have been a compound of complexity in breadth and complexity in depth, because of the need to integrate newer elements into the wider system.

The factors underlying this rising level of complexity include the following.

1. The spread of 'knowledge-intensive' production. This has led to an increase in complexity in depth through the inherent cognitive and practical difficulties that particularly characterise high-tech production and technology, e.g. in microprocessors, but also complexity in breadth through the rise (for instance) of what has been termed 'Mode 2' knowledge production (Gibbons *et al.*, 1994), involving a more diverse range of actors in knowledge production and a more extended degree of interaction among these more populous actors. The latter has affected all industries and many services, not just the high-tech ones (as emphasised in the EU's PILOT programme, *cf.* Hirsch-Kreinsen and Jacobson, 2008).
2. At the upstream end, so far as producer firms are concerned, technologies are accumulated over time, and are for the most part cumulative. The advent of a new technological paradigm rarely causes the old one to disappear, instead adding to the complexity of multiple interactions of association between old and

new technologies. To the extent that there is competition among them, we increasingly face a situation of 'hyperchoice' of a variety of ways of effecting similar — though often not identical — results.
3. At the other end, the products produced from these technologies face intensifying market pressures of competition, increasingly from global sources, even in many services. There are pressures for the *rapid* development of new products, especially those with advanced technological features, as product lifecycles allegedly shorten (von Tunzelmann and Acha, 2005). This reacts on the pressure to bring on new technologies more rapidly, notwithstanding their increasingly complex nature, as evident in, say, the somewhat disappointing progress of 'red' biotechnology (Hopkins *et al.*, 2007).
4. ICT networks have developed to try to cope with the associated problems of coordination arising from more complex delivery in shorter periods of time; however, these have raised coordination problems of their own at a variety of managerial levels.

To turn from the functions to the agents, we can see firms, at the fulcrum of the NSIs as in Fig. 1.3, themselves becoming more complex organisations over the longer term: first, in moving from production in one region to production in several regions or countries (multinational organisations), second in shifting from producing a single product to producing a range of products (multi-product organisations), and third in developing a range of core technologies that they utilise rather than a single core technology (multi-technology organisations). Multi-technology companies (Granstrand *et al.*, 1997) emerge from the growing relational complexity of modern technological systems. Firms 'know more than they make' (Brusoni *et al.*, 2001), partly for negative reasons of being unable to align the competencies that they possess, but also for more positive reasons of 'dynamic capabilities' to be expanded on below — in effect providing for a future of still greater complexity. Even in a number of industries dominated by SMEs the multi-technology context now prevails, e.g. in 'rapid prototyping' (Hwang, 2006). It goes almost without saying that this growing complexity increases the problems of integrating these dispersed technological competencies, and they are exacerbated by the pressures of time.

4. Capabilities and Learning

4.1. *Sources of learning*

An issue of growing importance has been that of whether the multiple technologies can be internally developed or instead externally acquired. Until the advent of the modern era of new technological development in ICTs, biotechnology and the rest — the so-called Third Industrial Revolution — the standard practice had been for large corporations to develop all their key technologies in-house. The rise of complexity in technologies, in products and geographically, tipped the balance towards external acquisition. On the external side this increased the complexity of inter-organisational linkages, through widening networks for technology among the diversifying types of agents already touched upon (universities, public R&D labs, hospitals, etc.). On the internal side it placed new burdens on assimilation, through enhancement of 'absorptive capacity' (Cohen and Levinthal, 1990), which could turn competencies into 'capabilities'.[4] Downstream as well as upstream firms developed 'system integration' capabilities, but in the context of the 'systems of systems' that we have previously adumbrated, the way each firm envisaged its system was likely to differ from the way its partners saw things.

In this complex structure, there is no *a priori* guarantee that the way in which the capabilities of one type of actor (say producers) evolve will go in the same direction as those of another type of actor (say, consumers). This is because (i) asymmetries of information may take them in different directions; (ii) even if asymmetries of information do not exist, *asymmetries of knowledge* may prevent them from even going in the same direction. Thus interaction among types of agents may be necessary: (i) *ex ante*, through knowledge exchanges; (ii) *ex post*, through market exchanges. It may be noted that a common pattern in such interactions as they evolve through time is to begin with a knowledge exchange (e.g. between component supplier and manufacturer), and to follow that up once component specifications are agreed with a set of market purchases/sales, thus as already noted adding market governance to knowledge network governance. Since different actors (e.g. different firms) have differing capabilities for interaction, we can therefore talk about differences in 'interactive capabilities'.

Note especially that all agents in systems variously act as producers, consumers and suppliers, but to different units of analysis. Thus, to revert to the view of the individual given in the Introduction to this chapter, university appointees 'produce' lectures and papers, in so doing 'consuming' IT equipment as well as basic necessities — not to mention the previous academic studies that we cite — and in the course of so doing, aim to 'supply' students, colleagues and perhaps policy-makers with the fruits of our knowledge. The same goes for all agents. 'Agents' are thus the individuals or organisations involved; 'actors' reflect their position in terms of how their activities are being envisaged.

---

[4] 'Competencies' and 'capabilities' are often used more or less interchangeably, but here we differentiate them. Put most simply, the former represent enhancements to productive resources of a particular organisation that are developed outside the organisation and then 'hired in' or otherwise acquired by that organisation. Thus a semiconductor company may hire graduates in solid-state physics on grounds of the potential they offer to improve output, technology, etc. in relation to its products. The actual enhancements are carried out in the universities from which those graduates originated. The firm would of course hope to convert the potential into actual improvements, in which case the competencies convert into the firm's own capabilities (von Tunzelmann and Wang, 2007).

The context of 'dynamic competition' (in the sense of Schumpeter) means the environment (landscape) may be constantly changing — there is a need for innovation in technologies, products, organisations, finance, etc. This entails interaction occurring in 'real time'. The extent to which the capabilities of producer firms are 'dynamic' is therefore dependent on the degree to which the resources and/or products are novel but also appropriate to the changing environments in which they are positioned (vis-à-vis their consumers and suppliers). Formally, the dynamic interactive capabilities of firms represent the extent to which the changes in their capabilities influence or are influenced by the changes in the capabilities of consumers and/or suppliers, all in real time.

The dynamic capabilities approach acts as a bridge between competing theories of innovation management: (i) the resource-based view (RBV) of non-imitable capacities, primarily for firms; and (ii) the strategic management view (e.g. Porter's 'diamond'), primarily for industries. The former looks mostly backwards, at the massing of competencies and (static) capabilities accumulated over past time ('resources'), while the latter looks mostly forwards, to the prospects for future development ('strategic'). Neither is complete in our context without the other — the RBV needs capacity for change in a context of Schumpeterian competition, while at the same time strategic management needs to be anchored in the existing strengths of an organisation.

Capabilities change as circumstances change — and to the extent that this is represented by changing regulation, standards, etc., it can fall to the role of other actors in the system as briefly indicated below — but especially as abilities change, which is mostly the consequence of 'learning'. Table 1.3 sets out a structure for sources of learning, adapted from the work of Malerba (1992), though a little differently arranged, and distinguishing in the columns as between internal sources of learning and external sources. The rows are arranged according to our threefold classification of actors as producers, consumers and suppliers. In the last-named, we adapt Malerba's specification of 'formal search' to include learning in human capital form as well as in technologies (R&D and S&T — Science & Technology).

The table strongly implies the need to blend together the internal and external sources of learning associated with each actor, and this relates again to the issue of 'absorptive capacity'. Implicitly the learning can arise not just in technologies, but in

Table 1.3. Channels of learning (after Malerba, 1992).

Sources as actors	Internal	External
Producers	Learning by doing	Learning from (horizontal) spillovers
Consumers	Learning by using	Learning from (vertical) interacting
Suppliers (formal search)	Learning from R&D and training	Learning from S&T and education

all the functions of the firm or other type of organisation, an issue to which we turn next.

4.2. *The functions of the firm*

In this section, we take the firm to be the relevant agent in the system, in view of the fulcrum role highlighted in Fig. 1.3 above. Other agents can be examined in similar ways, but the task of so doing is left mainly to future research, aside from the role of governments to be assessed in the sub-section to follow.

From the discussion immediately above, one can in the first place envisage the firm from the viewpoint of the various functions that it carries out. Figure 1.4 shows the layout of the functions of the firm in its core. The role of the producing firm is seen as one of transforming technologies into products (von Tunzelmann, 1995), involving the functions of techniques and marketing. To do this it can call on the functions of production processes and administration (financial and legal operations, etc.). These four functions are coordinated internally by management in terms of trying to optimise within given external constraints, and by entrepreneurship in dynamic contexts of bringing about changes in those constraints (Lazonick, 1991).

The functions of the firm at micro level each relate to functions of the national system of production and innovation at macro level. These go beyond the S&T system at national level to embrace national (or for that matter regional) systems of

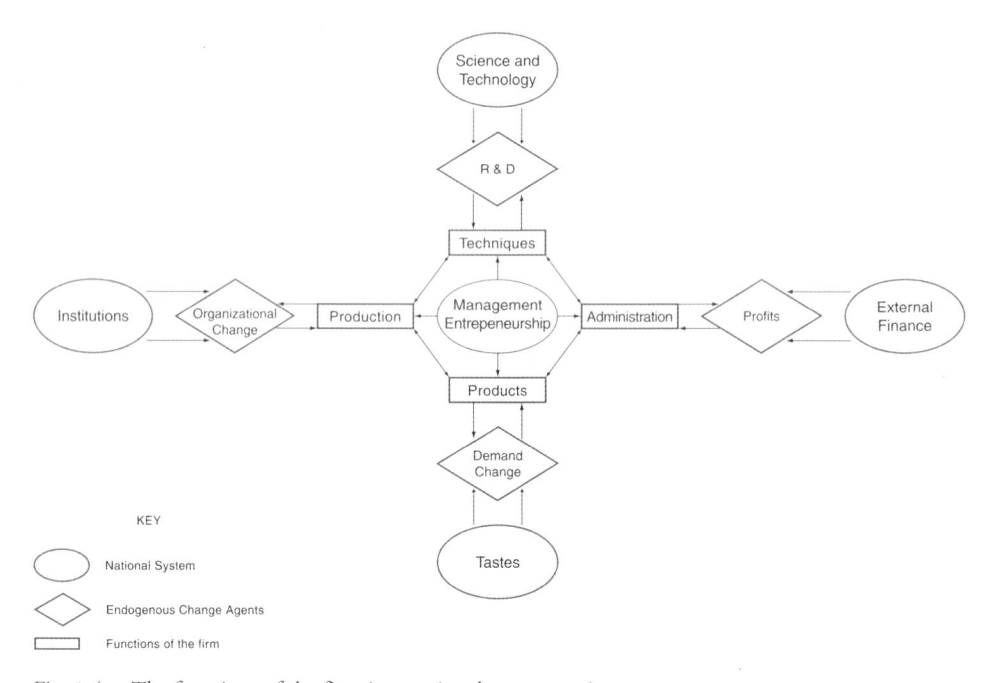

Fig. 1.4. The functions of the firm in a national system setting.

finance, consumption/taste patterns and 'institutions', with the latter here referring to the norms and rules of the game as they pertain to the organisation of production, broadly interpreted (*cf.* North, 1990).

The alignment of these national levels of functions is, of course, the central issue of the topic at large, executed through the various modes of governance outlined previously. The diagram, however, emphasises the interplay between macro and micro levels, conducted through the changes taking place at the various interfaces — in R&D as an interface for technology, and so on. The relationships between R&D and national S&T run in both directions, downward from the national level and upward from the firm level, as do those between the firm's techniques and its R&D. The same goes for the other functions. Again, issues of absorptive capacity in all functions remain paramount. Clearly the diagram is a simplification, in that the links between the macro and micro level are once again many-to-many rather than one-to-one, but the nature of the relationships to be observed is evident enough.

To bring these micro and macro levels of production and innovation into effect, interflows of resources are required. These operate at all levels, but will be illustrated in Fig. 1.5 from the situation of a particular firm, x, located in a particular industry, i.

Firm x appears as the nucleus of a hub-type network of supply chains, with each rectangle indicating a different type of input being supplied. The firm is taken to be in industry i located as a particular column in the meso-level input-output table. The table is shown in the same format for each type of input. The pattern shown focuses on inflows of labour and capital of various types, while the actual pattern for a firm should also include inflows of land and mineral resources, here excluded only to reduce the complexity of the figure. The primary source of each type of input is shown to differ: banks for physical capital, laboratories for R&D capital (technology), and so on. Once more, the pattern in reality is more complex, e.g. with governments supplying some external finance, technology, skilled labour, etc., to firms as well as infrastructural capital. The arrows as before run in both directions, inward from the supply side and outward from the demand side. The meso-level becomes highly complex when the range of firms and industries in the national/regional system is taken into account.

Finally we can show the spatial level of interactions, as set out in Fig. 1.6. This diagram makes use of the governance modes previously described to articulate the various geographical levels, though of course it can be done in other ways.

The political hierarchies are displayed at the top, here supranational (e.g. EU) and national governments, though regional and other levels could equally be shown. Markets and corporate hierarchies (firms) are shown at the bottom. In between are the various spatial levels of networks — here global, national and local networks, pictured as ovals. The two-headed arrows again simplify the multiplicity of real-world interactions. The networks are shown as partly (though only partly) overlapping.

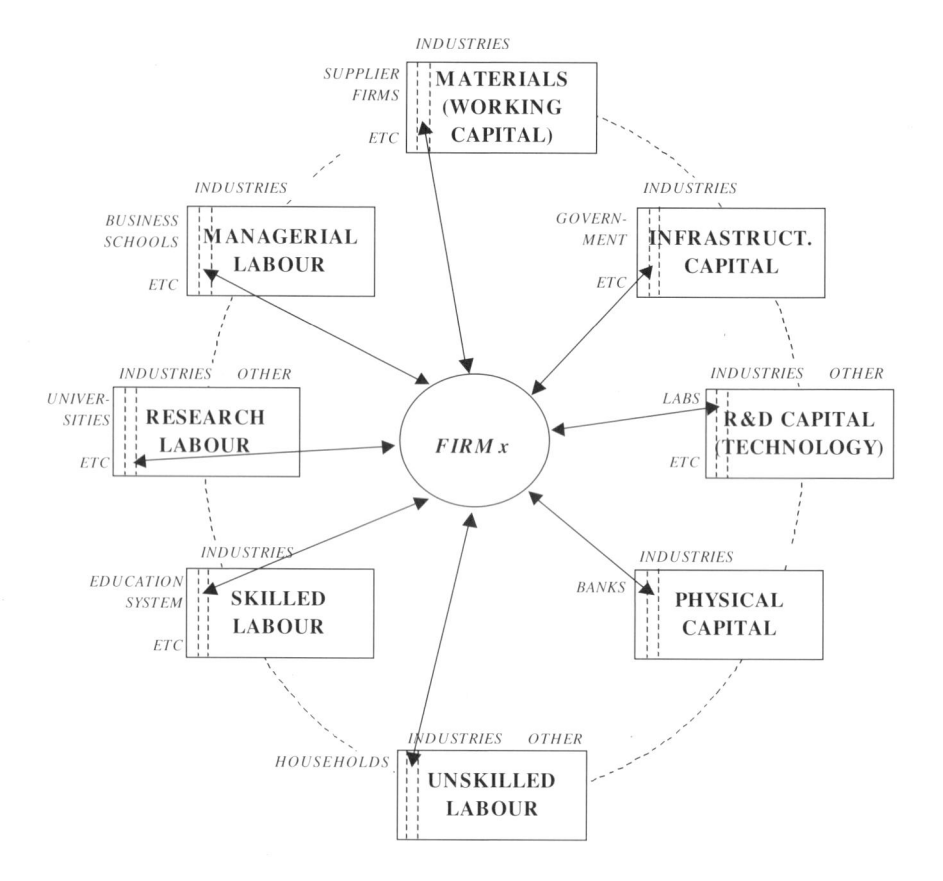

Notes: Each rectangle (box) represents an Input-Output relationship for the source specified.
Input agents (suppliers) are listed down the vertical axis of each box.
Directions of Output (demands) are listed across the boxes (same in each case).
The Industry relevant to Firm x is shown as the dotted column.

Fig. 1.5. Resource networks, from the viewpoint of the firm.

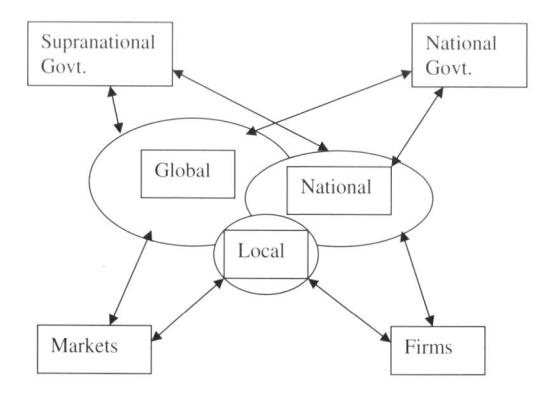

Fig. 1.6. Spatial interactions, viewed as modes of governance.

Once more, this spatial level of interaction in Fig. 1.6 intersects in many-to-many fashion with the functional networks of Fig. 1.4 and the resource networks of Fig. 1.5. Thus production in firm x is the simultaneous outcome of its functional structure (techniques etc.) and corresponding external relationships, its resource structure and corresponding external relationships (land, labour and capital), and the spatial structure of governance modes that it fits into (global, national and local). Naturally, any of these ties may be weak or strong depending on individual circumstances.

4.3. *The capabilities of government*

As compared with alignment at firm or individual organisation level, alignments at the meso level of industries and the macro level of countries are likely to be much more diffuse. Work on alignment at industry level is at an early stage of development, arising partly out of the recent work on sectoral systems of innovation (SSIs), though with antecedents in regional networks (e.g. for the 'Third Italy'). To the latter can be added work on industry associations and modes of governance (e.g. Cooke and Morgan, 1998), and the more analytical studies in the context of political scientists' approaches to governance as already mentioned.

Here we focus on the macro level, and particularly the role of governments in helping to bring about — or obstruct — the management and coordination of national systems ('social systems of accumulation'). Central to any success in this role are the needs for due alignment of governments within their social systems and for learning behaviour through all the internal and external channels of Table 1.3 — in this instance, 'policy learning'.

Some of the key requisites of adequate alignment on the part of governments include:

1. the need to operate through demand as well as supply factors, including (macro-) economic policy;
2. the need to enhance interactivity in space, e.g. through clusters;
3. the need to promote interactivity in 'real time', for global competition, e.g. building clusters into dynamically effective 'regional systems of innovation';
4. the need to align objectives of all types of agents, in both public and private spheres (if knowledge is substitutive, 'crowding out' can arise between public and private actions, if knowledge is complementary there should be 'crowding in');
5. the need to inculcate policy capabilities to make connections, through 'policy learning' (both internal and external).

Forging the links required for this demanding set of needs is in part an orthodox matter of targets and instruments — having common targets and sharp enough sets of instruments. The conventional requirement is for there to be as many instruments as targets, though it has long been known that this is not strictly the case. The tendency in the 1980s to 'roll back the frontiers of the state' left many governments with too few instruments and ones that were too blunt to cope (von Tunzelmann, 2009). In the modern era, national and supranational governments have to respond to the additional burdens imposed by the 'globalising learning economy' (Lundvall and Borrás, 1997), where the market sector is particularly unlikely to provide adequate resources and capabilities for proper alignment.

As complexity grows in depth as well as breadth, new pressures are thus placed on governments to sustain development processes. In this, they tend to be limited by the insufficient 'capabilities' of the state/authority to link its policy-making to client needs. As emerges from the list of requisites above, governments need to exert dynamic capabilities of their own, by keeping abreast or ahead of the game, but nowadays in a networked society potentially able to call on a wide range of talent and expertise rather than a hierarchically structured one.

4.4. *Gauging network alignment*

The problem of trying to measure the extent of network alignment — and hence trying to gauge how much misalignment is tolerable — begins at the beginning, with attempting to measure such notoriously elusive concepts as 'knowledge' and 'innovation'. The limitations of widely practised measures of the knowledge base and its diversity are well known — much can be said against each of the 'usual suspects', such as patents, R&D, skill levels or innovation surveys. The problems do not need to be laboured at this point. Nor is it a question of averaging out, since it is precisely the specificity of each measure that is likely to be valuable here. An immense amount of damage has already been done to the whole field of innovation studies by such elementary confusions as (crudely) measuring technologies from products, and so on. For example, the EU's Community Innovation Surveys have for a number of years been carried out in the absence of much semblance of a clear definition of what 'innovation' is, leading to often absurd results.

Without effective measures of these very basic concepts, it becomes difficult to assess in quantitative terms the goals or targets of a network structure. Yet network alignment must be about achieving common goals across a network or across networks of networks, without innate contradictions between the methods adopted in trying to attain them (the 'instruments'). We can, however, proceed to attempt to assess the targets of individual organisations in the network structure. Specifically we might wish to select the following list of targets for key agents:

1. for firms: one branch of literature, coming from international business studies, sees the goals of firms in diversification as market-seeking, cost-seeking or

knowledge-seeking, while that in strategic management has a somewhat different but reconcilable list of such goals;
2. for universities: widely observed targets tend to embrace research, teaching and revenues;
3. for governments: competing models in political science seeking to classify governmental behaviour list the regulatory, developmental and distributive states as viable choices.

The heterogeneity of these goals is highly suggestive of typical network alignment problems — how can this variety of aims and objectives be harnessed to the good of any visible purpose? This brings us back to the analogy with the invisible hand theorem in a network economy context, as mentioned at the start. In fact the 'developmental' goal was assumed for a national system of innovation (NSI) in our discussion of network failures; but this may have been simplistic or at least premature. To the extent it remains valid, one would need to see university–industry links as pro-developmental (contradicting the presuppositions of attempted measurement such as the UK's Research Assessment Exercise), and likewise for business–government links.

In trying to reap these rewards, agents are constrained by their capabilities, as explained above. Those that especially concern us here are the networking capabilities, i.e. the need for effective and efficient interaction between and among organisations. The diagrams presented in Figs. 1.4 to 1.6 suggested multiple agents interacting in both functional and resources respects in differing spatial contexts. These interactions give clues as to the economies of scale and scope ('synergies' in depth and breadth) present at system or network level, though again these are hard to quantify unless we are able to measure the knowledge itself, or (even less likely) how one piece of knowledge is ontologically related to another piece to achieve the synergies. In this context the contrast that Mokyr (2002) has drawn, to explain the historical evolution of NSIs, between learning focused on what and why (epistemic) as against how (technical, applications), could prove to be a very valuable insight.

The static scale and scope economies in any case probably pale alongside the potentials for dynamic scale and scope economies. These latter typically take the form of real-time economies in the short and medium term ('time-saving technical change') and increasing returns from learning in the medium-to-longer term. And this brings us back to assessing dynamic capabilities as real-time, learning-oriented expressions of the drivers of effective interactivity in conditions of 'dynamic competition'.

5. Conclusions and Implications

Establishing that a particular system of networks is or is not aligned is relatively straightforward, at least conceptually, in that it relates to the notions of various kinds of network failure previously listed. What is much harder to assess is the *extent* of network (mis)alignment. It seems obvious that the more restricted the goals or targets of a particular set of networks, and the smaller the number of relevant agents involved, the more likely it is that the structure will be fairly well aligned, *ceteris paribus*. But what degrees of misalignment are tolerable, and how can the amount of diversity needed in any system to maintain momentum be allowed for? In the CEE countries particularly, where at the time of writing newly emerging market-based mechanisms are being put under pressure by new waves of global market-based disruption, it would seem vital to know.

It is apparent from our currently limited information on this issue that no optimal solution is ever likely to be found, at least in the kind of real-time context that is relevant to practical situations confronting policy-makers at the macro level or strategic decision-takers at the micro level. Countries regarded as highly successful in recent times, e.g. China or South Korea, would seem to feature among those with quite extensive degrees of duplication in administrative circles, despite their periodic attempts to rein in the more excessive cases of overlap. Network misalignment would appear to be endemic in complex many-to-many environments. So does it matter?

The answer in our view is that, while the body politic — like the human body — can learn to adjust around the edges of minor setbacks, major weaknesses can be quite damaging. Localised and piecemeal improvements may end in an outcome that is far from acceptable, much less optimal. The East Asian governments alluded to above share with their nations some 'vision' of where they are heading, and this yields an outcome in terms of dynamic capabilities that may not be perfect but at least seems satisfactory. It is less clear that the countries described in the remaining chapters of this book do share such visions as to where they are going.

References

Bergek, A., Jacobsson, S., Carlsson, B., Lindmark, S. and Rickne, A. (2008). 'Analyzing the functional dynamics of technological innovation systems: A scheme of analysis', *Research Policy* 37: 407–429.

Brusoni, S., Prencipe, A. and Pavitt, K. (2001). 'Knowledge specialization, organizational coupling, and the boundaries of the firm: Why do firms know more than they make?', *Administrative Science Quarterly* 46: 597–621.

Burt, R.S. (1992). *Structural Holes: The Social Structure of Competition*, Cambridge, MA, Harvard University Press.

Carrington, P.J., Scott, J. and Wasserman, S. (eds.) (2005). *Models and Methods in Social Network Analysis*, Cambridge, Cambridge University Press.

Cohen, W.M. and Levinthal, D.A. (1990). 'Absorptive capacity: A new perspective on learning and innovation', *Administrative Science Quarterly* 35: 128–152.

Cooke, P. and Morgan, K. (1998). *The Associational Economy: Firms, Regions and Innovation*, Oxford, Oxford University Press.

Freeman, C. (1987). *Technology Policy and Economic Performance: Lessons from Japan*, London, Pinter.
Freeman, C. (2002). 'Continental, national and sub-national innovation systems: Complementarity and economic growth', *Research Policy* 31: 191–211.
Gibbons, M., Limoges, C., Nowotny, H., Schwartzman, S., Scott, P. and Trow, M. (1994). *The New Production of Knowledge: The Dynamics of Science and Research in Contemporary Societies*, London, Sage Publications.
Granstrand, Ö., Patel, P. and Pavitt, K. (1997). 'Multi-technology companies: Why they have "distributed" rather than "distinctive" core competence', *California Management Review* 39: 8–25.
Hanneman, R.A. and Riddle, M. (2005). *Introduction to Social Network Methods*. Riverside, CA, University of California, http://www.faculty.ucr.edu/~hanneman/nettext/.
Hirsch-Kreinsen, H. and Jacobson, D. (eds.) (2008). *Innovation in Low-Tech Firms and Industries*, Cheltenham, Edward Elgar.
Hopkins, M.M., Martin, P.A., Nightingale, P., Kraft, A. and Mahdi, S. (2007). 'The myth of the biotech revolution: An assessment of technological, clinical and organisational change', *Research Policy* 36: 566–589.
Hwang, J.-T. (2006). *The Role of Small Innovative Firms in Multi-Technology Innovation: The Case of Rapid Prototyping Industry*, DPhil Thesis, SPRU, University of Sussex.
Jessop, B. (ed.) (2001). *Regulation Theory and the Crisis of Capitalism*, Cheltenham, Edward Elgar.
Kenny, D.A., Kashy, D.A. and Cook, W.L. (2006). *Dyadic Data Analysis*, New York, Guilford Press.
Kim, S.-R. and von Tunzelmann, N. (1998). *Aligning Internal and External Networks: Taiwan's Specialization in IT*, SEWPS (SPRU Electronics Working Paper Series), No. 17, University of Sussex.
Larsen, M.T. and von Tunzelmann, N. (2006). 'Non-market failure: The role of public science in the development of generic technology', Aalborg, DRUID Summer Conference Paper.
Lazonick, W. (1991). *Business Organization and the Myth of the Market Economy*, Cambridge, Cambridge University Press.
Lee, T.-L. and von Tunzelmann, N. (2005). 'A dynamic analytic approach to National Innovation Systems: the IC industry in Taiwan', *Research Policy* 34: 425–440.
List, F. (1844). *The National System of Political Economy* (transl. S.S. Lloyd), London, Longmans, Green & Co. (1904).
Lundvall, B.-Å. (ed.) (1992). *National Systems of Innovation: Towards a Theory of Innovation and Interactive Learning*, London, Pinter.
Lundvall, B.-Å. and Borrás, S. (1997). *The Globalising Learning Economy, Implications for Innovation Policy*, DG Science, Research and Development, Brussels, European Commission.
Malerba, F. (1992). 'Learning by firms and incremental technical change', *Economic Journal* 102: 845–859.
Malerba, F. (ed.) (2004). *Sectoral Systems of Innovation: Concepts, Issues and Analyses of Six Major Sectors in Europe*, Cambridge, Cambridge University Press.

Marks, G., Scharpf, F.W., Schmitter, P.C. and Streeck, W. (eds.) (1996). *Governance in the European Union*, London, Sage Publications.

Mokyr, J. (2002). *The Gifts of Athena: Historical Origins of the Knowledge Economy*, Princeton, Princeton University Press.

Nelson, R.R. (ed.) (1993). *National Innovation Systems: A Comparative Analysis*, New York, Oxford University Press.

North, D.C. (1990). *Institutions, Institutional Change and Economic Performance*, Cambridge, Cambridge University Press.

Perini, F. (2009). *Organising Innovation between Multinational Companies and Innovation Systems*, DPhil thesis, SPRU, University of Sussex.

Porter, M.E. (1990). *The Competitive Advantage of Nations*, New York, Free Press.

Prakash, A. and Hart, J.A. (eds.) (1999). *Globalization and Governance*, London and New York, Routledge.

Sen, A.K. (1985). *Commodities and Capabilities*, Amsterdam, North-Holland.

Vanichseni, S. (2000). 'National systems of industrial technology development', in Arnold, E. et al. (eds.), *Enhancing Policy and Institutional Support for Industrial Technology Development in Thailand*, Brighton, Technopolis.

von Tunzelmann, G.N. (1995). *Technology and Industrial Progress: The Foundations of Economic Growth*, Aldershot, Edward Elgar.

von Tunzelmann, N. (2004). 'Network alignment in the catching-up economies of Europe', in F. McGowan, S. Radosevic and N. von Tunzelmann (eds.), *The Emerging Industrial Structure of the Wider Europe*, London, Routledge, pp. 23–37.

von Tunzelmann, N. (2009). 'Technology and technology policy in the post-war UK: "market failure" or "network failure"?', Revue d'Economie Industrielle, *forthcoming*.

von Tunzelmann, N. and Acha, V. (2005). 'Innovation in "low-tech" industries', in Fagerberg, J., Mowery, D. and Nelson, R. (eds.), *The Oxford Handbook of Innovation*, Oxford, Oxford University Press, pp. 407–432.

von Tunzelmann, N. and Wang, Q. (2007). 'Capabilities and production theory', *Structural Change & Economic Dynamics* 18: 192–211.

Wang, Q. and von Tunzelmann, N. (2000). 'Complexity and the functions of the firm: Breadth and depth', *Research Policy* 29: 805–818.

Welle, K. (2009). 'Monitoring access to rural water supply in Ethiopia', DPhil research outline, SPRU, University of Sussex.

SECTION 1

INNOVATION NETWORKS

CHAPTER 2

THE UK INNOVATION SYSTEM, FROM A MISALIGNMENT PERSPECTIVE

NICK VON TUNZELMANN

1. Introduction

For well over a century, scholars and many of the informed general public have been lamenting the UK's seemingly poor record in terms of technological performance, and more particularly how it has resigned itself to abandoning its one-time world leadership — during the mid nineteenth century when the country had come to be called the 'workshop of the world' — and to slipping ever further behind. Rival nations from, first, Western Europe, then North America, and most recently Asia, have pushed past and forged ahead, and perhaps nowhere more so than in just those sectors that had permitted Britain to call itself the world's workshop in those times now long ago. To be fair, this set of pessimistic viewpoints has by no means gone unchallenged, either in the past or nowadays, and due recognition should be given to the opposing optimists.[1] Nevertheless, the pessimists in this debate have long been in the ascendancy, and for the bulk of this chapter I shall suppose this standpoint to represent the orthodox, mainstream position.

Moreover I intend to confine the bulk of my attention to the most recent era — say the last four decades or thereabouts — that in a more global perspective has come to be thought of by some as 'post-industrial society' (e.g. Bell, 1973; Toffler, 1980), and by some others, a little less apocalyptically, as the 'Third Industrial Revolution'[2] or the fifth 'long wave' of industrialisation (e.g. Freeman and Louçã, 2001). To do so immediately raises the question of how different this latest stage of industrial development is from its predecessors, and whether the pessimist/optimist demarcations have shifted through time.

This chapter provides some preliminary thoughts as to how far misalignments at the network or system level (*cf.* Table 1.2 in Chapter 1) help to explain these

---

[1] A recent example is David Edgerton (1996), a fierce opponent of what he terms the 'declinist' position, though he is part of a longer legacy than he would readily admit to. Note also that a pessimist position does not necessarily imply declinism: from a counterfactual point of view, it merely requires an emphasis on the belief that the UK is not doing as well as it could, nor as well in these respects as some of its leading competitors.

[2] The present author is an advocate of this position, and thus far from unbiased.

seemingly endemic features of the UK's national innovation system — at least if one is prepared to accept the pessimists' story for the time being. The conclusions reached in Section 5 have to remain quite tentative, in the absence of either detailed historical investigation or adequate measures of the extent of misalignment (again see Chapter 1 for a discussion of the latter). In order to reach such interim conclusions, I shall next investigate the technological performance of the UK innovation system, then turn in Section 3 to the potential problems of network or systemic failure and misalignment in the private sector, and thence to policy problems and public–private links in Section 4.

2. The UK Record in Technology Performance Since the 1970s[3]

2.1. *Biases in technological change — Sectors, factor inputs and firm sizes*

The main emphasis in the 1950s and 1960s had been laid on capital-embodied technical progress, partly as a matter of reconstruction after the Second World War, relying principally on the heavy and chemical industries of the preceding 'Second Industrial Revolution' (coal-based electrification, steel, vehicles, heavy engineering, bulk chemicals, etc.). The focus for government support (either direct or indirect) thus had been directed towards large, capital-intensive firms like GEC (General Electric Company) in electrical manufactures or ICI in chemicals, and in particular to support their efforts towards monopolisation of their respective industries. At the meso-level, the focus on the consolidation of capital-intensive industries was intended to produce 'national champions'. This phase had coincided with an era of rising capital expenditure as a proportion of GDP, not just in the UK but across Western Europe more generally (for data and graphs, see von Tunzelmann, 1999, 28). However the competition in such sectors spread across continents, with the rising 'tigers' of Japan and a little later South Korea also targeting the heavy (e.g. steel, shipbuilding) and chemical industries at this time. Moreover growing integration among the economies of Western Europe via the Single European Market began to make the strategy of national champions look rather obsolete.

In practice, the rising intensity of gross capital formation that persisted until about 1973[4] gave way to a period in which investment ratios fell. This fall in physical capital formation was partly offset by rising investment in R&D, although the measures used for the latter (Frascati Manual definitions) reduced its magnitude as compared with some broader notion of 'intellectual capital'.

Associated with the shift from physical to intellectual capital was a shift in technological bias from 'embodied' to 'disembodied' technical change, i.e. to technical

---

[3] This section draws extensively on parts of my paper for the conference celebrating 30 years of the *Revue d'Economie Industrielle*, held in Juan-les-Pins, November 2008 (von Tunzelmann, 2009).
[4] For the more developed European countries, average capital intensity reached a plateau through most of the 1960s, before heading more sharply downwards after 1973.

change that was not so much embodied in capital equipment (machinery etc.) as it had been before, although more embodied in people. This aspect was epitomised by the expansion of software development, constituting a rising share of total investment in information and communication technologies (ICTs), though for a long time the emerging Third Industrial Revolution was identified with the hardware and manufacturing aspects of technology, especially of the electronics industry. In terms of products rather than technologies, the 'information' content of ICTs was largely equated with 'knowledge' — grossly oversimplifying the processes of technological and market learning.

The developments of the earlier post-Second World War years prior to the early 1970s thereby cast a long shadow over the late century years. The innovation system in the UK — and to be fair in many of its competitors, though perhaps not the larger rival countries — was having to deal with the new realities of the Third Industrial Revolution by using the tools developed for the Second Industrial Revolution. Hierarchical control at both corporate and political levels became very disjointed. Perhaps nowhere was this rift more evident — albeit only with hindsight — than in the arena of government policy which, being still framed largely in a national context, was often painfully slow to perceive any change of emphasis. It moved a little quicker into the newly emerging sectors like those based around IT, yet still for the most part retaining an assumption of the need for capital intensity and nationalistic fervour.

I shall return to the area of government policy-making in Section 4, meanwhile first summarising and updating previous findings on the empirics of technological performance in the UK economy in these years, and then coming to the question of failures and misalignments.

2.2. S&T performance and funding

The data available for the UK from the end of the Second World War to about the mid-1990s are collected and graphed in von Tunzelmann (2003), and the present summary will just survey and update these figures where necessary.

2.2.1. R&D performance — GERD, BERD and HERD

Figures on R&D expenditures have become the most widely cited of national indicators pertaining to technological performance. The attempt to construct a narrow consensual definition through the OECD's Frascati Manual means that much developmental work aimed at the commercialisation of innovations is left out of the figures for R&D. It is widely believed that the UK is stronger at 'upstream' science and technology than at 'downstream' adoption and diffusion, so if anything UK expenditures tend to overstate its relative international performance in technology. Figures for R&D intensity, i.e. GERD (Gross Expenditure on R&D) relative to the country's

GDP, suggest a rapid build-up to a plateau of around 2.3% from the late 1950s to the early 1990s, followed by some decline in the 1990s. These figures portray the UK as at best holding its level of R&D intensity, though failing to match the longer-term rises experienced in comparable European economies like France and (West) Germany. Over the decade from 1995 to 2004, average R&D intensity in the UK fell to about 1.8%, compared with 2.2% in France, 2.4% in Germany and 2.6% in the USA (figures from UK ONS database[5]).

In terms of BERD, i.e. business expenditure on R&D, there is in the long run again basic stability — from the late 1960s through to the late 1980s BERD sticks at about 1.5% of GDP, before declining in the 1990s, notwithstanding the (part-)privatisation of many government laboratories like those of the Atomic Energy Authority. Again, the UK did relatively badly compared with its main international rivals.

For HERD (Higher Education Expenditure on R&D) as a percentage of GDP the story is very different — here a positive performance by the UK not only features but almost dominates the picture. Until the cuts in university funding at the end of the 1970s the contribution of UK higher education institutions to the country's R&D was well below that in comparable countries. The cuts and the associated reorientation of university research towards applied objectives in order to secure non-governmental funding more than doubled the HERD contribution to UK GDP during the 1980s. By the mid-1980s the UK ratios were in the same ball-park as its rivals, and by the mid-1990s there had been strong convergence among the major countries. It can reasonably be claimed that the UK was successful in steering its universities into industrially relevant research. As of 2006, R&D performed by higher education (including the research councils) in the UK was half of that performed by the entire business sector (BERD), whereas in 1996 it had been little over one-third as much (ONS data).

Thus the pattern observed for the UK is rather different from that of most industrially advanced countries — instead of a slowdown in government R&D expenditure being more than offset by rising business expenditure, the UK witnessed a slowdown in business R&D expenditure, perhaps even a fall, and a rise in higher education R&D that was offset by a fall in government expenditure in other domains.

2.2.2. R&D funding

These figures on expenditures, reflecting amounts performed by the respective agents, must be clearly differentiated from the sources of funding. In most countries, and the UK is no exception, the government funds considerably more R&D than it performs. For instance, in 1996 private business in the UK funded about 47% of total domestic R&D but performed about 75% (Diederen *et al.*, 1999). By 2006, the respective

---

[5] Office of National Statistics.

proportions were 45% and 62% (ONS data). In the UK most of this 'subsidy' to industry has reflected military R&D, where the government contracts out a substantial portion of defence-related R&D.

Large changes occurred during the 1980s and early 1990s. At the beginning of the 1980s government funded around half of the total R&D performed in the country, but from 1983 this share fell away (Georghiou, 2001). Industry's share rose from just over 40% in 1981 to a maximum level about 10 points higher in 1988. Some part of the falling government share was compensated by a rising share funded by foreign sources, i.e. by increasing reliance on foreign-based multinational companies, and by other national sources (e.g. charities), especially after 1988. Charities were especially important in funding basic scientific research.

Overall the experiment of cutting UK government spending on R&D in the hope of boosting private R&D can hardly be judged a success. The growth in the UK R&D stock was the slowest of the G6 countries 1972–1989, and especially in 1990–1994 (Buxton *et al.*, 1998, 172).

2.2.3. *Patenting*

Patent figures are regularly, though sometimes inadvisably, used as a measure of the 'output' of technology. Most scholars are prepared to use them to gauge trends through time, if used with due care. The data for patents in the USA, chosen because it is the largest world market, relative to other advanced countries apart from the US, show UK patenting as declining in most periods from the 1880s onwards (when the data begin), except for the interwar period (Pavitt, 1980, 38–44). Having overtaken the UK in the late 1950s, at its peak on the eve of German reunification in 1990 the level for West Germany in per capita terms was about two and a half times that of the UK. France shows a slower rate of increase, but still caught up with the UK by the early 1980s, and rose somewhat above it in the early 1990s. The UK, by contrast, shows only a very slow trend increase in US patents per capita, reaching its peak in the early 1970s. All of these patterns are in fact dwarfed by Japan, which had dramatic rates of growth of US patenting per capita over these years.[6]

Alternative series are available for patenting at the European Patent Office (EPO) from the early 1980s. For the most recent years for which data are available (1995–2003), the average annual number granted to UK patentees was 112 (per million capita), compared with 127 for France, 149 for the USA, and 266 for Germany. Though this figure rose by 49% between 1995 and 2003 for the UK, the percentage increases were somewhat greater for the three comparator countries

---

[6] These figures cannot be simply compared with those for the USA itself, because it is the 'home nation'. For US comparisons, third-country data like those for the EPO (see below in the text) are more reliable, though showing, if anything, a reverse catching-up bias in terms of growth rates.

(ONS data). To the extent that patents do provide some indication of technological output, the data give little comfort to the view of a strong UK performance.

2.2.4. Science — Publications and citations

As a guide to the underlying strength of technology, the growth of the science base is an obvious pointer. Using data from the Science Citations Index for 1981/2000, the UK shares of both papers and citations thereto remain at respectably high levels, despite the global spread of science.

Overall, the numbers of publications, when compared to the material covered above, appear to indicate a much healthier state of British science than of British technology throughout the periods for which there exist reasonable data. A government report in 1997 showed the UK carrying out 5.5% of the total world research effort, producing 8.0% of the world's publications and 9.1% of all citations (May, 1997; Diederen *et al.*, 1999). The Office of Science & Technology thus showed high productivity for British science in terms of papers per amount spent on science, although it can be doubted whether like was being compared with like.[7] Even if valid, for many critics this simply reflected the low amounts spent in the denominator rather than the high outputs achieved in the numerator of the productivity calculation (Georghiou, 2001). The data do at the same time make the government attempts in the 1980s and early 1990s to blame universities rather than industry for Britain's economic woes rather implausible.

By the 1980s research funding had reached a stage which John Ziman captured in the title of the report, *Science in a 'Steady State'* (1987). His report contrasted the sustained growth in science funding of preceding decades with the levelling off of the 1980s, which he considered would continue. At the same time the need for science showed no sign of levelling off, and the costs of undertaking science were also on the rise. How could this circle be squared? Industry and government implored academia to adopt more business-like methods, which were partly pursued; but to critics within academia this was imposing on them the methods of an even more dubious UK business and financial system.

2.2.5. 'Hidden innovation'

A series of reports emanating from NESTA[8] (2006, 2007, 2008) have pointed out that 'historically, the UK has suffered from poor performance relative to its major competitors on traditional measures of innovation' (NESTA, 2007, 4), for instance R&D per capita, but better once what it calls measures of 'hidden innovation' are

---
[7] For instance, because of an evident bias in the data that favoured publications in the English language.
[8] The National Endowment for Science, Technology and the Arts.

taken into account. Sector-specific studies suggest the following indicators of such hidden innovation (*inter alia*):

i) 'Innovation that is identical or similar to activities that are measured by traditional indicators, but which is excluded from measurement...';
ii) 'Innovation without a major scientific and technological basis, such as innovation in organisational forms or business methods...';
iii) 'Innovation created from the novel combination of existing technologies and processes...';
iv) 'Locally-developed, small-scale innovations that take place "under the radar"' (*ibid.*, 5).

As these reports argue, the over-emphasis on traditional indicators has led to a situation in which, 'consequently, policymakers have responded by incentivising R&D, encouraging businesses to collaborate with universities and substantially increasing public investment in scientific research' (*ibid.*, 4), rather than promoting these sources flagged by due recognition of hidden innovation. However, the belief that the UK is particularly distinguished by such hidden forms of innovation remains largely an article of faith.

2.3. *Summary of the UK's technological performance*

With the admittedly important exception of this last consideration of hidden innovation, there seems little to disagree with on the basis of these and similar data as regards the orthodox pessimistic viewpoint, which contends that the UK has performed with some illustriousness in the field of upstream scientific research but has been relatively poor compared to its competitor countries in downstream applications. In such respects the contention converges upon the popular view that the UK is good at the preliminary stage of invention, but much weaker at the subsequent stages of innovation and commercialisation. Whether this is really the case is considered much less frequently; for instance there are some myths surrounding certain 'inventors', such as the Scotsman, John Logie Baird, touted as the true inventor of television.[9] To the extent that it can be upheld in terms of empirical evidence, the reasons why it should be the case are also relatively seldom assessed, despite there being an almost endless supply of possible explanations that might account for it. Besides, there is an inherent linearity in the popular argument that warrants more probing, especially when the growing role of universities (for HERD) is taken into the account.

---

[9] Baird's TV 'system' of circular scanning of the image was discarded in favour of line-by-line scanning from an early stage of development, including by the BBC.

Such matters are addressed in the next section of this chapter.

3. Misalignments in the UK System: The Private Sector

The primary deficiency of the British economy in regard to its innovative performance — at least so far as the technological dimension is concerned — over the years from the 1960s to the 1990s thus (according to the BERD data etc.) arose in relation to the private sector of industrial business. It is there that one must begin the search for sources of 'failure', even if, as already strongly implied, the failure turns out to be more broadly systemic at heart. Several candidates have proven popular in this respect.

3.1. 'Value chain' failures

This category picks up on a combination of the work of Porter (1985, 1990) on 'related and supporting industries' (Figure1.2 in Chapter 1), which uses the term 'value chain', and the more dynamic analysis of Lundvall (1992) in the spirit of 'learning by interacting' (Table 1.3 of Chapter 1). The analytical shortcoming of Porter's approach — which has regrettably spilled over into the recent literature on 'global value chains' — is that of confusing value chains, which are inherently about chains of functions, with ordinary supply chains of an input-output kind. I have no argument with the latter, as representing product-based flows of work-in-progress, but to include these among value chains is highly misleading. Supply chains are generally linear and uniquely defined, like the 'putting-out' system for processing textiles from raw materials to finished garments, which dates back to medieval times and possibly before. Value chains, by contrast, are typically non-linear and complex in structure — 'value networks' in effect (*cf.* Chapter 1, Figs. 1.4 and 1.5), though too often thought of as being high-end supply chains.

Such linear conceptualisations have permeated much UK strategic management and policy-making in relation to 'learning by interacting' in the national system of innovation (*cf.* Lundvall, 1992). The so-called 'linear model of innovation' is often traced back to the work of Vannevar Bush (1945) in the USA at the end of the Second World War, but in fact has older antecedents in the UK (at least). This one-directional model according to which more spending on science generates more discoveries and inventions, which in turn lead to innovations that become commercialised and then widely diffused, and hence at the far end of the line create the conditions for economic and productivity growth, has continued to enjoy popular support in the policy arena. Its supply-push simplicity was undermined by work on demand-pull influences on innovation in the 1960s and 1970s, such as the SAPPHO project in SPRU (Rothwell *et al.*, 1974), by more critical empirical assessments of what scientists and engineers actually do (Gibbons and Johnston, 1974; Vincenti, 1990), and by a flood of research in the field of 'innovation studies' that showed that in reality the procedures and the connecting interflows were vastly more complex.

In practice in the UK the linear model could serve as a reasonable approximation to the circumstances confronting industries such as pharmaceuticals, where the conditions in research labs of private firms to a great extent coincided with those encountered in universities. This may help account for the surge in R&D activity in pharmaceuticals that emerges from the ONS data (von Tunzelmann, 2003), alongside the national increase in HERD already observed. But in other technological fields such as ICTs, the linear model worked far less well, and here the UK success stories were more isolated, often in niches such as design stages for lightweight portable chips for mobile phones (ARM), or software applications such as video-games. These activities enshrined the interactive supply–demand nature of most innovation, yet remained largely untouched by directed government policies.

3.2. Spillovers and sectoral systems

There were, however, some benefits accruing from the indirect effects of policy in many such cases, like the spillovers from the 'Cambridge phenomenon' in the example of ARM semiconductors (Garnsey *et al.*, 2008). In Table 1.2 of Chapter 1 these are treated as 'horizontal' in nature, and can arise within a specific sector or across sectoral boundaries where there are no obvious input-output (i.e. vertical) linkages between them.

The literature on sectoral systems of innovation has not yet been able to demarcate clear boundaries for what it embraces by each sector — usually falling back on OECD definitions of 'industries', which are an inconsistent mixture of product-based and technology-based categories. Yet the work of Malerba (2005) and colleagues has adduced the main drivers of such systems, as summarised here under four sub-headings.

i) *Opportunity*: Most concern has been expressed in this connection as relating to technological opportunities, though market opportunities would seem to be more applicable to the given context of product-oriented sectors, and here the British situation was varied. There seems to be some agreement in the literature that government ownership and regulation of the National Health Service benefited the growth of the UK pharmaceuticals industry through its stability, whereas frequent changes induced by erratic governmental decision-making proved disruptive in some other high-tech markets (like nuclear power). In geographical terms, British producers have been criticised for restricting their exports largely to safe Empire and Commonwealth markets (e.g. Owen, 1999, for motor vehicles).

ii) *Appropriability*: Here the issues have tended to focus on patenting, or rather the lack of it (as the statistics previously cited demonstrate), by many British companies and other organisations. It is widely believed, for instance, that British success in patenting of pharmaceuticals boosted financial support for that industry. However it is conceivable that British companies were better at developing 'dynamic' modes of appropriability such as lead time, than 'static' modes such as patenting.

iii) *Cumulativeness*: In this aspect the issues focused on matters of size and concentration. It has already been observed how the 1960s and 1970s witnessed a quest for large corporations able to exert monopolistic muscle through becoming 'national champions'. This effort rather disintegrated thereafter, as forces of globalisation demanded the rise of 'international champions', leaving the old national monopolies stranded. Moreover, countervailing forces to do with anxieties about innovation, employment, autonomy, etc., appeared to warrant support for SMEs. Since the assessment by Kamien and Schwartz (1982), analysts have learnt to distinguish between matters of size and matters of concentration. Indeed, in the UK case, there is some evidence from admittedly rather confused data suggesting that both small and large firms may be best for innovation (e.g. Pavitt *et al.*, 1987, based on the SPRU innovation database for 1945–83), but medium levels of concentration could be best, to avoid the contrasting inefficiencies of lack of power in fragmented industries and lack of incentives in monopolistic industries.

iv) *Knowledge base*: There were belated concerns about declining numbers in STEM subjects (science, technology, engineering, mathematics), though attempts to solve the problem through government intervention were either inadequate — in the sense of having little visible impact — or in a few cases excessive, as students were lured into fields such as 'computer studies' in the later 1990s and early 2000s, only to find that the jobs to employ them were no longer present (*cf.* discussion of similar cases in Chapter 7).

The sectoral data provided in von Tunzelmann (2003) support many of the above findings, both positively and negatively. For the UK, the figures indicate a squeeze on R&D in high-tech sectors apart from pharmaceuticals — most evident in sectors like aerospace (facing some withdrawal of protected home markets as the government cut its defence budgets) and electronics (loss of innovative competitiveness), despite the production shares of the UK holding up in these sectors. The implication was one of a loss of power to foreign-based MNCs that took over much of the UK production.

Even more significantly, these figures overlook the rising share of R&D in services, amounting to maybe as much as one-quarter of the total by the later 1990s (Boden, 1998). The report from NESTA (2006) dwells on the importance of many service sectors to the UK economy, and the comparative unimportance of traditionally measured R&D in those sectors, though even here some impact has become evident.

Whether the UK success in innovative financial services outlives the current financial crisis remains to be seen.

3.3. Organisational/governance issues

The alleged weaknesses of British forms of industrial organisation, governance and management have been detected in a number of ways, apart from claims of sheer managerial incompetence that are hard to substantiate in terms of any aggregate impact. Among the arguments raised are the following:

i) Delayed introduction of the 'M-form' (multi-divisional) corporate style — this was the view put forward by the business historian Alfred Chandler (in Chandler *et al.*, 1999), viz. that British firms clung too long to obsolete corporate structures such as the 'U-form' (unitary), which were too unfocused for an era of multi-product companies selling their products to a variety of markets. However, while this may be a valid criticism of UK corporations in the early postwar years, in the days when large capital structures were dominant, the product-oriented multi-divisional form itself became too rigid for the ensuing years of the Third Industrial Revolution, when companies came to be not just multi-product and multi-regional, but multi-technology (Granstrand *et al.*, 1997). More specifically, the M-form could become a source of rigidity in a period when corporations were aiming to develop ICT-based systems.

ii) Short-termism through myopic decision-making systems (e.g. Patel and Pavitt, 1988) — this argument holds that UK companies were particularly prone to avoiding long-term strategic decisions such as those to invest in major new technologies, under the pressure of powerful financial capital interests together with voracious demands for dividends by their shareholders. Companies such as GEC preferred at times to accumulate monetary savings and place them in the stock market rather than reorient themselves to the new era of ICTs.

iii) The 'market for corporate control': such a market for corporate ownership led to aggressive takeovers and asset-stripping, as exemplified by the manoeuvres of wealthy industrialists such as Lord Hanson. In this case the kind of market involved, so far from failing, may have worked all too well. Only a concept such as systemic failure can properly account for the kinds of problems this caused for the governance of the private sector in UK industry.

3.4. Summary of private-sector weaknesses and strengths

From this kind of systemic point of view, the strengths of the British economy seemed to arise mainly in pockets of successes. From the mid-1990s until the financial meltdown in 2007–2008, to take the most obvious example, the apparent resurgence of the financial sector swept the country with a boost of confidence that had not been evident for many decades. At the same time, a more pessimistic perspective on this period might envisage it instead in terms of a much older schism between industrial capitalism, located mainly in the northern and Midlands regions of England as well as the chafing Wales and Scotland, and finance capitalism, emanating from its very restricted geographical base in the City of London. Both the Thatcher government of the 1980s and Blair's 'New Labour' administration at the turn of the century fuelled the restoration of the latter.

How much this refocusing on financial capitalism benefited the economy and its innovation system at large will no doubt be a leading subject for historical research in decades to come. On one side there is a dispiriting sameness about the 'fixes' to longer-term problems on offer, and an unwillingness to learn from the past (for the regularity of the finance–innovation cycle over successive long waves, see Perez, 2002). On the other side, there does emerge evidence of a growing fusion between manufacturing and service activities, with the service functions often carrying the manufacturing elements, if only from sheer weight of numbers in the modern economy. In innovation terms, these trends were reflected in the kinds of hidden innovation described previously, as well as steps towards more dynamic forms of interactive learning.

4. The Public Sector and Technology Policy

These conflicting drivers of change in the private sector carried major implications for reshaping public policy, which was, however, being pulled in yet other directions by the forces of 'multi-level governance' (Marks *et al.*, 1996); from above by EU technology policy, which remained rather conventionally supply-driven, and oriented towards high-tech industries, and from below, by pressures for decentralisation (political down to the regions, including Scotland, and economic down to clusters etc.). It is no great surprise to find the UK solution as one of 'muddling through', though whether such compromises betokened greater success than failure should be investigated.

4.1. *Changes in governance*

The most evident change in R&D governance over the period — in the UK as in many other leading countries — was the shift in its main thrust from being primarily government-led in the 1950s and 1960s to being primarily market-led in the 1970s and especially 1980s. Although the 1980s were associated with the pro-market Thatcher regime, these patterns were for the most part shared by both Labour and Conservative administrations. They were followed in turn by a more mixed set of views giving greater emphasis to collaboration in the 1990s, with decentralisation in the most recent decade, reversing the Thatcher trend towards increased centralisation, which had sat somewhat inconsistently alongside the pro-market stance.

The major shift of emphasis in the 1970s and 1980s implied that government technology projects then had to justify themselves using 'market-failure' or at least 'market-friendly' criteria. This went alongside a rather curious loss of popular faith in the properties of technology to redeem growth performance, which arose (at least in part) for the following reasons:

i) a continuing loss of British competitiveness in the 1960s and 1970s in what were regarded as technology-based industries;
ii) a sequence of public relations disasters, e.g. nuclear power, and later BSE ('mad cow disease'), for which the government was perhaps only partly to blame (Henderson, 1977; van Zwanenberg and Millstone, 2005);
iii) many high-tech companies turned into financial flops, i.e. became specific corporate failures, particularly as the dot.com bubble burst in the early years of the present century, though also earlier, as in the case of ICL in computers.

The correspondence between such loss of public respect for technology and an intensified desire by the UK government to obtain market-friendly outcomes led to a partial withdrawal of government support for technological objectives, after a high-water mark in the early 1980s. The consequences will be expanded on below.

4.2. *The 1970s and 1980s*

Technology had been envisaged by postwar governments as part of a drive to global dynamism at the macro level through a combination of Keynesian rationalism, partnership with both industry and trade unions, and mass education (Buxton *et al.*, 1998). The counterpart at the meso level was investment in technologically advanced manufacturing, and at the micro level of (static) economies of scale. These, as already observed, were seen as achievable through fostering large corporations, often with monopolistic control in the guise of the national champions.

In fact, no postwar government really succeeded in integrating all these components with technology in systemic fashion. As macroeconomic policies appeared to fail, industrial policy came to be increasingly directed at supporting 'lame duck' firms and industries, rather than setting the technological basis for a different future.

The new UK policy agenda for the 1980s tried to encourage deregulation, privatisation and enterprise — justified as representing 'working with the grain of market forces ... [assisting firms] without weakening their commercial responsibility for their own actions' (Barber and White, 1987, 26), and evidently preferable to working against the grain of market forces as in the lame ducks strategies of the 1970s. This, however, led to policy 'by default', of letting market and corporate failures take their own course towards destruction — contrasting sharply with the reality (though not the rhetoric) of US policy in the later 1980s (Branscomb and Keller, 1998).

Any government money for these purposes had to be justified on grounds of market failure (the market sector would not do such things unaided), 'additionality' (government money could not simply replace private expenditures), and especially of serving 'pre-commercialisation' research. Thus, according to a calculation by Baroness Margaret Sharp, industrial subsidies were cut from about £20bn in the late 1970s to just £0.5bn by the late 1990s (both measured in 1996 prices) (cited in Barber and Georghiou, forthcoming, 2).

Technology policy reached something of an impasse, as the new collaborative ventures set up even in the early 1980s were wound down, in a new vogue for enterprise as well as for rolling back the state. In practice, what this often meant was expanding the role for private-sector consultancy, funded if need be by the government, in lieu of leadership by the state. The most serious case in point was the 'Alvey Programme' to support fledgling developments in the UK's ICT sector, which although being highly ranked in evaluations by outside experts in its first phase (1983–1987), also fell victim to the cuts and diversions of public expenditures into the pockets of consultants thereafter.

More generally, the policy stances adopted in these years can be seen as including the following:

i) A shift from 'mission' towards 'diffusion' in the orientation of policies, to adopt the terminology of Ergas (1987), who had found the execution of such mission orientation weaker in the UK than in other primarily mission-focused countries like France or the USA.

ii) Despite this, a level of expenditure on military R&D that continued to be high, still some 36% of total GERD as late as 1997–1998 despite the ending of the Cold War at the start of the 1990s. Military R&D was characterised by a resort to 'baroque' technologies (Kaldor, 1982), increasingly limiting its 'dual-use' functionality for take-up by the civilian sector, e.g. in electronics.

iii) The relentless privatisation of nationalised industries cut R&D expenditures, which tended to be regarded as wasteful from a short-term commercial standpoint.

iv) Regulatory issues were compounded by governance problems, for instance in response to rising public awareness of environmental concerns, moving ahead of governmental action. Public support for science was shaken by a succession of scandals, especially in the area of food policy, where the role of the responsible ministry (MAFF, the Ministry for Agriculture, Fisheries and Food) was coming to be seen as deeply ambiguous — MAFF was replaced by DEFRA (the Department for the Environment, Food and Rural Affairs) in 2001.

4.3. Policy design in later years

'Policy design' represents the ways in which multiple layers of systems are individually and collectively structured and controlled to yield benefits — good policy design is, in part, the expression of a satisfactory alignment process. With this in mind, Freitas and von Tunzelmann (2008) tested a three-dimensional model of public support design — vertical/horizontal knowledge objectives, specific/general support provided, and local/central implementation — as a framework to characterise and compare national policy incentives. The paper compares 149 policy programmes in the UK and France from the early 1980s to 2002.

The investigation found that, despite the two countries having different national innovation systems, the role of policy-making in both became increasingly recognised as a provider of market incentives to new and/or better business-to-business services markets. In both countries public business support became more non-financial each time policy was redesigned, and increasingly concerned with innovation. More specifically, until the mid-1990s, the British portfolio of innovation policies showed a greater reliance on label creation (setting quality standards etc.) and central financial subsidies.

In the UK, the introduction of value-for-money and 'hands-off policy execution' principles in the public sector delayed the process of decentralisation of public business support — before the mid-1990s most horizontal public support consisted of specific types of support centrally delivered, but from the mid-90s a change can be observed towards more local implementation and the provision of general support. It is also worth observing that, at least in our dataset, most of the British programmes — unlike the French — did not last for more than one sub-period. Whether this implies a lesser stability in British policy-making or a greater willingness to take on new challenges (or both) must remain for others to assess.

To achieve this outcome implies in addition a need to enhance interactivity. In recent times this has led policy-makers to advocate approaches that involve support for 'clusters' — a view promoted further by the influence of advisers such as Michael Porter (Porter and Ketels, 2003). While these may help with the interactive side, they can sometimes be a hindering element as regards the pressure to act dynamically, since the notion of a cluster is inherently static. The dynamic counterpart of the cluster is indicated by the concept of 'regional system of innovation', designed to promote interactivity for change occurring in real time. Unfortunately, the Regional Development Agencies (RDAs) set up to divide the country with this in mind in 1999 have lacked an adequate knowledge base for effective policy-making (Barber and Georghiou, forthcoming).

The key issue that we keep coming back to is a need to align the objectives of all types of actors and agents. I am claiming in other words that the underlying source of policy inadequacy remains a matter of failure of both networks and systems[10] through misalignments. There is a need at governmental level to align the micro, meso and macro levels, which may involve positive interactions between, as well as within, local, regional, national and global systems of innovation. There is an associated need — as the defensible but underwhelming resort to RDAs shows — to inculcate policy capabilities to make the desired connections, through 'policy learning' (both internally within each government organisation, and externally through interaction with experts, evaluators, etc.).

5. Conclusions

The UK White Paper of 1988 (Cmnd 278) ended most support for single-company R&D and placed its emphasis on collaborative R&D, yet the underpinning economic analysis retreated deeper into the mystique of 'market failure'. Certainly, the latter may often have exacerbated the difficulties, as with recent financial problems, or in relation to the 'market for corporate control' (through encouraging myopic behaviour).[11] But we have argued that the basic failings are network failures, in terms of inadequate collaboration, and inter-systemic failures of breakdowns between national systems of science, industrial innovation, finance, workplace organisation, etc. (von Tunzelmann, 2003) — in other words, alignment failures. These breakdowns in turn gave rise to a blame culture, from mutual misunderstandings, for example as between the 'separate spheres' of finance and manufacturing industry. The resort to middlemen consultants achieved little, in that such people were not trusted by SMEs (Barber and Georghiou, forthcoming). Meanwhile, the rather incongruous adherence to the linear model involved a reliance on academic spin-offs for generating new technologies and also their diffusion. The split of the old DTI into the newly created departments called DIUS (for science and long-term technology development) and BERR (for business innovation) in 2007, if anything, seemed likely to perpetuate the inter-systemic failures that have characterised British technological development for over a century, while their re-amalgamation into BIS (Business, Innovation and Skills) at the time of writing in 2009 might simply be a case of 'papering over the cracks'.

The analysis of trends in UK technology policy in this chapter has suggested that narrowly economics-based views too often hampered good intentions to reform policy along more appropriate lines, and restricted development of any serious capabilities for policy learning in relation to innovation by UK governments, both national and regional. While probably no country gets all the relevant networks fully aligned to achieve optimal output, the argument here — one that I believe is

---

[10] For the differences between these two concepts, see Chapter 1.
[11] The arguments here are made more precisely in von Tunzelmann (2009).

consistent with a mildly optimistic as well as more pessimistic stances in relation to the debate observed in Section 1 — is that the UK could gain from adopting better practice approaches to improve its innovative performance.

References

Barber, J. and White, G. (1987). 'Current policy practice and problems from a UK perspective', in Dasgupta, P. and Stoneman, P. (eds.), *Economic Policy and Technological Performance*, Cambridge, Cambridge University Press, pp. 24–50.

Barber, J. and Georghiou, L. (forthcoming). 'Developments in UK technology and innovation policy and the formulation of policy rationales', mimeo draft, July 2008.

Bell, D. (1973). *The Coming of Post-Industrial Society*, London, Heinemann.

Boden, M. (1998). 'Science and technology in the private sector', in Cunningham, P. (ed.), *Science and Technology in the United Kingdom*, 2nd edn., London, Cartermill International.

Branscomb, L.M. and Keller, J. (eds.) (1998). *Investing in Innovation: Creating a Research and Innovation Policy that Works*, Cambridge, MA, MIT Press.

Bush, V. (1945). *Science: The Endless Frontier, A Report to the President*, Washington, DC, US Government Printing Office.

Buxton, T., Chapman, P. and Temple, P. (eds.) (1998). *Britain's Economic Performance*, 2nd edn, London, Routledge.

Chandler, A.D. Jr., Amatori, F. and Hikino, T. (eds.) (1999). *Big Business and the Wealth of Nations*, Cambridge, Cambridge University Press.

Diederen, P., Stoneman, P., Toivanen, O. and Wolters, A. (1999). *Innovation and Research Policies: An International Comparative Analysis*, Cheltenham, Edward Elgar.

Edgerton, D. (1996). *Science, Technology and British Industrial "Decline", 1870–1970*, Basingstoke, Economic History Society/Macmillan.

Ergas, H. (1987). 'The importance of technology policy', in Dasgupta, P. and Stoneman, P. (eds.), *Economic Policy and Technological Performance*, Cambridge, Cambridge University Press, pp. 51–96.

Freeman, C. and Louçã, F. (2001). *As Time Goes by: From the Industrial Revolutions to the Information Revolution*, Oxford, Oxford University Press.

Freitas, I.M.B. and von Tunzelmann, N. (2008). 'Mapping public support for innovation: A comparison of policy alignment in the UK and France', *Research Policy* 37: 1446–1464.

Garnsey, E., Lorenzoni, G. and Ferriani, S. (2008). 'Speciation through entrepreneurial spin-off: the Acorn-ARM story', *Research Policy* 37: 210–224.

Georghiou, L. (2001). 'The United Kingdom national system of research, technology and innovation', in Larédo, P. and Mustar, P. (eds.), *Research and Innovation Policies in the New Global Economy: An International Comparative Analysis*, Cheltenham, Edward Elgar.

Gibbons, M. and Johnston, R. (1974). 'The roles of science in technological innovation', *Research Policy* 3: 220–242.

Granstrand, Ö., Patel, P. and Pavitt, K. (1997). 'Multi-technology corporations: Why they have 'distributed' rather than 'distinctive core' competencies', *California Management Review* 39: 8–25.

Henderson, P.D. (1977). 'Two British errors: Their probable size and some possible lessons', *Oxford Economic Papers* 29: 159–205.
Kaldor, M. (1982). *The Baroque Arsenal*, London, Deutsch.
Kamien, M.I. and Schwartz, N.L. (1982). *Market Structure and Innovation*, Cambridge, MA, Cambridge University Press.
Malerba, F. (ed.) (2005). *Sectoral Systems of Innovation: Concepts, Issues and Analyses of Six Major Sectors in Europe*, Cambridge, Cambridge University Press.
Marks, G., Hooghe, L. and Blank, K. (1996). 'European integration since the 1980s: State-centric v. multi-level governance', *Journal of Common Market Studies* 34: 341–378.
May, R. (1997). 'The scientific wealth of nations', *Science* 275: 793–796.
NESTA (2006). *The Innovation Gap: Why Policy Needs to Reflect the Reality of Innovation in the UK*, London, NESTA.
NESTA (2007). *Hidden Innovation: How Innovation Happens in Six "Low Innovation" Sectors*, London, NESTA.
NESTA (2008). *Total Innovation: Why Harnessing the Hidden Innovation in High-Technology Sectors is Crucial to Retaining the UK's Innovation Edge*, London, NESTA.
Owen, G. (1999). *From Empire to Europe: The Decline and Revival of British Industry Since the Second World War*, London, HarperCollins.
Patel, P. and Pavitt, K. (1988). 'The international distribution and determinants of technological activities', *Oxford Review of Economic Policy* 4: 81–99.
Pavitt, K. (ed.) (1980). *Technical Innovation and British Economic Performance*, London, Palgrave Macmillan.
Pavitt, K., Robson, M. and Townsend, J. (1987). 'The size distribution of innovating firms in the UK, 1945–1983', *Journal of Industrial Economics* 35: 297–316.
Perez, C. (2002). *Technological Revolutions and Financial Capital: The Dynamics of Bubbles and Golden Ages*, Cheltenham, Edward Elgar.
Porter, M.E. (1985). *Competitive Advantage*, New York, Free Press.
Porter, M.E. (1990). *The Competitive Advantage of Nations*, New York, Free Press.
Porter, M.E. and Ketels, C.M. (2003). 'UK competitiveness: Moving to the next stage', *DTI Economics Paper No. 3*, May.
Rothwell, R., Freeman, C., Horsley, A., Jervis, V.T.P., Robertson, A.B. and Townsend, J. (1974). 'SAPPHO updated- Project Sappho phase II', *Research Policy* 3: 258–291.
Toffler, A. (1980). *The Third Wave*, New York, William Morrow.
UK Government (1988). *DTI — The Department for Enterprise*, White Paper (Cmnd 278), http://www.boperis.ac.uk/imgall/ref20518_1_1.html.
van Zwanenberg, P. and Millstone, E. (2005). *BSE: Risk, Science, and Governance*, Oxford, Oxford University Press.
Vincenti, W.G. (1990). *What Engineers Know and How They Know It*, Baltimore, Johns Hopkins University Press.
von Tunzelmann, N. (1999). 'Growth and the supply side in Europe since the Second World War', in Dyker, D.A. (ed.), *The European Economy*, 2nd edn, London, Longman, pp. 11–42.

von Tunzelmann, N. (2003). 'Technology in post-war Britain', in Floud, R. and Johnson, P. (eds.), *The Cambridge Economic History of Modern Britain, Volume III: Structural Change and Growth, 1939–2000*, Cambridge, Cambridge University Press, pp. 299–331.

von Tunzelmann, N. (2009). 'Technology and technology policy in the postwar UK: "Market failure" or "network failure"?', *Revue d'Economie Industrielle*, forthcoming.

Ziman, J. (1987). *Science in a 'Steady State': The Research System in Transition*, London, Science Policy Support Group.

CHAPTER 3

STILL DIVIDED BY TRANSFORMATION? CHARACTERISTIC FEATURES OF THE GERMAN INNOVATION SYSTEM AND THE BARRIERS TO EXTENDING IT TO EAST GERMANY

PETER FRANZ

1. Introduction

Since the economic shock caused by German unification and the breakdown of the firm structures characteristic of the socialist economies of the Soviet bloc, countless efforts have been made by political and economic actors to reconstitute a strong and self-supporting regional economy in East Germany. The economic recovery in the region since the 1990s indicates that it has, in some way, been integrated in the German economy, and indeed into the international division of labour. On the other hand, persistent deficits in productivity and innovation capability demonstrate that (at least some) economic shock effects have still not been overcome.

This chapter will concentrate on (1) describing the basic features of the German innovation system as a whole, and (2) discussing various factors preventing the establishment of an equally efficient regional innovation system in East Germany. For this purpose, after some preliminary remarks on methodology, we present in the third section a compact overview of the distinguishing features of the national German innovation system. The fourth section will deal with the development of new business structures in East Germany, the consequences thereof for the efficiency of the innovation system in the East, and the policy efforts implemented up to now to ameliorate the innovative performance of the East German economy. The fifth section turns to a discussion of diverse options for innovation policy a) in Germany as a whole, and b) for East Germany. The discussion here centres around the question of how the policy interventions aimed at improving the innovative performance of the East German economy might be re-oriented or rearranged for higher efficiency.

2. Preliminary Remarks on Methodology

Starting from the assumption that the advent of a knowledge-based society must be marked by the growing importance of high-tech innovations for the economies of such societies, we are still confronted with the problem of how to describe and analyse this trend towards innovation in an adequate way. The literature on innovation research and innovation economics currently offers a variety of approaches: national systems of innovation, sectoral systems of innovation (*cf.* Rothgang, 2008), regional systems of innovation, innovation within the framework of MNE activities and FDI, and so on. A decision to base the study on only one of these approaches might run the risk of missing important dimensions of the subject. Furthermore, the nature of innovation as an essentially dynamic object bids us beware of being too static in describing the features of innovation systems: an important aspect of any innovation system is its flexibility with regard to new evolving technologies. In the long run, the market success of an innovation from an earlier generation breeds path-dependency, and the risk of lock-ins in structures that have guaranteed prosperity in the past. From this particular standpoint on dynamics, it might perhaps be more appropriate to focus on sequences of new growth and decay in parts of innovation systems (Nero *et al.*, 2008), and to pay more attention to the life-cycle stages of industries. This chapter will accordingly refer to international, national and regional aspects in a systemic perspective, and will discuss sectoral aspects mainly through the case of the automotive industry. We will develop the dynamic aspect by looking at innovation activities at several points in time.

In the face of all this complexity, we have to be selective in our choice of dimensions and indicators. So the reader will learn but little about entrepreneurship, venture capital or the conditions of training highly qualified human capital in Germany in the pages that follow. The main form of empirical evidence used will be patent statistics, specifically the patent applications indicator. This indicator has been frequently criticised (*cf.* Schmoch, 1999; Franz, 2007, p. 346; Chapter 2 of this book), but is widely used in the absence of a better option.

3. Basic Features of the German Innovation System

The high proportion of German industrial output flowing into exports reflects a competitive German economy at the world level, and a deep degree of integration into the international division of labour. In spite of its continuous success in exporting, however, the German economy has, since the mid-1990s, suffered from weak economic growth, resulting in cumulative growth of just 20% between 1995 and 2007, whereas the aggregate economy of the EU-15 grew by 30% and that of the US by 45% in the same period (EFI, 2008, 64). These contradictory trends at the macro level conceal a recovery of economic growth in Germany since 2003, supported by a number of differentiated changes and processes starting in this period and still persisting up to 2008. Keeping track of and analysing these processes will help us to specify some basic features of the German innovation system and its weaknesses and strengths.

The first thing that we notice is that the value added stemming from research- and knowledge-intensive industries[1] increased from 40% to 46% of total value added in Germany between 1995 and 2005 (*ibid.*). In contrast to the pattern in many other Western countries, however, this trend was driven not by services but by industrial goods produced by automotive engineering, by the chemicals industry and by mechanical engineering. The German export surplus largely reflects consignments of vehicles, chemical products and machinery and equipment shipped to other countries. Products like these are technologically advanced, but they are not based on the cutting-edge technologies embodied in the products of the aerospace and space industries, in the computer, electronics and scientific instruments sectors, or in pharmaceuticals. In the industries applying cutting-edge technologies, the German trade balance is close to zero (BMBF, 2007; Schumacher, 2007).

Patent applications differentiated by technological field are a good indicator for showing the specialisation trends of German innovation activities (Table 3.1). The technological fields in Table 3.1 are ranked according to the number of patent applications in the year 2005.

The largest number of patent applications — 5,332 — come from the technological field 'Vehicles, Ships, Aircraft', this reflecting primarily the German strength in automotive engineering and production. In addition to that, the automotive industry is also responsible for the multitude of patent applications in the technological field 'Combustion Engines' (WIPO No. 22, Table 1). The automotive industry accounts for 33% of German manufacturing industry's total expenditures on innovation, which amounts to €27.5 bn in 2005 (Aschhoff *et al.*, 2007, 10). During the period 1995–2005 the German automotive industry increased its R&D staff by 50%, to 77,000 employees (Jürgens and Sablowski, 2008, 126). The growth in the number of patent applications in the Vehicles, Ships, Aircraft technological field — 99.6% between 1995 and 2005 (Table 3.1, last column) — can be interpreted as an output of these intensified innovation activities. Further effects include the size and share of sales of new products: in 2005 the automotive industry turned over €186 bn of sales of new products (28% of the total sales of new products in the whole economy), and these new products comprised 56% of the total sales of the automotive industry (Aschhoff *et al.*, 2007, 10).

As a result of imitating Japanese production models, the social organisation of R&D in the German automotive industry has changed. The high concentration of huge R&D departments at the headquarters of the (few) final producers has been restructured down the supplier chain in favour of R&D activities at the development centres of numerous suppliers. This restructuring should help to reduce final

---

[1] A detailed NACE Code list of the 2- and 3-digit industries subsumed under the category of 'knowledge and research and knowledge-intensive industries' is available in BMBF, 2007, pp. 168ff.

Table 3.1. German[a] patent applications differentiated by 31 technological fields, 1995, 2000 and 2005.

WIPO No.	Technological field (IPC)	Proportion in relation to all patent applications (%)[b]			Index (1995 = 100)				
		1995	2000	2005	1995	2000	2005	2000	2005
10	Vehicles, Ships, Aircraft	2671.8	4147.0	5332.2	9.0	10.3	11.9	155.2	199.6
30	Basic Electrical Elements and Technologies	2403.8	3637.9	4245.2	8.1	9.0	9.5	151.3	176.6
26	Measuring, Testing, Optics, Photography	2177.7	2894.5	3545.3	7.3	7.2	7.9	132.9	162.8
23	Machines and Engines in General	1689.3	2590.0	2852.6	5.7	6.4	6.4	153.3	168.9
22	Combustion Engines	1436.0	2062.1	2816.7	4.8	5.1	6.3	143.6	196.2
27	Horology, Controlling, Regulating, Computing	1004.1	1718.5	2487.0	3.4	4.3	5.6	171.1	247.7
31	Basic Electronic Circuitry, Electronic Communications Technology	1091.8	2009.5	2462.9	3.7	5.0	5.5	184.0	225.6
20	Building	1848.0	2288.9	2040.6	6.2	5.7	4.6	123.9	110.4
4	Health,[c] Leisure	1316.6	1826.9	1969.0	4.4	4.5	4.4	138.8	149.5
11	Hoisting, Lifting, Saddlery	1718.7	1823.5	1633.7	5.8	4.5	3.7	106.1	95.1
8	Mechanical Metal-Working, Punching	1180.9	1422.7	1463.2	4.0	3.5	3.3	120.5	123.9
7	Metal-Working, Lamination, Machine Tools	939.4	1265.7	1438.3	3.2	3.1	3.2	134.7	153.1
24	Lighting, Heating	1080.7	1336.2	1336.0	3.6	3.3	3.0	123.6	123.6
6	Separating, Sorting	1353.9	1474.9	1237.4	4.6	3.7	2.8	108.9	91.4
13	Organic Chemistry	1201.9	1256.8	1188.3	4.0	3.1	2.7	104.6	98.9
3	Personal and Domestic Articles	992.1	1252.6	1057.0	3.3	3.1	2.4	126.3	106.5
5	Medical and Veterinary Science	374.4	768.4	898.0	1.3	1.9	2.0	205.2	239.9
28	Education, Acoustics, Information Storage	400.3	628.9	794.5	1.3	1.6	1.8	157.1	198.5
14	Organic Macromolecular Compounds	777.4	841.5	779.7	2.6	2.1	1.7	108.3	100.3
15	Dyes, Petroleum Products, Oils, Fats	569.7	736.6	682.8	1.9	1.8	1.5	129.3	119.8
9	Printing	556.1	576.4	660.3	1.9	1.4	1.5	103.7	118.7
12	Inorganic Chemistry	667.5	661.1	590.1	2.2	1.6	1.3	99.0	88.4
18	Textiles, Flexible Materials	555.0	611.9	569.9	1.9	1.5	1.3	110.2	102.7
16	Biotechnology	200.1	471.6	558.7	0.7	1.2	1.3	235.7	279.3
17	Metallurgy	352.3	542.0	496.9	1.2	1.3	1.1	153.9	141.1
1	Agriculture	397.8	484.5	475.5	1.3	1.2	1.1	121.8	119.5
2	Foodstuffs, Tobacco	234.3	305.9	378.3	0.8	0.8	0.8	130.6	161.5
19	Paper	167.9	287.0	363.0	0.6	0.7	0.8	130.6	161.5

(Continued)

Table 3.1. (*Continued*)

WIPO No.	Technological field (IPC)	Proportion in relation to all patent applications (%)[b]			Index (1995 = 100)				
		1995	2000	2005	1995	2000	2005	2000	2005
25	Weapons, Blasting	160.0	238.4	179.6	0.5	0.6	0.4	149.0	112.3
21	Earth or Rock Drilling, Mining	127.8	116.8	86.4	0.4	0.3	0.2	91.4	67.6
29	Nuclear Physics and Engineering	42.3	95.8	71.2	0.1	0.2	0.2	226.3	168.1

[a] Applications by inventors located in Germany and submitted either to the German Patent and Trade Mark Office or the European Patent Office.
[b] The numbers contain decimal fractions because the shares of foreign applicants are factored out.
[c] Excluding medical or veterinary science (WIPO No. 5).
Source: DPMA, 2006; author's compilation.

Table 3.2. Patent applications[a] effective in Germany in selected fields of automotive technology, 2001–2007, from selected countries.

Country of origin	2001	2002	2003	2004	2005	2006	2007
Motor vehicle exhaust technology							
Total (all countries)	773	742	847	1117	1052	1139	1314
Germany	354	362	330	471	458	495	563
US	106	99	145	168	134	158	178
Japan	203	207	284	381	338	367	463
South Korea	6	8	6	3	10	6	5
France	32	29	24	39	58	71	60
Hybrid car technology							
Total (all countries)	385	372	376	414	429	474	562
Germany	75	73	104	95	92	131	219
US	29	76	53	40	94	101	110
Japan	258	205	200	248	223	213	203
South Korea	1	2	0	4	5	11	20
France	14	5	10	13	5	7	8

[a] Applications published by DPMA and EPO, avoiding double-counts, by applicant's place of residence. Applications filed by applicants having more than one seat are counted separately for each seat.
Source: DPMA, 2008; author's compilation.

producers' overheads, bottlenecks of specialists and 'time to market' lead-times for innovations (Jürgens and Sablowski, 2008, 126).

Table 3.2 compares the patent activities of the five nations with the largest automotive industries for the two cases of motor vehicle exhaust technology and hybrid car technology. The figures for motor vehicle exhaust technology illustrate the leading position of the German automotive industry, followed by Japan and the US.

The figures for hybrid car technology show that Japanese applicants have been at the forefront, but with German and US automotive firms increasingly active in this technology.

The total numbers of patent applications by German applicants increased from 29,690 in 1995 (index 100) to 44,690 in 2005 (index 150.5), which means an increment of 50% (last row in Table 3.3). With this number as a baseline, the dynamics of the patenting activities in the 31 technological fields listed in Table 3.1 can be assessed. The most dynamic field is biotechnology (increase of 279.3% as shown in the last column of Table 3.1), but still marked by relatively small total numbers. The seven highest-ranking technological fields in terms of number of patents also show an above-average growth rate, with 'Horology, Controlling, Regulating...' and 'Basic Electronic Circuitry' standing out. This pattern of growth concentrated upon the technological fields with the most intensive patent activities can also be interpreted as an indicator of the growing specialisation of the German system of innovation.

The innovation activities of the key export industry 'Manufacture of Machinery and Equipment' seem to be in line with the overall trend (technological fields 23, 26, 22 in Table 3.1). This does not hold true, however, for the chemicals industry. The three technological fields relevant for this industry (No. 13 — 'Organic Chemistry', No. 14 — 'Organic Macromolecular Compounds', No. 12 — 'Inorganic Chemistry' in Table 3.1) show a growth trend far below the average, and even signs of stagnation. At first sight this may suggest a weakness of innovation in the chemicals industry. At the same time it might reflect the depth of the international integration of this industry. Germany is the country with the second largest level of FDI in R&D worldwide (€12.6 bn in 2005), next to the United States (€25.5 bn) (EFI, 2008, 76). The chemicals industry is among the industries which have arrived at a high level of internationalisation. Foreign chemicals enterprises contribute 32% to R&D in this industry in Germany (*ibid.*), the highest proportion of all industries. This may mean that many patent applications are submitted at the headquarters of the MNE and not at the German R&D location. German chemicals and pharmaceutical firms in turn invested 40% of their FDI in R&D at locations in foreign countries, especially in North America and South-East Asia. Thus an assessment of the patent data has to consider the level of internationalisation of the industry in question, especially the extent of internationalisation of R&D activities.

Some additional figures may help to illustrate the general level of internationalisation in R&D activities. In 1995, 69% of German enterprises carrying out R&D also engaged in R&D at their foreign subsidiaries. Ten years later, this number had risen to 76% (EFI, 2008, 75). Over the same period, the proportion of firm-based R&D in Germany contributed by foreign firms rose from 15% to 26% (EFI, 2008, 76). The balance of German R&D activities abroad and of foreign R&D activities in Germany shows a surplus of €1.2 bn for the latter in 2005 (*ibid.*). The development of cross-border networks in R&D is predominantly a process involving Western

Europe and North America: 59% of the R&D investments from foreign subsidiaries in Germany come from European enterprises, and 38% from enterprises with a North American headquarters (EFI, 2008, 77).

4. The Evolution of the East German Innovation System

Within the Eastern Bloc, the East German planning economy had the image of an economy with outstanding innovative capabilities in various industries. In fact, in the last days of the GDR, many of the R&D departments of the huge socialist combines were for the most part busy with repairing the rotten machinery and equipment of their production plants. Only a few products manufactured in industries based on more advanced technologies (e.g. automobiles, computers, machinery) were able to compete with similar products developed in the Western economies. Against the background of this lack of technological competitiveness, the market position of East German firms deteriorated in the course of the unification process, in particular on account of monetary union and a wage policy oriented to the West German wage level. As a consequence, firm closures and insolvencies on a mass scale dissolved the East German business structure and brought its R&D activities to an end.

The first contours of a new (innovation-oriented) business structure replacing the old one became visible in the early 1990s (1) in the form of management buy-outs, where managers of the former combines tried to relaunch the most competitive parts of their former plants; (2) through start-ups created by scientists forced to leave their jobs at universities and at research institutes; and (3) through the direct investment activities of West German, West European and American MNEs. This FDI included acquiring and modernising existing production plants (e.g. the Leuna refinery by Total, the Buna chemical plant by Dow Chemical) as well as building completely new subsidiaries at greenfield locations (e.g. GM/Opel in Eisenach, BMW and Porsche in Leipzig).

The conditions of the subsidy programmes running at this time heavily favoured investment in capital goods. This had the effect that the modernised plants could be run with only a fraction of the workforce that had been employed in the former GDR. Besides these changes, the Federal government subsidised the redeployment of some remnants of the former large R&D departments of the combines as industrial research agencies (*Forschungs-GmbHs*). These agencies had the function of conducting industrial research for firms not disposing of sufficient own R&D capacities.

This newly evolving pattern of businesses proved to be a decisive cause of the lasting weakness of the East German innovation system. Many start-up firms were too small to pursue R&D activities on their own. The simultaneous emergence of a multitude of new firms created a business environment where trust as a precondition for networking, R&D cooperation and joint ventures proved to be in short supply.[2] The MNEs investing in East Germany relied on their R&D departments, usually located at or near their headquarters, and managed their East German subsidiaries as workbenches without or with only limited autonomy. Within the diverse value chains a large number of East German firms took up subordinate positions as suppliers for final producers. With regard to the automotive industry, the primary task for these supplier firms was to meet the manufacturing standards (e.g. narrow tolerances for the size of manufactured parts, organisation of production processes according to the requirements of just-in-time logistics) put forward by the large MNEs like Volkswagen, Daimler or BMW. This wide-ranging integration into the supplier chain of the MNEs conspired to lower East German export rates far below the German average. Another effect was the lasting low level of innovation activities which can be inferred from Table 3.3. (Note that the indicator presented in Table 3.3, the number of patent applications, may have a bias, because the 'headquarters advantage' mentioned above affects the patent statistics in that many large firms tend to submit their patent applications from their main location even if the innovation concerned originates at the location of a subsidiary.) Table 3.3 confronts the numbers, proportions and densities of patent applications in the ten West German *Länder* ('Old *Länder*', including Hamburg and Bremen as city states) with those in the five 'New *Länder*' (former territory of the GDR) and in Berlin (also a city state). The case of Berlin, having now regained the status as German capital, is a special one, because before 1990 the western half of its territory (West Berlin) belonged to West Germany and the eastern half (East Berlin) to that of the GDR. Thus its economy represents a mix of market economy and transformation economy.

The figures in Table 3.3 show that the percentage of patent applications submitted from East German locations stagnates at around 9% in the period under review. This proportion is far below the proportion of the East German employable population in the total German employable population — 17.5%. A closer inspection of the density columns reveals a wide range — between 18.0 and 112.2 (year 2005) — for the West German *Länder*, and values between 11.5 and 32.4 for the East German *Länder*. This means that some East German *Länder*, especially Saxony and Thuringia, have succeeded in catching up with the less inventive 'Old *Länder*'. In 1995 the bulk of patenting activity in East Germany was centered in Berlin. Ten years later, the largest number of patent applications came from Saxony, with Thuringia more than doubling its patent applications. These trends indicate a spatial concentration of innovative activities in the southern part of East Germany (Dohse, 2004; Franz, 2007), going hand-in-hand with a growth rate of regional Gross Regional Product (GRP) above, and an unemployment rate below, the East German average.

---

[2] A recent study about cluster effects in East Germany demonstrates that the knowledge spillovers to be expected beyond a certain threshold of regional concentration of a given industry still cannot be found in East German cluster locations (Hornych and Schwartz, 2008).

Table 3.3. German patent applications and patent density by *Länder* and region, 1995, 2000 and 2005.

Federal state	1995			2000			2005		
	Total	In %	Dens.[b]	Total	In %	Dens.[b]	Total	In %	Dens.[b]
Baden-Wuerttemberg	6957	23.4	67.6	9583	23.7	92.0	11963	26.8	112.2
Bavaria	6382	21.5	53.4	9361	23.2	77.5	10936	24.5	88.3
North-Rhine/Westphalia	6418	21.6	35.9	7965	19.7	44.3	7546	16.9	41.7
Hesse	2822	9.5	47.1	3295	8.2	54.6	3279	7.3	53.8
Rhineland-Palatinate	1434	4.8	36.2	1816	4.5	45.2	1848	4.1	45.5
Saarland	216	0.7	19.9	294	0.7	27.3	268	0.6	25.2
Lower Saxony	1799	6.1	23.2	2998	7.4	38.2	3257	7.3	40.8
Bremen	112	0.4	16.5	96	0.2	14.4	119	0.3	18.0
Hamburg	429	1.4	25.1	491	1.2	28.8	692	1.5	40.0
Schleswig-Holstein	537	1.8	19.8	789	2.0	28.6	811	1.8	28.8
West Germany	27106	91.3		36686	90.9		40719	91.1	
Berlin	960	3.2	27.6	1179	2.9	34.5	1100	2.5	32.4
Brandenburg	202	0.7	8.0	410	1.0	15.9	435	1.0	16.8
Mecklenburg-Western Pomerania	97	0.3	5.3	189	0.5	10.5	201	0.4	11.5
Saxony	763	2.6	16.7	1024	2.5	22.7	1247	2.8	28.7
Saxony-Anhalt	239	0.8	8.7	358	0.9	13.3	311	0.7	12.2
Thuringia	325	1.1	12.9	528	1.3	21.4	677	1.5	28.3
East Germany	2584	8.7		3688	9.1		3971	8.9	
Germany	29690	100.0	36.4	40374	100.0	49.2	44690	100.0	54.1

[a] Applications by inventors located in Germany and submitted either to the German Patent and Trade Mark Office or to the European Patent Office.
[b] Patent applications per 100,000 residents.
Source: DPMA, 2006; author's compilation.

Nevertheless these two forerunners are still far behind the top inventive *Länder* like Baden-Wuerttemberg and Bavaria (*cf.* Eickelpasch, 2008).

A further East-West difference, not shown in Table 3.3, is revealed when we look at different categories of applicants, e.g. private firms, scientific institutions and private individuals. In Baden-Wuerttemberg and other more inventive *Länder*, 85–89% of the applications stem from private firms, while in the East German *Länder* this percentage comes up to at most 70% (DPMA, 2006, 28). The proportion of patent applications submitted by universities and research institutes varies in the New *Länder* between 10 and 16%, but is significantly lower in the West German *Länder*: In Bavaria it comes to just 2.3% and in Baden-Wuerttemberg to 2.5% (*ibid.*).[3] These relationships signal

---

[3] Until 2002 inventors employed at German universities were entitled to retain and exploit the IPRs relating to their inventions. After the abolition of this 'professor's privilege', one would have expected a decreasing proportion of patent applications by private individuals in favour of applications by scientific institutions (*cf.* Fritsch and Slavtchev, 2006, 3). In fact, a comparison of these proportions for the years 2000 and 2005 shows a clear-cut reduction for patent applications submitted by individuals (from 21% to 13%), but at the same time a small reduction for patent applications submitted by scientific institutions (from 4% to 3.5%). By contrast, private firms and entrepreneurs increased their share from 75% to 83.5% over the same period (DPMA, 2006, 28).

relatively good performance on the part of the East German universities and research institutes.

The indicators in Table 3.4 were selected with a view to allowing a concise overview of the East-West differences in the publicly financed science and research institutions within the framework of the innovation system. The 100 universities located in East Germany amount to 25.6% of all German universities, and the 95 public research institutes to 36.8% of all German research institutes. The two cities with the largest number of scientific institutions are Berlin and Dresden (capital of Saxony), ahead of Munich, Hamburg and Stuttgart, and with Leipzig (Saxony) and Potsdam (Brandenburg) ranking sixth and seventh (Franz, 2008, 105). Among these cities of East Germany, Dresden stands out as the location of ten research institutes of the Fraunhofer Society that are well known for applied industrial research in new technologies. From the two first indicators presented in Table 3.4, the conclusion can be drawn that East German SMEs have a good chance of finding a university and/or research institute in their proximate environment, an important opportunity for R&D cooperation and knowledge spillovers (Lejpras and Stephan, 2008; Fritsch and Slavtchev, 2006).

A look at the third column of Table 3.4 shows marked *Länder* differences in R&D expenditures on public science institutions. The level of expenditure in the three city states, Bremen, Hamburg and Berlin, lies far above those of the other *Länder*. With the exception of Thuringia and Saxony-Anhalt, the level of public R&D expenditures in the New *Länder* is above the German average in 2006 of €99 per head. This relatively high overall level of expenditure partially reflects expenditure on universities, as presented (relative to regional GDP) in the fourth column of Table 3.4. But the patterns of the two indicators are not identical. Comparison reveals that Brandenburg spends little money on its universities, but quite a lot on its research institutes, concentrated mainly in and around Potsdam. However, the level of expenditure on universities for three new *Länder*, Saxony, Mecklenburg-Western Pomerania and Thuringia, exceeds the average value for Germany as a whole of 0.41% of GDP.

The two remaining indicators of Table 3.4, in the fifth and sixth columns, reflect the quality dimension of universities. The number of doctorates per professor tells us about the universities' performance and efficiency in training young academics; the amount of research money raised by professors is a proxy for the quality of research at the universities. Both indicators show a factor of variability of more than 50%. The East-West comparison shows that the universities of the new *Länder* rank below the German average on both indicators. The exception is Berlin, which has outstanding figures. So it is no surprise that Berlin's three large universities were the only East German winners in the 'Initiative for Excellence', an inter-university competition for additional grants from the federal government (*cf.* Franz, forthcoming). Altogether, the indicators in Table 3.4 suggest that East Germany has an endowment with public science institutions a bit above the average, but, with the exception of Berlin, still burdened with some quality problems.

Table 3.4. Selected indicators for the public-sector science and research system at the *Länder* and regional levels.

Land	Universities[a] (2007) Number	Public research institutes[b] (2007) Number	R&D expenditures of universities and research institutes per head (2006) €	Public expenditure on universities as proportion of regional GDP (2006) %	Doctorates per university professor (2006) Number	Research grants per university professor (2005) €
Baden-Wuerttemberg	68	35	127.8	0.41	1.01	232,700
Bavaria	49	25	83.2	0.34	0.95	174,600
North-Rhine/Westphalia	59	39	75.8	0.41	0.90	164,300
Hesse	28	13	57.8	0.36	0.86	149,400
Rhineland-Palatinate	20	8	40.8	0.35	0.71	124,500
Saarland	6	5	79.3	0.37	0.71	151,800
Lower Saxony	26	15	81.1	0.42	0.89	155,700
Bremen	7	7	270.0	0.58	0.62	186,000
Hamburg	15	7	179.2	0.37	0.79	125,200
Schleswig-Holstein	13	9	76.1	0.47	0.84	142,500
West Germany	291	163				160,700
Berlin	29	26	261.8	0.87	0.91	209,300
Brandenburg	13	16	131.6	0.27	0.70	108,500
Mecklenburg-Western Pomerania	9	7	107.3	0.55	0.66	91,600
Saxony	27	28	133.5	0.54	0.59	161,400
Saxony-Anhalt	10	11	86.6	0.35	0.55	116,900
Thuringia	12	7	75.8	0.47	0.50	107,600
East Germany	100	95	99.0		0.80	132,600
Germany	391	258		0.41		165,500

[a] Including universities of applied sciences (*fachhochschulen*), universities of fine arts, schools of administration and seminaries.
[b] Research institutes of the Max Planck Society, Fraunhofer Society, Leibniz Association and Helmholtz Association.
Sources: Federal Statistical Office; www.wgl.de; www.mpg.de; www.fhg.de; www.helmholtz.de; author's compilation and calculations.

The obvious weakness of innovation activities in the East German private sector (*cf.* also Fritsch and Slavtchev, 2008) prompted the federal government, and also the governments of the new *Länder*, to launch a multitude of programmes subsidising R&D and networking activities on the part of private firms, universities and regional officials. The coalition government of Social Democrats (SPD) and the Green Party (Die Grünen/Bündnis 90), which held office 1998–2005, launched in 1999 an 'Initiative for Innovation — The Region as Enterprise' (*Innovationsinitiative — Unternehmen Region*) comprising the following four programmes:

— *InnoRegio* (competition for regional initiatives delivering concepts for networking between private firms, universities, regional and/or local administrations, and institutions of secondary/vocational learning; the 23 winning initiatives were funded 1999–2006 to the sum of €250 m);
— *Innovative regional growth nuclei* ('Innovative regionale Wachstumskerne') (competition for regional initiatives in the form of business plans with a high chance of market success; thirteen winning initiatives have been awarded €1.5 m each since 2001);
— *Centres for competence in innovation* ('Zentren für Innovationskompetenz') (competition for centres of excellence at East German universities and research institutes engaged in knowledge transfer; twelve initiatives have been funded for a period of one year, including professional coaching; six of them have been selected for grants to the amount of €50 m in the period to 2009);
— *Interregional alliances for the markets of tomorrow* ('Interregionale Allianzen für die Märkte von morgen') (funding of market-oriented expert forums/specialist conferences with international participants aimed at developing knowledge transfer and contacts; €1 m yearly) (Bundesregierung, 2004, 43–47).

The coalition government of Christian Democrats (CDU/CSU) and Social Democrats (SPD), in office from late 2005 to 2009, initiated further programmes:

— *INNO-WATT* (funding of R&D joint ventures between SMEs; grants for 1,820 R&D projects so far);
— *Preliminary industrial research* ('Industrielle Vorlaufforschung') (R&D funding for East German external industrial research agencies);
— *Management of innovation* ('Innovationsmanagement') (funding for preparing and implementing process and product innovations in SMEs);
— *PRO INNO II* (funding for national and international R&D cooperation between SMEs, universities and research institutes);
— *Network management East* (NEMO) (subsidies for networking initiatives of SMEs — hiring professional technological and expertise in technology and business administration) (BMVBS, 2008, 58–60).

These funding programmes at the federal level were, and still are, supplemented by a variety of programmes at the *Länder* level. If we take the additional R&D programmes open for all German firms on top of it, the sheer number of programmes introduces a high risk of ending up with a 'jungle of subsidy programmes' (*Förderdschungel*). We return to the question of adequate policy strategies in the face of East German weakness in innovative activities at the end of the chapter.

5. Conclusions and Policy Options

As we arrive at the end of our analytical tour across the diverse features of the German innovation system by means of numbers, examples and (programme) titles, we face a crucial question concerning the sustainability of the innovation patterns described — the question of future trends. Is the existing automotive industry at a late stage of its product-cycle? Does it have enough inventive power and expertise to start new product-cycles? To what extent can new technologies, e.g. photovoltaics, contribute to a realignment of the innovation system? Do the East German *Länder* provide better preconditions for the rise of new technologies than the West German *Länder*, stamped as they are by the impress of established technologies? Answers to questions like these would indeed be helpful in formulating strategies in innovation policy on the national and the regional level. The fact is, however, that these questions require power of prognostication that exceed the capabilities of science. So the following concluding reflections on policy options in German innovation policy will be restricted to a rather short-run (present-day) and factually-oriented perspective. In all of this, the possibility of fundamental changes taking place along the lines of the questions listed above should not be forgotten.

Reports monitoring and analysing the German innovation system and predominant German innovation patterns (e.g. BMBF, 2007; EFI, 2008) frequently criticise the heavy orientation of that system to advanced technologies (e.g. automobiles, chemicals) at the expense of cutting-edge technologies (e.g. aerospace, space, computers, electronics and pharmaceuticals) and knowledge-based services. The benchmark for this critique comes from the comparison with other advanced economies like the US, where biotechnology (as an example of a cutting-edge technology) and a densely interwoven complex of computer software, IT services and financial services industries account for a much more pronounced share of patents and innovative products (*cf.* Fuentes *et al.*, 2004, 10ff.). In many cases, the analysts' penchant for laying stress on the weak points of the German innovation system leads to recommendations to intensify R&D in field where Germany has 'fallen behind', and to realign at least public research to these neglected technological fields. In many cases, recommendations like these go hand-in-hand with a skeptical view of the sustainability of the present economic success of the industries making automobiles, machinery, chemicals and electrical equipment. Critics refer to the high level of

German wages, and doubt Germany's competitiveness in face of the cheap labour from many catch-up economies. The mixed experience of a number of German manufacturing firms which have transferred or outsourced part of their production to such countries (offshoring) shows, however, that labour costs are not the sole factor that decides the success or failure of such ventures. Some firms have started to repatriate their offshoring activities, citing unreliability of the workforce, lack of technical expertise, and misjudgment on the part of management of cultural and mental differences, as reasons for reversing their decision (Kinkel *et al.*, 2007). A survey of German manufacturing firms with experience of offshoring and repatriating areas of their activities finds that within a period of four to five years, 15–25% of offshoring decisions will be revised in favour of repatriation (Kinkel and Maloca, 2008, 5).

The alternative option, namely focusing the policy recommendations on the admitted strengths of the innovation system in question, may seem less attractive.[4] But many of the assets of the German innovation system are in the field of automotive engineering and production. For the automotive industry, the German home car market takes on the function of a lead market, where the demand for and acceptance of innovations and of technically demanding automotive concepts can be tested. Within the framework conditions of such a lead market, state regulations on passenger security and environmental standards perform a fundamental stimulus function for the innovation activities of the automotive industry (Jürgens and Sablowski, 2008, 136). Designing such regulations and aligning the automobile industry to forward-looking standards is surely a more adequate innovation policy than subsidising specific R&D projects within technological fields where Germany does not show signs of specialisation.

A strategy like this is surely appropriate for an industry and a region that have already arrived at technological leadership, and dispose of powerful private R&D departments in the vicinity of firm headquarters. It does not seem to be appropriate in the case of East Germany. Configuring special programmes for the new *Länder* was justified in the early phase of transformation in order to diminish the specific handicaps for newly emerging small firms. Evaluations of some of these programmes, especially the InnoRegio programme, show that they have had moderate positive effects on regional economic growth (Eickelpasch and Fritsch, 2005; Emmrich and Brenner, 2008; Kauffeld-Monz and Fritsch, 2008). But now, with a stock of diverse subsidy programmes piling up from year to year, there is an increasing risk that a threshold will be passed after which more of the same (programmes) will not lead to more output (innovation), but to stagnation, as a result of unintended side effects. These include rising information costs for firms facing an non-transparent range of programmes (box of instruments), rising programme administration costs for the

---

[4] Some readers might have a strong suspicion that this tendency to emphasise the weak points and defects of the system under investigation, even when it is generally rated as successful, could be a typical German problem-solving trait.

government,[5] durable insider advantages for firms having successfully applied for funding (Fuentes et al., 2004, 28f.) and getting into the habit of subsidisation in a creeping way.

The incidence of these side effects would diminish if the federal government decided to shift its R&D support strategy away from specific subsidy programmes towards tax reliefs for firm R&D activities (cf. Fuentes et al., 2004, p. 27; BMBF, 2007; Franz, 2007, p. 349). Such a strategy would have been ineffectual for East German firms in the early phase of transformation, since many of them were taxed only moderately, if at all, because they made so little profit. A shift to tax reliefs for R&D by firms would reduce bureaucracy and free up a lot of resources currently absorbed by the process of submitting applications, especially in SMEs. It would also ease the pressure on officials to assess new technologies for support and to establish new programmes for them. In the past, there was substantial justification for a regionally differentiated innovation policy. This kind of policy will continue because the *Länder* will continue to have their own strategies in innovation policy. But at the federal level, the time has come for a policy shift.

This policy conclusion also contains an implicit answer to the question formulated in the title of this chapter: Is the German innovation system still divided by transformation effects? When we draw a map showing the German regions and insert indicators for the output of the regional innovation systems, we can still discern the old borderline separating East and West. There are some signs that at least in Saxony and Thuringia firms have found ways to continue the pre-war tradition of manufacturing sophisticated products requiring high expertise in engineering. Furthermore, many East German firms have been integrated into the supplier chains of MNEs, and now contribute to diverse production lines making competitive products. In public science the differences between East and West are very small, but the potential for innovation contained in universities and research institutes is still heavily underused by the East German private sector. Increasing absorptive capacities of the private sector and growing interest on the part of the science institutions in regional economic development may help to accelerate change in this pattern.

References

Aschhoff, B., Doherr, T., Löhlein, H., Peters, B., Rammer, C., Schmidt, T., Schubert, T. and Schwiebacher, F. (2007). *Innovationsverhalten der Deutschen Wirtschaft. Indikatorenbericht zur Innovationserhebung 2006*, Mannheim, ZEW.

Bundesministerium für Bildung und Forschung (BMBF) (ed.) (2007). *Bericht zur Technologischen Leistungsfähigkeit Deutschlands 2007*, Bonn/Berlin.

---

[5] The ministries responsible for the programmes usually outsource the handling of R&D-related subsidy programmes to special firms (*Projektträger* — project carriers) with expertise in different technologies and in process control.

Bundesministerium für Verkehr, Bau und Stadtentwicklung (BMVBS) (2008). *Jahresbericht der Bundesregierung zum Stand der Deutschen Einheit 2008. Die Neuen Länder — für ein Modernes und Soziales Deutschland*, Berlin.

Bundesregierung (2004). *Jahresbericht der Bundesregierung zum Stand der Deutschen Einheit*, Berlin.

Deutsches Patent- und Markenamt (DPMA) (ed.) (2006). *Patentatlas Deutschland. Regionaldaten der Erfindungstätigkeit*, München.

Deutsches Patent- und Markenamt (DPMA) (ed.) (2008). *Annual Report 2007*, München.

Dohse, D. (2004). *Regionale Verteilung Innovativer Aktivitäten in Ostdeutschland*, Kiel Discussion Papers, No. 411, University of Kiel.

Eickelpasch, A. (2008). 'Das industrielle Innovationspotential der Regionen: Stuttgart und München weiter vorn', *DIW-Wochenbericht* 75(39): 576–585.

Eickelpasch, A. and Fritsch, M. (2005). 'Contests for cooperation — A new approach in German innovation policy', DIW Berlin Discussion Papers No. 478.

Emmrich, C. and Brenner, T. (2008). 'An evaluation of the InnoRegio program in Germany on the basis of regional employment data', paper presented at the DIME WP 2.3 Workshop *Local and Sectoral Systems of Innovation — Policy Measures and Possibilities* in Marburg, Germany, 19–21 November.

Expertenkommission Forschung und Innovation (EFI) (ed.) (2008). *Gutachten zu Forschung, Innovation und Technologischer Leistungsfähigkeit* 2008, Berlin.

Franz, P. (2007). 'Räumliche Verteilung ostdeutscher innovativer Kompetenzen: deutlicher Zuwachs im südwestlichen Umland von Berlin und in den Zentren Sachsens und Thüringens', IWH, *Wirtschaft im Wandel* 12(9): 344–349.

Franz, P. (2008). 'From university town to knowledge city: Strategies and regulatory hurdles in Germany', in Yigitcanlar, T., Velibeyoglu, K. and Baum, S. (eds), *Knowledge-Based Urban Development. Planning and Applications in the Information Era*, Hershey, PA, IGI Global, pp. 101–115.

Franz, P. (forthcoming). 'Knowledge City Berlin? Potenziale und Risiken einer Stadtentwicklungsstrategie mit dem Fokus Wissenschaft', in Matthiesen, U. (ed.), *Das Wissen der Städte — Zur Koevolution von Raum, Wissen und Milieus sowie von Governanceformen in stadtregionalen Entwicklungsdynamiken Heute*, Wiesbaden, VS Verlag.

Fritsch, M. and Slavtchev, V. (2006). 'Universities and innovation in space', *Freiberg Working Papers* No. 15, University of Freiberg.

Fritsch, M. and Slavtchev, V. (2008). 'How does industry specialization affect the efficiency of regional innovation systems?', *Jena Economic Research Papers* No. 2008-58, University of Jena.

Fuentes, A., Wurzel, E. and Morgan, M. (2004). 'Improving the capacity to innovate in Germany', *Economics Department Working Paper* No. 407, Paris, OECD.

Hornych, C. and Schwartz, M. (2008). 'Räumliche Branchenschwerpunkte als Innovationsmotoren? Empirische Befunde aus Ostdeutschland', *Wirtschaft im Wandel* 14(9): 355–362.

Jürgens, U. and Sablowski, T. (2008). *Sektorale Innovationsprozesse und die Diskussion über Deutsche Innovationsschwächen*, Düsseldorf, Hans-Böckler-Stiftung 204.

Kauffeld-Monz, M. and Fritsch, M. (2008). 'Who are the brokers of knowledge in regional systems of innovation? A multi-actor network analysis', *Jena Economic Research Paper* No. 2008-089, University of Jena.

Kinkel, S., Lay, G. and Maloca, S. (2007). 'Development, motives and employment effects of manufacturing offshoring of German SMEs', *International Journal of Entrepreneurship and Small Business* 4: 256–276.

Kinkel, S. and Maloca, S. (2008). 'Produktionsverlagerungen rückläufig. Ausmaß und Motive von Produktionsverlagerungen und Rückverlagerungen im deutschen Verarbeitenden Gewerbe', Karlsruhe, Mitteilungen aus der ISI-Erhebung zur Modernisierung der Produktion, No. 45.

Lejpras, A. and Stephan, A. (2008). 'Locational conditions, cooperation, and innovativeness: evidence from research and company spin-offs', DIW Berlin Discussion Papers No. 804.

Negro, S.O., Hekkert, M.P. and Smits, R.E. (2008). 'Stimulating renewable energy technologies by innovation policy', *Innovation Studies Utrecht Working Paper Series* No. 08.13, University of Utrecht.

Rothgang, M. (2008). 'Sectoral innovation systems, corporate strategies, and competitiveness of the German economy in a globalised world', *Ruhr Economic Papers* No. 59, Essen, Rheinisch-Westfälisches Institut für Wirtschaftsforschung.

Schmoch, U. (1999). 'Impact of international patent applications on patent indicators', *Research Evaluation* 8: 119–131.

Schumacher, D. (2007). 'Wirtschaftsstrukturen und Außenhandel mit forschungsintensiven Waren im internationalen Vergleich', *Studien zum deutschen Innovationssystem* No. 16-2007, Berlin, BMBF.

CHAPTER 4

THE GOVERNANCE AND MANAGEMENT OF TECHNICAL CHANGE IN TRANSITION COUNTRIES

DAVID A. DYKER

1. Introduction

In no area of the production function is the standard paradigm of the market economy less applicable in the advanced economies than in that of R&D and innovation. Whereas conventional economic theory prescribes a clear-cut distinction between private and public sectors based on considerations of monopoly and competition, external economies and diseconomies, appropriable and non-appropriable goods and services etc., the reality of R&D sectors in the advanced economies is a sometimes bewildering mixture of public and private endeavour, not to mention the key role played by autonomous institutions — universities, research institutes etc. with mixed systems of funding. Competition is an important factor within the R&D sector, especially in relation to start-up companies and to government funding of non-core projects, but there are also strong elements of institutionalised monopoly, e.g. through patent systems. There is a strong and ancient tradition of collegiality and cooperation, especially among university researchers, but many R&D workers work within hierarchical systems — in both public and private sectors. R&D is in many respects deeply globalised. Most notably, recent decades have seen the emergence of *global innovation networks*, operating in ways similar to the global supply networks which have developed around key manufacturing sectors, notably the automotive and consumer electronics sectors.[1] Yet, 'in general, despite the large amounts of FDI in terms of capital values, TNCs still tend to largely concentrate their more strategic and core activities close to home. In other words, they remain more deeply embedded in their home country than elsewhere' (Narula, 2005, 47).

---

[1] Dieter Ernst (2005, 73) notes, in relation to the electronics sector, that 'the growing organizational and geographical mobility of innovation creates new challenges, but also provides new opportunities for innovation management. The challenge is that no firm, not even a global market leader like IBM, can mobilize all the diverse resources, capabilities and bodies of knowledge internally. Instead, both the sources and the use of knowledge become increasingly externalized. Now, firms must supplement the in-house creation of new knowledge and capabilities with external knowledge sourcing strategies. There are strong pressures to reduce in-house basic and applied research, and to focus primarily on product development and the absorption of external knowledge.'

Here, then, is a sector where socialism would surely show its strengths — where market disciplines were 'naturally' mixed with a more cooperative paradigm, but where at the same time the hierarchical principle was powerful and pervasive. Kenneth Arrow, hardly a champion of socialism, thought just that (Arrow, 1962). He was wrong. Socialism, certainly of its Soviet centrally-planned and Yugoslav/Hungarian market-socialist types, was actually *worse* at innovation and R&D activity than it was at ordinary, everyday production (it was not so good at that either) (Dyker, 1983; Radošević, 1999). This introduces the intriguing possibility that it was not the lack of market incentives that was the main failing of socialism (after all, the Hungarians and Yugoslavs did have a market), but rather the lack of some more general dimension of human endeavour. I do not intend to pursue that line of enquiry at this point, but rather simply to repeat and underline what is generally accepted — that by the end of the socialist era the countries concerned were spending on R&D proportions of their GDP comparable with those reported by the advanced countries, and apparently receiving nothing in return in terms of economic growth or any other indicator of human welfare. To the extent therefore that the socialist countries had National Innovation Systems, they were totally dysfunctional.

The next paradox appears when we start to look at the efforts on the part of the governments of these countries to make their R&D systems more effective — efforts which began in the late 1980s, some years before the end of socialism and the beginning of transition as such. From the start, the stress was on introduction of market forces, financial autonomy for research-active companies and R&D institutes, development of 'Academy-industry links', with, it seemed, little regard for the complexities and ambivalences of R&D governance structures as observed in the advanced countries. And yet (to risk a big generalisation), some 19 years after the start of transition, R&D sectors, and R&D activity in general, remain the least reformed of all the main sectors of the transition economies. But this is to run ahead of the argument. In the next section we describe the structure of R&D and technological governance in the transition countries right now, before looking critically at the pattern of development in key areas.

2. The Institutional Structure of R&D in the Transition Countries Today

In his path-breaking work on the concept of National Innovation System, Lundvall originally distinguished between narrow and broad definitions of an innovation system. The narrow definition covers only 'organisations and institutions involved in searching and exploring — such as R&D departments, technological institutes and universities'. The broad definition covers 'parts and aspects of the economic structure and the institutional set-up affecting learning as well as searching and adapting' (Lundvall, 1992, 12). In this book, we focus ultimately on the NIS in its broadest interpretation. At this stage, however, it is useful to focus more narrowly on 'organisations and institutions'. On that basis we can pick out the main actors within the NISs of the transition countries today as:

- Foreign companies with production facilities in the transition countries
- R&D-active domestic companies
- State-owned and financed research institutes (often operating under the aegis of national Academies of Sciences) and universities
- Privately-owned research institutes

We look at these in turn:

2.1. *Foreign companies*

The role of foreign companies in knowledge transfer in the transition countries can hardly be exaggerated. There are countries like Russia, where the activities of foreign companies are circumscribed by restrictive legislation. There are countries like Ukraine, Mongolia and Kyrgyzstan where foreign investors have, to date, perceived few opportunities for profitable operations. And there are countries like Turkmenistan and Uzbekistan where local political conditions have acted as a powerful disincentive to investment. But by and large, and even to some extent in Russia, it is FDI that has driven the process of productivity enhancement which has underpinned the dynamic of economic recovery in the transition region. The reasons are not hard to see:

> During the earlier socialist periods, many of these countries built up strong science bases and quite well trained industrial labour forces. That this had not led to competitive industries, based around local technology and creative capacities, reflected a lack of entrepreneurial risk taking in the absence of market forces… Here TNC R&D and innovation could provide a short cut through some stages of industrialization-oriented development (Pearce, 2005, 40).

Multinationals have typically gone into transition countries with large-scale investments, sometimes greenfield, sometimes on the basis of existing plants, establishing state-of-the-art production lines and aiming to raise local productivity to home country levels within three-to-five years (Dyker *et al.*, 2006). Here, technological governance at plant level is simply an extension of the technological governance system of the given multinational. *Operational and strategic technology and innovation decisions* are made at headquarters, key personnel (including production-line personnel) are trained by in-house training departments and teams, which may bring the workers to headquarters or themselves go the workers in the subsidiary plants in the host countries. Technology management in these cases is extremely tight, and the general aim is to produce subsidiaries which are essentially look-alikes to the main plant back home. While one or two multinationals have established main R&D laboratories in transition countries, the general pattern is for the seminal R&D work to be kept at headquarters. This pattern of technology and knowledge articulation and dissemination by multinationals in the transition region is exemplified by the case of Hungary, a country with a proportion of high-tech exports within total exports higher than the EU-15 average, but largely on the basis of multinational investment, with the know-how coming for the most part from the laboratories of the parent company in the home country.[2] That does not mean that there is no MNC R&D in Hungary. The list of multinationals that have set up main laboratories in Hungary includes General Electric,[3] Sanofi, Astra, Ericsson, IBM, Compaq, Nokia, Siemens, Motorola, Audi, Volkswagen, Michelin, Knorr-Bremse, Mannesmann, Novartis and Unilever (Inzelt, 2006, 5), and foreign companies account for half of total business R&D in Hungary (UNCTAD secretariat, 2005, 6). Nor is this simply low-level 'back-office' R&D. As many as 84.3% of Hungarian R&D workers work in high-tech sectors — the highest figure in the EU.[4] But the very fact that many of these exceptional facilities are 'internationally interdependent laboratories', tightly integrated into the global R&D networks of the given MNCs, means that they tend to reinforce the 'hub-and-spoke' pattern of technological governance. And their relationship with the general level of technology and productivity in the host economy may be as tenuous as that of laboratories in the MNC's home country.

> Internationally interdependent laboratories certainly have the potential to reinforce a country's developing strength at the phase of basic research and pure science. They can do this both by providing extra funding and by adding further dimensions to the research by positioning it in the wider technological perspectives of the TNC. However, there is no mechanism by which internationally interdependent laboratories necessarily strengthen the competitive scope of the host economy (Pearce, 2005, 38–39).

This tight technology management at the in-firm level is not matched at the supply network level. European and Japanese automotive and electronics firms are generally prepared for a fairly high degree of involvement in the governance of the hierarchies of supply networks that provide them with their components, at least within their home country.[5] As we saw earlier, this pattern has in recent years been

---

[2] Statement by P. Mogyorosi of Laser Consult at conference 'Research Centres for Knowledge-Based Economy', Warsaw, 26 January 2005.
[3] General Electric employs around 1,600 R&D workers at its home base in the US and a further c.400 in its two overseas research facilities. See Narula, 2005, 47.
[4] ITD Hungarian Investment and Trade Development Agency 2008, http://www.interaccessusa.com/14.html.
[5] NB US firms are generally less prepared to do this.

increasingly extended to R&D itself, particularly in electronic-based sectors. In the silicon chip industry, for instance:

> Over the past few years, a heavy concentration in a few centres of excellence has given way to growing organizational and geographical mobility. Vertical specialization within global design networks represents an important test case for the study of global innovation networks. Global design networks are shaped by the progressive *disintegration* of the design value chain and to its *geographical dispersion*. Vertical specialization within global design networks thus combines the 'outsourcing' of stages of chip design to specialized suppliers and its 'offshoring' across national boundaries (Ernst, 2005, 63).

However, the TNCs have tended, as a rule, to avoid this kind of development in the transition countries. In Central-East Europe, the most advanced transition region, multinationals rarely use local firms as first-tier suppliers, i.e. as suppliers making significant inputs into technology and design and the governance of the lower tiers of the supply network. Where they do, those local firms are nearly always partly foreign-owned, and many of the first-tier suppliers are simply subsidiaries of firms from the home country. In Ozatagan's sample of Polish supplier firms, over half are entirely or partly foreign owned, with 42.1% classified as wholly-owned subsidiaries of global suppliers (see Chapter 17 in this book). The multinationals obtain very little in the way of technology-oriented services from local companies or research institutes (Dyker *et al.*, 2006). In the extreme case of Slovakia, a very large foreign-owned sector generates negligible demand for local R&D services (*ERAWATCH Research Inventory Report for Slovakia;* see also Chapter 6 in this book). The big exception to the general rule here is software engineering. But even in this case, the potential for building sophisticated R&D networks remains largely unrealised.

> ICT-based information management creates new opportunities for globalization, enabling international production rather than exports to become the main vehicle for international market share expansion. Over time, the expansion of global production networks requires the parallel extension of engineering support services. This implies that knowledge diffusion among different network nodes becomes the necessary glue that enables global production networks to grow. At some stage, once an individual global production network node has reached a critical threshold, TNCs may need to upgrade these activities to include product development and design. *Much depends of course on the development of local innovation capabilities and systems.* (Ernst, 2005, 66, emphasis added)

The general tendency has been for the multinationals to view the level of development of local innovation capabilities and systems in the transition countries as inadequate to the task of such upgrading. Thus, once again, the issue of country-specific governance is simply avoided. While the multinationals play a key role in relation to *knowledge transfer* in the transition region, they contribute little to the more fundamental process of interactive *knowledge accumulation*.

2.2. *Domestic companies*

The majority of companies in the transition countries are not innovation-active. In the extreme case of Romania, only 5% of firms in manufacturing engage in any R&D activities (*ERAWATCH Research Inventory Report for Romania*). In Russia, industrial enterprises account for just 7% of the (modest) total for R&D (Kovaleva and Zaichenko, 2006, 5 and 8). Only *c*. 9% of manufacturing enterprises in Russia are innovation-active, and the figure is falling (Ivanova, 2009, Table 3). In 2001, only 9.2% of Russian industrial enterprises introduced new products or processes (Yegorov, 2006, 15). Strikingly, the rate of implementation of purely organisational innovations among Russian industrial firms is twice as high as that for technical innovations (Kovaleva and Zaichenko, 2006, 8). The only transition country where the rate of introduction of new and improved products is comparable to that of the EU-15 is Slovenia, with a figure of 19% (*Benchmarking…*, 2003, 133; *INNO-Policy TrendChart — Policy Trends and Appraisal Report Slovenia* 2008, 2). In Kazakhstan, a country which inherited a substantial proportion of the Soviet industrial capability, technical innovation within the key 'machine-building' sector is carried on at only a handful of companies (Dyker, 2005). But even in Poland and Estonia, two of the leading transition countries, most companies do not spend money on R&D (Jasinski, 2003, 5; Technopolis, 2006, 8). In Russia, no less than 69% of total R&D expenditure in 2003 was implemented at enterprise level (Kovaleva and Zaichenko, 2006, 7). But the great bulk of this was actually *financed* by the government.

There is a particular problem with SMEs. Thus in Hungary, another transition front-runner, 'despite the favourable trends since the end of the last decade, the weak R&D and innovation performance of the majority of small and medium-sized enterprises due to the lack of necessary resources still causes tensions. There are not many spin-off companies originating from knowledge centres (for example universities, research units), technological incubation is underdeveloped….' (National Office for Research and Technology, 2003; see also Inzelt, 2006, 10; Jasinski, 2003, 5). It is easy to find outstanding exceptions to this pattern throughout the transition region (see, for instance, Dyker, 1996; Jasinski, 2005). Country-wise, Slovenia stands out as an exception in that it boasts a number of domestic companies which are first-tier suppliers to multinationals (Dyker *et al.*, 2003). A shining example recently in the news is the Akrapovič exhaust system company, which supplies many of the top motorcycle manufacturers and also makes exhaust systems for Grand Prix cars.[6] Even in Slovenia, however, only 12.4% of small firms are innovation-active, compared to 58.8% for large firms (with more than 250 employees) and 32.6% for medium-sized firms (*Benchmarking...*, 2003, 134–135). Hungary is also a kind of exception, though in a slightly different way. While it does not boast first-tier suppliers within international supply networks, it has developed a genuine high-tech capability in the form of a competitive biotechnology sector (Inzelt, 2006, 10). In Estonia, though most SMEs do not innovate, 'SMEs that do innovate do so more intensively than large firms.' (Reid, 2003, 11; See also *INNO-Policy TrendChart — Policy Trends and Appraisal Report Estonia* 2008, 3) But these remain exceptions, and, Slovenia and possibly Hungary and Estonia apart, the exceptions have tended to become rarer as the first enthusiasm of transition has worn off. All of this presents a mirror image of the patterns we observed in the previous section in relation to multinational investment in the transition region. We will return to the question of the sequence of cause and effect in this pattern later on.

2.3. *State research institutes and universities*

Under socialism, by definition, all research institutes were in the public sector. In most countries, the great majority of institutes concerned with fundamental and theoretical research were under the aegis of *Academies of Sciences,* institutions which under socialism operated as *sui generis* ministries of science, but which in fact had much older histories, going back, in some cases, to the nineteenth century. Some applied science institutes were also under the Academies, but most formed part of the structure of branch ministries which formed the backbone of the system of plan implementation in the countries operating a Soviet-style, centrally planned system. It was this latter category of research institute which suffered most in the early transition period, as the majority of branch ministries were abolished, and state funding was simply withdrawn or very sharply cut back in the case of most such institutes.

The academy systems also suffered from financial cuts in the early period of transition. But academy institutes generally survived better than the old branch institutes. Overall academy budgets were cut less severely, and academicians were able to marshal their reduced resources in such a way as to ensure the survival of most of the institutes concerned, and even to finance the creation of a few new ones. As a

---

[6] Akrapovič is described on the *Laguna Motorcycles* website as a 'World leader for exhaust system technology'. The website goes on to claim that Akrapovič products 'constantly evolve through experience gained from partnerships with factory teams in Moto GP, Superbike, Supersport, Supermoto, Motocross, Enduro and Rally Raid. The Akrapovic philosophy is to understand and constantly innovate, to develop with the demands of the market. Their use of materials like carbon-fibre, titanium, stainless steel and now inconel, coupled with industry leading manufacturing techniques such as tube extrusion, bending, welding and hydro-forming ensure that all Akrapovic products live up to the quality expected and demanded at the highest level.' See http://www.lagunashop.co.uk/acatalog/Akrapovic_Exhausts.html.

result, in many transition countries today, there are more academy institutes than there were in 1990. The Academies are particularly important in the CIS countries, but in Hungary and the Czech Republic, two of the most advanced and 'westernised' transition countries, the Academy of Sciences and its subordinate institutes still claim some 30% of the total public R&D budget (*ERAWATCH Research Inventory Reports*). In Estonia and Latvia, most of the research institutes which operated under the aegis of the Academy of Sciences in the Soviet period have now been attached to universities, leaving the Academy of Sciences in a position rather more akin to the British Academy than to that of the traditional Central-East European model of the Academy. The situation is similar in Lithuania, though here the erstwhile Academy research institutes have been reconstituted as independent institutes (financed by the government). In only one transition country, Turkmenistan, has the Academy of Sciences actually been abolished. Survival elsewhere has not, however, meant high productivity. In Russia, for example, the institutes of the Academy of Sciences received 11.1% of total R&D funding in 2003, but took credit for just 8.9% of 'new technologies created' (it is unclear exactly how this category is defined) (Kovaleva and Zaichenko, 2006, 6). And in some cases it has been survival on the basis of the thinnest of shoe-strings. In Georgia, staffing levels at R&D establishments (mostly in the Academy of Sciences) have been maintained at well over half the 1991 level, although the proportion of GDP spent on R&D in that country fell from 1.1% in 1991, to 0.01% in 2004 (Yegorov, 2006, 2 and 3). In Armenia, the National Academy of Sciences continues to operate more or less as it did in Soviet times, with no fewer than 35 research institutes, while spending on R&D as a proportion of GDP fell from 2.5% in 1990 to 0.12% in 2006 (Arzumanyan and Khnkoyan, 2009, 7–8). The priority given to saving jobs has often meant draconian cuts in spending on equipment. The proportion of aggregate funding spent on equipment in the institutes of the Russian Academy of Sciences fell from 24.1% in 1990 to an average of 4–5% over the period 2000–2004 (Yegorov, 2006, 12). Ancillary staff, too, have often been cut to a level that must have deleteriously affected productivity, in the name of saving scientists' jobs. Thus in the Bulgarian Academy of Sciences between 1990 and 2001 the level of ancillary staffing was cut by 81.2%, while that of scientists was reduced by just 27.8% (Chobanova, 2005, 9). In Ukraine:

> According to the opinion of many prominent scientists, the number of 'inactive researchers' varies between 25 and 40% of the research institute's staff. On the other hand, according to our estimates, expenditures per scientist on R&D in Ukraine are substantially lower than in many developing countries, including India and China (measured in PPP terms). More than half of all research equipment is obsolete... and some institutes simply cannot do research, as their main 'means of production' do not work (Yegorov, 2009, 6).

The pattern of evolution of the industrial branch research institutes has varied a good deal from country to country. In the then Czechoslovakia they were slated for privatisation or liquidation as early as 1990, right at the start of the transition process. However, the government of the Czech Republic subsequently, in 1998, re-established the principle that branch research institutes could receive institutional financial support from the government (*National Research...*, 14). In 2006, there were nineteen ministry research institutes in the Czech Republic, fourteen of them located in Prague (*ERAWATCH Research Inventory Report for the Czech Republic*). In Russia, branch institutes suffered extreme financial privation in the mid-1990s, and many closed down (Yegorov, 2006, 8). A similar pattern was observed in Bulgaria, with the financial retrenchment accompanying the establishment of the currency board system in 1997 providing the final *coup de grâce* for many branch institutes (Chobanova, 2005, 17–18). In Poland, by contrast, there are still 190 branch research institutes in receipt of government financial support (an aggregate of around €120m annually, some 36% of total state expenditure on R&D, *c.*2004), and employing some 12,000 scientists, over 20% of the total number of scientists in Poland.[7] While these institutes are credited with a number of inventions, notably production of biosynthetic human insulin, a new kind of tram for urban transport systems and new types of machine for the coal-mining and non-ferrous metals industries,[8] they are widely seen as inefficient. A senior official of the Polish Economics Ministry has portrayed the situation in terms of 'a river with two banks but without a bridge, one being the Polish economy, the other being the RTOs [branch institutes]'.[9] The Polish government is now looking at a number of alternative strategies for the branch institutes, including privatisation, transferral of the institutes to the Academy of Sciences or the universities, or some kind of regrouping of the institutes into larger units. Thus the whole issue of the governance of the Polish branch institutes remains a completely open question. In Russia, as many as 266,000 R&D workers continue to work in branch research institutes — around one-third of the total number of R&D workers in that country. These institutes are now in the business sector, but their precise status in terms of governance and funding remains unclear (Kovaleva and Zaichenko, 2006, 6; Yegorov, 2006, 8).

Universities do not generally play the key role in R&D in the transition countries that they play in the advanced countries. In Russia, for example, just 40% of higher education institutions (HEIs) have research programmes (Dezhina, 2009, 2), and out of more than 300,000 teachers in higher education in 2003, only 29,000 were in receipt of research funding (Kovaleva and Zaichenko, 2006, 10). But 17% of university teachers conduct research (Dezhina, 2009, 2), and nearly 80% write

---

[7] *BerliNews*, 5 May 2005; *ERAWATCH Research Inventory Report for Poland*.
[8] *The Warsaw Voice*, 13 April 2005.
[9] *BerliNews*, 5 May 2005; see also *ERAWATCH Research Inventory Report for Poland*.

scientific papers, and the productivity of Russian university teachers in terms of 'creation of new technologies' is many times higher than that of their Academy of Sciences colleagues — they take credit for 32.1% of all new technologies created, while receiving only 4.3% of total R&D funding (Kovaleva and Zaichenko, 2006, 6). In Poland, the universities, especially the technical universities, have traditionally played a bigger role in the field of R&D, and there have been a number of high-profile spin-offs from, e.g. Warsaw Technical University and Lódź Technical University (see Dyker, 1996; Jasinski, 2005). As many as seven Polish universities have their own technology transfer offices, though these do not seem to be particularly effective (Jasinski, 2005, 6) — see further discussion below. In 2006 the university sector accounted for 23% of total GERD in Poland (*ERAWATCH Research Inventory Report for Poland*). In Estonia and Latvia, as noted above, the reform of the 1990s transferred the majority of research institutes from the Academy of Sciences to the universities (see also Reid, 2003, 19), thus creating a much more 'Western' model of R&D governance.

The system of governance in the state R&D sector has remained generally highly centralised. In Russia:

> The main administrative decisions are made at the government level — at the Ministry of Education and Science of the Russian Federation. These include the issues of the state priorities in the scientific sphere, the adoption and implementation of the state scientific programs, the state financing of science etc… At the present time the main instrument of state management in the field of science and technology is the system of orders and R&D financing in the directions that are of priority for the state. In this connection a significant management mechanism in this area is the system of federal economic programs approved by the Ministry of Finance and the Ministry of Economy of RF (Kovaleva and Zaichenko, 2006, 4).

In Poland the Ministry of Science and Computerisation (formerly KBN — the Committee on Scientific Research) operates in a similarly centralised fashion, certainly as far as finance is concerned. But funding is in all cases in the form of grants rather than the 'state orders' (*gosudarstvennye zakazy*) which remain so important in Russia, and there has in the past been less stress in Poland on government priorities. This may be changing with the formation of a National Research and Development Centre with the objective of 'reforming the system of financing R&D through the concentration of funding on a small number of large projects' (*ERAWATCH Research Inventory Report for Poland*). Allocation of funding in Poland is based on peer review, though the system does not always work perfectly (Jasinski, 2003, 2). The Hungarian system is more like the Polish than the Russian, with the Office for Technology and Research (KTIT) playing the key central administrative role. The role of the KTIT is, however, currently under fundamental review. The Hungarian government seeks to formulate and pursue an explicit technology and innovation strategy, but on the basis of a technology foresight exercise rather than Soviet-type priorities. Between one-half and two-thirds of total R&D expenditure in Hungary comes from the public sector (Inzelt, 2006; *ERAWATCH Research Inventory Report for Hungary*). The Bulgarian system, dominated at the administrative level by the Ministry of Education and Science and the Economics Ministry, is somewhere in between the Russian and Hungarian/Polish systems. The government accounts for some 70% of total R&D funding in Bulgaria (*ERAWATCH Research Inventory Report for Bulgaria*) — this high figure reflecting the paucity of private research funding, rather than the size of public research funding. In total, Bulgaria spent just 0.48% of its GDP on R&D in 2006 (*ERAWATCH Research Inventory Report for Bulgaria*). The Bulgarian ministries concerned seek to develop and impose a fairly clear-cut set of priorities for R&D as a whole (Chobanova, 2005, 5–6). It should be noted, however, that the Bulgarian Academy of Sciences obtains the great bulk of its funding from foreign organisations and companies, and from domestic Bulgarian companies and public-sector organisations (Chobanova, 2005, 12).

In Slovenia, the pattern is rather different, to a great extent because of the specifically Yugoslav legacy of market socialism. There is a Slovenian Academy of Sciences, but its role is more like that of the British Academy (and indeed the Estonian and Latvian Academy of Sciences), and it has no subordinate research institutes.

> In comparison with other CEE countries, Slovenia inherited some advantageous features of the former science and technology (S&T) system. Under self-management, decentralised research institutes and universities were not organisationally linked to the academy of sciences and government bodies. Institutes were open for contractual co-operation with the business sector and had many contacts with neighbouring Western research institutions. In the system of social ownership [the] business sector possessed relatively strong intramural R&D capacities (*Benchmarking…*, 2003, 127).

The Slovenian 'National Research and Development Programme', adopted in 2005, specifies priorities, but in fairly general terms (e.g. increasing the rate of high-tech start-ups and increasing high-tech exports), and in broad conformity with the priorities of the 6th Framework Programme (*ERAWATCH Research Inventory Report for Slovenia*).

The R&D sector in Slovenia is less dependent on government finance than in other transition countries. But there is no clear downward trend in the share of state funding in GERD. In 1993 the figure was 48.3%. By 1999 it had fallen to 36.8%, but then it rose again to 40% in 2000 (*Benchmarking*, 2003, 129). It seems to have remained at about the same level since then (*ERAWATCH Research Inventory Report for Slovenia*).

2.4. Private research institutes[10]

There are still very few of these in the transition region as a whole. In Russia there are about fifty private, non-profit scientific societies and organisations (Kovaleva and Zaichenko, 2006, 5). In Slovenia, where the private research sector has grown rapidly, it accounted for only 0.1% of total R&D funding in 2006 (*ERAWATCH Research Inventory Report for Slovenia*). In Lithuania there are just two private research institutes, plus a couple of R&D service companies that do research (*ERAWATCH Research Inventory Report for Lithuania*). In Estonia there are 20 companies registered as R&D organisations. There seems, however, to be some doubt as to the extent of their real contribution to Estonia's aggregate R&D effort (*ERAWATCH Research Inventory Report for Estonia*).

Where private research organisations do exist, they are often the product of specific, foreign-funded, technical assistance programmes. That means that they are under the joint governance of the funding agency and the local beneficiary — a system of dual power which often generates friction and problems for the staff of these programmes. When the programmes finish, the research organisation is automatically liquidated. There is, nevertheless, a permanent (if necessarily highly mobile) cadre of highly trained professionals who work in these private organisations. It is, however, too small to have a significant impact on general patterns of economic development.

3. Critical Weaknesses in the Chain of Governance in Transition R&D and Innovation Systems

To a considerable extent, the foregoing bald description tells the story. Foreign investors, local companies, local R&D institutes etc. run their own shows, paying little heed to the other major actors on the stage on which they play. The elements of a National System of Innovation are present, but there is no National System of Innovation. There is redeployment and absorption of assets (including of knowledge assets), but asset creation is limited. There is knowledge transfer, but little knowledge accumulation, at least knowledge accumulation that cuts across the boundaries of firms. There is supply networking and R&D networking, but the networks are incomplete and misaligned, and the higher levels of networking barely exist in most the countries of the region. Local R&D institutes have signally failed to take advantage of the development of global R&D networks in the period since communism collapsed.

Some of these shortcomings can be blamed on failures of *operational governance*, especially in the countries of the former Soviet Union. If we want to understand the

---

[10] NB not including R&D departments within business organisations.

big picture, however, we have to think more widely, in terms of *strategic governance,* and ask the question: why do company managers and institute directors not perceive the wider possibilities for exploiting their organisation-specific assets and advantages within the framework of an integrated National Innovation System? Let us now go back through our major categories of actor (missing out, this time, private research institutes) and pose the question to each of them in turn.

3.1. *The multinationals — The limits to corporate vision*

To repeat, multinational investment has had an enormous positive impact on the transition countries, in particular the CEEs. But in acknowledging this contribution, it is important to recognise that, in their operations in the transition region, multinationals have shown the same weaknesses and limitations, as also the same strengths and capacities, as in other regions of the world. Chief among those limitations is *fear of technological incongruence.* In building production capacities outside the home country, multinationals generally seek to implant clones of the production system they have developed at home. They may vary the system a little to take account of differences in factor prices (e.g. using less automation in countries where labour is relatively cheap), but technological congruence is nearly always a first priority. The operations of the big international car-makers in CEE during the 1990s and 2000s present prime examples of that pattern (Dyker *et al.*, 2006). This helps to explain why multinationals in manufacturing sectors generally prefer to invest in medium-developed countries rather than LDCs, despite the attractions of the latter, e.g. in relation to cheap labour. In these terms, former communist countries do, indeed, present almost ideal subjects for FDI. Labour is well educated and trained, and accustomed to the disciplines of factory life, but still relatively cheap. More specifically, factories in the socialist bloc were organised on a kind of *sui generis* Fordist model, based on highly specialised, linear production lines. While modern production lines in the advanced countries have moved on from Fordism to flexible production systems, the derivation is a direct one. It is not difficult to turn good Fordist workers and managers into good post-Fordist workers and managers — especially if you are prepared to invest a lot of time and resources in training and retraining them. This the multinationals have done to an exemplary degree in CEE, even in low-technology sectors like forestry and fish-processing (Dyker *et al.*, 2006). They have trained blue-collar and white-collar workers on the job, and they have brought both categories back to home base to deepen their knowledge and capabilities. In a word, they have sought, not just to absorb assets, but also to create new assets in the form of upgraded human capital.

As we saw earlier, the multinationals have generally shied away from close cooperation with supply partners in CEE. The reasons are straightforward — local companies are simply not able to maintain the levels of technology, quality and precision of supply that are essential conditions for key members of supply networks

(Dyker et al., 2006). What is more interesting from our standpoint is that the multinationals do very little to help actual or potential suppliers to raise their game. Thus their asset-creating activities end at the frontiers of the firm. In some cases, especially where US firms are involved, this makes perfect sense in terms of a corporate philosophy of keeping at arm's length from suppliers, working through short-term contracts and playing one off against the other to get the lowest price (Clark and Fujimoto, 1991, 137–138). Where the firms involved are German and Japanese, it goes against the dominant philosophy of doing business within the home country, based on long-term cooperation with first-tier suppliers. And indeed firms from those countries, when interviewed, will stress their commitment to developing local supply networks. That they do not generally succeed[11] seems to reflect something which stretches the concept of strategic governance to its utmost, and can only be described as a *failure of entrepreneurial vision*. Once multinationals move out of the familiar territory of technologically congruent Fordist and post-Fordist production lines, they seem unable, at least in the transition region, to articulate systems of joint network management, capable of handling key technology issues on a cross-company basis. And they are certainly not prepared to invest large-scale resources in solving the problem. Specifically in relation to the off-shoring of R&D, European MNCs, which are responsible for the bulk of FDI in Central-East Europe, seem to be particularly conservative (UNCTAD secretariat, 2005, 5). That the problem is in principle soluble is clear from the fact that those firms are perfectly capable of developing such network systems in their home countries. Of course, there are always two sides to any story. The multinationals may baulk at technological incongruence, but we have to ask why there is a problem of technological incongruence at the level of domestic firms in the first place. We return to this question in the next section.

3.2. *Domestic firms — The burden of the past and the limits to ambition*

Gazprom apart, the transition countries do not have home multinationals. This is one of the key respects in which those countries differ from other major categories of emerging economy, notably the East Asian countries, the leading Latin American countries and Turkey. That the situation is rooted in the history of an autarkic variant of socialism is obvious. But not much has changed in this regard since transition began. Thus there are no local models of international strategic governance which domestic firms can follow (and it must be said that Gazprom does not provide such a model in Russia), no big concentrations of international business managers who speak the same language, share the same cultural background and support the same football teams as managers of domestic companies. It is precisely these groups in the advanced countries that give domestic companies a lead in relation to exporting,

---

[11] A striking exception in the 1990s was Magyar Suzuki. See Havas (1997).

direct and indirect, and a yardstick in relation to technology and quality. It is these groups that, in sharing their tacit knowledge among people they view as colleagues and friends, maintain a constant stream of inter-firm technology transfer. But that process of technology transfer only works because the domestic firms involved are generally themselves innovation-active.

It is significant in all this that most of the Slovenian companies that are first-tier suppliers to multinationals are daughter-firms of the old *Iskra*, an electronics conglomerate which was already in the socialist period well-established in export markets, with stable and close links with a number of multinationals (Dyker *et al.*, 2003). And many of the Hungarian R&D units which have been taken over and developed by multinationals also already had established international positions in the socialist period. For the great majority of firms in the transition countries, however, the gap between the expectations of sceptical multinationals and the modest achievements of domestic innovation is simply too great. In the words of Havas, talking about the CEE automotive industry, 'it is not feasible to "raise" — or keep alive — "national" first-tier suppliers' (Havas, 1999, 37).

It must be stressed here that there is enormous variation between countries, and between main sub-regions of the transition region as a whole, in relation to strategic technological governance. Firms from CEE certainly do not devote enough time and resources to innovation. And even in the more advanced CEEs, the innovation activity that does take place is often oriented to short-term adaptation and improvisation, rather than to any strategic goal. Thus, in the Estonian case, 'while enterprises are relatively active in terms of in-house innovation and co-operation for innovation, product development across the economy is insufficient to sustain growth and competitiveness in the face of increased competition and rising costs.' (Technopolis, 2006, 31) In the countries of the former Soviet Union, the problems are more fundamental. In Kazakhstan, only a handful of companies carry out any meaningful innovation activities. Behind the bald statistics, furthermore, stand a range of attitudinal problems. Many managers in Kazakhstan are simply not aware of, or do not recognise, the importance of introducing new products. Often the understanding of supply-network-building does not go beyond the dimension of trying to rebuild old, Soviet supply links. And some Kazakh managers have difficulty with the very notion of generic, multi-purpose technologies. This is perfectly understandable, given the history of central planning, which excluded the idea of multiple purpose by definition. But it means that Kazakh managers today find it that much more difficult to see how the underlying capabilities of their companies and their staff can address the new challenges of international supply networking, coming, in this case, mainly from the oil and gas complex of the Caspian region (Dyker, 2005).

That there are failures of strategic governance, of entrepreneurial vision, on the part of local companies throughout the transition region is clear, and these failures form a perverse mirror image of the failures of strategic governance and entrepreneurial vision that we seen also at the level of multinationals investing in the region. But in some transition countries, notably those of the former Soviet Union, failures of governance go further than that. Many managers in these countries do not possess the full range of capabilities required to run their enterprises from day to day, to make short-term decisions about what to produce and who to try to sell to. Most optimistically, and with some justification, we can view these as essentially generational problems, which will resolve themselves as the process of natural wastage overtakes the cohort of managers whose views were formed under the Soviet system. That would bring the companies concerned up to the level that the typical CEE company is at right now, still with all the problems of strategic governance to sort out. It will clearly be a long time before such companies can take leading positions in international production networks. And it is striking indeed that two countries with much lower levels of GDP per head than the main CIS countries, but with very different economic histories — China and India — already boast a number of companies which are first-tier suppliers to the multinationals (Sutton, 2004).

3.3. *State research institutes and universities — A failure of restructuring*

As discussed above, the institutes of the Academies of Sciences of the transition countries have generally survived remarkably well in a purely bureaucratic sense. Some have been shifted to other parts of the bureaucratic hierarchy. Few have been closed down outright, and some new ones have been created. But this survival pattern has reflected a failure rather than a triumph of restructuring. Institutes have kept going through organisational and financial improvisation, by renting out parts of their premises, by 'moonlighting' in areas far removed from R&D, and by cutting ancillary services to the bone, while maintaining large numbers of (very poorly paid) researchers. Governments have connived at these improvisations by doling out (small) amounts of financial support across a wide range of institutes, thus reinforcing the pattern of bare survival. Interestingly, this pattern is as clearly delineated in countries where restructuring of R&D has been comparatively radical, such as Estonia and the Czech Republic, as in more conservative countries like Russia and Ukraine (Reid, 2003, 19–20; *National Research…,* 2000, 13). Academy researchers traditionally worked mainly in areas of basic science and, with the old branch institutes struggling to survive, the share of basic science in the (much reduced) figure for total R&D expenditure has actually tended to increase (Gokhberg, 1999; *ERAWATCH Research Inventory Reports*). Even in front-running Estonia, where most of the old Academy of Sciences institutes have been transferred to the universities, too much money is still spent on basic research and not enough on applied research and development work (Technopolis, 2006, 28). The pattern of 'disciplinary comparative advantage', as measured by bibliometric analysis of citations, remains heavily weighted in favour of the classic sciences — physics, chemistry and mathematics — the priorities of the heavily militarily-oriented research programmes of the communist period. 'New' sectors of science like life sciences and information and communications technology are still only weakly represented (Kozlowski and Ircha, 1999). In the Russian case, no less than 50.6% of publications registered on the Web of Science relate to physics and chemistry, compared to a figure for the whole world of 21.9%. And for clinical medicine the corresponding figures are 4.9% and 20.6% (Dezhina, 2009, 6). Even in the bench-mark case of Estonia, the old scientific priorities are still evident in the pattern of citations, though new sectors like biology and biochemistry are now pushing their way to the fore (Technopolis, 2006, 28). Patterns of disciplinary comparative advantage are important in their own right, to the extent that it is the new sectors of science and R&D that are currently growing rapidly, and therefore driving the overall rate of growth of science and R&D. But they also have a big indirect impact, because it is generally the new areas of R&D — microelectronics, biotechnology, pharmaceuticals and software (but also chemicals) that are most susceptible to globalisation (UNCTAD secretariat, 2005, 12). None of this should be taken to cast doubt on the value of the output of transition country S&T systems as such. In terms of productivity of science systems as measured by papers per $m of higher education R&D expenditure (HERD) and citations per $m of HERD, the Czech Republic, Hungary and Poland are all up with the leaders among the OECD countries, and well ahead of the United States. In terms of papers per researcher, however, they all rank near the bottom, this reflecting the degree of overmanning prevalent in these S&T systems (Katz, 2000, Table 8).

Behind these essentially negative trends in transition country S&T sectors lies a range of attitudinal problems. Particularly in the countries of the former Soviet Union, but also in some of the CEEs, the notion of 'big science' still survives, locking scientists and science administrators into a crude science-push mind-set, and reinforcing disciplinary conservatism as discussed above. Against that general background, some quite extraordinary specific problems of attitude continue to appear. In Kazakhstan, for instance, the Ministry of Science and Education proposed in 2006 that Kazakhstan, in seeking to restructure its science sector in post-Soviet conditions, should try to use Finland — the most science-intensive country in the world, with a level of GDP per head some six times that of Kazakhstan — as a model. That would mean introducing a number of familiar principles — a clear distinction between core and project funding, clear orientation towards final results even in relation to core funding, project funding on the basis of open competition and peer review with participation by international experts, and the introduction of a system of science and technology audit.[12] The response of the president of the Academy of Sciences of Kazakhstan, Murat Zhurenov, to this was that the Finnish model was not appropriate for 'the third scientific power in the

---

[12] A. Urmanov, Finansirovanie nauki, *Biznes & Vlast'* (Kazakhstan), 28 April 2006, 5.

CIS'. Zhurenov believes that science is more highly developed in Kazakhstan than in Finland, and contemptuously dismisses the latter as 'a small country, with no developed iron and steel industry, no chemical industry, no oil industry, and no real agricultural science....'[13] Zhurenov accepts the principle of establishing a clear distinction between core and project financing, but wants 70% of total funding to go to core financing.

Kazakhstan is an extreme example, but this kind of thinking is also present in Russia and Ukraine, and even, to a degree, in Poland, Hungary and Estonia. In that last country, even at the present time, 'R&D and innovation policies usually follow a linear approach to the role of knowledge (including scientific research) in socio-economic development, based upon the belief that massive investment in basic research and the resulting technological development would almost automatically lead to the efficient development of the economy.' (Tiits *et al.*, 2005, 160) Elements of pure fantasy apart, this residual science-push mentality is pernicious because it stops transition country R&D sectors, and in particular the basic science sub-sectors, from evolving in a way that would support the general work of restructuring the economy so as effectively to exploit the human capital resources of the region. Perhaps most important, it prevents the emergence of integrated systems of higher education and research such as are generally recognised in the advanced countries to be the most effective way of producing good research and good graduate students. Though, as noted earlier, Russian university teachers are very effective researchers, the number of research programmes at Russian universities open to participation by students has fallen sharply.

> While in the late 1980's and early 1990's over 70% of post-graduate students and almost 30% of full-time students took part in research and innovation activities, the current level of participation is 3–4 times lower (Kovaleva and Zaichenko, 2006, 10).

In Bulgaria, the number of people registered for doctoral degrees at institutes of the Academy of Sciences increased by 179% between 1996 and 2002. But in 2000 and 2001 only 4.0–4.5% of total doctoral students completed their degrees, compared to around 10% in the late 1990s. The Bulgarian Law on Higher Education of 1995 stipulated that universities should spend at least 10% of their state grant on research, but the law seems to have been widely disregarded. There was, indeed, a sharp fall in the amount of research being done in the higher education sector in Bulgaria through the mid- and late 1990s, with the number of FTE researchers falling from 3,460 in 1994 to 1,886 in 2000. (Chobanova, 2005, 12–13 and 17). But the leading Sofia universities have now emerged as significant research players, mainly on the

---

[13] Interview with Zhurenov in *Biznes & Vlast*', 28 April 2006, 5.

basis of FP6 funding (*ERAWATCH Research Inventory Report for Bulgaria*). There must be some presumption that this has had a positive impact on graduate teaching in those universities.

It is clear is that in all the transition countries, irrespective of the pattern of institutional restructuring, serious problems of mismatch between the demand for and supply of particular educational specialisations have emerged. While unemployment among people of under 24 years of age is over 20% in Estonia, companies complain constantly of the difficulty they have in recruiting qualified staff (Tiits *et al.*, 2005, 160). And even where there are no sectoral mismatches as such, fundamental problems of matching can still exist at the more general level:

> Simply providing tertiary level education and skilled manpower does not lead to increased R&D, nor is there a direct connexion between education and technological competence. The availability of a large stock of suitable qualified workers does not in itself result in efficient absorption of knowledge, as is well illustrated by the former centrally planned economies of Eastern Europe (Narula, 2005, 58).

It is not surprising, against the background of all this, that the governments of the transition countries — and in some cases the research institutes and universities themselves — have been anxious to develop bridging institutions, to channel the (often rather academic) outputs of the research community to commercial applications. Science parks, business incubators, innovation centres etc. have been established in most of the transition countries, with varying degrees of success. As in the advanced countries, some of these have tended to turn into speculative ventures in real estate. Often there has been little enough in the way of commercialisable intellectual capital to channel. Most fundamentally, however, there has been a problem of demand. As discussed earlier, the domestic firms which are in most cases the most obvious customers for local R&D outputs are simply not sufficiently involved in innovation to want to spend money on buying R&D services in the marketplace; and while the multinationals have the money and the will to spend on R&D, they do not generally look to transition country research institutes to supply their needs. Radoševic argues in this connection that the whole focus of transition country government policy has been wrong.

> Integration of local firms through value chains and FDI has been relatively undeveloped as a policy in CEECs... There has been much more policy focus on linkage mechanisms like S&T parks, innovation centers etc., i.e. on linkages for which weak and dependent local firms may not have immediate demand. This explains their irrelevance to local firms and their innovation activities, which are, primarily, value-chain driven (Radoševic, 2006, 138).

The key initial policy priority must, therefore, be to help firms to move closer to the productivity frontier through a developed innovation diffusion system, supported by an adequate knowledge base.

That reminds us of a theme that has, indeed, underlain the whole discussion. When we talk about governance, it is not enough to talk about governance of organisations. We have to talk about the governance of the relations between those organisations as well, about the governance of networks, and the alignment of those networks. It is the networks that make the difference between national innovation institutions and a National Innovation System. In all the transition countries there are serious mismatches, in particular between the technological needs of enterprises and the technological services being offered by the public sector. There is no clear evidence that the extent of these mismatches is diminishing. All in all, the experience of the transition countries with respect to technological governance echoes Andersson's dictum that 'an environment plagued by heavy distortions and a mix of certain strengths but severely lacking capabilities in other respects, is likely to experience one-sided knowledge flows and various undesirable consequences' (Andersson, 2005, 181).

4. Conclusions

The main points to emerge from the foregoing are as follows:

1. As a general rule, operational technological governance is not a major problem in the transition region. Multinational firms implement their own, tried-and-tested in-house systems of operational governance and maintain a high degree of control over technological variables. Local firms for the most part work on a much lower level of technological governance (not necessarily on a lower level of technology as such), but are able to control and develop technological variables within that constraint. There are two main exceptions to this generalisation, one sectoral, one regional. First, levels of operational technological governance, and indeed of governance in general, are unsatisfactory in most of the R&D institutes and units in the region. The managers of these organisations do not, on the whole, have any clear idea of how their activity does or should relate to the general process of economic catch-up, and tend to be focused rather on financial improvisation and/or considerations of scientific prestige. Second, in the former Soviet Union there is a significant number of domestic companies in which levels of operational technological governance are unsatisfactory. Managers of these companies do not have a clear understanding of how their in-house levels of technology relate to world levels, or of the relationship between specific and generic technologies and the requirements of modern global supply networks.

2. Levels of strategic technological governance are generally unsatisfactory throughout the region. Multinationals are hemmed in by their fear of technological incongruence, local firms by the weakness of their innovatory efforts, and local R&D organisations are of little help to either. Failures of strategic technological governance are as much network failures as failures of particular organisations. As such, they reflect critical network misalignments in the economies of the transition countries. These misalignments are not easing as the economies in question continue to grow and develop.

3. It is this last point that principally hampers the evolution of National Innovation Systems. In most of the transition countries all the elements of the NIS are present. But they do not hang together properly, they do not interact, even in the most advanced of these countries. The inevitable result is that innovation does not operate in the transition countries as an engine of growth in the way that aggregate growth analysis would suggest it should. This must ultimately pose the question of limits to the process of growth and development which might stop the transition economies well before the point of catch-up with Western Europe. There is no simple solution to the problem. Foreign models offer all the components of the NIS, but, as we have seen, the components are not the problem. Pressures from technology users are a sure way of improving the performance of public and public/private institutions of the NIS, but increases in technology demand cannot simply be manufactured by government. On the other hand, only government can build the kind of technology-diffusing and competence-building infrastructure which will ultimately generate technology demand. Different groups within the innovation/R&D community may interact (or not) for a whole range of sociological as well as economic reasons which may be deeply historical in origin. Quantitative targets are probably the least appropriate instruments for building a National Innovation System. That takes us outside the remit of the present chapter, but it is a challenge for Europe as a whole.

References

Andersson, T. (2005). 'Linking national science, technology and innovation policies with FDI policies', in UNCTAD, *Globalization of R&D and Developing Countries,* New York, United Nations.

Arrow, K. (1962). 'Economic welfare and the allocation of resources for innovation', in Nelson, R. (ed.), *The Rate and Direction of Inventive Activity*, Princeton University Press.

Arzumanyan, T. and Khnkoyan, A. (2009). 'On some aspects of S&T and innovation policy in Armenia during 2000s', Yerevan, mimeo.

Benchmarking Slovenia 2003. *An Evaluation of Slovenia's Competitiveness, Strengths and Weaknesses* (2003). Ljubljana, Republic of Slovenia, Ministry of the Economy, November.

Chobanova, R. (2005). *The Science, Technology and Innovation System in Bulgaria*, mimeo, October.
Clark, K.B. and Fujimoto, T. (1991). *Product Development Performance. Strategy, Organization, and Management in the World Auto Industry*, Boston, MA, Harvard Business School Press.
Dezhina, I. (2009). 'Recent Trends in Governance of Russian Science: Growing Policy Mix', Moscow, IMEMO, mimeo.
Dyker, D.A. (1983). *The Process of Investment in the Soviet Union*, CUP.
Dyker, D.A. (1996). 'The computer and software industries in the East European Economies — a bridgehead to the global economy', *Europe-Asia Studies* 48:6: 915–930.
Dyker, D.A. *et al.* (2003). '"East"-"West" networks and their alignment: industrial networks in Hungary and Slovenia', *Technovation* 23: 603–616.
Dyker, D.A. (2005). 'Technological change, network-building and dynamic competitiveness in the engineering industry in Kazakhstan', *Post-Communist Economies,* December.
Dyker, D.A., Higginbottom, K., Kofoed, N. and Stolberg, C. (2006). 'Analyzing FDI in Central-East Europe through case studies', in Dyker, D.A. (ed.), *Closing the EU East-West Productivity Gap. Foreign Direct Investment, Competitiveness and Public Policy*, London, Imperial College Press.
ERAWATCH Research Inventory Reports, European Communities, http://cordis.europa.eu/erawatch/.
Ernst, D. (2005). 'The complexity and internationalization of innovation: the root causes', in UNCTAD, *Globalization of R&D and Developing Countries,* New York and Geneva, United Nations.
Gokhberg, L. (1999). 'The transformation of R&D in the post-socialist countries: patterns and trends', in Dyker, D.A. and Radosevic, S. (eds.), *Innovation and Structural Change in Post-Socialist Countries*, Dordrecht, Kluwer.
Havas, A. (1997). 'Foreign direct investment and intra-industry trade: the case of the automotive industry in Central Europe', in Dyker, D.A. (ed.), *The Technology of Transition. Science and Technology Policies for Transition Countries*, Budapest, Central European University Press.
Havas, A. (1999). *Changing Patterns of Inter- and Intra-Regional Division of Labour: Central Europe's Long and Winding Road*, Budapest, mimeo.
INNO-Policy TrendChart — Policy Trends and Appraisal Report Estonia 2008.
INNO-Policy TrendChart — Policy Trends and Appraisal Report Slovenia 2008.
Inzelt, A. (2006). *Private Sector Interaction in the Decision Making Processes of Public Research. Country Profile: Hungary*, mimeo.
Ivanova, N. (2009). 'Russia's innovation policy in 2000s', Moscow, IMEMO, mimeo.
Jasinski, A. (2003). 'Has innovation policy an influence on innovation? The case of a country in transition', *Science and Public Policy* 30:6, December.
Jasinski, A. (2005). 'Infrastructure of scientific and technological knowledge flows in society: Polish experiences, 1989–2004', Warsaw, mimeo.
Katz, S. (2000). 'Scale-independent indicators and research evaluation', SPRU, University of Sussex, March, mimeo.

Kovaleva, N. and Zaichenko, S. (2006). 'The Russian system of higher education and its position in the NSI', paper presented to the 5th International Congress on Higher Education *UNIVERSIDAD* 2006, Cuba, 13–17 February.

Kozlowski, J. and Ircha, D. (1999). 'The structure of disciplinary comparative advantage in post-communist countries', in Dyker, D.A. and Radosevic, S. (eds.), *Innovation and Structural Change in Post-Socialist Countries*, Kluwer, Dordrecht.

Lundvall, B.-Å. (ed.) (1992). *National Systems of Innovation: Towards a Theory of Innovation and Interactive Learning*, London, Pinter Publishers.

Narula, R. (2005). 'Knowledge creation and why it matters for development: The role of TNCs', in UNCTAD, *Globalization of R&D and Developing Countries*, New York and Geneva, United Nations.

National Office for Research and Technology (2003). *R&D Programme,* www.nkth.gov.hu/main.php?folderID=158&articleID=1302&ctag=articlelist&iid=1.

National Research and Development Policy of the Czech Republic (2000). Ministry of Education, Youth and Sport of the Czech Republic.

Pearce, R. (2005). 'The globalization of R&D: key features and the role of TNCs in UNCTAD', *Globalization of R&D and Developing Countries,* New York and Geneva, United Nations.

Radošević, S. (1999). *International Technology Transfer and 'Catch Up' in Economic Development*, Cheltenham, Edward Elgar.

Radošević, S. (2006). 'Domestic innovation capacity — can CEE governments correct FDI-driven trends through R&D policy?', in Dyker, D.A. (ed.), *Closing the EU East-West Productivity Gap. Foreign Direct Investment, Competitiveness and Public Policy*, London, Imperial College Press.

Reid, A. (2003). *Optimising the Design and Delivery of Innovation Policy in Estonia*, Tallinn, Ministry of Economic Affairs and Communications of the Republic of Estonia.

Sutton, J. (2004). *The Auto-Component Supply Chain in China and India. A Benchmarking Study*, Annual Bank Conference on Development Economics — Europe, Brussels, 10–11 May.

Technopolis Consulting Group Belgium SPRL (2006). *Evaluation of the Design and Implementation of Estonian RTDI Policy*, Tallinn, Ministry of Economic Affairs and Communications of the Republic of Estonia.

Tiits, M., Kattel, R. and Kalver, T. (2005). 'Globalization of R&D and economic development: policy lessons from Estonia', in UNCTAD, *Globalization of R&D and Developing Countries*, New York and Geneva, United Nations.

UNCTAD secretariat (2005). 'An overview of the issues', in UNCTAD, *Globalization of R&D and Developing Countries,* New York and Geneva, United Nations.

Verblane, U., Dyker, D., Tamm, D. and von Tunzelmann, N. (2007). 'Can the national innovation systems of the new EU member-states be improved?', *Post-Communist Economies*, December.

Yegorov, I. (2006). 'Razvitie nauchnogo potentsiala Rossii i Drugikh Stran SNG', mimeo.

Yegorov, I. (2009). 'Ukrainian R&D: Continuing Decline in the Shadow of Political Instability', STEPS Centre, National Academy of Sciences of Ukraine, mimeo.

CHAPTER 5

MUTUAL PERCEPTION OF SCIENCE AND INDUSTRY IN INNOVATION NETWORKS — EVIDENCE FROM EAST GERMANY[1]

JUTTA GÜNTHER AND CORNELIA LANG

1. Introduction

Cooperation between scientific organisations and industrial companies in the field of research and development and innovation has increased greatly in recent decades. SMEs in particular, with fewer internal resources, can compensate in this way for the lack of economies of scale. Cooperation can take different forms, ranging from short-term contract research to long-term and strategic research consortia. Companies benefit from basic research findings, and scientific organisations in turn gain from third-party funding and application of their ideas.

This coming together of science and industry means changes and transformations on both sides, as summed up in the 'triple helix' and 'mode two' theoretical approaches (Etzkowitz and Leydesdorff, 2000; Gibbons, 1994). And there are many empirical studies focusing on different aspects of cooperation between science and industry (Hagedoorn, 2002; Powell and Grodal, 2005). Less attention has been paid to the question of how science and industry perceive one another. They operate in very different contexts with different self-perceptions. While industry is profit and short-term oriented, science is long-term oriented. Is science becoming more and more shaped and influenced by industry needs? Comprehensive empirical research on the mutual perception of science and industry is lacking so far. This paper seeks to fill this gap in undertaking explorative research based on a number of qualitative interviews investigating the mutual perception of science and industry with respect to cooperation in the field of research and development.

2. Introductory Remarks on the German Innovation System

The German science and innovation system has some particular features with respect to the range of scientific actors. Against this background, and following Edquist's (2005)

---

[1] The authors thank Isabel Büchsel for assistance in the implementation, transcription and reporting of interviews.

framework, this chapter will look at selected 'economic, social, political, organisational, institutional and other factors that influence the development, diffusion and use of innovations' in Germany. Some introductory remarks will also be made in relation to industry, insofar as it forms part of the innovation system.

2.1. *Scientific organisations*

2.1.1. *Universities and universities of applied sciences*

The universities and universities of applied sciences (*Fachhochschulen*) are important actors within the German innovation system, especially in terms of number. There are more than 100 universities and more than 200 universities of applied sciences in Germany. Universities are mainly concerned with teaching and basic research, while universities of applied sciences are mainly, but not exclusively, concerned with teaching. One important difference is that only universities have the right to award a doctoral degree. According to the *Hochschulrahmengesetz* (Framework Law for Higher Educational Institutions) all universities and universities of applied sciences are given a further task, namely the transfer of scientific knowledge to industry. This has led many (especially larger) universities and universities of applied sciences to install technology transfer offices in support of cooperation and exchange activities with industry.

2.1.2. *The extramural science institutes (Außeruniversitäre Forschungsinstitute)*

Extramural science institutes are a heterogeneous group of research institutes involved in either basic or applied research. Their budgets are partially or fully financed by the public authorities. The non-publicly financed part of the budget is covered through contract research with industry or public institutions (ministries, international organisations etc.).

There are four groups of institutes belonging to the group of *Außeruniversitäre Forschungsinstitute*: (a) Max Planck Institutes and (b) Helmholtz Institutes, both involved in basic research, mainly in the field of natural sciences, information technology and engineering. Then there are the (c) Fraunhofer Institutes, which perform applied research close to industry, often on a contract basis. Finally, there are the (d) Leibniz Institutes, which are a group of more than 80 institutes, in both applied and basic research, and ranging across all the academic fields (humanities, social sciences, natural sciences, engineering etc.). All these institutes are financially and legally independent from universities, but many cooperate with universities.

2.1.3. *University research centres (An-Institute)*

University research centres (*An-Institute*) emerged in the late 1990s with renewed significance as actors in the German innovation system. One important reform, the abolition of the 'professor's privilege' (*Hochschullehrerprivileg*) in 2002, provided fertile ground for university research centres to grow in influence and impact. In establishing that inventions by employees of the universities and universities of applied sciences would no longer be private property but become the property of the university,[2] the reform had two main effects on the structure of universities; first, it created incentives for them to encourage R&D activities. Second, it created the need for an institutionalised body to control these activities. Just like axons of a neuron reaching out to create synaptic connections that create motion in different limbs, research centres became the branches of German higher educational institutions, reaching out through strategic connections to stimulate R&D activities in industry. University research centres are financially and legally independent, but subordinated, through a cooperation contract, to their host university (Koschatzky, 2008, 12).

Universities and extramural science institutes comprise over 60% of the R&D facilities in Germany (Broekel and Brenner, 2005, 10). There is a wide range of science organisations, including universities, universities of applied science, extramural science institutes, as well as university research centres. Different actors fulfil different missions and pursue different strategies and goals, including with respect to industry linkages. Interviews with different types of scientific organisation are presented in a subsequent section.

2.2. *Industry*

For the purposes of this chapter, two industries have been picked out: (a) the chemicals industry as an example of a high-tech industry with a traditionally strong propensity to cooperate with science, and (b) the food-processing industry as an example of a low-tech sector with less emphasis on cooperation with science organisations.

In Germany, both chemicals and food processing are important industries within the manufacturing sector. In terms of sales, the chemicals industry accounts for 11% of total sales in manufacturing, after the car industry (21%) and machinery (13%). Food processing accounts for 8% of total sales. As regards employment, chemicals accounts for 7% of total employment in manufacturing industry, and food processing for about 10% (Source: *Statistisches Bundesamt*). Both industries have their own industry associations at national level, plus regional branches.

Many industrial companies in the chemicals industry in Germany belong to multinational groups, some with headquarters in Germany, some foreign subsidiaries located in Germany. There are several multinational companies in the food-processing industry, too, but this sector of the German economy is typically characterised by a high share of small and medium-sized companies.

Our choice of interviewees reflects these structural characteristics.

---

[2] www.paton.tu-ilmenau/pva/bmbf.pdf

2.3. *Policy framework*

The policy framework establishes parameters for the industrial and scientific actors within the innovation system. In general, these parameters take the shape of taxes, grants, *Länder*-level initiatives, federal-level initiatives, EU-level initiatives and the effect of the interaction of regulations at different levels. In Germany, there are no tax allowances for R&D-performing firms. Rather, the German innovation policy is strongly characterised by direct financial support for R&D and innovation projects (grants, allowances, loans etc.). Accordingly, the idea of cooperative projects (*Verbundprojekte*) plays an important role. A large number of programmes are in place specifically to support joint projects between science and industry, both at national and *Länder* level. According to a survey carried out in 2007 at the Halle Institute for Economic Research (IWH), there are 77 different programmes providing public support for R&D or innovation projects at the national level for which private firms are eligible. As many as 30 programmes are exclusively addressed to supporting joint (cooperative) projects, mostly between science and industry. Among these programmes, there are still a number of R&D and innovation support schemes which are specifically targeted at the former East Germany. This is because — according to policy-makers — there are still transition-related particularities in the East German economy which justify special support. Frequently mentioned aspects of the East German economy in this context are the strong dominance of small and medium-sized firms, and the weaker performance in terms of profit and capital of firms in East Germany compared to their West German counterparts.

3. Significance of the Economic Activities of the Central German Region

In East Germany, it was the region of Mitteldeutschland (Central Germany) that was the centre of manufacturing industry, especially of chemicals, including plastics, and process engineering, but also the car industry and machinery. After the privatisation and heavy restructuring of the early 1990s, this industrial tradition continued to develop through the transition period. Especially notable here is the Central German Chemical Triangle — the industrial agglomeration around the cities Halle/Merseburg, Bitterfeld and Leipzig. Related scientific organisations were also located in Mitteldeutschland under the old dispensation. After reunification many of these were re-established in a restructured form, and some new ones were created. In the chemicals industry of Mitteldeutschland there are now large West German investors like Bayer in Bitterfeld, as well as subsidiaries of foreign investors like Dow-Chemical. Science and industry actors in the region participating in the interviews belong to the group which successfully integrated the distinctive East-German industrial tradition with new and innovative best practices. These actors provide an opportunity to explore a combination of diverse organisational backgrounds interacting and changing in an environment of competitiveness.

The food industry in Saxony-Anhalt is strong and typical of the entire country. In 2008, nearly 19,000 people were employed at 115 companies in the food and beverage industry in the state, accounting for €575m in total sales revenues. The ratio of exports to total sales was 16.0% in 2006.

The chemicals industry has contributed enormously to economic performance in Saxony-Anhalt. The exports/total sales ratio is very high in this sector: 46.4% in 2008, compared to 30% across the board for East Germany as a whole. The turnover was nearly €557m in the same year. Currently there are 14,700 people employed in the chemicals industry of the *Land*. That represents nearly 14% of the workforce of Saxony-Anhalt.[3] Saxony-Anhalt ranks in the top ten among Germany's *Länder* in terms of production and exporting.

4. Empirical Data

The first step here was to look at secondary sources, such as documents of science organisations and trade associations focusing on cooperation between science and industry. The main results of this document analysis were articulated into a questionnaire for face-to-face interviews. The questionnaire was semi-structured, with an interview guide. Our interviews were designed to explore topics of cooperation in R&D activities, challenges in cooperative ventures, best-practice examples in cooperation, areas of improvement by government, areas of improvement by science and industry, and future expectations in terms of cooperative activities. The questionnaire was originally formulated and conducted in German, and was later transcribed and translated into English. Interviewees were selected according to the aforementioned taxonomy and significance within German innovation systems, following Edquist's model.

5. Results

5.1. *Scientific organisations*

The starting point for the interviews was a general question about conflicts of interest between the market orientation of industry and the pure scientific interest of science organisations. There was surprisingly little mention of the existence of such conflicts. There are slight differences here with respect to the type of science organisation: science organisations belonging to nationally and internationally active groups (e.g. Fraunhofer, Max Planck) have a different self-perception in this context from organisations with only a regional dimension. As a result, the two groups behave differently and perceive the other side (industry) differently. Regionally oriented

---

[3] *Source*: Statistisches Landesamt Sachsen-Anhalt, *Statistischer Bericht Produzierendes Gewerbe*, Handwerk, May 2008; authors' calculations.

science organisations look primarily for partners in local industry. They therefore depend on the existence of a prosperous industry landscape in the region. This is still a problem in East Germany. By contrast, institutes like *Fraunhofer,* with a national and international orientation and main activities in contract research for industry, have naturally a more broadly defined mission.

Independent of this, all interviewees mentioned that trust and personal relationships are extremely important for the initiation of collaboration and fruitful cooperation between science and industry. This process is often supported through formal and informal meetings during conferences etc. This stress on trust and personal relationships is reflected in the fact that nothing was mentioned by the interviewees about difficulties and hitches in running cooperative projects.

We then asked whether one of the two sides (science or industry) dominates agenda-setting. The answer we received was that it depends largely on the subject and nature of the cooperation. In the field of contract research, it is typically industry that dominates, while in other fields, for example in EU-funded projects, science and industry behave as equal partners in agenda-setting.

Within cooperative ventures, knowledge is produced which can be strategically important. The science organisations interviewed did not mention property rights as a point of conflict: cooperation contracts usually clearly regulate the issue of intellectual property rights in such a way that the publication interests of researchers are respected.

The German innovation system offers a variety of public support schemes for joint research projects between science and industry. The opinions of the interviewees about these vary slightly. None of them are completely against and none of them are altogether enthusiastic about the existing programmes. There is overall acceptance of the goals of the policy programmes and a general understanding in favour of public subsidies. However, the science organisations criticise the bureaucratic procedures, the very wide variety of programmes, and the heavy overlap between them. One way or another, it seems, everybody participates.

On the question of what science and industry themselves can do to improve the relationship, we found some interesting ideas. One idea is that scientific education in Germany should include aspects such as proposal writing, patent application, and supplementary skills important in academic work (e.g. how to plan, implement and document empirical and experimental field work). Industry, furthermore, should allow more freedom for employees involved in cooperative projects to take part in conferences and workshops relating to these projects. This should improve the mutual understanding of science and industry. Another suggested improvement for science–industry relations would come from a shift of the reward mechanisms for scientists. As long as industry cooperation is regarded as less valuable than cooperation with other science organisations within German universities, the incentive mechanisms do not really support science–industry relations. Scientific publications in refereed journals still count for more than contract research for industry.

At the end of the interviews we talked about future prospects for science–industry relations. Here again, the reward mechanisms were mentioned as an important factor. In general, it is expected that science and industry will come closer. Furthermore internationalisation *per se* could have an impact on science–industry relations, to the extent that once a scientific organisation starts cooperating with a partner from abroad, it tends to become more open to cooperation with industry.

5.2. *Industry*

In industry, we find a different pattern with respect to conflict of interest (market orientation vs. science orientation). Here, there is a stronger perception of potential conflicts and a greater awareness of competitive pressures than among science organisations. However, there is a difference between the two industries we looked at. In chemicals, cooperation with science has a long tradition, and the industry depends heavily on the results of basic research. The two food-processing companies in our sample are medium-sized, and producers of consumption goods. As a result, they face a different market and competition situation. The food-processing companies are much more oriented towards applied research and product testing, though they also look for potential partners in the field of production technology. Where companies are medium-size they are, of course, obliged to cooperate with research laboratories since they cannot provide everything in-house.

Like those in science, the interviewees in industry mentioned that trust and personal relationships are the most important factors for initiating collaboration and cooperation. Beyond that, spatial proximity is positive for cooperation, but also international contacts. Cooperation works only if the partners have a common level of scientific interest. In other words, if one party is making all the running, cooperation will not be fruitful. There must also be a good fit in the duration of the projects, which means that they should not be too long (for industry) or too short (for science).

Intellectual property rights are an important issue for industry. Everything is in principle fixed in the cooperation contracts, but interviewees also mentioned that trust in partners can be more important than a piece of paper. All interviewees stressed the importance of clear regulation. The closer it comes to product development, the less industry wants to continue with scientific partners, unless co-patenting is involved.

In contrast to science organisations, industry representatives have an ambiguous attitude towards public policy programmes. In general, industry is critical of R&D subsidies, for various reasons. Small enterprises feel disadvantaged vis-à-vis larger companies. Large, and especially multinational companies would prefer R&D tax allowances instead of direct subsidies. Both sides complain about bureaucratic procedures, transaction costs, the large number of programmes and the lack of transparency. Not surprisingly, the interviewees had no additional suggestions for further programmes to improve science–industry relations. The policy landscape is, it seems, already rich enough.

Finally, with respect to future developments, there is general agreement that cooperation will continue to play an important role. However, there is a difference in perception between small and large companies. Small and medium-sized firms will depend on cooperation because their R&D departments are too small or non-existent. While the quantity of projects will increase, the quality will not change. In contrast, large firms expect an increase in number and quality of cooperative projects. They believe that science and industry will come closer in the sense that universities will increasingly adopt topics or trends from industry, while industry will increasingly engage in strategic alliances with science organisations.

6. Interview Reports

6.1. *Scientific organisations*

Interview S1: Science institute

The interviewee had very little to say about conflicts in cooperation. The impression given by the interviewee was that cooperative projects between industrial partners and the research centre run smoothly.

Cooperative activities begin in a very informal way, through casual conversations which turn into purposeful communication. The exchange between the potential R&D partners develops; the research centre goes to present a project to the industrial partner; and the industrial partner visits the centre. This exchange continues for several weeks. A smaller project is initiated as a 'test drive'; if this project is successful, a trust base is established on which future cooperative ventures can be founded.

For our institute cooperative ventures come in different ways. It could be that the industrial partner gets in touch with us at a congress or conference; this kind of cooperation takes years to cultivate. We talk about common problems, or maybe it happens after we have provided consulting services etc., after a trust base has already been established.

First an exchange takes place; we come to the business partner and we talk about the things that are of interest. Then the representatives of the firm come to our institute. We speak about confidentiality and the other details of the possible contract; we show our equipment and the facilities in general; we introduce our specialists and our capacities. The rest of the process is a back and forth business which can take a long time. Then a small contract is signed, which is partially a test, a pilot project, and then if this cooperation works, the cooperation is extended.

Here the cooperation partners are local firms, and clusters play an important role for this research centre.

The direction of the research activity is established in conjunction with the industrial partner. The research centre has strict guidelines regarding research orientation, and such guidelines act as a selection criterion for industrial partnerships.

If we are offered a research project which is not in the interest of our institute or goes against the mission of our organisation, we do not take the offer up.

The interviewee expressed a clear vision of the cooperation process with industry.

Our task is to turn money into knowledge, while industry turns knowledge into money.

The chemicals industry has always worked in close collaboration with the university. There is a tradition of collaboration which is closer than with other scientific disciplines.

The role of personal contacts was again highlighted by the interviewee.

Personal contacts are very important; these issues cannot be underestimated.

Regarding publishing, the interviewee did not indicate any conflict between the research centre and the industry partner. One issue which was mentioned here is the different understanding of intellectual property rights in India and China. Thus the element of trust was brought to the forefront again.

The interviewee had very clear suggestions for government, under three main headings:

1. Debureaucratisation

The most important thing that politicians can do is to create space; this is the best thing they can do, but you can see that the tendency for years now is that politicians want to institutionalise things more and more.

2. Capacity building

They could help with know-how, instruments, equipment, so that institutes like ours can fulfill the needs for research that SMEs are not capable of performing on their own; especially in terms of the need for qualified personnel and infrastructure that they might lack.

3. Remove the restrictions and conditions attached to grant money

These caps and conditions on investments are one of the greatest stupidities of politicians, so that scientific personnel are not counted as investment in the eyes of the politicians. The institutes should be able to decide how they administer their money.

An important suggestion by this interviewee is that we should look for a market niche for extramural research centres as service providers for SMEs. This would enable SMEs to undertake research which they would not be able to perform otherwise.

The interviewee had concrete suggestions for universities and higher education institutions:

I think that one way would be to improve the curricula in education. The contents are deficient in some respects in my opinion. For example I think that students in professional

subjects should learn how to write patents and how to go about the legal aspects of these research activities. Also how to document research and protocol findings in the lab; I find that the majority of scientists are not trained in these tasks.

The interviewee referred to the pressures of globalisation as a driving force for the direction and the shape of future cooperative ventures.

Other Comments

It is worth stressing that personal contact was again mentioned as a key element in the establishment and success of R&D cooperative activities.

Interview S2: Science institute

The interviewee reported no conflicts regarding cooperative activities, this reflecting the clear mission and focus of the organisation.

Industry knows that we have this mission of applied research. We are quality-management certified, which means that companies can rest assured that we work in ways which are industry-compatible and ISO-certified, and do not present a risk for their prestige.

The interviewee explained that the organisation has a clear approach, which is significantly different from that of university research centres; they target industry and align their goals to those of the industrial partners.

It is very different from universities; there people make an invention and then think 'where is the market for this product?' — the so-called 'science-push approach'.

The interviewee expressed interest in workshops, fairs and cluster networks. The centre participates in networks at the local, national and international level. The interviewee stressed that networking needs to occur not just at the top level, but at every level; this is a key element for the effective exchange between organisations. It is also important to underscore that the research centre itself takes part in the initiation and leadership of cluster networks.

Our tools for reaching our customers are industry workshops; we go to fairs and conferences too but we are also part of networks. This is for us a very important option; we are also proactive in the creation of networks.

Given the character and mission of the research centre, it is not surprising that its research topics are basically set by the industrial partner. The ratio of contract to own research is 60/40.

The direction of the research, the topics etc. are given by our customers from industry. Our currency is not science or nature, but how many customers from industry we have.

These contract-based activities afford a certain degree of financial independence which enables the research centre to use the funds with greater freedom than other similar organisations. While the research centre still depends up to 40% on public funding, the profits from contract-based research can be used to fund bonuses and incentives for the employees.

There are very few conflicts regarding publishing because of the contract-based nature of the research activities. The research centre makes a concrete offer to the industrial partner, which is either accepted or turned down. Since the goal of the research centre is to 'sell', the offer needs to be attractive for the industrial partner as well.

Naturally, you have to respect the interests of each partner. Universities have very different interests and motivations from industry. There has to be a consensus. This is what we managed with this innovation-cluster. Colleagues from the universities are very motivated to participate, because they want to do something different. We use ideas from basic science in order to improve a product or vice-versa. This is a fascinating concept, and a modern project. In the immediate, this is a goal-oriented alliance.

With regards to government policy, the interviewee mentioned the complexity of the grant application process, which seriously hampers SMEs in their attempts to take advantage of such offers. The interviewee also had very concrete ideas of how this situation could be improved. He mentioned the voucher system as a tool for diminishing the transaction costs for every industrial organisation interested in applying for grants and participating in R&D partnerships.[4]

Large enterprises have no problem with this process; they have enough people to work in the application process. But this is not the case for SMEs.

The application process is difficult — it is necessary to adapt. It is better to get money from a foundation, the application process is simpler. Of course, it is not taxpayers' money. It is a pity, because the projects which are being financed are feasible for the SMEs. But the application process is too complicated and takes too much effort. This is where we sometimes take over the task of applying for the projects. I am a huge fan of the voucher system. 'I give you 10 and you give me 10 back'. This would be a great alternative measure, and would be feasible for the SMEs.

The interviewee indicated further that there needs to be greater specialisation in the activities targeted towards improving R&D cooperation, because industry differs from branch to branch, and this affects the R&D activities. The special challenges faced by SMEs should be given particular consideration. Furthermore, SMEs should be advised regarding specific possible market opportunities, in order to promote growth. The interviewee has had good experiences with clusters and considers them useful in such instances.

You have to differentiate. The chemicals industry is set up in a very unique way. The SMEs in the plastics industry grow at upwards of 10–15% annually, with a market volume of €15bn in total. In cars nowadays there are at least 100 plastic components. The SMEs need to address these issues strategically, and we need to help them support long-term

---

[4] The R&D voucher system, originally developed in the Netherlands, provides SMEs with vouchers which they can use to subcontract work to science organisations. SMEs apply for the vouchers at a state agency and use them for contract research with a science organisation of their choice. The bureaucratic procedures are reduced to a minimum for all parties involved.

development. This is where the research networks and clusters are useful. We need to think how to help the SMEs face the challenges of local and global markets. Innovation clusters are one way.

According to the interviewee, industry and science are in the future going to grow nearer to each other. They are going to be more reliant upon each other in seeking innovation through R&D activity.

They are going to be closer. The SMEs are going to realise that they need research and innovation, and that the only way to achieve this is though collaboration with research centres in universities and outside universities.

Other Comments

The interviewee expressed a clear understanding of the priorities of industry; the research centre capitalised on those priorities by providing the facilities and know-how to cater for the priorities of industry.

Industry wants to make a profit; they can only do this if they manage to bring innovative, high-value projects to the market, and they need the technology for this.

In our case, our employees are interested in applied research, and are excited when they see their ideas being accepted and implemented. We offer awards and bonuses as incentives to sharpen the interest.

Interview S3: University

The interviewee did not mention any conflicts emanating from the nature of the cooperative venture.

Most of the contracts that we get relate to finished products, so we stand at the end of the value chain. This keeps our lives simple. We investigate alternative products within a well-defined context, and we inspect the chemical reactions which take place in the technical production process.

The interviewee mentioned that cooperative ventures are in most cases initiated by industrial partners who seek the expertise of the research centre for quality-management and product-testing purposes.

Individual instances of cooperation as described by the interviewee come through as good, continuous, established partnerships of mutual benefit.

On the one side, there is a contract between the university and the non-university affiliated research institute, and then there is a contract between the institute and the company. This must all be consistent and acceptable to all parties involved.

The direction of research is generally set by the industry partner. Research in the form of consultancy services is directed by the company, as are certification and quality-management services. In other instances, the research centre initiates partnerships according to its own interests and determines the direction of the research activities.

Conflicts regarding cooperation ventures are averted through dialogue followed by agreement on key issues such as publishing and intellectual property rights prior to the initiation of the activities. The industrial partner, however, has veto power over publications.

This is all organised thoroughly through contracts. It is common procedure that publications are discussed in advance, and in some cases the industrial partner vetoes a publication. In the chemicals industry this is generally the case; only things which do not engender risk to patenting activities may be published.

The interviewee complained of 'cluster fatigue', an overload of offers and options for participation in network initiatives. The interviewee sees grants and monetary incentives as being counterproductive, because they bring partners together in an artificial way, i.e. the main incentive is the grant money, and not a common research interest.

Referring to the things which the scientific community could do to improve cooperation, the interviewee did not refer to concrete actions to be undertaken by members of the research centres, but rather referred to structural changes in universities. He argued that it is necessary to '*implement measures which include reward mechanisms for the universities.*'

Regarding the future of cooperation, the interviewee painted two different scenarios, both depending on the reward mechanisms implemented. If incentives are designed in favour of basic-research-oriented academic publishing, e.g. through the evaluation criteria of professors, cooperation with industry will play but a minor role, because science–industry cooperation produces more applied research. But if universities give greater acknowledgement to third-party funding from industry, and maybe even make it an evaluation criterion, cooperation with industry will be strengthened.

Other Comments

Another interesting comment made by the interviewee touched on the significance of the personal contacts and the background of cooperating partners. He provided a specific example:

The company has a research director, who is a former member of the Academy of the Sciences, and comes from a background of academic research and therefore knows how science works. I think that it is very important for someone to be present on the industry side who understands the other (academic) side. It is always difficult when someone who has no experience in academia comes and tries to evaluate things with very different standards. It is difficult because the industry partner will encounter things on the academic side that are not 100% controllable with strict timelines. This has improved recently, however.

Interview S4: University research centre

The interviewee indicated that there is a problem in cooperation regarding the transition times from one cooperative venture to the next. The intermediate phases are too long and there are no funds to support personnel in those times. This creates a challenge for both the centre and the employees.

The problem arises when the cooperative activity comes to an end, and our employees are left without a post. Even though these people are very highly qualified, this represents a challenge for them as well. That is why we are trying now to create more possibilities for ourselves as a school and institute, and for our employees.

The interviewee gave a clear picture of how cooperation originates. In seeking out possible partners, the research centre relies on good references from previous partnerships.

The centre goes actively to potential business partners, often working within clusters. The partners get to know us by word of mouth and publications. That is how cooperation ventures come into existence — they are established by a process which involves years of dialogue.

The interviewee indicated that the research centre has links with the food-processing industry and the cosmetics industry. They work primarily in the areas of quality management, issuing certificates of quality control. Government regulations play an important role, since they impose the guidelines on industry which result in contracts for the institute. The role of trust was also highlighted in this respect.

Who directs research activities is determined by the nature of the collaboration. In pure contract-based activities it is the industrial partner who is in charge. This is the dominant pattern in quality-control and product-testing procedures.

The interviewee indicated that conflicts in cooperation are regulated through contracts. There is an inverse relationship between grant money and the ability to keep information from the public:

... there is always the option of regulating things through contract — when, for example, the school and the institute can publish the results, and if this is OK with the business. There is also the issue of grant money; the more information that is given out for free, the higher the grant money. Nonetheless, we manage to work together.

As a suggestion for government, the interviewee stressed the need to encourage supra-regional exchange among cluster initiatives.

Under the heading of suggestions for science, the interviewee indicated that not many ideas come out of clusters, which makes participation in them less attractive. Cluster initiatives need direction and initiative.

The interviewee did not expect science and industry to melt into each other; nonetheless, the number of cooperative activities in R&D would continue to grow.

Other Comments

The interviewee noted that there is a limit to the scope of activity of East German research centres because most of the industrial headquarters are in West Germany, and they direct the location of research activities; West German research centres are often preferred to East German ones.

6.2. Industry

Interview I1: Large chemical company

According to our interviewee, there are relatively few conflicts in cooperation activities between science and the chemicals industry due to the nature of that industry, where there are several instances in which the production of marketable goods is a direct result of scientific research. This means that product development does not require any simplification of or deviation from pure scientific research.

A priori there are no differences in the mindset of our industry; there has always been research in our field. There is no conflict between science and industry, though there is sometimes tension.

The partner reported that they have both contract-based and purely scientific cooperative ventures. Applied research is conducted under contract research initiated by the industrial organisation. The scientific research is conducted in partnerships with universities. The universities of applied science therefore do not come into the equation, since the applied research is conducted under contract agreements. This results in lower transaction costs for the industrial organisation, since contract-based research requires no negotiation regarding intellectual property and patenting rights and licensing fees.

The interviewee also highlighted the role of personal contacts as a determining factor in the establishment and success of cooperative ventures.

The cooperative projects run without any trouble. Personal contacts are very important. It is also important to have our own research, and a director who is at the same level of the professors in the universities. The other institutes also have to bring capable, high-ranking individuals to the partnership.

The experience of cooperative projects has seen the successful establishment of working partnerships with university research centres. This success has translated into the creation of an in-house research centre which works under the dual supervision of university and industrial partners.

It (the organisation's research centre) works closely with the PhD candidates. It is a kind of university-affiliated institute, with the difference and the special quality that the partners work together each in their own premises and labs. There are no shared facilities, there is no common location.

The partner indicated that the pressures of the industry and the market dominate the management of joint research. But the leadership of industry has to keep asserting itself over the leadership of research institutes to maintain this pattern. Individual ability to assert one's own organisation's goals plays a determining role here.

The interviewee noted that conflicts over IPRs are avoided through sharing.

(The industrial organisation) patents together with colleagues from the universities and the institute. This is very important when the science is applied science.

IPRs are secured by industry. The company lawyers organise the contracts in this respect.

The interviewee expressed some disdain when referring to the political programmes aimed to fostering collaboration in R&D activities between science and industry, but saw an important role for government in relation to environmental research.

The partner stressed that it is important for industry to have its own capacities in R&D. This would improve the dynamics of collaboration between science and industry.

Good collaboration with the universities is possible because we have our own research. The cooperation within programmes of the BMBF (Ministry of Education and Research) is relatively successful. We have good access to the Ministry of Culture and Education of the Land. Next week we have a workshop there, and we are expecting approximately 100 participants.

The interviewee had strong ideas regarding the future of cooperation, and gave a very detailed wish list for the structure, financing and activities of future cooperative ventures.

- *No more institutes*
- *Limited Liability Companies to increase in number*
- *More bilateral cooperative ventures financed privately through banks*
- *A trialog based on the principle 'Academia meets business, meets government'*
- *More applied science*
- *Topics in research to be determined more by industry, but with some overall balance*
- *Universities of applied science to play a role in this dynamic as well, not only as research centres but also as sources for manpower and qualified workers.*

Other Comments

The interviewee indicated that the geographical location of the research institute plays a role in the availability of research opportunities. East Germany tends to be overlooked for research because West Germany holds the bulk of industry.

In East Germany the research is in general not very good. Often the relevant research activities are performed in the headquarters of the companies in West Germany and overseas.

Interview I2: Large chemical company

The interviewee recognised conflict in the cooperation between science and industry, since the goal of industry is to produce marketable goods, and this is not compatible with science's goal of publishing research results.

For industry, the prerogative over patent rights is one of the determining factors in evaluating possible cooperation partners. The interviewee used the illustration of American universities that patent themselves and market their own inventions; this factor creates a conflict and tension which industry seeks to avoid.

I personally have noticed discussions in our multinational enterprise where people say 'we would rather work with a university in Europe than one in the US, for this reason.'

The interviewee had a clear idea of how cooperative activities develop. He identified a historical factor, which tends to be more regional, and a branch-specific factor which tends to be supra-regional. The branch-specific factor is a more recent development, and exhibits a greater dependence on personal networking. The historical factor relies more on a tradition of organisational partnerships.

There are two components: there is a historical component which relies heavily on local links, concretely for example the collaboration with the institutes ...

The second component is the community in the field of Chemistry. It is relatively small and depends a lot on existing relationships and acquaintances; a lot of things result from these acquaintances and relationships. There is a relatively frequent exchange in which workers from the company R&D sector go to the universities and assume leadership positions in an institute, and vice-versa, for example PhD candidates come to work on the industry side.

Regarding experiences in cooperation, the interviewee indicated a preference for cooperating, in contract-based cooperation, with partners who have superior technical equipment and know-how. He also stressed that cooperative activities should have a manageable time-frame if they are to appeal to industry. These preconditions could give rise to conflict with scientific research institutions, because scientific activities stemming from pure scientific research often require longer lead-times.

Only in relation to [superior] equipment do they manage to cover exactly the needs of industry. Here the results of the research are quickly absorbed into the working practice of the industry.

Regarding the direction of research activities, the interviewee described the process of goal-setting as being determined by the initial conversations between the organisations participating in the R&D partnerships.

Often it is the case that a certain partner has a concrete idea, and the goals are then directed towards that concrete idea. We seek partners actively. We speak with people at conferences, or else ideas emerge in informal conversations in conferences; often one party takes the lead and follows through, and this is the way the goals are set.

The partner expressed a clear preference for contract-based research, due to the speed and simplicity of the process. In such instances the goal-setting is one-directional, dictated by industry. Partnerships with universities in government-sponsored projects tend to be lengthier and more complex; this complexity extends from goal-setting to ownership issues. In addition to the transaction costs, such partnerships are less attractive in that their output is often by nature not a marketable product. The significance of personal contacts was mentioned once again in this connection.

The interviewee emphasised the importance of contracts in regulating conflicts regarding publishing rights; however, he added that personal contacts and trust take precedence over contractual arrangements.

A contract is necessary in this case, but in my opinion you cannot specify all the details in a contract; the important thing is how well the project partners understand each other. A framework is necessary, but the decisive thing is a good basic trust between the cooperating partners; if that trust is present, the cooperative activities are going to be successful, regardless of the contract conditions. The contract does not play as important a role. As far as contract arrangements go, it is easier to work with a university or an institute than another industrial partner, because each company has their own legal department, and this tends to make things more difficult.

The interviewee expressed a clear overview and understanding of the scope of action of the programmes and the obstacles faced by different actors. He made a clear distinction between supra-national initiatives and local initiatives. But his key points on the programmes were lack of clarity and excessive complexity in the application process.

When I look at the state level, I find that there are too many different grant options. This starts with the BMBF and the different regional dimensions, and then new initiatives like the high-tech strategies etc. This is all rather unclear, and for each programme there are different conditions. In several of them, the emphasis is on pre-market-oriented research, and in this sense what you can do is really limited. We have already tried, but it is not a simple thing.

The interviewee mentioned the Netherlands as an example of best practice in terms of sponsoring R&D activities through tax incentives.

When I look at the other extreme, for example the Netherlands, I see so-called 'research incentives', where industry invests in research, and they get tax allowances from such activities. In my opinion this is a good way to support research, because it relieves people from the pressure of applying for grants, and makes it simple for us, an international corporation, to explain the process to our partners outside Germany.

The interviewee gave a positive evaluation of the state of affairs in the science/industry research landscape. He did not have any suggestions regarding activities which could be implemented to improve such cooperation.

Nonetheless, he did reiterate the point about the complexity of the German innovation policy system.

I see no need to go beyond what already exists; the BMBF has already made provisions relating to the topic 'Excellence Cluster', where the different options are shown and examples are given. Such things are very helpful, but they are in fact already happening. For me, the problem is mainly the lack of clarity and the multitude of layers in Germany.

But *in the future, the two sides will come closer together.*

The interviewee expressed very little interest in basic research, which he saw as having very few implications for market use. The future of research, in his view, is more applied and multidisciplinary, for market purposes.

Often the research does not happen exclusively in one discipline — it is multidisciplinary. You cannot just invent a molecule, you also need a scientist who will analyse what can be done with such molecules, and tell you what are the characteristics of this material. In the future there is going to be more cooperation.

Other Comments

The interviewee also expressed concern regarding the direction of R&D activities. He stressed the necessity for strategic intervention regarding the development of further branches of industry in the region. He remarked on the fact that there are very few universities of applied sciences with engineering schools in the region, which will mean a lack of qualified manpower in this area in the future. He insisted on the need for projects to be manageable in terms of time-frame.

Interview I3: Medium-sized food processor

The interviewee did not mention any conflicts in cooperation, and he stressed the importance of innovation for the company. Innovation is perceived as a result of R&D cooperation, and the company is mostly involved in contract-based activities.

Cooperation activities are initiated by the company. Partners for contract-based research are sought on an ad-hoc basis. In some instances research centres have approached the company, but these offers are considered only if they are aligned with the goals of the company.

…we give out the contract. Sometimes this or that institute comes with a proposal, … they are very keen to engage in cooperation. But we are a business, and such cooperation ventures have to fit our business strategy.

The interviewee stressed that the company does not have the facilities to undertake high-tech research, and in such instances they look to research partners (university/extramural research centres) to provide services for them. The manpower and facilities of the research centres are a great asset in this regard.

We have here at our facilities a small development department consisting of 3 employees. They work more intensively in the product area than in chemistry as such. We do not have the facilities for undertaking that kind of research. In those cases I turn to partners.

The interviewee identified a uni-directional approach for research. The company approaches the research centre with a specific request and the research centre's only role is that of service provider. There are established networks of cooperation on which the company relies heavily, which reduces uncertainty and risk. The lines of cooperation and roles that each partner will have in the R&D project are designated at the beginning, in order to avoid confusion once the project has started.

The interviewee indicated that conflicts regarding publishing rights are almost non-existent. Details are discussed and agreed on in advance. The industrial partner in this case allows for publishing after a period of time, and pays licensing fees. The ownership of the intellectual property remains with the research centre. Since the product is not highly specialised, intellectual property rights are crucial mostly in the short term.

There are no frictions. A scientific institute is very differently organised from an SME, and has different structures. However, details need to be agreed on in advance. This is essential. Take, for example, our current cooperative research project. The institute will receive licensing fees from us for a period of time. After this period of time, the institute can publish the results and sell the project to the highest bidder — but only after the period of time originally agreed on. Trust is a very important issue in this field.

The interviewee partner had very strong, specific and unfavorable opinions about government programmes to promote R&D activity.

There is a lot of big talk and I have mixed feelings about it. There are offers of lump sums, but the devil is in the detail — the application process is very complicated. If we look at the grant offers, we notice that there are several things they are asking for — too many, in fact. The offers are often too 'all-encompassing' and there is no consideration of the differences between SMEs and MNEs. I have just five or six people here who are in a position to think through and fill out all the application forms, and this is why I cannot take advantage of the offers.

I think that 80% of the programmes miss the goal for which they were intended.

The interviewee had nothing to say about what industry could do in order to improve R&D cooperation between science and industry, but rather referred to government initiatives in this area.

He did stress that SMEs have one advantage over MNEs — their ability to react and change with the market. This presents opportunities to SMEs to establish partnerships with research centres — to strengthen their chances of survival on the market.

This is the advantage of the SMEs — they practically only get the chance to beat the giants when they can bring to bear their speed and flexibility.

Other Comments

Interesting information was provided by the interviewee regarding the difference between East and West Germany, and how this shapes the market for and expectations of innovation, with East Germany showing less demand for innovative products than West Germany.

I have to differentiate between East and West Germany. Culture and history play a role in the expectations of people, and how much demand there is for innovation. East Germany, with its background of communism, registers lower demand for innovation than West Germany.

Interview I4: Medium-sized food processor

The interviewee did not mention specific conflicts in cooperation. Innovation activities are imperative for the food-processing industry, since the product life of food products is short and the appeal of novelties tends to fade away, and therefore they are actively pursued by the company. Nonetheless cooperative venture mostly takes the form of contract cooperation, or university graduates working in the industry — doing internships and working on their doctorates.

It says 'new' (on the package), and the consumer finds it attractive and buys it.

The interviewee stressed that the majority of cooperative activities are in the realm of product innovation; however, process innovation activities do also take place. Most of the research activities are dictated by the company.

The interviewee did not cite any specific instances of publication conflicts. Cooperative ventures are regulated by contracts based on consensus, and acceptable to all partners involved.

The interviewee had very clear opinions regarding existing government initiatives.

I see no use for them (clusters), certainly not in the food processing industry; they might be useful in other areas such as the automotive industry...

I am opposed to public financing, because it is a mistake when enterprises base their decisions on external public financial considerations.

The interviewee mentioned that scientific cooperation in his industry took place predominantly within the framework of branch-specific industrial associations, which organise meetings and conferences to help establish contacts and spread relevant information.

The interviewee said that he could see industry and science coming closer together in the future; nonetheless, science research centres and industrial firms would remain separate entities independent form each other.

I believe that cooperation between science and industry is going to increase, due to the market pressure for innovation.

Other Comments

The interviewee also commented on German culture, and the influence it has on the relationships between science and industry. He suggested that German scientific and industrial organisations need to be independent from each other and to have separate identities, because people have a sense of identification with their particular kind of organisation which needs to be maintained.

7. Conclusions

Overall, there is surprisingly little evidence of conflict of interest between market-oriented industry and science organisations in Germany. It seems to be self-evident that cooperation exists and works. The key issue is trust, based on personal relationships between the people on both sides. Patently good functioning is driven by a dense and recognised scientific infrastructure and an innovation system with a long tradition of science–industry cooperation. Although our field work took place in East Germany, a post-transition region, we did not observe any transformation-related disruption with respect to our subject (defined, of course, in terms of mutual perception rather than any 'objective' indicator). Misalignments are perceived, but there are seen as impinging on the regional (East Germany/West Germany) and macro-sectoral (government/private sector) dimensions rather than on the relationship between industry and science as such.

Originally, the selection of the two industries was motivated by the idea of having representatives of high-tech industry (chemicals) and low-tech industry (food processing). What we found was that food processing is in many ways also high-tech oriented, not only with respect to its goods, but also to production techniques and procedures. In this sense, the so-called low-tech sector absorbs and implements a lot of technology from other sectors.

References

Broekel, T. and Brenner, T. (2005). 'Local factors and innovativeness — An empirical analysis of German patents for five industries', *Papers on Economics and Evolution*, No. 2005–09, Jena, Max Planck Gesellschaft.

Edquist, J. (2005). 'National Innovation Systems' in Fagerberg, J. et al. (eds.), *The Oxford Handbook of Innovation*, Oxford University Press, 2005.

Etzkowitz, H. and Leydesdorff, L. (2000). 'The dynamics of innovation: From National Systems and 'Mode 2' to a Triple Helix of university-industry-government relations', *Research Policy*, 29: 109–123.

Gibbons, M. et al. (1994). *The New Production of Knowledge*, London, Sage.

Hagedoorn, J. (2002). 'Inter-firm R&D partnerships: an overview of major trends and patterns since 1960', *Research Policy*, 31: 477–492.

Koschatzky, K. et al. (2008). *An Institute und Neue Strategische Forschungspartnerschaften im deutschen Innovations System*, Stuttgart, Fraunhofer IRB Verlag.

Powell, W.W. and Grodal, S. (2005). 'Networks of innovators', in Fagerberg, J. et al. (eds.), *The Oxford Handbook of Innovation*, Oxford University Press.

CHAPTER 6

THE SLOVAKIAN INNOVATION SYSTEM — WHY DOES IT NOT WORK?

SILVESTER SALIS

1. Introduction

After the disintegration of the former Soviet Union the satellite countries such as Slovakia moved towards a market economy on the basis of the so-called 'Washington Consensus', with its key elements of trade liberalisation, liberalisation of inward foreign direct investment, privatisation of state enterprises and deregulation. The first three of these have determined the shape of the country today. Most sectors of the economy are today under foreign control, which has brought many positive things, as well as some negative. Most important of all, it has linked Slovakia with the rest of the world and built new channels for export. New methods of management were introduced and productivity was enhanced. The multinationals were, and still are, the main factor of high GDP growth. On the other hand, the economic policy of the country is very dependent on these companies. At the present time, foreign investors take maximum advantage of low-cost economies. However, this is not sustainable in the long-term for any individual country. The entry into the EU of new member states from Eastern Europe such as Bulgaria and Romania saps the competitiveness of countries such as Slovakia in terms of factor costs. Today, the key goal must be to transform the structure of the economy in the direction of production with higher added value, and start to build an effective system which will help with that task. Slovakia is a small country, and it seems that the only thing with export potential and the prospect of raising living standards is knowledge used effectively within the system of innovation. What has been done so far, and what needs to be done in the future, is the theme of this chapter.

2. Development in Market Conditions

The concept of innovation policy, in the context of the conditions of a modern market economy, is a new phenomenon in Slovakia. The previous period of development focused on solving problems related to macroeconomic imbalances. The disintegration and loss of former markets led to a decline in manufacturing production and an increase in the unemployment rate. Existing Slovak companies either went bankrupt or experienced financial crises. Moreover, new owners lacked experience of management in the new circumstances. In fact, this problem has persisted to the present day, which creates difficulties in terms of competitiveness and economic performance. Finding a solution involves learning from developed countries or systems, and from experts with experience in the field of knowledge-based economies. By looking at different systems and approaches to innovation policy, Slovakia may be able to implement its own system of innovation. This process has already started, and many policy-making initiatives are supported by consultation with foreign experts (see 'Policy Benchmarking and Transnational Learning' in *European Trend Chart on Innovation* for Slovakia). For example, the assessment of S&T policy is based on experience in developed OECD countries; many documents have been inspired by existing documents from other countries, and some institutions have been established in cooperation with foreign advisers. We stress the word 'advisers'. 'Learning how NSI works from the experiences of foreign systems might be useful if systems as a whole are properly understood. Naive copying should be avoided.'(Lundvall, 1992, p. 5)

The relatively high rate of economic growth in Slovakia (Fig. 6.1) is obviously not driven by the performance of indigenous subjects, nor by general conditions in the R&D or innovation fields. It is rather the result of the inflow of foreign direct investment (FDI), supported by infrastructural network-building, again in relation to FDI, which helped to improve the position of Slovakia among new EU member states (Fig. 6.2). The inflow of FDI has led to a positive shift in terms of labour productivity per person (GDP in PPS per person employed relative to the EU-25),[1] which increased by almost 7% 2000–2005. Over the period 1995–2003 Slovakia experienced annual average productivity growth of 5.4%.[2] (GDP growth per hour PPP), which was the

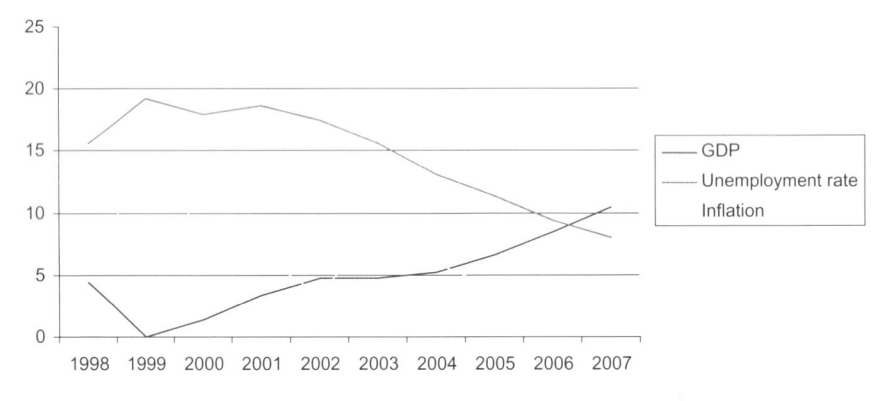

Fig. 6.1. GDP growth, unemployment rate and inflation 1998–2007 (%).
Source: Statistical Office of Slovakia.

---

[1] *Source*: Eurostat.
[2] Morvay, 2005, 15.

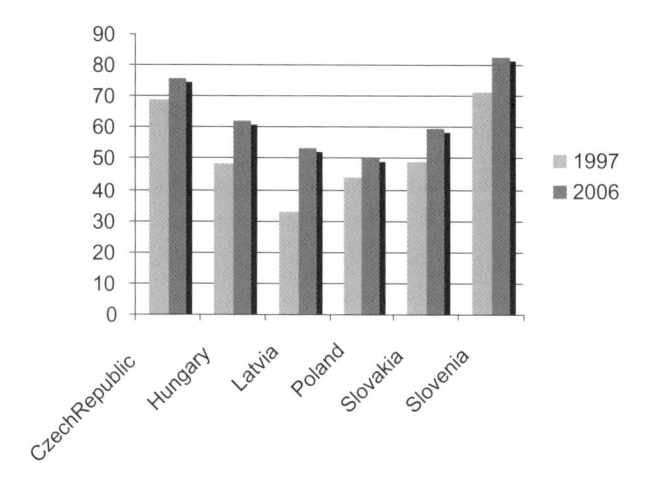

Fig. 6.2. Gross Domestic Product per capita in PPS (EU25 = 100).
Source: Eurostat.

highest rate among OECD countries. This was partly due to shrinkage in the labour force. Since 2003, however, productivity growth has accelerated, as FDI has produced real restructuring. Foreign direct investment has not brought the expected effect in terms of linkages between companies and R&D institutions, though. Foreign companies have contributed to technological upgrading in the form of transfer of technology, but not of connecting to existing networks.

Current patterns of globalisation allow governments and political representatives to neglect support for the institutions and mechanisms of general innovation systems, thus risking a negative impact on the competitiveness of a given country through banking too heavily on FDI and MNEs. Multinationals may, moreover, through the process of acquisition, exert subtle influences on other components of NSI. FDI can, of course, strengthen competitiveness and further develop the local market. However, this is not always the case. Entry of strong international players to emerging economies is not the same as entry to developed countries. Although the rules are the same for all firms, the strength of MNEs and their experience of free market management make it difficult for local companies to compete.

Among the key factors that attract FDI, natural resources are a weak point for Slovakia, while the opening-up of the economy has precluded firm-specific protectionism. What Slovakia has been able to offer is cheap labour, combined with other incentives in the form of tax cuts and free infrastructural facilities. The establishment of a stable political and macroeconomic environment by the government after 1998 had a positive impact on the level of trust in Slovakia on the part of foreign multinational companies, as well as international organisations such as the OECD (acceded in 2002) and the European Union (acceded in 2004). These factors have probably been the main stimuli for foreign companies to enter Slovakia, and the principal source of high GDP growth. Government policy over the last eight years has been largely aimed at macroeconomic stability, based on stability in public finance, employment and inflation. This can be seen in the smooth downward trend in the unemployment rate after 2001. However, that decline took place against the background, not only of FDI inflow, but also of outward economic migration after EU entry. New regulations in the labour market led to the exclusion of many unemployed from the labour force. Only in the past few years has the decline in unemployment been accompanied by employment growth.

Across-the-board cuts in government spending have had a negative impact on the situation in the education and R&D systems alike. Creating a more appropriate entrepreneurial background through change in the tax system has not so far had the desired effects in terms of boosting indigenous producers. Entering ERM II with a view to adopting the euro in the year 2009 was conditioned on stability in public finances and circumspection in public expenditures. Active policy towards the knowledge-based economy has been postponed, which implies a further lag in the catching-up process in terms of own technological upgrading. The policies pursued by the former government aimed at general improvements in the business environment. There was an expectation that the new government, which came to power in 2006, would continue in this direction, and add new elements and upgrade innovative awareness. The reality is that while terms like innovation or knowledge-based economy are often articulated at the highest levels, it is clear from the style and content of pronouncements that they are not fully understood.

It is, therefore, perhaps not surprising that in the recent past there has neither existed a complex innovation strategy nor a functional national innovation system comprising institutions, policies, programmes and tools for putting knowledge and new technologies into practice. Addressing macroeconomic imbalances in recent years has not left enough space to focus on qualitative factors of economic growth such as technological and innovation upgrading. The absence of a centrally coordinated innovation policy and piecemeal distribution of competencies among many government institutions and agencies are considered to be the main demerits of the innovation system in Slovakia. Such fragmentation leads to insufficient coordination and communication within the system and causes multiple misalignments. The role of coordinator properly belongs to the Government Council for Science and Technology Policy. However, despite involving members representing government, education, the science community and the private sector, this council focuses primarily on designing national science and technology policy, rather than providing an efficient communication system at the national or regional level. There is also the issue of the ideological approach to governance here. The liberal tendency among Slovak policy-makers would prefer to support general conditions rather than make direct interventions. The present government represents the opposite side of the policy spectrum. Its leftist tendency orients it not only to social issues programmes, but also to more direct or interventionist steps. Whereas the former government preferred privatisation and FDI in general as a main source of economic enhancement, the current government refuses to sell off indigenous property. As a result, some of the contracts from the previous administration (e.g. the privatisation of Bratislava Airport and railway goods transport) have been nullified. The official philosophy of the current leadership is support and assistance for domestic companies, or at least the equalisation of conditions with foreign companies.[3] Its approach is similar to the third policy approach mentioned in Chesnais's chapter in Lundvall (1992, 294): ' ... governments cannot view their role simply as providing decent externalities for MNEs and leave a free hand to the very strong processes working towards increased differentiation (both social and among regions) ... '.

The research environment in Slovakia faces a number of challenges. A significant shortcoming has been the progressive decline in expenditure on research and development as a percentage of GDP over the last ten years (Fig. 6.3). Slovakia is the only country of all the OECD countries experiencing such a trend. In recent years the negative trend can be put down to a higher growth of GDP. Even so, Slovakia lags behind all OECD countries except Mexico in terms of relative expenditures on R&D. The unfavourable situation in Slovak R&D has a negative impact on human relations within the system. A research career is, for financial and technical reasons, not

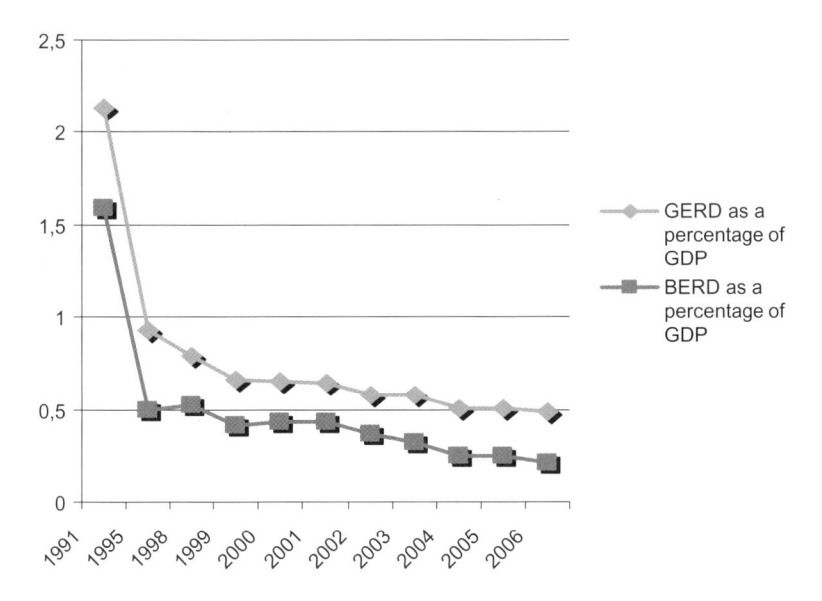

Fig. 6.3 GERD and BERD as a percentage of GDP.
Source: OECD, Main Science and Technology Indicators 2008/1.

---

[3] Over the past ten years only foreign companies have been offered investment incentives in the form of direct payments or tax reliefs. The few domestic companies which were able to invest and develop their businesses were discriminated against.

attractive, particularly for young people. Also the social status of researchers is low. Presentation of results to the public is poor, though some improvements have recently been made.

In present conditions just spending more on R&D would not solve the problem. The important part of R&D expenditures — expenditures by the business sector — should play a more significant role. The declining share of business enterprise expenditure on R&D (Fig. 6.3) has reflected low innovation activity in Slovak companies (Table 6.1), and this has had a negative impact on the overall situation in terms of linkages between public R&D institutions and the private sector. Lack of interest from the business sector may originate from:

- weak orientation of public R&D institutions to applied research;
- overall low demand for R&D outcomes from the side of private companies;
- communication and information barriers between science and business environment as well as insufficient innovation awareness and weak innovation management skills.

Channels for information flows, knowledge and prospective technology through general interactions or personnel mobility are not properly developed. There is also very low awareness of innovative entrepreneurship. The segment of the market (either private or public) which should be focused on providing valuable information about innovation possibilities and educating primarily small and medium companies in the ways of the system of innovation is simply missing.

It is difficult to find the right balance between basic and applied research, and every country needs to approach the issue in its own way on the basis of its needs, potential and affordability. This is strictly a subjective process, though. Slovak R&D consists mainly of basic rather than goal-specific research, financed predominantly

Table 6.1. Innovation in Slovakia.

Indicator	2001	2003	2004	2006
Share of innovation-active enterprises in total number of enterprises in industry and selected services, %	19.5	19.4	23.2	25.1
Small enterprises (10–49 employees)	15.1	14.6	16.3	19.2
Medium enterprises (50–249 employees)	24.4	24.2	34.8	34.4
Large enterprises (250 and more employees)	46.8	47.5	58	56
Share of innovation expenditure in total turnover, %	5.7	3.6	3.2	3
Structure of innovation expenditure, %				
Intramural R&D	6.8	6.6	8.1	8.3
Extramural R&D	2.5	2.8	2.2	3.8
Acquisition of machinery and equipment	77	60.9	84.5	85.5
Acquisition of other external knowledge	4.7	22.1	5.2	2.4
Marketing	9	7.6	—	—

Source: Statistical Office of Slovakia.

from the public budget, but on a minimal basis. The general view, as represented by the Academy of Sciences, tends towards the strategy of leaving basic research as the domain of the Academy, allowing applied research to shift towards the private sector on a self-financing basis. Institutes with no capability for innovation see organisations which are able to come up with marketable results as undeserving of public financial support. Three remarks can be made here. First, the academicians seem unable to grasp the complexities of applied research in the broader context. Problem-solving research often combines a high proportion of basic research and a high impact on the application side. Examples can be seen in medical science, where substances or methods developed in basic research lead to applied results in the form of drugs or healing techniques and many others. Second, there is a legitimate argument that society has the right to expect material results from the investment of public resources. Having an academy with a purely theoretical and cultural content is too expensive. Lastly, there is a serious issue in relation to the financing of basic or 'blue-skies' research. By and large, most companies prefer short or medium-term cooperation with R&D institutions oriented to broad spectrum applications. There are only few cases where companies are willing to finance long-term basic research. So measures to restructure science should be oriented towards better preparation for market needs. But public money, supplemented by income from applied research, is probably the only way to preserve and upgrade Slovak science in the future, and the research community should realise that.

The current approach to assessment of R&D results, in terms of numbers of publications and citations, induces a drive to publish in large amounts, regardless of the value of the papers and the pattern of citation. Moreover, if the paper has a potential invention in it, this is divulged to society for free. Given that the knowledge invented in a public organisation is the property of the state, this practice is at odds with the law, and with the requirements of an effective innovation system. The Slovak R&D assessment system has no way of picking out papers with direct innovation potential and thus higher value. Paradoxically, institutes with large volumes of publications, and thus disclosure, have higher rates of evaluation than those with better results in the field of application (cf. Chapter 5). Evaluation of research results seems, indeed, to be a science in itself, and therefore quite a complex issue. Some academy members argue for a system of criteria which would take into consideration problem-solving achievements as well as the specifics of blue-skies research. Certainly, it is vital to distinguish between top-class basic research institutes and those with weak performance. Current rules appear discriminatory for some very good research institutes.

3. Institutional Background

By any definition of 'national system of innovation', Slovakia does not have one. But taking a closer look, it is possible to recognise parts of it; however, they do not interact

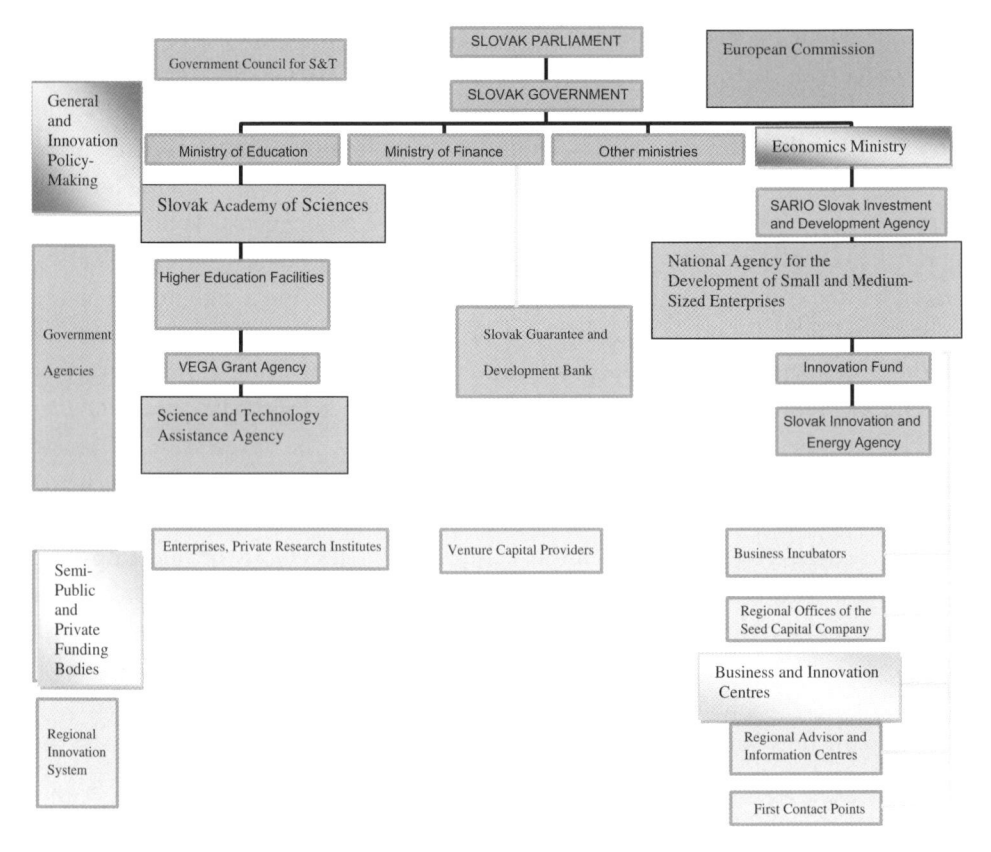

Fig. 6.4 Innovation system of Slovakia.
Source: European Trend Chart on Innovation — Slovakia 2006.

in terms of economically useful outcomes. To reach a satisfactory result in terms of innovation we must recognise the weak spots and bottlenecks, explaining why interactions among elements of the system do not work. Slovakia has a set of components that could make up a national system of innovation, ranging from government offices and research institutes to semi-public organisations meant to disseminate new knowledge (See Fig. 6.4). In terms of policy-making, however, the attention of responsible organisations is focused on the production of knowledge rather than putting it into practice. The main bodies are the Ministry of Education and the Economy Ministry. Their roles differ. Whereas the task of Ministry of Education is to produce knowledge, the role of the Economy Ministry is implementation and commercial use of knowledge. They use a range of tools and institutions for their mission. The Government Council for Science and Technology is the main contributor to policy-making. It operates within the Ministry of Education. The Government Council for Science and Technology is an advisory body to the government for science and technology matters, and also for S&T policy aimed at national security. Its principal role is to negotiate and assess mainly conceptual and strategic agreements concerning

S&T policy at national and EU level. It must be said that even in this narrow institutional sense, the national system of innovation is ineffective, because the institutions are not properly linked to each other, or to production and financial systems. They operate merely as individual elements with weak alignment between elements.

3.1. *Slovak Academy of Sciences*

The Slovak Academy of Sciences represents the backbone of basic research in Slovakia. It consists of 74 organisational units, dedicated to acquiring new knowledge of nature, society and technology, specifically targeted at building a scientific basis for the advancement of Slovakia. It was established in the year 1953. Its mission, in terms of the law, is systematic and organised work in the theoretical and applied sciences, and creative participation on the part of the science community in the economic and cultural development of Slovakia. This was supposed to be provided by the Academy's own institutes, and in collaboration with other R&D institutions. The Slovak Academy of Sciences (SAS) is closely linked with the Slovak Academy of Sciences and Arts. SAS covers natural and technical sciences, while the main focus of the Academy of Sciences and Arts is humanities.

SAS was originally divided into five sections: mathematical and natural sciences, technical sciences, biological and medical sciences, biological and agricultural sciences and humanities; later it was reorganised into three sections — physical and mathematical sciences, biological and chemical sciences and human sciences. In 1989 SAS had 6,252 employees. The physical and mathematical sciences section had 2,358 employees, the biological and chemical sciences section 2,240 employees, and the human sciences section 915 employees. They worked in 62 institutes — 51 scientific and 11 service. SAS has its own publishing house VEDA (Slovakian for *science*), which publishes 34 science journals, and also books and conference collections.

The break-up of the federation with the Czech Republic in 1992 and the establishment of a new country in 1993 — the Slovak Republic — led to the approval of a new law concerning the Slovak Academy of Sciences, under which the SAS was defined as an independent legal body, with budgetary status. In 1996 a process of accreditation ranked the institutes of the Academy by three categories: A — international standard (29 institutes), B — approaching international standard (26 institutes) and C — below international standard (1 institute). Distribution of (limited) financial resources is on the basis of accreditation. At present the Academy accordingly contains 56 institutes, in three sections.

SAS is the most successful actor in Slovakia in terms of obtaining international and foreign grants. A department for public relations has been established to further the popularisation of science. The research orientation of the Academy is influenced by integration into the European Research Area. Formation of Centres for Excellence in collaboration with top-ranking universities and research laboratories focused on applied research is calculated to lead to cooperation on the European level and to contribute to the creation of a European Network of Centres of Excellence (ERA-NET).

At the present time SAS publishes annually approximately 1,300 research papers in internationally-established journals and 100 monographs (one-fifth to one-quarter internationally). SAS researchers actively participate in the education process at universities and train around 900 PhD students. In 2006 SAS employed some 3,150 people (of which 1,350 held a scientific degree and 906 were PhD students), which represents more than one-fifth of total R&D personnel.

3.2. *The education system*

Slovakia has in recent years seen the opening of new universities. At the present time there are more than 30 universities or schools offering higher education, two-thirds of them in the public sector. This expansion has been accompanied by a decreasing level of R&D, and the universities are focused primarily on education and recruitment of new students owing to a financing system based on the number of students. In consequence, the average number of students per teacher is 100, in some cases even 500 and more. Teachers with hundreds of students have no time to conduct R&D activities. Conversely, the lack of research activity leads to weak students. Only 30 per cent of all PhD students studying at universities or SAS successfully graduate, suggesting that a research career has little appeal.

Among other issues that should be mentioned are weak orientation towards labour market needs and low level of communication between the education system and the private sector, which have a negative effect on the quality of educational institutions and the innovation system alike.

3.3. *The VEGA grant agency and the science and technology assistance agency*

The VEGA Grant Agency is an internal agency offering grants to finance research projects performed by the Slovak Academy of Science and the education system. VEGA is an advisory body of both the minister for education and the SAS chairman. The main tasks of the agency are the implementation of science and technology priorities, coordination and selection of submitted projects, audit of the utilisation of grants and coordination of teamwork among institutions of the educational system and SAS institutes. Research grants are aimed at solving basic research issues. The Agency proposes the amount of financial support that should be granted for new and on-going projects to the minister.

Like the VEGA agency, the Science and Technology Assistance Agency is focused on supporting research projects. The agency supports basic as well as applied research. Its other tasks are endorsing international R&D cooperation, developing and implementing new forms of research support in Slovakia (with particular consideration to the increase of interaction between basic and applied research), and developing support of R&D from EU funds. The Agency also seeks to promote dissemination of R&D results to the public, and to provide policy positions and analysis for public administration, advisory bodies and the National Council of Slovakia (the Slovakian parliament). In 2005 the volume of funds granted by the Science and Technology Agency was more than 429m Slovak crowns (€12.6m).

3.4. *The Slovak Investment and Trade Development Agency (SARIO)*

The mission of the SARIO Agency is to promote the Slovak Republic internationally and attract foreign direct investment. Its key activities are forming an appropriate business and investment environment, assistance to foreign direct investors with a view to simplifying activities related to their entry into Slovakia, and consultancy in the area of government support in terms of investment incentives. Other activities include cooperation between indigenous and foreign companies, joint ventures, services to small and medium-sized enterprises searching for foreign opportunities and services to companies and territorial authorities in the field of structural funds consultancy. The agency is divided into three sections — foreign direct investment, foreign trade and EU structural funds.

The foreign direct investment section provides complex consultancy services and information for potential foreign investors. This includes help with legislative, tax, customs and overall business conditions. The foreign trade section carries out activities aimed at export support and foreign trade development. Main priorities consist of participation in general and specialised exhibitions and expos, business missions abroad, educational programmes for exporters, providing advisory services for exporters and developing marketing studies. The EU structural funds section administers industrial and regional projects co-financed by the Slovak government and the European Commission in the investment field.

3.5. *The National Agency for the Development of Small and Medium Enterprises (NADSME)*

The National Agency for the Development of Small and Medium Enterprises was established as a joint venture of the European Union and the government of Slovakia for the support of SMEs. The agency coordinates international, national, regional and municipal activities as well as financial activities. Its main activities are the support of SME development by means of professional and financial assistance (returnable, non-returnable), creation of appropriate infrastructure for entrepreneurship (incubators) aimed at start-ups and innovative companies, networking and connecting the home environment to European information networks and databases with entrepreneurial content, publicity and promotion among the public at large (expos, conferences) and publication of promotional literature. Since May 2004 NADSME has taken part in the implementation of projects financed from structural funds under the heading of the Sector Operational Programme — Industry and Services.

3.6. *The Innovation Fund and Slovak Innovation and Energy Agency*

The purpose of the Innovation Fund is to support development in science and research, and speed up the innovation process in the Slovak Republic. The focus is on conceptual and development studies aimed at utilisation of scientific and R&D results. It helps to disseminate scientific, technical, economic and financial information at national and international levels, supports the protection of the IPRs and know-how of Slovak subjects, and develops technology policy instruments. Innovation Fund finance is offered on a returnable basis.

The activities of the Slovak Innovation and Energy Agency are conceptual, professional, systematic, coordinative, informative, educational and promotional; they are oriented towards decreasing the energy dependency of Slovakia in relation to creation and protection of biotopes and sustained development. The agency's public role is the implementation of structural funds projects aimed at entrepreneurship, innovation and applied research support as regards energy economy and renewable energy sources.

3.7. *Technology incubators as technology transfer institutions*

The mission of technology incubators is to facilitate the transfer of R&D results from a science environment to business by establishing innovative and technology-oriented companies. Their role within an economy is to support the knowledge-based economy by interlinking science, research and business companies with the aim of improving the competitiveness of the given region. Technology incubators operating in Slovakia are usually just ordinary business incubators, providing cheap premises, basic technical equipment like copy machines, cleaning services, secretariat and reception. They offer for the most part consulting services, including general business, accounting and tax counselling. Even so, they are generally not fully occupied. Although their mission is the dissemination of university knowledge and know-how, the element of closer relations between university and companies is essentially missing. There are several reasons for this.

First, the level of general interest in entrepreneurship from people with university degrees is low. With the entry of foreign direct investors, graduates prefer employment for an established company rather than starting their own businesses. Most companies located in technology incubators in Bratislava are from the IT sector, but operating at the level of routine web solutions, which do not require cooperation with academics. The general level of exploitation of university or research institute laboratories and interaction with researchers is very low. It is a two-way process. Low interest in science on the part of incubator tenants means little spin-off for the university in terms of assets for the research environment. It seems the only benefit for the university is prestige and higher visibility. However, this is not enough.

Another problem is the financing of the new technology transfer institutions. EU accession made it possible to obtain funding from the structural funds for these initiatives, and most related projects are financed wholly by these funds, usually on a short-to-medium term basis. This can give rise to a number of issues. Over its first two years of operation the technology incubator in Bratislava, for example, provided companies in the incubator with free advisory services, supplied by external companies. But this was funded by EU structural funds, and after the conclusion of the project the incubator could not afford to maintain it; as a result, the companies lost the service that was valued the most. Instability and irregularity of sources of financial support inevitably cause problems, so that structural funds are not an ideal way of supporting this kind of institution.

4. Imbalance in the Innovation Market

The Slovak national system of innovation needs to solve the problem of demand–supply imbalance for innovation to fulfill its mission. It needs to support the demand as well as the supply side of the innovative production process. It is clear that Slovak R&D is underfinanced, as witness the low level of funding from public budgets in comparison with other countries, including new member states. However, it is not clear that the situation would change if new sources of funding were accessed. Nobody can answer the question 'what is the money needed for', no one can guarantee that it will be used effectively. The truth is that the Slovak R&D needs more finance, but only in conditions where the line connecting R&D and final users is clear and properly aligned, and channels real benefits. Resources have to be oriented towards top-ranking institutes that can guarantee enhancement of their net value. That does not mean shutting down unprofitable institutes immediately. The idea is to finance basic overheads required for the functioning of an institute for a certain period. After that, unviable R&D capacities should be flushed away.

When we look at the *supply* issue, we are faced with the question 'are there are any usable or marketable results from Slovak R&D?' Certainly, most R&D institutions have something to offer, but the value is often doubtful. There are areas in Slovak science which are considered to be top-class as compared with other countries, but their utility needs to be examined. A first step to solve the supply problem would be an R&D capacity survey that would be looking for applicable results. It could be done for all areas of research, although the best strategy would be to look for likely growth areas of the future. But that would require an innovation strategy for the long term. The question arises: who should be responsible for such a survey, taking due account of national specificities? Would a top-down approach be feasible? Would bottom-up be better? The fact is that at present there is no element within the institutional architecture of the Slovak innovation system on the highest level which would have the authority — or indeed the skilled staff — to perform the role of sole adjudicator on R&D, technology and innovation matters. Innovation policy is currently divided between several government departments, and their activities are not harmonised or aligned. Sometimes, indeed, they are in conflict. In present conditions, therefore, a top-down approach would probably be inoperative.

Earlier, we discussed the lack of private or semi-private organisations connecting R&D with business in Slovakia. It is just such organisations that could take over the task of coordinating innovation policy and launch a bottom-up approach. Highly specialised teams of people concerned only with innovation and innovation practice might lay the foundations of the missing process, with support from and access to the highest level of government and the R&D institutes themselves. This process has, indeed, already begun, and two companies (one semi-public, one private) with this kind of approach now operate on the Slovak market. But both of them are brand new, so it is too early to assess their results.

Although the bottom-up approach seems more appropriate for Slovak conditions, it would be have to be backed up by initiatives from the top, to ensure that national interests were dovetailed with those of the private sphere. On the national level, the system needs full-time-employed representatives with just one task — to prepare a fully professional strategy, followed by steps for its implementation. It is no good if this is done by ordinary officials without adequate experience or understanding. And it has to be supported by a political will that is longer than one parliamentary session. In the end, therefore, bottom-up and top-down approaches probably need to be combined.

From the *demand* point of view, growth in numbers of new small and medium-sized companies is good for the economy in general. At the policy level, special attention should be given to technology-intensive companies which could be interlinked with R&D capacities from the beginning. This could be done through technology incubators, innovation centres or science parks. This is, indeed, a priority of the government's Innovation Strategy 2007–2013 (see below). But, as we have already seen, there are a number of pitfalls along this road. Establishment of an incubator or innovation centre is a financially demanding process. Building up such an institution with no certainty that its capacity will be filled and that there will be interest from potential customers is quite risky. But so is the whole innovation process. Examples from all around the world show successful as well as unsuccessful cases. What is clear is that spontaneous setting-up of innovation centres up and down the country, without proper appraisal, courts disaster. It can lead to vast expenditures without return. Yet this is what the Strategy aims to do. Technology incubators and the like require a professional approach, skilled personnel and organised management with experience. The first step should be to educate and train the people responsible for future tasks and acquaint them with innovation systems and innovation practice and management. The centres, parks and incubators of the future ought to be thriving and prosperous institutions on a par with business companies in any field. They should be innovative as well, and serve as an example for the companies they accommodate. At the same time, they should make profits for the university or research institute, to enhance equipment and facilities.

The key to successful cooperation is clearly that it must be beneficial for both sides. In that context, the basic problem is that Slovakian incubators barely cover their outlays, while universities receive nothing from them in financial terms. The solution may be for the universities to take a stake in the companies, providing free use of laboratory and other academic facilities, but sharing in the profits.

Another possible solution is the creation of spin-off companies. Here, the connection between science and application is much closer. Two obstacles need to be eliminated. The first is the perennial problem of finding a suitable management team. The founding institute needs qualified administration able to manage not only research activities but business as well. The answer is again training, as in the first case, or partnership with external entrepreneurs responsible for the business side of the project. The second obstacle is the law that forbids business activity to some research institutions, notably those of the Slovak Academy of Sciences. This law should be changed. Current practice allows institutes to market their research results, but the income thus generated belongs to the government, though the latter does give some of it back to the institutes. This is a deeply demotivating practice for research institutes and researchers alike.

The third way of solving the problem of the demand side of the innovation process is to offer potential R&D results to SMEs from abroad which are properly established on the market, have more experience with management, are interlinked with international or regional new technology networks and so forth. This could be done through existing institutions within the Slovak system such as the SARIO agency — one of its existing tasks is searching for partners from abroad. SARIO also supports attendance at international exhibitions where R&D suppliers can meet their partners. This approach would also attract support from the EU level, where cooperation between new member states and the rest of EU, and indeed the world, is highly valued.

If the formal and institutional issue of setting up an innovation centre or spin-off is solved, attention can turn towards practical considerations. There must be a reasonable probability that any given project has potential. This might be easier for spin-offs, where the founding research institute has usually received signals from the external environment that their product, process or service is in demand. Again, start-ups based in science parks or innovation centres face all the risks of the business environment. It is the role of the administration of the incubator or science centre to give the company a hand here. This is why understanding innovation centres etc. and their purpose is vital for the further development of innovative entrepreneurship in Slovakia.

5. Innovation Strategy

The vision of the Innovation Strategy 2007–2013 is: 'Innovation turns into the main instrument of knowledge-based economic development and high economic growth in Slovakia, meeting the target of catching up with the most developed countries of European Union'. Quantitative targets in 2013 are:

- number of successful projects (no specific number is specified)
- innovation will contribute 25% to the increment in gross domestic product in the given year (presently the contribution is about 8%)
- more than 50% of companies will be innovative
- more than 5% of innovations will be initiated by the Slovak Academy of Sciences and universities

These targets allow for proper appraisal and make it possible to draw a clear line between success and failure. The overall assessment system, and the actions envisaged for fulfilment of the strategy, are sound elements in the initiative, and ought to be emphasised. Previous documents on innovation policy — the National Development Plan, the Competitiveness Strategy for Slovakia — lacked these features, and failed to go beyond the dimension of theoretical framework.

The Innovation Strategy 2007–2013, based on the European Innovation Strategy, has three priorities:

1) High quality infrastructure and effective system of innovation — legal and substatutory standards and overall innovation legal framework; setting up an agency for innovation support
2) Human resources development — improvements in the educational system focused on linkages between academic and private spheres
3) Effective innovation instruments — direct and indirect tools such as purchase of licences, subsidies, loans, venture capital and simplified access to capital.

Under the *first priority*, the government offers financial support for establishment of innovation centres, and setting up an information portal aimed at boosting innovativeness in the private sector (see below). Further measures aim to improve cooperation between public and private sectors, mobility of researchers, and creation of appropriate conditions for spreading knowledge into the private sphere. The main task is to develop a supportive scheme to provide finance for the establishment of innovation centres. The measurable indicators are number of innovation centres, number of successful projects, value added of implemented projects and proportion of public to private financial sources. This measure is inspired by the Swedish National Board for Technological and Industrial Development initiative. It must be said that establishment of number of innovation centres as an indicator is a weakness. The authors of the Strategy understandably see EU funds as a good opportunity to tap resources for underdeveloped areas like science, technology and innovation policy. The question remains, for whom are the centres built? There is a real danger that the buildings will remain empty or simply turn into office blocks. In this case the quantitative approach is simply inappropriate, because it fails to address the underlying problem of low or no interest in innovative entrepreneurship.

Other measures envisaged by the Strategy include passing a law on innovation, defining comprehensively the system of development and support of innovation — innovation infrastructure, competences, responsibilities and conditions, and the setting-up of a central information portal for R&D by the Ministry of Education. The purpose of the portal is to provide information about innovations, innovative institutions and financial opportunities for research projects. The quantitative indicators for the portal are number of visits and level of satisfaction of visitors. The idea of the portal is taken from the EU Innovating Regions in Europe (IRE) network. Some R&D institutions already have their own portals, but a centralised one would certainly be better.

In order to achieve coordinated progress in science, technology and innovation policy, new competencies are being designed for the government Science and Technology Council in the area of innovation. The new council is to be composed of government representatives, entrepreneurs, members of parliament and representatives of basic and applied research. The main task of the council would be development and coordination of science, technology and innovation policy and coordination of the national system of innovation, as well as coordination of implementation agencies, and programmes and instruments aimed at research, development and innovation support. The model used is the Science and Technology Policy Council of Finland. But Slovakia is not Finland, and creation of new competencies for the Slovakian Science and Technology Council is in current conditions of dubious value. Its members have only consultative privileges, and their main responsibilities lie within other institutions. The essential problem is precisely that the Slovak NSI lacks institutions with full-time staff focused only on innovation and S&T policy. Adding new competencies to current representatives means more responsibilities with a poor prospect of significant positive outcomes.

An important step under the first priority of the Strategy is creation of an assessment system for regular appraisal of innovation development, to assess the effectiveness of expenditure on the basis of innovation indicators. Within the framework of the assessment system it is proposed to measure indicators on a national level as well as company, agency and ministry level. This initiative is based on general OECD country indicators.

The last measure within the first priority is to set up a specialised institution dealing with implementation of innovation support and assessment, within the framework of the Economics Ministry, possibly in one of its existing agencies, with new extended competencies. It will also prepare background documents for public tenders for innovation programmes and participate in selection and approval procedures. The agency's tasks will include, for example, training and promotion in the field of innovation business activities, with the cooperation of the Ministry of Education and the Ministry of Labour, Social Affairs and Family. Quantitative indicators are establishment of the agency, number of projects managed by the agency, and number of activities supported by the agency. Popularisation of science and support of projects or researchers with high potential are key long-term goals, hitherto neglected. So this is an important initiative.

The *second priority* of the Strategy deals with two measures. The first is support of media initiatives related to innovation promotion. The purpose of the measure is to popularise innovations among the broader public. It includes competitions for research teams aimed at applied research, international exchange of experience through conferences, seminars aimed at applied research and other PR campaigns. The target group should be not only R&D members but also enterprise sphere workers, and it is intended to include amateur inventors as well. Quantitative targets here are number of registered projects, number of conducted PR activities and number of conference participants.

The next measure under the second priority is aimed at entrepreneurs, researchers, students with exceptional potential, development engineers, who could be supported by scholarships, targeted vouchers (innovation vouchers), grants supporting education and scientific activity, through stays abroad with the purpose of gaining experience and new knowledge concerning applied research, or new innovation methods implemented in both business and public spheres. The measure addresses the problem of persistent low mobility of scientific research staff, entrepreneurs and their employees who work on innovation. The purpose of the measure is creation of a supportive programme to gain new experience and international exchange of experience in the innovation area. Applicants could be entrepreneurs, research institutes, universities as well as individuals. The grants might be in the form of support for participation in conferences, seminars, specialised exhibitions aimed at innovation, scholarships, support for educational stays or other educational and scientific activity. The quantitative indicators are number of participants in educational activities and number of activities.

The first measure within the *third priority* aims at increasing innovation activity of private companies, increasing the value added of their output, increasing production effectiveness and decreasing negative impacts on the environment. This measure addresses the issue of low company innovativeness, low investment in innovation, insufficient commercialisation of R&D results into practice and low level of innovation management capability. The goal is to create a support system for innovative activities, including transfer of modern technology and provision of venture capital from public, EU and private sources. Examples in this area indicate that this is a very frequently used tool of explicit policy in France, the United Kingdom, Belgium, Latvia, Luxembourg and Israel. The quantitative indicators are number of successful projects, the value of venture capital funds and the ratio of public to private sources within the funds.

The next measure deals with the improvement of the innovative environment. It aims to increase the competitiveness of private companies by way of applied research support and innovation activities from public, private and EU financial sources, in the form of co-financing for selected activities relating to the implementation of innovation. Within the framework of the measure, support will be provided for the development of business infrastructure in brown-field industrial parks (eligible costs to include environmental audits, rehabilitation of contaminated industrial locations, etc.), incubators for starting off entrepreneurs and sole traders in industry and services, and incubators focused on innovative business, supporting the building of innovation business centres for entrepreneurs to foster cooperation between universities, R&D organisations and the business sector with the aim of improving access to highly technical information, to applied research results, and to new advanced technologies. The main indicator here is the number of companies located in the parks.

The last measure focuses on acceleration of commercialisation of innovations, specifically on patent registration support, protection of intellectual property, building quality management systems, certification and progressive technology transfer. An important part of this tool will be the programme supporting spin-off activities in the enterprise as well as in the academic and research sphere. This will enable new ideas formed in companies, universities or research institutes to find their way into the life of a new company. It will enable support for the implementation of the results of innovation projects for which the originators lack sufficient funds of their own, and for which there is no guarantee of immediate profits, so that they are not suitable for support through indirect financial tools. The quantitative indicators here are number of supported patents, number of processes of certification, number of acquired licenses, value added of projects and number of spin-off companies.

Innovation projects generally focus on the organisation of events and training programmes, and the setting up of any number of knowledge-based activities. What is usually missing is the feedback element or assessment process indicating acomplishment of designated goal. In this context, it must be stressed that the Innovation Strategy has two dominant features which make it better than previous, similar documents. The first is the mission to serve as a manual or 'road-map' for the creation of a Slovakian NSI. The second positive side is the assessment system, including quantitative targets. But its main imperfection is that in its present form, and in current institutional conditions, it is unworkable, as witness the inactivity of the competent institutions over the last two years. So far, the related initiatives have not been implemented, or even started. The Strategy remains just one more document concerning the development plans of Slovakia.

6. Conclusion

While developed countries have been focusing on technological progress and development and creation of qualitative competitive instruments, Slovakia has been dealing with economic imbalances and the transformation process. That process has brought a positive perception from foreign investors, and has been an essential condition for subsequent high economic growth. This high economic growth was created by the national workforce, but the other factors of production have been largely foreign. Building an economy just on cheap labour seems in the long term unsustainable.

Slovakia does not currently have a national system of innovation. But, taking a closer look, it is possible to recognise the elements of one, though they do not interact in terms of economically useful outcomes. Responsibility for science, technology and innovation policy are shared among the Government Council for Science and Technology, the Ministry of Education and the Ministry of Economy, with help from the Ministry of Finance. Such fragmentation leads to mismatches and misalignments, and often contradictory results. Institutions from sub-levels of the NSI just conduct activities as approved by their mother institutions, since they have no authority to do more.

Innovation system bottlenecks in Slovakia can be assessed from two opposite but complementary viewpoints. From the *supply* side, the main faults are the dominant orientation to basic research in narrowly defined areas which might be very important within highly complex problems, but are not directly exploitable for market needs. Where the situation is the opposite, the current practice of releasing results through publications leads to exploitation of the results without benefits to the inventors and their institutes. Even where results could in principle be commercialised, market conditions may make them unattractive for private companies. On the other hand, the promotional activities of R&D institutions are generally weak, so that firms may be left unaware of potential opportunities.

From the *demand* side, the interest of indigenous subjects in R&D, innovation and innovative entrepreneurship is very low, as are managerial skills and the overall business culture associated with future development. Foreign direct investors are oriented towards cost advantages, and are unwilling to link up with a formal innovation system that is in fact not functional. Efforts to interlink R&D with the economy through innovation centres and technology incubators have not attained their goal yet. Most of these are struggling to survive, and often abandon their claims to the status of technology institute to that end.

The Innovation Strategy 2007–2013 is trying to solve some of these problems. Its targets are high-quality infrastructure and an effective system of innovation, improvements in the educational system focused on linkages between the academic and private spheres, and the creation of effective innovation instruments. The idea is good and the strategy appropriate. The document has some imperfections, though. If we agree with Edquist's dictum (2000, 16) that a national system of innovation cannot be created but only its constituent parts, the efforts of Slovakian plans will be fruitless. The strategic aim of the Innovation Strategy is stated thus: `In the period 2007–2013 a national system of innovation will be created … '. But there is no definition of how the innovation system is understood. The system is a complex issue, and the Strategy addresses only parts of it. It does not take note of national particularities, and most of the measures are simply taken over from the systems of other countries — another mistake according to the theory of innovation systems. The positive side is more frequent discussion of innovation and innovation strategy. In the end that will lead to higher innovation awareness.

References

Balzat, M. (2006). *An Economic Analysis of Innovation*, Cheltenham, Edward Elgar Publishing.

Economics Ministry of the Slovak Republic (2006). *Innovation Strategy 2007–2013*, Bratislava.

Edquist, C.H. and McKelvey, M. (2000). *System of Innovation: Growth, Competitiveness and Employment*, Cheltenham, Edward Elgar Publishing.

Klas, A. *et al.* (2005). *Technologický a inovačný rozvoj v Slovenskej republike, Ustav slovenskej a svetovej ekonomiky SAV*, Bratislava.

Klas, A. (2006). *Vývoj inštitúcií výskumu a vyššieho vzdelávania na Slovensku (860–2005), Ekonomický ústav SAV*, Bratislava.

Lundvall, B.A. (ed.). (1992). *National System of Innovation*, London, Pinter Publishers.

McGowan, F., Radosevic, S. and von Tunzelmann, N. (2004). *The Emerging Industrial Structure of the Wider Europe*, London, Routledge.

Morvay, K. (2005). *Výkonnosť a konkurencieschopnosť Slovenska v integrovanej Európe — otázky, mýty, odpovede*, M.E.S.A. 10, Bratislava.

OECD working papers (1996). *National Innovation Systems.*

OECD: *Main Science and Technology Indicators, 2000–2006.*

www.statistics.sk (Statistical Office of Slovakia).

www.nbs.sk (National Bank of Slovakia).

www.ec.europa.eu/eurostat (Eurostat).

www.sav.sk (Slovak Academy of Sciences).

www.sario.sk (Slovak Investment and Trade Development Agency (SARIO)).

www.nadsme.sk (National Agency for the Development of Small and Medium Enterprises (NADSME)).

www.apvv.sk (Slovak Research and Development Agency (APVV)).

SECTION 2

LABOUR MARKETS, JOB MATCHING AND SOCIAL NETWORKING

CHAPTER 7

JOB MATCHING, HUMAN CAPITAL ACCUMULATION
AND ECONOMIC DEVELOPMENT

DAVID A. DYKER

1. Introduction

In no area of policy studies is there greater scope for confusion and subjectivity, and for divergence in the interpretation of (sometimes apparently contradictory) statistical data, than in that of job matching. Let us begin by listing some of the most prominent such difficulties.

- The 'conventional wisdom', widely propagated by politicians in particular, and by some business managers, is that job matching, or rather failures of job matching, reflect essential weaknesses in national education systems. Yet the conclusion of a recent, major study of job matching in the UK is that 'it is difficult to conclude that policies to improve the quality of labour supply in the UK — including the expansion of Higher Education — are substantially to blame for the job mismatches which exist in the UK labour market. Indeed, this report includes evidence that there are significant demand-side factors which explain some of the job matching problems which the UK faces.' (Bevan and Cowling, 2007, 51.)
- Overall rates of job matching in the EU, as measured by the *European Working Conditions Survey*, are generally quite high — 85% on average across the whole Union in 2000, compared to 84% in 1996. In Denmark it was as high as 92% in 2000. And half of the respondents reporting mismatching specified over-skilling rather than under-skilling.[1] Yet when companies are asked about the key business problems facing them they are strongly inclined to cite shortages of skilled labour. Thus the *Observatory of European SMEs* found for the period 2005–2006 that 35% of SMEs (and incidentally 42% of LSEs) cited shortage of skilled labour as a major constraint. Comparable figures for SMEs in the new member states are considerably higher — as high as 72% in Lithuania and 39% on average over the 12 new member states (The Gallup Organisation, 2007, 25). It should be noted, however,

---
[1] A further *European Working Conditions Survey* was conducted in 2005. However, it does not appear to have included questions about job matching.

that detailed analysis of the *European Working Conditions Survey* data for the UK reveals that under-skilling problems are particularly high for the category of 'plant and machine operatives', i.e. skilled industrial workers, a key category of labour demand for manufacturing SMEs.
- Most of the job-matching data is subjective. Thus the *European Working Conditions Survey* is based on worker interviews, while the *Observatory of European SMEs* puts its questions to management.
- While perfect job matching is clearly, *a priori*, a 'good thing', it is difficult to demonstrate its impact on overall economic performance with reference to aggregate economic statistics. Thus the UK, the flexible labour markets of which are widely cited as one of the main factors behind relatively strong GDP growth performance in recent years, has the lowest rate of job matching (77% in 1996 and 80% in 2000) in the EU, according to the *European Working Conditions Survey.*

We cannot hope to resolve all of these issues in this short chapter. What we will try to do is to go through some of the generally available empirical material in greater detail, seeking at the very least to clarify some of the taxonomical and factual questions surrounding the subject, and providing on this basis a more focused introduction to the empirical work in the succeeding chapters.

2. Job Matching — Which Segments of the Labour Market Should We Focus On?

Do aggregate figures on job matching conceal more than they reveal? How useful are they for a book focusing on the knowledge economy? Some of the most notorious and recalcitrant labour shortages relate to traditional trades based on skills (in the old-fashioned sense) rather than knowledge in the Lisbon Agenda sense. Famously the UK has suffered from a shortage of plumbers ever since I can remember. Good plumbers can make a great deal of money in the UK, and British technical colleges offer excellent courses in plumbing, but those things in themselves have not been enough to solve the problem. In the last two or three years the problem has finally been, to a degree, solved, through the phenomenon of the 'Polish plumber', who has attained almost legendary status, and come to symbolise the impact on the British labour market of EU eastwards enlargement. The story tells us something about the integration of the European labour market, about the phenomenon of 'the foreigner doing the jobs that no one else wants to do', but virtually nothing about job matching in a knowledge economy.

The situation at the other end of the labour supply spectrum is even more complex and confusing. In recruiting for management jobs, what are companies looking for? Do they want graduates in economics, finance, business studies etc.? Do they want specialists in the field of the company's specialisation (e.g. chemistry graduates for chemicals firms)? Do they just want good graduates in any subject? It is very difficult to give a clear-cut answer to this question, for two reasons. Firstly, many companies find it difficult to project their business plans more than a year or two into the future, so that it is very hard for them to have any clearly defined strategy for recruitment to management positions (Bevan and Cowling, 2007, 41–42). Secondly, and within that constraint, companies may pursue recruitment strategies which explicitly de-emphasise precise job matching. Bevan and Cowling (2007, 48) pick out two such strategies, namely:

1. *Credentialism*, under which the firm or organisation will aim explicitly to recruit personnel overqualified in strict job-matching terms, on the assumption that the best qualified people are ultimately the best matched to the job. A UK example from the government sector is the 'Teach-First' scheme, which seeks to channel brilliant young graduates into teaching in bottleneck disciplines like mathematics in 'difficult' inner-London schools.
2. *The 'Magnet' employer*, whereby a company or organisation with a high-profile image uses its 'brand' to attract top graduates, not because it thinks that they are the best job matches, but because it thinks they are the best material for training 'on the job'. The company may also believe that having 'high-flyers' on its staff reinforces the image of the company. Many top Japanese companies fit into this category.

We leave the question of whether these strategies are well-taken or mistaken to a later section. Suffice to say for the present that they make nonsense of any attempt to assess job matching in strict, quantitative terms.

In between the plumbers and the high-flyers we have a broad swathe of occupations, many of them IT-based, which are not management jobs, which may not require higher-educational qualifications, but which are skill-intensive, and clearly central to the knowledge economy. When SME managers talk about acute skill shortages, it is probably mainly this kind of occupational group that they have in mind. Partly in function of the pattern of technological change, partly because of (related) changes in management style, there has over recent decades been a tendency to move away in these occupational areas from rigidly bounded 'Fordist' skill profiles (which rarely offered any opportunities for incremental up-skilling) to more flexible employment patterns, based on multi-skilling and continuous training. Once again, therefore, we have to be careful about how we interpret aggregate job-matching statistics. The implicit theory lying behind those statistics is essentially a Fordist one, so they may not be well designed to pick up emerging patterns of multi-skilling. That might help us to understand the paradox of the UK, with its flexible working patterns and (relatively) poor job-matching statistics.

3. The Supply Side — Is There a Problem, or Isn't There?

The above material must incline us to agree with Bevan and Cowling's assessment of the relative importance of supply-side and demand-side problems in relation to job matching. If companies only want the best graduates for management jobs, irrespective of their specialisation, and if multi-skilling is the pattern of the future in relation to the more humble positions within the knowledge economy, why worry about the supply side? While accepting Bevan and Cowling's argument in general terms, we would suggest the following reasons why we should not forget about the supply side altogether.

1. There is evidence that some university specialisations provide a better foundation for management work, even where there is no direct matching of specialisation to job as such. The most striking example is radio astronomy, in itself a rather abstruse area of science with few direct spin-offs for business in terms of equipment and hard technology. 'Much more important were the economic benefits associated with the skills embodied in the postgraduates trained in radio astronomy who later moved on to other occupations. A survey of these former students revealed that their training in such tasks as the construction of receiver equipment, the development of computer programmes, and the devising of mathematical techniques for processing and analysing data was found to be extremely useful in their subsequent careers. About 30% of those surveyed had at some stage occupied a post involving "research, design and development" in industry.' (Martin and Salter, 1996, 27, quoting research reported in Irvine and Martin, 1984, 113)

2. There are serious supply-side problems in the form of imbalances in the pattern of specialisation in higher education in all of the European economies. Pål Børing, in his chapter on job-matching issues in Norway in this section, demonstrates that mismatches are much more common with graduates in generic disciplines than with graduates in vocational disciplines. The problem is particularly acute in the transition countries. Partly as a reaction against the 'engineeringism' of communism, partly because young people in particular felt the need to position themselves within the new market economy, there was a rush into economics and business courses in the 1990s, with the excess demand being met through the creation of dozens of new private universities and business schools. In Kazakhstan, for example, there are now 750,000 university students and just 500,000 technical college students. Of the total number of technical college students, only 1% study mechanical engineering and only 2% electrical engineering, with the majority of students studying humanities and social sciences.[2] In a similar vein, but more strikingly, 'the education system

---

[2] Report on conference 'The status and problems of training of specialists in the education system and companies of the Republic of Kazakhstan. Prospects for integration of production and technical education', organised by the Confederation of Employers of the Republic of Kazakhstan, May, 2006. See *Panorama* 17, 2006, 3 (in Russian).

[in Estonia] is fragmented and unbalanced: the higher education system is oversized and does not sufficiently take into account the needs of the labour market. Over production takes place in the so-called soft areas (economics, law and management education) while specialists in physical sciences or engineering are lacking.' (Technopolis, 2006, 29). As we will see in the following chapters, the situation is similar in Hungary and Romania. The problem is if anything even more serious in relation to the training of technicians. In many transition countries the system of technical colleges has virtually collapsed, creating severe shortages of electricians, specialist installation workers and the like. Some of this may be marginal to the knowledge economy in a direct sense, but it may have serious knock-on effects — you cannot install an IT system without electricians.

4. What is the Relationship Between Job-Matching and S&T?

As we have seen in Section 1 of this book, there are plenty of problems of alignment between S&T systems and the business sector in transition countries. Can we pinpoint specific problems of job matching in those countries that spin off from those alignment problems? Two points come immediately to mind:

1. The training of graduates is one of the most important ways in which S&T contributes to economic development, and specifically to the governance of the economy. 'New graduates entering industry bring not only knowledge of recent scientific research, but also abilities to solve complex problems, perform research and develop ideas. Instrumentation skills and techniques are especially valuable.' (Salter *et al.*, 2000, p. 32.) Transition region S&T organisations tend, however, to be weak in relation to the training of graduates. In the socialist period, the general pattern was for teaching to be concentrated in the universities, research in the institutes of the Academies of Sciences, with graduate students unevenly spread across the whole system. The transition period has witnessed changes here, but it is difficult to say to what extent they represent progress. Thus in Russia the number of research students (*aspiranty*) in institutes of the Academy of Sciences grew by 230% over the 1990s. But only 10–12% of students actually complete their dissertations (Yegorov, 2006, 10). As we saw in Chapter 6, Ph.D. completion rates in Slovakia are slightly better than that. And in the more advanced transition economies, notably in Estonia and the Czech Republic, significant progress has been made towards establishing a Western-style system where postgraduate education, and specifically Ph.D. programmes, are closely integrated into R&D programmes. No detailed information on the impact of these changes has come to hand. In the case of Estonia, however, a recent, authoritative study gauges that 'the continued pursuit of higher quality and a greater range and number of doctoral study programmes with appropriate postgraduate possibilities to continue research *needs to be assured.*' (Technopolis,

2006, 29, emphasis added.) In Romania, a law of June 2004 made provision for the creation of *consortia of universities and R&D institutions*, to offer masters' and doctoral programmes within the framework of high-level research programmes. The Romanian Ministry of Education and Research has also instituted a system of postdoctoral programmes for young researchers (*ERAWATCH Research Inventory Report for Romania*). Implementation of this programme has, however, been hampered by a lack of clear specialisation among universities, a related shortage of good postdoctoral programmes, and a dearth of adequate supervisors. (Miclea, 2008.)

2. The highly conservative pattern of 'disciplinary comparative advantage' in transition country S&T systems highlighted by successive research reports means that the general orientation of S&T workers in these countries is still towards the priorities of the defunct centrally-planned economy, rather than those of a dynamic market economy. We should be careful here, however. As noted above, training in particular areas of the classic hard sciences — maths, physics and chemistry — is acknowledged to be the best preparation for business management in any part of the world. Asian tigers like Taiwan and Korea also show disciplinary comparative advantage in physics and chemistry, along with engineering (Lattimore and Ravesz, 1996, Table 4.1). Many of the specific skill shortages reported in transition countries relate to physics and chemistry, precisely the areas, along with maths, in which transition region science remains strongest. That suggests that it is weaknesses in graduate training rather than in science itself that lie at the bottom of at least some of the skill shortages in the transition countries. But in the sunrise sectors like ICT and biotechnology, transition region science is weak. Where employers need young people with specific skills in these areas, transition region S&T is often not in a position to supply those needs, even where there is a general willingness to develop graduate training.

All of this needs to understood against the background of the general problem of subjectivity in the job-matching area, and indeed in the area of the general relationship between S&T and economic development as a whole. Public perceptions of this relationship are largely filtered through the prism of government, and we must in turn be ready to filter out political 'noise'. Pavitt notes, in relation to the general issue of the relationship between fundamental science and business, that:

> It is not clear that the pressure in European countries for more practical relevance in government-funded basic research comes from business firms, many of whose managers in fact fully understand the benefits of basic research activities complementary to their own applied research and development activities. It often comes instead from those in governments (and particularly in

Ministries of Finance) who are responsible for the accountability and effectiveness of public expenditures, and who cannot (or do not want to) understand the complexities of tracing the benefits of basic research. (Pavitt, 2000, 13.)

This brings us back to the issue of how well business managers understand their own needs specifically in the job-matching area, and on to the next section in this chapter.

5. Do Managers Know What They Want?

One of Bevan and Cowling's main conclusions is that employers are more to blame for job-matching problems than teachers and educational organisations. They pin-point employer resourcing practices as one of the reasons for over-skilling and the underutilisation of skills (Bevan and Cowling, 2007, 16). They question the rationale of company training programmes, pointing out that in the UK around 40% of under-skilled workers receive no training, while about the same percentage of over-skilled workers *do* receive training (*ibidem*, 33).[3] They dismiss credentialism as being based on a 'mistaken belief' (*ibidem*, 48). Quoting a recent British government report (Leitch, 2006), they define the major challenge of job matching in terms of 'developing and sustaining a robust, demand-led approach to skill formation and utilisation, with employers playing a more prominent role' (Bevan and Cowling, 2007, 10). We should be sceptical about the strength of these assertions, if not about their essential correctness, on two grounds:

1. There are strong empirical grounds for being more positive about credentialism. The Teach-First programme in the UK has been a successful one. And the material cited earlier about the contribution of radio astronomy graduates to business management suggests that intentionally recruiting over-qualified people may be a very good business strategy indeed.
2. Bevan and Cowling's conclusions are largely based on the UK experience, which may not be typical.

On that second point, it is worth stressing that, as we shall see in detail in Chapter 8, there is evidence of similar problems on the demand side in Hungary. We should, nevertheless, keep an open mind on the relative importance of supply-side and demand-side problems in the job-matching domain. Bevan and Cowling have certainly done us a great service in stressing (perhaps overstressing) that job-matching problems are not all the fault of teachers.

---

[3] But they also note that training reduces the level of over-skilling. It is difficult to interpret this finding unless we are prepared to dismiss over-skilling as an essentially subjective category, reflecting exaggerated ideas of own capability on the part of workers.

6. What About the Informal Labour Market?

All our discussion up to now has been based on the assumption that the labour market is populated exclusively by people who have a proper job, pay national insurance etc., and people who would like to have such a job. This is a palpably inaccurate assumption. All EU economies have substantial grey economies, therefore grey labour forces, and this, indeed, is one of the reasons why the British authorities find it so difficult to give precise figures for immigration into the UK. In the CEE countries and applicant countries like Turkey and Croatia the grey economy is relatively that much bigger. In Hungary there are around 100,000 people who operate as 'sub-contractors' to big firms on a regular basis, i.e. effectively work for those firms, but without paying social security contributions.[4] In Turkey, in 2003, according to OECD estimates, over 60% of the workers in construction were unregistered, and over 40% of workers in trade and transport. Even in finance, some 20% of workers were unregistered![5] In some CIS countries, e.g. Georgia and Armenia, the grey economy is very large indeed, and in parts of the former Yugoslavia, e.g. Macedonia and Kosovo, it is predominant. In striving, as we do in this book, to look beyond the EU heartland to the European periphery, we clearly cannot afford to neglect the informal labour market.

If the informal economy is predominantly populated by unskilled workers, peeling potatoes in restaurant kitchens, picking seasonal crops etc., then we do not have to worry too much about it in a knowledge economy context. Certainly many grey economy workers in the UK are doing precisely those types of jobs. No doubt the same is true of CEE. But the most striking thing to emerge from the literature on the informal economy in CEE is that many knowledge workers work in that economy, too. In Poland, according to the State Statistical Administration (GUS) survey of 1995, grey employment was concentrated in the skilled worker category (11.0% of the total number of people in that category), but as high as 5.5% among university graduates (and only 6.7% among workers with only primary education) (Grabowski, 2002, 5). And even within the sub-group of foreign workers, many grey economy workers in Poland work in professional positions (Grabowski, 2002, 13). Mroczkowski's study, based on a survey conducted about the same time as the GUS survey, also found evidence of a substantial presence on informal labour markets of graduate workers, especially in Warsaw (Mroczkowski, 1997, 28). All of this data is rather out of date, especially the GUS survey data. But the 2003 data from Turkey, with its surprisingly high figure for unregistered employment in the financial sector, suggests that, in that country at least, there are still a lot of knowledge workers

---

[4] 'Piac és Profit', *Százezer színlelt szerzoeődés*, 20/6/06. I am indebted to Andrea Szalavetz for providing me with this reference.
[5] OECD, *Economic Policy Reforms*, Paris, 2005, 115. I am indebted to Özge Aktas for providing me with this reference.

working in the grey economy. There are no hard data from Hungary on grey knowledge workers, but many journalists, actors/actresses, doctors, consultants and IT-specialists operate in that country on a sub-contracting basis as discussed above.[6]

We can only guess at how informality in employment relations might impact on the overall job-matching picture. University graduates peeling potatoes could hardly be cited as an example of successful job-matching. But university graduates working informally for a number of employers, offering specialised skills just-in-time and only as required (as many university teachers do in their spare time in the old EU countries), could be viewed as the epitome of flexible working patterns and multi-skilling. We should be careful not to idealise the informal labour market as a praiseworthy 'flight from Fordism'. All grey economy workers are by definition highly vulnerable to bullying, and in many cases bullying turns into gross exploitation (NB. less so if the worker is effectively self-employed). But we have to ask the question: in economies which report acute skill shortages, like Lithuania, as discussed above, does the informal economy come in as a compensating factor, alleviating these shortages? It is simply not possible to answer this question on the basis of currently available information. Rather it must stand as a signpost to a future major research project which would investigate the sectoral pattern of grey employment in a selected group of European countries.

References

Bevan, S. and Cowling, M. (2007). *Job Matching in the UK and Europe,* London, Skills for Business, Sector Skills Development Agency, Department for Education and Skills, Research Report 25, July.

ERAWATCH *Research Inventory Reports,* European Communities, http://cordis.europa.eu/erawatch/.

European Foundation for the Improvement of Living and Working Conditions (various years), *European Working Conditions Survey.*

Grabowski, M. (2002). *Informal Labour Market and Informal Economy during Transition — The Polish Perspective*, Gdansk Institute for Market Economies.

Irvine, J. and Martin, B. (1984). *Foresight in Science. Picking the Winners*, London, Pinter Publishers.

Lattimore, R. and Ravesz, J. (1996). *Australian Science: Performance from Public Papers*, Canberra, Bureau of Industry Economics, Report 96/3, Australian Government Printing Office.

Leitch, S. (2006). *Prosperity for All in the Global Economy — World-Class Skills*, London, HM Treasury.

Martin, B and Salter, A. (1996). *The Relationship between Publicly Funded Basic Research and Economic Performance. A SPRU Review*, Report prepared for HM Treasury, April.

---

[6] Communication from Andrea Szalavetz.

Miclea, Mircea (2008). 'Doctoral studies in Romania: admissions procedures, social and legal aspects of doctoral training', *Higher Education in Europe* 33(1): 89–92.

Mroczkowski, T. (1997). 'Informal employment in the transition economy of Poland: the case for policies leading to legalization', *Journal of East-West Studies* 3(2): 23–42.

Pavitt, K. (2000). 'Public policies to support basic research: what can the rest of the world learn from US theory and practice? (And what they should not learn)', *SPRU Electronic Working Paper Series* No. 53.

Salter, A. *et al.* (2000). *Talent, not Technology. Publicly Funded Research and Innovation in the UK,* London, CVCP, July.

The Gallup Organisation (2007). *Observatory of European SMEs, Analytical Report,* Flash Eurobarometer No. 196.

Technopolis Consulting Group Belgium SPRL (2006). *Evaluation of the Design and Implementation of Estonian RTDI Policy,* Tallinn, Ministry of Economic Affairs and Communications of the Republic of Estonia.

Yegorov, I. (2006). 'Razvitie nauchnogo potentsiala Rossii i drugikh stran SNG', mimeo.

CHAPTER 8

HUMAN CAPITAL AND SKILLS IN HUNGARY — MATCHING DEMAND AND SUPPLY

ANDREA SZALAVETZ

1. Introduction

The Hungarian labour market has been afflicted by a range of severe problems and distortions ever since the change of regime. Persistent low employment or rather high inactivity,[1] low labour mobility, excessive heterogeneity (in terms of regional and skill-related differences) of workers, sluggish rates of productivity increase and the high number of unregistered employees[2] are among the most frequently cited difficulties.[3]

> The Hungarian labour market has been stuck in a steady unfavourable state for many years, while the level of employment is extremely low…employment difficulties are concentrated in certain layers of society and certain regions of Hungary …The polarization of the Hungarian labour market[4] and the extreme and permanent territorial differences result from the low territorial mobility of the labour force... (Fazekas, 2006, 199–202)

Despite rapid growth in the supply of graduates, the Hungarian education system has been unable to give an adequate response to the challenges triggered by economic transformation and skill-biased technical change. Instead of demand-led adjustment

---

[1] The total number of employed (in the population of males (15–59) and females (15–54)) was 3.7 million in 2005, while the total number of inactive people was 2.1 million within the same age groups. The number of pensioners and other inactive people above 55 (female) and 60 (male) was 2.3 million. The activity rate in 2005 was 54.5%. *Source:* Fazekas and Kézdi, 2007.

[2] Published surveys of the widespread practice of unregistered employment relate mainly to the situation in the agricultural and rural manufacturing sectors (Kun , 2004a and 2004b, 2005). In his sociological surveys, Kun details the difficulties manufacturing firms in the eastern, unemployment-ridden part of Hungary have in finding, hiring and retaining blue-collar employees.

[3] The annual joint publication of the Institute of Economics and the Hungarian Employment Foundation *The Hungarian Labour Market* provides regularly updated, thorough analyses of the evolution and prevalent problems of the labour market situation. See also Fazekas, 2006; Kőrösi, 2005; Laki, 2007; Balla *et al.*, 2008.

[4] According to a 1998 Hungarian Central Statistical Office survey, 27% (!) of the working age population is unskilled (with no more than primary school completed). (Quoted by Karvalics and Kollányi, 2006). According to the calculations of Dávid *et al.* (2005), the corresponding share in 2001 was 20.4%.

and skill upgrading, educational expansion has rather produced a supply shock,[5] and has led to the devaluation of the value of certain diplomas, and to some decrease in the return to education (decrease of the wage premium to university degree). The extent of this decrease is still debated among analysts.[6]

The worsening performance of the educational system is documented both by hard facts, and by the results of 'soft' sociological investigations. In terms of the former, international comparisons suggest that the pattern of education by field of specialisation in Hungary is not conducive to the process of catching-up and staying competitive in a knowledge-based global economy. While Finland or Ireland both have 34% of total graduates in the fields of science and engineering, the corresponding Hungarian figure was just 25% in 2004 (OECD Education at a Glance, 2007[7]) As for retention rates in higher education, the Hungarian rate (62% in 2004) is lower than that of the advanced economies.[8] The OECD Programme for International Student Assessment has documented Hungarian students' worsening performance over the years, and the persistent and increasing inequalities within the Hungarian schooling system.[9] The system fails to enhance social mobility and catching-up: student performance is strongly linked to their social background.

In relation to the latter point, the Public Employment Service, an organisation created by the amended Employment Act of 2001, commissioned a Hungarian consulting firm (3K Consens Bureau) to prepare a comprehensive survey of the state and evolution of labour demand and supply relations in Hungary (Dávid et al., 2005, 2007).

---

[5] The total number of graduates was 640,000 in 1993 and 850,000 in 2003. The share of new graduates in the total number of graduates was as high as 30.1% in the 2001–2005 period. (Source: Kertesi and Köllő, 2007, 80). In the early 2000s the annual number of new graduates was 2.5 times higher (!) than the aggregate demand for graduates from the labour market (Dávid et al., 2005).

[6] In relation to the pre-2002 period, Galasi (2004) discovered no evidence of university graduates increasingly filling jobs that require only secondary education. According to Galasi, although the proportion of overqualified workers increased in the second half of the 1990s, the market rewarded the extra years of education, so that the return to education did not diminish. Later investigations however, found convincing evidence of a worsening negative trend (i.e. increasing numbers of overqualified workers; worsening employment prospects for job seekers with higher education; declining wage premium and returns to education) (Kertesi and Köllő, 2007). It should be borne in mind that the Hungarian wage premium used to be among the highest, so that even with a small decrease it is still higher than the OECD average (OECD Education at a Glance, 2007). According to the calculations of Dávid et al. (2005, 8), 8% of employees with higher educational attainment were employed in occupations that did not require a diploma in 2001. On the other hand, there were 72,500 employees without diploma in occupations that require higher educational attainment. This number is approximately 10% of the total number of diploma holders.

[7] In its country briefing the OECD formulated this conclusion even more harshly: 'Relative to population, Hungary produces a lower number of science graduates (695 per 100,000 of the employed population aged 25–34 years) than any other OECD country and less than half the rate for the OECD on average. Social sciences, business, law and services are the most common subjects of graduates, with these subjects representing more than 50% of the annual university level graduate output.' (OECD Education at a Glance, 2007).

[8] Finland: 71%; France: 79%; Germany: 75%; Ireland: 78%; Netherlands: 76%; UK: 71% (OECD Education at a Glance, 2007).

[9] The social segregation index in educational institutions among 15-year-old students in Hungary is the highest among 30 OECD economies (as of 2003) (Source: Field et al., 2007, 59).

These studies found that the traditional relations between the key players of the system (employers, educational institutions, students) had been disrupted after the change of regime, and have not recovered since. *Parents, students and educational institutions disregard the messages of the labour market.* (2005, 5) Educational institutions are financed according to the number of students admitted, thus are not forced to establish 'business-oriented' relations with firms and take employers' needs into consideration when determining their curriculum. Decision-makers are too timid to intervene in educational institutions that insist on their autonomy. This has led to the emergence of *extreme and worsening imbalances: on the one hand shortages of specific skills keep building up, and on the other the stock of holders of superfluous degrees for which no demand exists also keeps growing* (2007, 14–15, 25, 37).

It is in this context that we have carried out our field investigations on job matching. Job matching has been a favourite topic in mainstream labour economics, with papers surveying trends in (i) job-requirements-related qualification levels; (ii) wage premium; (iii) mobility and educated labour force reallocation issues.[10] They have also looked at the empirical data on:

- returns to schooling at various levels;
- evolution of the number of jobs at various educational levels;
- tendencies in the gap between observed and required education;
- the proportion of workers with higher education diplomas working in occupations requiring higher education etc.

A common research methodology is interviewing larger or smaller samples of job holders about their perceptions concerning their qualification levels (overqualified, properly qualified, underqualified, related to the requirements of their current occupations). Another common research question in interviews is the relation between individual qualification levels and the frequency of participation in job-related training schemes.

An alternative, similar method is to interview a sample of recently graduated students about the process and outcomes of their labour market entrance. Students are asked to assess the usefulness of their studies, the skills they miss most at their workplace, as well as the most useful skills they had acquired at their higher educational institutions. This approach generates data about wage levels, the difficulties in finding a job, training efforts on the part of companies and overall levels of satisfaction etc. (Hajdú *et al.*, 2005; Kabai *et al.*, 2007)

A third analytical approach takes as its point of departure the analysis of employers' expectations, the difficulties they have in finding adequately qualified

---

[10] For a comprehensive survey of the Hungarian situation and literature overview see Galasi and Varga, 2005.

employees, and the evolution and costs of employers' efforts to help the newly hired meet job-related requirements.[11]

However, to our knowledge, there has been no investigation in Hungary focusing on the matching of supply and demand in a key specific segment of the labour market, namely that of graduates with higher education.[12] Our investigation tries to fill this gap, by exploring:

- company perceptions of difficulties in recruiting suitable employees for occupations requiring high levels of skill/educational attainment, and their selection methods and practices;
- company training efforts and methods;
- aspects of company relations with higher educational institutions.

Our analysis is based on data compiled from several sources: field investigations (knowledge- based local SMEs and MNCs' local subsidiaries); interviews with representatives of higher educational institutions; and surveys of university and MNC homepages.

The aim of this chapter is to provide a broad overview on job matching in the upper segment of the labour market, to identify the main problems, and to draw competitiveness-related conclusions and formulate policy recommendations. The main focus of our investigations is ICT-related (software and programming) skills, which allows for the selection of sample companies from a broad range of industries. Nevertheless, we shall also elaborate on some other fields (e.g. research and technical development skills; practical engineering skills), where our interviews offered interesting lessons. The paper deliberately details anecdotal corporate cases, since our goal is to provide insights into the multifaceted process of job matching, i.e. to illustrate issues rather than simply mobilise quantitative evidence.

---

[11] One recent example is Polónyi (2007) who carried out, in one of Hungary's NUTS II regions, a questionnaire-based survey of a sample of 146 companies about employers' expectations vis-à-vis individual levels of higher education, their relations to higher educational institutions and their views about ways to improve this relationship. The author identified some mismatch between companies' skill expectations and the focus of higher educational institutions' curricula (excessively theory-oriented education at all levels, disappointing level of command of foreign languages). Another example is Laki's (2001) field interviews of a sample of 15 companies and six vocational training institutions, about the human resource management practices and expectations and problems of the former group, and performance, industry relations and problems of the latter group.

[12] The only exception is Selmeczy and Tóth (2006). Here, the authors carried out field interviews about company demand for graduate job entrants, and whether employers are satisfied with supply. According to their findings, electrical and mechanical engineers and IT-specialists with adequate qualities and skills are the most difficult to find (poor command of languages and lack of practical experience were the most frequently mentioned problems). Of the interviewed 121 firms, 40% provided some kind of training to the newly hired employees (the larger the firm, the more likely it is that new recruits receive training). As many as 52% of the interviewed firms had some relations with higher educational institutions, but only six of them participated in the elaboration of the academic curriculum. The authors repeated the survey in 2007, and this time interviewed 1,000 firms. Results were basically similar to the previous survey. In the larger sample, every fourth firm maintained some form of relation with at least one institution of higher education (www.gvi.hu).

Section 2 overviews companies' recruitment practices and problems, as well as the skills and abilities they consider indispensable. It also tries to identify differences between MNC and SME practice. Section 3 is concerned with ex-post job matching in the light of companies' training efforts and methods. Section 4 surveys the state and the evolution of industry–university interactions, companies' involvement in determining university curricula, and the support they provide to universities with a view to improving the match between the supply and demand for graduates. Section 5 concludes.

2. Recruitment Practices and Problems

Both the MNC subsidiaries and the SMEs interviewed were unanimous in claiming that it is extremely difficult to find talented, interested, ambitious and hard-working new employees, and that this is one of the most significant obstacles of growth. The other side of the coin is that it is becoming increasingly difficult for graduates to find employment, even in occupations with substantial labour shortage. Personal acquaintances matter more and more.

Problems with supply are manifest in relation to both quantity and quality. Career advertisements are posted continuously (i.e. IT-specialists can submit applications on a continuous basis, rather than up to a predetermined deadline) and all of the interviewed companies had vacancies (some of them as many as 15–20 positions) at the time of interview.[13]

The recruitment strategy of both groups was to hire recently graduated persons. Some experience was, of course, considered an asset, but firms were not willing to pay much more to 'poach' experienced professionals from competitors; they rather opted for hiring relatively inexperienced new employees and training them internally.[14] One exception was the position of top manager. In this case 'poaching someone from the competitors' seemed to be the dominant strategy at the two SMEs where this issue had arisen.

The recruitment process MNCs apply is a highly formalised one, including several selection rounds during which various skills are tested. Many of the MNCs centralise the first step of recruitment: applicants have to send their CVs to the company's global HR office, not the Hungarian one. The selection process typically takes several months, and includes language tests, job knowledge tests, cognitive tests and personality tests (aptitude, intelligence, trainability, interest, behaviour, capability to work in a team etc.), interviews, sample tasks etc.

---

[13] In 2005 3444 IT-specialists graduated, which substantially exceeds demand at the aggregate level, but at the same time there is a labour shortage in terms of specific IT-skills (Source: Dávid et al., 2007).
[14] On the other hand nearly all of the companies mentioned the steadily rising turnover rate, and confirmed that their employees are increasingly being attracted away by competitors, which shows that competition in the talent market is on the increase.

One thing that comes through very clearly from the interview material is that MNCs consider applicants' personal characteristics (values, motivations) to be as important as, sometimes more important than, their professional and vocational knowledge and skills. Capabilities including ability to work in a team, communication skills, decision-making capability, ability to work independently, responsibility, capacity to bear stress and high workloads, flexibility, learning capacity etc. are among the personal qualities in highest demand, and often limited supply.

Audi proceeded as follows: a list containing the requirements for 15 occupations the local subsidiary intended to recruit manpower for was prepared. The HR manager sent these lists to secondary and higher educational institutions in the region. Interestingly, the main part of the requirements consisted of the above-mentioned personal attributes (plus command of languages or software programming/using skills). Upon receipt of this list, professors at Széchenyi University Győr organised a brainstorming session on how to include the 'transfer' of these previously neglected skills into the curriculum, since — as they admitted — educational institutions can hardly pass these behavioural features on to students in the course of conventional programmes of professional and vocational education. These attributes and values may, in fact, be more readily acquired and assimilated in the course of elementary and secondary education.

After each round of the personnel selection process, applicants are shortlisted, and only a few of them participate in the final interviews. It also happens sometimes that on conclusion of this long selection process no one is selected, and the company launches a new recruitment campaign. Sometimes, it seems, not even managers know what they want, in managing or supervising the recruitment process. In reality, they have a clear picture about the ideal candidate, his/her vocational, language and communication skills, autonomy, commitment and values, though their expectations seem somewhat exaggerated. As one representative of a professional HR firm (the companies interviewed frequently also resort to the services of these firms) put it: *managers want to recruit employees with Chinese/Korean work culture, American autonomy, independence and decision-making capability, and Finnish language skills.*

Interviews revealed certain signs of credentialism, with employers requiring university-level diplomas for jobs that do not require the specific training or skills that make up these credentials. In Hungary, there is substantial oversupply of business graduates, and employers take advantage of new graduates' difficulties in finding work, hiring people with higher education for occupations (e.g. personal assistant, secretary etc.) that do not require a university degree. Their considerations are twofold. One is that someone with higher education may be more reliable and committed, and may be better suited to the task of answering the phone (if important customers call) than employees with secondary or vocational education. The second reason is that there are really wide discrepancies in the performance of graduates of different higher educational institutions. Some of these institutions are only a little more advanced than secondary schools, giving only the most basic skills to graduates but no serious professional knowledge. Employers are more or less aware of the differences among individual educational institutions and the values of the degrees they offer, so they tend to employ graduates from the relatively weaker institutions for tasks requiring only secondary educational attainment.

According to the HR officials interviewed, applicants consider the selection process very strenuous and tiring: language skills, for example, were tested more rigorously than they had been previously at the official language exam. The other side of the coin is that employers were highly dissatisfied with applicants' language skills. Especially in the case of software programmers, serious deficiencies in the command of languages were revealed. Even worse, it was not only in the case of job seekers specialised in science and engineering that the command of foreign languages was found to be inferior to expectations. In the case of graduates in humanities and social sciences, 'they have already passed a language exam when they are admitted to the university, and they start forgetting the language right away. It seems that university students are not required to read education-related academic papers in foreign languages: they are absolutely incapable of doing so.' (interview excerpt)

Companies also complained about job entrants' inferior-to-expectation communication skills and low confidence, as well as about the excessively theory-oriented education they seemed to have received at higher educational institutions. 'When asked to define the term "cash flow" most of them can give an answer. However, if I ask them what they use the cash flow for, what a cash flow suggests at first sight — very few of them know.' As for IT-specialists, according to one of the interviewed HR officials, 'If they can demonstrate good practical skills, it usually turns out they have acquired them during some previous work experience — practical skills are not acquired at the university.'

IBM Hungary commissioned a Hungarian research institute (GKI eNet) to prepare a survey about innovation trends in Hungary and factors influencing these trends. (Innovációs trendek, 2007). Researchers surveyed, among other things, the quality of IT-related higher education. They interviewed 500 graduating students in seven Hungarian universities and colleges (90% of them had received IT-related education). Students were basically satisfied with the quality and quantity of the theoretical education they had received, but were highly dissatisfied with the quality and quantity of practical experience they were able to access during their years of study.

One exemplary initiative that contributes to the alleviation of this deficiency is the PRACTING programme, launched by Széchenyi University Győr in 1996 with PHARE support, and still going strong. This programme not only grants students the possibility of gaining practical experience, but also contributes to job matching in the region both for SMEs and for large companies. For the modest amount of €400 (paid to the PRACTING Foundation) companies can employ an undergraduate student for half a year (the university integrates this sandwich course into its curriculum at its engineering faculties). Future engineers participate in companies' research efforts, and can thereby demonstrate their innovativeness and other capabilities, which helps them find employment later at the given company. Companies (especially SMEs) are enthusiastic about this costless way of getting acquainted with their future employees. Within the framework of the PRACTING programme, companies have to give formal feedback to the university, and assess not only the students' performance, but also the prevalent gaps in skills.

By comparison with MNC procedures, the recruitment practices of the interviewed SMEs were less formal and much simpler. The SMEs seemed to be in a better situation than the MNCs. Implementing formal HRM practices is costly in terms of time and money for small firms, but they felt they could get along without them: they benefited from their informal relations with educational institutions, or from the fact that in most cases SME CEOs were university professors themselves (the SMEs in our sample were all knowledge-based companies). They could spot talented students and attract them, and hire them without any previous formal recruitment procedure. For all that, however, MNCs are more successful in attracting the most talented graduates. As the HR manager of Siemens underlined, the huge amount they spend on public relations and image building is also beneficial for the HR department; students all know very well that Siemens is one of the top blue chip companies; they are more or less acquainted with career development possibilities in the company, and this corporate image helps Siemens attract talent. So Siemens is a classic 'magnet'-employer, as discussed in the last chapter.

3. Company Training Initiatives and Methods

Our interviews revealed that MNCs apply their company-specific HR management and development models in Hungary. They have developed a standardised company-specific system of training newly recruited employees and providing regular training for their existing ones. This way, MNCs contribute to the general improvement of the bleak assessment in the OECD *Education at a Glance* (2007) study that 'in Hungary, participation in job-related education and training is low compared with other OECD countries.'

GE has a portfolio of compulsory training programmes for all new recruits, including quality assurance and work security issues, and a so called 'Integrity Programme' about corporate culture, values, rules etc. Employees receive task-specific training and participate in professional workshops, team-building etc. Many of them receive training in communication and negotiation techniques, conflict management, ergonomics, and language courses. During their initial training period most of the newly hired people undergo a predetermined rotation process, which contributes to their integration as well as to their competence in carrying out cross-functional tasks. Managers receive training in leadership skills, management of change and various other coaching programmes.

MNCs have a system of regular, formal performance review, and elaborate programmes for their employees' career development. They encourage newly hired employees to rotate between different functional areas and divisions, and offer the possibility of transfers across locations and regional subsidiaries. Part of the training is online, with company-specific intranet courseware and exams. A good channel of knowledge acquisition is the purchase of MNC services in terms of software systems and course content. The international business software company SAP sells its own 'Learning Solution' system, which is employee-tailored and allows for flexible time management (employees can decide themselves how they share their time between working and learning). Software systems also make virtual classroom training available, where employees at various locations participate in courses sitting in front of their computers. (They may ask questions using a web camera and a microphone.)

In contrast to the formalised training processes of MNCs, Hungarian SMEs provide training to their employees in an ad hoc manner. Training is mostly in-house. SME training commitment is, however, greatly enhanced by government-sponsored programmes that support employees training. Grant schemes are announced within the framework of the National Development Plan Human Resource Development Operational Programme. Megatrend (on the borderline between SME and large-company status) has won a sizeable amount of public funding for human resource development, and launched a comprehensive programme including language courses, ECDL (European Computer Driving License) and project management courses, stress management and executive coaching, as well as EU-specific courses (EU-institutions, decision-making in the EU, the consequences of accession etc.)

Software companies, whether small or medium-sized, are an exception to the rule that SMEs devote less than average resources and attention to employees' internal training — they cannot survive without the continuous training of their employees. Many such companies have established training centres themselves, partly for their own employees, partly for their customers and their partners, but increasingly also for outsiders (as an additional source of income). Magyar Telekom offers a wide range of training services for outsiders (private persons, but in particular firms), and rents out its training premises, conference halls and seminar rooms. Magyar Telekom's business unit, the Educational and Knowledge Management Directorate, has developed various (online) curricula and makes them available for outsiders as well. Its executive coaching experts and internal organisational development experts offer consultancy services on a market basis.

4. Relations with Higher Educational Institutions

Our interviews revealed that the main difference between the local subsidiaries of large MNCs and local SMEs is the degree of formality in company relations with higher educational institutions. Local SMEs tend to rely on informal relations: managers maintain contact with their old professors.[15] In contrast to SMEs, local subsidiaries of MNCs establish formal relations with universities they intend to recruit workforce from — often with several, in some cases up to half a dozen, educational institutions.

As a rule, SME–university relations become more and more formalised in the course of their development: MNC practice has a non-negligible demonstration effect on how to manage these relations. The main obstacle for SMEs in formalising their relations with higher educational institutions is lack of finance, since establishing and maintaining a horizontal network requires a sizeable amount of money, which may be beyond the means of SMEs.

The first stage of formal relationship-building is commitment on the part of companies to grant summer placement possibilities to students. Beyond that, both MNCs and local SMEs attend annual job matching events organised by universities, where they distribute information about the company, announce vacancies, collect CVs etc. Some companies organise or participate in summer schools, where managers make presentations about the company, its evolution, its technology and its expectations about future employees.

Széchényi University Győr has been running a course entitled 'Audi: the modern company' for five years now. Here, local, regional (European) and global leaders of Audi make presentations about the company, and about organisational and business issues. While this course targets business administration students, the courses planned by Opel and Suzuki are rather about manufacturing technology issues, targeting students in Mechanical Engineering and Mechatronic Engineering faculties.

Occasionally, MNCs announce and sponsor research competitions for students. For example, IBM regularly announces a software programming competition, while Microsoft Hungary and Cisco Hungary sponsored an international IT competition 'EuroSkills', the final round of which was in Debrecen in 2008.

At a higher level of commitment, companies — usually local subsidiaries of MNCs — provide universities/colleges with in-kind support in the form of instruments, computers, software,[16] machinery, testing equipment etc. The other side of the

---

[15] According to the founder of AAM Ltd., at least 40 of his employees are his own students. His colleagues also teach at various universities; he even encourages them to provide free courses (if necessary, even during working time), in order to be able to spot talent. Balabit Ltd.'s representatives also give seminars on security solutions, and participate in and sponsor workshops organised by the Budapest University of Technology and Economics (BUTE).

[16] As much as 2–3% of Microsoft Hungary's sales revenue is devoted each year to supporting education (through a subscription licensing programme for educational institutions, Campus Agreements, scholarships, programming competitions etc.). Microsoft Hungary has opened a teacher training laboratory at Eötvös Loránd University of Sciences.

coin is that companies pay a fee to universities for using their expensive research equipment (acquired by the universities on the basis of public research grants) for company purposes. Companies sponsor university conferences related to their activities and research interests.

The next commitment level is characterised by industry–university research cooperation and regular research grants, offered either to university professors and researchers or to students.[17] MNC subsidiaries delegate specific research tasks to university professors, the tasks to be carried out together with talented students. Furthermore, they set up research competitions for the students of the given university and grant scholarships to the university's students.

General Electric regularly announces research competitions for students of the University of Miskolc. The company nominates a contact person, who supervises the student's work. Announcements contain a description of the technological background, a list of the tasks to be performed by the student (e.g. literature survey, design, testing and measuring tasks, analysis etc.) His or her work is monitored and supported also by a nominated university professor, in some cases a professor from another university, which in itself contributes to inter-university knowledge spillover. Students compete for the given topics; they hand in CVs and abstracts outlining the planned work. Applications undergo a pre-selection mechanism. The next step is that representatives of the company, together with university professors, discuss the plans of the short-listed students. The final selection is made, and the selected students are asked to hand in a more formalised and detailed work plan. They receive the grant, called the Aschner Lipót Grant,[18] for four semesters. The amount of the grant more or less corresponds to that of the minimum wage in Hungary. After the third semester, students spend one month in a summer placement at GE, where they continue working on their research topic. Following successful graduation and completion of the research task, students may receive an award amounting to three months' scholarship. They are offered a position at GE which they may take or reject. The student may also opt to participate in a GE-supported PhD programme.

GE Hungary has also launched an Edison Engineering Development Programme, which offers work experience in four diverse positions (altogether two years) within GE's global network. Selected students receive theoretical and practical training. Another programme bears the name of a famous Hungarian professor of physics, József Öveges (1895–1979), who popularised science for a generation of young Hungarians. This programme, launched by GE Healthcare, involves students in individual development teams working on GE's global development initiatives.

---

[17] One example is the E.ON Scientific Awards for students and professors of BUTE, which reward outstanding publications in the field of energetics. Siemens also offers an award (the Werner Siemens Excellence Award) to honour outstanding dissertation and PhD work at BUTE. Ericsson's HSN (High Speed Networks) Lab provides scholarships for students of various technical universities to conduct research activities related to Ericsson's interests.

[18] Lipót Aschner (1872–1952) was the first CEO of the forerunner of Tungsram (the company taken over by GE).

Participants thus obtain deeper insights into a specific R&D project, and also into the work culture and methods of GE, and can develop their own dissertation work in the process. The duration of the programme is two semesters, but GE also supports, under the same name, longer programmes oriented to PhD students.

The GE Foundation Scholar-Leaders Programme, with a scholarship of €1,000 annually for three years, is designed for students in the fields of economics, management, engineering and technology. It assists students in accumulating personal human capital.

In some cases universities/faculties/researchers benefit from MNCs' global (not Hungary- or CEE-specific) programmes. For example, BUTE benefited from the IBM Faculty Award, a competitive worldwide programme intended to foster collaboration between researchers at leading universities worldwide and those in IBM research, development and services organisations.

The strength of the demonstration effect from this kind of MNC initiative shows up clearly in the way that one fast-growing Hungarian SME has decided to follow suit and announce its own support scheme. Balabit Ltd., a software company (with 30 employees), has set up a yearly scholarship named after its main product. This scholarship is a useful channel for industry–university links, and it also generates good PR for the firm. According to the CEO, granting a scholarship is a much cheaper solution than hiring someone who turns out to be inadequate after three months. Balabit can assess the student's performance when evaluating his work during the period of the scholarship. They thereby gain better knowledge about the student's capabilities, and can better decide whether to hire him or not. Balabit has also offered BUTE financial support for a laboratory, where students can learn about its security solutions, and about security systems and firewalls in general.

Some of the interviewed companies participate in special research network initiatives, including Cooperation Research Centres (CRCs) and Regional University Knowledge Centres (RUKCs),[19] programmes initiated by the National Office for Research and Technology. These programmes involve universities with the status of centre of excellence, which establish a tight network with companies. Network members share the costs of expensive research infrastructure and initiate a range of joint research activities, which facilitates technology transfer on the one hand, and

---

[19] One example (there are 14 CRCs altogether) is the Inter-University Cooperation Research Centre for Telecommunications and Informatics centred around Budapest University of Technology and Economics, with corporate members including Ericsson Hungary, T-Com Hungary, Sun Microsystems and others. An example of a RUKC is the Regional University Knowledge Centre for the Vehicle Industry centred around the Széchenyi University of Győr, with partners including Rába Axle Manufacturing Ltd. and Shefenacker Automotive Parts Ungarn. Another example is the IT Innovation and Knowledge Centre at BUTE. This consortium includes multinational companies (T-Systems, Nuance-Recognita, Hewlett Packard — these MNCs all have substantial local R&D expenditures), as well as innovative SMEs (including Megatrend, DSS, e-Group, etc.) In addition to joint development projects, the stated aim of the centre is to involve PhD, MSc and BSc students in its work, and give them the possibility of acquiring practical experience.

increases the practical (business) orientation of university research on the other. RUKC and CRC programmes co-finance industry–university joint research and universities' investment in research-related infrastructure.[20]

At an even more intense level of industry–university relations, companies get involved in the formulation of academic curricula. They establish 'faculties' at the universities, which either means that a representative of the company's management takes the post of head of the faculty, or that the dean, and/or some academics or lecturers, are given monthly allowances by the company in return for the investment of faculty time in developing company-specific human resources.

Audi established an 'Audi Faculty' at the Széchenyi University of Győr with an initial investment of €40,000 (assuming at the same time also further contributions to the faculty's operational expenses as well as to the expenses of inviting foreign guest lecturers). The academic curriculum includes production technology, aspects of product development, mechatronics etc. In this case, therefore, the company is looking to the faculty to provide specific operational training for prospective employees.

In 2000, Corvinus University Budapest (the former Budapest University of Economics) signed an agreement with various companies to create 'corporate chairs'. Among the companies were Bábolna Plc., Magyar Külkereskedelmi Bank (Hungarian Foreign Trade Bank), Magyar Villamos Művek, McKinsey & Co., Mol, Siemens, Alcoa Köfém Ltd., Antenna Hungária, BAT Hungary, Gresco Plc. and System Consulting Plc. They selected activity-specific research topics, and funded chairs (one per company) the incumbents of which assumed responsibility for implementing and coordinating the given topic-related research projects. Each chair is funded to the tune of €28,000 annually for five years.

The Robert Bosch Group (Bosch has 12 factories/facilities in Hungary, including an Engineering Development Centre, and more than 7,000 employees) established a Bosch Faculty of Mechatronics at the University of Miskolc in 2006. The agreement included the establishment of a well-equipped laboratory (transfer of machinery, testing equipment etc.) and the training of university professors according to the group's global training curriculum to familiarise them with Bosch's skill requirements. Professors use Bosch's equipment in the course of their practical teaching of future engineers. Bosch supports other Hungarian universities as well. For example, in 2008 it offered BUTE the sum of €300,000 as a non-refundable grant, for infrastructure

---

[20] The RUKC and CRC programmes have similar objectives (promoting industry–university cooperation, creating centres of excellences, fostering innovation and commercialisation activities on the part of higher educational institutions), and they operate in parallel. Programme announcement, however, is not coordinated. Most higher educational institutions try to obtain funding from both programmes (Széchenyi University of Győr participates in both, and has also applied to receive support from the City Growth Pole Development Programme). Consortium members are often the same in each of the individual programmes. Coherence of the individual support programmes is the responsibility of the grant recipients); CRC and RUKC participants try to rationalise their activities within the framework of these programmes so that they are complementary rather than overlapping.

development and scholarships. The university has signed similar agreements with other multinational companies (E.ON, for €120,000; Continental Temic Telefunken; Siemens etc.)

In 2006 Mentor Graphics (the local subsidiary of a US-based multinational corporation specialising in electronic design automation) invested as much as US$20m in the creation of a chip design laboratory (equipped with up-to-date software) at BUTE and the funding of related university scholarships. Another company-sponsored laboratory at BUTE is the HSN Lab (High Speed Networks Laboratory), which started operating as early as 1992 at the department of telecommunications and telematics. HSN Lab has cooperated closely with Ericsson right from the outset. Basic and applied research is performed in the lab in the field of network configuration and routing optimisation, asynchronous transfer mode (ATM) networks etc.

Under a 2006 agreement, SAP Hungary undertook to support BUTE by providing free software licenses to the value of €200,000. In addition, the company agreed to sponsor scholarships, commission applied research programmes, and offer the possibility to selected talented students of participation in the company's own training programmes. BUTE, for its part, agreed to include SAP-specific courses relating to business solution systems in the university curriculum. According to company data, the support (in various forms) Siemens has so far given to BUTE amounts to €800,000. Siemens also supports Corvinus University (corporate chair and e-government faculty programmes) and several other educational institutions.

The sums of money quoted in the above paragraphs make it clear that the provision of high-quality, state-of-the-art technical education that meets the current requirements of companies requires huge investments[21] that are beyond the means, not only of local universities, but also of SMEs. Without such investments, university curricula simply cannot adjust to corporate needs, and complaints from prospective employers about the disappointing level of graduates' practical skills will become more and more vociferous.

5. Conclusions

Our investigations have revealed that problems with labour supply are manifest on both qualitative and quantitative dimensions in Hungary, and that this is an increasingly serious limitation on the scope for economic policy directed at modernisation and increased competitiveness, and on the expansion plans of companies themselves.

---

[21] The other side of the coin is that, according to one of the interviewed companies, representatives of some higher educational institutions consider MNCs to be 'cash cows', from time to time asking them for sponsorship without any commitment to establish formal partnership relations. One of the colleges even asked for money in return for publishing the company's internship offer, in spite of the fact that many of its graduating students find it difficult to get a proper job.

We found that MNC subsidiaries apply their standard, formalised personnel policy (in terms of selection, recruitment and training) in Hungary, which exerts a non-negligible demonstration effect on local SMEs. Competition in the talent market keeps increasing. MNCs' local subsidiaries can compensate for their weakness in informal relations with universities, and for the lack of a network of local acquaintances, by establishing tight formal relations with universities and supporting higher educational institutions in various ways. This support is crucially important for universities, not only for financial reasons, but also from the point of view of keeping pace with technical progress and staying up-to-date on new technological trends, technological problems and the educational requirements of companies.

In-house company training programmes help to compensate for the deficiencies in the curricula of higher educational institutions. But this is not enough. The qualitative upgrading of the factors of production (in this case of human capital), a prerequisite of staying competitive in the knowledge economy era, requires conscious educational reform steps, such as would alter the structure and quality of labour supply, and result in better job matching. In all of this, Hungary ought to consider the related experience of high-performance catch-up economies, e.g. the human-capital push that contributed to the emergence and rapid strengthening of the Indian software industry (Arora and Bagde, 2006), and the expansion and qualitative upgrading in Ireland's educational system that was one of the key elements of the country's spectacularly successful development policy (OECD, 2006).

References

Arora, A. and Bagde, S. (2006). 'The Indian Software Industry: The Human Capital Story', Paper presented at *DRUID Summer Conference 2006 on Knowledge, Innovation and Competitiveness: Dynamics of Firms, Networks, Regions and Institutions*, mimeo.
Balla, K., Köllő, J. and Simonovits, A. (2008). 'Transition with heterogeneous labor. Structural change and economic dynamics', mimeo.
Berde, É., Czenky, K., Györgyi, Z., Híves, T., Morvay, E. and Szerepi, A. (2006). 'Diplomával a munkaerőpiacon' (Graduates in the labour market), mimeo.
Dávid, J., Fülöp, E., Mód, P. and Tajti, J. (2005). 'A munka-erőpiaci keresletet és kínálatot meghatározó tényezők. 3K Consens Bureau', mimeo.
Dávid, J., Debreczeny, T., Fülöp, E., Glofák, P., Gyöngyösi, K., Holczer, G., Horvát, K., Mód, P. and Tajti, J. (2007). 'NEM EGYEZNEK... A munkaerőpiaci kereslet és kínálat előrejelzése: 2005–2015. A feszültségpontok és a közelítés lehetőségei és eszközei.' (THEY DO NOT MATCH... Forecasting demand and supply in the labour market. Tension points and perspectives and ways of diminishing the gap), mimeo.
Fazekas, K. (2006). 'Employment prospects in Hungary: Present and future', *Public Finance Quarterly* 51(2): 199–212.
Fazekas, K. and Kézdi, G. (eds.) (2007). *The Hungarian Labour Market. Review and Analysis 2007*, Budapest, Institute of Economics, Hungarian Employment Foundation.

Field, S., Kuczera, M. and Pont, B. (2007). *En Finir avec l' Échec Scolaire*, Paris, OECD.
Galasi, P. (2004). 'Túlképzés, alulképzés és kereset a munkaerőpiacokon (1994–2002)' (Overqualification underqualification and earnings in the Hungarian labour market between 1994 to 2002), *Közgazdasági Szemle* 51(5): 449–471.
Galasi, P. and Varga, J. (2005). *Munkaerőpiac és Oktatás*, Budapest, MTA KTI.
Hajdú, C., Finna, H., Fortuna, Z., Szabó, I. and Veres, G. (2005). 'A Budapesti Mőszaki és Gazdaságtudományi Egyetem friss diplomásainak elhelyezkedési esélyei' [Employment perspectives of BUTE's recently graduated students], Budapest, BME Diákközpont, mimeo.
IBM Hungary (2007). 'Innovációs trendek' (Innovation trends), GKIeNet, mimeo.
Kabai, I., Wölcz, J., Winkler, M., Béki, O. and Tóth, G. (2007). *Mi Lesz Velünk a Diploma Után? (What Happens after Graduation?)*, Budapest, Zsigmond Király Főiskola.
Karvalics, L. and Kollányi, B. (2006). 'Humán tőke és versenyképesség' (Human capital and competitiveness), in Vértes, A. and Viszt, E. (eds.), *Tanulmányok Magyarország versenyképességéről (Papers on Hungary's Competitiveness)*, Budapest, Ú.M.K.
Kertesi, G. and Köllő, J. (2007). 'Graduate earnings in 1992–2005', in Fazekas and Kézdi (2007, 78–85).
Kőrösi, G. (2005). *A Versenyszféra Munkapiacának Mőködése* (The Functioning of the Labour Market in the Private Sector), Budapest, KTI könyvek.
Kun, I. (2005). 'A feketemunka felmorzsolása' (Eliminating black labour), *Mozgó Világ* 31(7): 25–29.
Kun, I. (2004a). 'Gyár a keleti végeken' (Factory in the East), *Mozgó Világ* 30(9): 71–95.
Kun, I. (2004b). 'Pacuha ország' (The sloppy country), *Beszélő* 9(5): 42–49.
Laki, L. (2007). 'Mit is jelent a szegénység a krízishelyzetű kistérségekben?' (What poverty really means in crisis-ridden small regions), *Egyenlítő* 5(12): 2–7.
Laki, L. (2001). *Vállalatok és Vállalkozások Igényeinek Változásai a Munkaerő Képzésével-Képzettségével Kapcsolatban* (Changes in Companies' Requirements concerning Workforce Qualifications), Budapest, MTA PTI.
OECD (2006). *Higher Education in Ireland*, Paris, OECD.
Polónyi, I. (2007). 'A gazdaságőés a felsőoktatás kapcsolatának néhány jellemzője — egy empirikus kutatás néhány megállapítása' (Some aspects of the relation between the economy and higher education — findings of a piece of field research), *Competitio* 6(2): 149–178.
Selmeczy, I. and Tóth, I.J. (2006). 'Az üzleti szféra fels?fokú végzettségű pályakezdők iránti kereslete, ennek várható alakulása és a pályakezdők tudásával való elégedettség 2005-ben' (Current and expected corporate demand for graduate job entrants, and companies' level of satisfaction with job entrants' knowledge in 2005), MKIK GVI (Research Institute of Economics and Enterprises — Hungarian Chamber of Commerce and Industry), mimeo.
Szűcs, I. (2005). 'Kényszerből a felsőoktatásba' (Forced participation in higher education), *Echo Survey*, Szociológiai Kutatóintézet, mimeo.

CHAPTER 9

LABOUR MARKET CONSTRAINTS IN ROMANIA: THE CHALLENGE OF SKILL MISMATCH IN A TRANSFORMING ECONOMY

DRAGOS PISLARU

1. Introduction: The Market for Skills

Balancing the skill availability with the current and anticipated needs of the economy is an ever increasing challenge of any government, particularly in the context of a complex, transnational labour market. More difficult still is to achieve this in a transforming country, the economy of which has undergone repeated and dramatic shake-ups. As Jack Keating (2007, 10) notes:

> A perfect skills market would achieve relative equilibrium in the short and longer term such that it continued to encourage workers to invest in skills, and encouraged employers and the labour market to provide sufficient but not excessive wage and occupational or career incentives for workers to invest. It also would encourage employers to invest in skills, and in particular, would encourage them to maximize the capacity for technology transfer, through the availability of skills at a reasonable price, and the associated labour productivity gains in increasingly competitive global markets. [...] However, training markets are imperfect, as training systems are subject to other demands and interventions, and productivity and wage levels are also influenced by other factors. Therefore, virtually all countries have some form of government intervention, frequently in conjunction with industry partners, in their national training or skills development systems.

Three key issues emerge from this statement:

1. Workers — current and future — should not be considered only passive suppliers of labour and skills; rather they should be regarded as active players on the market;
2. Employers — the demanders — also play an important role in developing a suitable pattern of labour and skill supply;

3. The state — the regulatory mechanism — should seek to balance the supply of and demand for skills and labour, particularly through the education system.

Skill availability has become almost synonymous with competitiveness (be it at local, regional or national level). Knowledge transfer and acquisition, and the ability to apply knowledge in economic activity, are impossible when workers do not have the necessary skills and capabilities to understand the information they receive.

Recent developments show patterns of underinvestment in skills (Brunello and De Paola, 2004), throughout the European Union. This is attributed to various reasons across countries, ranging from imperfect labour markets to lack of incentives for public and especially private investment in education and skills development. Relating to the three key components of the market highlighted above, the disincentives are supply-driven (workers are not interested in acquiring education, or lack the financial means to do so), demand-driven (training costs are too high, propensity to poaching etc. is too strong) or state-driven (overregulated labour markets or non-compulsory training regulations). Besides these reasons, other external factors, such as migration, contribute to an overall underinvestment in training. Against that background, in the context of globalisation, and given the high premium set on labour productivity and the supply of matching skills for industry, the need for common strategies for the supply of skills across countries is self-evident. Of course, these strategies need to be mediated by local circumstances in the form of, or expressed through, the institutional structures that define, in each country, skills formation systems, and which in turn provide many of the levers for policy in this area. There are many different types of education system. These different types are all the products of particular national histories, economies and social and political cultures.

2. The Romanian Context

Romania's accession to the European Union and the vibrant economic growth enjoyed by the country in the last seven years appear to have triggered large and increasing shortages of labour and skills. These have placed the issue of labour market balance, and indeed the efficiency of the Romanian education system, under sharp scrutiny and criticism. At first sight paradoxically, shortages coexist with low participation rates and excess supply of labour in the declining sectors, mainly in agriculture. And high unemployment persists among some labour categories, such as the unskilled and the young. *This suggests a substantial mismatch between the skills of the workers released in the restructuring process and the shift in labour demand, visible in recent years, and raises questions about the relevance of education for the needs of the labour market.*

The issue of skill mismatch is not new to the labour market, and extensive research has been done in the field; one of the first studies, and still the most appropriate to describe the Romanian situation today, was edited by Fiorella Padoa-Schioppa and published in 1991. Basically, the book presents four key interpretations of skill mismatch. The first is *turbulence in the economy*, namely, the collapse of some industries and the growth of new forms of entrepreneurship, generating economic shocks. This process has its origin in technological innovation, changes in the pattern of foreign competition and changes in relative prices of resources, all of which in turn affect the structure of employment. Declining sectors experience progressive job loss, and at the same time vacancies increase in number in the sunrise sectors. The same line of reasoning is valid on a regional level. The Padoa-Schioppa book also looks at *problems of equilibrium in regional and sectoral markets, inefficient allocation of labour and the NAIRU (non-accelerating inflation rate of unemployment) model* as possible sources of skill mismatch problems. But in developing the Padoa-Schioppa approach for application to the Central-East European countries (specifically in the case of Poland), Izabela Grabowska-Lusinska found the turbulence interpretation the most useful. The state of affairs in Poland is in fact very similar to that in Romania: as in Poland, the present employment situation in Romania has been exacerbated by large external migration flows. It is estimated that over two million Romanians have left the country in search of better opportunities abroad, especially within the EU.

Poland also experiences pedal mobility — a typical phenomenon of the transition period. Like the movement of a person on a swing, people are pushed out of their home countries in order to earn good money in the destination country, and then quickly pulled back home in order to spend the money. This movement generates the bulk of the household's income, and also means that the majority of the people involved in the movement are economically inactive in their country of origin (Grabowska-Lusinska, 2007). Similar patterns can be observed in Romania.

Unsurprisingly, these trends have pushed wages above productivity gains and inflated labour costs, eroding external competitiveness. The expectation is that the imbalances will continue to grow rapidly in the absence of coherent and timely policy responses.

It must be recognised, however, it may prove difficult to come up with efficient and opportune solutions to these problems. Even if solutions are found and implemented, the time-lag before their effects are seen could be long enough to create serious strains in the Romanian economy. While solid economic growth, expected to continue for the foreseeable future, should create favourable conditions for increasing participation and fostering sustainable job creation, policy reforms need to focus on bringing back into employment those labour categories which are unable to take advantage of growth, and on reducing the transaction costs for companies. The young, older workers, women and the long-term unemployed are particularly affected by high unemployment and/or low participation. The skills with which the education system endows graduates appear often to be out of line with the expectations of the employers. A better alignment of the curricula with the demand for labour is therefore imperative. Non-wage labour costs, among the highest in Europe, need to be reduced, while employment protection legislation, among the most rigid in the EU, should be made more flexible, to allow companies to respond effectively to economic opportunities. Opening up segments of the labour market to foreign workers should also be considered, as a way of filling the gap between the existing supply of labour and the expanding demand.

3. Recent Trends in Participation, Employment and the Demand for Labour

Following seven years of robust economic growth, Romania's employment rate for the population aged between 15 and 64 years picked up slightly in 2006, after a significant period of quasi-stagnation (see Fig. 9.1). Casual empiricism indicates that the introduction of the flat rate income and profit tax in early 2005 has been a contributory factor here, although a direct causal link has yet to be established. But whatever the cause of the recent increase, the overall employment rate in Romania remains modest relative to the Lisbon Agenda target, the EU-27 average and the best performers in the new member states, such as Latvia, Slovenia and Estonia (see Fig. 9.2).

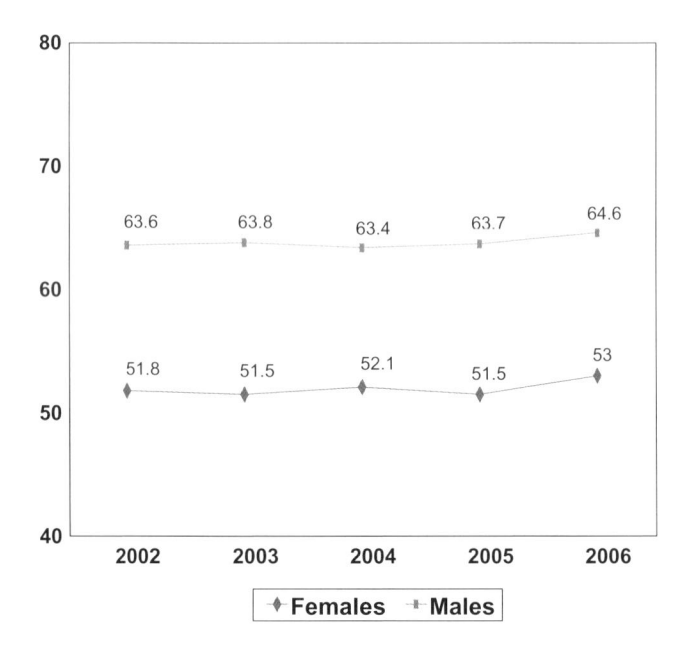

Fig. 9.1. Romania: Male and female employment rates (%).
Source: EUROSTAT.

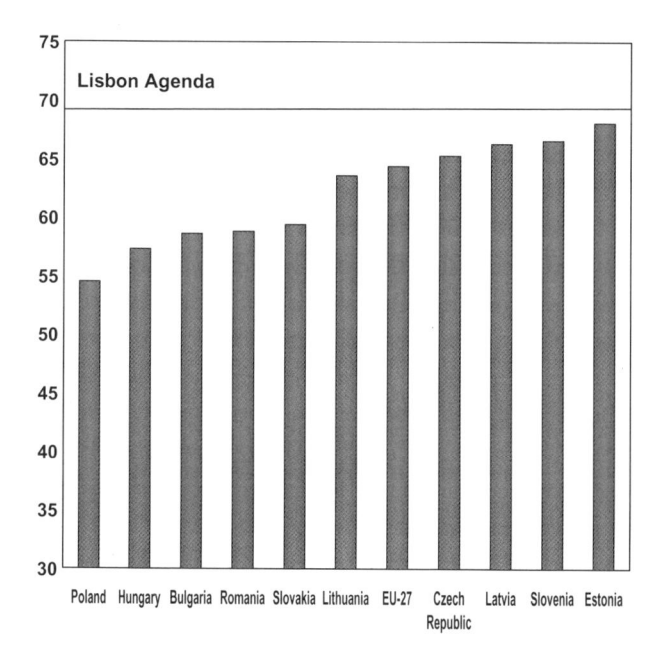

Fig. 9.2. Total employment rate, 2006 (%).
Source: EUROSTAT.

The stubborn flatness of the trend visible in recent years suggests that the economy remains deficient in developing appropriate incentive systems to attract people back into employment, especially labour categories which have particularly low participation rates, as we shall see below. Observers attribute the slowness of the process of reversal of the trend in employment to the protracted enterprise restructuring process, which continues to lead to labour shedding, and the slow pace of structural reform in the public sector. The still high social contributions and the rigidity of the employment protection legislation might have an offsetting effect vis-à-vis the drivers of employment expansion, namely the consolidation of economic growth and income tax relaxation. The large external migration flows constitute another factor explaining the inertia in employment trends, as many working-age people seem to have found that the easiest route to better job opportunities is to go abroad.

Available evidence suggests that some labour market categories have particularly low participation rates. These categories are primarily women, older workers outside agriculture and young people. Their employment rates are significantly below the Lisbon targets. The female employment rate was, for example, at 53% in 2006, around 10% below that of males, which was 64.6% in the same year, and one of the lowest in Europe (see Fig. 9.1). As the chart shows, the figure was fairly stable from 2002 to 2005, then rose slightly in 2006. On the same pattern, the employment rate of older workers averages around 40%, well below its Lisbon target.

One has to be cautious in interpreting the employment rates of women and older workers. The two rates decreased rapidly in the early stages of transition, before stabilising at the current rates. Romania, unlike most of the EU countries, had a tradition of high female participation rates. The drop in the activity rates of women in the 1990s was largely involuntary, attributable to the decline in output and employment opportunities following the collapse of socialism, and the concomitant severe deterioration in living standards and increase in long-term unemployment. We would expect, therefore, a percentage of inactive women to return to work when labour market conditions start to improve. At the same time, the participation of women and older workers in the subsistence agricultural sector is even higher than in the case of men of prime working age. The correlation between the decrease in agricultural employment on the one hand, and the decrease in female and older worker participation, on the other, cannot be coincidental. This suggests that the employment figures in the two cases hide bigger imbalances than appear at first glance.

The significant expansion in European employment during the 1990s was to a large extent attributable to the relaxation of labour legislation to promote part-time and temporary employment. In the case of Romania, as Fig. 9.3 suggests, the introduction of provisions allowing for part-time employment in the 2003 Labour Code appear to have yielded positive results. In 2006, according to Eurostat, around 10% of employment in Romania is part-time, one of the highest rates in Central and Eastern Europe, after Lithuania and Poland, although still well below the EU-27

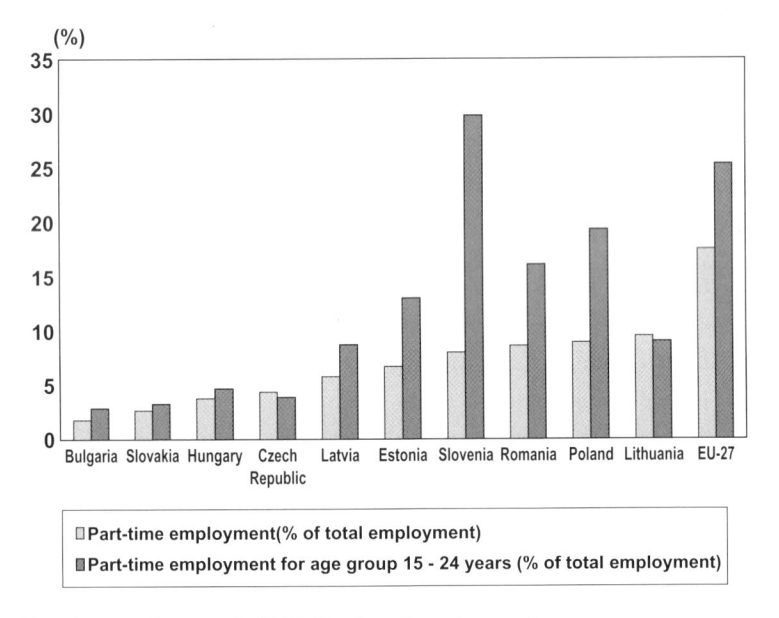

Fig. 9.3. Part-time employment in 2006 (% of total employment).
Source: EUROSTAT.

average and the top European performers. What is particularly encouraging is the fact that the share of part-time employment for the 15–25 age group is significantly higher, at over 15% of total employment for this category. This group does, of course, have a low participation rate and a high unemployment rate.

A phenomenon which has become increasingly evident in recent years in Romania, as well as in most of the new EU member states, is the coexistence of labour and skills shortages in some sectors with excess supply in other areas of the economy (see Figs. 9.4 and 9.5). While labour participation remains low by European levels

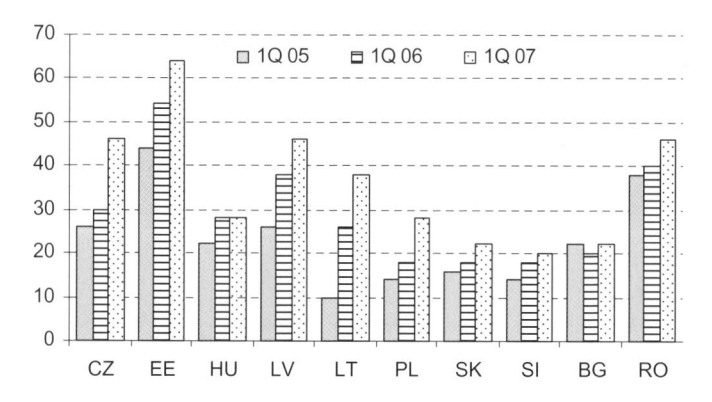

Fig. 9.4: Vacancy rates in the new EU member states 2005–2007 (%).
Source: World Bank, EUROSTAT.
Note: Data for enterprises employing more than 10 workers.

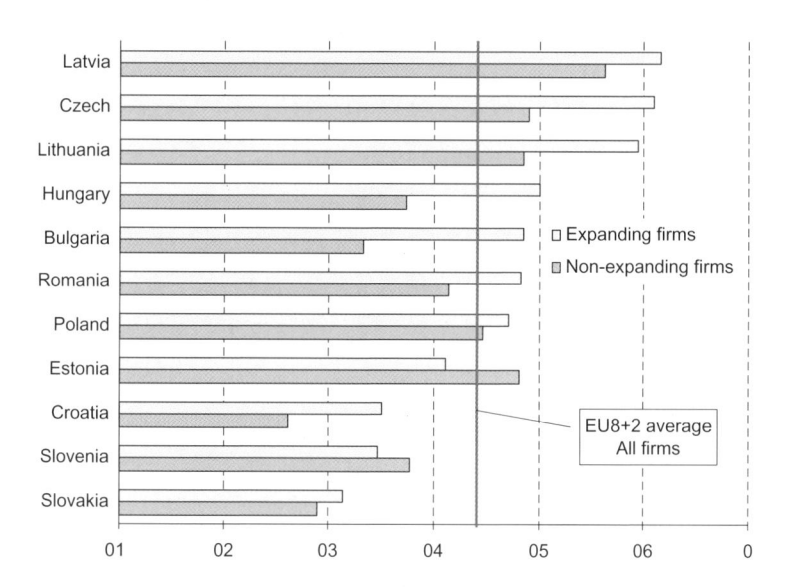

Fig. 9.5. Percentage of firms reporting deficiencies in worker skills as an important obstacle to firm operation and growth (2005).
Source: World Bank.

and is only slowly picking up, labour demand has expanded substantially in recent years. This has led to significant shortages of labour and skills in some segments of the labour market, and has exacerbated imbalances by pushing wages above levels of productivity, affecting competitiveness and augmenting inflationary pressures. While there is no systematic evidence on the magnitude of these labour shortages, sectoral studies and casual empiricism seem to suggest that they affect both skilled and unskilled segments of the labour force. Industries ranging from construction and manufacturing to ICT, as well as services ranging from retail trade to public services, including health and education, seem to be affected, and the imbalances appear to be intensifying.

The year 2008 was one of particular stress in terms of the overall Romanian macroeconomic situation because of the elections. As one of Romania's leading economic analysts noted, 'in this period, the tendency is to increase salaries heavily in the public sector, which creates the feeling that everything is all right, the economy is healthy, and people will be tempted to borrow as much as possible, without being aware of the risk. Thus, the authorities introduce morphine in the system. [...] In 2008, too, the deficit of skilled labourers remained, the most sought-after employees continuing to be in construction, textiles, hotels and restaurants and in the financial-banking system.'[1]

Romanian net wage growth, which is one of the main drivers of inflation at the present time, slowed somewhat in February 2008 when compared with January of that year (see Fig. 9.6), but remained very strong. Net wages rose at an annual 20.5% rate in that month, as compared with 30.7% in January, bringing the average net monthly wage to 1,134 lei ($493), according to data from the National Statistics Institute.

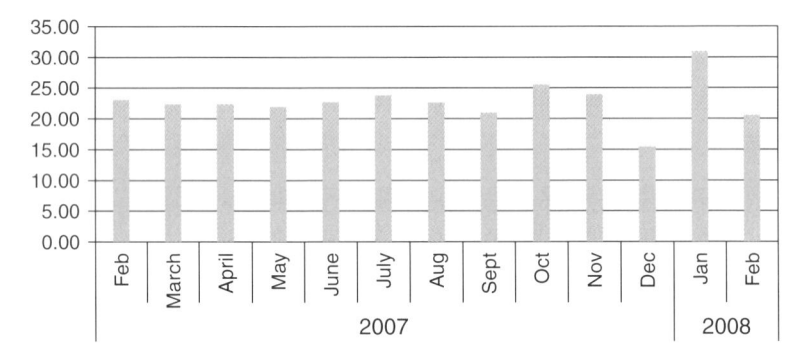

Fig. 9.6. Romania: Net average earnings (Monthly, year on year % change).
Source: INSSE.

---

[1] Florin Cîţu in an interview given on 22 February 2008, available at http://www.curierulnational.ro/In%20brief/2008-02-22/Romanian+labour+market+to+regulate+itself+within+three-four+years.

Table 9.1. Youth unemployment rates in the EU.

	2006q3	2006q4	2007q1	2007q2	2007q3	2007q4	2007q4 change on previous quarter	2007q4 change on previous year
BE	21.2	20.5	19.6	20.1	17.6	18.4	0.8	-2.1
BG	18.8	16.6	16.5	14.5	15.3	12.1	-3.2	-4.5
CZ	17.6	14.8	11.7	11.9	10.3	9.2	-1.1	-5.6
DK	6.7	7.5	7.7	7.9	8.8	8.3	-0.5	0.8
DE	12.4	12.0	11.2	11.1	11.0	10.7	-0.3	-1.3
EE	11.4	10.3	11.5	10.8	10.7	11.4	0.7	1.1
IE	8.5	8.2	8.7	8.6	9.2	8.5	-0.7	0.3
GR	24.9	25.5	24.5	22.9	22.6	:	-0.3	-2.3
ES	17.6	17.6	17.4	18.1	18.5	18.7	0.2	1.1
FR	21.7	21.6	20.4	19.8	18.7	18.1	-0.6	-3.5
IT	20.2	21.7	20.1	18.6	20.2	:	1.6	0.0
CY	10.1	9.8	9.8	9.6	9.3	9.1	-0.2	-0.7
LV	11.9	11.4	11.4	10.7	11.8	11.0	-0.8	-0.4
LT	10.5	8.1	9.4	7.6	8.9	8.1	-0.8	0.0
LU	16.0	17.1	17.3	16.6	16.3	16.3	0.0	-0.8
HU	19.5	19.4	18.0	17.4	17.7	18.4	0.7	-1.0
MT	16.0	14.8	13.9	13.2	12.3	11.0	-1.3	-3.8
NL	6.6	6.6	6.4	6.1	5.8	5.2	-0.6	-1.4
AT	8.9	8.6	8.6	8.5	8.4	8.2	-0.2	-0.4
PL	28.7	26.9	24.3	22.4	21.2	19.2	-2.0	-7.7
PT	16.5	16.9	17.7	16.5	16.2	16.0	-0.2	-0.9
RO	22.3	21.1	20.4	20.8	21.1	21.6	0.5	0.5
SI	12.5	10.8	10.0	9.5	9.8	7.9	-1.9	-2.9
SK	25.8	23.6	21.9	20.6	19.4	18.2	-1.2	-5.4
FI	18.8	17.9	17.2	16.4	16.3	16.4	0.1	-1.5
SE	21.0	19.4	20.9	18.9	17.8	18.3	0.5	-1.1
UK	14.5	14.1	14.6	14.6	14.6		0.0	0.1
EU27	16.9	16.5	15.8	15.4	15.2	14.9	-0.3	-1.6
Male	16.5	16.1	15.4	15.2	15.1	15.0	-0.1	1.1
Female	17.3	16.9	16.4	15.7	15.3	14.8	-0.5	-2.1

Source: Eurostat, harmonized series on unemployment.
Note: ":" Data not available. Data seasonally adjusted. For GR, IT and UK changes 2007q3/2007q2 and 2007q3/2007q3.

The situation is thus somewhat paradoxical. Inactivity rates in Romania are comparatively high, including among the young population (See Table 9.1), and there is a large under-employed pool of labour in rural areas. Around 45% of the population live in rural zones, and there is significant unemployment, with rates often in double digits, in small urban mono-industrial localities where traditional industries collapsed in the early stage of transition. Why has this substantial labour potential not been appropriately exploited yet?

Available evidence points to several explanatory factors. First, there is a substantial mismatch between the skill profiles of the labour released in the process of enterprise restructuring and the new jobs that have emerged over recent years. Put simply, the large cohorts of workers who lost their jobs through the transition in the declining sectors have not been absorbed by the expanding ones, and have rather been pushed into unemployment, usually long-term, into agriculture, or out of the labour force altogether. These outflows of labour, predominantly from traditional heavy industries, have been very large, as the rate of job destruction in Romania was among the highest in the former socialist bloc relative to the size of its labour force.

A second explanation relates to the relevance of education to the needs of the labour market. Labour force surveys point to a significant number of graduates, at all levels of education, going directly into unemployment and out of the labour force, often simply through discouragement.

The Household Labour Force Survey (AMIGO) for 2006 shows that, within the total number of unemployed, most had high-school education (32.5%), followed by graduates of vocational schools (31.7%), while 19.6% had only primary school education. People with higher education (up to master's and PhD level) accounted for only 6.8% of total unemployed. Looking closely at these figures, we observe that the group most affected by unemployment are those with upper-secondary/tertiary education, with an unemployment rate of 7.8%, almost double that for graduates of higher educational institutions (3.8%) (See Table 9.2).

In order to have a more comprehensive view of the pattern of unemployment rates relative to level of education, let us briefly analyse the educational structure of the population (age 15 and over). Thus, in 2006, more than half the total population (51.6%) had a medium level of education, 39.7% only elementary education, and no more than 8.7% higher education. Furthermore, when looking at residence areas, we notice the huge discrepancy between rural and urban areas: most of the population having medium and higher levels of education come from urban areas — 66.1% and 90.3% respectively. The fact that the number of students in higher education coming from rural areas is so low suggests the existence of major obstacles to access to education which could only lead to labour market imbalances.

Table 9.2. Unemployment rate, ILO definition, by level of education, gender and rural/urban residence, 2006.

	Total	Male	Female	Urban	Rural
Level of education/Total	7.3	8.2	6.1	8.6	5.6
Higher (university)	3.8	3.3	4.3	3.7	4.4
Medium (high school, tertiary, upper secondary, specialised post-high school, vocational)	7.8	8.4	7.1	8.6	6.5
Low (primary and secondary school, no education)	7.6	10.1	4.9	19.4	4.6

Source: AMIGO Survey.

All the above-mentioned figures suggest that there are important gaps in the education system which current curricula fail to address in terms of endowing students with the appropriate mix of general and specific skills to make them attractive to employers. The evidence is particularly strong in relation to people with a medium level of education, i.e. the majority of the total population, which has the highest rate of unemployment (7.8%).

If we look at the unemployed (males and females) with a medium level of education we can observe that the vocational schools are the most inefficient in terms of preparing students for the labour market, even more inefficient than the high schools, where men are concerned (see Fig. 9.7). For women, the situation is the opposite: the high school prepares them poorly for the labour market; 41.3% of total unemployed women have a high school education, compared to 23% for women with vocational education. As regards post-high school education and technical education the situation is better: only 2.4% of unemployed men and 3.9% of unemployed women have this level of education.

In addition, the low scores registered by Romania in standard cross-country tests, such as PISA or TIMSS, indicate that not only the focus but also the quality of education remains an unresolved issue. Romania's position relative to the Lisbon Agenda educational indicators, as highlighted in the 2007 Presidential Commission Report on Education, is presented in Table 9.3.

A third factor explaining the currently widening imbalances in the labour market is the low level of internal labour mobility, particularly between rural areas, where the

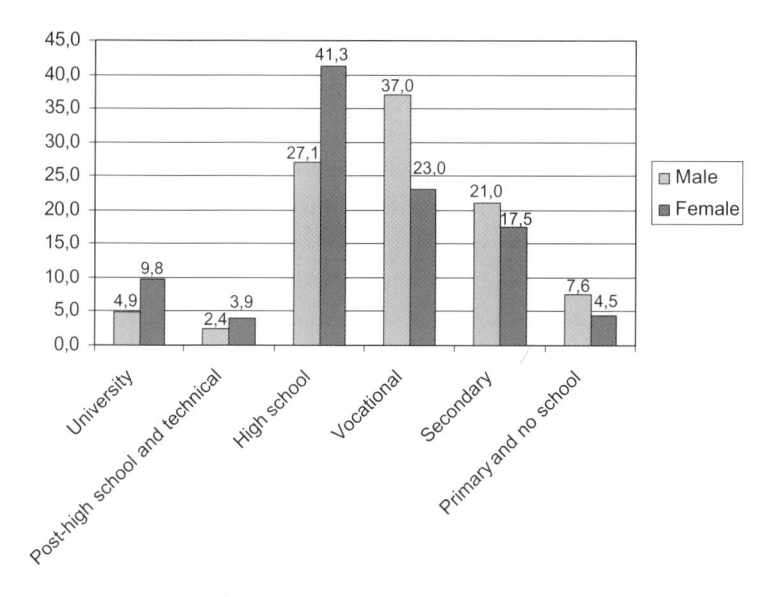

Fig. 9.7. Unemployment by education and gender, 2006 (% of total unemployment).
Source: AMIGO Survey.

Table 9.3. Romania and the Lisbon educational indicators

Lisbon Indicators	Romania	EU	EU Target 2010
Early school dropout	23.6%	14.9%	Max. 10%
% of the 22-year old population with at least upper secondary qualifications	66.5%	77.3%	Min. 85%
% of 15-year old pupils that cannot reach even the lowest score on PISA 2001	41%	19.4%	15%
% of graduates in Maths, Sciences and Technology	23%	24.1%	+10%
Adults' participation in life-long learning (% of total adult population)	1.6%	10.8%	12.5%

Source: România Educaţiei, România Cercetării, July 2007.

surplus of labour is largely located, and the growing urban regions, the engines of growth, where the demand for labour comes from. The complex transition Romania has gone through has seen large outflows of labour from the declining urban industries into agriculture and rural areas, while the migration from the latter to the former has been relatively modest. This situation is partly explained by the large external migration, as people judge that they will be better off leaving the country and working in the old EU member states than moving to Romanian cities. While there is migration from rural to urban areas, the inflows do not seem sufficient enough to keep up with the expansion of demand. Cultural factors also seem to be at play here as, traditionally, Romanians do not move to where the jobs are — a feature characteristic of much of Europe.

External migration intensifies ever-widening labour market shortages. The number of Romanians working abroad is estimated at over 2 million. (NB. the data in Fig. 9.8 reflects only those working abroad legally, as registered by the Italian and Spanish authorities.)

These workers sent back to their families remittances totalling over €5bn, equivalent to around 5–6% of GDP, in 2006. Romanian workers seem to be concentrated in countries experiencing both shortages of labour and tight labour market regulations, in particular Spain and Italy. Cultural affinities clearly influence the migrants, who seem to prefer Latin countries as destinations. The potential for migration after Romania's accession to the EU remains high. A World Bank study (2007b) finds that around 88% of young Romanians aged 15–24 would consider leaving the country in search for better job opportunities abroad. Only 20% of them, however, would consider migrating permanently. As the opportunity cost of migrating or commuting to urban localities, where most of the new jobs are expected to be created, is still high, external migration seems to remain a better option for the unskilled.

Whatever the cause, the situation is reaching critical dimensions. According to a recent study by the National Council for SMEs in Romania conducted early in 2008,

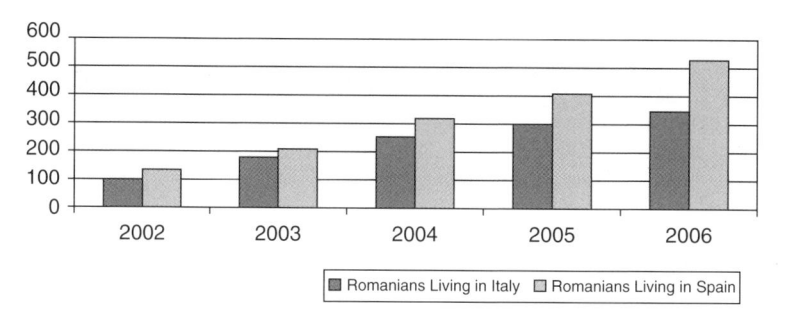

Fig. 9.8. Romanians in Spain and Italy (thousands)
Source: ISTAT and Spanish National Statistics Office.

the average SME is short of 17 workers; during 2009, the number is expected to increase to 29. In 2007, about 71% of Romanian SMEs were confronted with manpower shortages, more than double the percentage from the previous year (32%). Problems relating to lack of personnel were the main cause of bankruptcy for one-third of the total number of registered bankruptcies in the SME sector (almost 40,000 SMEs) in that year.[2]

4. The Challenge of Unemployment

Stabilising at between 7–8% of the labour force,[3] and on a downward trend, Romanian unemployment is not high relative to European levels. It is actually slightly below the average rate for the EU-27 (see Fig. 9.9). Registered unemployment, which measures the number of unemployment benefit claimants, is even lower, at around 4% on average, and even less than that in the fast-growing regions and cities. Men are more affected than women by unemployment, with a rate over two percentage points higher than that of women, suggesting that the decline of the male-dominated heavy industries has taken a significant toll among male workers (see Fig. 9.10). Female unemployment has declined steadily since 2004, to around 6% of the labour force in 2006. While the overall level of joblessness is not high, the unemployment situation nevertheless has several important characteristics that need to be highlighted.

First, the decline in unemployment has not been matched by a proportional rise in formal employment, suggesting that external migration and other factors are playing a role in driving unemployment down. In the absence of job opportunities at home,

---

[2] The study was based on a survey of 234 SMEs.
[3] LFS figures, following broadly the ILO definition of unemployment.

172   D. Pislaru

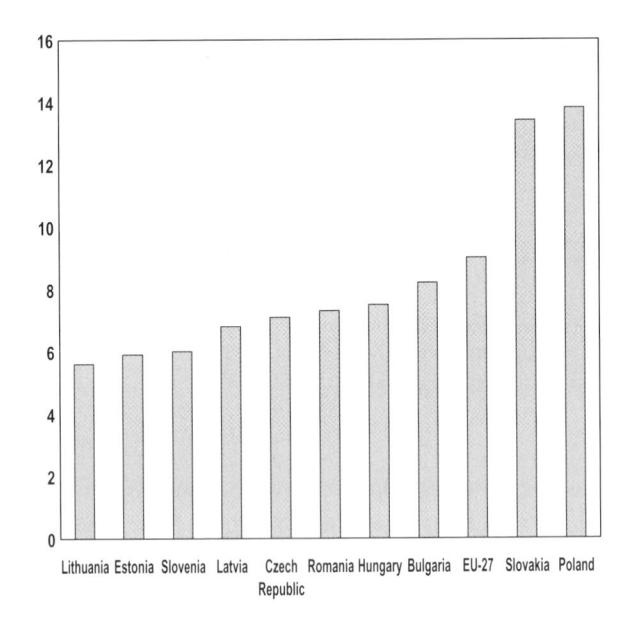

Fig. 9.9.   Total unemployment rate, 2006 (%, LFS).
Source: EUROSTAT.

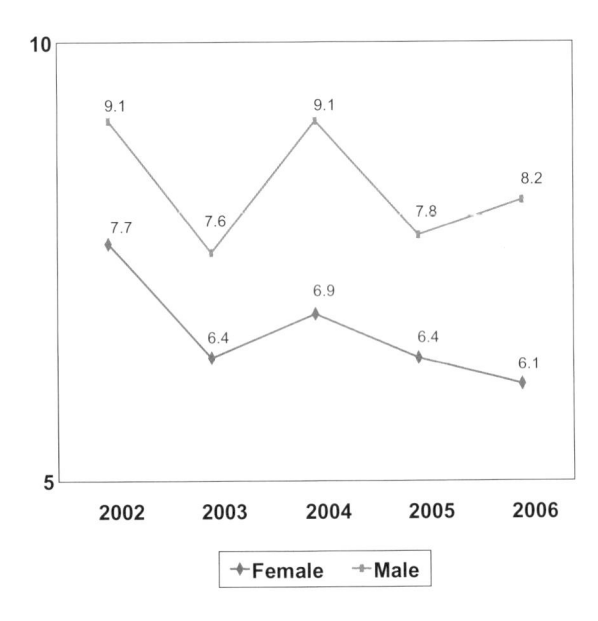

Fig. 9.10.   Romania: Male and female unemployment rates (%, LFS).
Source: EUROSTAT.

many have preferred to migrate rather than face unemployment. The large informal economic sector, estimated at least 20% of GDP, may also help to explain the paradox of low formal employment figures and low unemployment. The grey economy appears to provide a large number of low-paid jobs to mostly unskilled individuals who cannot find formal employment. This phenomenon is evidenced by the large discrepancy between unemployment as estimated by labour force surveys (LFS) and registered unemployment, which indicates that a large number of ILO-unemployed do not actually qualify for unemployment benefits. At the same time, a large number of claimants are not actually unemployed on the ILO definition, that is, they are not actively searching for work, one reason being probably that they are already informally employed. Limited quality job opportunities and long spells of unemployment discourage people from actively looking for jobs, and push them out of the labour force or into subsistence agriculture. The number of discouraged workers seems to be large, especially among the young.

Second, unemployment disproportionately affects the young population. The unemployment rates of the 15–24 group are particularly and stubbornly high, at around 22% for males and 20% for females (see Fig. 9.11). These are among the highest in the new member states. Only Poland and Slovakia, two countries characterised by generally high unemployment, above the EU-27 average, quote higher corresponding figures (Fig. 9.12). Available evidence suggests that youth unemployment

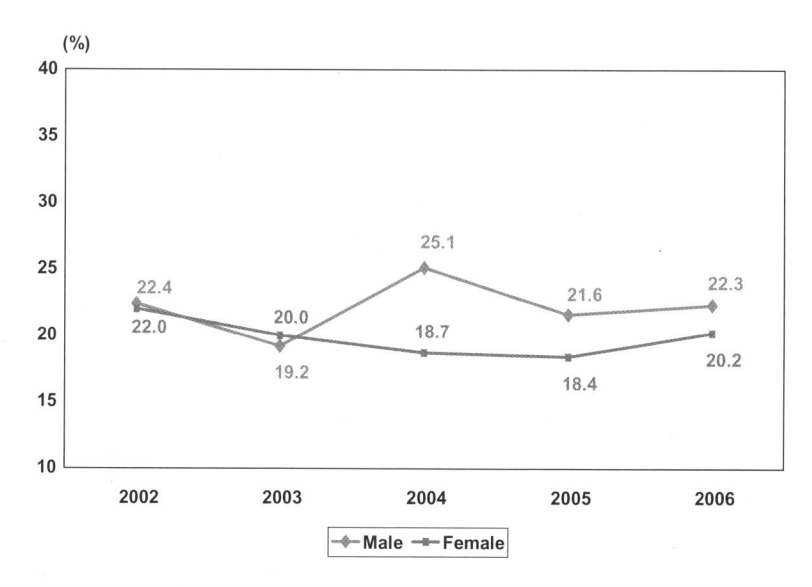

Fig. 9.11. Romania: Male and female unemployment rates for age group 15–24 years, 2006 (%, LFS). *Source*: EUROSTAT.

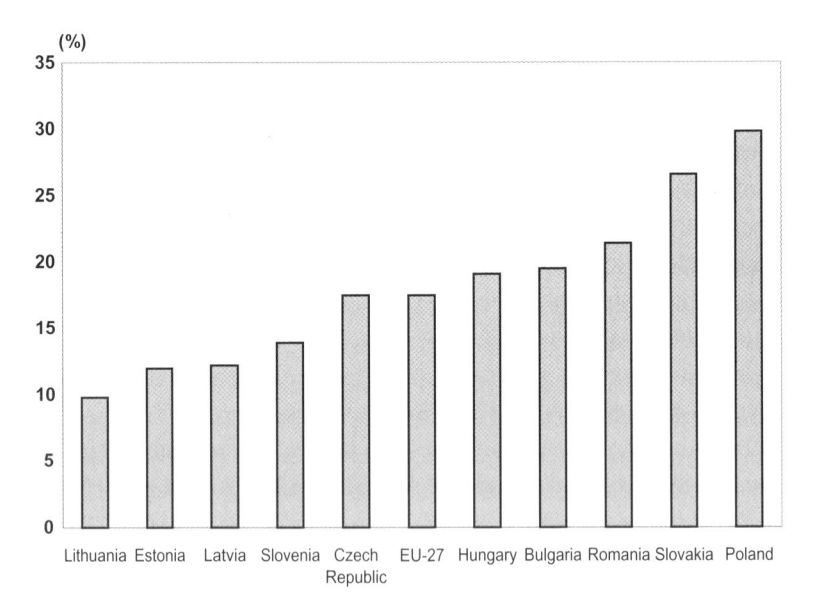

Fig. 9.12. EU: Unemployment rates for age group 15–24 years, 2006 (%).
Source: EUROSTAT.

is high for practically all educational attainment levels, primary, secondary and tertiary, indicating low employment opportunities for the young irrespective of their level of formal education. The figures point again to the limited relevance of education to recent trends in the structure of the demand for labour and skills. This situation is particularly detrimental insofar as it affects the long-term human development potential of the country and encourages external migration.

Third, Romanian unemployment is long-term, characterised by relatively low entry and exit rates and high average duration. Over 50% of the unemployed have been in the unemployment pool for more than one year, above the EU-27 average (see Fig. 9.13). There is also no indication that the numbers will decline in the future, as the current levels have persisted for years. Older workers, the unskilled, those with lower levels of education and those with untransferable specific skills are particularly affected. As the demand for labour has picked up strongly in recent years, the incidence of long-term unemployment imposes an effective labour supply constraint. The problem seems to be therefore not so much related to the availability of jobs as to the incentives to take advantage of those, and the skills that are required for them. This situation is, of course, not unique to Romania. Many EU countries face similar conditions.

5. Productivity, Labour Costs and Labour Market Flexibility

Labour productivity in Romania is converging rapidly towards the EU average, although the gap remains large. As a result of substantial investments, labour

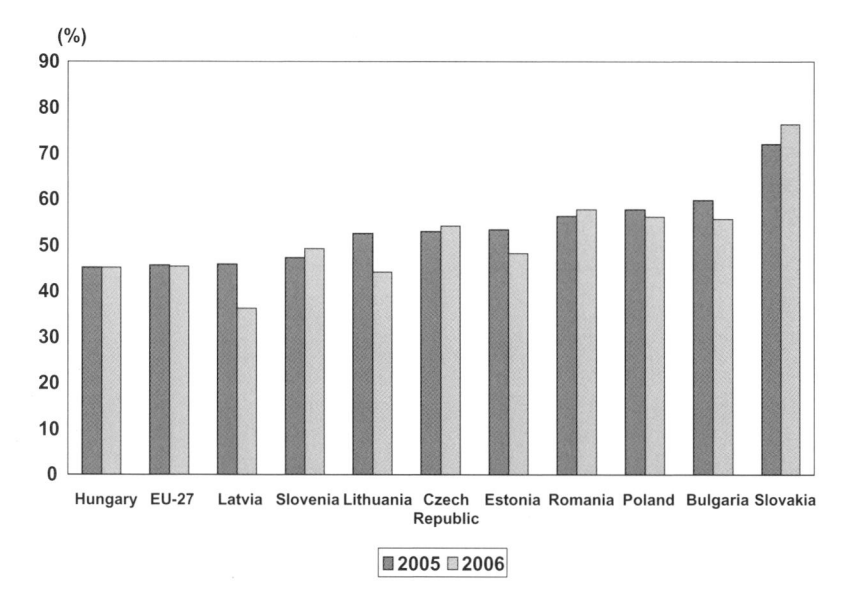

Fig. 9.13. Long-term unemployment (% of total unemployment).
Source: EUROSTAT.

shedding, reallocation of resources towards more productive ends, and also to improved corporate governance and business climate,[4] productivity in industry has recently been growing at around 11% per annum, one of the fastest rates in the new member states. This has helped close the gap with the EU, although, overall, GDP per person employed is still only around 40% of the EU-27 average (see Fig. 9.14). At the same time, real wages are growing even faster, at an average rate of around 19–20% per annum in real terms, eroding external competitiveness and augmenting inflationary pressures. As a result, overall labour costs increased by around 50% in real terms between January 2005 and June 2007 (Fig. 9.15). Nevertheless, real labour costs remain substantially below the EU average. Average annual gross earnings in Romania, measured at PPP, represented 20% of those in Spain and around 48% of those in Poland in 2006.

Contemporary research (World Bank, 2007a, Chapter 2) suggests that the largest share of the recent productivity gains in the transition region as a whole is attributable to within-sector productivity growth, while the contribution of the reallocation across sectors component has been modest. As the contribution to both output and employment of the services sector, the engine of growth in mature market economies, remains low in Romania, there is a suggestion that there may in that country be

---

[4] Romania was ranked 48th in the world in terms of ease of doing business in 2007 by the World Bank *Doing Business 2008*, 30 places higher than in 2005.

176   D. Pislaru

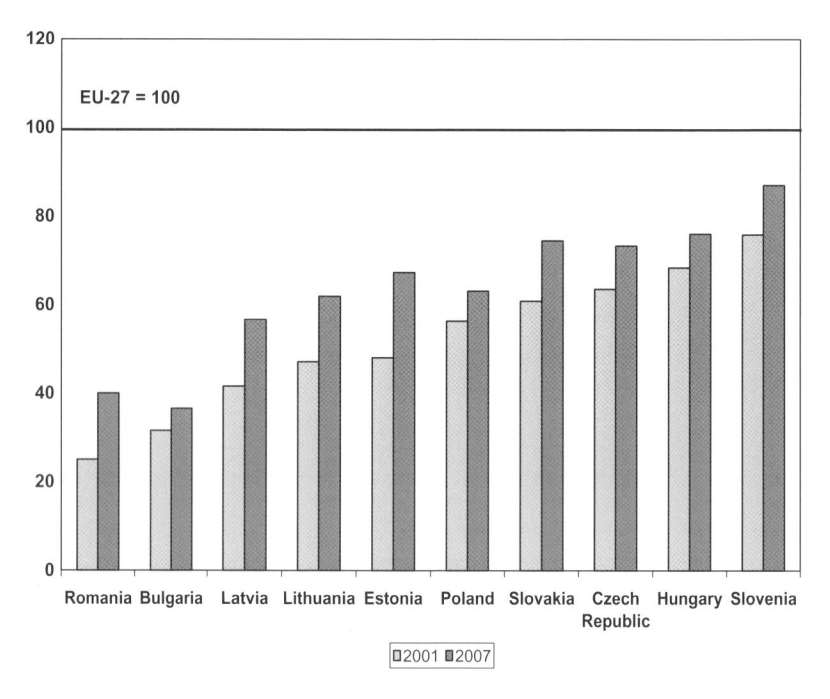

Fig. 9.14.   GDP per person employed (EU-27 = 100, PPS).
Source: EUROSTAT.

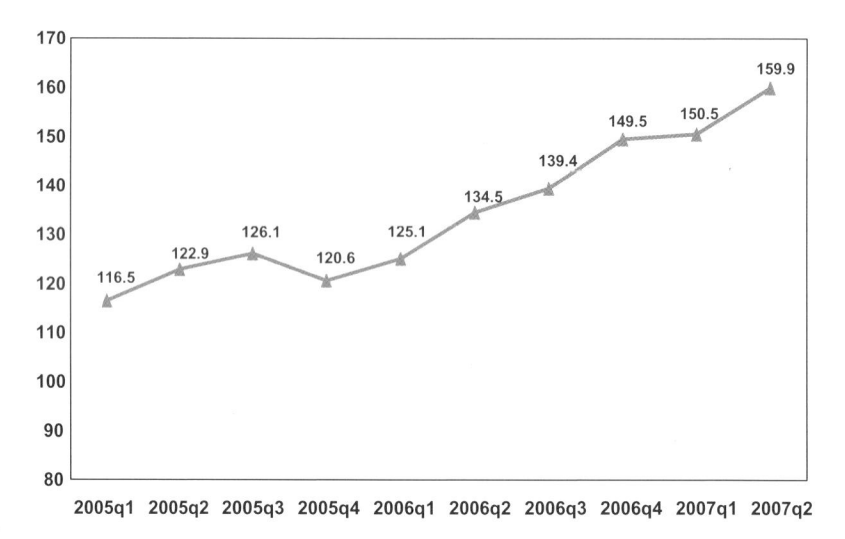

Fig. 9.15.   Romania: Labour cost index (2000 = 100, constant prices).
Source: EUROSTAT.

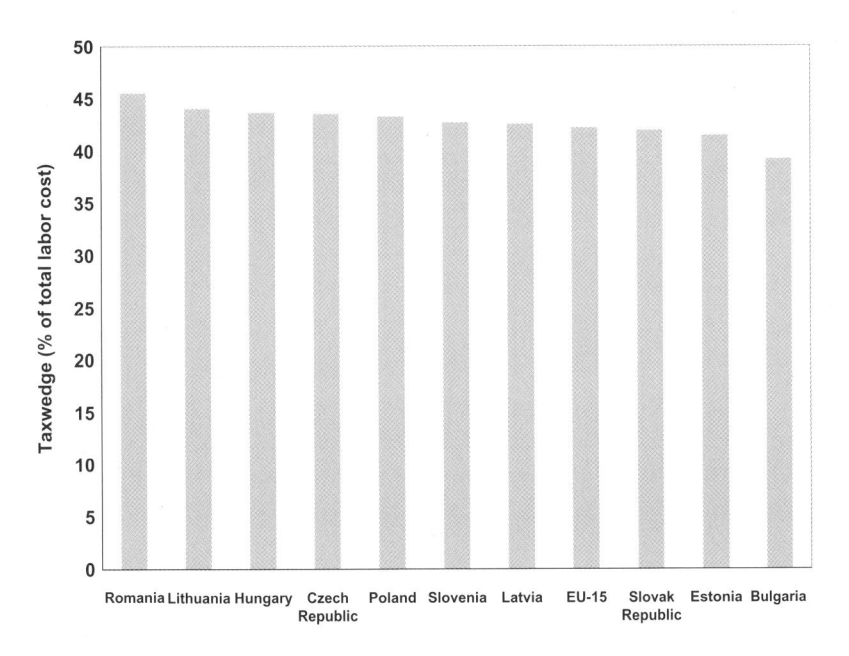

Fig. 9.16. Tax wedge on labour, 2006.
Source: World Bank.

additional obstacles to a more rapid reallocation of labour across sectors, and especially towards services.

Observers identify the still high taxes on labour and the rigidity of the employment protection legislation as important barriers affecting labour participation and impeding a more rapid reallocation of labour resources to better ends in Romania. As Fig. 9.16 shows, the tax wedge on labour in Romania is higher than the EU-15 average, and indeed the highest among the new member states, after Hungary. The high social security contributions (PAYG pensions, unemployment fund, health insurance, etc.) create a distortion affecting both the supply and the demand sides of the labour market and increase transaction costs for companies. The authorities also recognise that the high contribution rates encourage migration into the informal sector in a manner that undercuts tax collection and complicates tax administration. In recent years, the government has introduced a series of reductions in payroll taxes, and plans additional cuts (up to 6% by the end of 2008) to align them with regional standards. However, in the short-run, the scope for large social tax rate reductions is limited by budgetary constraints.

Employment protection legislation is also rigid by European standards, as Fig. 9.17 suggests. Among the EU new member states, only Latvia, Estonia and Slovenia have

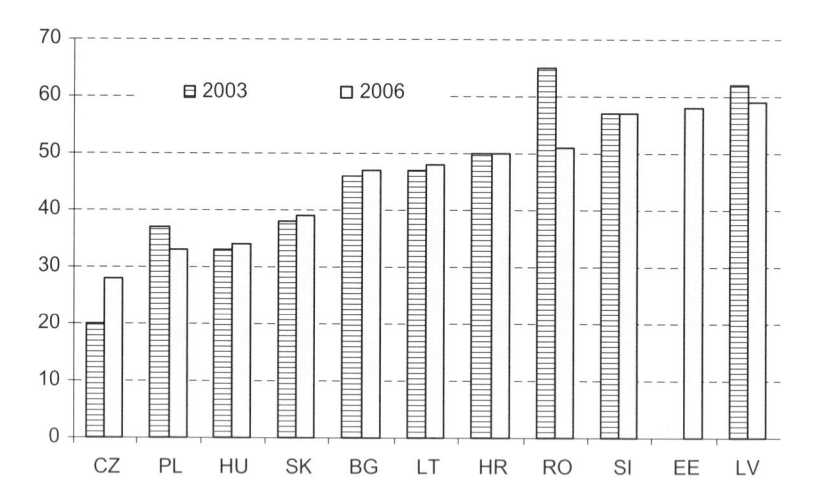

Fig. 9.17. Rigidity of employment index.
Source: EUROSTAT, World Bank.

employment laws more restrictive than Romania's. Flexibility in the area of labour and labour relations means allowing companies to employ, adjust, distribute and dismiss workers on the basis of job requirements, to ensure their capacity to adjust to external market criteria like changes in the economic environment and maintain competitiveness by means of cost control. While there has been an increase in the flexibility of the legislation in recent years, following the relaxation of some of the provisions of the 2003 Labour Code, more needs to be done to facilitate the mobility of labour, enhance sustainable job creation and preserve the cost competitiveness of Romania on the internal European market, taking due account of the experience of old EU members, such as Spain and the Netherlands, where recent growth in employment is clearly attributable to relaxation of employment protection legislation.

6. Skill Mismatch and the Education Reform

While the creation of new jobs is important *per se*, the quality of the human capital they embody is equally central. The distribution by levels of education of the labour force is positively correlated with value added, and hence with the overall competitiveness of an economy. It is clear that in Romania the quality and relevance of education to the needs of the labour market affects participation and exacerbates skills shortages. To address this challenge, the education system is undergoing a comprehensive reform. The reform has already produced changes, especially in compulsory education.

The process of decentralisation of pre-university education was initiated at the end of 2005, and is currently being piloted in 50 schools. Positive results in this pilot phase will allow the extension of decentralisation in pre-university education. Decentralisation in education addresses issues like financing, HR management at local level, improved relevance of curricula for local development needs, and competence requirements.

From a financial perspective, decentralisation measures enhancing the role of local budgets, especially in the case of pre-university education, were introduced in 2001. Thus, local budgets now account for approximately 60% of education spending. Furthermore, the last few years have seen an increase in the importance of alternative financial resources for education, such as external credits, European programmes, and own funding (tuition taxes, sponsorships, consultancy etc.) (*Tendinte Sociale*, 2007)

Regarding the university level, the restructuring process was started in the academic year 2005/2006, following the Bologna Accords. As part of the restructuring and modernisation of university education, progress has been made recently in terms of the institutional framework and the methodology supporting the development of a National Qualifications Framework (NQF) in Higher Education. In 2005 a National Agency for Qualifications in Higher Education and Partnership with the Social and Economic Environment was set up, and development of a National Register of Qualifications for Higher Education is currently under way.

Reform measures have also been piloted in the vocational education and training system (VET). One of the objectives of the restructured education system, in force since the school year 2003/2004, has been to enhance access to initial VET. Measures undertaken by the Ministry of Education, Research and Youth have targeted issues such as access to initial education and training, the attractiveness of VET, and providing equal opportunities for access to VET in disadvantaged areas. Data show that the number of students enrolled in vocational education increased by 3.1% in 2004/2005 as compared to 2003/2004, but decreased by 1.5% in 2005/2006 year-on-year. Schooling capacity for initial VET reached 1,495 units in 2005/2006, as compared to 844 in 2002/2003 (with a significant increase in rural areas), mostly due, it must be said, to the reclassification of educational facilities.

Measures undertaken for the further restructuring of the VET schools network — the introduction of bussing facilities for students, as well as the development of institutional capacities for VET schools, with a view to ensuring inclusive education and training for students with special educational needs — produced a total of 1,367 VET school units (of which 611 are in rural areas) in 2006/2007. Furthermore, a system of quality assurance based on the Common Quality Assurance Framework (CQAF) agreed at European level has already been introduced, and implementation of quality assurance instruments within the whole VET system is underway.

The restructuring of the VET system was conducted with a view to improving co-operation with employers, and addressing individual educational and training needs. The VET curriculum has been developed on the basis of training standards validated by Sectoral Committees. Methodologies and mechanisms for updating training standards and VET curricula have been developed and applied in the course of the implementation of Phare TVET (Technical and Vocational Education and Training) projects, and will be kept up-to-date through the institutional development of the National Authority for Qualifications (NAQ), supported by Phare projects.

The new curriculum, which is based on building up competences and a transferable credits system, seeks to develop learner-based teaching methodologies and individually tailored educational options. A major component of the curriculum is entrepreneurial education, which is already present at gymnasium level, in the 10th grade and in the high school lower cycle, as well as at upper secondary level. In the context of all this, it is clear that further improvement of the targeted training of teachers is now a top priority.

Increased relevance of education and initial VET to labour market requirements remains a major goal in the policy-making and activities of education providers against the background of a high rate of youth unemployment. Several measures aimed at improving initial VET supply responsiveness to labour market needs, and improving the strategic planning of initial VET provision and delivery of career guidance and key competences, have been instituted. Key remaining problems include:

— Still insufficient involvement of relevant stakeholders in the participatory planning of educational activities/offers;
— Insufficient training provided to stakeholders in education and VET planning;
— Insufficient up-to-date information and studies on long-term labour market needs affecting initial VET planning and responsiveness;
— Insufficient development and appraisal of partnership in education and training, and limited cooperation in developing continuing education programmes and work-based learning programmes etc.

Some of these issues (e.g. involvement of social partners, local authorities, and other stakeholders) will be addressed through the implementation of NQF and new instruments for quality assurance in education. It is clear that new graduates need a longer period of time to adapt to job requirements than people with longer working experience. This situation is directly related to the weakness of the link between education and initial VET provision and labour market needs. In order to be able to practice, and to adapt to the requirements of a specific occupation/job, graduates need to be integrated into programmes for transition from school to work. Current programmes do not support graduates' effective insertion into the labour market, and work-based learning and career counselling are not yet responding to the requirements of individual study programmes. In this respect, specific actions for increasing the relevance of qualifications provided by initial education and training have been undertaken, and some progress has been made.

Over recent years, a major priority of the reforms in education has been to ensure compatibility with European standards. Romania's post-accession strategy, published in January 2007, focuses on the following objectives[5]:

1. ensuring equal opportunities and increasing participation in the educational process
2. expanding compulsory education
3. decentralisation and autonomy of the pre-university level
4. strengthening economic competitiveness through investment and promotion of R&D
5. upgrading the education system in rural areas
6. developing continuous education from an institutional perspective
7. matching the education and Researcher Development Initiative (RDI) systems to European objectives/standards
8. increasing the quality of education and research through human resources development (HRD)

Furthermore, the Ministry of Education, Research and Youth in Romania has drafted a set of new regulations, which are currently posted on the official website of the Ministry, and are open for public debate. These new regulations include:

1. *The law on pre-university level education*
   This law will bring about some major changes in the structure of the pre-university education system, and of high school final examinations. The high school admissions procedure is also to be changed. It is predicated that compulsory education should include pre-school, primary and lower secondary cycles, covering the 3–18 age group.[6]

2. *The law on university education*
   The main provisions of this draft law focus on the election and mandate of rectors and deans, and on the compulsory evaluation of teachers by students.[7]

3. *The law on the teachers' statute*
   According to this law, teachers applying for management positions within the education system must have a master's degree or a degree in educational science. Teachers involved in research activities should be entitled to a 12-month sabbatical every nine years of teaching.[8]

---

[5] *Post-accession Strategy 2007–2013* (draft), Ministry of Education and Research, January 2007.
[6] http://www.euractiv.ro/uniunea-europeana/articles|displayArticle/articleID_12135/.html.
[7] http://www.hotnews.ro/stiri-esential-2104806-legea_invatamantului_superior_studentii_dau_note_profesorilor_rectorii_greu_de_schimbat.htm.
[8] http://www.hotnews.ro/stiri-esential-2105785-statutul_cadrului_didactic_profesorii_cercetatori_concediu_luni_fiecare_este_interzisa_filmarea_profesorului.htm.

4. *The Government Decision on the total number of student places in public education institutions*

   While this act does not introduce any major changes, it does aim to increase the number of university students, specifically master's degree students. The draft regulations seek to respond to the call for implementation of the three-cycle academic degree structure,[9] as well as to the provisions of the Lisbon Agenda and the HRD Sectoral Operational Programme.[10]

7. Conclusions and Policy Recommendations

Romania has promoted, in recent years, a series of reforms aimed at enhancing the flexibility of the labour market and increasing participation and sustainable job creation. This includes the introduction of the flat 16% income and corporate profit tax, one of the lowest in Europe, the revision of the Labour Code, more emphasis on active labour market policies and improvements in the business environment to reduce transactions costs for companies, including by simplifying company registration. The effects have been beneficial, with increased employment and lower unemployment. In this context one should not, of course, forget the safety valve represented by the massive migration of workers abroad, which has helped to keep unemployment relatively low.

A common understanding has been reached, and revised regulations and reform measures have been adopted. It is nevertheless difficult to conclude that there is a common conception of the policy and mechanisms that should be implemented. Romania still lacks a strategic view of how to match the education and qualifications of the labour force to the demands of the business environment, and indeed the conceptual, methodological and planning instruments needed to integrate and align existing, separate, strategic documents. Several reasons could be cited to explain this fact: the failure systematically to observe patterns of demand for labour from the point of view of labour force quality, the lack of an integrated system of professional careers advice and information; the need for closer involvement of employers in labour market projections; the shortage of resources in schools, and the difficulty older people have in accessing vocational training and education.

The high economic growth enjoyed since 2000, and which is expected to be maintained over the next few years, should make job creation easier, so that the increasing trend in participation is likely to continue. At the same time, major labour market categories — particularly young people, older workers and the long-term unemployed — are not taking advantage of the enhanced employment opportunities

---

[9] Batchelor's, master's and PhD.
[10] Draft Decision regarding the number of student places in pre-university and university education for the year 2008/2009, Framework Note.

offered by economic growth. Female participation is also low by European standards. This suggests that, in addition to promoting growth as a means of increasing employment, Romania needs policies targeted at improving the labour supply incentives of these categories of workers. Such measures would include more flexible work arrangements, such as part-time and temporary contracts, improved job search assistance and counselling, and targeted programmes, including job subsidisation, where required.

Limiting the scope of early retirement programmes, with a view to increasing the effective retirement age of workers, should help gradually to correct the imbalance in the ratio between pension contributors and beneficiaries, enhance the revenues of the pension fund, and increase replacement rates[11] without resorting to transfers from other public budgets. Financial incentives to encourage workers to stay longer in employment should be considered. The statutory retirement age should also gradually increase, while the eligibility rules for disability pensions should be reviewed. Retraining and skills upgrading programmes should be made available to older workers and the long-term unemployed, and the performance of the schemes should be monitored, in terms of achieving the objective of bringing people back into work.

Beyond that, more needs to be done at the level of the education system as a whole, in particular by better aligning curricula with the demand for graduate skills. Improving the effectiveness of public spending on education, including by introducing performance-related incentives, such as per capita financing, should be part of the reform agenda. Expanding the use of lifelong learning opportunities should better link the provision of skills to the fast changing sectoral and occupational profile of the demand for labour. Connecting schools and employers is also paramount in helping young people to manage the transition from school to work; more resources need to be allocated to school-work experience programmes, and to better promotion of these programmes among students, parents, teachers and business; greater involvement of employers in their design and delivery should also be encouraged, as well as up-to-date training for teachers.

Reduction of the administrative and regulatory obstacles to business should have a major positive impact on sustainable job creation. Further effort is therefore needed to improve the transparency, stability and predictability of the business environment. Recent assessments (World Bank, 2008) indicate that in Romania the process of dealing with licenses, especially for small businesses, continues to be cumbersome, while registering property and closing a business require lengthy procedures, unnecessarily increasing transaction costs for companies. In addition, employers should be allowed greater flexibility in adjusting employment to respond to opportunities for economic development. Hiring and firing costs should be reduced, and the use of

---

[11] The ratio of the initial pension payment to the wage in the last year of employment.

flexible labour contracts should be further encouraged. The level of labour taxation should be further gradually reduced, though at a pace which does not put fiscal balances at risk.

References

AMIGO Survey (2006). National Institute of Statistics, Bucharest.
Brunello, G. and de Paola, M. (2004). *Market Failures and the Under-Provision of Training*, CESIFO WP No. 1286, September.
Grabowska-Lusinska, I. (2007). 'Skill shortages, emigration and unemployment in Poland — causes and implications', migrationonline.cz, May.
Keating, J. (2007). *Matching Supply of and Demand for Skills: International Perspectives*, Final report, 1 May, Centre for Post-Compulsory Education and Lifelong Learning, NCVER.
Padua-Schioppa, F. (ed.) (1991). *Mismatch and Labour Mobility*, Cambridge, Cambridge University Press.
Tendinte sociale (various years). National Institute of Statistics, Bucharest.
World Bank (2007a). *Unleashing Prosperity: Productivity Growth in Eastern Europe and the Former Soviet Union*, Washington, DC.
World Bank (2007b). *Development and the Next Generation*, World Development Report 2007, Washington, DC.
World Bank (2008). *Doing Business 2008*, Washington, DC.

CHAPTER 10

HORIZONTAL AND VERTICAL MISMATCH IN THE LABOUR MARKET AMONG GRADUATE STUDENTS WITH GENERIC OR VOCATIONAL HIGHER EDUCATION

PÅL BØRING

1. Introduction

A primary task of higher educational institutions (HEIs) is to provide society with particular skills and knowledge. This task has important implications for the science–industry link, since it has long been recognised by both academics and policy-makers that one of the key contributions to industrial innovation is the development of skills and knowledge (Lambert Review, 2003). Phrased in economic terms, two narrow but important goals of HEIs are to produce graduates and research output. We focus on the first of these goals.

Higher education is organised around disciplines or higher professional fields, and hence around the learning of discipline- or field-specific (i.e. vocational) competencies. However, in higher education students acquire not only vocational knowledge and skills, but also generic competencies. Generic competencies can be defined as a combination of competencies which provide a strong basis for further learning. This indicates that generic competencies include more than just learning abilities in a strict sense: they can also include problem-solving or analytical competencies.

The effectiveness with which different higher educational groups are able to adjust or improve their competencies in the labour market is determined by the types of competency acquired, and especially the extent to which their study programmes are generic or vocationally oriented. Heijke *et al.* (2003) examine the role of generic and vocational competencies in the transition to the labour market, using survey data for Dutch higher education graduates. The survey was conducted three years after graduation. They classify the group of graduates into two clusters, having either generic or vocational education, and find that those with vocational competencies have an occupation inside their own educational domain (i.e. are not horizontally mismatched) more often than those with generic competencies.

Green and McIntosh (2002) find that business and management studies, together with social sciences, have the highest rates of over-qualification (i.e. vertical mismatch) among graduates. They note that the reason may be that these subject areas are among the most heavily populated at HEIs, and that there is simply an insufficient number of appropriate jobs for the number of graduates in business and management studies coming through. In their view, however, a more likely explanation is that graduates in these subject areas are quite heterogeneous in terms of quality.[1]

Støren and Arnesen (2007) study the labour market situation five to six years after graduation. Their sample consists of graduates from 13 European countries.[2] They find that a vocationally oriented course of study greatly reduces the risk of being horizontally mismatched, or both horizontally and vertically mismatched (i.e. double-mismatched). The former result is a confirmation of the results of Heijke *et al.* (2003). Detailed discussion of the analysis in Støren and Arnesen (2007) can be found in the 2008 report (in Norwegian) by Støren.

The aim of our study is to investigate the role of generic and vocational education in the transition from higher education to the labour market. We examine to what extent the variation in the mismatch level in the labour market among persons with different educational qualifications can be explained by type of education (generic or vocational). Our study is based on the analysis in Støren and Arnesen (2007). However, and in contrast to their analysis and the paper by Heijke *et al.* (2003), we focus on individuals' labour market situation in the period immediately after graduation.

We use Norwegian survey data on recent graduates. The mismatch measure reflects the relevance of the graduate student's education to the labour market, and thus goes beyond the numerous studies of higher education which concentrate on the effects within the educational system itself — for example the flow of students, degree performance and student learning (Naylor and Smith, 2004; Johnes and McNabb, 2004; Dancer and Fiebig, 2004; Toutkoushian and Smart, 2001).

In the next two sections, the data set and the different types of mismatch are described. Then the empirical results are presented. This is followed by an analysis of possible effects of non-response. Finally, we present our conclusions.

2. Data

Our data set is culled from the *NIFU STEP Graduate Surveys*, which were conducted in 1995–1997, 1999–2001, 2003 and 2005.[3] These surveys contain information

---

[1] Green and McIntosh (2002) argue that comparatively few employers specify the subject of job applicants' degrees; they are often more interested in the quality of the degree, including the institution where the degree was obtained. See discussion of credentialism in Chapter 7.
[2] The countries are: Austria, Belgium-Flanders, Czech Republic, Estonia, Finland, France, Germany, Italy, the Netherlands, Norway, Spain, Switzerland and the UK.
[3] No surveys were conducted in 1998, 2002 or 2004.

about the subsequent labour market status of recent graduates.[4] All students who graduated during the spring term of the given year were asked to complete a questionnaire six months later.

The Graduate Surveys include all graduates with higher degrees (masters' degrees), and all first degree (bachelor's degree) graduates in business administration from public (i.e. state) HEIs, with some few exceptions.[5] First degree graduates from university colleges, coming out as school teachers, pre-school teachers, teachers in further and continuing education, child welfare workers, social workers, engineers, bioengineers, electronic data processing (EDP)/computer science graduates, nurses, graduates in business administration from private university colleges, and graduates in transport logistics and security, have on one or more occasions been included in these surveys,[6] but usually only a sample has been drawn from each group due to capacity limitations.[7] Information about the graduates is gathered directly from the HEIs.

A total of 40,875 graduates received the questionnaire in the Graduate Surveys from 1995 to 2005. Among this group there are 24,243 graduates with higher degrees (including 89 people with higher degrees in health and safety) and 3,121 first degree graduates in business administration (public HEIs), which makes a total of 27,364.[8] In addition, there are 13,511 other first degree university college graduates. Due to the very low number of graduates with higher degrees in health and safety, they are excluded from the analysis.

In the analysis we include only graduates with higher degrees, and first degree graduates in business administration from public HEIs, since only these groups of graduates are included in all the surveys. Figure 10.1 gives information about graduates in these groups — those who received the questionnaire, those who answered the questionnaire (i.e. the gross sample), and the sample of graduates used in the analysis (i.e. the net sample). The response rate is high among the graduates in the gross

---

[4] The Graduate Surveys have also been used in Børing (2005), Try (2004, 2005), Støren (2004), Try and Grøgaard (2003) and Arnesen (2000).

[5] For the 1995 Graduate Survey, a sample was drawn from the following groups: Higher degree graduates in law (2/3 of all graduates), and first degree graduates in business administration from both state and private HEIs (1/2 of males, 2/3 of females). Note also that doctors are not included in the Graduate Surveys. The reason is that the labour market for recent graduated doctors is highly regulated, in that these students must complete a further one-and-a-half years of internship (turnustjeneste) after graduation.

[6] These subject fields all require either three or four years of study.

[7] University graduates with a bachelor's degree are not included in the Graduate Surveys, since the universities have difficulty in identifying these groups of graduates. There are also difficulties in identifying business administration graduates from private university colleges, and they are therefore excluded from the surveys from 1999 onwards.

[8] This sample covers 3% of the total Norwegian population of graduates with either higher degrees (masters' degrees) or first degrees in business administration in the age group 20–66 years for the period 1995–2005, 2% for those completing higher degrees and 4% for first degree graduates in business administration. *Source*: Register data from Statistics Norway. Note that the whole population of first degree graduates in business administration includes graduates from both public and private HEIs, since the register data do not contain any information about type of HEI.

188 P. Børing

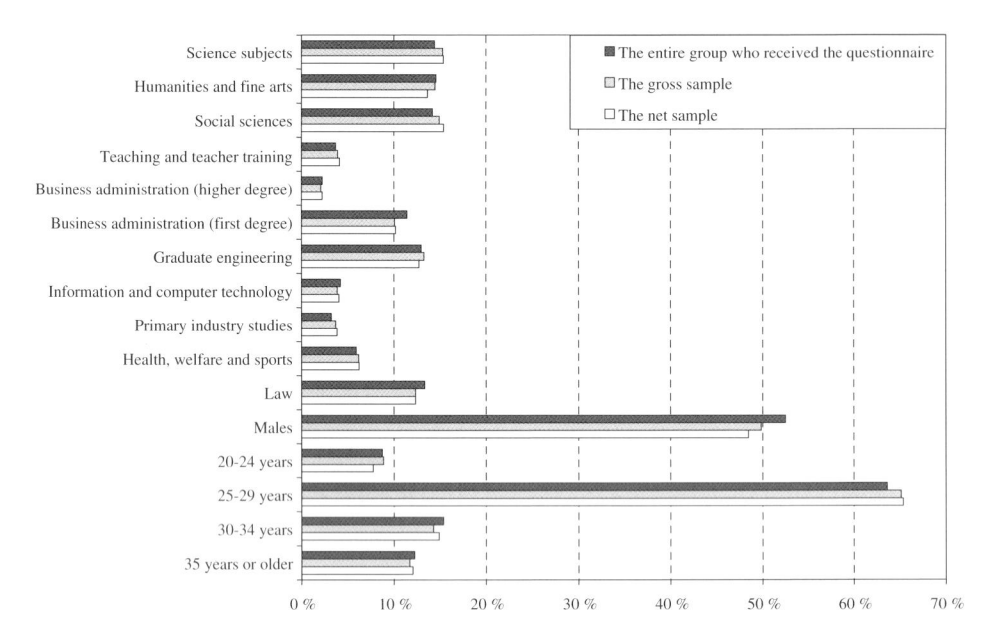

Fig. 10.1. Graduates with higher degrees and all first degree graduates in business administration from public HEIs.

Notes: 1) Excluding graduates with higher degrees in health and safety. 2) The response rate (%) among graduates in the gross sample was: 70 (1995), 77 (1996), 78 (1997), 74 (1999), 69 (2000), 70 (2001), 71 (2003), 66 (2005), and 72 for the whole period 1995–2005. 3) The entire group who received the questionnaire: N = 27,275. The gross sample: N = 19,607. The net sample: N = 16,834.

sample — between 66% in 2005 and 78% in 1997. Since our analysis focuses on the transition to the labour market, we exclude from the net sample graduates who left the labour force after graduation.[9] In total our net sample consists of 16,834 graduates (see Table 10.1). Each person in the net sample is either employed or unemployed, i.e. all persons in this sample are included in the labour force.

Figure 10.1 shows how the graduates are divided into different subject fields for the whole period from 1995 to 2005, i.e. using all cohorts within this period. We see that higher degree graduates are grouped into ten main subject fields, where the science and humanities subject groups are the largest fields of study, and business administration (higher degree) is the smallest (based on the number of graduates). Business administration (first degree) is the shortest degree, requiring four years of study.[10] Subjects offering higher degrees generally require at least five years of study.

---

[9] We have also excluded graduates with unknown labour force status (18) and those with unknown type of mismatch (961) from the net sample; adding in graduates outside the labour force (1,794 persons) makes a total of 2,773 exclusions. Graduates outside the labour force are neither employed nor unemployed.

[10] The 4-year course on business administration (first degree) is in the process of being replaced by a 5-year master's degree course.

Table 10.1. Descriptive statistics for the new graduates who answered the questionnaire in the Graduate Surveys: The net sample.

Type of education[1]	1995	1996	1997	1999	2000	2001	2003	2005	Total	%
The generic group	1,047	1,145	1,322	1,318	1,254	1,283	1,333	1,545	10,247	61
Science subjects	333	346	368	337	295	291	294	321	2,585	15
Humanities and fine arts	199	238	309	296	288	301	293	368	2,292	14
Social sciences	285	275	282	324	325	324	360	416	2,591	15
Teaching and teacher training	49	43	63	77	91	61	115	191	690	4
Business administration (higher degree)	35	37	31	24	21	46	42	137	373	2
Business administration (first degree)	146	206	269	260	234	260	229	112	1,716	10
The vocational group	753	897	984	853	808	783	757	752	6,587	39
Graduate engineering	351	372	385	229	197	169	239	202	2,144	13
Information and computer technology	70	65	63	55	59	93	103	169	677	4
Primary industry studies	80	53	95	116	111	88	52	47	642	4
Health, welfare and sports	76	90	145	123	152	142	155	159	1,042	6
Law	176	317	296	330	289	291	208	175	2,082	12
Gender										
Males	920	1,033	1,200	1,050	983	1,005	964	1,000	8,155	48
Females	880	1,009	1,106	1,121	1,079	1,061	1,126	1,297	8,679	52
Age group[2]										
20–24 years	173	183	187	171	151	154	136	143	1,298	8
25–29 years	1,156	1,381	1,553	1,447	1,346	1,328	1,356	1,433	11,000	65
30–34 years	272	295	329	345	297	313	324	333	2,508	15
35 years or older	199	183	237	208	268	271	274	388	2,028	12
Married or cohabitant	995	1,069	1,235	1,182	1,101	1,172	1,204	1,403	9,361	56
Graduates with children	380	393	446	444	433	446	423	467	3,432	20
Females with children	184	207	214	252	251	243	247	280	1,878	11
Father with primary and secondary school or without any education	362	370	420	393	367	367	333	307	2,919	17
Father with upper secondary education	531	578	626	573	557	568	524	609	4,566	27
Father with higher education	874	1,056	1,208	1,156	1,084	1,090	1,200	1,329	8,997	53
Father with unknown education	33	38	52	49	54	41	33	52	352	2
Mother with primary and secondary school or without any education	564	583	627	543	500	512	470	457	4,256	25
Mother with upper secondary education	630	707	761	704	667	644	599	640	5,352	32
Mother with higher education	569	723	869	888	858	879	996	1,156	6,938	41
Mother with unknown education	37	29	49	36	37	31	25	44	288	2
Grade level unknown	192	225	276	219	67	119	849	166	2,113	13
Previous educational experience	259	296	405	419	465	496	583	700	3,623	22
Earlier work experience	1,136	1,303	1,465	1,437	1,427	1,442	1,627	1,852	11,689	69
Some earlier relevant work experience	520	703	765	770	805	767	1,006	1,119	6,455	38
Contacted family and acquaintances	311	393	306	343	301	298	624	602	3,178	19

(*Continued*)

Table 10.1. (*Continued*)

Type of education[1]	1995	1996	1997	1999	2000	2001	2003	2005	Total	%
Outcomes after graduation										
Employed without being mismatched	1,008	1,142	1,390	1,182	1,133	1,111	973	1,146	9,085	54
Horizontally mismatched	22	15	21	19	19	22	12	19	149	1
Vertically mismatched	361	437	487	502	535	500	487	553	3,862	23
Double-mismatched	175	228	256	344	268	288	377	392	2,328	14
Unemployed	234	220	152	124	107	145	241	187	1,410	8
All graduates	1,800	2,042	2,306	2,171	2,062	2,066	2,090	2,297	16,834	100

Notes: [1] Excluding graduates with higher degrees in health and safety. [2] At time of graduation.

The categorisation of generic and vocational education in Fig. 10.1 and Table 10.1 is based on our evaluation of the educational system, and our assessment of the extent to which different types of higher education are linked to particular occupations or professions.[11] Some comments on our categorisation are in order. First, we include everyone with a higher degree in humanities and fine arts, social sciences, teaching and teacher training, and business administration (both higher and first degree graduates), in the generic group. Second, we consider all educational programmes in law, primary industry studies, and health, welfare and sports, to be vocational education. We also split the group of graduates in natural sciences and technical subjects into one generic group (graduates in science subjects) and two vocational groups (graduate engineers and graduates in information and computer technology).

It is clear from Fig. 10.1 that there are missing data because of non-response, which can affect our analysis and conclusions. From the figure we see, moreover, that there are small differences in the proportions between our net sample, the gross sample and all those who received the questionnaire in the surveys with respect to their main subject fields and the selected age intervals for the whole period 1995–2005.[12] Finally, the gross sample contains a lower fraction of males (50%) than the entire group receiving the questionnaire (52%), and this fraction is again lower for the net sample (48%) than for the gross sample. In the section on possible effects of non-response we will discuss how these gender differences may affect our conclusions.

The Graduate Surveys include not only information on individual characteristics such as gender, age and subject field, but also marital status, children, socio-economic

---

[11] The categorisation in Heijke *et al.* (2003) is based on the respondents' assessment of their competencies at time of graduation, while Støren and Arnesen (2007) include an educational background variable in their multivariate analyses which measures to what extent the study programme was vocationally oriented.

[12] The difference between the three groups for each main subject field and age interval is at the most one percentage point.

background, degree classification, previous educational and work experience, job search strategy, and county of residence. Previous educational experience is defined in terms of completion of any other university or college educational programme with a full-time duration of at least one year before the one they completed in the spring term of the given survey year. A student with previous work experience is one that has been gainfully employed since (s)he turned 18 years, and before the time of graduation.[13] If the earlier work experience is related to the education a student completed in the spring term of the survey year, the person is judged to have had earlier relevant work experience as long as the earlier work experience was not compulsory educational placement. The gender, marital status, children, socio-economic background, job search strategy and county of residence characteristics are measured at the time each survey was conducted. Age is measured in years at the time of graduation, which is in the same year as the survey week. Socio-economic background measures whether a student's father or mother has completed a higher educational programme, has only completed primary and secondary school or upper secondary education, or has not completed any educational programmes at all. The job search strategy measures whether a person has contacted family and acquaintances in order to find a job. Achieved grade levels are numerical grades, and alphabetical grades are converted to numerical grades.[14]

We see from Table 10.1 that 52% of the people in the net sample are females for all cohorts taken together, and most of them are under 30 years old (73%). More than half of them are married or cohabiting (56%), but few have children (20%). Just 60% of the graduates have a father or mother (or both) with higher education (statistics not shown in the table). Most of them have earlier work experience (69%), and among these people there is a high fraction with some earlier relevant work experience (38% of all graduates).

In Norway there are 68 HEIs, of which 33 are represented in the net sample. Among these we find all seven universities, all six specialised university institutions, both the national institutions for the arts, 15 of the 24 state university colleges, but only three of the 29 private university colleges. In the period 2001–2005, under 20% of the total number of students who completed either a bachelor's, master's or PhD degree (*ferdige kandidater*) in the relevant spring terms were from private university

---

[13] Excluding vacation work, jobs lasting less than three months without interruption, and compulsory educational placement.

[14] Grades are normalised within the subject fields. The reason is that there may be different grade standards across subjects (Arnesen and Try, 2001). For example, the numerical grade level 2.2 is more difficult to obtain in law than in a science subject. We normalise the grades by subtracting the grade average within the field and dividing it by the standard deviation within the field. The normalised grade variable is then defined as a z-score, with an average equal to 0 and a standard deviation equal to 1. We have also inverted the scale, so that the better the grade level, the higher is the value. The z-score for a student with unknown grade level is set to the average 0, and in that case the dummy variable 'Grade level unknown' is equal to 1 (and equal to 0 if a student's grade level is known). This procedure has the advantage that there are no missing data on observed covariates.

colleges.[15] This fraction varies from 10% in 2001 to 19% in 2003. As many as 82% of the people in the net sample graduated from one of the universities, but just 9% from one of the specialised university institutions, and 8% from one of the state university colleges. Very few people graduated from either of the national institutions for the arts (0.2%), or from one of the private university colleges (0.7%). Note that only Norwegian HEIs are included in the Graduate Surveys.

3. Types of Mismatch and Hypotheses

For our sample there are five possible outcomes after graduation: employed without being mismatched, (only) horizontally mismatched, (only) vertically mismatched, double-mismatched (i.e. both horizontally and vertically mismatched), and unemployed. These outcomes are defined as follows:

1. *Employed without being mismatched*: Respondents included in groups (i) and (iii).
2. *Horizontally mismatched*: Respondents included in groups (i) and (iv).
3. *Vertically mismatched*: Respondents included in groups (ii) and (iii).
4. *Double-mismatched*: Respondents included in groups (ii) and (iv).
5. *Unemployed*: Respondents without gainful work (i.e. non-employed) who also fulfilled at least one of the following conditions:
   (a) They considered themselves as mainly unemployed and had applied for work.
   (b) They did not consider themselves as either mainly employed or unemployed, but had applied for work within the last four weeks prior to the survey week, and could have taken a job in this week.
   (c) They had participated in certain labour market programmes.

The different groups used here are:

(i) Graduates who answered that their work required higher education either at the same level as or at a higher level than the one they completed in the spring term of the survey year.
(ii) Graduates who answered that their work required higher education either at a lower level than the one they completed in the given spring term, or that the work did not require higher education but it was an advantage to have it, or that higher education was irrelevant.

---

[15] Source: Norwegian Social Science Data Services (NSD); see the web site http://dbh.nsd.uib.no. Note that there are missing values for private university colleges for this kind of information in the NSD database before 2001.

(iii) Graduates who answered that the content of the education they completed corresponded to a greater or lesser extent with their work.
(iv) Graduates who answered that the content of the education they had completed did not correspond at all with their work.

Mismatched persons include those who are unemployed, and persons who are horizontally or vertically mismatched (or both). All horizontally or vertically mismatched persons are employed.

In our opinion, horizontal and vertical mismatch are two very different forms of mismatch. It can be argued that being vertically mismatched is more damaging, and thus more important to individuals, than being horizontally mismatched. If graduates are failing to obtain a graduate level job, this may have important implications for their labour market success in the longer term. For example, Arnesen (2006) examines the labour market situation for persons having completed higher degrees in a follow-up survey of a sample of the 2000 cohort from the NIFU STEP Graduate Surveys. She finds that, among the different groups of mismatched persons, only those who were in jobs for which they were overqualified six months after graduation have a significantly higher probability of being mismatched four and a half years later (i.e. in autumn 2004), compared with those who were employed without being mismatched. Moreover, the analysis in Arnesen (2006) clearly shows that being mismatched six months after graduation has significant negative effects on graduates' wage levels four and a half years later.

On the other hand, if graduates move into a graduate job where the content of the education they completed does not correspond at all with their job, this situation seems to be of less concern than in the case of vertical mismatch. Indeed, it can be argued that the very point of generic education is to provide individuals with general skills which they can use in a whole range of jobs. An individual with, for example, a history degree might not actually end up working in a job requiring historical knowledge, but could fill a number of graduate level jobs requiring the ability to reason analytically, prepare coherent arguments, gather evidence, communicate effectively, etc.

As a rule, generic competencies are seen as transferable between different educational domains. In line with the results of Heijke *et al.* (2003) and Støren and Arnesen (2007), we therefore expect that those with a generic education will show a stronger tendency to have a job outside their own field of study (i.e. be horizontally mismatched) than those with a vocational education. However, it is not possible to argue *a priori* that graduates with generic education will experience vertical mismatch problems to a greater extent than graduates with vocational educational qualifications.

4. Average Mismatch Levels by Type of Education in the Period 1995–2005

From Table 10.1 we see that 54% of the graduates in the net sample are not mismatched on the labour market, which implies that 46% are mismatched. Among mismatched

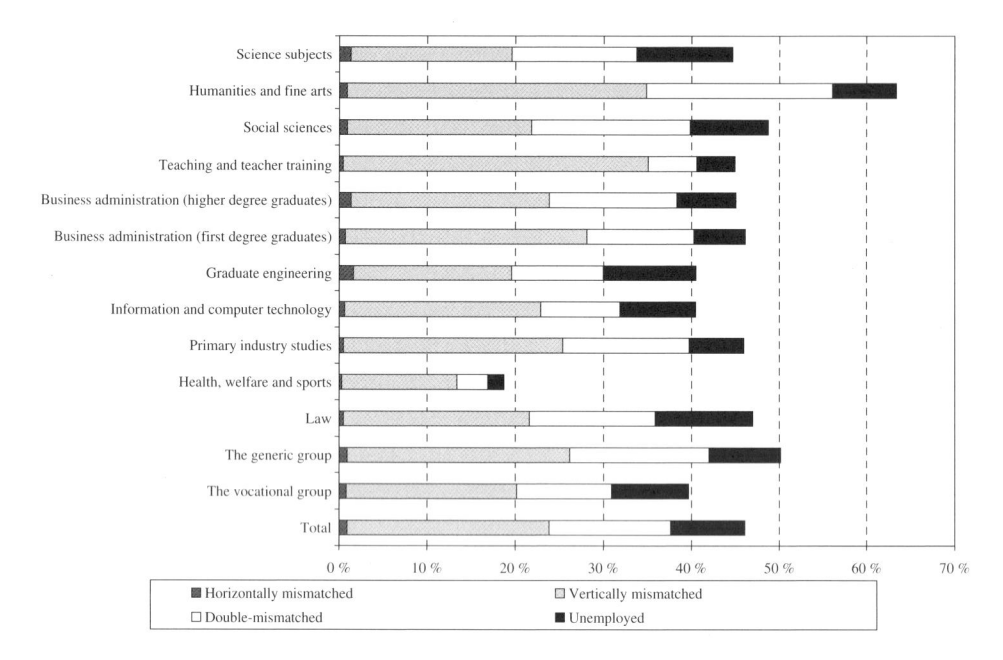

Fig. 10.2. Mismatched graduates as a percentage of the labour force six months after graduation, by type of education: The net sample.

Note: The figure shows the average proportions for the whole period 1995–2005. N = 16,834.

persons, most are vertically mismatched (23%), while very few graduates are horizontally mismatched (1%). Unemployed persons represent 8% of the net sample.

Figure 10.2 shows the number of mismatched persons, in per cent of the labour force, for all cohorts taken together. The proportions of mismatched persons by type of education can be considered as an average measure of educational mismatch. From the figure we see that the generic group has a higher average mismatch level than the vocational group, with respective average mismatch rates of 50% and 40%. The generic group of graduates in humanities has the highest average level of mismatch, with a rate of 63%, while graduates in social sciences also have a high average level (49%). We find educational groups with low average mismatch levels only within vocational education. The lowest level of mismatch is among those completing courses in health, welfare and sports — only 19%.

From Fig. 10.2 we also see the four types of mismatch in the labour market. The generic group has a higher vertical mismatch level (25%) and a higher double-mismatch level (16%) than the vocational group (19 and 11% respectively). However, the horizontal mismatch levels are the same for both groups (1%), and the unemployment rates are also about the same (generic group: 8%, vocational group: 9%). The highest vertical mismatch levels are among the generic groups of teaching and teacher training (35%) and humanities (34%). Those having completed courses in the humanities also have the highest proportion of double-mismatched (21%), but this fraction is also high among social scientists (18%). Unemployment rates are highest among lawyers and engineers (both 11%).

5. The Probability of Being Mismatched by Type of Education in the Period 1995–2005

We have found that generic graduates are more vertically mismatched and more double-mismatched than vocational graduates, while there are only small differences in the unemployment levels between the two groups, on average. The average proportions of horizontally mismatched persons are the same for both groups. These results, however, are based solely on descriptive statistics. Individual patterns of mismatch may depend not only on institutional settings such as type of education, but also on individual characteristics and other factors such as labour market conditions.[16]

In the Graduate Surveys we have information on several individual characteristics (see Table 10.1). The question is whether some types of mismatch levels are still higher for the generic group than for the vocational group when we take account of these individual characteristics, and of variations in labour market conditions between graduates.

Table 10.2 shows the results from multinomial logistic regressions based on the Graduate Surveys from 1995 to 2005. The explanatory variables for educational groups and individual characteristics in the table are dummy variables (including the variable 'Grade level unknown'), except for three variables — age, achieved grade (z-score) and county-specific unemployment rates, which are continuous variables.[17] We measure the differences in the county-specific unemployment rates between the graduates by using the proportion of registered unemployed and people in labour market programmes, in per cent of the labour force, in a student's county of residence at the time of graduation; these unemployment rates are measured as annual averages. The dependent variable has five values: 1 if a person is horizontally mismatched, 2 if (s)he is vertically mismatched, 3 if (s)he is double-mismatched, 4 if (s)he is unemployed, and 0 if (s)he is employed without being mismatched, which is the reference category. In both regressions we have also included dummies for regions of residence (estimation results not shown in the table), which are based on the 19 Norwegian counties. However, in this section we do not try to estimate possible variations in the mismatch outcomes across different cohorts. Consequently, we do not include any cohort dummies in the regressions.[18]

---

[16] For example, the proportion of graduates with previous work experience may vary between different educational groups (Børing, 2005).
[17] See the specification of the achieved grade (z-score) in the data section.
[18] The reference person in Table 10.2 is, therefore, considered to be included in an 'average cohort'.

Table 10.2. Estimates of multinomial logistic regressions: The probability of being mismatched as opposed to being employed without being mismatched six months after graduation: The net sample.

		Model 1		Model 2	
	Type of variable	Coeff.	St.dev.	Coeff.	St.dev.
Horizontally mismatched					
Constant		−3.550*	1.924	−4.571**	1.959
Female	Dummy	−0.314*	0.186	−0.149	0.191
Age	Continuous	−0.008	0.108	0.041	0.110
Age squared	Continuous	0.000	0.001	0.000	0.001
Married or cohabitant	Dummy	−0.007	0.178	0.034	0.179
Graduates with children	Dummy	−0.265	0.331	−0.269	0.332
Females with children	Dummy	−0.037	0.448	−0.065	0.449
Father with primary and secondary school or without any education	Dummy	−0.225	0.284	−0.226	0.285
Father with higher education	Dummy	−0.032	0.210	−0.033	0.210
Mother with primary and secondary school or without any education	Dummy	−0.001	0.244	−0.005	0.243
Mother with higher education	Dummy	−0.016	0.208	-0.023	0.209
The vocational group		−0.354**	0.176		
Graduate engineering	Dummy			0.494**	0.226
Information and computer technology	Dummy			−0.662	0.520
Primary industry studies	Dummy			−0.722	0.597
Health, welfare and sports	Dummy			−1.614***	0.593
Law	Dummy			−0.817**	0.337
Grade level (z-score)	Continuous	−0.280***	0.100	−0.238**	0.097
Grade level unknown	Dummy	−0.174	0.258	−0.042	0.260
Previous educational experience	Dummy	0.035	0.205	0.080	0.206
Earlier work experience	Dummy	0.129	0.242	0.205	0.244
Some earlier relevant work experience	Dummy	−0.029	0.220	−0.041	0.222
Contacted family and acquaintances	Dummy	0.493**	0.215	0.488**	0.215
County-specific unemployment rates	Continuous	−0.055	0.057	−0.078	0.057
Vertically mismatched					
Constant		−2.527***	0.484	−2.801***	0.489
Female	Dummy	0.127***	0.045	0.173***	0.046
Age	Continuous	0.095***	0.027	0.104***	0.028
Age squared	Continuous	−0.001***	0.000	−0.001***	0.000
Married or cohabitant	Dummy	−0.008	0.043	−0.008	0.043
Graduates with children	Dummy	0.087	0.076	0.072	0.076
Females with children	Dummy	−0.176*	0.095	−0.147	0.096
Father with primary and secondary school or without any education	Dummy	0.038	0.062	0.044	0.062
Father with higher education	Dummy	−0.059	0.050	−0.048	0.050
Mother with primary and secondary school or without any education	Dummy	0.101*	0.055	0.105*	0.055
Mother with higher education	Dummy	−0.033	0.050	−0.031	0.050
The vocational group		−0.427***	0.042		
Graduate engineering	Dummy			−0.370***	0.068
Information and computer technology	Dummy			−0.244**	0.101

(Continued)

Table 10.2. (*Continued*)

	Type of variable	Model 1 Coeff.	Model 1 St.dev.	Model 2 Coeff.	Model 2 St.dev.
Primary industry studies	Dummy			−0.034	0.102
Health, welfare and sports	Dummy			−1.214***	0.098
Law	Dummy			−0.237***	0.063
Grade level (z-score)	Continuous	−0.084***	0.022	−0.083***	0.022
Grade level unknown	Dummy	−0.179***	0.060	−0.085	0.061
Previous educational experience	Dummy	−0.168***	0.050	−0.159***	0.050
Earlier work experience	Dummy	0.061	0.058	0.059	0.059
Some earlier relevant work experience	Dummy	0.005	0.053	0.014	0.053
Contacted family and acquaintances	Dummy	0.546***	0.052	0.527***	0.053
County-specific unemployment rates	Continuous	−0.053***	0.014	−0.055***	0.014
Double-mismatched					
Constant		−6.428***	0.727	−6.632***	0.734
Female	Dummy	0.147***	0.054	0.181***	0.055
Age	Continuous	0.320***	0.043	0.324***	0.043
Age squared	Continuous	−0.004***	0.001	−0.004***	0.001
Married or cohabitant	Dummy	−0.076	0.052	−0.074	0.052
Graduates with children	Dummy	−0.091	0.098	−0.109	0.098
Females with children	Dummy	−0.285**	0.126	−0.255**	0.127
Father with primary and secondary school or without any education	Dummy	−0.022	0.078	−0.012	0.079
Father with higher education	Dummy	−0.071	0.061	−0.057	0.061
Mother with primary and secondary school or without any education	Dummy	0.064	0.069	0.067	0.070
Mother with higher education	Dummy	0.006	0.060	0.009	0.060
The vocational group		−0.572***	0.052		
Graduate engineering	Dummy			−0.473***	0.085
Information and computer technology	Dummy			−0.709***	0.146
Primary industry studies	Dummy			−0.072	0.126
Health, welfare and sports	Dummy			−1.872***	0.176
Law	Dummy			−0.318***	0.075
Grade level (z-score)	Continuous	−0.077***	0.027	−0.076***	0.027
Grade level unknown	Dummy	−0.193***	0.074	−0.072	0.075
Previous educational experience	Dummy	−0.286***	0.064	−0.268***	0.064
Earlier work experience	Dummy	0.490***	0.066	0.493***	0.067
Some earlier relevant work experience	Dummy	−0.934***	0.064	−0.914***	0.065
Contacted family and acquaintances	Dummy	1.007***	0.057	0.985***	0.057
County-specific unemployment rates	Continuous	−0.077***	0.017	−0.078***	0.017
Unemployed					
Constant		−11.418***	0.926	−11.543***	0.934
Female	Dummy	0.020	0.068	0.089	0.070
Age	Continuous	0.504***	0.055	0.502***	0.055
Age squared	Continuous	−0.007***	0.001	−0.006***	0.001
Married or cohabitant	Dummy	−0.350***	0.065	−0.358***	0.065
Graduates with children	Dummy	−0.164	0.125	−0.175	0.125

(*Continued*)

Table 10.2. (*Continued*)

	Type of variable	Model 1 Coeff.	St.dev.	Model 2 Coeff.	St.dev.
Females with children	Dummy	0.312**	0.152	0.329**	0.152
Father with primary and secondary school or without any education	Dummy	0.022	0.095	0.033	0.096
Father with higher education	Dummy	0.021	0.076	0.020	0.076
Mother with primary and secondary school or without any education	Dummy	0.110	0.083	0.099	0.083
Mother with higher education	Dummy	−0.110	0.075	−0.108	0.076
The vocational group		−0.145**	0.062		
Graduate engineering	Dummy			0.009	0.092
Information and computer technology	Dummy			−0.036	0.154
Primary industry studies	Dummy			−0.183	0.179
Health, welfare and sports	Dummy			−1.988***	0.239
Law	Dummy			0.253***	0.087
Grade level (z-score)	Continuous	−0.088***	0.033	−0.079**	0.033
Grade level unknown	Dummy	0.033	0.085	0.199**	0.087
Previous educational experience	Dummy	−0.249***	0.079	−0.239***	0.079
Earlier work experience	Dummy	−0.271***	0.082	−0.288***	0.082
Some earlier relevant work experience	Dummy	−0.745***	0.085	−0.701***	0.086
Contacted family and acquaintances	Dummy	1.438***	0.065	1.399***	0.066
County-specific unemployment rates	Continuous	0.126***	0.020	0.118***	0.020
Cox & Snell R Squared			0.121		0.137
Nagelkerke R Squared			0.134		0.151
McFadden R Squared			0.054		0.062
Number of graduates			16,834		16,834

Notes: 1) For the dependent variable we use the following outcome as the reference category: *employed without being mismatched*. 2) The age variable is measured in years at time of graduation. A county-specific unemployment rate is the fraction of registered unemployed and people in labour market programmes, in per cent of the labour force, in a student's county of residence at time of graduation, and is measured as an annual average. See the data section for descriptions of other explanatory variables. 3) The difference between the two models is as follows: In Model 1 a dummy variable ('the vocational group') for the aggregated group of all the vocational educational programmes is included in the regression, while in Model 2 dummies for each of the vocational educational programmes are included. The generic group is used as the reference category in both models. 4) ***Significant at the 1% level, **significant at the 5% level, *significant at the 10% level. 5) In the regressions we have also controlled for regional dummies of residence (not shown in the table), which are based on the 19 Norwegian counties. 6) The reference person: *male, unmarried, without children, generic education, known grade level, no previous educational or work experience, has not contacted family and acquaintances to find a job, and both parents with upper secondary education*.

The only difference between the two models in Table 10.2 is the way in which different educational groups are included in each model. In Model 1 we use a dummy variable ('the vocational group') in the regression, which is equal to 1 if a person has a vocational education, and 0 if a person has a generic education. Dummy variables for each of the vocational subjects are included separately in Model 2. For both Model 1 and Model 2 the generic group of subjects as a whole is used as the reference category.

5.1. *Type of education*

We see from Model 1 that persons who have completed vocational courses not only have a lower probability of being horizontally mismatched on the labour market (as compared to getting a job without being mismatched) than those who have completed generic courses, which is to be expected, but also that they have a relatively lower probability of being vertically mismatched, double-mismatched and unemployed. In fact, the vocational group has an even lower probability of being double-mismatched or vertically mismatched than of being horizontally mismatched or unemployed, compared with the generic group.

The results from Model 2 show that there are large differences in the mismatch probabilities among graduates from different vocational educational programmes. Graduates in health, welfare and sports and law graduates have a lower probability of being horizontally mismatched, vertically mismatched and double-mismatched (as opposed to being employed without being mismatched) than the generic group. The probability of being unemployed is also relatively lower for graduates in health, welfare and sports, but this probability is relatively higher for law graduates. Among all the vocational subjects, the largest differences in the mismatch probabilities are between graduates in health, welfare and sports and the generic group, except for the probability of being horizontally mismatched, where there are only small differences between the educational groups.

We see also from Model 2 that graduate engineers and graduates in information and computer technology have a lower probability of being vertically mismatched and double-mismatched than the group of generic graduates. However, graduate engineers have a relatively higher probability of being horizontally mismatched, while there are no significant differences in this probability between graduates in information and computer technology and the group of generic educational specialisations. There are also no significant differences in the probability of being unemployed between graduates with one of these two vocational subjects and generic graduates as a whole. We find no significant differences in the mismatch probabilities between people having completed courses in primary industry studies and graduates in the generic group.

We found earlier that the generic group of humanities specialists has the highest average mismatch level. Accordingly, we carried out a multinomial logistic regression analysis (results not shown), where dummy variables for the generic subjects are also included in the regression separately, except for the reference category humanities and fine arts. All other explanatory variables are the same as in the two models in Table 10.2. This analysis shows that graduates from all other subjects have a lower probability of being vertically mismatched and double-mismatched than graduates in humanities. We find, further, that graduates in teaching and teacher training, business administration (both higher and first degree graduates), and graduates in health, welfare and sports, have a significantly lower probability of being unemployed than graduates in the humanities and fine arts (at the 5% level of significance). But only graduates in health, welfare and sports and law graduates have a significantly lower probability of being horizontally mismatched than humanities specialists (5% level), though none of the other subjects have a significantly higher probability in this connection. The largest differences in the mismatch probabilities (excluding the horizontal mismatch probability) between graduates in humanities and those from other educational groups are with graduates in health, welfare and sports.

Our results from Model 1 show that the vocational group as a whole has a lower probability of being vertically mismatched and double-mismatched than the generic group as a whole. But are these results driven by the higher mismatch level among graduates from one of the generic subjects, namely humanities and fine arts? We find that even if we either exclude the group of humanities specialists (which has the highest mismatch level) or the vocational group of graduates in health, welfare and sports (which has the lowest mismatch level) from our sample, the generic group still has a higher probability of being vertically mismatched or double-mismatched than the vocational group, while there are no significant differences in the probability of being horizontally mismatched or unemployed (results from this multinomial logistic regression analysis not shown).[19] It follows that the differences in the vertical and double-mismatch probabilities between the generic and vocational group are not driven by the higher mismatch level among graduates in humanities: these differences are still significant if we exclude the group of humanities specialists from the sample.

5.2. *Individual characteristics and county-specific unemployment rates*

From Models 1 and 2 in Table 10.2 we see that the probability of being vertically mismatched and double-mismatched is significantly higher among females than among males, while there are no significant gender differences in the probability of being horizontally mismatched and unemployed (based on the 5% level). The results from both models also show that all types of mismatch probabilities, except for the probability of being horizontally mismatched, are estimated to increase with increasing age at time of graduation.

Married or cohabitant graduates have a lower probability of being unemployed than unmarried graduates, while there are no significant differences between these

---

[19] These results also hold if both groups are excluded from the sample, except that in this case the generic group has a relatively lower probability of being unemployed.

groups for the other mismatch probabilities. Marital status indicates the degree of economic dependency, and may affect both graduates' reservation wage and their employability. But in our analysis it affects only the probability of being unemployed.

Males with children have no significantly higher or lower mismatch probabilities than males without children. However, females with children have a lower probability of being double-mismatched, but a higher probability of being unemployed, than with males without children (the reference individual).

We do not find significant direct effects of graduates' socio-economic background on any of the probabilities of being mismatched. On the other hand, degree classification has a significant negative effect on each of these probabilities.

Graduates with earlier educational or some relevant work experience have a significant lower probability of being double-mismatched and unemployed than other persons. Those with earlier educational experience also have a lower probability of being vertically mismatched. The dummy variable measuring whether a person has earlier work experience or not has a significant negative effect on the probability of being unemployed, but a positive effect on the probability of being double-mismatched. There are no significant effects on the probability of being vertically mismatched with respect to earlier work (including relevant work) experience. We do not find any significant effects of earlier educational or work (including relevant work) experience on the probability of being horizontally mismatched either.

Persons who contact family and acquaintances to find a job have higher mismatch probabilities than others. The reason may be that those who use this job search method are a selected group of job searchers with lower relevant employability than other persons, and who encounter problems in finding a relevant job on their own account.

Finally, the probability of being vertically mismatched and double-mismatched is negatively affected by county-specific unemployment rates, while those rates have a positive effect on the probability of being unemployed. The impact of county-specific unemployment rates on the probability of being horizontally mismatched is non-significant. It is not a surprising result that a person's probability of being unemployed is positively affected by the unemployment rate in his/her county of residence, but it is less obvious that this rate should have a negative effect on the probability of being vertically and double-mismatched. If, for example, graduates prefer to be employed rather than being unemployed, even if they fail to obtain a graduate-level job, we would expect that the unemployment rate would have a positive impact on the vertical mismatch probability. However, suppose that graduates with a high risk of being vertically mismatched also have a high risk of being unemployed, compared with those who have high relevant employability. Then their probability of getting a non-graduate job (compared to being employed without being mismatched) could decrease with an increasing unemployment rate.

6. Possible Effects of Non-Response

In the data section we noted that there are missing data on account of non-response, though there are no missing data on observed covariates. In order to investigate the nature of non-response, we compared the following three groups with respect to some individual characteristics: the net sample, the gross sample and the entire group who received the questionnaire. We found that there were small differences in the average proportions of the main subject fields and the selected age intervals between these three groups for the whole period 1995–2005. The proportion of males, moreover, was lower among graduates in the net sample than among persons in the gross sample and among the entire group who received the questionnaire. How might these gender differences affect our analysis and conclusions?

Figure 10.3 shows that there are small differences in the mismatch level between males and females as two separate groups, and this is also the situation for each of the four types of mismatch taken separately. While 45% of the male group within the net sample is mismatched on the labour market, the corresponding proportion for females is 47%. Among females we find that 24% are vertically mismatched, while 14% are double-mismatched. For males these fractions are 22 and 13% respectively.

We also see from Fig. 10.3 that the fraction of mismatched graduates with a generic education is higher among females (52%) than among males (48%), and

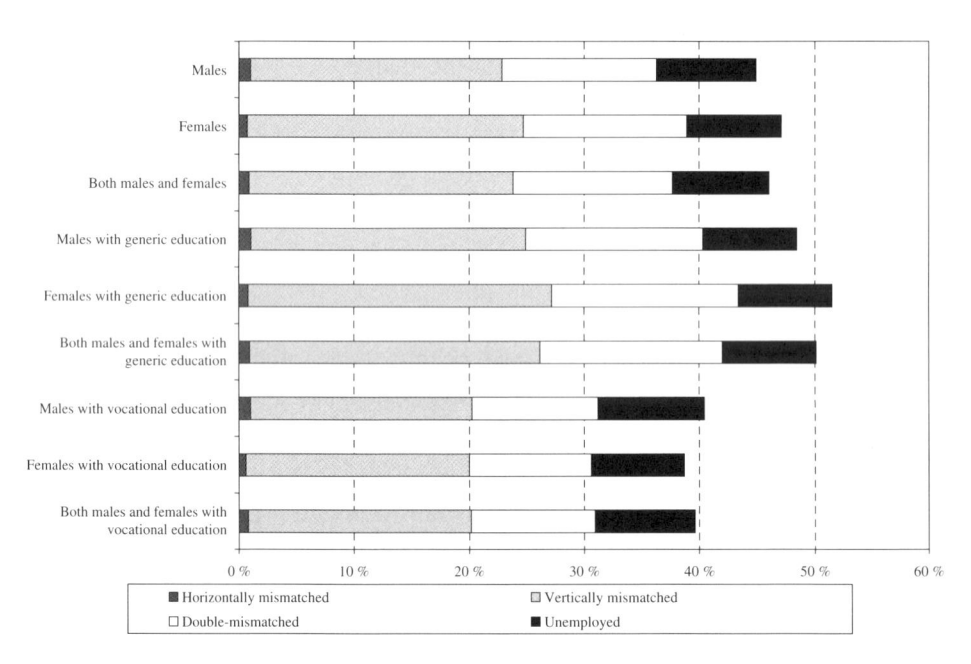

Fig. 10.3. Mismatched graduates as a percentage of the labour force six months after graduation, by gender and type of education: The net sample.

Note: The figure shows the average proportions for the whole period 1995–2005. N = 16,834.

there are small gender differences in this proportion for each of the mismatch categories. Among those with a vocational education, the fraction of mismatched females (39%) is approximately the same as for mismatched males (40%).

For each gender we have carried out a multinomial logistic regression analysis (results not shown). The estimation results from these regressions are based solely on Model 1, where we compare the generic group as a whole with the vocational group as a whole. We find that each of the various mismatch probabilities is lower for females with vocational education than for females with generic education, and that the relative differences in the double-mismatch and vertical mismatch probabilities are also stronger among females than among both genders taken together (the estimates for both males and females are presented in Table 10.2). Males in the vocational group have a significantly lower probability of being mismatched only in relation to vertical and double-mismatching compared with males in the generic group, and these effects are also weaker than for males and females taken together. Since males are overrepresented in the non-response group, we may thus overestimate the effects of type of education on each of the mismatch probabilities.

7. Conclusions

We focus on the role of type of education, defined in terms of generic and vocational education, in the transition from higher education to the labour market. Our study is based on the analysis in Støren and Arnesen (2007). NIFU STEP Graduate Surveys from 1995 to 2005 are used to examine to what extent the variation in each of four possible mismatch outcomes is explained by type of education six months after graduation. The four mismatch outcomes are: a graduate student may be either horizontally mismatched, vertically mismatched, double-mismatched (i.e. both horizontally and vertically mismatched), or unemployed.

Descriptive statistics show that graduates in generic subjects have a higher observed average mismatch level than graduates in vocational subjects. This is due to the fact that the proportions of vertically mismatched and double-mismatched persons are relatively higher among graduates in the generic group; there are only small differences in the proportions of horizontally mismatched and unemployed persons between the generic and vocational group. The individual mismatch levels may, however, depend not only on institutional settings such as type of education, but also on individual characteristics and other factors such as labour market conditions. Using multinomial logistic regressions, we find that the levels of all four types of mismatch are higher for the generic group than for the vocational group when we take account of personal characteristics and differences in county-specific unemployment rates between graduates.

The result that generic graduates have a higher probability of being horizontally mismatched than vocational graduates is to be expected, and is in line with previous research by Heijke *et al.* (2003) and Støren and Arnesen (2007). On the other hand, the finding that graduates in the generic group also have a relatively higher probability of being vertically mismatched and double-mismatched, i.e. that generic graduates find it more difficult than vocational graduates to obtain graduate level jobs, is a much more important finding. In addition, the generic group has a relatively higher probability of being unemployed. Our analysis also shows that if we exclude the educational group with the highest or lowest mismatch level from our sample, we still find that the generic group has a higher probability of being vertically mismatched or double-mismatched than the vocational group, while there are no significant differences in the probability of being horizontally mismatched or unemployed.

It is important to emphasise that we focus exclusively on graduates' mismatch levels over a short period after graduation. A follow-up survey of a sample of the 2000 cohort from the NIFU STEP Graduate Surveys shows that almost all of those who graduated in spring 2000 had entered the labour market by autumn 2004, and were in relevant jobs at that time. However, Arnesen (2006) analyses the labour market situation for higher degree graduates in this follow-up survey, and finds that being mismatched six months after graduation had significant negative effects on graduates' wage levels in autumn 2004. Thus mismatch problems in the period immediately after graduation may have consequences for graduates' career opportunities in the longer term.

Acknowledgements

I thank David Dyker and Clara Åse Arnesen for helpful comments on earlier drafts of the paper. Remaining errors, omissions and opinions are my own.

References

Arnesen, C.Å. (2000). 'Higher education and graduate employment in Norway', *European Journal of Education* 35(2): 221–228.

Arnesen, C.Å. (2006). 'Har etableringsfasen i arbeidsmarkedet betydning for senere yrkeskarriere?', *Søkelys på Arbeidsmarkedet* 2: 149–158.

Arnesen, C.Å. and Try, S. (2001). 'Karakterers betydning for overgangen fra høyere utdanning til arbeidsmarkedet', *NIFU Rapport*, No. 6, Oslo, NIFU.

Børing, P. (2005). 'Har arbeidserfaring betydning for studentenes jobbmuligheter etter avsluttet utdanning?', *NIFU STEP Skriftserie*, No. 1, Oslo, NIFU STEP.

Dancer, D.M. and Fiebig, D.G. (2004). 'Modelling students at risk', Australian Economic Papers 43: 158–173.

Green, F. and McIntosh, S. (2002). *Is There a Genuine Underutilisation of Skills amongst the Over-Qualified?*, SKOPE Research Paper No. 30, Coventry, University of Warwick.

Heijke, H., Meng, C. and Ris, C. (2003). 'Fitting to the job: The role of generic and vocational competencies in adjustment and performance', *Labour Economics* 10(2): 215–229.

Johnes, G. and McNabb, R. (2004). 'Never give up on the good times: student attrition in the UK', *Oxford Bulletin of Economics and Statistics* 66(1): 23–47.

Lambert Review (2003). *Lambert Review of Business-University Collaboration*, HM Treasury, http://www.hm-treasury.gov.uk/media/DDE/65/lambert_review_final_450.pdf.

Naylor, R. and Smith, J. (2004). 'Degree performance of economics students in UK universities: Absolute and relative performance in prior qualifications', *Scottish Journal of Political Economy* 51: 250–265.

Støren, L.A. (2004). 'Unemployment experiences during early career of immigrants and non-immigrants graduates', *Journal of Education and Work* 17(1): 71–93.

Støren, L.A. (2008). 'Høyere utdanning og arbeidsmarked — i Norge og Europa. Norsk rapportering fra EU-prosjektet «REFLEX»', *NIFU STEP Rapport*, No. 6, Oslo, NIFU STEP.

Støren, L.A. and Arnesen, C.Å. (2007). 'Winners and Losers', in Allen, J. and van der Velden, R. (eds.), *The Flexible Professional in the Knowledge Society: General Results of the REFLEX Project*, Research Centre for Education and the Labour Market, Report to the EU Commission, Maastricht University.

Toutkoushian, R.K. and Smart, J.C. (2001). 'Do institutional characteristics affect student gains from college?', *The Review of Higher Education* 25(1): 39–61.

Try, S. (2004). 'The role of flexible work in the transition from higher education into the labour market', *Journal of Education and Work* 17(1): 27–45.

Try, S. (2005). 'The use of job search strategies among university graduates', *The Journal of Socio-Economics* 34(2): 223–243.

Try, S. and Grøgaard, J.B. (2003). 'Measuring the relationship between resources and outcomes in higher education in Norway', *NIFU Skriftserie* No. 27, Oslo, NIFU STEP.

CHAPTER 11

HUMAN RESOURCES AND SKILLS GAP IN A REGIONAL CONTEXT: THE CASE OF CAMPANIA[1,2]

MARIA DEL SORBO

> The most valuable of all capital is that invested in human beings
> (Marshall [1890], 1922, 564)

1. Introduction

This chapter aims to analyse the role of human capital in a spatial context, where public actors at different levels — national, regional, provincial and local — seek to interact and communicate to meet the community's needs. In this context it is necessary to identify and manage appropriate human and financial resources, with a view to understanding and fulfilling the real demands of the citizens, families and organisations that take part in the socio-economic system, thus helping them to attain their objectives. It is in turn essential to have available an infrastructure that supports them and the required set of competences or *skills* to address the needs that present themselves in both private and public sectors.

The development and growth gap in the southern regions of Italy is an expression of a varied socio-economic system that finds its roots in different styles of governance, accessibility to infrastructure, industrial framework and human capital, which are translated into a variety of capacities to create and implement innovation. Assessing the wide variations of technological development and innovation demands some understanding of the real commitment of all the stakeholders acting in the territory concerned, at national, regional and local levels.

As the private and public sectors need specific competences that new graduates do not always possess, job–education patterns need to be developed and drawn into line with the labour market. Universities and research centres have to interpret national

---

[1] An earlier version of this paper was presented to the PRIME conference, 'EU-US Early Career Researcher Conference on Research and Innovation Studies', University of Twente, Enschede, Netherlands, July 2008.
[2] I am grateful to Professor Nick von Tunzelmann and Dr Simona Iammarino of SPRU for their valuable comments on and support for this research.

and local demands and support policy decisions through appropriate deployment of R&D activity, coordinated with those specific local needs (Bonaccorsi and Nesci, 2006). As argued in the UK Lambert Report (Lambert, 2003, 84), the recruitment of *knowledge workers* to the technology transfer field can be a successful strategy, where training collaborations between public and private sector channel PhD students, post-doctoral students and researchers into firm-level R&D projects.

In this chapter we attempt to set out ways of measuring the level of knowledge and skills production on the basis of some main indicators for the region of Campania, in Southern Italy. In this region, according to secondary data provided by the Italian National Institute of Statistics (ISTAT), the International Labour Organization (ILO) and EUROSTAT, it seems that there has been an increase in the number of knowledge workers over the last decade or so. If this is so, why, then, is Campania's level of development still far below the average of the rest of Europe, and why, indeed, is the gap increasing? (See Fig. 11.1.) The study aims to reveal the true nature of the knowledge worker gap in Italy, and particularly in Campania, and to suggest what policies might address it.

Section 2 of the paper sets out the theoretical context of the study, by way of a literature review of a number of apparently contradictory theories of development, technological change and skills. Section 3 establishes the corresponding empirical context, by developing the notion of regional systems of innovation. Section 4 presents our results, leading to some conclusions in Section 5.

2. Theoretical Context

How is it possible to quantify and analyse knowledge and skills production in a regional context? Does knowledge and skills production express the innovative capacity of a regional innovation system? How is it possible to determine and

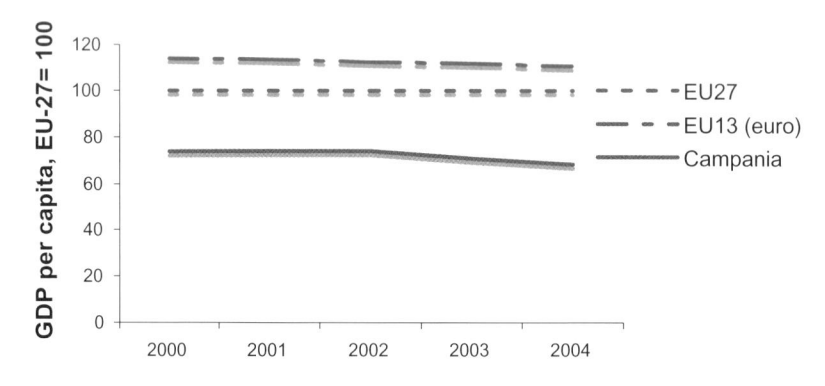

Fig. 11.1. GDP per capita in Campania and the EU, 2000–2004.
Source: EUROSTAT, 2007.

therefore measure the skills and knowledge production in a region? What is the role of universities in the learning process: are they innovation *makers*? Is it possible to evaluate the scientific and technological skills gap at regional and national level? Is it possible to measure the regional innovation level? What indicators are appropriate? What are the policy implications? Against the background of the extensive scope of the topic and the practical difficulty of gathering more significant data, we aim to find at least partial answers to most of these questions.

The theoretical underpinnings to this chapter are derived from the following approaches: human capital theory, economic growth theory, and regional innovation systems. These have been chosen because of the necessity of understanding the existing, and rather complex, relationships between technology transfer, economic growth, knowledge and skills production, and labour market dynamics.

2.1. *Human capital theory and human resource development*

The reasons that might explain the social and economic differences between regions or countries can be linked to differences in levels of assets production and productivity. An investment in 'human capital' could lead to an accumulation process of inputs and could thereby yield better future performance (Gori, 2003).

There are many theories that seek to link the knowledge and skills possessed by individuals with success in their job-life. Human capital (HC) theory stresses job productivity, so that the reward system should reflect the skills of individuals, such as talents, education and degree of expertise (Becker, 1964). The 'labour queue' or 'job competition' model attaches greater importance to educational attainments as 'screening devices' or 'signals' of trainability, implying lower training costs in the future (Thurow, 1975; Del Sorbo *et al.*, 2007). Both these theories consider the individual requirements, the job and the working environment. Sattinger (1993) considers the personal aspects related to the specific job context in his 'assignment' theory. Here, the job typology depends on a corresponding typology of *skills and capability*. This helps to explain why graduates in specific fields have more job chances in sectors related to their studies.

All these theories valorise the quality of the skills and competences required by labour markets. As numerous authors have observed, it seems that formal and experimental learning may both yield an efficient pattern of learning. HC theory considers the learning abilities of the workers as a precious production resource (Lucas, 1990; Schultz, 1961). Growth in levels of education and training are expressions of a policy of investing in *human resources* seen as 'a form of capital for development', to address the labour market and boost individual and organisational productivity. In addition, they may promote general growth in productivity and 'global' development (Aliaga, 2001). Hence, while HC theory focuses on the productivity of people, the human resource development perspective aims specifically to enhance *workforce quality* through education and training (Nafukho, Hairston and Brooks, 2004, 547).

Some Italian authors (Dagum, Lovaglio and Vittadini, 2000; Gori, 2003) argue, for the Italian case, that educational human capital has an impact on production through the medium of 'working HC', and that the salary level depends more on this working HC (i.e. 'capabilities') than HC linked purely to education. Human capital in different regions of Italy depends more on the type of job and the proficiency accumulated through learning by doing, by observing and by interacting, than the level and the years dedicated to education.

We can propose that the accumulation of HC requires:

- Universities, government and industry to act in concert to invest in the educational system;
- Scientific, technical and professional information to be provided to families, students, potential students and the employers;
- An incentive system to finance the education system, especially for higher educational levels such as the doctoral, including the opportunity to insert PhD students into business-oriented research projects on topics similar to their own research; also the chance to go abroad and/or carry out fieldwork to acquire information on better practice and data for research;
- Investment in R&D to allow the private and public sectors to employ the skills of universities and research centres.

At the same time, investment in infrastructure and physical capital has to be at a level to guarantee a suitable technological base to sustain a proper deployment of skills (Dagum, Lovaglio and Vittadini, 2000).

Gori (2003, 10) argues that there exist three different categories of competences:

- *Academic competences*, acquired at university level;
- *Specific competences*, acquired at educational and working levels;
- *Managerial competences*, acquired mainly through experience in the field.

It can be argued that these 'competences' confuse the distinction between competences and capabilities, though those boundaries can be reconfigured (von Tunzelmann and Wang, 2007). Table 11.1 sets out some of the relevant aspects of competences in this stricter sense.

Heijke *et al.* (2002, 5) argued that academic skills possess a key relevance 'as they increase the effectiveness with which occupation-specific skills are generated or maintained, thereby reducing training costs', even where specific skills and learnt capabilities play a significant role (Del Sorbo, 2007). This kind of argument is often referred to under the heading of 'learning to learn'.

Table 11.1. Competences classification, examples.

Academic competences, general	Educational competences, specific	Management competences, taught
Broad general knowledge	Specific theoretical knowledge	Coursework from management education
Cross-disciplinary thinking	Specific knowledge of methods and techniques	Project work
Problem-solving ability	Taught craft skills	Planning procedures
Analytical competences		
Reflective thinking, self-assessment		
Critical thinking and evaluation		
Power of concentration		
Writing and communication skills		

Source: Gori, 2003,10, based on Heijke, H., Meng, C. and Ramaekers, G. (2002). Reconfigured by the author to eliminate instances of 'capabilities' and instead to highlight taught elements of 'competences'.

2.2. *Economic growth: Neoclassical and post-neoclassical views*

An important contribution was provided by the form of neoclassical growth theory advanced by Robert Solow (1957), who found that up to 87.5% of economic growth in the US 1909–49 could be explained by 'exogenous' technological change. In addition, according to the neoclassical growth model, if the same technological know-how were universally available, in the long term 'all countries' economic growth rates and living standards would, under certain conditions, eventually converge' (ETB [Engineering and Technology Board], 2004, 51).

Subsequent to Solow's contribution, which stresses how much observed growth owes to 'exogenous' technological change, other 'endogenous' ('new growth theory') models were formulated, where human capital (or knowledge) is introduced into the production function; in some of these models the level of technological change relies on human capital (in others it rests more on 'endogenous' R&D). The accumulation of human capital is, however, not enough to account for the significant increases in the standard of living observed in the developed world over the last couple of centuries (ETB, 2004). As Romer states: 'Our knowledge of economic history, of what production looked like one hundred years ago, and of current events convinces us beyond any doubt that discovery, invention, and innovation are of overwhelming importance in economic growth and that the economic goods that come from these activities are different in a fundamental way from ordinary objects. We could produce statistical evidence suggesting that all growth came from capital accumulation with no room for anything called technological change. But we would not believe it' (Romer, 1993, 562).

Technological change is related to innovation and technology transfer; new economic growth theories directly involve government policies, taxes and subsidies. Institutional reforms might accordingly bring more consistent, if indirect, consequences for growth than the 'exogenous' factors proposed by the neoclassical model that Solow propounded. In this context, policies aimed at acquisition of skills, improvement of technical standards and encouragement of foreign direct investment (FDI) may be key factors reducing the 'ideas gap' and the 'technological gap' in the 'knowledge economy'.

2.3. *Structuralist approaches*

According to the structuralist approach, economic growth is led by technological change, following a direct path in a micro-economic context. Institutions and modes of organisational behaviour may influence it; hence 'historical accidents' like the invention of writing (ca. 4000 BC), the printing press, irrigation/sanitation, wind and steam power and the invention of railways may have powerful impacts on the macro-structure. The evolution of technologies and the framework that binds them into one body is an indispensable element in the understanding of economic growth. Schumpeter argued, like others, that history influences growth through a path-dependent process. Lipsey and Bekar (1995) argue that 'growth creating technological change occurs in large jumps causing deep structural adjustments'. Therefore the changes cannot be represented as a series of continuous small shocks as reflected in the usual neoclassical models. Rather each strong structural adjustment has common features, and the special role of current information and communications technologies in the modern and strongest period of technological change is self-evident. In turn, the opportunity to use new materials is vital in assuring the development of the key growth sectors, such as microelectronics, transportation, architecture, construction, energy systems, aerospace engineering and production processes in the automobile industry (ETB, 2004, 52).

The new growth and structuralist approaches both incorporate paradigms of technological change that are partially endogenous. Nevertheless, the structuralist approach considers different policy implications from the post-neoclassical point of view, based on the observation that thriving innovation policies strengthen the existing facilitating structure. The latter includes factors at the firm level (such as geographical allocation of production units), at industry level, and on an economy-wide dimension (such as social policy, facilitating job mobility). An economy's infrastructure may be influenced by macro policies that help to train people through elementary schools, trade schools, universities and on-the-job training. This aspect of the structuralist approach appears similar to the human capital concept found in those 'endogenous growth models' that underline the importance of skilled labour in the technologically driven knowledge economy (ETB, 2004, 52).

2.4. Triple Helix view

The Triple Helix model helps to identify, formalise and understand the relationships between university, industry and government. This model has a double dimension: the diversity between science and the market and the importance of combining them, and the institutional difference between private and public sectors. 'Universities, business and government should work in a climate of reciprocal trust and should be free from every form of prejudice, debating every issue that may occur, because the goal should be to solve the problems faced and overcoming the obstacles' (Del Sorbo, 2007, 11). Therefore '…unfavourable research results must not be suppressed in return for future contract or consultancy income. Even the perception of possible conflict of interest could prove to be extremely damaging to the reputation of the university and company' (Lambert, 2003, 34–37).

For the present study, this model has relevance to the assessment of the opportunities of recruiting very professional, well-skilled and well-qualified staff to the technology transfer field. A collaborative training approach might allow businesses to benefit significantly by taking on PhD students to undertake R&D projects, and recruiting skilled people who may offer access to academic contacts and knowledge. The Triple Helix may be seen as a game where university, industry and government assume a dynamic role and each player should be clear in defining its specific tasks. For instance, universities should 'explain the kind of collaboration provided and how they will participate in the business plan.' (Del Sorbo, 2007, 10)

According to the UK Lambert Report, the roles of the three actors of the Triple Helix should be shared out as follows:

- *University:* definition of the research agenda and development of competitive skills;
- *Government:* strong support to guarantee useful business–university collaboration;
- *Business:* employing the innovative ideas of the university and its networks in a productive way.

As Lambert suggests, it is appropriate to provide continuing professional development for business employees, as many universities are already doing. 'Businesses can raise the skill levels of their workforce and learn about the latest academic ideas, while universities gain access to the latest developments in professional practice. Moreover, universities may keep profitable returns from their courses' (Lambert, 2003, 114). Successful performance at individual, organisational and social level may be achieved by joining together several types of knowledge: explicit and tacit knowledge, know-how, know-why, know-what (Tidd *et al.*, 2005; Isaksen, 2006). In all of this, it is crucial not to forget to take into account the sustainability of the business in the planning processes involving the different dynamic players.

3. Regional Innovation Systems, Human Capital and Skills

As Faggian (2006) argues, it is the job of the university system to transfer the high quality of the national human capital stock to the regions. In this way, the university can be seen as a bridge connecting with the local system to increase the employability of the human capital of the region. However, students may have study and quality-of-life standards that are sensitive to the degree of development of the local system in which the universities are located geographically, since the existence and perception of a strong local and regional economy are important factors underlying future job chances.

Faggian and McCann (2006) try to assess the link between the regional innovation level and the probability of finding a future job. The only positive spillover from university to industry they find relates to the increase of human capital availability, to the extent that it produces positive effects on local economic development. Specifically, the quality of the research led by local universities has a positive influence on students' choice among the local universities. Faggian and McCann observe different factors that link the human capital availability to 'regional knowledge assets': innovation in the local economic system, concentration of universities in the same location, the presence of innovative departments and high quality of research. They examine primarily the relationship between knowledge resources and inter-regional human capital/knowledge flows, and find little support from UK material for the argument that human capital migration generates informal spillovers from university to industry and consequent regional learning effects.

Human capital, skills, knowledge and strategic intelligence all play a crucial role for economic development, and within institutions and organisations. The over-lapping of national and regional interests requires a combination of science, innovation, higher education and regional policy. The merging of organisations for science and innovation at regional and national level may cause conflicts of interest in the decision-making processes, especially in the distribution of the resources, such as the location of infrastructure and services to support science (Cooke, 2004). In this context a combined top-down and bottom-up approach may be fundamental in the decision-making processes and in consequential implementation; national initiatives in science policy can hardly be executed without linked local action aiming to realise planned objectives.

There are two perspectives on the relationship between innovation and geographical location. The first, in the Marshallian tradition, tends to see the benefits of geographical agglomeration and its effects on economic growth. The 'industrial atmosphere' is generated by the availability of the skills and know-how in specific contexts that support economic growth and encourage the creation and dissemination of new ideas. The local dimension is seen as a key factor for development and as an exogenous variable. The availability of data related to firms, institutions, organisations and universities that explain why national performance in innovation is better than regional becomes crucial to any effective analysis.

The second perspective stems from specific models of organisations at subnational level, such as innovative milieux (Aydalot, 1986), new industrial districts (Becattini, 1987), technological districts (Markusen, 1985, 1996; Storper, 1998), learning regions (Asheim, 1995; Morgan, 1997), and the regional systems of innovation (RSI) approach itself (Braczyk, Cooke and Heidenreich, 1998; Cooke, 1992; Cooke, Gomez Uraga and Etxebarria, 1997; Howells, 1996). RSIs are defined as 'located networks of actors and institutions in the public and private sector, which generate activities and interactions, import, modify and diffuse new technologies within and outside the regions' (Iammarino, 2005, 4).

The RSI can be seen as a framework within which to analyse economic and innovative performance, and at the same time as a tool for enhancing localised learning. It comprises a set of private and public institutions and generates systemic effects to encourage the firms inside the regions to embrace common rules, expectations, values, attitudes and practices, producing an environment where the culture of innovation is strengthened and learning processes are enhanced (Asheim, 1995). As also happens within the National System of Innovation (NSI), RSIs are characterised by systemic interactions between the stakeholders that generate, employ and diffuse innovations and support regional technological and economic performance.

In Italy, a number of regional models coexist. They are based on diverse firm structures, aims, strategies and performance, systemic and contextual characteristics, density and quality of interactions and functional effectiveness. The south of Italy is the most backward Italian area in terms of innovation and technological indicators, and we can hardly talk about RSI status in this context. Path dependency, economic differentiation and political fragmentation throughout its history have prevented the development of a 'natural dimension' in Southern Italy, to which can be added an anti-developmental mode of governance managed by the southern barons in the nineteenth century and more recently by the Mafia. It should be added that the southern regions of Italy possess fewer natural endowments than the northern and central regions (Iammarino, 2005, 22).

How can the older regional trajectories be discarded? Is it possible to break free from the socio-economic and institutional past? How can a structural and localised framework for change be planned and managed? Is there a role for regional policy at every governance level?

Local strategies should not diverge from the local context, and equally so for regional policy. Policy aims must be strongly based in historical and local circumstances (Iammarino, 2005). The regions need a budget and a plan: the larger its scope, the higher will be their capacity to manage innovative resources (Cooke *et al.*, 1997). The financial capacity of the regions depends on the availability of a budget out of which a local government can spend. Hence, regions that face a reduced budget will have a lower capacity to manage their resources and will find it difficult to gain any kind of innovative advantage. As the majority of regions do not have the budgetary capacity to build infrastructure, we have to pose the question: does the region have the power to design and establish the basic infrastructure for an RSI? In this context Cooke analyses the RSI by using a dual approach:

- Regionalisation:
  The region has specific competences and capacities that it employs to fashion and guide policy, based on a certain degree of autonomy, such as the financial capacity for basic infrastructure and the necessary investments for development and innovation;
- Regionalism:
  This considers the role of 'learning milieux', collaborations and partnerships between actors at national, regional and local levels (Cooke *et al.*, 1997, pp. 480–481).

Institutional changes oriented to active policies may enhance the learning environment. An RSI cannot operate outside the context of a set of rules based on trust, reliability, reciprocity and interaction (Cooke, 1992). However, over-dependency on public support can undermine the existence of a healthy RSI. An *ad hoc* mix between public and private governance at regional level may be desirable to promote an innovation system.

De Laurentis (2006) shows how the RSI can undergo evolution and the region might develop *knowledge laboratories* able to influence labour market conditions. She sees innovative firms working inside regional networks, through cooperation and interaction with other firms, such as suppliers, clients and competitors. But even with technology and research organisations, innovation support agencies and venture capital funding may be required by regional and local governments. Innovation is a learning process that benefits from the proximity of organisations that can activate this process. Furthermore, regional authorities have a significant role to play to support that learning process through supplying services and other mechanisms that strengthen the links among the actors that are involved across the whole territory (De Laurentis, 2006, 1061).

It is clear that networks involving firms and the institutions that support innovative activities have to be inserted into the RSI framework, if economic and innovation performance is to be improved and localised learning processes strengthened. Let us see now how these principles work out in practice in the Southern Italian case.

4. 'Measuring' Regional Innovation

The theories and empirical literature discussed in Section 3 provide a basis for understanding the meaning of technological change, innovation, learning processes, skills and knowledge production in terms of the Triple Helix and the RSI frameworks. Our attention now shifts to the secondary data, as collected by ISTAT, the ILO and EUROSTAT. In analysing the data, we seek to quantify the level of innovation and knowledge production at regional and national level by benchmarking a number of innovation indicators. A simple comparison between the *supply of skills* provided by universities and the *demand for skills* emanating from industry highlights the importance of the gap between the two. However it is difficult to test directly for this gap; for this reason indirect quantitative methods will be adopted to assess its magnitude.

Regional innovative capacity can be expressed in terms of the following indicators: number of graduates in science and technology disciplines; number employed in science and technology; number of employed R&D researchers; patent intensity; public and private R&D expenditure. However, the data available from the sources mentioned do not fit exactly with the comparisons required. There is no data on the regional skills gap, and the ILO does not provide regional data. The data refer to 'competences' rather than capabilities (in the sense of Table 11.1), since they look at the *potential* for innovation, rather than the level of innovative activity itself. Against this background, we have tried to adapt the available data to meet the aims of our research.

The data are organised at the national, Mezzogiorno and regional levels. The Mezzogiorno includes the following southern regions: Abruzzo,[3] Molise, Campania, Calabria, Puglia and Basilicata; additionally, insular Italy is included: Sicily and Sardinia. There are six indicators, and they are organised in three groups: the first two are averages (Figures a and b), while the third represents growth rates (Figures c). These rates are based on just the first and last available years for each dataset, as the simplest way of computing growth performance. It should be noted that in each case (Figs. 11.2, and 11.3, etc.) the footnotes and sources for the 'a' graph also apply to the 'b' and 'c' graphs.

Figure 11.2 displays the average number of Science and Technology graduates aged 20–29 per 1,000 inhabitants in all the Italian regions during the period 1998–2006. The x-axis represents geographical areas, while the y-axis measures the average number of S&T graduates. From the data, it can be seen that there is great variability in the average number of graduates. In particular, it is clear that there are not as many graduates in the Mezzogiorno compared to the rest of the country; however, Campania could be considered an exception within the Mezzogiorno, since it is closer to the national average, ranking 12th out of 20 regions (Figs. 11.2a and 11.2b).

Surprisingly, the number of graduates in Italy had been growing consistently and rapidly (nearly 192% cumulatively for the whole period). It is interesting to note that the Mezzogiorno experienced the highest growth rates (222%), followed by Campania taken by itself (211%), and then the rest of the country. This demonstrates that Italy is adjusting in accordance with the European Structural Funding planning cycle from

---

[3] There are very substantial variations within Mezzogiorno. Abruzzo, while undoubtedly qualifying in terms of geography as part of the Mezzogiorno, comes first in the region and even above some of the North Italian regions by many of the indicators used: S&T graduates, employment in R&D, firms' expenditure on R&D, patents registered at the EPO, etc.

218   M. Del Sorbo

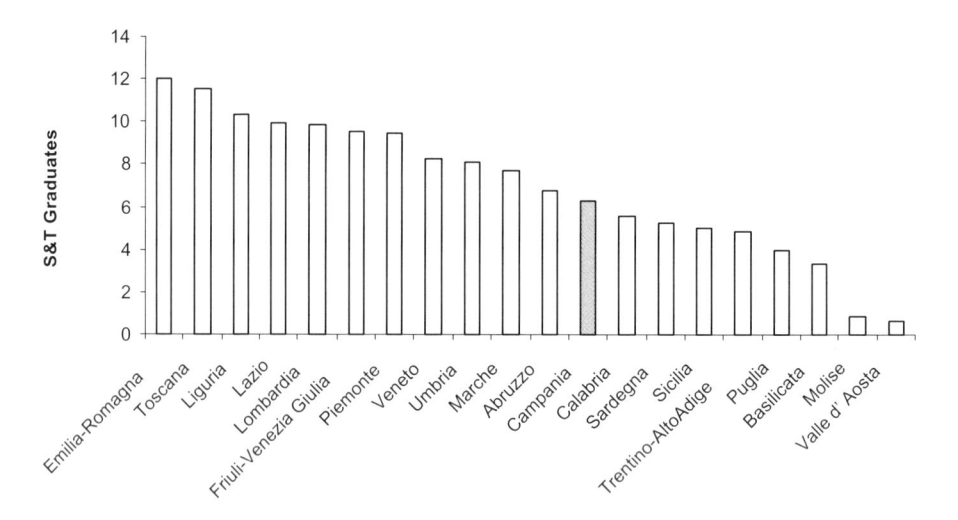

Fig. 11.2a. S&T graduates aged 20–29 years per 1,000 inhabitants, all regions, average 1998–2006.
Source: Based on ISTAT, 2008.

(a) The subjects included are: Engineering, Information Technology Science, Mathematics, Physics, Statistics, Industrial Chemistry, Environmental Sciences and Biotechnology, and Architecture (Disciplines Isced 42, 44, 46, 48, 52, 54 and 58). The degrees included are: bachelor's, master's (1st and 2nd level), doctorate and specialisation school qualification (Isced 5A, 5B and 6).
(b) From 2002 the data also include graduates of single cycle (combined bachelor's and master's) degrees.
(c) The data for 1998 are for graduates in the academic year 1997/98.
(d) For 2005–2006, there may be a discrepancy between the data used and the Eurostat data, owing to the delay in updating population data.

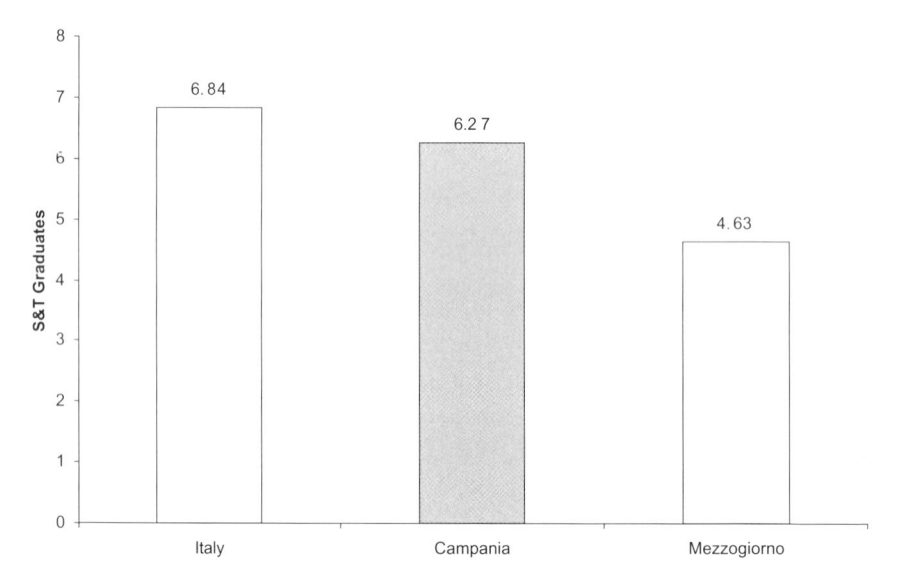

Fig. 11.2b. S&T graduates aged 20–29 per 1,000 inhabitants, Campania, the Mezzogiorno and Italy, average 1998–2006.

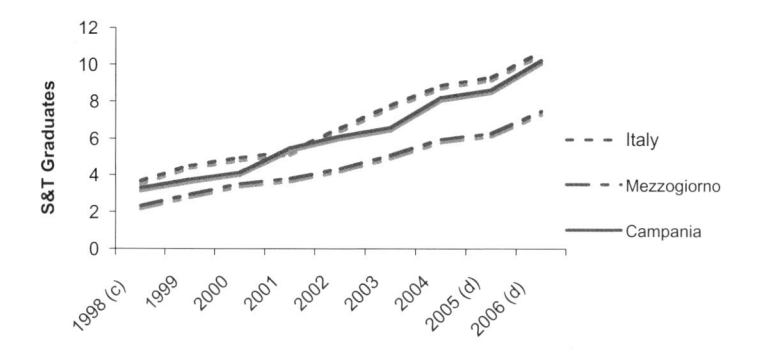

Fig. 11.2c. S&T graduates aged 20–29 per 1,000 inhabitants, Campania, the Mezzogiorno and Italy, trend 1998–2006.

2000–2006 to 2007–2013, except for one region, Valle d'Aosta. All of this is in line with the Lisbon Strategy, to increase European innovation capacity and competitiveness.

The next two figures (11.3a and 11.3b) show average employment in R&D (research and development) per 1,000 inhabitants per region and area from 1995 to 2005. The first thing that stands out here is that there is a highly uneven distribution of employment in R&D by region. Although Campania is in 12th position by R&D employment ranking, it only employs one third (1.78 per 1,000) the number of R&D workers in the highest performing Italian region (Fig. 11.3a). The Italian average is equal to 2.24, while the average for Mezzogiorno is 1.34, with Campania coming in between (Fig. 11.3b). Figure 11.3c shows that the evolution of R&D employment of Italy as a whole has been fairly uniform, especially from 2000. The growth rate of R&D employment for Campania is 32.7% for 1995–2005, this time above both the Italian average (26.8%) and the Mezzogiorno average (31.0%).

Taking Figs. 11.2 and 11.3 together, we can argue that the supply of S&T graduates in the less developed regions is more than the labour market is absorbing (in terms of R&D employment). On the other hand, the higher growth rates in numbers of graduates and employment in the Mezzogiorno and Campania are expressions of their efforts to catch up with the rest of Italy in terms of skills and knowledge production for development.

Next, Fig. 11.4a shows the average intramural R&D expenditure carried out by the public sector and universities as a percentage of GDP. Public efforts to reactivate the regions based upon public R&D expenditures have, indeed, been considerable. In fact, Campania is the region with the third highest ratio of public R&D expenditure to GDP. Moreover, it is not surprising that Campania is better positioned in terms of public R&D expenditures to GDP than either Italy as a whole or the Mezzogiorno (Fig. 11.4b). As can be seen from Fig. 11.4c, public expenditure on R&D as a percentage of GDP did not change much between 2000 and 2005 in Italy as a whole.

220 M. Del Sorbo

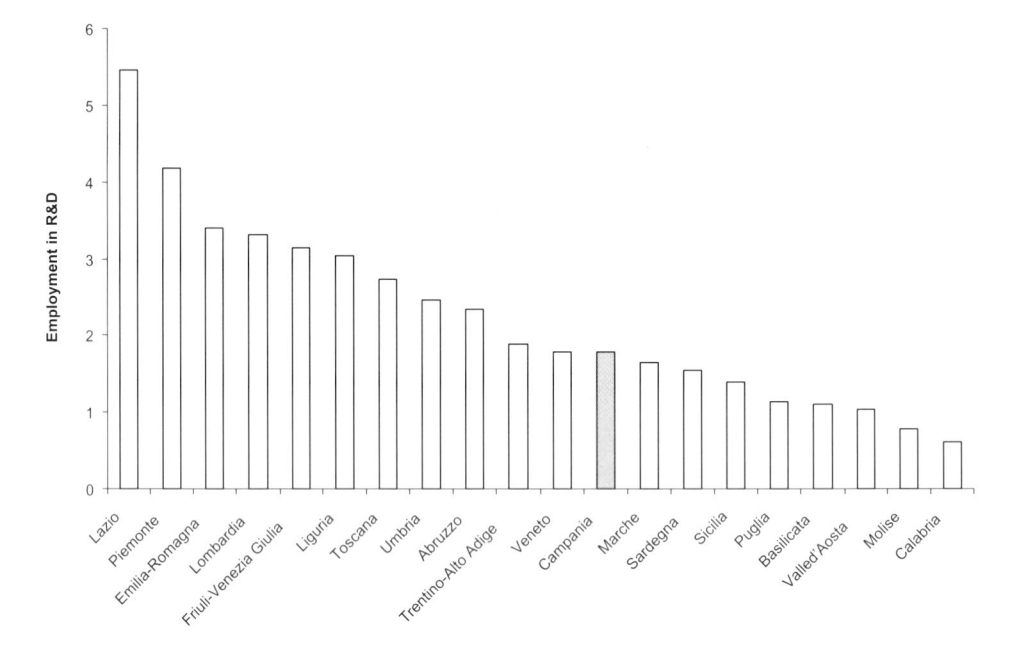

Fig. 11.3a. Employment in R&D per 1,000 inhabitants, all regions, average 1995–2005.

Source: Based on ISTAT, 2008.

Notes:
a) The data cover researchers, technicians and R&D personnel in public administration, universities and public and private firms; numbers are expressed in full-time equivalents.
b) For 1997, the data for Piemonte include company personnel from Valle d'Aosta, and those for Basilicata include company personnel from Calabria.
c) For 1998, the data for Piemonte include personnel in public administration from Valle d'Aosta, while the figures for Abruzzo include company personnel from Molise.
d) For 2000, the data for Abruzzo include company personnel from Molise.
e) From 2002, the data include personnel from private non-profit organisations, previously not surveyed.

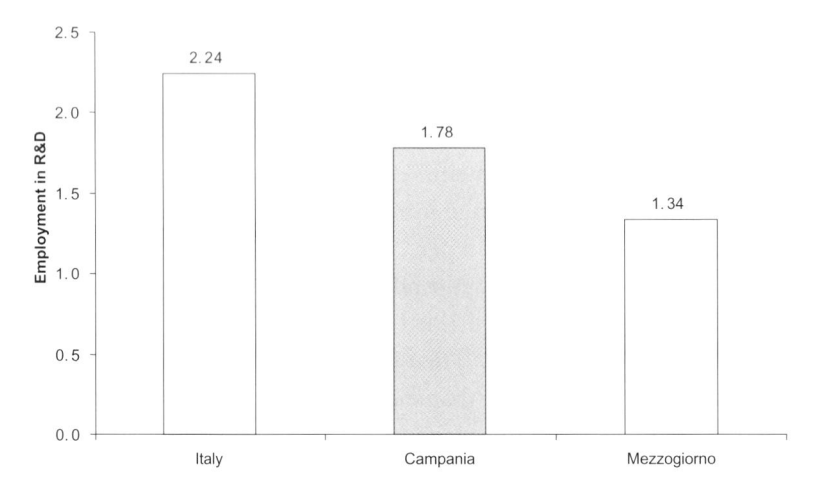

Fig. 11.3b. Employment in R&D per 1,000 inhabitants, Campania, the Mezzogiorno and Italy, average 1995–2005.

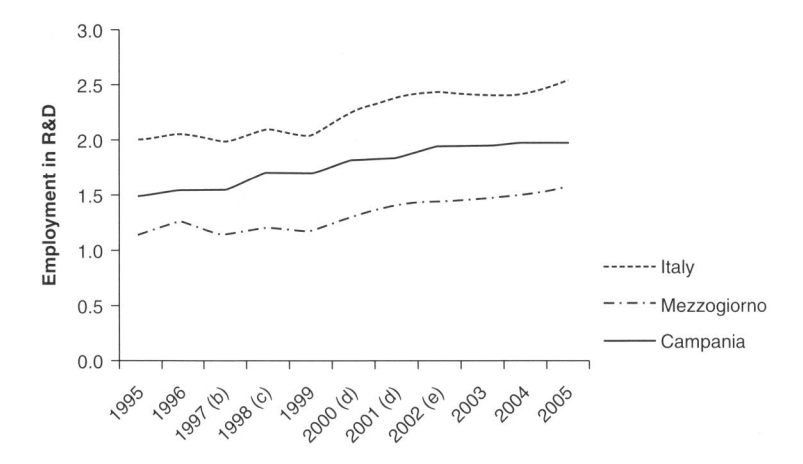

Fig. 11.3c. Employment in R&D per 1,000 inhabitants, Campania, the Mezzogiorno and Italy, trend 1995–2005.

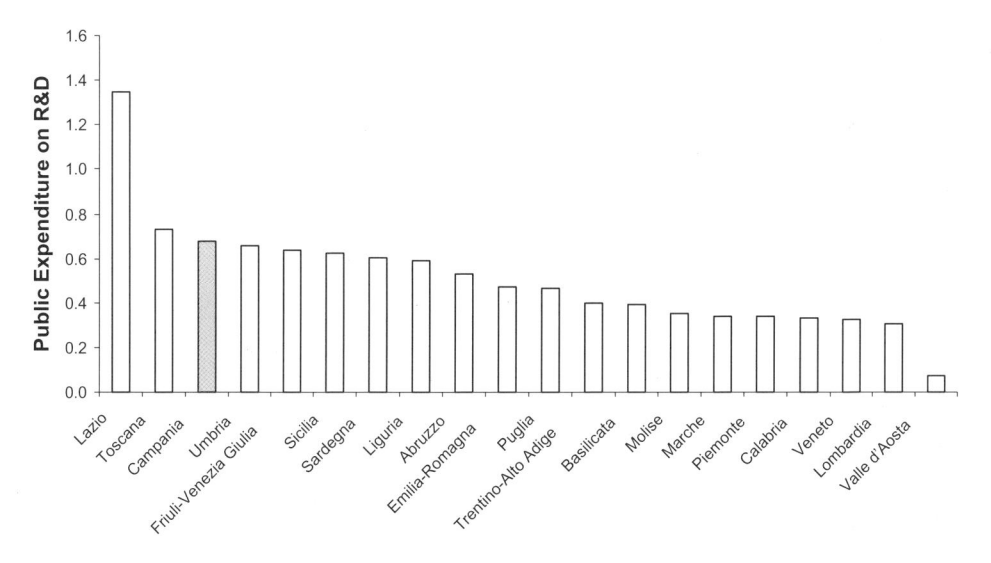

Fig. 11.4a. Public expenditure on R&D (% of GDP), all regions, average 2000–2005.
Source: Based on ISTAT, 2008.

Campania, however, saw a rise from around 0.65% to 0.68% over that period. What is surprising is the systematic withdrawal of public investment in R&D, except for Campania, with drops in related expenditure proportional to GDP at national and Mezzogiorno levels of 2.79% and 5.47% respectively 2000–2005, while the corresponding figure for Campania increased by 4.62% over the same period.

In terms of expenditure on R&D by firms, private and public, there is again wide dispersion across the regions. It is difficult to argue that the Italian average is

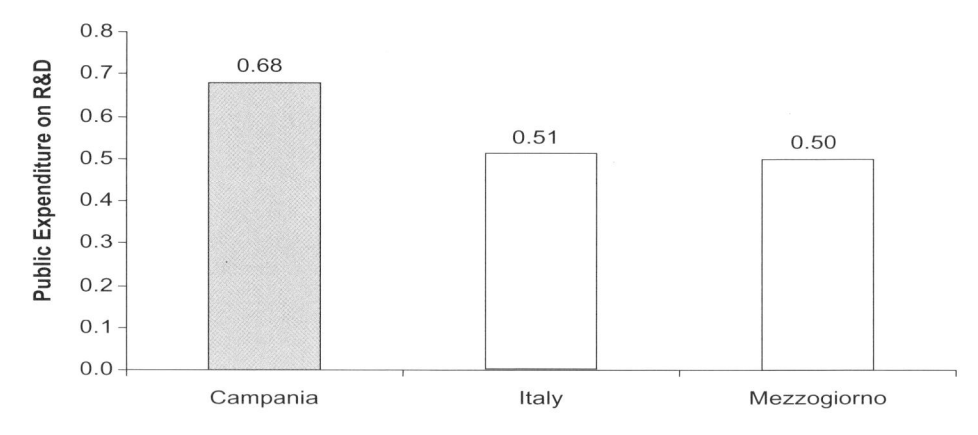

Fig. 11.4b. Public expenditure on R&D (% of GDP), Campania, the Mezzogiorno and Italy, average 2000–2005.

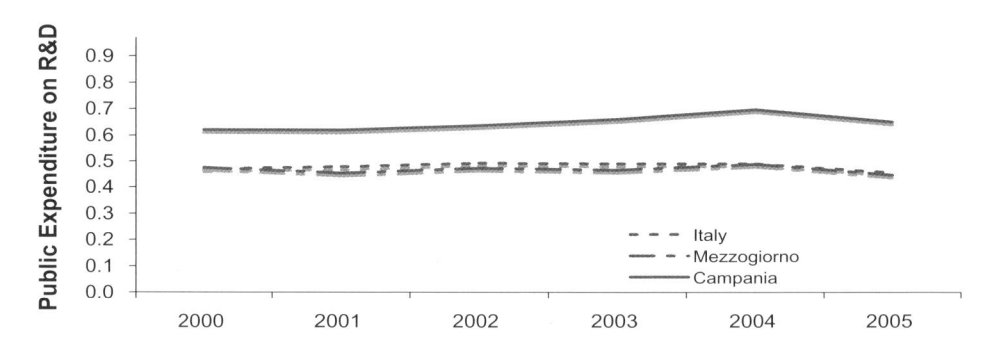

Fig. 11.4c. Public expenditure on R&D (% of GDP), Campania, the Mezzogiorno and Italy, trend 2000–2005.

representative of the nation, since the better performing regions are clearly extreme cases. Campania is in 9th position, with a share of company R&D expenditure of 0.35% of GDP, which represents only around one-third of Piemonte's share, at 1.35% (Fig. 11.5a). The great variability here is very evident from the difference between the Mezzogiorno and the Italian average; yet again Campania is not far below the mean (Fig. 11.5b). This has not always been the case; Campania's stronger position is the result of more rapid growth in company expenditures on R&D from 2002 onwards. The growth rate of company R&D expenditure relative to GDP in Campania 2000–2005 was 20.8%, while it stood at 15% and just 3.5% for the Mezzogiorno and Italy as a whole respectively (Fig. 11.5c). These trends are encouraging in terms of catching up, since at these growth rates, company R&D expenditures will exceed public expenditures on R&D by 2010.

Total public and private expenditure on R&D include expenditure by universities and public administration, and by public and private firms. In terms of that magnitude as a share of GDP, Campania is in 8th position, with a share of 1.03% (Fig. 11.6a). And as with the previous indicator, Campania is ahead of the Italian average, and, of course, the figure for the Mezzogiorno (Fig. 11.6b). Total R&D expenditure relative to GDP

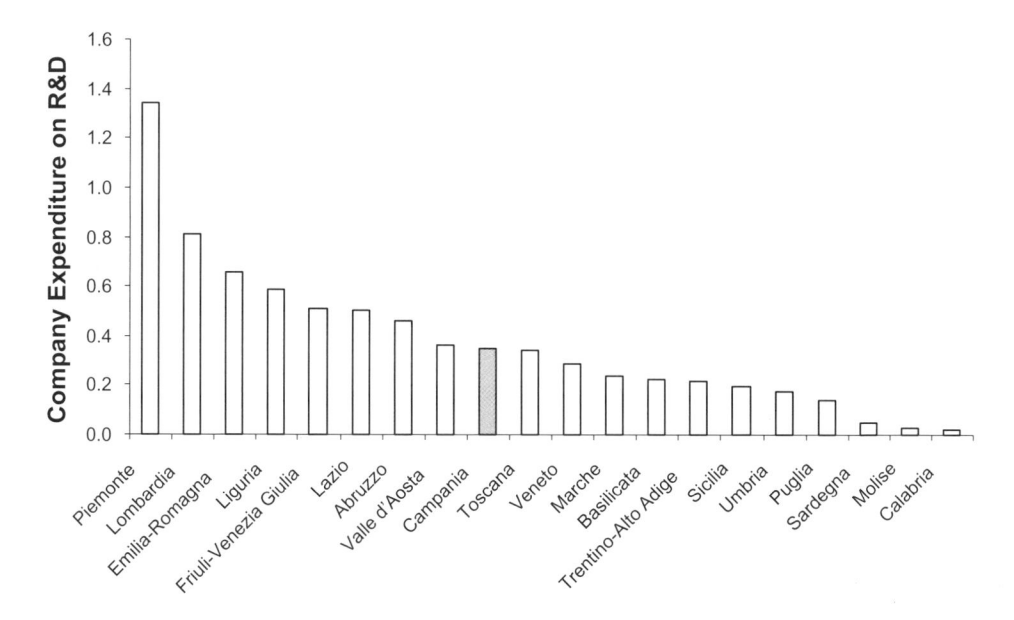

Fig. 11.5a. Company expenditure on R&D (% of GDP), all regions, average 2000–2005.
Source: Based on ISTAT, 2008.
Note:
(a) The data for Molise are included in Abruzzo for reasons of confidentiality.

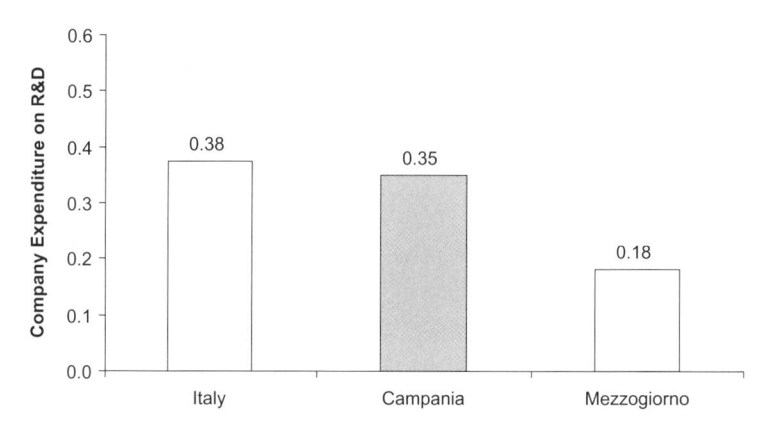

Fig. 11.5b. Company expenditure on R&D (% of GDP), Campania, the Mezzogiorno and Italy, average 2000–2005.

224   M. Del Sorbo

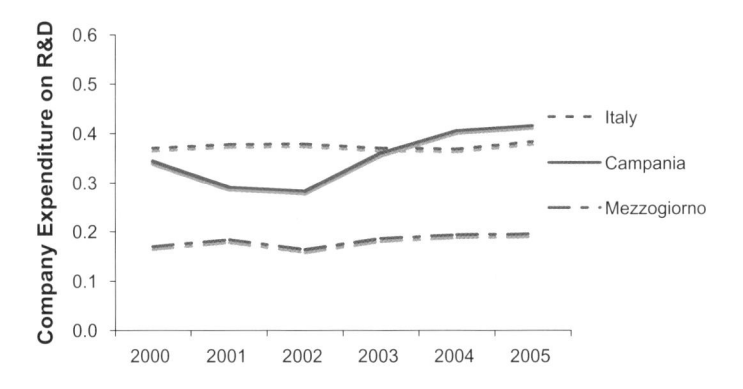

Fig. 11.5c. Company expenditure on R&D (% of GDP), trend 2000–2005.

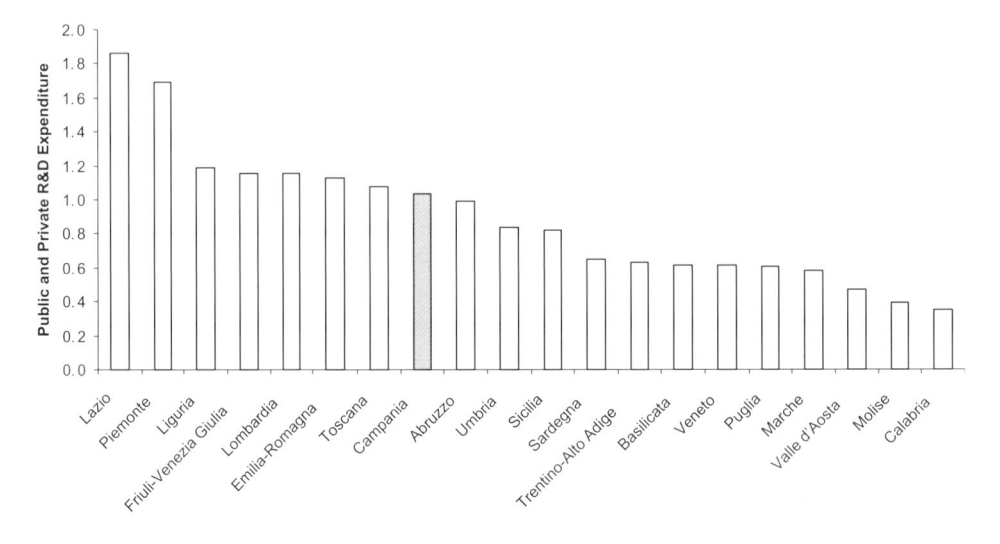

Fig. 11.6a. Total public and private expenditure on R&D (% of GDP), all regions, average 2000–2005.

Source: Based on ISTAT, 2008.

Note:

(a) From 2002 the data include the intra-mural R&D expenditures of non-profit private organisations, previously not counted.

rose at all levels between 2000 and 2005, and again Campania outperformed Italy as a whole and the Mezzogiorno, with an increase of 11.8%, as compared to 5.8% and 2.1% respectively for Italy and the Mezzogiorno (Fig. 11.6c).

Unfortunately, the innovative efforts by Campania do not seem to have paid off in terms of outputs. One of the most frequently used indicators of innovation output is patenting. Using data from the European Patent Office (EPO), we can distinguish three groups of regions in terms of outcomes of innovative efforts — high, middle and low performers. Campania registered 8.75 patents per million inhabitants

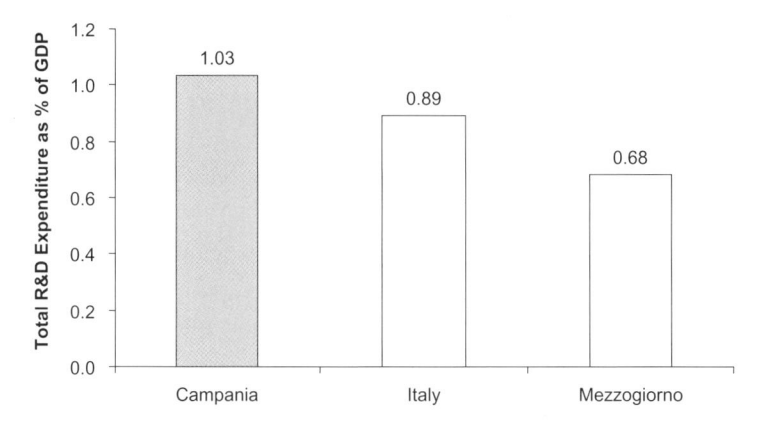

Fig. 11.6b. Total public and private expenditure on R&D (% of GDP), Campania, the Mezzogiorno and Italy, average 2000–2005.

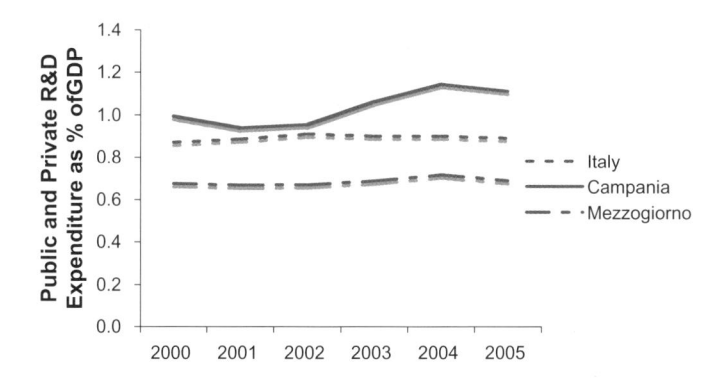

Fig. 11.6c. Total public and private expenditure on R&D (% of GDP), Campania, the Mezzogiorno and Italy, trend 2000–2005.

1995–2002, ranking 16th among the Italian regions, and this puts it among the low-performing regions (Fig. 11.7a). Thus, strikingly, while in terms of innovative inputs Campania has in some respects performed better than the rest of Italy, including the Mezzogiorno, in terms of the outcomes of those efforts it falls far behind (Fig. 11.7b).

Figure 11.7c shows how Italy developed its patenting capacity from 1995 to 2002. At national and Mezzogiorno level numbers of patents increased by 83.8% and 58.9% respectively. The rate of growth for Campania was far higher at 176.3% for this period. But it was from a very low starting point, so that the gap between Campania and the Italian average remained very large.

The patent figures could be taken to argue that the quantity of innovative efforts may not necessarily be related to the quality of such efforts. On the other hand, it may also be the case that innovative activities in a given region opt for other types of protection of intellectual property, such us faster product life cycles, certificates of origin etc. But if we use just patents as a measure of innovative output, we may conclude that Campania needs to capitalise more on its innovative efforts, and perhaps rethink its strategies for a better quality of R&D. Again, however, it may be too early to judge on these matters, since patenting activity has only recently begun to take off in the region.

We have demonstrated that Campania and the Mezzogiorno are below average for Italy as a whole in terms of number of S&T graduates, employment in R&D, and company R&D expenditures and patents; while for public R&D expenditure

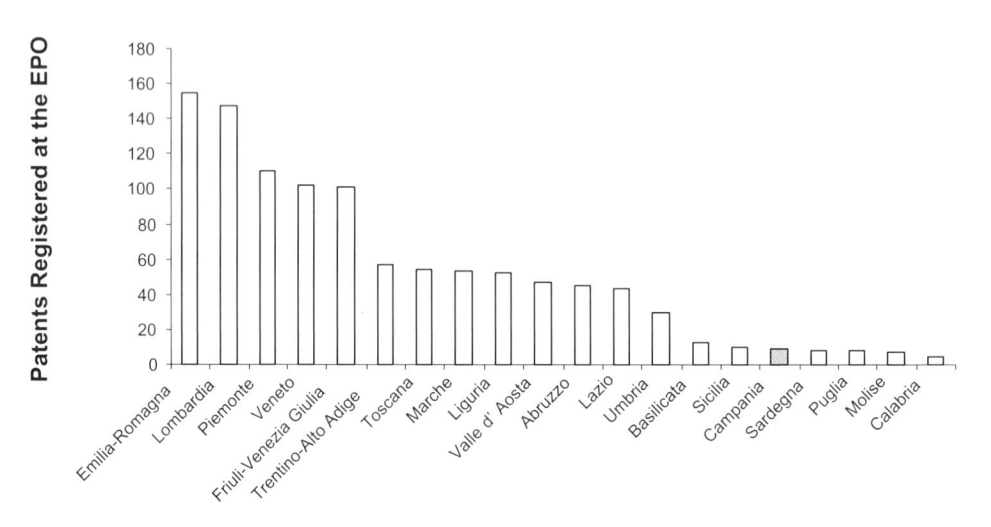

Fig. 11.7a. Patents registered at the EPO per million inhabitants, all regions, average 1995–2002.
Source: Based on European Patent Office data; ISTAT, 2008.
Note:
(a) The data are disaggregated at territorial level according to the postcode of the inventor's home.

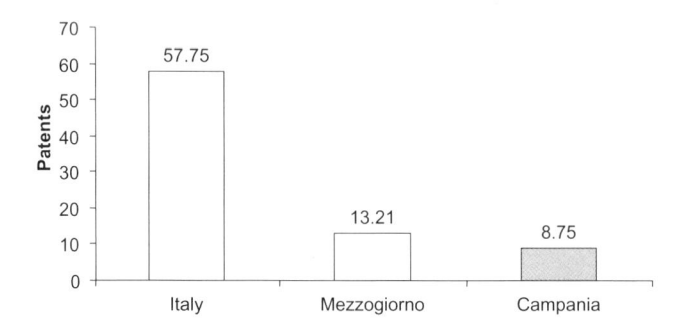

Fig. 11.7b. Patents registered at the EPO per million inhabitants, Campania, the Mezzogiorno and Italy, average 1995–2002.

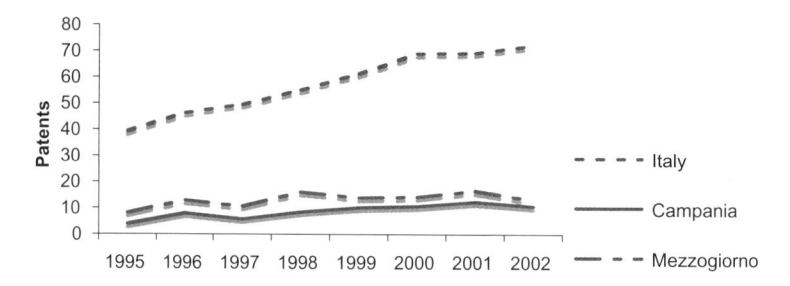

Fig. 11.7c. Patents registered at the EPO per million inhabitants, Campania, the Mezzogiorno and Italy, trend 1995–2002.

Campania fares better than the average Italian region. The Mezzogiorno, though, performs better than Campania in levels of patenting. It is worth emphasising in all this that the regions with the highest EU patent registrations are those which not only report the highest levels of company expenditure on R&D, but also *invest in skills* in education and R&D and in terms of reinforcing the absorptive capacity of the firms, so that they also employ R&D human resources more intensively than the Mezzogiorno and Campania. This is notably true, for instance, in the case of Emilia Romagna, which occupies first place for the number of S&T graduates and patents and third place for R&D employment and expenditure by firms. More firm-level R&D investment in Campania and the Mezzogiorno may be necessary — with public support — to see more consistent results in educational and patents levels.

We should not forget, of course, that in terms of *growth rates* for key innovation indicators, Campania is ahead of the national averages every time (S&T graduates, knowledge employees in R&D, R&D expenditures from both public and private sectors, patents), while the Mezzogiorno is ahead of the national average for S&T graduates, knowledge employees in R&D (for which the growth rates are both slightly higher than in Campania too) and company R&D expenditure (ISTAT, 2008). So a process of *catch-up* is clearly in process. We are left trying to explain the relatively low absolute output from innovative efforts in Campania. Possible explanations include poor resource management, the difficulty of employing the existing networks in the best way, the need to wait for the long-term effects of the strategy of investing in knowledge workers to show up, or more simply the results of old historical trajectories as discussed in the theoretical part of this chapter.

A propos of long-term trends, we present in Fig. 11.8 some figures from the International Labour Organisation (ILO), which illustrate patterns in the number of S&T knowledge workers by decade from the 1970s to the 2000s for the whole of Italy. (The figures for the earlier period are estimated relative to the total employed population; from the 1980s they are based on data for the economically active proportion of the population.) The figure shows that the growth in S&T employment in Italy 1971-2000 was 32.4%, with an apparent decline between 1981 and 1991 of

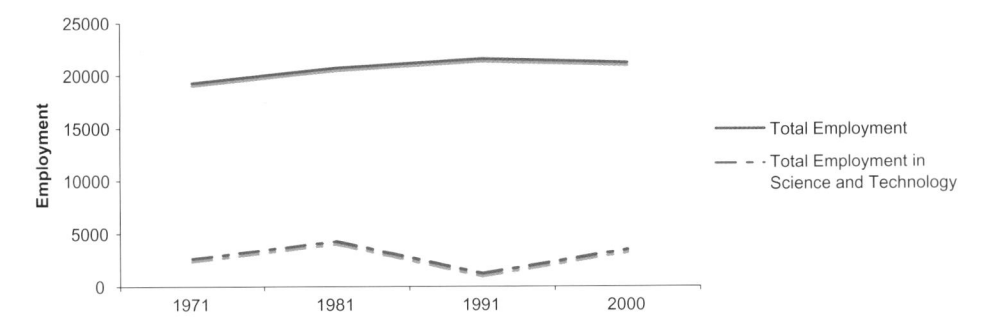

Fig. 11.8. S&T employees in Italy, 1971–2000 (thousands).
Source: Based on ILO, 2007, 2009.

71%. The causes of this fall remain unclear, though the change in the basis of calculation obviously plays some part. Even so, the reported share in S&T employment in total employment rose from 13.6% in 1971 to 16.4% in 2000, with the highest rates of growth coming during the 1990s (ILO, 2007, 2009).

5. Policy Implications and Conclusions

While the aims of universities are public ones, and therefore not subsumable to profit maximisation, the universities do need to get more involved in training and consultancy work. Indeed, this perspective offers them a good opportunity to fit better into labour market requirements, and at the same time to find new sources of funding. The universities, in concert with industry and government, should open dialogues to support decision-making processes; the ministers responsible for science policy should interact with ministries of industry and employment, so that they are aware of the profound changes going on in organisations and firms, and in order to create synergies and avoid duplication.

The benchmarking of innovative performance by region could be a means of improving practice in the European and national context. 'RIS policy fine-tuning must be practised by sub-national development agencies to better integrate system interaction and improved knowledge flows.' (Cooke, 2006, 28) To this end, it is necessary to acquire data related to the research world, through surveys, missions, teamwork projects and mobility, to assess the knowledge and skills production inside the RSI. Other possible desirable interventions include: technical and financial private–public support; intra- and inter-university mobility of researchers, PhD students and knowledge workers; and incentive systems to guarantee not only their mobility, but the possibility of returning to their own countries and regions.

What is clear is that the regions are becoming knowledge and learning development centres, requiring a research infrastructure that is technologically advanced, a highly qualified labour force and an innovative culture. The proximity and support of institutions, skills and experts is a valuable asset for designing specific competences for firms and for the other organisations, to create synergies and local development in the RSI. To enhance individual, local, regional and therefore national performance, regional policies should be based on specific local needs and take into account *regional path dependency* (De Laurentis, 2006). The universities should be led by a multi-dimensional vision, based on a simultaneous awareness of the past, present and future. Human capital accumulation, and the fit and proper employment of the human capital stock, should be pursued through updating, changing (if required), and acquiring new know-how, new skills, i.e. being ready for technological change and innovation. In this way it will be possible to aim, not only at economic growth, but at an economically sustainable form of development.

References

Aliaga, O.A. (2001). 'Human capital, HRD and the knowledge organization', *paper presented at* Academy of Human Resource Development 2001 conference, Tulsa, OK.

Asheim, B.T. (1995). 'Industrial districts as learning regions: A condition for prosperity?' Oslo, STEP Group.

Aydalot, P. (1986). *Milieux Innovateurs en Europe*, Paris, Gremi.

Becattini, G. (1987). *Mercato e Forze Locali. Il Distretto Industriale*, Bologna, Il Mulino.

Becker, G.S. (1964). *Human Capital: A Theoretical and Empirical Analysis with Special Reference to Education*, New York, NBER.

Bonaccorsi, A. and Nesci, F. (2006). *Bacini di Competenze e Processi di Agglomerazione. I Distretti Tecnologici in Europa*, Unioncamere, Milan, Angeli.

Braczyk, H.J., Cooke, P. and Heidenreich, M. (1998). *Regional Innovation Systems*, London, UCL Press.

Cooke, P. (1992). 'Regional innovation systems: competitive regulation in the New Europe', *Geoforum* 23: 365–382.

Cooke, P. (2006). 'Regional innovation systems as public goods', Unpublished Working Paper, UNIDO.

Cooke, P. (2004). 'Introduction: regional innovation systems — an evolutionary approach', in Braczyk, H.J. *et al.* (eds.), *Regional Innovation Systems*, London, UCL Press, pp. 1–18.

Cooke, P., Gomez Uraga M. and Etxebarria G. (1997). 'Regional innovation systems: Institutional and organizational dimensions', *Research Policy* 26: 475–491.

Dagum, C., Lovaglio, P.G. and Vittadini, G. (2000). 'Il capitale umano in Italia: Analisi della distribuzione', http://ww.statistica.unimib.it/utenti/vittadini/pubblicazioni/pubblicazion/il%20capitale%20umano%20in%20italia%20analisi%20della%20distribuzione%20dagum%20lovaglio%20vittadini,%20mulino%2023.3.05.pdf.

De Laurentis, C. (2006). 'Regional innovation systems and the labour market: a comparison of five regions', *European Planning Studies* 14(8): 1059–1085.

Del Sorbo, M. (2007). *How Can We Account for the So-Called 'Skills Gap' in Engineering, and what are the Differences in the Approaches to Tackle the Problem Between the UK and Italy in Recent Years?*, Unpublished MSc Dissertation. SPRU, University of Sussex.

Del Sorbo, M., Ibarzabal, M., Lee, G.C., Chen, M.Y. and Plancarte, C. (2007). *Research and Development Organizational Project*, Doosan Babcock Energy Limited Consultancy Report.

ETB (The Engineering and Technology Board) (2004). *Digest of Engineering Statistics* 2003/4 Report, London.

Eurostat (2007). Regional Gross Domestic Product (PPS per inhabitant as % of the EU-27 average), http://epp.eurostat.ec.europa.eu/tgm/table.do?tab=table&init=1&plugin=0&language=en&pcode=fab11536.

Faggian, A. and McCann, P. (2006). 'Human capital flows and regional knowledge assets: A simultaneous equation approach', *Oxford Economic Papers* 26(1).

Gori, E. (2003). 'L'investimento in capitale umano attraverso l'istruzione', www.acton.org/ital/publicat/gori.pdf.

Heijke, H., Meng, C. and Ramaekers, G. (2002). 'An investigation into the role of human capital competences and their pay-off', ROA Research Centre for Education and the Labour Market, Maastricht, ROA-RM-2002/3E.

Howells, J. (1996). 'Tacit knowledge, innovation and technology transfer', *Technology Analysis & Strategic Management* 8: 91–106.

Iammarino, S. (2005). 'An evolutionary integrated view of regional systems of innovation: Concepts, measures and historical perspectives', *European Planning Studies* 13(4): 495–517.

ILO (2007, 2009). *Employment by Sex and Detailed Occupational Group*, ILO: http://laborsta.ilo.org/cgi-bin/brokerv8.exe.

Isaksen, S.G. (2006). *Meeting the Innovation Challenge: Leadership for Transformation and Growth*, Chichester, John Wiley.

ISTAT (2008). *Tavole Produttività dei Fattori*, www.istat.it.

Lambert, R. (2003). Lambert Review of Business-University Collaboration, Final Report, London, HM Treasury.

Lipsey, R. and Bekar, C. (1995). 'A structuralist view of technical change and economic growth', *Bell Canada Papers on Economic and Public Policy* 3; *Technology, Information and Public Policy*, John Deutsch Institute for the Study of Economic Policy, Queens University.

Lucas, R.E. (1990). 'Why doesn't capital flow from rich to poor countries?', *American Economic Review* 80(6): 92–96.

Markusen, A. (1985). *Profit Cycles, Oligopoly, and Regional Development,* Cambridge, MA, MIT Press.

Markusen, A. (1996). 'Sticky places in slippery space: A typology of industrial districts', *Economic Geography* 72: 293–313.

Marshall, A. (1922). *Principles of Economics: An Introductory Volume*, London, Macmillan (1st edn. 1890).

Morgan, K. (1997). 'The learning region: Institutions, innovation and regional renewal', *Regional Studies* 31: 491–504.

Nafukho, F.M., Hairston, N. and Brooks, K. (2004). 'Human capital theory: Implications for human resource development', *Human Resource Development International* 7(4): 545–551.

Romer, P.M. (1993). 'Ideas gaps and object gaps in economic development', *Journal of Monetary Economics* 32(3): 543–573.

Sattinger, M. (1993). 'Assignment models of the distribution of earnings', *Journal of Economic Literature* 31(2): 831–880.
Schultz, T.W. (1961). 'Education and economic growth', in Henry, N.B. (ed.), *Social Forces Influencing American Education*, Chicago, University of Chicago Press.
Solow, R.M. (1957). 'Technical change and the aggregate production function', *Review of Economics and Statistics* 39: 312–320.
Storper, M. (1998). *The Regional World: Territorial Development in a Global Economy*, New York, Guilford.
Thurow, L.C. (1975). *Generating Inequality*, New York, Basic Books.
Tidd, J., Bessant, J. and Pavitt, K. (2005). *Managing Innovation: Integrating Technological, Market and Organizational Change* (3rd edn), London, Wiley.
von Tunzelmann, N. and Wang, Q. (2007). 'Capabilities and production theory', *Structural Change and Economic Dynamics* 18(2): 192–211.

CHAPTER 12

URBANISATION AND NETWORK ALIGNMENT ISSUES IN ISTANBUL: INFORMAL NETWORKS IN HOUSING AND LABOUR MARKETS

OZGE AKTAS

1. Introduction

Not surprisingly, and congruous with the trend in developing countries, Turkey went through a period of rapid urbanisation after 1945 that is intertwined with internal migration, leading to growth of large metropolises, and particularly Istanbul. The dynamics of rapid — and unexpected — growth, such as proliferating squatter neighbourhoods/slums, inadequate infrastructural services and welfare provision, the dimension of internal migration, the growing informal economy, and the changing dimensions of poverty, brought together lots of issues in the urban sphere that demanded active urban and economic policy-making from the governing bodies. The fact that Istanbul is still experiencing many social and economic problems related to urbanisation confirms that these issues have never been satisfactorily dealt with, whether at the peak of urbanisation in the 1950s or subsequently.

In this chapter, I will seek to explain both the inefficiencies and the potential capacities of the networks of urbanisation, focusing on the two major actors within them, namely households, i.e. internal migrants, and the government, i.e. governing bodies that deal with urban policy and labour markets. I seek primarily to evaluate these agents as part of a 'network', and to analyse how the particular networking relations (alignment) observed might have played a role in the urbanisation process in Turkey. I will first present evidence regarding the widely accepted view that these networks have been largely blocked, and have not functioned efficiently in terms of enabling a sustainable urbanisation. At the same time I will try, based on my fieldwork done over the period 2006–2008 with the Istanbul migrants, to present a picture of the capabilities that exist within the informal networks — such as kinship and hometown networks[1] — highlighting their potential power to *transform* by

---

[1] In Turkey, having the same hometown (in Turkish *hemseri*) involves a high degree of solidarity among people, particularly among internal migrants, as they also share the same sense of destiny.

providing households with rights and command over certain goods. The data presented in these chapters are based on 24 in-depth interviews (Autumn 2006) and 94 questionnaires (Summer 2008) conducted with migrants in the Yesiltepe squatter settlement. In addition, nine in-depth interviews conducted with local authority officers in 2006 and 2008 are analysed. Based on this, I will first argue that the spontaneous, informal networks are intertwined with the formal ones, constantly seeking to decongest the blockages arising within formal networking relations — but also, ironically, leading to informalisation of the formal. Second, I will present cases in which this very potential also poses a threat in terms of closed informal networks that act as a barrier, excluding its members from certain resources such as employment that they might otherwise access. Overall, the main focus will be on two major issues of urbanisation: the housing market and the labour market.

2. Population Figures

Between 1927 and 2000, the population of Turkey grew approximately five times, while the population of Istanbul grew 12.4 times (Table 12.1). Between 1990 and 2000 the annual population growth rate of Istanbul was 3.31%, while that of Turkey as a whole increased by 1.83% annually during the same period. Turkey's population more than tripled between 1950 and 1997, but the urban population grew nine times within the same period (Levent Baycan, 2002).[2]

Table 12.1. Population of Istanbul, 1927–2000.

1927	806,863
1935	883,599
1940	991,237
1945	1,078,399
1950	1,166,477
1955	1,533,822
1960	1,882,092
1965	2,293,823
1970	3,019,032
1975	3,904,588
1980	4,741,890
1985	5,842,985
1990	7,390,190
2000	10,018,735

Source: Turkish Statistical Institute (TURKSTAT) 2000.

---

[2] The first population census in Turkey was held in 1927, the second in 1935, and after that censuses were conducted every five years, until 1990, when the state decided thenceforth to hold a census every ten years. The next one was done in 2000. The figures for 1997 are based on the population count (it was not a full census including socio-economic variables) that was held on account of upcoming elections.

In 1950, Istanbul was one of the 86 cities in the world with a population above 1 million. Istanbul's population grew from 1 million in 1950 to 5 million in 1980 and 10 million in 2000. Today, with an estimated population of 15 million, it is well beyond the UN Population Division's mega city threshold of 8 million. The projected population for 2030 is above 20 million, which will make it a hyper city.

The two main topics central to an understanding of the dynamics of the rapid urbanisation of Istanbul are: the informal housing market, with its historical heritage and (lack of) urban planning policies; and the labour market.

3. Brief History of the Housing Market in Istanbul

The discussion starts off with the proposition that the rapid population growth in Istanbul is based on the possibility and ubiquity of informal housing (Keyder, 1997). During the 1950s, with state industrialisation plans that needed a substantial labour force, rural–urban migration started to boom; the settlement of the rural population created a nightmare for the urban planners due to the complexity of land property rights (Keyder, 1997). Squatter houses, called *gecekondu*[3] in Turkish, started to appear in areas that were effectively 'no man's land'. Land previously owned by Greeks and Armenians who left the country right after the republic was founded, property formerly belonging to the Ottoman state, and various types of public land were intertwined in the urban space, which allowed squatter houses to be built even in the wealthiest parts of the city. Nevertheless the major clusters of squatter houses were erected in the peripheral regions of the city, as these were the main areas of public land where state regulation was inadequate, and this opened the doors for squatter settlement. Most of the time, the public land was expropriated through bribery of the authorities by relatively wealthy migrants, who then sold this land in parcels to other migrants, acting almost as informal estate agents. This process helped to postpone the regularisation of the ambiguous status of these houses. Such delays empowered the squatter dwellers against the state, as they managed to create a massive physical presence of buildings, as well as establishing themselves as a political force within the area. That discouraged the state from taking radical eviction plans that would go against its populist politics. Thus the demand side of the housing network gained enormous bargaining power through mass settlements, and the exercise of such power led to the expansion of the informal household network because it constituted a pull-factor for more rural migrants who felt secure about settling in the city, since they were already informed of the possibilities of housing by their kin or fellow townsmen.

---

[3] The literal translation of the term is 'built overnight'. One of the earlier definitions of the term is 'hastily erected buildings, lacking in most cases elementary comfort conditions, not conforming to construction regulations and being developed regardless of the land owner's rights' (Yavuz, 1954). The term today is loaded — or maybe overloaded — to imply urban poverty, internal migration, ambiguous urban land ownership, social movements, housing policies or self-construction practices. Studies about rural migrants and squatter settlements are also known as 'gecekondu studies'.

4. (Lack of) Urban Planning Measures in Turkey

Inadequate urban planning policies made the rapid urbanisation of Istanbul a highly problematic issue; the city is overcrowded, with insufficient and unequally distributed public services and a massive number of houses that were built without reference to building codes or public standards. Let us look at these weaknesses in urban planning policies in detail. First, due to lack of funds and the inadequate urban planning capacity of the government, public services in Turkey have rarely been provided in advance of the development of a region. On the other hand, the absence of public services did not have much impact on settlement patterns. That is to say, illegal housing has pushed out the borders of urban areas before any systematic urbanisation policy was implemented or even projected. Public services had to follow *de facto* settlements, and were often heavily skewed in favour of high-income areas. It is also true that it becomes very costly to provide infrastructure and services after irregular and unplanned growth has occurred, reducing the power of the urban planner to control and direct urban development. Second, a highly centralised government long denied to cities the power to meet the demand for public services, instead disbursing funds through central planning (Keles, 1984). It was also the case that the municipal services were divided among local jurisdictions, resulting in an uneven distribution and quality of public services due to the uneven distribution and redistribution of the central public services fund. Nevertheless, there were continuous attempts to tackle squatter houses, and urban planning problems in general, through new laws and policies based mostly, however, on inaccurate assumptions and projections. Let us look at these in detail in order to explain the blockages that prevented an efficient flow of resources within the government networks.

In 1924 (one year after the republic was founded), the state initiated a law that enabled municipalities to demolish any property on unowned land. However, applying this law was extremely difficult, since it required a court order, the issue of which took a very long time. Long before urbanisation had started to pose problems, the government had an ill-functioning law enforcement system. When the urban population in the squatter neighbourhoods increased, the government had great difficulties deciding how to treat these urban squatters. This was due both to the pressure of votes, and also to the fact that the shortage of low-cost housing increased each time a unit was demolished (Keles, 1984). As long as the government did not offer any alternatives, it was not easy to justify demolishing squatter housing. Even poorly paid municipal officials, who were delegated to enforce the laws on demolition, were themselves moving into squatter houses (Keles, 1984). In any case, by the 1950s, the state increasingly perceived squatter settlers as positive signs of the urbanisation, industrialisation and modernisation of Turkey, despite the problems they posed. The government had enacted new laws in 1948 that delegated to the municipalities responsibility for the improvement of squatter settlements, generating title deeds in return for minimal payment, and also developing cooperatives with easy credit and tax exemptions provided by the Bank of Real Property. However, only the migrants that had been living in the city for more than one year were eligible, and, ironically, in those years newcomers were increasing in number. The first half of the 1960s did not see many urban planning policy initiatives in Turkey. It can be argued that the liberal politics of that period, which replaced the earlier statism, was in a way 'misinterpreted' to imply hostility towards any attempt at urban planning in the name of favouring free entrepreneurship and individual benefit (Ekinci, 1994). In 1958, the Ministry of Reconstruction and Resettlement was established, and mandated to control various urban functions, reinforcing central control (Yonder, 1998). By 1960, the number of *gecekondus* had increased to approximately 60,000, from only 5,000 in 1949. On a broader level, unauthorised housing (including houses without planning permission and occupancy permits) increased from 600,000 units in 1970 to a total of 2 million units in 1990 (Pamuk, 1996). The sharp increase in numbers was partly due to the determination of earlier migrants, who simply rebuilt (informally), after each demolition (Yonder, 1998).

In 1966, the state enacted the Gecekondu Law, 'Turkey's most comprehensive attempt to deal with squatters' (Keles, 1984) within the framework of the first five-year state development plan. The law proposed ways of improving rather than demolishing the settlements, by formalising both old and new settlements, improving the living conditions of existing housing, site preparation for the development of low-cost housing, prohibition of new squatters and finally demolition of some of the existing *gecekondus*. The law was unrealistic, primarily because it assumed that no new houses would be established, and the problem would come to an end. In 1976, just before the elections, the government legalised all the informal houses that had been built between 1966 and 1976. During this period, however, insufficient funding meant that only three out of twelve *gecekondu* prevention areas were actually made ready for new housing (Danielson and Keles, 1985). Many people preferred to use *the self-help mechanism* of *gecekondus* rather than participating in the government's scheme, which would make them indebted to state financial institutions for many years (Danielson and Keles, 1985). In other words, people preferred to utilise informal networks that helped them own a house in a much easier way than that offered by the government. By the mid-1960s the informal networks had developed a power structure, where some local strongmen controlled the rights over even public land. New migrants who wanted a *gecekondu* had to pay these people, who were mostly connected to entrepreneurs with underworld connections (Yonder, 1998). In that sense, being part of informal networks gained huge significance as the urban space came increasingly under the control of these (informal) networks, which had their own, particular distribution of power within them.

During the late 1970s, the government made a few more attempts to solve the housing problem and implement an effective squatter policy, yet once again failed to meet the demands of the public. One major problem common to all these attempts was the failure of the government to fund housing project initiatives properly, always trying to facilitate low-cost housing with credit adjustments and tax exemptions rather than actual financial support. Most of the time these adjustments or schemes of payment failed to target the urban poor, as they required a certain amount of capital to start with. In other words, housing policies and laws were not well targeted to heal the wounds. On the contrary, they unintentionally accelerated the process of informal housing construction, and actually fostered informal institutional arrangements.

In 1975, 52% of all urban households in Turkey lacked running water, and 43% had no electricity; these figures largely representing the squatter settlements in Istanbul and Ankara. At first, city councils were under no pressure or obligation to provide services to newly built squatter houses on the outskirts of the city, since they were illegal constructions. Yet, in the long run, not only could the law not manage to solve existing urban problems but it actually added new ones. The supply of public services remained at very low levels, which motivated the squatter dwellers to follow their rural practice of helping themselves. As one of the squatter dwellers clearly stated at that time, 'If the state doesn't help, then we dig our own trenches and get our own water' (Karpat, 1976); thus *self-help* also emerged as a strategy to cope with inadequacy of services.[4]

Here it is also crucial to mention that self-help housing generated new networks of construction suppliers, for both buildings and infrastructure. Informal institutional arrangements such as the 'build and sell system', which links the informal to the formal, have emerged (Pamuk, 1996). This system rests on informal agreements between landowners and builders to build a multi-storey house on legally owned land without an occupancy permit. The builders are mostly small-scale, but reliable, with a good reputation in the community, and they finance the construction through pre-sale of the flats. The multi-storey flats are then shared between land owner and builder, typically half and half. The municipal services can in most cases be received without an occupancy permit, resulting in quasi-formal housing. This process of building and selling is completely in line with the formal commercial housing market, while the recruitment of the builders relies heavily on informal ties. In a way this type of informal institution cuts across informal and formal networks, indicating a convergence of the two.

The military regime of 1980–1983, high rates of inflation, and the commercial bank crash of 1982, slowed down market activity in Turkey significantly in that period, which directly influenced the housing sector (Yonder, 1998). Urban reforms increased the planning and enforcement capacity of local governments, expanding the

---

[4] Many of the migrants I interviewed mentioned that initially their quality of life declined in Istanbul compared to their hometowns, and that they had to improvise legal and illegal strategies to cope. The most common of these was tapping illegal electricity from legal buildings around them at night-time.

jurisdiction of municipalities as they started to increase their revenues through real estate taxes. Municipal control also sharply reduced the scope for informal housing as the public land within municipal boundaries was set aside for large-scale projects with increased controls. The *gecekondus* did not disappear, but some of them were pushed further out beyond municipal boundaries, resulting in outer city squatter settlements. The new 1982 Constitution extended housing rights to all citizens, leading to the establishment of a National Housing Authority and a Mass Housing Fund (now known as TOKI), resulting in the construction of 350,000 new houses between 1982 and 1984. However these cooperative housing initiatives again targeted middle-income households, and efforts to provide low-income housing were directed away from Istanbul (Yonder, 1998).

Over the period 1985–2000 approximately three million new migrants arrived in Istanbul. In terms of housing policy, the new era started after the 1990s and was marked by 'urban transformation projects', which in the main meant demolishing inner-city *gecekondu* settlements in particular. In addition, up until 2001, TOKI was receiving state funds to build relatively cheap housing that was also offered as an alternative to people whose houses were demolished. However, as with earlier initiatives, TOKI houses were not generally affordable by the target population.

In sum, Turkey had started to urbanise while retaining a 'feudal' structure in the urban areas (Kiray, 1998). In economic terms, the industrial structure and pattern of specialisation remained very limited up to the mid-twentieth century, undermining the basis for a flourishing economy and advanced industrialisation. This constraint had a direct influence on the way urban space was organised, in that the site of the city was not well adapted for mainstream industrial location and development. When the population increased under this type of social order, smooth organic growth of the city could hardly have been expected. The city was simply not ready to accommodate newcomers, or provide them with employment. It has been argued that this model of urban development — 'urbanisation without industrialisation' — is specific to the 'semi-peripheral' (developing) Mediterranean region, and distinct from urbanisation patterns in the core (developed world) or periphery (undeveloped world) (Leontidou, 1990). The pattern can be explained by the interaction of 'popular spontaneity', economic forces and state control as discussed in detail above. It was popular creativity, in this particular case *gecekondus*, that set the pace for the urbanisation process. This popular creativity can be traced back to the *informal networks*, which generated powerful informational and resource channels to solve the issue of housing for migrants, partly due to their articulation with the formal networks.

5. Informal and Formal Housing Networks Among Yesiltepe Migrants

Yesiltepe is an informal housing settlement located within a predominantly upper-middle- class municipality, Bahcesehir, which is 50km from Istanbul city centre. All the houses are built on privately owned land, with 54 out of 56 house owners having title deeds for the land, but none of the houses comply with the building codes established by the municipality. In other words, they are all informal. The municipality is aware of the situation, but nevertheless provides infrastructure to the area. Besides, the municipality helps the migrants living in the area by providing periodic financial and food aid to all the households. At the same time — and ironically — the municipal urban planners has recently sent a project proposal to TOKI for including the area in an 'urban transformation project', i.e. demolishing the houses and replacing them with multi-storey apartments, by paying the value of the land to the occupants. For the time being, TOKI is hesitant about taking on the project because of the cost of the sewage systems required for multi-storeys. If the project is accepted, however, the people will have to leave their houses, and will not be given a sufficient sum to buy an apartment in the multi-storey buildings. Therefore they will be forced to leave the area. In this respect, the current situation not only provides an ideal platform to observe the interaction of formal and informal networks, where formal networks act informally despite their efforts to formalise the area; but also demonstrates how informal information channels supply initial access to housing resources, in a context where these demands are not met by the formal networks.

Yesiltepe is populated by internal migrants who have arrived over a long time-span, starting in 1972. Out of 94 households, 35 had settled in another neighbourhood before coming to Yesiltepe; for the rest, it is their initial settlement. When asked how they heard about the neighbourhood, 84% specified very close ties such as family and relatives, and when we include friends and fellow townspeople it goes up to 94%. Only six said they found their current house on their own (see Table 12.2).

During the interviews it was revealed that 'on their own' actually meant through an estate agent they had heard of through their close ties, and usually through fellow townspeople. Almost all the house owners, i.e. more than half of the respondents (see Table 12.3), built their houses on their own; with the help of relatives and neighbours; or else they employed a small building contractor. The rest of the house owners bought their houses from previous owners. When building their houses, the migrants

Table 12.2. Housing information networks in Yesiltepe: How they heard about their current neighbourhood.

	Frequency	Percent
Family	54	57.4
Relatives	25	26.6
Friends	5	5.3
Fellow Townspeople	4	4.3
On their own	6	6.4
Total	94	100.0

Table 12.3. House ownership in Yesiltepe.

	Frequency	Percent
House owner	56	59.6
Rent	34	36.2
Temporary residence	2	2.1
Other	2	2.1
Total	94	100.0

did not engage in any government housing scheme or take out any credits. However, most of them borrowed money within their close networks.

The area was not part of the current municipality until 1999. The respondents reported that since then living conditions in the area have improved. Also some interview passages show that the enhanced living conditions were due not only to the municipality's aid programme for the area, but also to a certain solidarity that cut across the formal and informal networks. During the incumbency of a Bahcesehir mayor who was from Kars, two particular cases demonstrate both the upside and downside of fellow-townspeople networks, and also highlight the informal behaviour of the municipality.

> In earlier times it was easier to build houses here. After 1999 they did not allow that, but thanks to Gurbuz Capan, the previous mayor of Yesiltepe, who was from Kars, my fellow townsman, he helped me to extend this one, he didn't send out people to investigate the process of building.
>
> (Huseyin, 85 years old, migrant from Kars)

> In earlier times it was better, but Gurbuz Capan (the mayor back then) didn't let us build more, he said I will demolish them, so we can't move forward; what I earn now is just enough for us. I got this place as 175 square metres but Capan left us with just 135, and that's not enough to build a legal house. I told him I paid 40 million for the land and asked him to give my 40 million back, but he didn't. So we boycotted for a while. Somebody sued me as he got two plots next to mine and also wanted mine. I have been here for 15 years, even when there was nothing here. Then people started to come here and the land got more valuable, so they sued me. I've got 12 people living in this house, and what am I supposed to do. If the government showed me a new place to fit this many people in, then it would be OK, but they don't. What are we supposed to do? Become homeless?
>
> (Satilmis, 62 years old, from Tokat, gardener)

Most of the respondents mentioned that they accessed information on housing resources through migrants who had previously settled in Istanbul — in most cases family and relatives.

> My brother persuaded me to come here. We thought there was lots of land available, because everybody who came here before us managed to settle in the city centre. But it wasn't like that any more. My brother said we should go to the periphery, and he found us this land. It was cheap. At that time there was nothing here — no electricity, no water; but if it hadn't been for my brother, we wouldn't have found any place.
>
> (Mustafa, 43 years old, migrant from Gumushane)

Most of the tenants in the area reported that they knew the landlord before renting their house, which also shows that informal ties tend to replace the commercial rental market. In some cases, these informal ties have put pressure on network members by loading them with the responsibility of looking after the close ties. Thus in some cases migrants had to give up superior housing and living conditions in order to accommodate their extended family and relatives — and that meant finding a bigger plot of land in an area with looser housing laws, such as Yesiltepe, rather than a more central location with better infrastructure, but which would be sufficient only for their immediate family.

In a way, the social capital of the Yesiltepe migrants consists of the housing resources embedded within informal housing networks and formal networks, where both can lead to unequal distribution of resources, in a context where the informal interacts with the formal on an almost daily basis, and where the formal networks operate to some extent informally.

6. Labour Force Participation and Unemployment in Turkey

The picture of serious network misalignment is reinforced when we look at labour and employment dynamics. The annual rate of population growth in Turkey declined over the 1990s to 1.5% in 2000. In the same year, the working-age population (15–64)[5] growth rate was 2.6%, while the rate of growth of employment was approximately 1.7% (Auer and Popova, 2003). Thus the labour force was increasing at a slower pace than the working-age population. Today, the working-age population (15–64 years) of Turkey is approximately 50 million people, i.e. 70% of the total population. However, only half of these people are in the labour force, of which

---

[5] In Turkey the working-age population was defined as aged 12–64 until 2000. However, most of the data is adjusted to the OECD definition of 15–64.

22.5 million are employed and 2.5 million are unemployed, which gives us a relatively low official unemployment rate of around 10%. The employment rate — 45%[6] — is one of the lowest in the world. This represents a sharp change from the past. In 1975 Turkey's employment rate was the highest among OECD countries (except for Japan), and in 1997 it was the lowest in the OECD (except for Spain).[7] Out of the total labour force, only 25% is female. Strikingly, there are no significant differences between male and female unemployment rates, in overall terms. However if we look at non-agricultural unemployment, the rate of unemployment for women is 17.9%, which is much higher than for men, with 11.3% (TUIK HLFS, 2008). While this could indicate that there are limited employment opportunities for women in the cities, it does not explain why there is such low overall labour force participation in Turkey. When we look at the working-age population that does not participate in the labour force, however, we see that three-fourths of it is female, i.e. approximately 20 million. The main reason cited for not participating is 'doing domestic work', well ahead of other reasons such as 'being disabled or sick', 'attending school', or 'not seeking a job but prepared to work' (TUIK HLFS, Periodical results 2006). Here 'doing domestic work' reflects various socio-cultural factors, particularly in Eastern Turkey, that do not allow women to work outside their homes, while loading them with all the household responsibilities. In addition, a large proportion of the working-age population is not looking for work, either because they have given up hope, or because they are discouraged ex-workers. It must be stressed at the same time that the fact that Turkey does not have a satisfactory unemployment insurance scheme forces people to work for very low returns, which leads to underemployment and underutilisation of the labour force, while keeping official unemployment rates relatively low.

There are other supply-driven factors that have contributed to the declining trend of labour force participation. First, the social security law of 1993 replaced the minimum retirement age with time spent in employment as the key determinant of pension rights, and the participation rate of the 55+ age group started to fall, as its members began to drop out of the labour force to take up their entitlement to retirement benefits.[8] Second, more people are staying longer at school. Third, more people and particularly women, tend to stay at home rather than joining the labour force. (World Bank, 2006) The declining rates for women relate partly to the conditions of

---

[6] November 2008, Turkish Statistics Institute (TUIK), Household Labour Force Statistics (HLFS).
[7] See *Turkey Labour Market Study* by the World Bank for further comparisons.
[8] Until May 2006, the Turkish social security system was made up of three separate social institutions: SSK for private and public sector workers; ES for civil servants; and Bag-Kur for self-employed workers and farmers. The system gave rise to enormous deficits, and the cumulative value of these deficits for the period 1994–2004 was equal to approximately 110% of annual GDP. The government passed a new law in May 2006 that unifies the three social security institutions, aiming to improve the administration thereof, and in the long run to close these deficits and advance the pension system. See Brook and Whitehouse (2006) for further discussion. The law was changed again in 2006, introducing a minimum retirement age of 60 for women and 65 for men for people starting work from 2007 onwards. For details (in Turkish) see www.sgk.gov.tr.

rural migrant women who were previously involved in agriculture, but lacked the necessary skills to get any kind of job in the urban industrial centres, or were simply not allowed to work by their families. The skills deficit point is also related to relatively low educational attainment of women compared to men, which again is partly due to family pressure on women in the rural areas. Consistent with the low female participation rate, there is a high dependency rate, where usually there is only one bread-winner within a household, particularly among the new migrants.

The shares of part-time and fixed-term employment are still very low in Turkey, which reduces labour market flexibility. The labour market has very long working hours. Because of severance requirements, employers tend to increase working hours for existing workers rather than hiring new workers in times of high labour demand. This blockage leads to relatively high unemployment rates for young educated people. Another way of reducing employment costs, when economic conditions are uncertain, is to use informal workers. In this situation the informal economy has a better chance of creating jobs than the formal economy. The rate of job creation has, indeed, been very moderate since 1980, particularly in the services sector, despite relatively strong economic growth.

7. The Informal Economy in Turkey

The informal economy concept remains as an ambiguous one. In the literature there are various definitions, e.g. 'specific form of income-generating production relationships, unregulated by the institutions of society in a legal and social environment in which similar activities are regulated' (Castells *et al.*, 1989). One approach seeks to develop the concept on the basis of the older concepts of unorganised sector and non-monetary sector, encompassing small-scale production units such as the household. Another approach is to analyse the concept in relation to the traditional–modern (agriculture–manufacture) dichotomy of the dual economy, which conceptualises economic development in terms of growth of the modern sector absorbing the labour freed up from the traditional sector. In this argument, the traditional sector is considered as a temporary state of the economy that would gradually be absorbed into the modern (Blunch *et al.*, 2001). Hart (1973) redefined the traditional urban sector as an informal sector that created a permanent type of employment in less developed countries. One of the earlier uses of the term was in the *Kenya Report* prepared by the World Employment Programme of the International Labour Organization (ILO), in 1970. Here, the informal sector concept was utilised to explain unexpectedly low unemployment figures following a rapid rural–urban migration era in Kenya. The surplus labour force that could not be absorbed by the formal labour market was shifting to a (rapidly growing) informal labour market. This report clearly underlines the organic relation between migration and the informal sector.

A number of terms such as unrecorded, unofficial, shadow, illegal and black are sometimes used interchangeably with informal economy. The latest report of the State Planning Organization in Turkey (DPT, 2003), uses the umbrella concept 'unrecorded economy', and clearly distinguishes three main parts to it: the illegal economy (criminal economy), which engages in economic activities that are outside the law; the underground (hidden) economy, which engages in legal economic production but does not report to social security institutions and/or does not fulfill the tax requirements; and, third, the informal economy as defined in the Fifteenth International Conference of Labour Statisticians (ICLS) (1993). The definition used in this report is based on the characteristics of the enterprises (production units) in which the activities take place, rather than in terms of the characteristics of the persons involved or of their jobs. Production units of the informal sector are defined as a:

> subset of unincorporated enterprises owned by households i.e. as a subset of production units which are not constituted as separate legal entities independently of the households or household members who own them, and for which no complete sets of accounts (including balance sheets of assets and liabilities) are available which would permit a clear distinction of the production activities of the enterprises from the other activities of their owners and the identification of any flows of capital and income between the enterprises and the owners.
>
> (Hussmanns and Mehran, 2003, 2)

The informal economy is embedded in a wider socio-economic framework, and should therefore be evaluated as an outcome of this particular matrix, with its advantages as well as its widely reviewed disadvantages. In the Turkish context, the main advantage is creating employment opportunities where otherwise unemployment rates would be much higher than 10%. The main disadvantages are a deteriorating labour environment in terms of various elements of the work process such as the status of labour (undeclared, no social benefits, paid less than minimum wage), and conditions of work (health conditions, safety hazards). It has been argued that rapid industrial growth should theoretically lead to labour absorption, and thus to a decline in the informal sector. Yet Latin America has proved this assumption wrong (Castells *et al.*, 1989). By the same token, the figures for Turkey[9] also challenge the theory. In reality, rapid industrial growth has gone parallel with an even more rapidly increasing urban population that could not be absorbed by the labour market, which has stimulated the rise of the informal economy. It is certainly hard to measure informality

---

[9] Turkish Household Labour Force Statistics define the informal sector as all non-agricultural economic units comprising establishments whose legal position is individual ownership, paying basic tax or no tax at all, and working with 1–9 engaged people.

accurately, given that it can be defined in various different ways, and given that it is unrecorded most of the time. According to the World Bank criterion of informal economy, which counts the workers who are not registered with social security institutions, Turkey has a large informal economy, with one-third of the working population in urban areas in the informal sector. However, this figure fluctuates depending on the method of measuring the informal economy.[10] In line with the World Bank criterion, Lordoglu (1999) measures the informal labour based on registration to social security institutions and finds that in 1999 89% of the working population in agriculture worked informally. We can argue that such a high rate of informality in agriculture is another push factor to the urban informal sector from the rural areas. The migrants feel that they have nothing to lose, since they already feel insecure and instable. At the same time, the fact that they were not registered with the social security institutions in their rural employment makes it seem acceptable for them to get informal jobs in the city as well.

As discussed throughout the chapter, Istanbul has had the best possible conditions for the growth of an informal sector, such as surplus labour force coming from rural areas, lack of a sound social security system, and also the weakness of government policies and inspections. It has been argued, furthermore, that the dynamic nature of the informal sector was a very important factor keeping the rate of absolute poverty low in Turkey compared to other countries going through severe economic crises (Isik and Pinarcioglu, 2003). It is also important to note that the dynamic nature of the informal sector partly emanates from urbanisation patterns in Turkey. As discussed above in detail, the process and the institutions of urbanisation in Turkey enabled small/medium capital owners and enterprises to survive in the urban economy. If we consider the informal sector of the economy as another 'self-help' mechanism that operates within the web of informal networks, we should recognise the significant role played here by rural–urban migrants. The dynamics of urbanisation and economic development have enabled the newcomers to find jobs in the informal economy and/or through informal channels, as well as providing them with housing, if they could manage to articulate themselves with the already established networks of the earlier migrants. These informal networks in Turkey are based on family/kin networks, ethnic networks, and, most importantly, being from the same city of origin. Such ties not only motivated the original migration, but also facilitated the development of migrant survival mechanisms in the city, by establishing a very strong incentive for migrants to belong to particular networks. That is to say, the first challenge of the self-help mechanism was being part of an informal network — with its

---

[10] According to the Informal Economy Report published by the State Planning Organization of Turkey (2001), there are ten different methods of measuring the informal economy, including the tax-based method, the social security method, the macro-economic method, the labour-force method, and the cash flow method. The results vary widely depending on which method is used. For instance the report shows that in 1989, based on the cash flow method, the informal economy covered 61% of the whole economy, whereas based on the macro-economic method it was only 13%.

specific power relations — such as would provide a basis for enhancing and transforming living conditions. People provided themselves with what the state could not provide them. The informal economy expanded through these informal networks and constituted a major weapon in the fight against poverty. Besides the informal economic network at the general level, the channels that were used to access jobs were almost exclusively informal for the migrants. Let us look now at the potential of informal employment information networks to break down the blockages within the labour market.

8. Informal Employment Networks in Yesiltepe

Out of 47 women respondents in our study, 33 are neither working nor seeking work, 10 women are employed, and 4 women are unemployed, prepared to work but not looking for work. By contrast, out of 47 men, 45 of them are working, one man is unemployed and looking for work and one man is unemployed and not looking for work due to age (see Table 12.4).

Out of 10 employed women and 45 employed men, only one man said that he found his current job with the help of the Employment Centre (ISKUR). As many as 88% of men and all of the employed women reported fellow townspeople, family/relatives and friends and neighbours as helping them find their current job. However, it is interesting to note that, later in the survey, when asked if they knew anybody who could help them to find a job, 62% of men[11] said they did not know anybody. And when asked if anybody helped them find work right after settlement, 64% of men said nobody helped them. There might be various reasons behind the difference in responses here. Based on the interview responses, it seems that the definition of 'getting help' can be explained with reference to the cultural conceptions surrounding the proximity of social ties, particularly in the rural areas. The help

Table 12.4. Employment status

Gender	Frequency	Percent
Female		
Employed	10	21.3
Unemployed	37	78.7
Total	47	100.0
Male		
Employed	45	95.7
Unemployed	2	4.3
Total	47	100.0

---

[11] Since there are only ten employed women in the survey, most of the quantitative analysis has been carried out for men only.

coming from very close ties such as the family is almost always 'taken for granted', i.e. it is not recognised as help or viewed as anything to be grateful for, nor is it reciprocated. For instance within the family — or sometimes even within the extended family — the money flow is not regulated by common codes such as loans or borrowing. The loans are not identified as debts within the family even for mature children. That is to say, there is little expectation of getting a loan back, and little notion of identifying such loans as 'help'. In a way, people tend to take for granted this type of intimate network, which they are born into, rather than giving credit to the social ties that indeed generate resources for them. Secondly, the first question might have generated more positive responses than the latter two questions because it asks about the *current* job, whereas, of the latter two questions, one is seeking to find out the *potential* informational resources for future jobs, and the other one is asking about the *actualised* information resources right after settlement, but not necessarily the present job. What already happened (for some of them many years ago) or what might happen in the future are challenging questions in terms of getting accurate responses. However, in terms of informal networks, it is also crucial to note that the actualised resources match the potential resources within the social networks, showing us that the expectations of resources have a basis in fact.

When we look at the national survey statistics, we find that around 30% of the unemployed are looking for work through informal ties. Ironically, even ISKUR, in its 'Looking for Work Guide', 'highly' recommends the unemployed to ask their relatives, friends or neighbours for help in finding work. It is also interesting that only one of the people I spoke to had applied to this institution in seeking employment, and most of the respondents had never even heard of it. Bearing in mind that ISKUR is also in charge of unemployment benefits, it is not surprising that only one person (out of 94) is receiving unemployment benefit — and he is the same person that is looking for employment through ISKUR.

Here the interview data give us more detailed insights into the influence of social networks and resources on finding employment. Most migrants stated that they followed an already established and employed relative or fellow townsperson to Istanbul, and that actually they would not 'dare to come' otherwise.

> When I first came, it was 1986, I came to stay with my uncles in Sariyer; the idea was to go back; work here, earn here, and for instance get a fridge and take it back to the village, or a coloured TV — some people in the village had it, and we didn't. So I worked hard and really earned — that's how I got to know Istanbul. My relatives helped me find a job in construction…. Then I went back….Then my brother came here and convinced me to come here; he had a job, told me I could work here…
>
> (Satilmis, 62 years old, from Tokat, gardener)

Besides providing employment information before and right after arrival, the informal networks are also the main resource of job seeking in Istanbul. Some of the ties are so close and binding that sometimes the 'pioneer' migrant takes over the demanding responsibility of finding employment for the rest of the family and relatives. In fact, in some cases this responsibility acts as a barrier to social mobility, imposing tight constraints on individuals.

> Actually, my husband could have come here years ago. He passed the exams for the police academy, but he didn't enrol because he could not leave the rest of his family, his parents and brothers. He thought that if he were to go to the academy, then he could only take me and our children to Istanbul, and it would be like abandoning his brothers. So we came here when he found a job through relatives, and then brought all his brothers and found a job for each of them. And then he went bankrupt; sometimes I wonder what our life would have been like if he had attended the police academy….
>
> (Cigdem, 42 years old, from Kars, housewife)

Currently, the perceived scarcity of jobs also seems to put more pressure on the social networks.

> In the past you could just come here and find employment soon after; now I wouldn't recommend anybody to come like that unless they have relatives or something here that can help them to find a job. If you don't know anyone this city will swallow you, you will starve; you can't find a job on your own.
>
> (Sultan, 40 years old, from Tokat, housewife)

More of the earlier migrants stated they had strong informal networks where they could hear about new job openings compared to relatively newer migrants (who arrived after 1990). Although most respondents agreed on the general scarcity of jobs, particularly after 2000, for some new migrants, strong social networks also compensated for the disadvantages of the labour market on a broader scale.

> My husband was lucky enough to get a job two days after we arrived. People look for work for years here and can't find it. There are not so many jobs around. We had relatives here, and they knew an opening for a night guard and told us immediately. Thanks to them, we are better off than we were in the village now…
>
> (Sukran, migrated a month ago, housewife)

Among the employed migrants, when we look at figures of registration with a social security institution, we see that 13 men and 7 employed women are not registered with one, therefore working informally. Of these informal workers 13 are self-employed or part-time workers, which for women is exclusively domestic cleaning jobs. The interviews reveal that these informal workers feel very insecure about their jobs, and consequently about their lives in general. In some instances they had to work for months without being paid by their employers, in which case they again turned to their close networks for help.

> I worked at a textile shop for three months and they didn't pay me a penny. The firm was doing badly, and they kept on telling me one day they would pay. Then they fired me. I was completely broke, my parents didn't have money, I had to borrow from my neighbours in order to pay my debts. Otherwise I wouldn't be able go on really...
>
> (Fatma, 22 years old, migrant from Mus)

9. Conclusion

The process of urbanisation in Istanbul is to a great extent marked by the interaction between and the misalignment of the informal and the formal networks of housing and employment. Initially, the informal networks emerged as a strategy to cope with the lack of formal networks of urban planning, in terms of creating *gecekondu* settlements that benefited from ambiguous urban land supply patterns and laws, in order to meet the needs of the newly arrived rural migrants. In terms of employment, they also played a crucial role by disseminating job information for the informal sector in a context where formal employment opportunities were not enough to absorb the migrant labour force. Later the informal housing networks to a degree intertwined with the formal networks on various levels, private and public (notably the municipality), sometimes resulting in formal networks acting informally and vice versa.

Informal networks, while posing an alternative to formal distribution of resources, are, indeed, often misaligned among themselves. For instance, old migrant networks have established stronger ties with the urban resources and thus have more embedded resources to redistribute to its members. In addition, within an informal network, such as a hometown network, there are better connected network positions that generate more resources for some individuals and fewer for some others. It is also important to note that, when the informal networks are based on very close ties, they generate a certain solidarity, constraining members to take care of the other members of the network and therefore creating barriers against their own socio-economic mobilisation.

Overall, the informal networks seem like the only reliable resource for migrants, for fighting against poverty, homelessness, unemployment and also coping with general economic downturns. However, this resource is also a breeding ground for new inequalities, and unequal distribution of resources among the informal networks; making some of them more advantageous due to their size, density, embeddedness and access to information channels.

References

Auer, P. and Popova, N. (2003). 'Labour market policy for restructuring in Turkey: The need for more active policies', *International Labour Office*, Employment Paper.

Blunch, N.H., Canagarajah, S. and Raju, D. (2001). 'The informal sector revisited: A synthesis across space and time', *World Bank*, Social Protection Discussion Paper Series, No. 0119.

Brook, A.M. and Whitehouse, E. (2006). 'The Turkish pension system: Further reforms to help solve the informality problem', *OECD Economics Department*, WKP 57.

Bugra, A. (1998). 'The immoral economy of housing in Turkey', *International Journal of Urban & Regional Research* 22(2): 303–317.

———— and Keyder, C. (2003). *New Poverty and the Changing Welfare Regime of Turkey*, United Nations Development Programme.

———— (2005). *Poverty and Social Policy in Contemporary Turkey*, Bogazici University Social Policy Forum.

Bulutay, T. and Tasti, E. (2004). 'Informal sector in the Turkish labour market', *Turkish Economic Association*, Discussion Paper 2004/22.

Castells, M., Portes, A. and Benton, L.A. (1989). *The Informal Economy: Studies in Advanced and Less Developed Countries*, Baltimore, Johns Hopkins.

Danielson, M.N. and Keles, R. (1985). *The Politics of Rapid Urbanization: Government and Growth in Modern Turkey*, New Jersey, Holmes & Meier.

Davis, M. (2006). *Planet of Slums*, New York, Verso.

DPT (2003). *Kayit Disi Ekonomi Ozel Ihtisas Komisyonu Raporu* (Informal Economy Commission Report), Devlet Planlama Teskilati, Ankara, http://ekutup.dpt.gov.tr/ekonomi/kayitdis/oik614.pdf.

Ekinci, O. (1994). *Istanbul"u Sarsan On Yıl 1983–1993* (Ten Years that Changed Istanbul 1983–1993), Istanbul, Anahtar Kitaplar.

Guloglu, T. (2005). 'The reality of informal employment in Turkey', *Cornell University*, Visiting Fellow Working Papers.

Hart, K. (1973). 'Informal income opportunities and urban employment in Ghana', *The Journal of Modern African Studies* 11(2): 61–89.

Hussmanns, R. and Mehran, F. (2003). 'Statistical definition of the informal sector: international standards and national practices', *International Labour Office*, Bureau of Statistics.

Isik, O. and Pinarcioglu, M. (2001). *Nobetlese Yoksulluk: Sultanbeyli Ornegi* (Poverty in Turns: the Example of Sultanbeyli), Istanbul, Iletisim Yayinlari.

———— (2003). 'Yoksullugun degisen yuzu' (Poverty changing its face). *Gorus*, July.

Karpat, K. (1976). *The Gecekondu: Rural Migration and Urbanization,* Cambridge, Cambridge University Press.

―――――― (2004). 'The Genesis of Gecekondu: Rural migration and urbanization (1976)' *European Journal of Turkish Studies*, Thematic Issue No. 1.

Keles, R. (1972). *Turkiye"de Sehirlesme, Konut ve Gecekondu* (Urbanisation, Housing and Gecekondu in Turkey), Istanbul, Gercek Yayinevi.

―――――― (1984). *Kentlesme Politikasi* (Urbanisation Policy), Ankara, Imge Kitabevi.

Keyder, C. (1997). *Istanbul: Kuresel ile Yerel Arasinda* (Istanbul: Between the Local and the Global), Istanbul, Metis.

―――――― (2005). 'Globalization and social exclusion in Istanbul', *International Journal of Urban and Regional Research* 29(1): 124–134.

Kiray, M. (1970). 'Squatter housing: Fast depeasantization and slow workerization in underdeveloped countries,' *Research Committee on Urban Sociology of the 7th World Congress of Sociology.*

―――――― (1998). *Kentlesme Yazilari* (Urbanisation Notes), Istanbul, Baglam.

Leontidou, L. (1990). *The Mediterranean City in Transition: Social Change and Urban Development,* Cambridge, Cambridge University Press.

Levent Baycan, T. (2002). 'The demographic transition and urban development in Turkey', in Geyer, H.S. (ed.), *International Handbook of Urban Systems*: *Studies of Urbanization and Migration in Advanced and Developing Countries,* Cheltenham, Edward Elgar, pp. 329–365.

Lordoglu, K. (1998). 'Türkiye"de enformal istihdam ve bir boyut' (Informal employment in Turkey and one particular dimension) *TUHIS*, pp. 243–244.

Martin, P., Midgley, E. and Teitelbaum, M. (2001). 'Migration and development: focus on Turkey', *International Migration Review* 35(2): 596–605.

Pamuk, A. (1996). 'Convergence trends in formal and informal housing markets: The case of Turkey', *Journal of Planning Education and Research* 16(2): 103–113.

Saracoglu, S. (2005). 'The informal sector and tax on employment: A dynamic general equilibrium investigation', *Turkish Economic Association*, Discussion Paper 2005/7.

Sencer, Y. (1979). *Türkiye"de Kentleşme: Bir Toplumsal ve Kültürel Değişme Süreci* (Urbanisation in Turkey: A Social and Cultural Transformation Process), Ankara, Kültür Bakanlığı Yayını.

Yonder, A. (1998). 'Implications of double standards in housing policy: Development of informal settlements in Istanbul, Turkey', in Fernandes, E. and Varley, A. (eds.), *Illegal Cities: Law and Urban Change in Developing Countries,* London, Zed Books.

World Bank (2006). *Turkey Labour Market Study,* The World Bank, Washington, DC www.worldbank.org.tr/labor2006.

SECTION 3

INDUSTRIAL NETWORKS AND INTERNATIONAL SPILLOVERS

CHAPTER 13

KNOWLEDGE SPILLOVERS, INNOVATION AND FIRM-LEVEL PRODUCTIVITY GROWTH IN SLOVENIA

JOŽE P. DAMIJAN, ČRT KOSTEVC, MATIJA ROJEC
AND ANDREJA JAKLIČ

1. Introduction

According to the endogenous growth literature, innovation is central to the growth of the firm. Early empirical research concentrated on estimating either the rate of return to firm own R&D expenditures of firms or the impact of external knowledge spillovers on firm productivity growth. The objective of this chapter is to analyse the link between factors determining the ability of the firm to innovate, and, in particular, the subsequent impact of innovation on productivity growth. In using firm-level data on innovation activity (based on CIS1, CIS2 and CIS3) combined with firm financial data for a large sample of Slovenian firms in the period 1996–2002, we first study the relative importance of factors determining the ability of the firm to innovate. Specifically, we analyse to what extent the innovative ability of the firm is formed by own R&D activity of the firm, by factors external to the firm, and what are the most important channels of external knowledge spillovers. These can be in the form of direct technology transfer (through FDI, trade, licensing, importing etc.), learning effects (innovation spillovers and learning-by-exporting), and public R&D subsidies. So far, most of these channels have been studied separately. Here, we use an integrated dynamic model to analyse the impact and determine the relative importance for the innovation activity of firms of direct and indirect knowledge transfer through inward FDI and trade, as opposed to that of R&D subsidies and own R&D activity of firms. In the second step, we study the effectiveness of firm-level innovation, i.e. we estimate the impact of innovations by firms on firm-level productivity growth. In doing so, we apply two approaches — simple OLS regressions and matching techniques.

Innovation activity and productivity growth: Our exercise is conceptually based on endogenous growth theory, which suggests that technological progress is driven by a deliberate investment of resources by profit-seeking firms (Smolny, 2000). The innovation activity of the firm is found to be central to its technological progress and productivity growth. Griliches (1979) was the first to introduce R&D capital stock as a factor of production into the residual computational framework pioneered by Solow (1957). In this approach, R&D activities add to the existing stock of accumulated knowledge of firms, leading to productivity growth through product and process innovation. Romer's (1990) model predicts a link between R&D activity and productivity growth, and Cohen and Leventhal (1989) point to the importance that R&D activity can have in absorbing technology produced in other firms. Empirical work in favour of the positive influence of R&D on productivity growth includes Cameron, Proudman and Redding (2003), Griliches (1980), Griliches and Lichtenberg (1984), Mansfield and Romero (1980), Hall and Mairesse (1995), Griffith, Redding and Simpson (2004).

One of the most influential studies on innovation and productivity growth is that of Crepon, Duguet and Mairesse (1998), who combine a knowledge-production function, relating R&D activity to patenting or innovative activities, with economic performance as measured by labour productivity. The paper by Crepon, Duguet and Mairesse has influenced a new and burgeoning literature on the relationship between innovation output and firm performance. The main finding of these studies is that, regardless of how performance is measured, innovation output positively and significantly affects firm performance. The exception to this is the study by Klomp and van Leeuwen (2001), which finds a negative but insignificant effect of innovation output on employment growth.

Determinants of firm-level innovation activity: Innovation activity by firms is the result of own R&D and absorption capacity, of external knowledge spillovers and public R&D subsidies, and of a number of control variables, such as the technological intensity of the sectors in which the firm operates, which co-determine the innovation activity of the firm, and the extent of absorption of external knowledge spillovers. Own R&D is the crucial determinant of the innovation capacity of the firm. R&D has two complementary effects on innovation activity and productivity growth: first, it increases the technology level of the firm through new innovations; second, it increases the absorptive capacity of the firm — the ability to identify, assimilate and exploit outside knowledge (Cohen and Levinthal, 1989). Theoretical foundations for the positive impact of own R&D are supplied by the literature on endogenous innovation and growth (see, for instance, Aghion and Howitt, 1992, 1998; Grossman and Helpman, 1991; Romer, 1990).

Own R&D apart, the innovation activities of the firm depend heavily on external sources (see, for instance, Fagerberg, 2005; Keller, 2002a; Keller, 2004; Eaton and Kortum, 1999). Economic analysis of innovation identifies international knowledge flows (through FDI, trade, licensing and international technological collaboration) as important determinants of the development and the diffusion of innovations. Here, the notion of technology and knowledge spillovers is central. It is based on the theories of endogenous technical change of the early 1990s (see, for instance, Aghion and Howitt, 1998; Grossman and Helpman, 1991; Romer, 1990), claiming that the return to technological investments is partly private and partly public (Keller, 2004). Because of the non-exclusive character of technology and innovation, which is produced by one firm, it can also be used by another firm without incurring very much additional cost (Smolny, 2000). These are technology or knowledge spillovers. The literature identifies three principal channels of international knowledge spillovers. The first is a direct transfer of technology via international licensing agreements (Eaton and Kortum, 1996; UNCTAD, 2000),[1] the second is FDI and the third channel is international trade.

In dealing with FDI as a source of foreign technology and productivity growth, we should distinguish between direct effects of FDI and FDI spillovers. Direct effects of FDI relate to the impact of foreign ownership on the technology transfer to and productivity of foreign subsidiaries. There is ample empirical evidence on positive direct technology transfer from MNCs to their local affiliates in terms of higher productivity levels and growth. These studies, using firm-level panel data, include developed as well as developing countries (see, for instance, Haddad and Harrison, 1993; Blomström and Wolff, 1994; Blomström and Sjöholm, 1999; Aitken and Harrison, 1999; Girma, Greenaway and Wakelin, 2001; Barry, Görg and Strobl, 2002; Alverez, Damijan and Knell, 2002; Blalock, 2001; Damijan, Knell, Majcen and Rojec, 2003 etc.).

FDI spillovers are the second channel of technology transfer via FDI. Knowledge spillovers from FDI take place when the entry or presence of foreign subsidiaries, which typically have better technologies and organisational skills than domestic firms, increases the knowledge of domestic firms, and MNCs do not fully internalise the value of these benefits (Smarzynska, 2003). Empirical literature on spillovers from foreign subsidiaries to domestic firms has produced mixed results; it shows positive, neutral, and negative spillovers. For transition countries, the firm-level panel data analysis, as the most relevant methodological approach, suggest that there are few intra-industry spillovers from FDI, or that they are restricted to certain countries and categories of firms (Konings, 2001; Djankov and Hoekman, 2000; Kinoshita, 2000; Damijan, Knell, Majcen and Rojec 2003). The main reasons for the lack of evidence on FDI spillovers in firm-level analysis are: (i) there may really be no or even negative spillovers; (ii) lack of absorption capacity in host countries; (iii) spillovers may not occur horizontally (intra-industry) but rather through vertical (inter-industry) relationships; (iv) firm heterogeneity, where positive spillovers may only affect a sub-set of firms. The literature says that horizontal intra-industry spillovers are probably less likely to take place than vertical spillovers (Blalock, 2001; Schoors and van der Tool, 2001; Kugler, 2006; Smarzynska-Javorcik, 2004; Damijan, Knell, Majcen and Rojec 2003; Gorodnichenko, Svejnar and Terrell, 2007; Halpern and

---

[1] Licensing agreements have recently fallen in importance as a source of technology transfer, as the latest and most valuable technologies are often not available on license.

Murakozy, 2007), that geographical distance between foreign subsidiaries and domestic firms impacts on the scope of spillovers (Griliches, 1979, 1992; Gőrg and Greenaway, 2004; Audretsch, 1998; Jacobs, 1993; Branstetter, 1996; Girma and Wakelin, 2002; Sgard, 2001; Halpern and Murakozy, 2007); that knowledge spillovers occur more frequently if the technology gap between domestic and foreign firms is not too large (Perez, 1998; Halpern and Murakozy, 2007; Ben Hamida and Gugler, 2007; Abraham, Konings and Slootmaekers, 2006; Girma, Gong and Gőrg, 2006), and that human capital capacity increases the ability of domestic firms to benefit from positive spillovers (Borensztein, De Gregorio and Lee, 1998; Meyer and Sinani, 2005; Ben Hamida and Gugler, 2007; Girma et al., 2006).

International trade works as a channel of technology transfer through either imports of intermediate products and capital equipment (Feenstra, Markusen and Zeile, 1992) or learning-by-exporting into industrial countries (Clerides, Lach and Tybout, 1998). According to Keller (2004), overall evidence supports the notion that importing is associated with technology spillovers, but we do not know how strong diffusion through embodied technology in intermediate goods as opposed to other forms of technology diffusion associated with imports are (see, Keller and Yeaple, 2003; Eaton and Kortum, 2001; Coe and Helpman, 1995; Coe, Helpman and Hoffmaister, 1997; Xu and Wang, 1999; Keller, 2000; Lumenga-Neso, Olarreaga and Schiff, 2001; Keller, 2002b; Kraay, Soloaga and Tybout, 2001). There is much less evidence for knowledge spillovers via learning-by-exporting. The conventional wisdom is that learning-by-exporting effects are non-existent, and this is consistent with available evidence. According to Keller (2004), learning-by-exporting effects have been found in the case study literature, whereas authors of econometric studies take a much more sceptical view. In a meta analysis of recent studies, Wagner (2007) finds no conclusive evidence in favour of the learning-by-exporting hypothesis.

Yet another possible factor of firm-level innovation activity is R&D subsidies. The crucial issue here is, whether there are any positive spillovers from public to private R&D expenditures, i.e. from R&D subsidies given by the government to own R&D expenditures of firms (David, Hall and Toole, 1999). Is public spending complementary and thus 'additional' to private R&D spending, or does it substitute for and tend to 'crowd out' private R&D? The standard rationale for government support of R&D is rooted in the belief that some form of market failure exists that leads the private sector to underinvest in R&D (Arrow, 1962; Nelson, 1959). Underinvestment in R&D occurs because the social benefits from new technologies are difficult to appropriate by the private firms bearing the costs of their discovery, and because imperfect capital markets may inhibit firms from investing in socially valuable R&D projects (Griliches, 1998; Romer, 1990). Economic incentives therefore do not generally lead firms to undertake the first best level of R&D spending. The aim of government intervention in R&D activity is to establish efficiency. Therefore, publicly supported R&D is supposed to augment or complement private R&D

expenditures. Yet the empirical evidence suggests that there is some substitution between private and government funded R&D (Wallsten, 2000; Busom, 2000; Klette and Moen, 1997; Lach, 2000). David, Hall and Toole (1999) survey the body of available econometric evidence and also find ambivalent results. They do not offer a definite empirical conclusion regarding the sign and magnitude of the relationship between public and private R&D.

The remainder of this chapter is structured as follows. Section 2 presents empirical analysis of the determinants of innovation activity of Slovenian firms, while Section 3 provides estimations of the effect of innovation activity on firm-level productivity growth. The last section concludes.

2. Determinants of Firm-Level Innovation in Slovenia

In this sub-section, we explore the factors driving innovation activity of Slovenian firms through the official Community Innovation Surveys (CIS1, CIS2, CIS3). Table 13.1 describes the sample characteristics with respect to the determinants of innovation activity. It is revealed that innovation activity by firms is persistent over time, i.e. firms that have innovated two years ago are more likely to innovate in the present. Table 13.1 also demonstrates that innovative firms are likely to be larger in terms of employment, invest much more in R&D and also attract a higher proportion of subsidies, either public or foreign.[2] At the same time, innovative firms also export a larger share of their sales and are more likely to be foreign-owned. Surprisingly, innovative firms do not seem to be more productive in terms of value added per employee (measured in terms of the individual sector average).

In order to reveal the importance of these individual factors on firms' innovation activity we estimate the probability to innovate of a firm i in period t ($INOV_{it}$):

$$\Pr(INOV_{it}) = 1 | \mathbf{M}_{it} = G(\omega \mathbf{M}_{it}), \tag{1}$$

where $\mathbf{M}_{it}$ is a matrix of operational characteristics of firms. We assume that errors are IID distributed and have an independent extreme-value distribution. The dependent variable $INOV_{it}$ is equal to 1 if a firm has made any innovation in products (services) or production processes in period t, and 0 otherwise. The control variables contained in $\mathbf{M}_{it}$ are those listed in Table 13.1, i.e. a dummy for past innovation activity (lagged one period, i.e. two years), firm size (number of employees), relative productivity (firm value added per employee relative to the average productivity of the particular sector), share of R&D expenditures in total sales, export propensity and a dummy for foreign ownership, plus three variables for the importance

---

[2] However, R&D subsidies on average do not represent a significant share of R&D expenditure. According to the innovation surveys, innovation expenditure are mostly covered by own funds.

Table 13.1. Determinants of firm-level innovation in Slovenia, 1996–2002.

	N (No of firms)	INOV_t-2 (Proportion of firms being innovative two years ago; %)	rVA/Emp (Value added per employee as compared to sectoral average; ratio)	Emp (Average no of employees per firm)	R&D/Sales (Ratio of R&D expenditures to sales; %)	R&D/VA (Ratio of R&D expenditures to value added; %)	Total sub./R&D (Ratio of total subsidies to R&D expenditures; %)	Public sub./R&D (Ratio of public subsidies to R&D expenditures; %)	Foreign sub./R&D (Ratio of foreign subsidies to R&D expenditures; %)	EX/Sales (Ratio of exports to sales; %)	IFDI (Proportion of foreign-owned firms; %)
Innovative firms											
1996	316	—	1.26	346.7	1.55	5.39	5.39	3.12	0.27	43.9	38.8
1998	409	64.3	0.84	312.9	1.62	5.96	4.07	2.42	0.85	43.1	39.7
2000	533	55.4	1.11	278.5	6.02	19.22	4.33	3.42	0.59	38.1	36.8
2002	527	69.4	1.09	283.6	6.47	18.42	4.98	3.14	1.08	43.7	36.4
Non-Innovative firms											
1996	1138	—	1.19	122.8	0.026	0.101	0.180	0.066	0.054	25.7	25.4
1998	1368	9.5	1.11	96.5	0.003	0.006	0.004	0.004	0.000	27.3	23.7
2000	1985	12.2	1.01	68.5	0.021	0.047	0.013	0.013	0.000	21.6	20.1
2002	2037	11.3	0.99	67.5	0.015	0.038	0.016	0.000	0.001	22.8	21.5

Source: Statistical Office of Slovenia; own calculations.
Note: IFDI = inward foreign direct investment.

of R&D subsidies (total R&D subsidies, public R&D subsidies and R&D subsidies received from abroad, all as a share of total firm R&D expenditures). In the model we also include horizontal and vertical spillovers from the innovation activity of other firms. Horizontal spillovers are measured by the number of innovations done in the sector of the given firm. Vertical spillover indicators are constructed as the number of innovations conducted in a related sector multiplied by the respective input–output coefficient, where the latter reflects the strength of input–output relationship between the sectors. In other words, the more interlinked the two sectors are through bilateral supply and demand links and the higher the innovation activity in both sectors, the greater is the scope for positive vertical knowledge spillovers between the two sectors. The model also takes into account the technology intensity of the sectors. It is expected that firms operating in more technologically intensive sectors will be more likely to innovate in order to remain competitive or to build up their technological competitive advantage over their competitors. Owing to a short and non-balanced panel, we do not include time dummies.

We estimate a probit model using biannual data for a set of manufacturing and non-manufacturing firms in Slovenia in the period 1996–2002. Results for two

Table 13.2. The probability of a firm innovating* in Slovenia, 1996–2002 (results of a probit model).

	Model 1		Model 2	
	Coef.	z-stat	Coef.	z-stat
$INOV_{t-2}$	0.821	11.5[†††]	0.822	11.5[†††]
Size	0.495	10.0[†††]	0.497	10.0[†††]
rVA/Emp	0.003	0.4	0.003	0.4
R&D/Sales	117.259	25.2[†††]	118.173	25.2[†††]
Total sub./R&D	7.217	5.1[†††]		
Public sub./R&D			8.497	4.3[†††]
Foreign sub./R&D			17.678	1.7[†]
IFDI	0.119	1.7[†]	0.117	1.7[†]
EX/Sales	0.112	1.1	0.103	1.0
HS_INOV	0.008	3.3[†††]	0.009	3.4[†††]
VS_INOV	−0.003	−0.4	−0.002	−0.4
Med-Low-tech	−0.043	−0.4	−0.056	−0.5
Med-High-tech	−0.035	−0.3	−0.045	−0.4
High-tech	−0.133	−1.0	−0.162	−1.2
Const.	−2.602	−18.7[†††]	−2.603	−18.7[†††]
Number of obs	4167		4167	
LR chi²(12)	2888.5		2897.6	
Prob > chi²	0.00		0.00	
Pseudo R²	0.616		0.618	

Dependent variable: $INOV_t$

* Product and process innovation are treated equally.

[†], [††] and [†††] denote significance of coefficients at the 10%, 5% and 1%, respectively.

separate probit estimations are given in Table 13.2. The first model includes only an aggregate figure for subsidies, while the second model distinguishes between public and foreign subsidies. Both estimations show that the current innovation activity of firms is heavily dependent on previous innovation activity. More specifically, there is an 82% probability that a firm innovates a product or a process if it was innovative in the previous period. Firm size positively affects the ability of the firm to innovate, most likely due to the scale effect, i.e. large-scale sales permit the funding of substantial R&D expenditures. This is confirmed by a highly significant and positive sign for own R&D expenditures. While the literature is inconclusive regarding the importance of R&D subsidies, our results indicate that both public R&D subsidies and R&D subsidies received from abroad (measured as a share of firm's total R&D subsidies) significantly improve the ability to innovate of the firm.

Foreign ownership stimulates firms to innovate, but exporting is not revealed as having a significant impact on firm-level innovation activity. Horizontal knowledge spillovers seem to be a driver of firm innovation activity, while vertical knowledge spillovers are shown not to be important. This can be interpreted in the sense that a highly competitive environment in terms of high innovation activity of competitors pushes individual firm to engage in R&D and innovation activity. On the other hand, technological linkages to other sectors seem to be rather weak.

Endogenous growth theory suggests that innovating firms base their productivity on innovative effort, which could, given high serial correlation of productivity measures, translate into more productive firms also being more innovative. Our finding is that, contrary to expectations, labour productivity does not affect innovation activity. Nor does the technological intensity of the sector in which the firm operates. Surprisingly, given that the share of innovation expenditure in sales was considerably higher in the high-technology class,[3] firms engaged in medium-high and high-technology-intensive sectors are no more likely to be innovative than their counterparts from less technologically intensive sectors.

In addition to the above estimations, where we do not distinguish between product and process innovations, we also run separate estimations for each of these types of innovation activity. However, the results (see Table 13.A1 in Appendix) are almost identical for both types of innovation activity, which justifies our decision to treat both types of innovation under one common variable. There are only some minor differences in the separate estimations in the sense that process innovations require a slightly larger firm size, while product innovations seem to be more pronounced in foreign-owned firms and seem to give slightly higher returns to public subsidies.

---

[3] 8.5%, compared to 2.5% for medium-high-, 2.7% for medium-low- and 1.4% for low-technology sectors for the total sample.

3. Impact of Innovative Activity on Firm-Level Productivity Growth in Slovenia

This section is aimed at exploring the efficiency of innovation in terms of firm-level total factor productivity (TFP) growth. We apply two different empirical and econometric approaches in order to verify the robustness of the link between firm-level innovation and productivity growth. First, we estimate the growth accounting model, including R&D capital, by applying the OLS approach. In the second approach we use matching techniques and propensity scores to discriminate among innovating and non-innovating firms, and to explore whether innovation activity is the decisive factor driving firm productivity growth.

3.1. *Effect of innovation on productivity growth using OLS estimations*

In our empirical work we are following a great body of literature on the contribution of R&D to firm-level TFP growth. Typically, a growth accounting approach in the form of a standard Cobb–Douglas production function is used in this type of analysis (see Griliches, 1992 and Mairesse and Sassenou, 1991 for comprehensive overviews of the empirical studies on the contribution of R&D to growth). We start from the following production function:

$$Y_{it} = A e^{\lambda t} K_{it}^{\alpha} L_{it}^{\beta} R_{it}^{\gamma} e^{\varepsilon it}, \tag{2}$$

where Y_{it} is value added in firm i at time t, and K, L, and R represent, respectively, the capital stock, employment and research capital used in production. A is a constant and λ represents the rate of disembodied technical change; e is the error term capturing all firm-specific disturbances as well as measurement errors, etc. The production function is homogenous of degree r in K, L and R, such that $g = \alpha + \beta + \gamma \neq 1$, which implies that Y may have non-constant returns to scale. α, β and γ are the elasticities of output with respect to capital, labor and R&D capital. Our main focus is on the estimated elasticity γ, which reflects the marginal productivity or rate of return in terms of output to R&D capital.

By log-linearising one can easily rewrite (2) in the form of first differences:

$$\Delta y_{it} = 1 + \alpha \Delta k_{it} + \beta \Delta l_{it} + \gamma \Delta r_{it} + \Delta \varepsilon_{it}. \tag{3}$$

Note that after controlling for standard inputs (labour and capital) the estimate of γ gives the contribution of R&D capital to total factor productivity (TFP) growth. We assume that R&D capital contains a set of factors that enhance innovation activity, and are either internal or external to the firm. Hence, we can write R as a function of firm's internal R&D capital $\mathbf{F}_{it}$ and of various spillover effects $\mathbf{Z}_{it}$:

$$R_{it} = f^i(\mathbf{F}_{it}, \mathbf{Z}_{it}), \tag{4}$$

where $\mathbf{F}_{it}$ contains firm own R&D expenditures, measured as a share of R&D expenditures relative to total sales. $\mathbf{Z}_{it}$ captures all spillover effects that enhance the firm's ability to innovate, such as foreign ownership, learning by exporting (exports to sales ratio), public R&D subsidies received either from national or international sources, and innovation spillovers received from other firms within the same sector or from other sectors.

Note that in a panel data framework, Eq. (2) is typically subject to firm-specific time invariant disturbances, which can be controlled by using one of the standard panel data estimation techniques (within or between estimators). Alternatively, one can get rid of firm-specific effects by estimating the equation as in (3), where by first-differencing the time-invariant firm-specific effects are simply eliminated. Another problem with the time-series cross-section specification of (2) is the potential endogeneity between the inputs and the output, which may lead to biased estimation of input coefficients. However, in such a short and unbalanced panel dataset, with mostly two to three observations per firm, there is little we can do about this. Correcting for such endogeneity, whether by using the Olley-Pakes method or the general method of moments (GMM), requires longer time series of input and output data if they are to be effective as lagged instruments for the present performance of the firm.

In the first specification, we follow other empirical studies and estimate (3) by including only R&D expenditures (relative to sales) as a measure of R&D capital. This estimate gives us the upper bound of possible return of output to R&D capital. Indeed, as shown in Table 13.3 (see Model 1), the estimated elasticity of R&D capital with respect to TPF growth for Slovenian firms in the period 1996–2002 is about 0.24. This estimate is within the bounds of returns — between 0.04 and 0.56 — found by other empirical studies with similar model specification (see Griliches, 1998).

In our second specification (see Model 2 in Table 13.3) we go one step further by estimating the impact of innovations, which is the effective result of R&D, on firm TFP growth. This is our preferred estimation, returning an estimate of the rate of return to innovation of 0.069. It demonstrates that in an average Slovenian firm innovation resulted in TFP growth of 6.9% over the period 1996–2002. In addition to that, foreign ownership enhanced firm's TFP growth by an additional 6.2%. Our results also show that foreign ownership does additionally impact on TFP growth through innovations (see interaction term INOV∗IFDI). Thus foreign ownership enhances the ability of a firm to innovate, as was demonstrated in the previous

Table 13.3. Impact of R&D and innovation on TFP growth of Slovenian firms, 1996–2002.

	Model 1		Model 2		Model 3	
	Coef.	t-stat	Coef.	t-stat	Coef.	t-stat
ΔCapital	0.029	4.5***	0.025	3.4*	0.021	3.0***
ΔLabour	0.446	13.4***	0.446	13.2***	0.451	13.4***
ΔR&D/Sales	0.238	1.9*				
INOV			0.069	1.8*		
p[INOV]					0.083	2.2**
IFDI			0.062	1.8*	0.051	1.8*
INOV * IFDI			−0.051	−0.8		
EX/Sales			0.052	1.3		
HS_INOV			0.001	1.5		
VS_INOV			0.002	1.4		
Med-Low-tech			−0.055	−1.2		
Med-High-tech			0.036	0.7		
High-tech			0.054	0.5		
Const.	−0.205	−3.0***	−0.302	−3.6***	−0.185	−2.6***
Time dummies	No		Yes		Yes	
Number of obs	3144		3073		3073	
F-test	72.81		21.63		45.65	
Adj R².	0.064		0.069		0.068	

Dependent variable: ΔVA

*, ** and *** denote significance of coefficients at the 10%, 5% and 1%, respectively.

section, but also contributes additionally to firm-level TFP growth via superior organisation techniques, etc.

Other external spillover variables included in our specification of Model 2, such as export propensity and vertical innovation spillovers, do not seem to have any further impact on firm-level TFP growth. As was demonstrated in the previous section, it is very likely that these external knowledge spillovers only enhance the ability of the firm to innovate, but do not affect firm's TFP growth *per se*. We check for this by including the predicted value of innovation that we have estimated in the probit model of 'innovation production' (we take predicted values of Model 1 in Table 13.2). The effect of including this predicted innovation variable (see Model 3 in Table 13.3) is a somewhat higher estimate of the return to innovation (the estimate of γ increases to 0.83). But again, foreign ownership is shown to contribute additionally 5.1% to firm TFP growth.

According to the above findings, we can draw three important conclusions for Slovenian firms. First, firm-level own R&D expenditures as well as external knowledge spillovers, such as national and international public R&D subsidies, foreign ownership and intra-sector innovation spillovers, do enhance the ability of the firm to innovate. Second, innovations resulting from a firm's R&D seem to contribute substantially to firm-level total factor productivity growth. And third, foreign ownership has a dual impact on firm-level TFP growth — it enhances the ability of the firm to innovate, but then it also contributes additionally to TFP growth via superior organisation techniques, etc.

3.2. *Effect of innovation on productivity growth using nearest neighbour matching and average treatment effects*

The results presented above indicate that innovation and R&D expenditure may be of crucial importance as determinants of firm productivity dynamics. However, our approach so far has not controlled for the exact differences between innovative and non-innovative firms. In order to determine the actual effect that innovative activity has on firm productivity growth, we should estimate the effect of innovative activity on firm performance by comparing a sample of very similar firms. One way of doing this is to employ matching techniques to construct a controlled experiment. Using the propensity of firms to innovate, we match innovating firms with otherwise similar non-innovating firms to evaluate the importance of innovation on productivity growth.[4] In order to ascertain the probability of a given firm innovating, we run a probit regression similar to the one presented in Table 13.2:

$$\Pr(\text{INOV}_{it} = 1)$$
$$= \alpha + \beta_1 \text{INOV}_{it-2} + \beta_2 \text{Size}_{it} + \beta_3 \frac{rVA}{\text{Emp}_{it}} + \beta_4 \frac{RD}{\text{Sales}_{it}} + \beta_5 \frac{EX}{\text{Sales}_{it}} + \beta_6 \text{IFDI}_{it} + \varepsilon_{it}$$

(5)

Conditional on satisfying the balancing property of the propensity score, the fitted values obtained from estimating the above equation (probit estimation) are used to pair up innovators with non-innovators, and those matched pairs are subsequently used to estimate the average treatment effect of innovation on firm productivity growth. The balancing property ensures that once the observations have been stratified into blocks according to the propensity score, the right hand side variables of (5) do not differ significantly between the groups of treated and non-treated observations within a block. The more closely the firms are matched with respect to regressors in (5), the more likely it is that the observed productivity differences reflect the fact that some firms managed to innovate while others did not. We match innovating firms with their non-innovating counterparts using nearest neighbour matching (with random draws), which pairs up treated observations with the non-treated observations closest with respect to the

---

[4] Ideally, one would observe the same subject with and without the treatment action to pinpoint the impact of the treatment.

propensity score. Given that our sample size is very small in some instances, all the standard errors reported were generated by bootstrapping with 100 repetitions.

Tables 13.4–13.9 present the results of average treatment effects estimates of innovation on different specifications of growth in value added per employee. In each

Table 13.4. Growth in VA/Emp (difference in logs) two periods after innovation $(t + 2) - t$.

Firm size	Manufacturing (NACE 15–37)			Services (NACE 45–90)		
	ATT	SE	No. of obs. treatm. (control)	ATT	SE	No. of obs. treatm. (control)
Emp ≤ 50	−0.295	0.330	73 (19)	−0.045	0.199	49 (16)
50 < Emp ≤ 100	0.097	0.179	91 (20)	−0.325	0.384	8 (4)
100 < Emp ≤ 200	−0.034	0.233	105 (18)	−0.327***	0.119	6 (4)
Emp > 200	0.225	0.238	403 (71)	0.195	0.250	70 (28)

Note: ***,**,* denote statistical significance at 10%, 5% and 1% level. The number of observations is given in terms of both the number of treatment observations and the number of control observations (the latter is in parentheses). ATT = Average effect of treatment on the treated. SE = bootstrapped standard errors.

Table 13.5. Growth in VA/Emp (difference in logs) between two and four periods after innovation $(t + 4) - (t + 2)$.

Firm size	Manufacturing (NACE 15–37)			Services (NACE 45–90)		
	ATT	SE	No. of obs. treatm. (control)	ATT	SE	No. of obs. treatm. (control)
Emp ≤ 50	0.205	0.341	73 (7)	−0.068	0.327	49 (8)
50 < Emp ≤ 100	0.303	0.285	91 (14)	0.635	1.725	8 (1)
100 < Emp ≤ 200	0.150	0.240	105 (12)	0.150	0.489	6 (2)
Emp > 200	0.052	0.187	403 (54)	−0.324**	0.155	70 (14)

Note: As for Table 13.4.

Table 13.6. Growth in VA/Emp (difference in logs) two periods after innovation $(t + 2) - t$ [Process innovation].

Firm size	Manufacturing (NACE 15–37)			Services (NACE 45–90)		
	ATT	SE	No. of obs. treatm. (control)	ATT	SE	No. of obs. treatm. (control)
Emp ≤ 50	−0.174	0.130	73 (19)	−0.252	0.173	49 (16)
50 < Emp ≤ 100	−0.263	0.283	91 (20)	−0.639***	0.244	8 (4)
100 < Emp ≤ 200	0.031	0.067	105 (18)	−0.207	0.213	6 (4)
Emp > 200	0.065	0.072	403 (71)	−0.012	0.119	70 (28)

Note: As for Table 13.4.

Table 13.7. Growth in VA/Emp (difference in logs) between two and four periods after innovation $(t + 4) - (t + 2)$ [Process innovation].

Firm size	Manufacturing (NACE 15–37)			Services (NACE 45–90)		
	ATT	SE	No. of obs. treatm. (control)	ATT	SE	No. of obs. treatm. (control)
Emp ≤ 50	0.671**	0.316	73 (7)	−0.374*	0.230	49 (8)
50 < Emp ≤ 100	0.259	0.242	91 (14)	0.027	2.576	8 (1)
100 < Emp ≤ 200	0.087	0.097	105 (12)	0.041	0.220	6 (2)
Emp > 200	0.125	0.090	403 (54)	−0.305**	0.153	70 (14)

Note: As for Table 13.4.

Table 13.8. Growth in VA/Emp (difference in logs) two periods after innovation $(t + 2) - t$ [Product innovation].

Firm size	Manufacturing (NACE 15–37)			Services (NACE 45–90)		
	ATT	SE	No. of obs. treatm. (control)	ATT	SE	No. of obs. treatm. (control)
Emp ≤ 50	−0.118	0.515	73 (19)	0.076	0.280	49 (16)
50 < Emp ≤ 100	−0.009	0.223	91 (20)	−0.451	0.378	8 (4)
100 < Emp ≤ 200	−0.204	0.169	105 (18)	−0.002	0.188	6 (4)
Emp > 200.	0.033	0.076	403 (71)	0.163	0.275	70 (28)

Note: As for Table 13.4.

Table 13.9. Growth in VA/Emp (difference in logs) between two and four periods after innovation $(t + 4) - (t + 2)$ [Product innovation].

Firm size	Manufacturing (NACE 15–37)			Services (NACE 45–90)		
	ATT	SE	No. of obs. treatm. (control)	ATT	SE	No. of obs. treatm. (control)
Emp ≤ 50	0.300	0.232	73 (19)	0.151	2.859	49 (8)
50 < Emp ≤ 100	0.269	0.266	91 (20)	0.432	0.364	8 (1)
100 < Emp < 200	0.126	0.100	105 (18)	−0.260	0.265	6 (2)
Emp > 200	0.014	0.319	403 (71)	−0.463***	0.038	70 (14)

Note: As for Table 13.4.

of the tables, we differentiate between manufacturing and services firms and take explicit account of firm size classes. Table 13.4 presents the average treatment effects of innovation on labour productivity growth in the first two years after the innovation was introduced.

$$\text{growth}[(t+2)-t] = \ln\left(\frac{VA}{\text{Emp}}\right)_{t+2} - \ln\left(\frac{VA}{\text{Emp}}\right)_t \qquad (6)$$

At this stage, we do not discriminate between product and process innovation.

Contrary to expectations, no significant positive effects of innovation on labour productivity growth are revealed in Table 13.4. Moreover, service firms with between 100 and 200 employees even experienced a significant negative 'treatment' effect of innovation on labour productivity growth. Given the very small number of actual respondents in that cohort of services firms, one should not put too much emphasis on this result, as it may be driven by specific circumstances in one or two of the firms in question. These factors may not be adequately controlled for within our propensity score specification. The other possible issue driving the results is that we are not capturing the real growth period. It may take longer than two years after the initial innovation for firms to internalise all its benefits. To control for this issue, we redefined productivity growth so that we explore the growth in labour productivity between the second and fourth year after the innovation:

$$\text{growth}[(t+4)-(t+2)] = \ln\left(\frac{VA}{\text{Emp}}\right)_{t+4} - \ln\left(\frac{VA}{\text{Emp}}\right)_{t+2} \qquad (7)$$

Table 13.5 presents estimates of the average treatment effect of innovation on labour productivity growth between the second and fourth years after the innovation was initially made. By changing the period of observation, we hope to capture effects of innovation on productivity that were not apparent in the first two years after the moment of innovation. As before, however, we see that innovating firms do not grow significantly faster (in terms of productivity) than comparable non-innovating firms. And as before, we observe a significant negative effect of innovation in the case of large service firms.

In order further to disentangle the cause of this lack of evidence on the effects of innovation on productivity growth, we opt for a more specific definition of innovation, by explicitly discriminating between product and process innovations — see Tables 13.6–13.9. Namely, Parisi, Schiantarelli and Sembenelli (2006) find that process innovations significantly impacted on the productivity growth of Italian firms in the late 1990s, while product innovations had a much less significant effect. Tables 13.6 and 13.7 present estimates of the average treatment effect of process innovation on labour productivity growth. It should be noted that the change in the definition of innovation has to be reflected in the propensity score specification in Eq. (7). In this case, the propensity score actually represents the probability of producing a new or improved production process.

In the event, results do not differ substantially from those presented for innovation as a whole so there is, again, little evidence of innovations positively affecting productivity growth. As with the previous case, most of the estimates are not significantly different from zero, and in some instances innovating service firms actually grew slower than their non-innovating counterparts.

Finally, we present results using product innovation as the treatment indicator (Tables 13.8 and 13.9), and find that this makes hardly any difference, as the results fail to yield any indication of a significantly positive effect of innovation on firm productivity growth. Again, the only somewhat robust finding is the slower productivity growth of larger service firms that innovated compared with those that did not.

Possible reasons for the lack of results may be that the effects of innovation are not adequately captured by labour productivity; perhaps total factor productivity should have been used instead. Additionally, our productivity proxy fails to control for contemporaneous growth in inputs which may conceal the actual productivity dynamics. Finally, perhaps an even longer period of observation is needed to observe the complete spectrum of innovation effects.

4. Conclusions

The objective of this chapter has been to analyse the link between factors determining the ability of firms to innovate, and, in particular, the subsequent impact of innovation on productivity growth. We analyse the impact of innovation on firm-level productivity growth using firm-level innovation (CIS) and financial data for a large sample of Slovenian firms for 1996–2002. Two different methods, simple OLS and matching techniques are used to check for the robustness of the results. We also distinguish between product and process innovations.

In the first part we estimate the importance of internal and external sources of innovation and evaluate their impact on productivity growth. Own R&D expenditures and past innovation activity — treated as variables of internal sources — are consistently confirmed as significant determinants of innovation activity. However, they turn out to be much more efficient when accompanied by diffusion of knowledge from outside sources. External knowledge spillovers, whether domestic or international, are thus found to be important and innovation-enhancing. R&D subsidies, both domestic and from international sources, and intra-sectoral innovation spillovers, complement internal sources and significantly increase the ability of Slovenian firms to innovate. Inward FDI also significantly increases the ability to innovate. Exporting, on the other hand, was not found to be an important spur to innovation.

In the second part, we explore the relationship between innovation activity and the performance of firms, applying various empirical approaches. While in applying a simple OLS we find some evidence of positive impact of innovation on productivity growth, these results are not confirmed when we use the alternative empirical approach of matching techniques (average treatment effects). Matching techniques produce no conclusive evidence that more innovative firms have higher productivity growth. Some recent research suggests that product and process innovation may have opposite impact on employment levels, and thus differentially affect labour productivity in innovating firms. For Slovenian firms, however, we find no divergent effects for the two groups of innovating firms.

References

Abraham, F., Konings, J. and Slootmaekers, V. (2006). 'FDI spillovers, firm heterogeneity and degree of ownership from Chinese manufacturing'. Leuven, Catholic University Leuven, mimeo.

Aghion, P. and Howitt, P. (1992). 'A model of growth through creative destruction', *Econometrica* 60: 323–351.

Aghion, P. and Howitt, P. (1998). *Endogenous Growth Theory*. Cambridge, MA, MIT Press.

Aitken, B.J. and Harrison, A.E. (1999). 'Do domestic firms benefit from direct foreign investments? Evidence from Venezuela', *American Economic Review* 89: 605–618.

Alverez, I., Damijan, J.P. and Knell, M. (2002). 'Do Spanish firms get technology through FDI and trade?', Madrid, University of Madrid, mimeo.

Arrow, K. (1962). 'Economic welfare and the allocation of resources to invention', in Nelson, R. (ed.), *The Rate and Direction of Inventive Activity*. Princeton, Princeton University Press, pp. 609–625.

Audretsch, D.B. (1998). 'Agglomeration and the location of innovative activity' *Oxford Review of Economic Policy* 14: 18–29.

Barry, F., Görg, H. and Strobl, E. (2002). 'Productivity spillovers and labour-market crowding out: Interactions between foreign and domestic firms in Irish manufacturing', Dublin, University College Dublin, mimeo.

Ben Hamida, L. and Gugler, P. (2007). 'FDI and spillovers in Switzerland: Interaction effects between spillover mechanisms and domestic technological capabilities', Fribourg, University of Fribourg, Department of Economics, mimeo.

Blalock, G. (2001). 'Technology from foreign direct investment: Strategic transfer through supply chains', Berkeley, University of California, mimeo.

Blomström, M.F. and Sjöholm, F. (1999). 'Technology transfer and spillovers: Does local participation with multinationals matter?', *European Economic Review* 43: 915–923.

Blomström, M. and Wolff, E. (1994). 'Multinational corporations and productivity convergence in Mexico', in Baumol, W., Nelson, R. and Wolff, E. (eds.), *Convergence of Productivity: Cross-National Studies and Historical Evidence*, Oxford, Oxford University Press, pp. 263–284.

Borensztein, E., De Gregorio, J. and Lee, J.W. (1998). 'How does foreign direct investment affect economic growth?', *Journal of International Economics* 45: 115–135.

Branstetter, L. (1996). 'Are knowledge spillovers international or intranational in scope? Microeconometric evidence from the U.S and Japan', *NBER Working Paper Series, Working Paper 5800*. Cambridge, MA, National Bureau of Economic Research.

Busom, I. (2000). 'An empirical evaluation of the effects of R&D subsidies' *Economics of Innovation and New Technology* 9(2): 111–148.

Cameron, Proudman, G.J. and Redding, S. (2003). 'Technological convergence, R&D, trade and productivity growth', *European Economic Review* 49(3): 775–807.

Clerides, S., Lach, S. and Tybout, J. (1998). 'Is learning-by-exporting important? Microdynamic evidence from Colombia, Mexico and Morocco', *Quarterly Journal of Economics* 113: 903–947.

Coe, D. and Helpman, E. (1995). 'International R&D spillovers', *European Economic Review* 9: 859–887.

Coe, D., Helpman, E. and Hoffmaister, A. (1997). 'North-south R&D spillovers', *Economic Journal* 107: 134–149.

Cohen, W. and Levinthal, D (1989). 'Innovation and learning: The two faces of R&D', *Economic Journal* 99: 569–596.

Crépon, B., Duguet, E. and Mairesse, J. (1998). 'Research, innovation, and productivity: An econometric analysis at the firm level', *NBER Working Paper Series, Working Paper 6696*, Cambridge, MA, National Bureau of Economic Research.

Damijan, J.P., Knell, M., Majcen, B and Rojec, M. (2003). 'Technology transfer through FDI in top-10 transition countries: How important are direct effects, horizontal and vertical spillovers?', *William Davidson Working Paper Number 549*, Ann Arbor, The William Davidson Institute at the University of Michigan Business School.

David, P.A., Hall, B.H. and Toole, A.A. (1999). 'Is public R&D a complement or a substitute to private R&D? A review of the econometric evidence', *NBER Working Paper Series, Working Paper 7373*, Cambridge, MA, National Bureau of Economic Research.

Djankov, S. and Hoekman, B. (2000). 'Foreign investment and productivity growth in Czech enterprises', *World Bank Economic Review* 14(1): 49–64.

Eaton, J. and Kortum, S. (1996). 'Trade in ideas: Patenting and productivity in the OECD' *Journal of International Economics* 40: 251–271.

Eaton, J. and Kortum, S. (1999). 'International patenting and technology diffusion: Theory and measurement', *International Economic Review* 40: 537–570.

Eaton, J. and Kortum, S. (2001). 'Trade in capital goods', *European Economic Review* 45: 1195–1235.

Fagerberg, J. (2005). 'Innovation: A guide to the literature', in Fagerberg, J., Mowery, D.C. and Nelson, R.R. (eds.), *The Oxford Handbook of Innovation*. Oxford, Oxford University Press.

Feenstra, R., Markusen, J. and Zeile, W. (1992). 'Accounting for growth with new inputs: Theory and evidence', *American Economic Review* 82: 415–421.

Girma, S., Gong, Y. and Görg, H. (2006). 'Can you teach old dragons new tricks? FDI and innovation activity in Chinese state-owned enterprises', Nottingham, University of Nottingham, mimeo.

Girma, S., Greenaway, D. and Wakelin, K. (2001). 'Who benefits from foreign direct investment in the UK?', *Scottish Journal of Political Economy* 48: 119–133.

Girma, S. and Wakelin, K. (2002). 'Are there regional spillovers from FDI in the UK?', in Greenaway, D., Upward, R. and Wakelin, K. (eds.), *Trade, Investment, Migration and Labour Markets*, Basingstoke, Macmillan, pp. 172–186.

Gőrg, H. and Greenaway, D. (2004). 'Much ado about nothing: Do domestic firms really benefit from foreign direct investment?', *World Bank Research Observer* 19: 171–197.

Gorodnichenko, Y., Svejnar, J. and Terrell, K. (2006). 'Vertical and horizontal FDI spillovers in transition economies: Do institutions matter?', mimeo.

Griffith, R., Redding, S. and Simpson, H. (2004). 'Foreign ownership and productivity: New evidence from the service sector and the R&D lab', *CEP Discussion Paper No 649*, London, Centre for Economic Performance, London School of Economics and Political Science.

Griliches, Z. (1979). 'Issues in assessing the contribution of R&D to productivity growth', *Bell Journal of Economics* 10: 92–116.

Griliches, Z. (1980). 'Returns to R&D expenditures in the private sector', in Kendrick, K. and Vaccara, B. (eds.), *New Developments in Productivity Measurement*. Chicago, Chicago University Press.

Griliches, Z. (1992). 'The search for R&D spillovers', *Scandinavian Journal of Economics* 94: 29–47.

Griliches, Z. (1998). *R&D and Productivity*, Chicago, University of Chicago Press.

Griliches, Z. and Lichtenberg, F. (1984). 'R&D and productivity growth at the industry level: Is there still a relationship?', in Griliches, Z. (ed.), R&D, Patents and Productivity, Chicago, NBER and Chicago University Press, pp. 465–496.

Grossman, G. and Helpman, E. (1991). *Innovation and Growth in the World Economy*, Cambridge, MA, MIT Press.

Haddad, M. and Harrison, A. (1993). 'Are there positive spillovers from direct foreign investments? Evidence from panel data for Morocco', *Journal of Development Economics* 42: 51–74.

Hall, B. and Mairesse, J. (1995). 'Exploring the relationship between R&D and productivity in French manufacturing firms', *Journal of Econometrics* 65: 263–294.

Halpern, L. and Murakozy, B. (2007). 'Does distance matter in spillover?', *The Economics of Transition* 15: 781–805.

Jacobs, J. (1993). *The Economy of Cities*, New York, Random House.

Keller, W. (2000). 'Do trade patterns and technology flows affect productivity growth?', *World Bank Economic Review* 14: 17–47.

Keller, W. (2002a). 'Geographical localization of international technology diffusion', *American Economic Review* 92: 120–142.

Keller, W. (2002b). 'Trade and the transmission of technology', *Journal of Economic Growth* 7: 5–24.

Keller, W. (2004). 'International technology diffusion', University of Texas, National Bureau of Economic Research, Centre for Economic Policy Research, mimeo.

Keller, W. and Yeaple, S.R. (2003). 'Multinational enterprises, international trade, and productivity growth: Firm level evidence from the United States', *NBER Working Paper Series, Working Paper 9504*, Cambridge, MA, National Bureau of Economic Research.

Kinoshita, Y. (2000). 'R&D and technology spillovers via FDI: Innovation and absorptive capacity', CERGE-EI, Prague, mimeo.

Klette, T.J. and Moen, J. (1997). 'R&D investment responses to R&D Subsidies: A theoretical analysis and microeconomic study', mimeo.

Klomp, L. and van Leeuwen, G. (2001). 'Linking innovation and firm performance: A new approach', *International Journal of the Economics of Business* 8: 343–364.

Konings, J. (2001). 'The effects of foreign direct investment on domestic firms: Evidence from firm level panel data in emerging economies' *CEPR Discussion Paper 2586*, London.

Kraay, A., Soloaga, I. And Tybout, J. (2001). 'Product, quality, productive effciency, and international technology diffusion: Evidence from plant-level panel data', *Paper presented at* The NBER Summer Institute.

Kugler, M. (2006). 'Spillovers from foreign direct investment: Within or between industries?', *Journal of Development Economics* 80: 444–477.

Lach, S. (2000). 'Do R&D subsidies stimulate or displace private R&D? Evidence from Israel', *NBER Working Paper Series, Working Paper 7043*, Cambridge, MA, National Bureau of Economic Research.

Lumenga-Neso, O., Olarreaga, M. and Schiff, M. (2001). 'On "indirect" trade-related R&D spillovers', The World Bank, Washington, DC, mimeo.

Mairesse, J. and Sassenou, M. (1991). 'R&D productivity: A survey of econometric studies at the firm level', *NBER Working Paper Series, Working Paper 3666*, Cambridge, MA, National Bureau of Economic Research.

Mansfield, E. and Romero, M. (1980). 'Technology transfer to overseas subsidiaries by U.S. based firms', *Quarterly Journal of Economics* 95: 737–750.

Meyer, K. and Sinani, E. (2005). 'Spillovers from foreign direct investment: A meta-analysis', *Working Paper*, Department of Economics, University of Reading, Reading.

Nelson, R.R. (1959). 'The simple economics of basic scientific research' *The Journal of Political Economy* 7: 297–306.

Parisi, M.L., Schiantarelli, F. and Sembenelli, A. (2006). 'Productivity, innovation and R&D: Micro evidence for Italy', *European Economic Review* 50: 2037–2061.

Perez, T. (1998). *Multinational Enterprises and Technological Spillovers*, Amsterdam, Harwood Academic Publishers.

Romer, P. (1990). 'Endogenous Technological Change', *Journal of Political Economy* 98: S71–S102.

Schoors, K. and van der Tol, B. (2001). 'The productivity effect of foreign ownership on domestic firms in Hungary', Gent, University of Gent, mimeo.

Sgard, J. (2001). 'Direct foreign investments and productivity growth in Hungarian firms, 1992–1999', *Document de Travail No 01.19* (Decembre), Paris, CEPII — Centre d'etudes prospectives et d'informations internationals.

Smarzynska-Javorcik, B.K. (2004). 'Does foreign direct investment increase the productivity of domestic firms? In search of spillovers through backward linkages', *American Economic Review* 94: 605–662.

Smarzynska, B.K. (2003). 'Does foreign direct investment increase the productivity of domestic firms? In search of spillovers through backward linkages'. *William Davidson Working Paper Number 548 (March)*, Ann Arbor, The William Davidson Institute at the University of Michigan Business School.

Smolny, W. (2000). *Endogenous Innovations and Knowledge Spillovers*, Heidelberg, Physica-Verlag.

Solow, R.M. (1956). 'A contribution to the theory of economic growth', *Quarterly Journal of Economics* 70: 65–94.

UNCTAD (2000). *World Investment Report 2000*, New York and Geneva, United Nations.

Xu, B. and Wang, J. (1999). 'Capital goods trade and R&D spillovers in the OECD', *Canadian Journal of Economics* 32: 1258–1274.

Wagner, J. (2007). 'Exports and productivity: A survey of the evidence from firm-level data', *The World Economy* 30(1): 60–82.

Wallsten, S.J. (2000). 'The effects of government-industry R&D programs on private R&D: The case of the DSmall Business Innovation Research Program', *Rand Journal of Economics*, Spring.

Appendix

Table 13.A1. The probability of firms innovating products and processes in Slovenia, 1996–2002 (Results of a probit model).

	Product innovation				Process innovation			
	1		2		3		4	
	Coef.	z	Coef.	z	Coef.	z	Coef.	z
INOV_t-2	1.136	18.5	1.137	18.5	0.868	13.1	0.866	13.1
Size	0.438	9.9	0.442	10.0	0.532	12.1	0.531	12.0
rVA/Emp	0.003	0.4	0.003	0.4	0.007	1.0	0.007	1.0
R&D/Sales	18.842	18.0	19.217	18.4	18.489	17.4	18.504	17.5
Total sub./R&D	4.413	6.9			2.851	7.3		
Public sub./R&D			5.115	6.4			3.268	6.2
Foreign sub./R&D			4.771	2.5			2.273	3.5
IFDI	0.146	2.4	0.140	2.3	0.106	1.7	0.103	1.7
EX/Sales	0.241	2.8	0.228	2.6	0.175	2.0	0.171	1.9
HS_INOV	0.007	3.4	0.008	3.4	0.011	5.0	0.011	5.1
VS_INOV	−0.008	−1.5	−0.008	−1.5	0.002	0.3	0.001	0.3
ML tech	−0.030	−0.3	−0.035	−0.4	−0.206	−2.1	−0.214	−2.2
MH tech	0.144	1.5	0.135	1.4	−0.150	−1.5	−0.158	−1.6
H tech	0.188	1.6	0.177	1.5	−0.184	−1.6	−0.183	−1.6
Const.	−2.426	−19.8	−2.424	−19.8	−2.612	−21.2	−2.596	−21.2
Number of obs	4166		4166		4166		4166	
LR chi^2(12)	1931.6		1938.3		1536.4		1527.5	
Prob > chi^2	0.00		0.00		0.00		0.00	
Pseudo R^2	0.438		0.440		0.382		0.380	

Dependent variable: INOV$_t$.

CHAPTER 14

THE IMPACT OF TECHNOLOGY ON SKILLS IN ESTONIAN WOOD-BASED INDUSTRIES[1]

KADRI UKRAINSKI

1. Introduction

The impact of rapidly changing technology on employment, skills and wages has interested researchers for many years, but there is no consensus on the direction and the magnitude of the impact. Earlier studies claimed that technology is leading to the 'de-skilling' of workers, meaning that an automated factory would replace skilled workers with workers who perform simple repetitive tasks (Edwards, 1979). Braverman (1974) argued that new technologies would raise skill levels initially but lead to deskilling later. Recent works, however, show that modern technologies are generally biased towards more skilled workers. There is a range of empirical research on this matter (see the reviews in Handel, 2003; Machin, 2004; and Chennells and Van Reenen, 1999). The empirical research has been conducted mostly at industry level, and the case studies and sector-specific analyses have been limited in range. The results show that across the same industries in different countries the proportions of skilled workers has increased despite generally rising (or stable) relative wages (Machin, 2004). The case studies reviewed in Handel (2003), covering manufacturing and services, show that 'technological change works mostly in the direction of skill upgrading, but the magnitude of these effects is unclear and may be gradual enough that their impacts are easily absorbed' (Handel, 2003, 69). Chennels and Van Reenen (1999) and Handel (2003) accordingly highlight the research gap in terms of both methodology and empirical evidence concerning the impact of technology on skills.

Great sectoral diversity regarding the sources and modes of technological change (see the review of studies in Peneder, 2003) would mean that sectoral evidence could differ regarding the effects of specific technologies on jobs and skills in the particular context. As far as the wood industries are concerned,[2] the pattern has been one of

---

[1] In addition to the EU 6th FP *U-Know* Project, this research has been supported by ESF Grants 6853 and Estonian Ministry of Education and Research Target Funding SF0180037s08.

[2] In this paper, 'wood industries' covers forestry, the wood-processing industry, and the paper and furniture industries.

applying advanced technologies and innovating continuously, while at the same time having quite low R&D expenditures and relatively low educational levels in the work force. As a result, they have been classified among 'low-tech' industries.[3]

The basic technologies and practices in the wood-based industries seem to have undergone no drastic changes in recent times. New developments are mainly connected with the use of new ICT-based solutions in timber processing and logistics, widening applications of chemical engineering to structural analysis and modification of durability of wood, but also new combinations of composites, polymers and wood for use in construction. The Estonian wood sector has experienced even more extensive changes in technologies in recent years as it has emerged from the backwardness engendered by the Soviet regime. The main developments include modern mechanised timber harvesting systems, improved sawmill, wood panel and paper technology, and changes in the mode of construction of wooden houses and in technologies for making windows. Some less dramatic technological upgrading has occurred also in the furniture industry. Behind these changes lies the export demand that these industries are meeting; a significant part of the technological upgrading has occurred through FDI.

The aim of this chapter is to find out how these rapid changes in technology have altered the demand for labour demand by skill types and levels in the Estonian wood sector. The chapter opens with an analysis of the general development of technologies in wood-based sectors, and the related impact on the demand for skills. Thereafter, measurement issues relating to technology and skills are discussed. We then analyse Estonian wood sectors with a view to identifying changes in technology and skill patterns. In the final sections the results are discussed, conclusions drawn, and policy implications assessed.

2. Changes in Technology in Wood-Based Industries

There seem at first sight to have been no radical changes in wood technology over recent decades. For example, in forestry, tree harvesters and forwarders with automated control systems have been generally employed since the early 1990s (Blombäck *et al.*, 2003). The first walking harvester was produced in 1995, and was in use in harvesting in Germany by 1997. In 2000, the combination of harvester and forwarder functions in one machine (harwarder) was achieved (Kurvits, 2003). In the wood-processing industry, log sawmilling, computerised scheduling, and multiple circular saws and edgers for the processing of small-sized logs, were introduced already in the 1980s (ILO, 2001, 49). Advanced pulp and paper mills with digital process control of almost all of the production parameters, and with very low labour

---

[3] The problem of this misleading classification has been raised by several authors studying wood-related sectors: (Hirsch-Kreinsen *et al.*, 2003; Laestadius, 1998a, 1998b; Palmberg, 2002).

participation in the process, have been used since the 1960s (Laestadius, 2000). Computer-aided manufacturing systems (CAM), design systems (CAD) and automated coating systems have also gone through only minor changes recently. Rather than radical changes, there have been constant incremental improvements of technological processes in the sectors under consideration. The analysis of case studies in Palmberg (2002) reveals a very close interrelationship between product and process innovation. He finds that in the glue-lam timber industry incremental innovations related to sawing, gluing and jointing techniques have added important new characteristics to the end product. The same results are shown by Laestadius (2000) for pulp and paper industry technologies. However, these incremental changes in products and processes have been based on recent advances in a range of 'high-tech' sectors. The cases where technological advances in other industries have been used to develop technologies in the wood sector are brought together in Table 14.1.

As can be seen from the table, the underlying technological advances are connected with chemical and mechanical engineering, but also with biotechnology and ICT. The latter covers a remarkably wide range of technologies used in the wood sector. As discussed by Schienstock *et al.* (1998, 25), modern ICTs have a wide range of roles to play: they can function as tools, automation technologies and control devices; as organisational strategies and technologies; as a medium connecting machines and people; and finally as a process to be developed. ICTs are general purpose technologies (GPTs) — they introduce radical changes into many other technologies, and are also generally seen as complements to more skilled labour (see also Murphy, Riddell and Romer, 1998). Alternatively, ICTs can be considered as

Table 14.1. Examples of technological advance in the wood sector.

Underlying technological advance	Technology used in wood sector	Motives and results for wood sector
Mechanical, electronic engineering	Automation and control systems, valves, transmission systems, pumps, dryers for pulp and paper mills etc.	To develop new machine concepts, components, systems, equipment, tools aimed at optimising costs and improving environmental performance
Chemical engineering	Chemical modification of wood, fibre etc.	New conversion techniques
	Development of paints, adhesives etc.	New application concepts
		New/improved qualities of products
Biotechnology	Genetically modified wood	Better handling (storage, transportation)
	Enzymes for bleaching processes	Higher product quality, some cost-cutting
ICT	Application software (GIS etc.)	Increased use of scale-economy processes
	Production systems (CNC, CAM etc.)	Optimised service functions (KIBS, including logistics, e-commerce)

Source: Author's compilation, based on Pavitt (2005).

pervasive technologies embracing a wide range of particular technologies, each of which can be viewed as a GPT (as in Freeman and Perez, 1988).

Traditionally, the pace of advance in the technological development of the various sectors in the economy are assessed through R&D intensities. In forest industries, the R&D intensity, and the related educational level of employees, is relatively low. The markets where wood sector firms operate are classed as very competitive ones, where technology and innovation are only weakly appropriable, because in many cases the products are relatively easy to imitate, at least at first sight (Palmberg, 2002, 25). The low R&D levels in these sectors are to some extent explained by depleted technological opportunities and saturated markets. Most of the research for these industries is done by other sectors, like equipment manufacturers or biotechnology firms. Often those firms are highly specialised, concentrated, and operate worldwide (for example, harvester and forwarder producers or paper mill equipment producers), so they make the latest technology available everywhere (ILO, 2001, 50). State-of-the-art technology is generally diffused to developing and transition countries by FDI — but not always. In the literature (e.g. ILO, 2001) there are examples of large firms in developing countries that do well without that kind of help from foreign capital.

Additional to the process technologies used in production, many larger and more specialised firms in the forest, wood and paper industries are gradually converting to e-commerce, because there are some real gains to be made here in terms of production and distribution costs through improved planning and management of procurement processes, transport and storage. Deeper analysis for all different kind of knowledge-intensive business services (KIBS) in the Finnish wood sector is given in Viitamo (2003).

To sum up on technological change, one can say that today's forest, wood and paper sectors represent a knowledge-intensive sector that continuously uses the latest developments in information and communication technology, process control and environmental technology to respond to demand in terms of properties and function, but also new applications and solutions. All these technological changes have been the result of gradual improvement in technology, but have had strong impacts on employment (ILO, 2001, 49).

3. Demand for Skills in the Wood-Based Industries

Wood-based industries are rarely analysed from the skills perspective; the attention has always been focused more on the job losses caused by the efficiency gains of technological change. However, many technologies used in wood-based industries overlap in general terms with other manufacturing industries (CAM, computer numerically controlled [CNC], chemical process technologies like pumping, drying and other technologies). So let us look at some relevant studies concerning other manufacturing industries.

Authors analysing the demand for different skills and competencies have concluded that, since the 1970s, the required level of skills in manufacturing has risen constantly (Berman *et al.*, 1998). This reflects not only upgrading of skill levels, but also changes in types of skills needed. It is associated with the development of technology and emergence of flexible production systems, but at the same time with the globalisation of production and marketing. Different levels of industrial development and competitiveness require more diverse and changing skills. In general, the more advanced an economy is, the greater and more diverse are its human capital needs (Lall, 1999, 20).

The ability of firms in a given sector to take in outside knowledge and technology is denoted as absorptive capacity (Cohen and Levinthal, 1989, 1990). This capacity includes, from the one side, basic skills of employees, but also broader knowledge of modern scientific and technological developments. Since technological learning entails a great deal of learning by doing (producing) and learning by using (the technology or materials), the capacity to adapt and improve technology is as important as the capacity to absorb. As discussed by Helpman and Rangel (1999) and Caselli (1999), skilled workers generate lower costs in terms of use of new machines than unskilled, and therefore new machines are more likely to be assigned to skilled workers, who will further increase their productivity and hence the demand for skilled workers. The adoption of new technology is hence easier for skilled workers. However, the increase in demand for skilled workers during the adoption process will disappear as the implementation of the technology is completed (Chum, 2003).

A significant role in the above-described technological processes is played by so-called 'technological gatekeepers' within the firm (Klobas and McGill, 1995). They may be appointed individuals with formal dissemination responsibilities, influential persons in the firm or 'gatekeepers', recognised as experts to whom others can turn to for reliable information. They are the key persons within the firm with the personal ability to translate and disseminate relevant external scientific or technological knowledge throughout the firm. In the literature, these gatekeepers have quite high status; they have a supervisory role *vis-à-vis* product and process development, as well as a long employment history with extensive contacts within the firm (Palmberg, 2002, 30). The role of such gatekeepers is often crucial for technological development of the sectors not having high shares of technically skilled workers, since the gatekeepers are able to obtain necessary knowledge from outside the firm through networks. In wood-based industries, the most important role of gatekeepers could hence be seen in terms of adapting new technologies and facilitating the process and product innovation through networks of suppliers, customers, but also research institutions.

There is a kind of technological capability that is especially relevant to firms in 'low-tech' industries. This is the ability, sometimes called architectural capability, to introduce new combinations of existing technologies (see Henderson and Clark, 1990). Competitive markets force companies to be very creative in running and readjusting their machinery and equipment. Laestadius (1998a) discusses the issue through the example of the pulp and paper industry. As shown by Laestadius (1995, 1998b) and Hirsch-Kreisner *et al.* (2003), this demands from firms different, non-R&D-based types of knowledge. This type of knowledge is tacit, and entails practical engineering problem-solving by engineers and technicians, but also shop-floor workers. Laestadius (1995) argues that such knowledge within the firm also supports innovation flowing from external sources to the firm (through collaboration with universities, R&D institutions or suppliers of machinery and equipment).

As discussed by Handel (2003, 1–2) computers in general, and through various production technology systems, influence skills in a variety of ways:

(1) IT may raise skill requirements through changing the content of existing jobs; the character of the job changes from manual/routine to a more conceptual/abstract set of tasks; therefore information becomes more decentralised, leading workers to take on more decision-making and problem-solving responsibilities previously carried out by more skilled workers.
(2) IT may increase overall skill levels by changing the occupational distribution of workers — increasing the share of high-skilled occupations (because IT requires more skilled workers to manage the technology itself (e.g. programmers, technicians, maintenance workers) or to analyse the information it generates); and by decreasing the share of less-skilled workers (because of automation).
(3) IT may change the occupational distribution across industries in favour of skilled workers in more skill-intensive manufacturing or service industries, even if the distribution within a given industry remains relatively unchanged.

Empirical studies of changes in specific technologies show that automated process control systems have upgraded general skill levels, because they have increased the share of skilled maintenance workers, specifically of electricians (Handel, 2003). Computerised process control systems have, on the other hand, increased skill demands within existing jobs. This is shown by Zuboff (1988) for pulp and paper industry operators. The rise in skill demands has been caused by the reintegration of tasks to other systems, the need for more conceptual understanding of the whole production process, and a higher level of responsibility for expensive equipment (Handel, 2003). CNC technology setup in the factories has demanded of machinists more problem-solving and conceptual skills (Giordano, 1992); they need quite often to correct unforeseen problems by implementing programming tasks beyond their traditional skills (a change towards multi-skilling). Kelley (1989, 303) found that about two-thirds of CNC-technology users had occasionally to perform some relatively simple programming responsibilities. Milkman and Pullman (1991, 140) found that process automation did decrease some skill requirements in manufacturing processes (like precision, concentration, judgement, memory, reading, maths and problem-solving) for low-skilled workers, but increased them for skilled workers.

Even where skill increase is identified as a requirement, the workers need relatively short training times to be able to handle these new technologies. The US Survey of Manufacturing Technology reviewed in Handel (2003) revealed that only 10% of surveyed plants reported the need for increased training activities due to advanced technology. As evidenced by Hunt and Hunt (1983, 121), experienced machine repairers and electricians require only three months' training to be able to handle robots they had never used and repaired before.

Additional impact of technology on skills can accrue via organisational changes. New technologies require new organisational structures (as shown by Caroli and van Reenen, 2001; and Aghion, Caroli and Garcia Peñalosa, 1999), reflecting the procedures governing how innovative activities and production activities are organised at the firm level. In the literature, it is argued that the introduction of new organisational structures and management practices has required more skilled employees. For example, Dickerson and Green (2004) show the growth of a wide spectrum of different generic and specific skills used in workplaces in the US and Canada.

Not much work has been done in relation specifically to the skill needs of the wood sector. Using general analysis for other manufacturing sectors, however, we can summarise in Table 14.2 the skills that are becoming increasingly necessary as a result of the technological and organisational changes that have been reviewed in this section.

Stemming from the increased need for skilled workers, as reported to the European Parliament in 2000 (but also in more recent documents), skilled labour shortage could become a major impediment and threat to the competitiveness of the wood-based industries in the future. There are many issues underlying this development — as higher requirements for skills makes recruitment more difficult for companies around Europe, the intensive competition in wood markets is narrowing the scope for paying higher wages. We return to this issue later.

Table 14.2. Increased skill requirements and underlying changes in wood technology.

Skills, knowledge, qualifications	Underlying changes in wood technology
Theoretical knowledge	Work as a process of problem-solving
Technical (digital) knowledge	Introduction of modern ICT, use of CAM, CNC technologies
Practical, tacit knowledge	Increased uncertainty and competition, risk situations caused by technical integration, architectural capabilities important for combining existing technologies with new ones
Professional skills (multi-skilling)	Integration of tasks of operators, de-specialisation, group work
International skills	Globalisation of technology and markets, wide use of state-of-the-art imported technology
Social skills	Direct interaction within and between work groups, customisation, direct interaction with (foreign) suppliers/customers
Management skills (information and technology management)	Flat hierarchies, decentralisation, increased information exchange

Source: Author's elaboration of Schienstock *et al.* (1999).

4. Data and Methods

There are number of problems related to the empirical assessment of both technology and skills. In empirical analysis technological changes cannot be captured by simple and uniform variables, and therefore a wide range of proxies are used. Three main groups of variables are used in industry-level studies to describe technological changes: R&D activities, patents and technology diffusion measures such as the use of computers in a firm (see the review in Handel, 2003). However, most of these measures also capture other effects, and therefore include potential biases. These biases arise because of conceptual problems, but are also due to pure measurement issues. The potential biases, according to Sanders and ter Weel (2000), arise first of all from the difficulty in capturing the effects of learning from production technology (learning by doing) and the unresponsiveness (in the short and medium term) of skill supply to wage signals. Additionally, innovation (especially process innovation) is by nature skill-biased endogenously, because high-skilled labour is more likely to identify and implement possible improvements in processes and products. Bearing in mind all these problems, a variety of statistical measures are used to identify technological change in this study.

First, in order to analyse the dynamics of technological advances at the sectoral level, the aggregated time-series data from the Statistical Office of Estonia (2008) and the UN Commodity Trade Statistics (2006) are used. The data include the investments of Estonian companies in transportation machinery and computers, and also import data on selected commodity groups like paper mill machinery or pressers for particle-board. Those data are aggregated at the sectoral level, but their weakness for current purposes is that the novelty of technology is not directly measurable from them, and the numbers of firms that have invested in technology are not identifiable.

In order to analyse whether the technology utilised is new to the firm, the surveys 'Innovation in Estonian Enterprises 1998–2000' and 'Innovation in Estonian Enterprises 2002–2004'[4] are used. Here, only wood processing, paper and furniture manufacturing enterprises are included, and hence the samples consist, respectively, of just 335 and 216 companies. New technology is understood in these data as process innovation involving additionally organisational changes.

Palmberg (2002) showed that often innovation stems from changes in technologies leading to changes in products; for the analysis, wood sector companies are accordingly grouped as following:

(1) Firms that did not undertake product and/or process innovation (in the respective surveys 66.6% and 47.2% of the sample),

---

[4] These surveys are generally known as Community Innovation Survey 3 and 4 (CIS3 and CIS4), because they are based on the methodology developed by the European Commission and Eurostat.

(2) Firms that implemented process innovation without product innovation (9.3% and 14.4% of the sample),
(3) Firms that implemented product innovations without process innovation (10.1% and 14.8% of the sample) and
(4) Firms that implemented both process and product innovation (14% and 23.6% of the sample).

This distribution of firms enables us to study the behaviour of skill indicators in those companies which actually made significant changes in their technologies. The disadvantage of the approach lies in the rather short period covered by the data, and hence lack of dynamic analysis, but also in missing opportunities to address the causality issue.

In addition to process innovation, expenditures on R&D (both internal and external), share of total expenditure on equipment and machinery (including computer hardware), share of total expenditure on obtaining patents, licences, trademarks, software and other sources of external knowledge are included, because those indicators are often taken as proxies for technological change in other studies, and can shed some light on potential problems and probabilities for selected variables describing technological upgrading.

For the measurement of skills, two broad groups of indicators are usually used: occupation- and education-based measures. The problem with both measures lies in an excessive level of generalisation — belonging to the elementary occupations category does not necessarily mean having a low level of skill, and belonging to the highly educated group does not mean being employed in a job that demands high skills. There have also been attempts to divide up different aspects of job content and task complexity, but usually those studies are not comparable across time and different countries (see Wolff, 1997).

In this study, aggregate occupational and educational data from Estonian Labour Force Surveys based on ILO methodology[5] and covering the period of 1989–2007 are used. The surveys are representative for all sectors under discussion except for the paper industry, where in some years (1993–1999) the sub-sample covered fewer than 20 residents. The occupational profiles are described in terms of ISCO-88 occupational groups[6] and ISCED-97 educational levels.[7] Both of these indicators are generally used to denote skill levels, whereby it is assumed that higher levels of education are appropriate for groups of occupations demanding higher skills. However, this

---

[5] Fore a detailed description of this survey see Labour Force Survey... (2004).
[6] Includes the following occupational groups: legislators, senior officials and managers; professionals; technicians and associate professionals; clerks; service workers and shop and market sales workers; skilled workers; craft and related workers; plant and machine operators and assemblers; elementary occupations.
[7] The ISCED-97 level I comprises basic level of education or lower (with no vocational education); level II comprises primary education with vocational education, and level III post-secondary vocational education and also tertiary education.

link is not straightforward,[8] and therefore changes in occupation and education are examined separately.

These aggregated data show general trends, but they do not pick out technologically dynamic companies. Therefore indicators from the CIS surveys are added, to help us connect skill data with technological change. Data available in CIS3 cover the share of R&D specialists, the share of other specialists with ISCED third level education, and the share of training expenses in total sales, as indicating the resources dedicated to general upgrading of skills (not necessarily directly related to the use of technology) at the firm level. Unfortunately, these indicators were left out of the Estonian CIS4 survey.

Earlier studies have found that skill requirements and job content have been changed by technology. Since these aspects are not covered by aggregate data, the gap is filled by a survey and interviews. The survey was conducted in 2002 by the Ministry of Environmental Affairs (Lamp, 2002),[9] and covered only forestry companies and employees. The purpose of this survey was to identify the status and perspectives of forestry vocational and higher education. An interesting feature of this survey is that both employers and employees were surveyed, and workers with forestry education with a job directly connected with their educational profile were exclusively targeted. Additionally, interviews with eight industry leaders carried out in 2003 are used to indicate the range of needs in skill types.[10]

The large number of different data sources for empirical analysis stems only partly from the complex concepts that are analysed, but also from the fact that forestry and wood processing/manufacturing, which are connected by strong material flows and by same educational and scientific research fields, are separated in many statistical classifications. Thus, for example, forestry is not included in the CIS surveys.

Table 14.3 describes the coverage and representativeness of all the different data sources. As can be seen, the CIS survey sample strata and the corresponding population strata deviate within boundaries of 12–13%. However, the mean deviance is 6.7% and 5% respectively for the two sets, so that the CIS samples are quite reliable representations of the populations.

Since forestry was not covered by the more detailed sources, the survey covering 10% of forestry employees was added. Finally, the interviews, which cover about 4% of employees, were done with the larger and more successful companies, so they are not representative for the whole industry. But they give some indication of the trend of development of leading companies in the sector. For the pulp and paper industry,

---

[8] The issue of matching occupational and educational profiles is considered in Ahola (1999).
[9] Major divisions of the state forest company (32), municipal offices of environmental affairs (11), private wood and forestry companies (13 — the response rate was very low) and workers with degrees in forestry specialities (55), were surveyed.
[10] Since technology and skill requirements were not the main topics of the interviews, and were only occasionally mentioned in nine interviews, the structure of the interviews and other details are not presented here.

Table 14.3. Coverage of data sources by number of employees.

	Population in 2002 N	% break-down	CIS (1998–2000) N	% break-down of the sample	% of the population	Population in 2005 N	% break-down	CIS (2002–2004) N	% break-down of the sample	% of the population	Lamp survey (2002) N	% break-down of the sample	% of the population	Interview data (2003) N	% break-down of the sample	% of the population
Forestry	8668	20	—	—	—	6016	15	—	—	—	876	100	10	—	—	—
Wood Processing	19775	47	8878	51	45	18860	48	9322	50	50	—	—	—	514	29	3
Pulp and Paper	1457	3	1257	7	86	1832	5	863	5	47	—	—	—	528	29	36
Furniture	12551	30	7421	42	59	12264	32	8418	45	67	—	—	—	760	42	6
Total	42451	100	17556	100	41	38972	100	18603	100	57	876	100	10	1802	100	4

Sources: Statistical Office... (2006), Innovation in... 1998–2000, Innovation in... 2002–2004, Lamp (2002); Agasild (2003); Arula (2003); Botvinkina (2003); Kull (2003); Kukk (2003); Kolk (2003); Kuldkepp (2003); Karjus (2003).

the interviews cover one company with more than a third of the employees and half the output of the sub-sector. These latter data sources used for identifying skill changes are not representative in the sectoral sense, and also with regards to methodology; generalisations about sectors cannot be made on the sole basis of interviews. The interview results are accordingly used here merely as indications of general trends.

5. Development of Technology and Skills in Wood Industries in Estonia

The industries under discussion form a large and growing part of the entire Estonian economy: forestry generates about 1.7% of Estonia's GDP, and wood, paper and furniture-making more than 25% of total manufacturing output. All those industries are much more oriented towards foreign markets than manufacturing in general; they also have higher than average productivity (the exception is the furniture industry) (Ukrainski and Vahter, 2004, 187). A considerable amount of FDI has flowed into wood processing companies, but the share of foreign capital is still below the average level for manufacturing. The superiority in productivity of foreign-owned companies over domestically-owned firms is much lower in the wood sector than the average for Estonian manufacturing (except, again, for the furniture industry) (ibid, 186).

The Estonian forest and wood sector firms have made significant technological advances in the last 15 years. Technology absorption (mainly in the form of FDI-dependent technology import) started in the early 1990s, and had matured by 1995 (Kolk, 2003). Here, strong information and technology flows can be observed from the forest clusters in Finland and Sweden, but also from the other Nordic countries — thus the Estonian wood industries have taken technological advances from the existing regional pool of technology and knowledge.

As illustrated in Figs. 14.1 and 14.2, investment in machinery and computer-related systems show a generally increasing trend in the period 2000–2006. The procurement of IT-related systems shows different peak years by sub-sectors. In the early 2000s, it was the forestry and furniture industries that invested most heavily, but the paper industry spent more than €230 per employee on computers in 2005. The transportation machinery situation has significantly improved in forestry, where it plays a crucial role in determining the productivity of the sector. Since 1994 modern tree harvesters and forwarders have been imported, and today about 100 harvesters and 300 forwarders are harvesting about 40% of all fellings in Estonia. In 2002 (two years after its original launch), the first harwarder was also employed in Estonia (Kurvits, 2003). In recent years, the capacity of all the machinery acquired is way above local needs, and therefore harvesting services are also occasionally exported to other countries (Russia and Sweden). It is interesting to note that, as with transport machinery, it is forestry that has invested most heavily in IT-related systems compared to other sub-sectors.

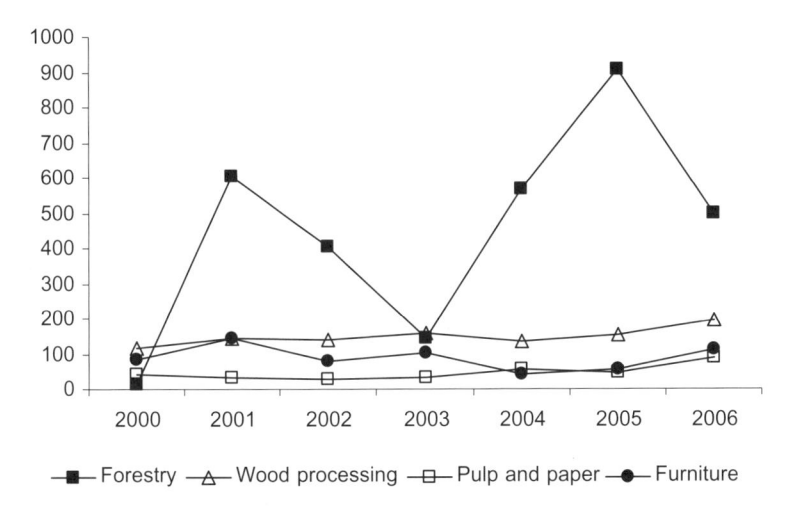

Fig. 14.1. Trends in investment in transportation equipment per employee (€, adjusted for PPP)
Source: Author's calculations, based on Statistical Office of Estonia (2008).

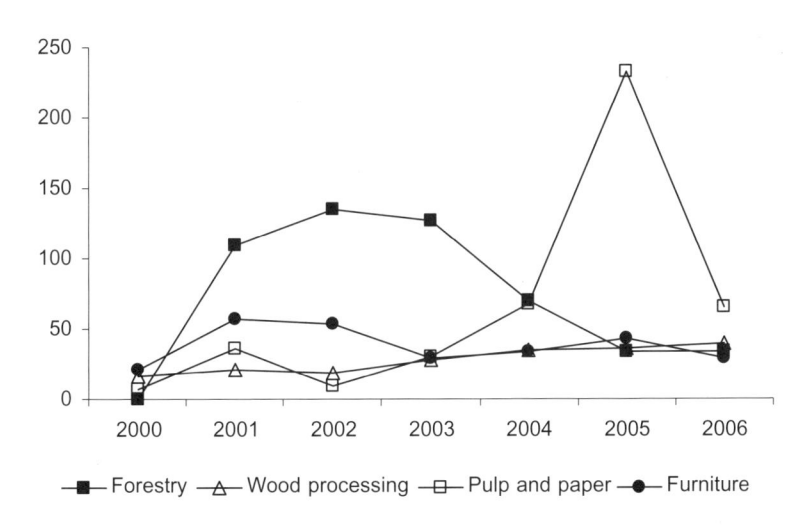

Fig. 14.2. Trends in investment in computers and related systems per employee (€, adjusted for PPP)
Source: Author's calculations, based on Statistical Office of Estonia (2008).

The observed trends in technological investments in the paper industry have been stable in recent years, and more incremental in terms of machinery. Since paper-producing machinery is very expensive, some parts of the production process are replaced with modern machines, working with second-hand imported equipment or existing old technology in other parts (Botvinkina, 2003). The same pattern has been revealed by other studies of pulp and paper industries (e.g. Rundh, 2003, on the Swedish industry). According to UN Comtrade Statistics data, Estonia has imported about US$ 3m annually of paper and pulp mill machinery since 1998. The figure peaked in 2000 at almost US$5m (*c.* US$2,000 per employee).

In wood processing, a greater degree of technological diversity can be found. With the acquisition of several sawmills, Stora Enso has modernised most of its Estonian mills up to the frontier of this technology (*Stora Enso's...*, 2006), as reflected also by the import data. The import of machine-tools for working with wood, cork or similar hard materials jumped from US$15m in 2002 to US$23m in both 2003 and 2004 (*c.* US$1,000 per employee). In addition, the import of saws (handsaws, blades for all kinds) expanded from US$3m to US$5m over the same period. Presses for the manufacturing of particle- or fibreboard were imported to the value of US$1–2m annually 2002–2004.

In the wood-based panel and furniture industries, modern factories co-exist with old Soviet-technology producers. When we look at the general trends, however, we see that the acquisition of technology has been quite extensive. As can be generally concluded from the interviews, most leading wood sector companies are in the adaptation phase in relation to modern imported technology (Agasild, 2003; Kolk, 2003); but there are also some firms that are creating novel technologies at world standards (Kuldkepp, 2003).

All these rapid technological changes have driven the companies to a position where they feel the need of skilled employees sharply, against the background of considerable competition for such employees on the labour market. As can be seen from Fig. 14.3, the forestry and pulp and paper industries are characterised by relatively high productivity levels, permitting the payment of higher wages compared to the rest of economy. The wood-processing and furniture industries remain at lower levels in this respect.

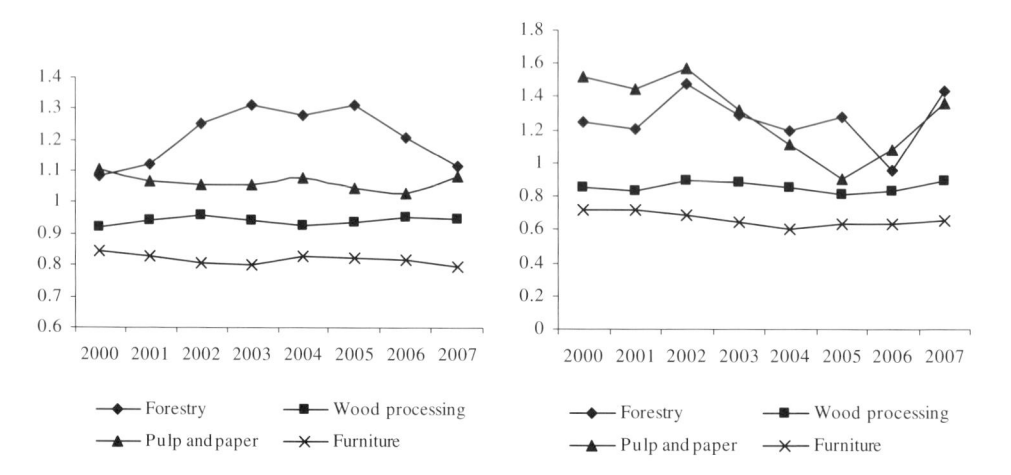

Fig. 14.3. Relative wages (left) and productivity (based on value added, right).
Source: Statistical Office of Estonia.

By taking a closer look at the distribution of employees by occupational group, we can see that the dynamics have varied between sub-sectors (see Figs. 14.4–14.7). In forestry, the share of elementary occupations and occupational profiles demanding higher education increased in 2001, but compared with the early transition years the share of highly-skilled employees decreased. One reason behind this development is certainly the restructuring of forestry (privatisation of forests, but also passing procurement activities over to the bigger wood companies). It is interesting to note that in forestry the peak shares for elementary occupations — in 2001 and 2005 — coincide with the peaks of investments in transportation machinery.

In terms of educational levels, the share of employees with the lowest level has decreased. Connecting these trends, we can see that the elementary occupations

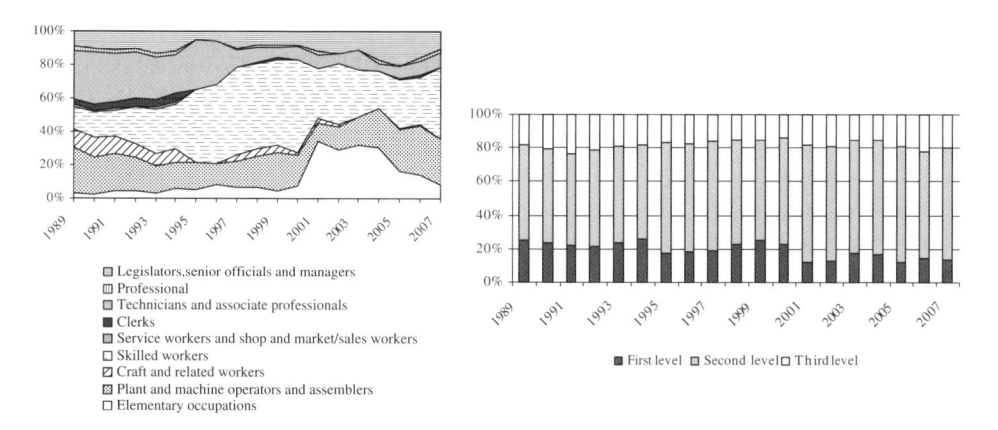

Fig. 14.4. The distribution of employees by ISCO-88 occupational groups and ISCED-97 educational levels in forestry.
Source: Statistical Office LFS Data.

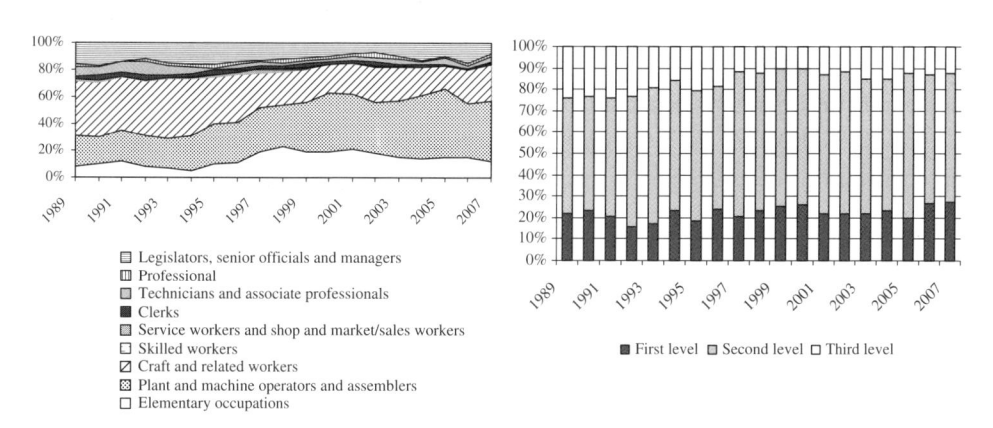

Fig. 14.5. The distribution of employees by ISCO-88 occupational groups and ISCED-97 educational levels in the wood-processing industry.
Source: Statistical Office LFS Data.

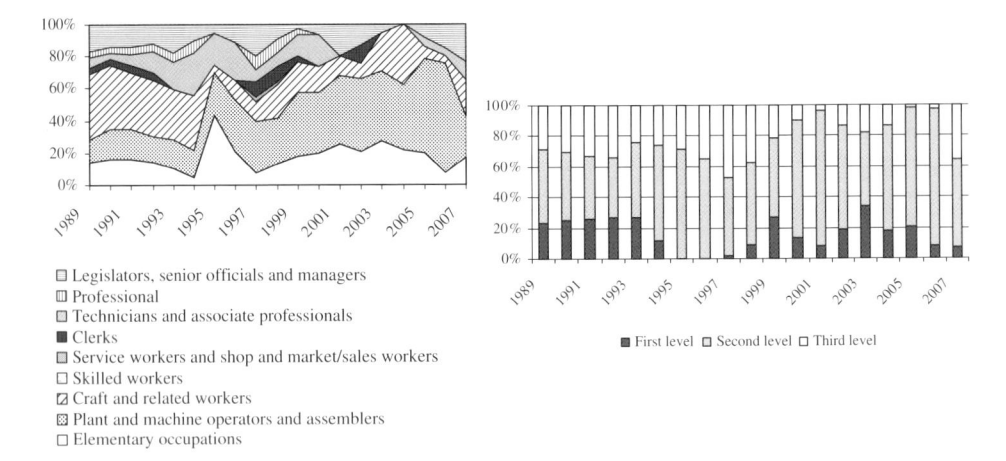

Fig. 14.6. The distribution of employees by ISCO-88 occupational groups and ISCED-97 educational levels in the pulp and paper industry.
Source: Statistical Office LFS Data.

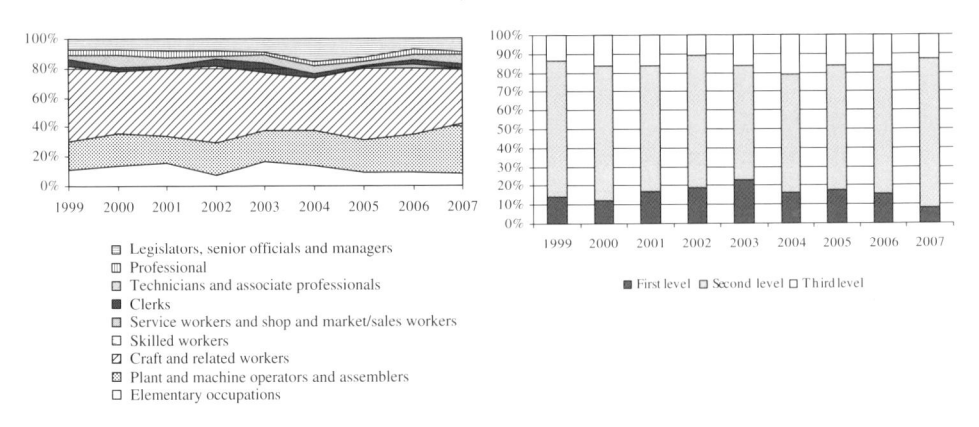

Fig. 14.7. The distribution of employees by ISCO-88 occupational groups in the furniture industry.
Source: Statistical Office LFS Data.

(lowest 30% in 2003) are increasingly manned by people with the second level of education (the first educational level comprised only slightly more than 10%), which could reflect the growing level of skills needed in these elementary professions.

The trends in the wood-processing industries reflected in Fig. 14.5 have been dominated by an increasing share of plant and machine operators and assemblers, which reflects concentration in the sawmilling industry and establishment of new large sawmills. The share of elementary occupations and professionals has been relatively stable in recent years, but has grown since the beginning of transition. When we look at educational levels, we see that the share of employees with the third educational level has decreased, while the share with the first level has increased.

This pattern does not support the skill upgrading hypothesis. It seems that this is the opposite case to forestry — more plant operators or craft workers with only basic education have been employed.

The pulp and paper industry is a very special case, because it is small and extremely concentrated (two large paper mills account for most of the industry). Here, one can see that the share of professionals with higher education is close to zero in some years. This can be explained by the small sample, but also at least to some extent by the fact that in Estonia the specialists concerned are not formally educated at all, and the enterprises have to train the workers themselves (which does not show up in the statistics of educational levels). The educational levels chart shows that the share of employees with the third level of education has decreased since 1989, but suddenly increased again in 2007. The empirical evidence here remains inconclusive, although the trends in occupational and educational profiles are similar.

The furniture industry has been relatively stable in recent years, but, of course, here the time span covered by the data is shorter. Not much productivity improvement is seen in this industry, and the technology has not been changed so drastically (compared to, for example, forestry or wood processing). A similar stability can be observed with respect to educational levels. However, it seems that employment of the lowest and highest educational levels has been decreasing, while the share of higher occupational groups has expanded slightly. Interviews with managers suggest that there may be specific supply-side explanations like shortage of wood-related specialists with higher education here (Botvinkina, 2003).

Summarising the dynamics of educational and occupational shares, we can say that the share of occupational profiles demanding higher education (legislators, professionals, technicians) has decreased in forestry and wood processing. At the same time, the share of elementary occupations has grown. In most cases, the changes in shares are not radical, but in the case of forestry, the movements in the share of elementary occupations have been quite extensive and volatile (from less than 5% to about 30% and thereafter to 12% of the work force). In the pulp and paper and furniture industries, the trends have been the contrary — the shares of the highest occupational profiles have grown and those of the lowest decreased or remained stable. In terms of changes in educational levels, the highest level shows a decreasing share in wood processing, while in other industries this share has been stable or even increased a little. The share of the lowest educational level has been decreasing in all sectors in recent years (most notably in forestry), except for the wood-processing industries. On the basis of these results, it seems that it is only in forestry that there is a shift in required skill levels, as a large and growing share of elementary occupations are filled with employees with second level education.

In the previous sections, very broad aggregate indicators of skills and technology were used for analysis, and these have shown quite different trends across industries. The results reveal a certain stability in educational and occupational distribution.

This could reflect the fact that the firms using new technologies are not numerous enough to have an impact on aggregated skill data. To elaborate this aspect, we now group the firms according to changes in their technologies. The purpose is to identify whether in the companies with significant technological changes the average skill levels are higher. A simple ANOVA[11] is performed by using process innovation indicators as a proxy for technological change. The results of the estimations are presented in Table 14.4. It has to be stressed here that no causality issues can be addressed on the basis of these results.

All the indicators relating to changes in technology are in accordance with each other: the companies with process and product innovations have a higher share of R&D expenditure, investments in equipment and external knowledge flows from patents, licences etc. compared to non-innovators. However, for those who performed product and process innovations at the same time, the shares of internal R&D and expenditure on external knowledge are significantly higher compared to only product and only process innovators. This result suggests that changes in technological processes together with improvement of product characteristics demand significantly higher investments in internal R&D and external knowledge from patents and licences.

Considering the respective skill indicators, we can see that the share of specialists with higher education (ISCED third category), does not differ between groups of firms. However, the share of R&D specialists is higher for those companies that did undertake process and product innovations at the same time, and for those who undertook only product innovation without changing the processes. The share of training expenses is higher for product innovators and seems not to be associated with process innovation. In summarising these results, we can see that the educational levels are not generally related to changes in technologies, but rather specific R&D-related skills matter for changes in products and technologies.

While the levels of skills in all statistical categories analysed seem to have only limited response to changes in technologies, there is a need to study the skill demand problem in terms of types of skills more closely. Some information can be obtained from Lamp's small-scale survey and from statements by industry leaders. Table 14.5 summarises the different skill aspects stressed in interviews and in Lamp's forestry survey.

The companies in the wood industry seem to need the same skills that come up in the literature generally. From Table 14.5 it can be seen that foreign languages, IT and experience of using different interactive databases are relevant, but also multi-skilling

---

[11] The model used is simple analysis of variance (ANOVA). For each dependent variable, the means are tested among the four groups. The null hypothesis tested is the following: $H_0: \mu_1 = \mu_2 = \cdots = \mu_k$, where μ_i is the mean of the given indicator in group i. The F statistic for this comparison is constructed as follows: $F = $ *variation among the sample means/variation within the samples*. If the means of samples are far apart from each other, the F statistic becomes large and the null hypothesis is rejected.

Table 14.4. Differences in mean values of indicators across groups of firms by innovative activities.

Model/dependent variable	Innovation type: (1) no innovations, (2) process only, (3) product only, (4) process and product					
	CIS3 (1998–2000)				CIS4 (2002–2004)	
	Multiple comparisons of group means[a]				Multiple comparisons of group means[γ]	
	Types of innovation groups compared	Difference in means	K-W test[β] p-value	Types of innovation groups compared	Difference in means	K-W test[δ] p-value
Share of internal R&D	(4)-(1)	0.0043*	0.000	(4)-(1)	0.0025*	0.000
	(4)-(2)	0.0041*	0.002			
	(4)-(3)	0.0042*	0.009			
Share of external R&D	(4)-(1)	0.0646*	0.000	No differences between groups identified		
Share of equipment investments	(4)-(1)	0.0218*	0.000	(2)-(1)	0.0775*	0.000
Share of external knowledge	(4)-(1)	0.0003*	0.000	No differences between groups identified		
	(4)-(2)	0.0003*	0.013			
	(4)-(3)	0.0003*	0.032			
Share of R&D specialists	(4)-(1)	0.0296*	0.000	The variable was not included in the questionnaire		
	(3)-(1)	0.0253*	0.000			
Share of other specialists	No differences between groups identified			The variable was not included in the questionnaire		
	(3)-(2)	0.1729*	0.609			
Share of training	(3)-(1)	0.1730*	0.001	The variable was not included in the questionnaire		

*Significant at the 0.05 level (Levene's test).
[a] Here we use the Bonferroni method of determining multiple comparisons, which employs t-tests to perform pairwise comparisons between group means, but controls the overall error rate by setting the error rate for each test to the overall error rate divided by the total number of tests. In cases where the assumption of homogeneity is violated, we use the Tamhane's T2, Dunnett's T3 and C-test rather than the Bonferroni method.
[β] There are several assumptions that should be fulfilled in order to perform the ANOVA — the samples should be normally distributed and the variances within samples equal (homogenous), and all observations should be independent. To assess whether or not the sample standard deviations vary significantly across the groups, a Levene's test has to be conducted. Because the Levene's test is considered unduly sensitive, especially if the data are not normally distributed, alpha should be set to 0.001 (see Tabachnick and Fidell, 1996). If $p < 0.001$, we conclude that the standard deviation or variances vary significantly across the groups, and thus there is a violation of the assumption of homogeneity of variance. If $p > 0.001$, we conclude that insufficient evidence is available to prove that the standard deviation or variances vary significantly across the groups. With our data, the violation of the homogeneity of variance requirement is present in some models. For models with heterogeneous variance, the Kruskal-Wallis test (indicated as K-W test) is performed. It does not assume the normal distribution.
[γ] See fn.α.
[δ] See fn.β.

Table 14.5 Skill demand by types of skill in the Estonian wood sector.

Skills, knowledge, qualifications	Skills required in wood processing, paper manufacturing and furniture manufacturing industries (interview data, 2003)	Need for additional training or lack of existing skills in forestry occupations (% of respondents) (survey data, Lamp, 2002)
Theoretical knowledge	Theoretical knowledge of forestry and wood material science (Arula, 2003; Kukk, 2003; Agasild, 2003)	Forest and environmental protection (Employees: 7.3%; Companies: 12.5%) Legislation (Employees: 9.5%; Companies: 15.7%)
Technical (digital) knowledge		General IT (Employees: 3.6%; Companies: 9.4%) Forestry Information System (Employees: 3.2%; Companies: 10.5%) Geographical Information System (Employees: 5.9%; Companies: 5.3%) Harvesting machinery (Employees: 4.5%; Companies: 1%)
Practical, tacit knowledge	Analytical capabilities (Arula, 2003; Karjus, 2003) Experience in working in the field, work safety (Kull, 2003; Botvinkina, 2003; Arula, 2003; Kukk 2003)	
Professional skills (multi-skilling)	Multi-skilling (Karjus, 2003; Agasild, 2003)	Business (Employees: 3.6%; Companies: 6.0%) Accounting, (Employees: 4.5%; Companies: 4%) Logistics (Employees: 6.8%; Companies: 1.4%) Documentation (Employees: 2.7%; Companies: 8.3%)
International skills	Foreign languages (Kukk, 2003)	Foreign languages (Employees: 11.7%; Companies: 20.6%)
Social skills	Suitability for team-work (Arula, 2003)	

Sources: Schienstock *et al.* (1999, 84); Lamp (2002); Agasild (2003); Arula (2003); Botvinkina (2003); Kull (2003); Kukk (2003); Kolk (2003); Kuldkepp (2003); Karjus (2003).

(forestry specialists need a wide range of skills: business, accounting, law etc.). The main skill problems stressed in interviews are, again, lack of computer skills and skill in working with electronics, knowledge of languages (which is very important in the case of fitters working abroad with clients, but also for technicians servicing imported machinery and equipment, for example), multiple professional skills, but also motivation (Kull, 2003; Kukk, 2003; Agasild, 2003). The most urgent skill requirements for forestry firms and employees relate to international skills (foreign languages), environmental protection and general legislation.

The forestry survey does, however, show that rapid changes in technology have raised only modestly the need for different types of skills (in most cases fewer than 20% of the firms and employees surveyed specified the lack of a given skill type). This shows that rapidly changing technology has only a modest impact for given skills. Table 14.5 hence affirms the pattern of muted effect obtained by analysing broad indicators of occupational and educational distribution.

6. Discussion

The above analysis reveals that the educational levels and occupational profiles have hardly changed alongside quite rapid changes in technology. Certainly, when we look more closely at skill types, we see somewhat increased demand for multiple skills. Considering the shared pattern of development of these industries in recent years, we can see that the wood sector has had to cope with global competition using complicated new technologies in combination with old ones. However, these changes in technology do not imply that all of the employees using new technologies have to know all the technical details about them. Advanced technology can increase the need for maintenance workers and electricians, who do really need to know more about the functioning of this technology (as discussed by Handel, 2003). But since some of the new technologies are imported, wood industry firms can rely on foreign assistance in maintenance and repair works from e.g. Finnish and Danish firms, as shown by some of the interviews (Kukk, 2003; Agasild, 2003). In this case, then, an increase in skills needed is not reflected in indicators of occupations and education.

Another part of the explanation for the stability of occupational and educational shares could stem from the fact that most changes in skill demands occur within existing jobs (*cf.* Zuboff, 1988; Giordano, 1992), and are therefore not reflected in occupational statistics. As revealed by interviews, companies cope with the need for multi-skilled workers by switching operators between multiple stages of the production process, thereby increasing their conceptual understanding of the whole process (Botvinkina, 2003; Kukk, 2003). Additionally, more complex skills concerning specific processes and technologies seem often to be obtained by self-education (Kukk, 2003; Karjus, 2003) or by employing a 'technological gatekeeper' in the firm (Agasild, 2003). These kinds of changes in skills are again not reflected in indicators of occupations, educational levels and training costs.

Demand-side indicators for skills are also influenced by the supply-side's reaction to changes in the skills needed in the economy. Thus the skill demand problem cannot be correctly addressed without studying the related educational system (this issue has also been raised by Chennels and van Reenen, 1999, 3). The view that blue-collar education is generally not satisfactory in Estonia is supported by the interviews with wood sector managers. The skill levels of employees (especially those of factory workers) are actually picked out by one of the managers interviewed as the main impediment to rapid technological upgrading (Kukk, 2003). However, the supply of wood-related skills is difficult to analyse,[12] because the relevant specialists are grouped in very different educational profiles (agriculture, engineering, manufacturing and construction). At the moment, one general issue concerning vocational education is the duplication of many specialities in different schools. Because of this fragmentation, enrolment has been very low and the average dropout rate very high — wood-related training institutions in Estonia (but also in other EU countries according to the ILO, 2001, 68) face difficulties in attracting enough students. At the same time, all schools are short of funding to ensure education of good quality (equipment, practical training) and also short of qualified teachers. When we take a closer look at wood-related higher education, we see that there is only one specialised wood-processing programme, in which the number of graduates has decreased drastically in recent years, and which is therefore not sufficient to satisfy the needs of the industry. A lack of university educated technicians in key fields can cause a drop in numbers of workers with higher education in the long run (unless it is compensated for by using suitable specialists from abroad, as is currently done by the paper mill included in the interviews, where highly skilled paper technology specialists are called in from Russia [Botvinkina, 2003]). Thus it is clear that there are serious misalignments between the Estonian wood-based industries and the educational and training systems that are meant to serve them.

7. Conclusions and Policy Implications

In recent years, there has been steady growth in all of the wood-based industries in Estonia, and that has been made possible by rapid technological change in the sector. However, these changes in technology have generated only modest changes in the skill levels observed. This result is generally in line with the findings of other studies reviewed in Handel (2003). The up-skilling tendency is supported only in some lower educational profiles, where growing shares of elementary jobs are occupied by people with vocational education. Significant improvements in technology, however, are primarily associated with the R&D-related specialists and technicians who assimilate rather than use the technology.

The supply of labour in this field is far from meeting industry needs. State action could provide part of the solution to these misalignments — pinpointing key areas of labour shortage and then launching a grant system, which could be tied in with subsequent placement work in the industry. But such initiatives would not be enough by themselves to solve the skill problem in the industry. There is a big job to be done in improving the image of wood-related professions in cooperation with companies and

---

[12] This section rests on the analysis of the system of wood-related education in Estonia by Ukrainski (2004).

industry associations. From the other side, vocational schools and companies do not actively cooperate, which means that the link between education and practical training remains weak. This issue could also be addressed by public policy. At the same time, the most important thing here is for the companies to ensure the quality of the apprenticeship. Of the skill and knowledge types analysed, only some can be developed from formal education (theoretical, technical, international skills). There is also a group of skills that is impossible to develop outside production processes or work participation (knowledge of practical work processes, multi-skilling, communication etc.).

For the wood-based industries, it is very important that the educational system encourages the preparation of specialists who are able to develop dynamically. In a very fluid and unpredictable economic and technological environment, companies do not know exactly which kind of knowledge and skills they might need in the future. Our analysis shows the importance of high-quality general education, IT training and language skills, but also of encouraging creativity and problem-solving skills during the work process.

References

Agasild, T. (2003). 'Viking Windows', recorded interview by U. Varblane, T. Roolaht and T. Vissak, 10 November, in Estonian.

Aghion, P., Caroli, E. and Garcia Peñalosa, C. (1999). 'Inequality and economic growth: The perspectives of new growth theories' *Journal of Economic Literature* 37(4): 1615–1660.

Ahola, S. (1999). *The Matching of Educational and Occupational Structures in Finland and Sweden*, Final Report, Thessaloniki, CEDEFOP.

Arula, M. (2003). 'Vara Saeveski OÜ', recorded interview by U. Varblane, T. Roolaht and T. Vissak, 29 October, in Estonian.

Berman, E., Bound, J. and Machin, S. (1998). 'Implications of skill-based technological change: International evidence', *Quarterly Journal of Economics* 113(4): 1245–1279.

Blombäck, P., Poschen, P. and Lövgren, M. (2003). *Employment Trends and Prospects in the European Forest Sector*, New York and Geneva, UN.

Botvinkina, Z. (2003). 'Horizon Pulp and Paper', interview by U. Varblane, T. Roolaht and T. Vissak, 30 October, in Estonian.

Braverman, H. (1974). *Labour and Monopoly Capital: The Degradation of Work in the Twentieth Century*, New York, Monthly Review Press.

Caroli, E. and Van Reenen, J. (2001). 'Skill biased organisational change? Evidence of a panel of British and French establishments', *Quarterly Journal of Economics* 116: 1449–1492.

Caselli, F. (1999). 'Technological revolutions', *American Economic Review* 89(1): 78–103.

Chennels, L. and Van Reenen, J. (1999). 'Has technology hurt less skilled workers? An econometric survey of the effects of technical change on the structure of pay and jobs', *The Institute for Fiscal Studies Working Paper Series*, W99/27.

Chun, H. (2003). 'Information technology and the demand for educated workers: Disentangling the impacts of adoption versus use', *The Review of Economics and Statistics* 85(1): 1–8.

Cohen, W.M. and Levinthal, D.A. (1990). 'Absorptive capacity: A new perspective on learning and innovation', *Administrative Science Quarterly* 35: 128–152.
Cohen, W.M. and Levinthal, D.A. (1989). 'Innovation and learning: The two faces of R&D', *The Economic Journal* 99: 569–596.
Dickerson, A. and Green, F. (2004). 'The growth and valuation of computing and other generic skills', *Oxford Economic Papers* 56: 371–406.
Edwards, R. (1979). *Contested Terrain: The Transformation of the Workplace in the Twentieth Century*, New York, Basic Books.
European Parliament (2000). *Report on the Commission Communication on the State of the Competitiveness of the EU Forest-Based and Related Industries,* A5–0384.
Freeman, C. and Perez, C. (1988). 'Structural crises of adjustment, business cycles and investment behaviour', in Dosi, G., Freeman, C., Nelson, R., Silverberg, G. and Soete, L. (eds.). *Technical Change and Economic Theory*, London and New York, Pinter Publishers, pp. 38–66.
Giordano, L. (1992). *Beyond Taylorism: Computerization and the New Industrial Relations.* New York, St. Martin's Press.
Green, F., Ashton, B., Burchell, B., Davies, B. and Felstead, A. (2000). 'Are British workers becoming more skilled?', in Borghans, L. and De Grip, A. (eds.), *The Overeducated Worker? The Economics of Skill Utilization,* Cheltenham, Edward Elgar, pp. 77–106.
Handel, M.J. (2003). *Implications of Information Technology for Employment, Skills, and Wages: A review of Recent Research,* Arlington, VA: SRI International, http://wwwsri.com/policy/csted/reports/sand/it.
Helpman, E. and Rangel, A. (1999). 'Adjusting to a new technology: Experience and training program', *Journal of Economic Growth* 4(4): 359–383.
Henderson, R. and Clark, K. (1990). 'Architectural innovation: The reconfiguration of existing product technologies and the failure of established firms', *Administrative Science Quarterly* 35: 9–30.
Hirsch-Kreinser, H., Jacobson, D., Laestadius, S. and Smith, K. (2003). 'Low-tech industries and the knowledge economy: State of the art and research challenges', *PILOT: Policy and Innovation in Low-Tech,* European Commission, Key-Action 'Improving the Socio-Economic Knowledge Base'.
Hunt, H.A. and Hunt, T.L. (1983). *Human Resource Implications of Robotics.* Kalamazoo, MI, W.E. Upjohn Institute for Employment Research.
ILO (2001). *Globalization and Sustainability: The Forest and Wood Industries on the Move,* ILO, Geneva.
Innovation in Estonian Enterprises in 1998–2000, Database of Statistical Office of Estonia, CD-ROM.
Innovation in Estonian Enterprises in 2002–2004, Database of Statistical Office of Estonia, CD-ROM.
Karjus, T. (2003). 'Scanhouse OY', recorded interview by U. Varblane, T. Roolaht and T. Vissak, 10 November, in Estonian.
Kelley, M.R. (1989). 'An assessment of the skill upgrading and training opportunities for blue-collar workers under programmable automation', in Dennis, B.S. (ed.), *Industrial*

Relations Research Association Proceedings of the Forty-First Annual Meetings, Madison, WI: IRRA, pp. 301–308.

Klobas, J. and McGill, T. (1995). 'Identification of technological gatekeepers in the information technology profession', *Journal of the American Society for Information Science* 46: 581–589.

Kolk, T. (2003). 'Toftan', recorded interview by U. Varblane, T. Roolaht and T. Vissak, 7 October, in Estonian.

Kukk, K. (2003). 'FSS Plywood', Recorded interview by U. Varblane, T. Roolaht and T. Vissak, 13 November, in Estonian.

Kuldkepp, E. (2003). 'RPM', interview by U. Varblane, T. Roolaht and T. Vissak, 14 October, in Estonian.

Kull, A. (2003). 'Estonian Woodworking Federation', recorded interview by U. Varblane, T. Roolaht and T. Vissak, 29 October, in Estonian.

Kurik, S., Lumiste, R., Terk, E. and Heinlo, A. (2002). *Innovation in Estonian Enterprises 1998–2000,* Tallinn, Foundation Enterprise Estonia, http://www.esis.ee/ist2004/text/images/128.pdf.

Kurvits, V. (2003). 'Rapidly changing forest harvesting technology', *Eesti Mets* 4, http://www.loodusajakiri.ee/eesti_mets/artikkel228_212.html, in Estonian.

Labour Force Survey in Acceding Countries: Methods and Definitions 2002 (2004). Luxemburg, Office of Official Publications of the European Communities, http://epp.eurostat.cec.eu.int/cache/ITY_OFFPUB/KS-BF-04-001/EN/KS-BF-04-001-EN.PDF.

Laestadius, S. (1995). 'Tacit knowledge in a low-tech firm', *European Journal of Vocational Training* 6: 27–33.

Laestadius, S. (2000). 'Biotechnology and the potential for radical shift of technology in the forest industry', *Technology Analysis & Strategic Management* 12(2): 193–212.

Laestadius, S. (1998a). 'Technology level, knowledge formation and industrial competence in paper manufacturing', in Eliasson, G. and Green, C. (eds.), *Microfoundations of Economic Growth — A Schumpeterian Perspective*, Ann Arbor, The University of Michigan Press.

Laestadius, S. (1998b). 'The relevance of science and technology indicators: The case of pulp and paper', *Research Policy* 27(4): 385–395.

Lall, S. (1999). 'Competing with labour: Skills and competitiveness in developing countries', *Issues in Development Discussion Paper*, Queen Elizabeth House, Oxford, 31.

Lamp, M. (2002). *Metsandusliku ja Puidutöötlemisalase Hariduse Hetkeseis ja Tulevik. Ankeetlüsitlus ja Tulemused*, Tallinn, EV Keskkonnaministeerium Metsaosakond.

Love, J. and Roper, S. (1999). 'The determinants of innovation: R&D, technology transfer and networking effects', *Review of Industrial Organisations* 15: 43–64.

Machin, S. (2004). 'Skill-biased technical change and educational outcomes', in Johnes, G. and Johnes, J. (eds.), *International Handbook on the Economics of Education,* Cheltenham, UK; Northampton, MA, USA: Edward Elgar Publishing, pp. 189–210.

Manasse, L., Stanca, L. and Turrini, A. (2004). 'Wage premia and skill upgrading in Italy: Why didn't the hound bark?', *Labour Economics* 11: 59–83.

Milkman, R. and Pullman, C. (1991). 'Technological change in an auto assembly plant: The impact on workers' tasks and skills', *Work and Occupations* 18: 123–147.

Ministry of Environmental Affairs (2003). *The Strategy of Estonian Forestry to 2010*, Tallinn, Ministry of Environmental Affairs, in Estonian.

Murnane, R.J., Willett, J.B. and Levy, F. (1995). 'The growing importance of cognitive skills in wage determination', *Review of Economics and Statistics*, 77: 251–266.

Murphy, K.L., Riddell, W.G. and Romer, P.M. (1998). 'Wages, skills, and technology in the United States and Canada', *NBER Working Paper* 6638.

Palmberg, C. (2002). 'The many faces of absorptive capability in low-tech industries — The case of glue-lam timber and foodstuffs', Paper presented at the DRUID Summer Conference on *Industrial Dynamics of the New and Old Economy — Who embracing whom?* Copenhagen/Elsinore 6–8 June.

Pavitt, K. (2005). 'Innovation processes', in Fragerberg, J., Mowery, D.C. and Nelson, R.R. (eds.), *The Oxford Handbook of Innovation.* Oxford, Oxford University Press.

Peneder, M. (2003). 'Industry classifications: Aim, scope and techniques', *Journal of Industry, Competition and Trade* 3(1–2): 109–129.

Rundh, B. (2003). 'The impact of product technology on the marketing issue: New development within the paper supply chain', paper presented to the 19th *IMP conference* in Lugano, Switzerland, http://www.impgroup.org/papers.

Sanders, M. and ter Weel, B. (2000). 'Skill/biased technical change. Theoretical concepts, empirical problems and a survey of the evidence', *DRUID Working Paper,* No 00/8.

Schienstock, G. et al. (1999). *Information Society, Work and Generation of New Forms of Social Exclusion (Sowing): Literature Review,* Tampere, Finland, University of Tampere, Work Research Centre.

Statistical Office of Estonia (2006). *Statistical Database,* http://pub.stat.ee/px-web.2001/I_Databas/Economy/Economy.asp.

Statistical Office of Estonia (1989–2008). *Databases of Labour Force Surveys.*

Stora Enso's Mills in Estonia (2006). http://www.storaenso.com/CDAvgn/main/0,,1_-6513–14321-,00.html.

Tabachnik, B.G. and Fidell, L.S. (1996). *Using Multivariate Statistics* (3rd edn.), New York, Harper Collins Wilkinson.

Ukrainski, K. (2004). 'The role of labour force and education in forming the competitiveness of Estonian wood industries', in Varblane, U. and Ukrainski, K. (eds.), *The Competitiveness of the Estonian Wood Industry,* Tartu, Tartu University Press, in Estonian, pp. 307–324.

Ukrainski, K. and Vahter, P. (2004). 'The Competitiveness of the Estonian furniture industry', in Varblane, U.and Ukrainski, K. (eds.), *The Competitiveness of the Estonian Wood Industry,* Tartu, Tartu University Press, pp. 185–207.

UN Commodity Trade Statistics Database (2006). http://unstats.un.org/unsd/comtrade/.

Viitamo, E. (2003). 'Knowledge-intensive services and competitiveness of the forest cluster — case of Finland', *ETLA Discussion Paper,* 845.

Zuboff, S. (1988). *In the Age of the Smart Machine: The Future of Work and Power,* New York, Basic Books.

Zwick, T. (2004). 'Training — A strategic enterprise decision?', in Fandel, G., Backes-Gellner, U., Schlüter, M. and Staufenbiel, J. (eds.), *Modern Concepts of the Theory of the Firm — Managing Enterprises of the New Economy*, Heidelberg, Springer-Verlag, pp. 355–366.

CHAPTER 15

FDI AND THE NATIONAL INNOVATION SYSTEM — EVIDENCE FROM CENTRAL AND EASTERN EUROPE

JUTTA GÜNTHER, BJÖRN JINDRA AND JOHANNES STEPHAN

1. Introduction and Motivation of Analysis

In catching-up regions, policy-makers in charge of economic development actively promote foreign direct investment (FDI). This is related to the expectation that foreign direct investors build up modern production capability, create new employment and stimulate demand. Economists as well as policy-makers also emphasise knowledge transfer and spillover effects induced by FDI.

In principle, one could argue that such technological effects could derive from any investment without consideration of ownership or origin. However, one of the important particularities of post-transition countries in Central-East Europe (CEE) is that their socialist past has delinked their companies from the international division of labour and active participation in technological development, resulting in significant productivity gaps at the outset of systemic transformation. After nearly two decades into the process of restructuring and catching-up in the transition phase, all CEE countries still face significant technology gaps compared to Western Europe. Post-transition countries still often lack indigenously owned firms that operate internationally through a network of own subsidiaries. Hence the importance attached to FDI in CEE countries. Foreign investors in these economies typically provide the link to globally operating firms with a strong endowment in terms of financial and human resources as well as access to an international network of knowledge creation. The operations of such multinationals have the potential to affect significantly the competitiveness and economic performance of regions within host economies. Against this background, we tend to see considerable competition between countries and regions for FDI. In order to attract foreign investors and to leverage positive effects, policy-makers resort to fiscal incentives, improve local infrastructure, and bolster human capital and science and technology.

Policy-makers and economists dealing with these issues are thus faced with two fundamental, but very different questions: how to attract foreign investors, and how to upgrade existing operations to create more sustainable effects from FDI. That in turn gives rise to a number of secondary questions, such as: how attractive is the region for international investors? What kind of investors does the region attract? Are the FDI projects dominated by 'extended work benches'? Do FDI projects by and large constitute modern, well-equipped production sites fully integrated into the international corporation, but still isolated from the domestic economy? Or do affiliates of foreign investors engage in own technological activities such as R&D and innovation? Do they exchange knowledge and technology with local partners in the regional innovation system? And finally, which firm- and region-specific factors influence a foreign investor's decision to locate technological activities in a particular region, and to source technology locally?

Those questions all lie at the heart of the developmental role of FDI, and require analysis at the level of both the host economies and the firm. This chapter argues that whether or not FDI can support economic catching-up in CEE host economies depends — inter alia — upon their technological capability, and the intensity of technological linkage with other actors from the national innovation system (NIS), such as scientific research institutions, suppliers, or customers. The empirical analysis described here is based on the new 'IWH FDI micro database'. This unique database forms a representative survey of foreign investment enterprises (FIEs) in a selection of CEE countries and regions, namely East Germany, Slovenia, Poland, Croatia and Romania. The survey was conducted in Spring 2007 by an international consortium involving national teams in the respective countries and regions. The database provides a rich resource of internationally accepted technological indicators as well as a number of organisational variables that are not available in other datasets for FDI projects in these FDI-hosting economies. All the data presented in this chapter reflect the situation in 2007, unless otherwise stated.

The chapter continues with a theoretical overview of the organisation of technological activities in international firms, followed by a description of the IWH FDI micro database. The subsequent section offers a comparative assessment of strategic motives of foreign investors across the individual host economies and the technological capabilities and activities of their FIEs. Finally, we develop a set of hypotheses with regard to the determinants of the technology sourcing of foreign affiliates and of their interaction with their host economies. These hypotheses are tested within the framework of correlation analysis and ordered probit estimation. The article closes with a discussion of the results and concludes with an outlook for future research avenues.

2. Theoretical Background and Development of Hypothesis

From an organisational perspective, the locus of technological innovation resides not only within the boundaries of the firm, but also outside them, at the interfaces between firms, universities, research laboratories, suppliers and customers

(Powell *et al.*, 1996). Many innovations intrinsically demand collective efforts, requiring different stakeholders to act cooperatively to generate new knowledge and ideas (Chesbrough, 2003). This is related to the idea that innovation proceeds by the recombination of existing knowledge (Kogut and Zander, 1992; Nonaka, 1994). The use of multiple sources for technological knowledge leads to both increases in technological opportunity (Klevorick *et al.*, 1995) and to complementarities and synergies between knowledge sources (Leiponen and Helfat, 2004). For example, academic research provides knowledge central to industrial innovative activity, yet it generally does not provide solutions to the more applied sort of problems on which firms tend to focus on (Mansfield, 1991; Pavitt, 1998). Agreements between firms tend to concentrate more on product-specific developments of basic research discoveries (Arora and Gambardella, 1990). Users, i.e., firms or individual consumers, that expect to benefit from using a product are potentially able to provide knowledge regarding problems with, or desired modifications of, existing products (von Hippel, 1976, 2005). Suppliers provide producers with knowledge regarding inputs, including raw materials, plants and equipment, product components and subsystems relevant to technological processes.

What does this mean for technological processes in foreign subsidiaries of internationalised firms? It has been suggested that the traditional advantages of centralisation of R&D and innovation activities in home economies — often connected to economies of scale and scope in R&D — seem to be increasingly counterbalanced by the competing advantages associated with decentralisation of technological activities (Pearce and Singh, 1992; Howells and Wood, 1993; Miller, 1994). Decentralisation offers linkages between technological activity and foreign production, local markets, suppliers and clients, as well as the exploitation of technological fields of excellence in host economies of subsidiaries (Dunning and Wymb, 1999; von Zedtwitz and Gassmann, 2002; Cantwell and Iammarino, 2003; Cantwell, 1992, 1993). However, firms have not internationalised their innovative activity proportionally to the growth in their overall production activities (Zanfei, 2000; Patel and Pavitt, 1999). This could be associated — inter alia — with the complex nature of systems of innovation, the embeddedness of the technological activities of the firms in the home environment (Narula, 2002), and the need for internal cohesion within the firms (Blanc and Sierra, 1999; Zanfei, 2000).

Overseas technological activities, on the one hand, can be associated with adapting and modifying the existing technological assets of firms in response to demand conditions. This has been labelled as 'home-base exploiting' (Kuemmerle, 1997) or 'competence exploiting' behaviour (Cantwell and Piscitello, 1999; Cantwell and Mudambi, 2005). On the other hand, foreign subsidiaries can be used to augment existing technological assets by actively absorbing technological spillovers, either from the local knowledge base in general (public infrastructure or agglomerative effects in a specific sector), or from specific firms (see for example Dunning and Narula, 1995; Cantwell and Janne, 1999; Patel and Vega, 1999). This strategy has been labelled as 'home-base augmenting' (Kuemmerle, 1997), or 'competence augmenting' (Cantwell and Piscitello, 1999; Cantwell and Mudambi, 2005). Criscuelo *et al.* (2002) hold that most foreign firms simultaneously engage in both competence-exploiting and competence-augmenting activities, because products are multi-technology based, and therefore any given foreign affiliate has a need for a variety of technologies, so that any given host location may possess a relative technological advantage in one area but not in another. In sum, the capacity of subsidiaries to exploit or augment technological competences is a function not only of their own resources, but also of their ability to utilise complementary resources associated with the relevant local innovation system (Criscuelo *et al.*, 2002).

For a home-base-augmenting strategy to take effect, foreign investment affiliates drawing from the host economy knowledge base obviously need some degree of autonomy over their own business functions, as they have access to information about the best sources of local knowledge and the most productive mode of tapping those resources. The literature on the roles and embeddedness of foreign investment affiliates accordingly suggests that the greater the extent of autonomy of the affiliate, the better its ability to form external network linkages with other companies and institutions in its own local environment (Birkinshaw *et al.*, 1998; Andersson and Forsgren, 2000). It is hence the most strategically independent foreign affiliates that cooperate most intensively and productively with other firms, and so utilise their autonomy as a means of leveraging local technological assets to enhance the competitive advantages of their enterprise group as a whole (Andersson, Forsgren and Holm, 2002; Cantwell and Mudambi, 2005).

The existing theory on the conditions on which foreign subsidiaries draw on local knowledge sources is still fairly limited (Frost, 2001; Criscuelo *et al.*, 2002). First and foremost, for local host economy knowledge assets to be utilised, the technological activity of FDI operations has to be sufficiently decentralised to grant the FIEs some mandate to be technologically active: Frost (2001) proposes that the greater the innovation activity of a foreign subsidiary, the greater the likelihood that its innovations will draw upon technical ideas originating in the host economy. However, there are also studies arguing that the reverse is true, i.e., that the existence of local external innovation networks fosters the technological capability of foreign subsidiaries (Holm and Fratocchi, 1998; Birkinshaw and Ridderstrale, 1999) and innovation activity (Pearce and Papanastassiou, 1999; Andersson *et al.*, 2002; Yamin and Otto, 2004). There seems, therefore, to be an unresolved issue in the literature with regard to whether the causality runs from the technological capability of subsidiaries (R&D and innovation) to external technological sourcing or vice versa. Here, we refrain from assuming a particular direction of causality: for our correlation analyses (which does not imply any particular direction of causality), we use the hypothesis:

H(1) *Technologically active FIEs are more likely to source technological knowledge from local scientific institutions.*

Because a regression analysis would assume a particular direction of causality (endogeneity problem), we decided not to include this hypothesis in the regression analysis. Rather, we reduce our sample of FIEs to the group of technologically active FIEs, to get around the problem of endogeneity. H(1) can still be tested in the framework of a pairwise correlation analysis.

Criscuelo *et al.* (2002) state that home-base-augmenting activities are primarily undertaken with the intention of acquiring and internalising technological spillovers that are location-specific to the host economy. This objective is secondary for competence-exploiting subsidiaries. Similarly, Frost (2001) argues that an exploitive strategy reinforces the existing knowledge base of the corporation through reproduction and incremental extension. A focus on refinement and adaptation is more likely to preserve the existing search routines of the whole corporation, which are strongly associated with internal knowledge flows and the parent firm's existing external network in the home country. In contrast, with an augmenting strategy, subsidiaries may broaden their scope of search, and are more likely to incorporate resources that lie outside the existing network of the parent company (ibid). Both authors provide sufficient ground to hypothesise that.

H(2) *An FIE following a competence-augmenting strategy is more likely to source technological knowledge from local scientific institutions.*

The primary function of subsidiaries with competence-exploiting mandates is to serve the local market. Their role is predominantly demand-driven. Thus, Frost (2001) argues that a home-base-exploiting innovation strategy that simply adapts the foreign parent technological base of the foreign subsidiary has a negative effect on external technology sourcing by subsidiaries from the host economy environment. Therefore, we hypothesise.

H(3) *An FIE following a competence-exploiting strategy is less likely to source technological knowledge from local scientific institutions.*

Related to the issue of tapping knowledge and skills from external networks (Kogut and Zander, 1993) is the question of autonomy: the literature holds that a high level of autonomy of FIEs allows them to make best use of local technological assets (Birkinshaw *et al.*, 1998, Andersson and Forsgren, 2000). Therefore, we hypothesise.

H(4) *The higher the autonomy of an FIE, the more likely it is to source technological knowledge from local scientific institutions.*

Frost (2001) argues that older foreign subsidiaries, i.e., those with more time and resources to gain a reputation for cooperative behaviour, are more likely to have access to local sources of knowledge than their younger counterparts, which might suffer from the 'curse of newness' (Stinchcombe, 1965; Venkataraman and Van de Ven, 1998) in the host economy environment. Therefore, we hypothesise that:

H(5) *The longer the FIE is established in the host economy, the more likely it is to source technological knowledge from local scientific institutions.*

In our analysis, we hence focus on the level of the FIE, and examine its developmental implications by assessing the strategic motive of the foreign investor, the technological activity of the foreign affiliates, the extent and nature of their interaction with their host economies, and compare these determinants across our set of four post-socialist host economies in CEE, plus East Germany.

3. The IWH — FDI Micro Database

In order to provide some answers to those questions, information at the level of the firm the FIE, is needed. In late 2002 to early 2003, a European consortium, financially supported by the EU in its 5th Framework Programme, conducted coordinated field work projects, questionnairing manufacturing FIEs in a selection of CEE countries: Estonia (73), Slovenia (69), Poland (153), Slovakia (78), Hungary (85).

In 2007, a follow-up on the first wave was conducted, again financially supported by the EU in its 6th Framework Programme, this time focusing on East Germany (295), Slovenia (40), Poland (110), and Romania (220). Without financial support, Croatia also joined our field work and collected 144 filled-out questionnaires.

In both waves, the questionnaires were centrally designed (first wave in 2002, second wave in 2007), whereas the implementation of the surveys was organised on a decentralised basis. All firms from the population were approached in writing or by phone, and invited to participate in the survey. Firms received the questionnaire by post, fax, or in an electronic version. In Romania, due to the large size of the population, a random sub-sample was drawn from it. Here, all firms in the sub-sample received the questionnaire by post, and the interviews were carried out face-to-face. In East Germany, all firms from the population were contacted by phone and invited to take part in the survey. Most interviews were done directly by phone; only a few FIEs preferred to fill in the questionnaire in its written form. The project deliberately allowed the country teams to choose the most appropriate method and timing individually.

For East Germany, a complementary survey (also conducted by the IWH and using the same questionnaire) focused upon West German multinationals (industrial firms that undertook FDI in at least one country outside Germany) that own at least ten per cent of equity and/or are the ultimate owners of a legally independent firm located in East Germany. As formerly centrally planned economies, the countries and regions analysed here were virtually closed to foreign investment from the West before 1989 (Meyer, 1995; Dunning and Rojec, 1993; Hunya, 1997). Our dataset hence consists predominately of investments undertaken after 1989: in fact, only eight investments in our dataset were made before 1989 (of which five in East Germany in the second half of the 1980s): amongst our countries, Slovenia was probably the most protective *vis-à-vis* FDI, but had nevertheless accumulated an FDI stock of nearly 9.5% of GDP by 1995 and nearly 21% by 2003. Romania started to receive noticeable amounts only after 1996 and had accumulated a stock comparable to Slovenia's by 2003. Poland experienced large FDI inflows right from the start of the transition process, while Croatia started to receive significant amounts only after 1995. Still, Croatia's FDI stock/GDP ratio in 2003 was nearly 32%, compared to a comparable figure for Poland of just 24%.[1] Of course, Poland and Romania are much larger economies than Croatia and Slovenia, with Croatia and Slovenia having GDPs of around half the size of Romania's and around one-eighth of Poland's.

3.1. Definition of subjects of analysis: Foreign investment enterprises (FIEs)

Proceeding from the theories and related literature sketched above, we target in our analysis FIEs in our selection of CEE host economies. The database includes only manufacturing industries. No explicit distinction was made in any of the country-specific sub-samples between affiliates of foreign investors with, and without further affiliates in other foreign host economies.

An FIE is defined as a legally independent enterprise with a foreign equity participation of at least ten per cent and/or an ultimate owner located abroad.

In principal, no restriction in terms of firm size was introduced. However, the Croatian and Romanian participants decided to include only foreign-owned firms with at least ten employees in their population.

3.2. The main areas of interest in the questionnaires

In the first wave, the focus was mainly on three sets of issues: first, we asked FIEs to characterise their own firm (size, sector, age, etc.). Second, we placed considerably

---
[1] While Slovenia and Croatia both belonged to the former Yugoslavia, and therefore had more elements of a market economy than Poland and Romania, Croatia's economic development and systemic transformation were held back significantly by the wars of the early 1990s.

stress on the corporate governance issue, i.e., the relationship between subsidiaries and headquarters. Finally, we devised a set of questions on the extent of integration of FIEs into their host economies in terms of trade (inputs, sales) and technological linkages with the host economy (embeddedness or role of FDI in local innovation system issues).

In the second wave, we retained the questions pertaining to FIE characterisation and the corporate governance issue, but also changed the focus somewhat, to probe deeper into own technological activities (R&D and innovation) of FIEs, and significantly broadened the treatment of the issue of embeddedness or role of the FIE in its local innovation system.

The two waves are hence comparable in some respects, but no real panel structure could be established; first, because of the differences in country composition (owing to the different designs of the two EU projects involved), and second, because the questions differ. Finally, and most importantly, the death and birth rates of FIEs in those countries between the two waves exclude the possibility of conducting large-scale, representative fieldwork in a panel-structure. In the following analysis, we use only the data from the second wave.

3.3. Comparing total population and sample

The total population of our second wave field work consists of FIEs located in Croatia, Slovenia, Poland, Romania and East Germany in 2006. In selecting these regions in economic transition, we tried to balance country size, geographic location, and level of economic development. The population includes different types of foreign investors apart from industrial companies, such as mutual and pension funds, banks, foundations, individuals/families, and combinations of these.

The populations of FIEs in Poland, Romania, and East Germany were drawn from the Amadeus database. The Polish and East German populations were supplemented with data from the respective foreign investment agencies (Invest in Germany — IIG, Invest in Poland — PAIZ). The East German population data was additionally supplemented with information from the European Investment Monitor (2006) and the EU's industrial R&D investment scoreboard (2005).[2] The Croatian population of FIEs was compiled using information provided by the Institute for Business Intelligence (Zagreb). In the Slovenian case, the population was drawn from statistics provided by the Bank of Slovenia. The cumulated total population across our five host economies consists of 6,833 manufacturing firms with foreign investors, employing about 1.1 million employees (see Table 15.1).

The resulting total sample of FIEs in the second wave holds information from 809 enterprises that account for employment of over 214,000 people across the

---

[2] For a detailed description of the East German sample see also Günther *et al.* (2008).

Table 15.1. Country composition of total population of manufacturing firms with foreign investors.

	Nr of FIEs	In % of total population	Employment	In % of total population
East Germany	1090	16.74	195,429	18.55
Slovenia	365	5.61	40,791	3.87
Poland	1511	23.21	211,055	20.03
Croatia	220	3.38	56,033	5.32
Romania	3325	51.07	550,361	52.23
Total	6511	100.00	1,053,669	100.00

Source: IWH FDI micro database.

Note: The extraordinarily large share of Romanian FIEs in the total population probably represents an upward distortion: even the latest editions of the Amadeus database include firms that have ceased to exist. This was particularly problematic in the Romanian case; the databases for the total populations of the other countries were cleaned up more thoroughly.

Table 15.2. The IWH FDI micro database — country composition and response rates.

	Nr of FIEs	In % of total	Employment	In % of total	Response rate for nr of FIEs (%)	Response rate for employment (%)
East Germany	295	36.46	39,876	18.61	27.06	20.40
Slovenia	40	4.94	9686	4.52	10.96	23.75
Poland	110	13.60	38,408	17.93	7.28	18.20
Croatia	144	17.80	36,963	17.25	65.45	65.97
Romania	220	27.29	89,292	41.68	6.62	16.22
Total	809	100.00	214,225	100.00	12.43	20.33

Source: IWH FDI micro database.

five countries surveyed (see Table 15.2). In terms of number of FIEs, the sample constitutes 12.43% of the total population, and in terms of employment 20.33%.

The sample response rates vary across countries. In terms of number of firms, it ranges from 6.62% in Romania to 65.45% in Croatia. In terms of employment, it ranges from 16.22% for the Romanian sample to 65.97% in Croatia. Such differences in response rates are mainly explained by the differences in the size of the respective populations of FIEs and the financial means available to collect completed questionnaires. The larger populations of Romania, Poland and East Germany hence tend to have reduced response rates. In the cases of Romania and Poland, this results in an underrepresentation within the sample in terms both of numbers of FIEs and employment. Strikingly, the response rates for Poland and Romania differ markedly between the response rate according to the number of FIEs (much lower) and that according to the number of employees (much higher). This indicates that the FIEs in the sample are larger than the average firm in the respective populations of the two countries, so that we have a bias towards large firms. In fact, the total sample is underrepresented for micro enterprises

(1–9 employees) and small enterprises (10–49), and consequently overrepresents medium-sized (50–249) and large (above 250) firms.

In general, the samples generated in the second wave are representative of the total population in terms of NACE-2 industrial branches. In the East German case, representativeness was also verified for the regional aggregate of *Raumordnungsregionen* (ROR) (a functional aggregate of 97 regions with a size range between NUTS2 and NUTS3), and for the size of FIEs.

4. Method and Results of Explorative Analysis of Technological Activity and Local Embeddedness of FIEs

The explorative analysis in this chapter starts with a description of stylised facts, and is focused on the main theoretical ideas introduced above: with a view on the developmental character of foreign direct investment in CEECs as post-transition countries, we are interested in the kind and extent of interaction of FIEs with actors of their NISs. We provide some stylised facts on the dominant investment motives, on the technological activity of FIEs, on the degree of autonomy of FIEs *vis-à-vis* their foreign investors (corporate governance issue), and on the degree of integration of FIEs into their host economies (embeddedness issue). We close this chapter with some correlation analyses and linear logistic regressions, testing the relationships between the interaction of our FIEs with one particular actor in the NISs (i.e., research institutions) and other firm-specific determinants. This allows us not only to make comparisons between our different host economies, but also tells us about the kind of FDI project or FIE that are most likely to provide a positive developmental impact on their host economies.

4.1. *Stylised facts: Investment motives of foreign investors*

As a first step, we want to find out what strategies are dominant amongst the foreign investors in our selection of post-transition economies. We distinguish between five strategic motives, and asked the FIEs to rank the importance of each of the 'strategic motives pursued by the foreign investor at initial entry and today':

- to access a new market or increase the existing share of the host market
- to follow key foreign clients that moved to the host country
- to increase efficiency across the foreign owner network
- to access location-bound natural resources, and
- to access location-bound knowledge, skills, technology.

The ranks range from 1 for 'not important' to 2 for 'of little importance', 3 for 'important', 4 for 'very important' and 5 for 'extremely important'. Table 15.3 lists

Table 15.3: Average importance of strategic motives for investment, by host economy.

	Market	Follow client	Efficiency	Natural resources	Knowledge, skills, techn.
East Germany	3.3	1.9	2.8	1.7	3.0
sd	*1.3*	*1.3*	*1.3*	*1.2*	*1.3*
Slovenia	3.0	2.0	3.2	1.5	2.7
sd	*1.6*	*1.2*	*1.4*	*1.0*	*1.2*
Poland	3.8	2.3	3.3	2.5	2.5
sd	*1.1*	*1.3*	*1.1*	*1.4*	*1.0*
Croatia	3.5	2.1	3.5	2.2	3.1
sd	*1.4*	*1.2*	*1.3*	*1.4*	*1.2*
Romania	3.4	2.6	3.3	2.5	3.0
sd	*1.4*	*1.4*	*1.3*	*1.5*	*1.4*
Total	3.4	2.2	3.2	2.1	2.9
sd	*1.4*	*1.3*	*1.3*	*1.4*	*1.3*

Notes: Averages are calculated as means over the country-groups of FIEs, without individual weights for FIEs. Large and small FIEs are treated equally.
sd = standard deviations.
The number of firms are for East Germany 257; Slovenia 40; Poland 107; Croatia 106; and for Romania 213.
Source: IWH FDI micro database.

averages and the corresponding standard deviations of averages in FIE groups according to host economies. From the perspective of today, access to new markets or increase of an existing market share turn out to be the dominant strategic motive in all economies except Slovenia. Here, the motive of increasing efficiency across the foreign owner network is slightly higher than the host market motive. This latter motive turns out to be the second most important one for Poland, Croatia (by a very small margin), and Romania.

Our main interest here is in the strategic motive of tapping the local host economy knowledge base in terms of existing knowledge, skills of personnel and available technology. This motive appears to be particularly important for East German FIEs (second only to the market motive), but less so for Slovenia, Croatia, and Romania (all third rank). For foreign investors in Polish FIEs, with their large home market and low labour costs, access to local knowledge and skills and technology appears to be the least important one on average. Over all FIEs in our country-samples, this motive is third after market access and increasing efficiency. Importantly, the pattern of strategic motives has not changed much since the time when the foreign investor first invested in the foreign affiliate: the mean for knowledge base was at that time slightly lower — 2.2 for foreign investors into Poland, 2.8 in Croatia, and 2.8 in Romania. The ranking, however, was the same in these latter cases. Standard deviations appear to be low enough to warrant robust interpretation of results.

4.2. *Stylised facts: Technological activity of FIEs in a cross-country comparison*

The second focus of our analysis pertains to the technological activity of FIEs, which helps us to distinguish between foreign investment projects that are, from a developmental perspective, (potentially) positive contributors to technological catch-up by the host economies and others that may rather effect some form of lock-in of host economies in lower technological trajectories.

With our database, we are able to compare across host economies both the share of FIEs that are technologically active and the intensity of technological activity. For technological activity, we use R&D activity, both in expenditure and personnel ('Number of R&D personnel' greater than 0), and also innovation ('whether the FIE has undertaken any innovations over the last three years'). We use two indicators for R&D activity, because we assume that for significant R&D activity FIEs should both invest financial resources in R&D and at the same time have explicitly dedicated personnel to work on R&D.

R&D activity is typically interpreted as an input of innovation, which is in turn treated as output of technological activity. Contemporary research, however, indicates that R&D may or may not effect this linear causation, but in any case has a wider set of roles: most importantly, we learn from Cohen and Levinthal (1989) that R&D not only stimulates innovation but also develops the ability of the firm to identify, assimilate, and exploit outside knowledge likely to increase the incidence of technology diffusion. Moreover, the literature on decentralisation of R&D in foreign direct investment shows that foreign investment networks allocate parts of their R&D projects amongst their foreign affiliates rather than centralising R&D at headquarters. This assigns FIEs an active role in the foreign investors' technological activities, even if the strategic motives followed by the foreign investor are focused mainly on markets and key clients. We hence expect to observe technological activity with a degree of independence from strategic motives amongst our CEE FIEs.

From Fig. 15.1, there emerge two classes of country-specific FIEs: the share of FIEs that undertake R&D turns out to be around 50–60% for East German, Slovenian, and Polish FIEs. R&D activity appears to be less common in the cases of our Croatian and Romanian FIEs; here the share of active FIEs is around 40%. In the cases of East German and Croatian FIEs, the non-response rates, for R&D expenditure and R&D employment respectively, are quite high.

We complement the picture provided by the statistics on the share of R&D-active FIEs with statistics on the R&D intensity of those FIEs that are, in fact, active with respect to R&D. From our field work, we can derive three indicators for R&D intensity: R&D employment in per cent of total employment (measured as the sum of R&D employment in FIEs over the sum of total FIE employment, for each host economy, obviously considering only FIEs that have provided information on both data), the share of R&D expenditure in total turnover (measured again in aggregates),

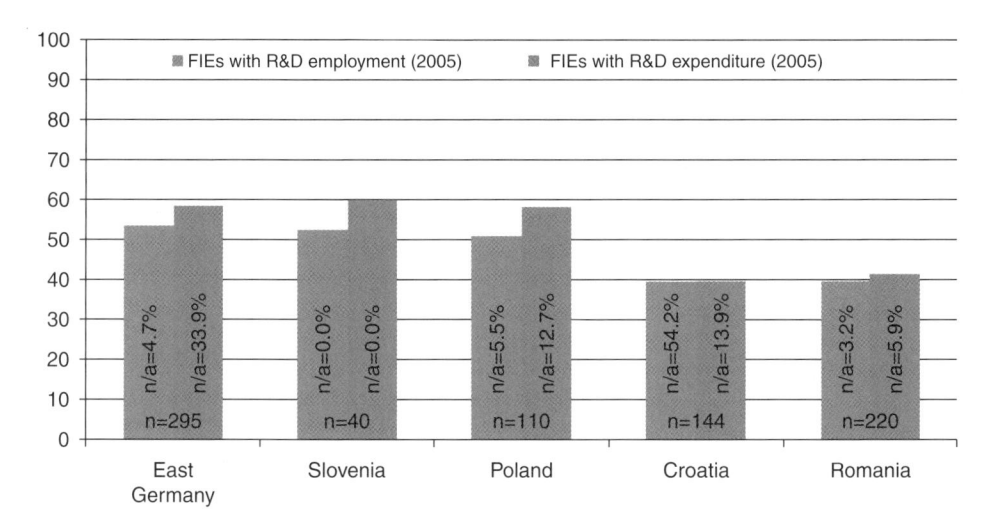

Fig. 15.1. Share of FIEs with R&D activity across host economies (%).

Note: The shares presented here are for the firms that reported that they do have R&D employment and R&D expenditure.

n/a denotes the share of FIEs that did not provide information with respect to R&D employment or R&D expenditure, and are not included in the shares of R&D-active FIEs.

n = total number of FIEs per host economy.

Source: IWH FDI micro database.

and finally the share of R&D expenditure in gross value added (calculated again in aggregates, where value added is calculated as 'Value of total sales' reduced by the 'Share of intermediate inputs/supplies'). While the two former indicators are complementary and should convey a comparable ranking between host economies, the latter indicator is intended to correct for differences in firm-sizes: R&D expenditure shares in total turnover tend to become under-proportional with increasing firm-size, i.e., underestimate R&D intensity amongst groups of larger FIEs.

The indicators for the intensity of R&D activity amongst groups of R&D-active and country-specific FIEs (see Fig. 15.2) largely confirm the weakness of Romanian FIEs in R&D; not so, however, with Croatian FIEs. The intensity of R&D activity in Polish FIEs is also out of line. While a relatively low share of Croatian FIEs are actually active in R&D, those that are active appear to spend rather a lot on R&D (standard deviations are high, but markedly lower than for, e.g., East German FIEs). For our Polish FIEs, the opposite applies: while a high proportion are R&D-active, they seems to spend rather little on R&D.

In sum, we can conclude that Croatian FIEs that are active in terms of R&D appear to have the highest intensities of R&D, i.e., are best endowed with R&D employee shares, and spend the most on R&D as a proportion of turnover and of gross value added. Second to Croatian FIEs are East German foreign investment affiliates. For both these country-specific groups of FIEs, the aggregate indicators

316   *J. Günther, B. Jindra and J. Stephan*

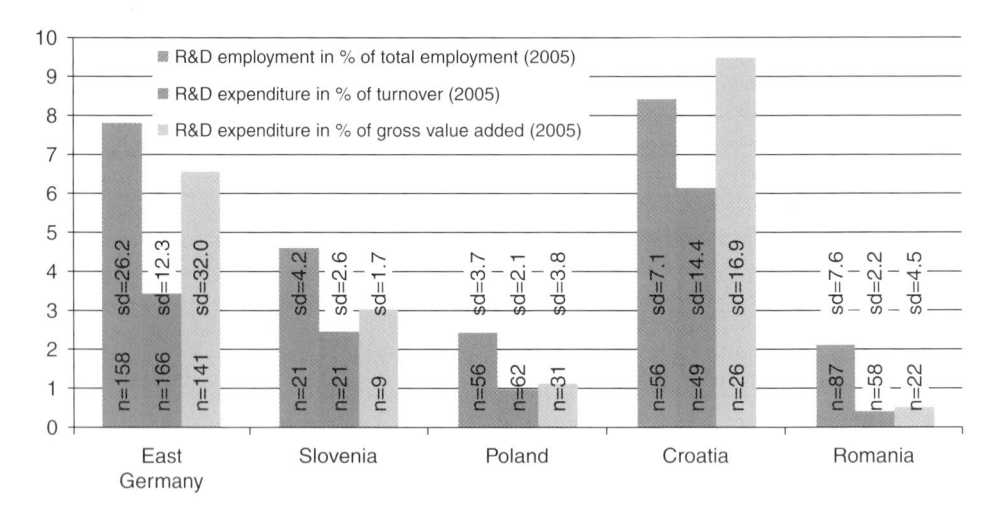

Fig. 15.2. R&D intensities of R&D-active FIEs: aggregated averages over three indicators across host economies

Note: Averages are calculated as aggregated means over the country groups of FIEs that provided information on R&D activity (i.e., with individual weights for FIEs and excluding n/a).

n = the number of R&D-active FIEs per host economy.

sd = standard deviation.

In the cases of East Germany and Romania, one statistical outlier each had to be removed.

Source: IWH FDI micro database.

are, however, not very robust; standard deviations in firm-specific indicators for R&D intensities are quite high. Slovenian FIEs assume third place, and Polish and Romanian FIEs have the lowest intensity of R&D.

This order of ranking largely confirms expectations, bar the high results of Croatia: East Germany is generally considered technologically the most advanced host economy among the transition economies, Slovenia has the highest level of economic (and likewise technological) development in CEE, Poland is mainly interesting for foreign investors on account of its large market and low wages, and Romania has only recently started to pick up the pace with respect to FDI and technological catching up.

To measure innovative activity of FIEs from our group of countries, we split the innovation-questions into the Oslo Manual classifications of product, process, marketing, and organisational innovations (OECD, 2005). The former two are classified as technological innovations, the latter two as non-technological innovations. Also with reference to the Oslo-manual, innovations were defined to be not necessarily new to the market but new to the firm. We generated data on the share of FIEs that 'have undertaken innovations over the last three years' and the intensity of product innovations produced by firms (measured in terms of 'product-innovation intensity in comparison to your competitors in the relevant market' with possible

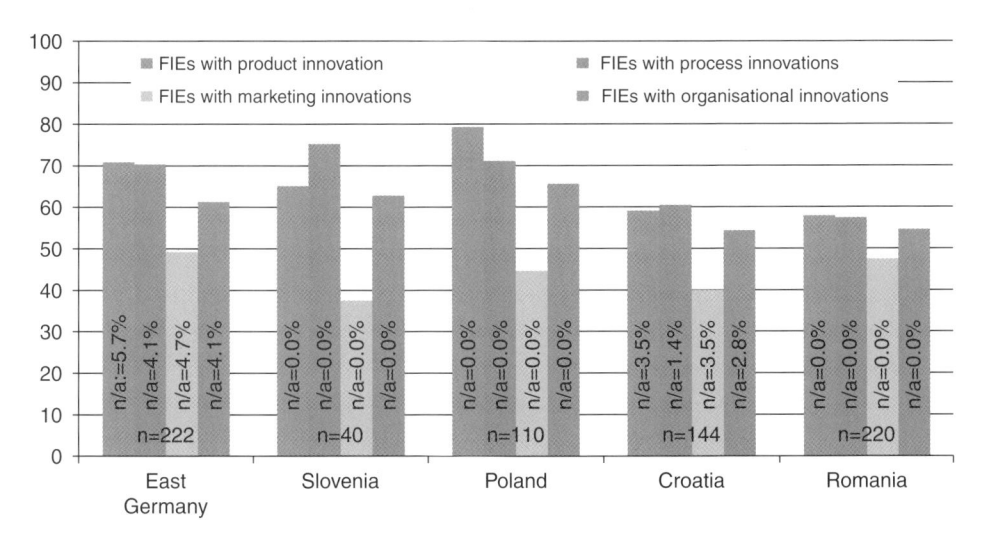

Fig. 15.3. Share of FIEs with innovative activity across countries and types of innovation (%).

Note: The shares presented here are for the firms that reported that they had undertaken innovations.

n/a = the share of FIEs that have not provided information with respect to innovations, and are not included in the shares of innovation-active FIEs.

n = the total number of FIEs per host economy.

Source: IWH FDI micro database.

answers: 1 = very low, 2 = below average, 3 = average, 4 = above average, 5 = very high). The proxy hence assumes values between 1 and 5 (See Fig. 15.3).

What is particularly interesting is that the Polish FIEs appear to consider themselves as particularly innovative, not least in comparison with competitors: nearly 80% of the Polish FIEs had undertaken product innovations in the three years preceding the field work, a share much higher than for FIEs of other countries (East Germany 71%, Slovenia 65%, Croatia 59%, Romania 58%). For process innovations, the Polish FIEs are second only after Slovenian FIEs, for marketing innovations third after East German FIEs and Romanian FIEs and for organisational innovations again with the highest share.

With respect to innovation intensity, we only use FIEs that have 'undertaken product innovations over the last three years'. The share of firms that consider their own innovative activity as 'above average' or even as 'very high' are marked in cumulative positive bars in Fig. 15.4; the share of firms with 'average', 'below average' and 'very low' comparative innovation intensities are marked in cumulative negative bars.

The results again show Poland with the highest share of FIEs with above-average product innovation intensities (cumulated positive bars) and likewise the lowest share of average and below-average intensity FIEs (cumulated negative bars). This positive result appears, however, to be mainly driven by a high share of FIEs with

318   *J. Günther, B. Jindra and J. Stephan*

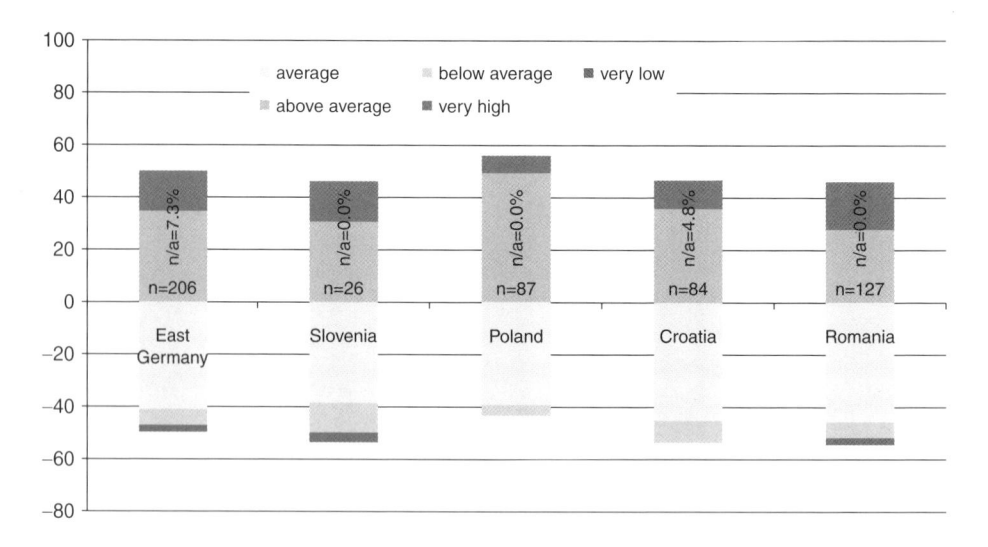

Fig. 15.4. Innovation intensities of FIEs with product innovation across host economies.

Note: Cumulative bars represent the shares of product innovation-active FIEs that consider their intensity of product innovations with those of their competitors in the relevant markets to be very low, below average, and average in negative bars, and as above average and very high in positive bars.

n/a = the share of product-innovation-active FIEs that have not provided information with respect to their comparative innovation performance.

Source: IWH FDI micro database.

above-average intensities, not by a high share of 'very high' comparative intensities: on this latter indicator, the share of Polish FIEs is in fact particularly low (less than half the corresponding shares for any of the other country-groups of FIEs). Thus the Polish FIEs appear to assume a rather comfortable upper-middle-ground in their own comparison with competitors, while a larger share of FIEs in the other countries appear to belong to the technological envelope. The average innovation intensity category accounts for approximately 40% of FIEs in all countries, with Croatia and Romania slightly higher. More marked differences appear again for the categories of below average and very low product innovation intensities: while the latter does not exist amongst Polish and Croatian FIEs, it is highest amongst Slovenian FIEs followed by Romanian and East German ones.

If we were to amalgamate this information on country-groups and classifications of FIEs into one composite indicator which imputes increasing values to the categories according to their implied intensities, and in equal steps (weights are for 'very low': 0.1, 'below average': 0.2, 'average': 0.3, 'above average': 0.4, 'very high': 0.5), then Polish FIEs would achieve the highest intensities for product innovations with an indicator value of 35.9, followed by East German (35.4) and Romanian (35.3), and finally Croatian (34.9) and Slovenian (34.2).

Apart from the technological characterisation of FIEs across the host economies, the results also tell us that R&D and innovation do not necessarily follow a linear relationship: R&D-activity may follow objectives quite independent of innovation. In fact, in additional pairwise correlation analysis between R&D expenditure (both in absolute values and as per cent of turnover) and product, process, marketing, and organisational innovations, not one coefficient turned out to be high (the highest significant coefficient of correlation is 16.6, between R&D as a share of turnover and product innovation intensity).

Finally, we collected data to measure the effect of innovation on the performance of FIEs with product innovations under the heading of 'share of new or significantly improved products in total sales' (Fig. 15.5: again the statistics are calculated in the aggregate, not the average over individual shares). To add some information on dynamics, we asked firms to estimate the share of sales for the years 2002 and 2005. The descriptive statistics show that, among product-innovation-active FIEs, product innovation activities in East German, Slovenian, and Polish FIEs appear to be most productive in terms of increasing sales, i.e., firm growth. For 2005, the data for Romania also suggest high innovation productiveness in terms of firm growth, but only after a sharp jump from a very low level in 2002. Croatian FIEs here come at the bottom of the list. As a matter of fact, the productiveness of

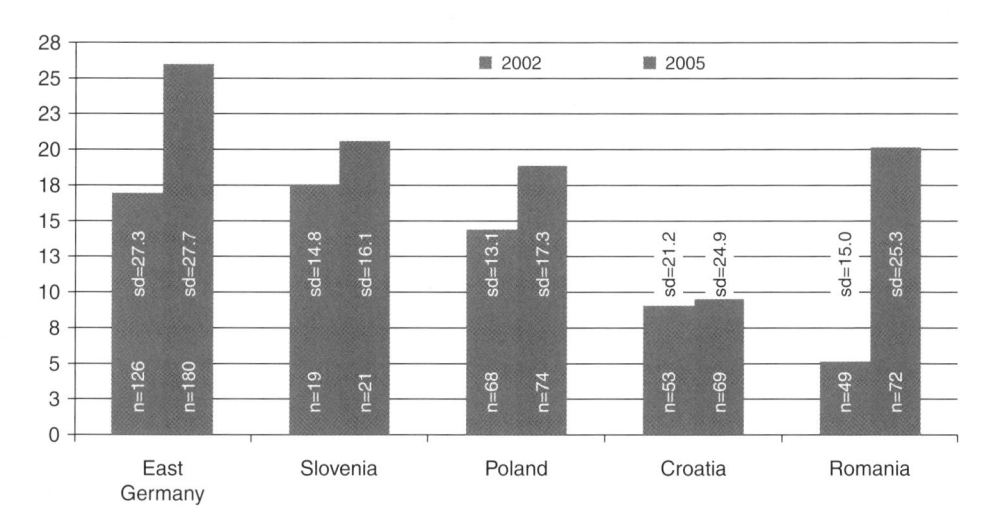

Fig. 15.5. Aggregated share of sales attributable to new or significantly improved products across countries (%).

Note: The aggregate shares presented here are the sum of sales attributable to new or significantly improved products as a percentage of the sum of sales of the population of firms (n) that have reported both figures.

sd = standard deviation.

Source: IWH FDI micro database.

product innovative activity seems to have increased between 2002 and 2005 for all country-groups of FIEs. The high intensity of innovation of Polish FIEs observed above did not fully translate into FIE performance; in 2005 that country's FIEs fall behind even Romania's FIEs in terms of new products as a share of total sales. It is worth noticing that (a) standard deviations are in some cases very high indeed; (b) the populations of FIEs that make up these aggregated shares are not identical between 2002 and 2005.

4.3. *Stylised facts: Autonomy of FIEs vis-à-vis foreign parents*

The literature on subsidiary roles and embeddedness raises the issue of corporate control and autonomy of FIEs with respect to embeddedness (e.g. Birkinshaw *et al.*, 1998; Andersson and Forsgren, 2000). The obvious conclusion to be drawn from this literature is that, with increasing autonomy from parent companies, FIEs can have a larger development impact on the host economy in terms of technology transfer and hence technological development of the host economy.

In relation to this issue, we collected data on the level of autonomy enjoyed by the FIE *vis-à-vis* the foreign owner, asking them the question 'to what degree are the following business functions currently undertaken either by your firm or the foreign owner network (HQ/other unit)'. The possible answers range from 1 = only your firm, 2 = mainly your firm, 3 = mainly foreign investor network, 4 = only foreign network. We asked firms to specify their degree of autonomy in a set of seven business functions: (i) production and operational management; (ii) market research and marketing; (iii) basic and applied research; (iv) product development[3]; (v) process engineering[4]; (vi) strategic management and planning; and finally (vii) investment projects and finance.

Because we are here mainly interested in technological activities of foreign affiliates, and in order to allow comparison across FIE country-groups in a stylised manner, we reduced the information available to an unweighted average over the three technology-oriented business functions (iii) to (v).

The results are interesting indeed (see Fig. 15.6): rather unexpectedly, FIEs in Romania appear to be the most autonomous *vis-à-vis* foreign parents in the business functions of basic and applied research, product development and process engineering, which is mainly due to much greater autonomy in 'basic and applied

---

[3] The questionnaire specifies 'product development' as referring to product innovations which represent new or significantly improved goods or services with respect to their characteristics (technical specifications, components, materials, incorporated software) or intended uses (user-friendliness etc.). The product has to be new to the FIE, but not necessarily to the market.

[4] Process engineering is defined as referring to new or improved production methods (e.g. computer-assisted design) or delivery methods (e.g. bar-coded goods-tracking system), including changes in techniques, equipment and/or software.

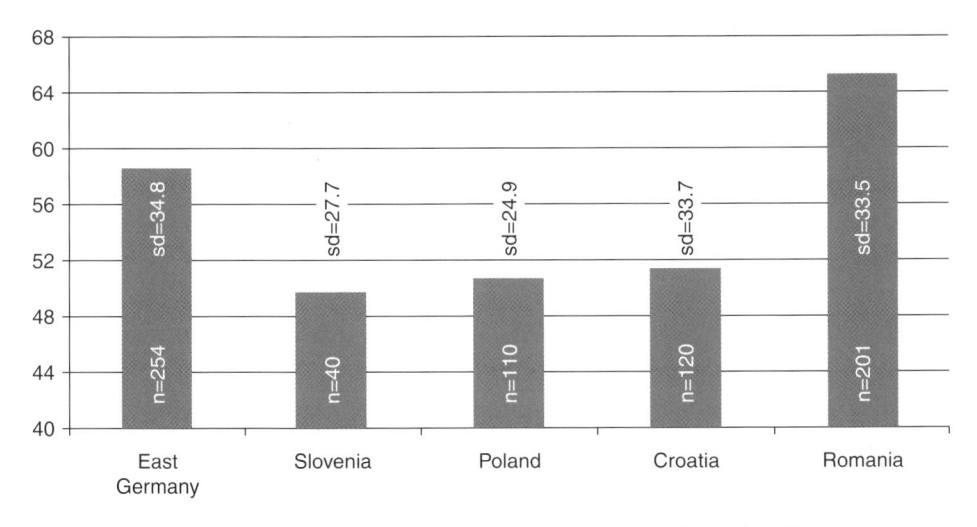

Fig. 15.6. Average levels of autonomy from foreign investors in technology-related business functions of FIEs across countries.

Note: Autonomy levels are coded as 0 for no autonomy and 100 for full autonomy over the three technology-oriented business functions of basic and applied research, product development, and process engineering.

n = the number of firms that reported on all these business functions.

sd = standard deviation.

Source: IWH FDI micro database.

research' (incidentally the average level of autonomy of Romanian FIEs is also higher than in the other host economies if all seven business functions are considered). This seems to suggests that Romanian FIEs have a high degree of independence in deciding about own R&D, even if they have the lowest R&D intensity of all the other countries (see above). Slovenian, Polish, and Croatian FIEs command much lower levels of autonomy, while East German FIEs are somewhere in the middle. Further analysis (see below) will address the question of whether the high level of autonomy for Romanian FIEs and the low level for, in particular, Polish FIEs in fact have the kind of repercussions on local host economy embeddedness that the literature suggests.

4.4. *Stylised facts: Importance of augmenting and exploiting strategies*

With respect to the two possible strategies of foreign investors, our data allows us to distinguish which strategy is dominant and/or whether the strategies are in fact complementary. Using the data from our survey, we proxy the importance of the augmenting strategy by the 'importance of the FIE as a source of technological knowledge for R&D or innovation for others'. The possible answers range among 1 = not important; 2 = of little importance; 3 = important; 4 = very important; 5 = extremely important, and we use the average of the answers for 'Headquarters of your MNE group' and for 'Other units or subsidiaries of your MNE group': where the average is greater than 3 (i.e., on average 'important' or higher), the FIE is assumed to follow an augmenting strategy. The proxy for the exploiting strategy is defined as the 'importance of the following sources of technological knowledge for R&D or innovation in the firm', and again the possible answers range among 1 = not important; 2 = of little importance; 3 = important; 4 = very important; 5 = extremely important. The two sources of technological knowledge considered for the exploiting strategy are 'R&D carried out at the headquarters of your foreign investor network' and 'R&D carried out by another unit of the foreign investor network', and we use the average level of importance between the two. Where the average is greater than 3, the FIE is assumed to follow an exploiting strategy.

For Fig. 15.7, we calculated the share of FIEs that have either the exploiting strategy as their dominant strategy (i.e., the proxy for exploiting is greater than 3 and that for the augmenting is lower than 3), or the augmenting strategy as the dominant strategy (i.e., the proxy for augmenting greater than 3 and exploiting lower than 3), or both strategies as important, very important, or extremely important (i.e., both proxies greater than 3), or, finally, neither of the strategies (i.e., both proxies lower than 3).

The results show that FDI projects in our host economies in fact often envisage both strategies as important: the shares of FIEs attaching importance to both strategies

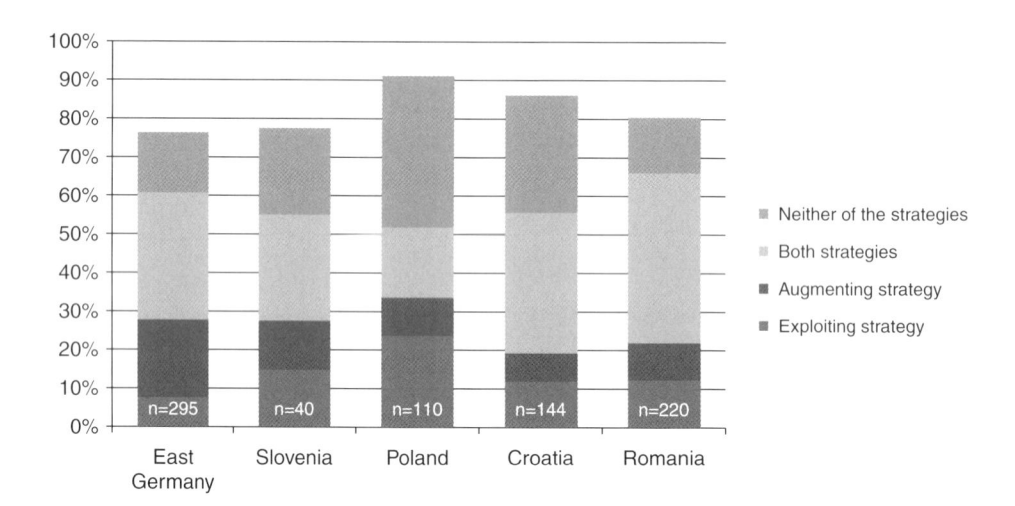

Fig. 15.7. Importance of exploiting and augmenting strategies across countries.

Note: Based on shares of firms per host economy that evaluate the exploiting or the augmenting strategies as important, very important, or extremely important. Shares not adding up to 100% reflect firms that did not provide the information.

n = the number of firms that reported on the questions used to proxy the strategies.

Source: IWH FDI micro database.

at the same time revolve around 30% amongst East German and Slovenian FIEs, around 20% for Polish FIEs, around 35% for Croatian, and around 45% (the highest share) amongst Romanian FIEs.

Other important differences on the country-specific dimension emerge: FIEs with a dominant exploiting strategy can be found mainly in Polish and Croatian FDI initiatives; FIEs with a dominant augmenting strategy are mainly located in East Germany. It is interesting also that amongst Polish FDI initiatives a large share, around 40% (around 30% for Croatia), do not attach any particular importance to either augmenting or exploiting strategies — clearly there is little knowledge transfer here.

4.5. *Stylised facts: Integration of FIEs into host economies*

Again, we draw from the literature the proposition that the developmental impact of FIEs increases with the extent of embeddedness of FIEs in the national innovation system: where technological activity of transnational corporations is decentralised, the host economy will benefit most intensively from technology transfer if the technologically active foreign affiliate is firmly embedded in its host economy.

As a first set of indicators denoting the degree of embeddedness of FIEs into their host economies,[5] we use data on the structure of sales and supplies according to the location of buyers and customers. In the questionnaire, the firms were asked to estimate those shares directly: the possible sources of supplies suggested in the questionnaire were 'Imports from your foreign investor network (headquarters and other foreign units)', 'Imports from other foreign suppliers', 'Supplies from other domestic subsidiaries of your foreign investor', and 'Supplies from other domestic suppliers'. The possible direction of sales were 'Exports to your foreign investor network (headquarters and other foreign units)', 'Exports to other foreign buyers', 'Sales to other domestic subsidiaries of your foreign investor', and 'Sales to other domestic buyers'. For the descriptive analysis, we compare the share of sales and supplies contracted with other actors in the host economies, the shares of trade with the foreign parent and members of the parent network, and the shares of trade with non-network actors from outside the host economy.

In line with the strategic motive of the foreign investors to access a new market or to increase the existing share of the host-country market (see Table 15.3), the share of sales to host economy markets are highest amongst Polish and East German FIEs, followed by Croatia, Romania and, finally, with the lowest share, Slovenia. (See Fig. 15.8.) While these shares of sales to the host economy reflect the degree of embeddedness of FIEs in terms of trade, the shares of sales to the foreign investor's

---

[5] In the East German case, 'host economy' was defined as East Germany rather than Germany as a whole.

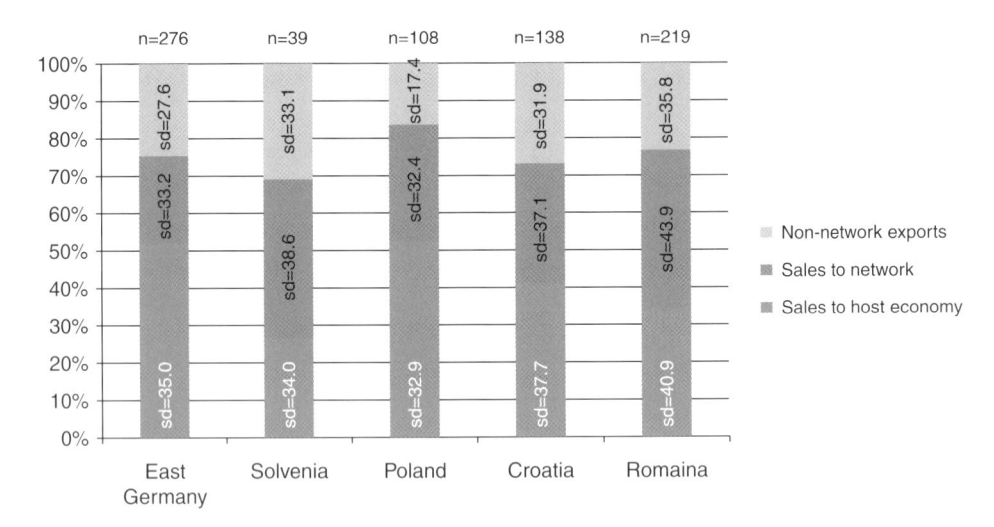

Fig. 15.8. Structure of sales across countries: averages of destinations of sales.

Note: The bars represent the host-economy-specific unweighted means of shares of sales amongst the respective groups of FIEs.

sd = standard deviation.

Source: IWH FDI micro database.

network partners (both domestically and abroad) may serve as some indication of the 'closedness' of the FDI initiative. This latter indicator is, in fact, highest for Romanian and Slovenian FIEs and lowest for East German FIEs. Unfortunately, standard deviations are quite high, suggesting that embeddedness is less country-specific than firm-specific — yet another indication of heterogeneity.

Exports of FIEs to non-network partners are typically treated as a performance indicator for FIE development (see for example Filatotchev *et al.*, 2008). Here, we find the highest shares for Slovenian, Croatian, and East German FIEs. The lowest shares are recorded amongst Polish FIEs.

Vis-à-vis the supplier-structure of our country-specific FIE-groups, FIEs tend to procure predominantly from their host economies in the cases of East Germany and Poland, but much less so in those of Romania, Croatia and Slovenia (see Fig. 15.9). Correspondingly, the shares of supplies from foreign investors' networks are highest amongst Romanian and, with a bit of a gap, Polish and Slovenian FIEs. The shares of imports from outside the foreign investors' networks are particularly high for Croatian, Slovenian, and Romanian FIEs, suggesting that the kind of intermediate products and raw materials needed by FIEs are not as abundantly available in these host economies.

The second set of data denoting the degree of embeddedness of FIEs in their host economies relates to technological interaction. As the most promising amongst the various actors in the national innovation systems of the host economies, we expected

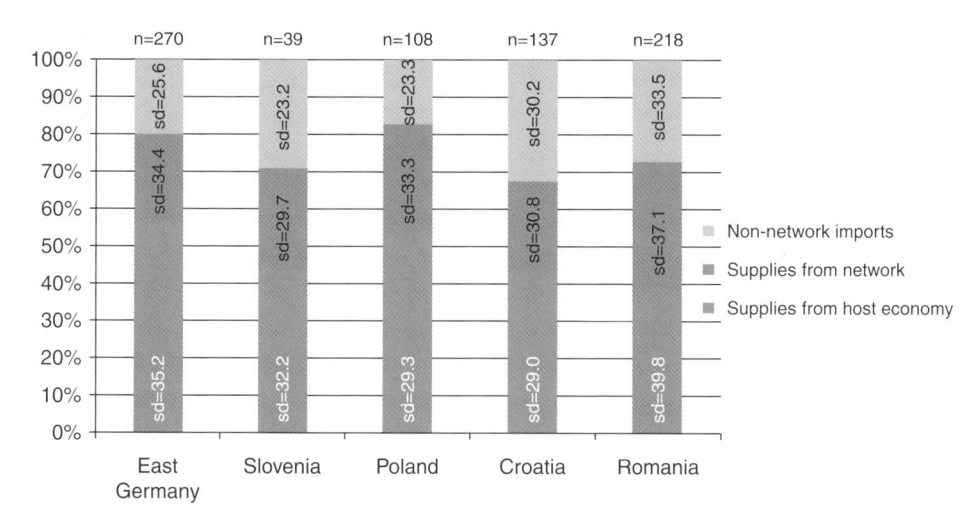

Fig. 15.9. Structure of supplies across countries: averages of origins of supplies.

Note: The bars represent the host economy-specific unweighted means of shares of supplies amongst the respective groups of FIEs.

sd = standard deviation.

Source: IWH FDI micro database.

local scientific institutions to be particularly important for own R&D and innovation by FIEs. From our database, we used the 'importance of R&D carried out in collaboration with local scientific institutions as sources of technological knowledge for R&D or innovation', and as possible answers we again suggested 1 = not important; 2 = of little importance; 3 = important; 4 = very important; 5 = extremely important.

In the presentation of the results in Fig. 15.10, we calculated the shares of product innovation-active FIEs in groups according to the five possible answers, and depict those shares in cumulative bars: the shares for FIEs that consider their local scientific research institutions as being either 'not important' or 'of little importance' are presented in negative bars, the shares for the others are presented in positive bars.

Polish FIEs appear to value Polish research institutions as comparatively the most important for their own technological activities, followed by East German and Croatian FIEs. While the differences between countries are not very pronounced, we have no information about the actual content of cooperation: we would assume that the research institutions in East Germany (e.g. Fraunhofer, Max Planck, Leibniz) are better endowed financially, being funded by West Germany. Additionally, they may have better access to qualified personnel, with standards of living and, last but not least, wages much higher in East Germany than in the countries of CEE. We would assume that this would lead to better qualified cooperation in the East German case than in CEE. More research using additional data is necessary to shed more light on

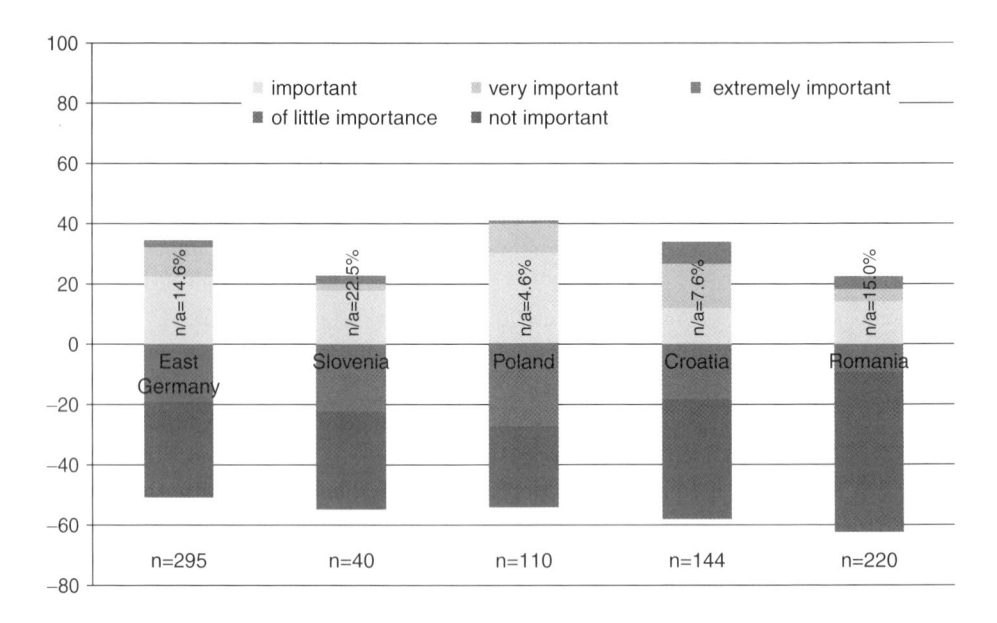

Fig. 15.10. Intensity of cooperation with local scientific institutions across host economies.

Note: Cumulative bars represent the shares of product-innovation-active FIEs that consider local research institutions to be not important, of little importance (negative bars), important, very important, or extremely important (positive bars) for their own technological activities.

n/a = the share of product innovation-active FIEs that did not answer this question.

sd = standard deviation.

Source: IWH FDI micro database.

this issue. What is absolutely clear is that there is a major and deep-seated network misalignment here. The results suggest that the majority of FIEs in fact consider national research institutions as having either no or minor importance — and this holds across all countries. Clearly the national Academies of Sciences in post-socialist countries have so far not been able to overcome their unfavourable reputation to play a vital role in national innovation systems (*cf.* Chapter 4)

The results in any case contain one very important policy implication, namely that in order to increase the developmental impact of FDI in the host economies, the interaction of FIEs with scientific institutions has to be improved. This involves not only behavioural incentives for both partners, but also the empowerment of scientific institutions to be valuable partners for FIEs.

4.6. *Firm-specific determinants of technological interaction of FIEs with host economies*

In the final step of the analysis, we depart from the country-specific comparative analysis to try to account for the problem of heterogeneity found in several instances in our analysis so far. We test our set of hypothesis pertaining to the determinants of technological interaction of FIEs with their host economies, and focus here again on scientific institutions.

Because we have no theory of determinants of technological interaction that would determine a particular direction of causality and hence allow us to distinguish between dependent and independent variables, we apply pairwise correlation analysis rather than a regression model. Any analysis, hence, has to remain rather explorative.

Because we measure the importance of scientific institutions as a source for technological knowledge on a five-point rating scale, the correlation analysis is specified in terms of Spearman rank correlations. The results are presented in Table 15.4. All correlation coefficients turn out to be rather low: the highest coefficient is reported for the determinants of the extent of the augmenting nature of the strategy of the FDI initiative. Because correlation coefficients are often quite low for field work data using discrete data, we can still conclude that, while the relationships are not very strong, they do test positive, and all relationships but the one with the age of the FIE in fact turn out to be significant.

With regard to our hypotheses, we can find support for H(1) namely that technologically active FIEs are more likely to source technological knowledge from local scientific institutions — though a large number of FIEs are not considered in the analysis, because the question on innovation intensity in comparison to competitors in the relevant market was left unanswered on many occasions. We also find support for H(2), and can safely conclude that the more important the competence-augmenting strategy, the more do FIEs interact with local scientific institutions as a source of technological knowledge. This implies that FIEs actively search for new

Table 15.4. Correlation between interaction with scientific institutions and determinants of degree of embeddedness.

	Intensity of innovation	Extent of augmenting nature of strategy	Extent of exploiting nature of strategy	Level of autonomy	Age of FIE
Extent of interaction with local scientific institutions	0.1835* 425 0.0001	0.3512* 668 0.0000	0.3613* 670 0.0000	0.1109* 651 0.0091	−0.0468 688 0.2198

Note: Correlations are specified a Spearman pairwise rank correlations, whereby all pairwise correlation coefficients are calculated by using all available data. The first line in each cell shows the correlation coefficient, the second the number of FIEs considered in the analysis, and the third line is the p-value, denoting the significance level. Stars indicate that the correlation coefficient is significant at the 1% level. Only correlations of determinants of the extent of embeddedness are displayed.

Source: IWH FDI micro database.

knowledge beyond the established knowledge base of the foreign investor (Frost, 2001), and furthermore that foreign parents mandate FIEs with a home-base-augmenting approach to innovation and technology development in order to enhance the firm- specific advantages of the whole corporation (Cantwell and Mudambi, 2005). H(3) proposed that an FIE following a competence-exploiting strategy is less likely to source technological knowledge from local scientific institutions. Our results, however, refute this hypothesis by finding significant support for the opposite. This evidence may reinforce the argument of Criscuelo *et al.* (2002), namely that foreign subsidiaries can follow both competence-augmenting and -exploiting strategies for different technologies at the same time. In other words, sourcing knowledge from the parent in one technological field does not exclude external technological interaction in another.

We proposed, following the literature, that higher FIE autonomy should result in an increased ability to form external technology linkages. H(4) on FIE autonomy does in fact test positive on our pairwise analysis. (Here, again, we use the average between autonomy levels on three technology-related business functions.) Certainly, the correlation coefficient is particularly low. Still, we can conclude that more autonomous FIEs appear also to interact more intensively with local scientific research institutions.

Frost (2001) argued that older subsidiaries should be more likely to source technology from the host economy. Using our data, we proxy the age of the FIE as the years that passed since the 'year of the entry of the foreign investor into the firm'. Our Spearman pairwise test for the age of the foreign affiliate in fact provides no information. The (negative) coefficient is far too low to be able to conclude anything. H(5) hence remains an open issue.

5. Conclusions and Outlook for Future Research

Above all, our analysis of this unique micro-database clearly shows that FDI initiatives in Central-East Europe and East Germany are not dominated by extended workbench scenarios: first, the market access investment motive dominates over the efficiency motive, and the motive of tapping localised knowledge skills and technology even comes second after market access in the East German sample. Second, around half of the FIEs in the region are in fact technologically active in terms of conducting own R&D, and more than 50% of FIEs generated product and process innovations during the three-year period preceding our field work.

Countries, however, differ in terms of the performance of their FIEs: East German FIEs appear to have a higher intensity of R&D activity than the other host economies considered (bar the surprising results for Croatian FIEs). The differences between countries in terms of innovative activities are less pronounced, with Polish and East German FIEs leading the ranks. The most pronounced differences between the countries are recorded for the economic effect of innovations, where East German FIEs clearly dominate over the other FIEs in terms of sales attributable to new or significantly improved products in 2005. Across all those descriptive indicators for technological activity, the Slovenian FIEs turn out to be surprisingly active, while the data for the Croatian and Romanian FIEs remain somewhat inconclusive (the former for R&D intensities and the latter for the sales effect of product innovations in 2005).

To some extent, these results correspond with the conventional wisdom about the countries, and hence are quite in line with expectations: East Germany can be considered the technologically most advanced host economy in the group of transition economies, because German reunification allowed early access to the EU and heavy transfers from West Germany. Slovenia has the highest level of economic (and likewise technological) development in CEE; Poland is attractive for foreign investors due to its large market and low wages, and Romania has just started catching up.

The results, however, also show that the characterisation of FIEs often does not follow host economy-specific patterns — rather firm heterogeneity prevails. Our firm-specific correlation analysis shows that FIE innovativeness, both home-base augmenting and competence-exploiting strategies, and the level of autonomy from parent investors, all raise the probability that the foreign affiliate is firmly embedded in the host economy innovation system, here exemplified by local scientific institutions. In respect of the developmental implications of FDI initiatives, this has a very important policy implication, namely that in order to increase the developmental impact of FDI in the host economies, the interaction of FIEs with scientific institutions has to be improved. This involves not only behavioural incentives for both partners, but also the empowerment of scientific institutions to be valuable partners for FIEs and leading actors in national innovation systems. While in East Germany, the public science sector has been fundamentally transformed since reunification, and a rich and highly modernised science infrastructure is available today, Central-East European countries still lag behind in this respect (McGowan *et al.*, 2004; Meske, 2004).

Although the database used for this analysis is unique and offers many avenues for explorative research on FDI projects in emerging host economies, it so far offers little data that would allow us to conduct a more dynamic analysis. Further waves of field work are needed, using the same or a very similar questionnaire, possibly even resulting in a panel structure, to allow a time-series content in the analysis.

References

Andersson, U. and Forsgren, M. (2000). 'In search of centre of excellence: Network embeddedness and subsidiary roles in multinational corporations', *Management International Review* 40(4): 329–350.

Andersson, U., Forsgren, M. and Holm, U. (2002). 'The strategic impact of external networks: Subsidiary performance and competence development in the multinational corporation', *Strategic Management Journal* 23(11): 979–996.

Arora, A. and Gambardella, A. (1990). 'Complementarities and external linkages: The strategies of large firms in biotechnology', *Journal of Industrial Economics* 38(4): 361–379.

Birkinshaw, J.M., Hood, N. and Jonsson, S. (1998). 'Building firm specific advantages in multinational corporations: The role of subsidiary initiative', *Strategic Management Journal* 19(3): 221–241.

Birkinshaw, J. and Ridderstrale, J. (1999). 'Fighting the corporate immune system: A process study of subsidiary initiatives in multinational corporations', *International Business Review* 8: 149–180.

Blanc, H. and Sierra, C. (1999). 'The internationalisation of R&D by multinationals: A trade-off between external and internal proximity', *Cambridge Journal of Economics* 23: 187–206.

Cantwell, J. (1992). 'The theory of technological competence and its application to international production'. In McFeteridge, D.G. (ed.) *Foreign Investment, Technology and Economic Growth*, Calgary, University of Calgary Press, pp. 33–67.

Cantwell, J. (1993). 'The internationalization of technological activity and its implications for competitiveness'. In Granstrand, O. *et al.* (eds.), *Technology Management and International Business*, Wiley, Chichester, pp. 137–162.

Cantwell, J. and Iammarino, S. (2003). *Multinational Corporations and European Regional Systems of Innovation*, London, Routledge.

Cantwell, J. and Janne, O.E.M., (1999). 'The role of multinational corporations and national states in the globalisation of innovatory capacity', *The European Perspective, Technology Analysis & Strategic Management* 12(2): 155–172.

Cantwell, J. and Piscitello, L. (1999). 'The emergence of corporate international networks for the accumulation of dispersed technological competences', *Management International Review* 39: 123–147.

Cantwell, J. and Mudambi, R. (2005). 'MNE competence creating subsidiary mandates', *Strategic Management Journal* 26: 1109–1128.

Criscuelo, P., Narula, R. and Verspagen, B. (2002). 'The relative importance of home and host innovation systems in the internationalisation of MNE R&D: A patent citation analysis', MERIT-Infonomics Research Memorandum Series, 26.

Cohen, W. and Levinthal, D. (1990). 'Absorptive capacity: A new perspective on learning and innovation', *Administrative Science Quarterly* 35(1): 128–152.

Dunning, J. and Narula, R. (1995). 'The R&D activities of foreign firms in the United States', *International Studies of Management and Organization* 25(1–2): 39–73.

Dunning, J.H. and Wymbs, C. (1999). 'The geographical sourcing of technology-based assets by multinational enterprises'. In Archibugi, D. *et al.* (eds.) *Innovation Policy in a Global Economy*, Cambridge, Cambridge University Press, pp. 185–224.

Dunning, J.H. (1993). *Multinational Enterprises and the Global Economy*, Wokingham, England, Addison-Wesley Publishing Company.

Frost, T. (2001). 'The geographic sources of foreign subsidiaries' innovation', *Strategic Management Journal* 22: 101–123.

Greene, W.H. (2003). *Econometric Analysis*, Upper Saddle River, New Jersey, Pearson Education International.

Günther, J., Stephan, J. and Jindra, B. (2008). 'Foreign subsidiaries in the East German innovation system — Evidence from manufacturing industries', *Applied Economics Quarterly Supplement* 59: 137–165.

Holm, U. and Fratocchi, L. (1998). 'Centres of excellence in the international firm'. In Birkinshaw, J. *et al.* (eds.) *Multinational Corporate Evolution and Subsidiary Development*, London, McMillan, pp. 189–209.

Howells, J. and Wood, M. (1993). *The Globalisation of Production and Technology*, London, Belhaven Press.

Hunya, G. (1997). 'Large privatisation, restructuring and foreign direct investment'. In Zecchini. S. (ed.) *Lessons from the Economic Transition. Central and Eastern Europe in the 1990s*, Dordrecht, Kluwer Academic Publishers, pp. 275–300.

Filatotchev, I., Stephan, J. and Jindra, B. (2008). 'Ownership structure, strategic controls and export intensity of foreign-invested firms in transition economies'. *Journal of International Business Studies* 39(7): 1133–1148.

Klevorick, A.K., Levin, R.C., Nelson, R.R. and Winter, S.G. (1995). 'On the sources and significance of inter-industry differences in technological opportunities', *Research Policy* 24: 185–205.

Kogut, B. and Zander, U. (1993). 'Knowledge of the firm, combinative capabilities, and the replication of technology', *Organization Science* 3(3): 383–397.

Kuemmerle, W. (1997). 'Building effective R&D capabilities abroad', *Harvard Business Review* 3(4): 61–70.

Leiponen, A. and Helfat, C.E. (2004). *Innovation Objectives, Knowledge Sources, and the Benefits of Breadth*, Cornell, Cornell University.

Mansfield, E. (1991). 'Academic research and industrial innovation', *Research Policy* 20: 1–12.

McGowan, F., Radosevic, S. and Von Tunzelmann, N. (2004). *The Emerging Structure of the Wider Europe*, London, Routledge.

Meske, W. (2004). *From System Transformation to European Integration. Science and Technology in Central and Eastern Europe at the Beginning of the 21st Century*, Münster, Lit Verlag.

Miller, R. (1994). 'Global R&D networks and large-scale innovations: The case of the automobile industry', *Research Policy* 23: 27–46.

Narula, R. (2002). 'Innovation systems and 'inertia' in R&D location: Norwegian firms and the role of systemic lock-in', *Research Policy* 31: 795–816.

Nonaka, I. (1994). 'Dynamic theory of organizational knowledge creation', *Organization Science* 5(1): 14–37.

Organisation for Economic Co-operation and Development (OECD) and European Commission, Eurostat (2005). *The Measurement of Scientific and Technological Activities — Proposed Guidelines for Collecting and Interpreting Technological Innovation Data. Oslo Manual.*

Pavitt, K. (1998). 'The social shaping of the national science base', *Research Policy* 27: 793–805.

Patel, P. and Pavitt, K. (1999). 'Global corporations & national systems of innovation: Who dominates whom?'. In Archibugi, D. *et al.* (eds.), *Innovation Policy in a Global Economy*, Cambridge, Cambridge University Press.

Patel, P. and Vega, M. (1999). 'Patterns of internationalisation and corporate technology: Location versus home country advantages', *Research Policy* 28: 145–155.

Pearce, R.D and Papanastassiou, M. (1999). 'Overseas R&D and the strategic evolution of MNEs: Evidence from laboratories in the UK', *Research Policy* 28: 23–41.

Pearce, R.D and Singh, S. (1992). *Globalizing Research and Development*, London, Macmillan.

Powell, W., Koput, K. and Smith-Doerr, L. (1996). 'Interorganizational collaboration and the locus of innovation: Networks of learning in biotechnology'. *Administrative Science Quarterly* 41(1): 116–145.

Stinchcombe, A.L. (1965). 'Social structure and organizations'. In March, J.G. (ed.), *Handbook of Organizations*, Chicago, Rand-McNally, pp. 142–193.

Venkataraman, S. and Van de Ven, A. (1998). 'Hostile environmental jolts, transaction set, and new business', *Journal of Business Venturing* 13(3): 231–255.

Von Hippel, E. (1976). 'The dominant role of users in the scientific instrument innovation process', *Research Policy* 5(3): 212–239.

Von Hippel, E. (2005). *Democratizing Innovation*, Cambridge MA and London, MIT Press.

Von Zedtwitz, M. and Gassmann, O. (2002). 'Market versus technology drive in R&D internationalization: Four different patterns of managing research and development', *Research Policy* 31: 569–588.

White, H. (1982). 'Maximum likelihood estimation of misspecified models', *Econometrica* 1: 1–26.

Yamin, M. and Otto, J. (2004). 'Patterns of knowledge flows and MNE innovative performance', *Journal of International Management* 10: 239–258.

Zanfei, A. (2000). 'Transnational firms and the changing organisation of innovative activities', *Cambridge Journal of Economics* 24: 515–542.

CHAPTER 16

THE IMPACT OF OUTWARD FDI ON HOME-COUNTRY EMPLOYMENT IN A LOW-COST TRANSITION ECONOMY[1]

JAAN MASSO, URMAS VARBLANE AND PRIIT VAHTER

1. Introduction

Until recently, outward foreign direct investment (OFDI) has been made mainly by firms originating from high-income economies. However, the growing importance of OFDI from the Asian emerging economies and new EU member states in Central-East Europe (CEE) has fostered the need to analyse the impact of OFDI on the parent firms from those countries, and more broadly on their home economies.

The present chapter studies the impact of outward investment on employment in the home country. This has for some time been among the most delicate issues for policy-makers and labour organisations in the high-income home economies of investors. Public opinion is highly sensitive to the risk of job losses in the metropolitan countries to the target countries of outward investment. We argue in this chapter that the whole logic of outward investment from the relatively low-cost economies is different, so that the employment effect is different too. There are relatively few cases of FDI from catch-up countries to high-income economies (so-called South–North investment) and the major target countries here have a similar or lower level of economic development, so that we are generally talking about South-South investment (Svetlicic and Jaklic, 2003). The likely reason is that firms investing abroad from the catch-up economies have only a few firm-specific advantages based on technologies, intellectual property, brand names etc. that could be exploited profitably in developed markets (Kokko, 2006; Varblane *et al.*, 2003). Rather, the particular competence of those firms lies in their market-specific knowledge about neighbouring catch-up economies, their better access to international channels of distribution, and their superior methods of doing business in a transitional higher-risk environment (Svetlicic and Jaklic, 2003). For example, Estonian firms have built up this type of

---

[1] The authors acknowledge financial support from the Estonian Science Foundation grants 5840, 6493 and 6853, and Estonian Ministry of Education and Research target funding projects SF0182588s03 and SF0182588s03, in addition to support from the EU through the *U-Know* project. The study started while Priit Vahter was working at the Research Department of Eesti Pank.

competence from their long experience in the neighbouring markets of Latvia, Lithuania, Russia and Ukraine (Varblane *et al.*, 2003). Additional motives for foreign market entry by firms from catch-up countries include gaining a market share and, in the case of services, following the customers.

In this context, we would expect that vertical FDI would not be used extensively, owing to the small wage differential between the host and home countries; horizontal investments tend to be in the non-tradable sectors like services (so that production in foreign affiliates cannot substitute for home country exports), and therefore short-run job losses in the home country due to outward FDI would be unlikely. It would be reasonable to expect the horizontal type of FDI to dominate in the given context, so that cost reduction as a motive to invest would play a smaller role. In general, the expectation is that the complementary effect will prevail, which means that investments abroad will create additional jobs at home. Horizontal FDI in neighbouring catch-up economies is likely to help increase the market share in the host country, which requires increased production at home and thereby facilitates employment growth. Thus we would expect that outward investments from catch-up economies would affect home employment positively.

This study estimates the home country employment effects of FDI by using data from Estonia, which is an interesting case, as Estonia ranks ahead of other CEE countries in terms of its inward FDI per capita, and ahead of most other CEE countries also in terms of its outward FDI relative to the size of the economy (see, for example, World Investment Report, 2005). In 2005, inward FDI stock constituted 102% of Estonian GDP (own calculations based on data from the Bank of Estonia). In the same year, OFDI amounted to 16.1% of Estonia's gross fixed capital formation, which is the third highest figure among new EU members, after Cyprus and Malta. The relatively big role of OFDI in the Estonian economy, and specifically of indirect investors[2] and investment in services (see Table 16.1), highlight Estonia as an interesting case for studying the home-country effects of FDI from low-income economies. (Vahter and Masso, 2005; Masso *et al.*, 2007).

There are very few studies analysing OFDI home country employment effects in the case of developing and transition economies. The only one we know is the study by Svetlicic *et al.* (2007), which found a positive home country employment effect in the case of Slovenian firms (especially in that of SMEs). In the light of this, and of our *a priori* reasoning, our research proposition would be that outward investments from Estonia (and other catch-up economies) affect home employment positively. Our specific contribution to the existing literature lies also in the distinction we make between the manufacturing and services sectors. Owing to data limitations, the majority of previous studies have focused on manufacturing; but in fact services appear to play the dominant role in the structure of outward investment, not only

---

[2] I.e. foreign-owned firms located in Estonia.

Table 16.1. Number of firms by sector, and presence of inward and outward FDI, 1996–2002.

Inward FDI	Outward FDI	Sector	Number of firms			Percent of firms		
			1996	1999	2002	1995	1999	2002
No	No	Manufacturing	2778	3715	4391	91	88.6	88.5
No	Yes		13	26	33	0.4	0.6	0.7
Yes	No		257	428	517	8.4	10.2	10.4
Yes	Yes		5	24	23	0.2	0.6	0.5
No	No	Construction	1470	2091	2606	97	97.4	97.2
No	Yes		5	8	8	0.3	0.4	0.3
Yes	No		40	47	63	2.6	2.2	2.4
Yes	Yes		0	1	3	0	0	0.1
No	No	Business services	10925	18148	22864	93.1	92.7	92.1
No	Yes		29	92	151	0.2	0.5	0.6
Yes	No		769	1294	1751	6.6	6.6	7.1
Yes	Yes		8	42	67	0.1	0.2	0.3

Source: Authors' calculations based on Estonian firm-level panel data 1995–2002.

from Estonia, but also from other new EU member states (Svetlicic and Jaklic, 2003). The stylised view is that horizontal South-South FDI is more commonly found in services like construction and hotels than in manufacturing (Kokko, 2006). But it has traditional been believed that the flows of intermediate inputs in those activities are relatively limited, and that production in the home country will benefit relatively little from them; we propose that investments in services between catch-up economies may influence home employment positively as well. Firms in services in catch-up economies are typically rather small, which means that investments in neighbouring economies will require additional white-collar jobs — in order to manage the process of increasing the complexity of service provision. However there are local reasons why we should not expect a negative effect in manufacturing either. Many of the Estonian outward investments are in the two other Baltic States — Latvia and Lithuania. Because the Baltic markets are small and well integrated, most producers have chosen to concentrate their production into one country to achieve economies of scale (Varblane *et al.*, 2001). Thus, the purpose of investing abroad here is probably not to *off-shore* as such.

Third, we distinguish between direct investors (domestic firms investing abroad) and indirect investors (foreign-owned firms investing abroad). Many outward investors in the transition economies are foreign-owned firms; however, in analyses of home-country effects of employment in general, this distinction seems to have been neglected (one exception is the study by Altzinger and Bellak, 1999). A previous study on motivation of outward investments from Estonia also revealed differences between direct and indirect investors (Varblane *et al.*, 2003). Additionally, there is evidence from the late 1990s that, in conjunction with the growing political and economic stability in Central European transition economies, multinationals from the EU were already pushing vertical FDI into these countries (Radosevic *et al.*, 2003). All of this gives us reason to expect that the impact of outward investment on employment in Estonia may differ between indirect and direct investors. As indirect investors can rely more on the global resources of their mother companies, and since their motives may be more orientated towards vertical FDI, their employment effect in Estonia could be weaker than that of direct investors.

The rest of the chapter is organised as follows. The next sub-section reviews the existing literature on the home-country employment effects of OFDI. Section 2 describes the research methods used, and Section 3 contains an overview of the data and a descriptive analysis. Section 4 presents the results of the regression analysis and propensity score matching. The last section concludes with policy implications.

2. Overview of the Existing Literature on the Home-Country Employment Effect of FDI

The impact of OFDI on the home economy has been attracting researchers' attention for a couple of decades (see a recent literature review in Kokko, 2006 and Appendix 1 in Masso *et al.*, 2007). An important motivation behind the majority of the resulting studies was the quest for an answer to the widespread fear of policy-makers and labour organisations that FDI, especially in the developing and transition countries, would replace home country production and exports, and consequently lead to loss of jobs at home, through a process of off-shoring.

When analysing the home-country employment effect of FDI, it is crucial to take into consideration the motives of foreign investors moving abroad. Most basic is the distinction between horizontal and vertical FDI. Vertical FDI is made by firms that geographically fragment their production into stages, typically on the basis of factor intensities, exploiting lower factor prices abroad or reducing transaction costs by internalising upstream or downstream activities (i.e., suppliers, marketing channels) (Ekholm and Markusen, 2002; Kokko, 2006). If different stages of the production process are characterised by different levels of labour intensity, a reasonable strategy would be to allocate the stages with high labour intensity to countries with low levels of labour costs, and the stages requiring lots of skills or capital to high-income countries. With vertical investments, there is a complementarity between foreign and home operations, because both are needed to produce the good. When one of the activities expands, it accordingly causes the expansion of the other activity (Brainard and Riker, 1997, use the term 'technological synergy'). However, in the short run, substitution between employment levels at home and abroad may also take place, if an activity previously conducted at home is relocated abroad (Braconier and Ekholm, 1999). Vertical OFDI is a classic vehicle of off-shoring.

Horizontal multinational enterprises (MNEs) are multi-plant firms that seek to exploit their existing advantages and replicate roughly the same activities in many locations. In this model, the major trigger for moving outward is the desire to reap the benefits of foreign market opportunities and use the economies of scale effect. If the produced good is tradable, we would expect a substitution between foreign and home employment: the firm either exports the good produced at home to other locations, or produces it in its foreign affiliates (Braconier and Ekholm, 1999). However, in the case of non-tradables, no such substitution is possible.

The question whether outward FDI substitutes or complements domestic employment has been the subject of a large number of empirical studies, which can be divided into two major groups on the basis of their findings. The first group consists of mainly earlier studies using aggregate level data — imports, wage level etc. (Sachs and Shatz, 1994; Feenstra and Hanson, 1996). The other group of studies is based on cross-section or panel data from multinational firms investing abroad (Kravis and Lipsey, 1988; Slaughter, 1995; Konings and Murphy, 2003; Braconier and Ekholm, 2001). Studies on the home-country employment effect of FDI have produced diverse conclusions. The first group of studies found a substitution effect between the activity of the foreign subsidiary and that of its parent (Kravis and Lipsey, 1988; Brainard and Riker, 1997; Braconier and Ekholm, 2001; Konings and Murphy, 2001; and Cuyvers *et al.*, 2005). Some concluded that substitution occurs between countries with comparable factor endowments, which means that low-wage countries are better employment substitutes for one another than for parent (high-income) economy employment (Brainard and Riker, 1997; Slaughter, 2000; Braconier and Ekholm, 2001; Konings and Murphy, 2003; Hansson, 2005). Others showed that US multinationals using the vertical FDI model appear to reduce employment at home, relative to production, by allocating labour-intensive stages of their production to their affiliates in developing countries (Brainard and Riker, 1997; Slaughter, 2000; Blomström *et al.*, 1997). Konings and Murphy (2003) also concluded that labour substitution is more likely to take place when factor proportions are different in various locations and vertical FDI prevails.

The second group of empirical investigations has concluded that the complementary effect prevails, which means that the activity of the foreign affiliate has a positive employment effect (Lopez-de-Silanes *et al.*, 1996; Feenstra and Hanson, 1996; Lipsey *et al.*, 2000; Markusen, 2002). The logic behind this is that the opportunity to invest in a low-cost host country can increase the firm's competitiveness, promote its use of economies of scale, and reduce its costs, which may lead to an increase in home-country employment even in the case of vertical investments. Thus there is a 'scale effect', which dominates over the 'substitution effect' for the parent country firms and employment (Ekholm and Markusen, 2002). This pattern was revealed, for example, in the North American car industry by Lopez-de-Silanes *et al.* (1996). Research on Japanese firms likewise revealed that their home-country employment grew when they invested abroad (Lipsey *et al.,* 2000). This is explained in terms of a process of of allocating labour-intensive production to developing countries, which allows the development of increasing supervisory and ancillary employment at home to service foreign operations. Braunerhjelm and Oxelheim (2000) found that in industries based on Swedish raw materials, horizontal OFDI has a complementary effect on home employment.

Finally, there is a third group of studies providing an interesting variation on the win–win employment effect (Feenstra and Hanson, 1996; Markusen, 2002), based on the notion that outward investments can raise the demand and wages for skilled labour in both the parent and host country. This stems from the differences in the pattern of labour demand in the two countries. Activities transferred by multinationals to low-cost countries are unskilled-labour intensive from the point of view of the home economy, but skilled-labour intensive from the point of view of the host country.

Thus the analysis of the employment effect of horizontal and vertical type of investments has produced mixed results. We can summarise thus: the effect of outward investment on home employment depends on at least eight groups of factors: the motive of investment (horizontal *versus* vertical); the income gap between the home and host country (North–North, North–South, South–South and South–North types of investment — Kokko, 2006); differences in factor intensities (Braconier and Ekholm, 2000); the size of the parent company (Pennings and Sleuwaegen, 2000; Svetlicic *et al.*, 2007); sector-specific aspects (Braunerhjelm *et al.*, 2005); the home country's labour market regulations (Dewit *et al.*, 2004); the size of the home economy; and access to global networks (Pennings and Sleuwaegen, 2000).

3. Framework for the Empirical Analysis

We next present our regression model for analysing the impact of outward and inward FDI on firm-level employment growth. In the existing literature, different approaches have been used to estimate these impacts. First, in some studies the inference is based on the regression of the employment growth at firm level derived from the firm growth model of Jovanovic (1982) and Evans (1987); the independent variables include firm size, age and other controls (Heshmati, 2001). Here a positive coefficient indicates that firms with inward or outward FDI experience faster than average growth. Second, many studies have followed the static labour demand model, where employment depends on the value added and wage (in many cases both in the parent and the affiliates). In a number of studies, the list of independent variables includes just the sales or value added of the parent, but not wages (Blomström *et al.*, 1997; Mariotti *et al.*, 2003). In this case, if the dependent variable is (growth of) parent employment, a positive coefficient for the OFDI dummy, or the number of employees in foreign affiliates, indicates that outward FDI increases the labour intensity of the parent's operations (Mariotti et al., 2003). Many studies have focused their inferences about the employment effects of FDI on the elasticities of parent employment to wages in its affiliates and in the parent itself (e.g. Konings and Murphy, 2001; Braconier and Ekholm, 1999). A positive impact for wages in the foreign affiliate on home-country employment indicates a substitution effect, while a negative coefficient indicates that employment in the affiliate and the parent are complementary.

Our estimation strategy was driven by the particular data available to us — the dataset includes no exact information on the affiliates, i.e. we did not know the wages and employment level of the affiliate, what type it was (whether it was a production or selling unit), etc. Given that, our interpretation of the employment effect of OFDI follows from the sign of the OFDI dummy variable in the regression. Thus we first estimated the following regression model, where the dependent variable is the logarithmic growth in employment, $\Delta n_{i,t} = \log N_{i,t} - \log N_{i,t-1}$, where $N_{i,t}$ is the number of employees in firm i at time t, and the lower-case letters denote the natural logs of variables, i.e. $n_{i,t} = \log N_{i,t}$. The model of the growth of a firm in Jovanovic (1982) and Evans (1987) implies that the growth of a firm at time t is a function of its size and age (labelled as A, $a_{i,t} = \log A_{i,t}$) at time $t-\tau$, i.e., if we measure a firm's size by its number of employees, then $\Delta n_{i,t} = \ln F(A_{i,t-\tau}, N_{i,t-\tau}) + u_{it}$, where F is some twice differentiable function and $u_{i,t}$ is the error term. We regress firm-level employment growth on various firm characteristics (age, size, etc.) lagged by two periods (i.e. $\tau = 2$). According to Faggio and Konings (2003), this specification is particularly robust to possible measurement errors in the size of the firm (e.g. in terms of employment). Using a flexible translog functional form for the function F ()(e.g. the second-order approximation), the relationship can be written as

$$\Delta n_{i,t} = \alpha_0 + \alpha_1 n_{i,t-2} + \alpha_2 n_{i,t-2}^2 + \alpha_3 n_{i,t-2} + \alpha_4 n_{i,t-2}^2 + \alpha_5 n_{i,t-2} \alpha_{i,t-2}. \qquad (1)$$

When we add various other firm-level and industry-level variables that are likely to affect the employment decision as well as various dummies, the equation to be estimated becomes as follows:

$$\Delta n_{i,t} = \alpha_0 + \alpha_1 n_{i,t-2} + \alpha_2 n_{i,t-2}^2 + \alpha_3 \log a_{i,t-2} + \alpha_4 a_{i,t-2}^2 + \alpha_5 n_{i,t-2} a_{i,t-2} + \alpha_6 \text{OUTFDI}_{i,t}$$
$$+ \alpha_7 \text{INFDI}_{i,t} + \alpha_8 \text{OUTFDI}_{i,t} \times \text{INFDI}_{i,t} + \alpha_9 \text{STATE}_{i,t} + \beta X_{i,t} + u_{i,t}. \qquad (2)$$

In this equation, OUTFDI and INFDI are dummies that equal 1 if, and only if, the firm has, respectively, made outward FDI or has received inward FDI. The interaction term of the two variables distinguishes the intermediated FDI (indirect FDI) from the outward FDI made by domestic companies (direct FDI). STATE is the dummy for state firms. Thus the comparison group is domestic private firms without FDI. Note that we do not include in the equation the change in the output of the firm, so that the value of the dummy for outward investment indicates the effect on growth in employment at the parent firm; otherwise, if the parent's output growth were included, the OFDI parameter would show the impact of OFDI on the change in the parent's labour intensity. The vector $X_{i,t} = (Z_{i,t}, I_i, T_t, R_i)$ includes the vector of firm-level variables $(Z_{i,t})$, dummies for 1-digit industries (I_i), years (T_t) and 5 geographical regions of Estonia (R_i), while $u_{i,t}$ is the error term. The vector of firm-level variables $Z_{i,t}$ includes the dummy for exports, the log of average labour costs per employee, the log of labour productivity calculated as the ratio of value added (sales minus intermediate inputs) to the number of employees, and capital intensity (log of the ratio of fixed capital to the number of employees). The definitions of the variables can be found in Table 16.A1.

In making our estimates, we had to consider a number of estimation issues. First, a 2-step selection model was also estimated, in order to control for the selection bias resulting from non-random entry and exit from the sample. Given that our dataset includes the population of Estonian firms, the inclusions in and exclusions from the sample are due to 'true' entry and exit; in other studies the selection bias has also been due to the construction of the sample, e.g. the application of size threshold to the firms to be included in the sample (Heshmati, 2001). In our case, controlling for entry and exit is motivated by the stylised fact that the survival probabilities of a firm depend on such characteristics as its age, size, etc. Therefore an analysis of the growth rate based only on surviving firms would give biased results. In the first step, the survival model of the firm was estimated as $z^*_{i,t} = \gamma w_{i,t} + \eta_{i,t}$, where γ is the vector of parameters, $w_{i,t}$ is the vector of explanatory variables, $\eta_{i,t}$ is the error term and $z^*_{i,t}$ is a latent variable; $\Delta n_{i,t}$ is observable only in cases when $z^*_{i,t} > 0$. Then, using the estimated parameter values, the inverse Mill's ratio was calculated. The inverse Mill's ratio was then added to a regression that included only the surviving firms (*viz.*- those observed at both times t and $t - 2$, i.e. without entrants or exits). Another estimation issue we needed to resolve was how to reduce the impact on the estimation results of the small number of outliers that are likely to exist in firm-level micro data. For that purpose we used robust regression analysis.[3]

In addition to regression analysis, we followed a number of earlier studies in using propensity score matching. This allows us to consider the possibility that, FDI being

---

[3] The robust method for regression begins by fitting the regression, calculating Cook's D statistic, and excluding any observation with D larger than 1. Thereafter an iterative procedure is applied, through which weights are calculated on the basis of absolute residuals and the regression is run again using these weights; the procedure stops when the weights converge (StataCorp, 2003). In the probit model, the possible impact of a small number of outliers on the results was taken into account by excluding from the dataset observations that fell below the lower 0.5% or above the 99.5% of the size distribution of the continuous independent variables.

generally implemented by relatively more successful firms, changes in the performance of the firm after undertaking FDI (increased productivity, growth of employment or skill level of labour) need not have been caused by the FDI, but might have occurred in any case owing to some other observable or unobservable characteristics of the firm (size, managerial excellence, etc.). Thus merely comparing the change in the employment growth pattern of a firm after it acquires MNE status with its earlier employment growth pattern does not provide evidence of the causal effects of outward FDI, as the firm may have been affected by factors other than FDI. Similarly, regression methods such as OLS will results in inconsistent estimates of the effect of engaging in OFDI, since the variable OUTFDI$_{i,t}$, above, is correlated with the error term (Smarzynska Javorcik, 2004; Arnold and Smarzynska Javorcik, 2005). The fundamental problem in the evaluation literature is that the counterfactual outcome — in our paper, the case where a firm had not invested abroad — is not observable. That selectivity issue is tackled by constructing an appropriate control group for the foreign investment firms from among firms without foreign investments which are as similar as possible on a range of dimensions. Inevitably, due to the non-experimental nature of our data, this is not a true counterfactual, but simply a step that allows us to go a bit beyond a simple comparison of means, or a simple least squares regression analysis. Usually, propensity score matching (hereafter PSM) is used for that purpose (Rosenbaum and Rubin, 1983; Caliendo and Kopeinig, 2005). There is an increasing number of papers addressing the effects of FDI by using PSM (e.g. Barba Navaretti and Castellani, 2004; Huttunen, 2005). (Another possibility would be to use the instrumental variable approach. However, good instruments for FDI decisions are hard to find.)

The PSM method gives a way of summarising a number of characteristics of firms into a single variable — the propensity score — indicating the probability of making OFDI. The propensity score is estimated by using a probit model where the dependent variable is a dummy variable (at time t) indicating new outward investors (NEWOUTFDI$_{i,t}$),[4] and independent variables are included in the above-mentioned vector of observable variables $X_{i,t-1}$ (at time $t-1$) that may affect the choice of investing abroad:

$$P(\text{NEWOUTFDI}_{i,t} = 1) = F(X_{i,t-1}). \tag{3}$$

This new variable is computed both for the firms switching from the status of 'national' to 'multinational', and for the firms that stay 'national'. Then each new multinational firm is paired with its nearest neighbour(s) among the national firms in

---

[4] This means that we focus exclusively on the first time that an investment in a foreign country is made, leaving out the cases where an additional investment is made in another location. The earlier papers seem to have followed the same approach.

terms of propensity score. In this way, the counterfactual 'what if' is built. Different matching algorithms have been proposed. We use nearest neighbour matching (the treated firm is matched with the firm from the comparison group that is closest in terms of propensity score) and the kernel matching algorithm (weighted averages of all firms in the comparison group are used to construct the counterfactual[5]). At the next step, the average effect of treatment on the treated (ATT) is calculated (Caliendo and Kopeinig, 2005); it can be written down as

$$\text{ATT}_{PSM} = \overline{\Delta^s n_{t+s}^{treated}} - \overline{\Delta^s n_{t+s}^{control}}, \qquad (4)$$

where the first term on the right-hand side is the mean employment growth of treated firms (new multinationals) and the second term is the weighted mean of employment growth for the counterfactuals over the same period of time. The symbol s denotes the time over which the employment change is calculated (e.g. $\Delta^2 n_{t+2} = n_{t+2} - n_t$).

Arnold and Smarzynska Javorcik (2005) also specify that the matched control observations should come from the same industry and year. It is, indeed, reasonable to specify that manufacturing firms should be matched with other manufacturing firms, not with firms from other sectors. We did not, however, use the Arnold and Smarzynska Javorcik approach. Instead, we implemented matching in a panel, and controlled for time and sector dummies in the propensity score estimation. In this way, we indirectly controlled for years and sectors in the matching.[6] As a robustness check, we also implemented the matching and calculation of ATT separately year by year, and separately for the manufacturing and services sectors. However, the number of treatment observations (firms with new OFDI) is not really large enough in any particular year. For the implementation of the propensity score matching we used the programme psmatch2 by Leuven and Sianesi (2003).

4. Data Description and Preliminary Data Analysis

The firm-level panel dataset we used combines the Estonian Business Register balance sheet and income statement data of all Estonian firms with the dataset from the Bank of Estonia on firms with OFDI. Our dataset covers the years 1995–2002, and has information about the whole population of Estonian firms — up to 41,000 firms per year, including the primary sector, manufacturing, construction and services. Our panel data also includes information about the type of ownership and the presence of

---

[5] The Epanechnikov kernel has been used, with the bandwidth set at 0.06.
[6] We thank Holger Görg from the University of Nottingham for discussions on these issues.

outward investments, which allows us to distinguish between four main types of firms in Estonia:

(a) Domestically owned firms that have not invested abroad;
(b) Domestically owned firms that have invested abroad (direct investors);
(c) foreign-owned firms that have not invested abroad from Estonia;
(d) foreign-owned firms that have invested abroad from Estonia (indirect investors).

Many of the previous studies on the home country effect of FDI have had access to better data, including more detailed information on the affiliates, e.g., employment and wages in affiliates at different locations (Braconier and Ekholm, 1999; Konings and Murphy, 2001). We can calculate just a foreign investment dummy variable. However, the uniqueness of our dataset is that it originates from a low-cost (middle-income) transition economy, whereas in previous studies the parents have always been from relatively high-income countries.

The descriptive statistics of the variables used in the regression analysis are presented in Table 16.A1. Note the rather wide variation of firm-level employment growth relative to its mean value. This means that the growth rates of individual firms differ markedly (even in declining industries there are growing firms and vice versa). The same can be said about the profit-to-sales ratio. About 15% of the firms in our dataset have at least some exports, 7% are foreign-owned, and 1% are state-owned. The average annual wage of €2321 per employee indicates a rather low level of labour costs; however, we should mention that this figure is not adjusted for working hours.

Table 16.1 provides a summary of the investing status of Estonian firms at the beginning, in the middle and at the end of the sample period. The number of firms with direct or indirect OFDI (second and fourth row respectively within each section of the table) increased during the period analysed (1996–2002) 4.4-fold, from 63 to 274 firms. Even in the case of the latter figure, we can consider our sample of outward investment firms to be rather small. Striking growth occurred among the business service group, where between 1996 and 2002 the number of firms with OFDI increased from 43 to 218. In 2002, 56 outward investors belonged to manufacturing, 11 to construction and 218 to services. The low share of manufacturing firms investing abroad is probably a consequence of the relatively small differences in production cost levels between Estonia and its main FDI host countries — Latvia and Lithuania.[7] However, outward investing firms in manufacturing

---

[7] In 2002, according to our database, Estonian firms had in total 463 affiliates abroad, of which 182 (39%) were in Latvia and 112 (24%) in Lithuania. The share of affiliates in the EU15 countries was a mere 12.5%. Thus it is not possible to make a comparison of the South-South type of investment and the South-North type using Estonian material, because there is simply not enough variation by destination country at present.

Table 16.2. The role of the four groups of firms in the Estonian economy in 2002 (% of sector totals).

Inward FDI	Outward FDI	Sector	Employees	Exports	Imports	Annual labour productivity, €000	Annual wages, €000
No	No	Manufacturing	63.9	34.8	28.2	20.2	2.4
No	Yes		3.9	3.5	3.3	43.6	4.9
Yes	No		28.1	52.6	59.7	39.6	4.6
Yes	Yes		4.2	9.0	8.8	74.0	6.1
No	No	Construction	89.6	30.9	41.5	21.5	2.3
No	Yes		1.9	3.7	8.5	58.9	4.4
Yes	No		5.9	63.4	44.5	97.4	6.7
Yes	Yes		2.7	2.0	5.4	100.5	
No	No	Business services	83.7	62.8	56.1	35.9	2.2
No	Yes		4.2	8.2	7.5	153.3	7.4
Yes	No		11.2	27.0	32.4	100.4	5.9
Yes	Yes		1.0	1.9	4.0	133.7	9.3

industry tend to be larger than those in the services sector in terms of number of employees based in Estonia (Table 16.2). Roughly one-third of the population are indirect outward investors and two-thirds direct outward investors. The proportion of direct investors is somewhat lower in manufacturing (59% of all investors) and higher in construction and services (67–73%).

Table 16.2 helps us to get a better understanding of the importance of firms with OFDI within the Estonian economy. It reveals that the share of firms with OFDI by employment or exports is several times higher than their share by number of firms. In manufacturing, 1.2% of firms has OFDI, but their share in employment is 8.9%, and in exports 12.5%. A similar picture emerges in services, where the 0.9% of firms with OFDI has an employment share of 5.2%. Indirect investors have a higher employment share in manufacturing and construction, direct investors in services. Thus the preliminary analysis of data tells us that outward investors' employment (firm size) is above the average level of the corresponding economic sector. In manufacturing, the shares of exports or imports of outward investors (respectively 12.5 and 12.1%) are not very much higher than their share in value added (9%). These numbers suggest horizontal investments, because with vertical investments we would expect intensive trade flows between the parent and its affiliates.

As concerns the ranking of the four groups of firms in terms of labour productivity, wages and capital intensity (see Table 16.2, and Vahter and Masso, 2005), both indirect and direct outward investors outperform both foreign-owned and domestic firms, having 1.5–4.0-fold higher productivity, wages and capital intensity. A similar pattern appears in the services industries. These numbers are evidence that the

Table 16.3. Annual average employment growth rate of firms with inward or outward FDI.

Industry	Period	No inward or outward FDI Domestic firm (%)	Inward FDI, no outward FDI Foreign firm (%)	No inward FDI, outward FDI Direct investors (%)	Inward & outward FDI Indirect investors (%)
Manufacturing	1995–99	−0.48	0.26	**8.38**	−1.51
	2000–02	2.98	0.82	**7.23**	6.93
Construction	1995–99	−2.38	**14.43**	−0.36	−27.55
	2000–02	2.87	5.49	**9.71**	−3.29
Wholesale and retail trade; hotels and restaurants	1995–99	0.25	3.27	**8.76**	2.75
	2000–02	0.57	6.37	3.41	**6.75**
Transport, storage and communications	1995–99	1.59	−0.47	**9.54**	−0.88
	2000–02	4.51	**6.21**	4.42	−19.86
Financial intermediation, real estate and business services	1995–99	−0.81	15.80	4.69	**28.03**
	2000–02	0.22	**14.77**	−3.03	−16.17

Note: For each sector and period, the figures in bold indicate the group with the highest rate of employment growth.

outward investors are relatively successful firms. Although there is some evidence that some foreign-owned firms have located their production in Estonia to take advantage of cheap labour, the productivity figures for OFDI suggest that this does not apply so much in the case of outward investors.

Table 16.3 presents the results of employment changes in different groups of Estonian firms. In order to give a clearer picture of the dynamics of employment, the data were split into two periods: 1995–1999 and 2000–2002. The first period is associated with the restructuring period in the Estonian economy and it ends with the breaking of the Russian crisis. The second period is one of rapid economic growth, with extensive use of OFDI as a market entry method. The average GDP growth rates in the two periods were respectively 5.1% and 8.8% (*Source*: Bank of Estonia).

The first and most general finding is that home employment growth of firms performing OFDI (in manufacturing, construction, and trade) is much higher, which supports our first research proposition (positive impact of outward investment on the parent's employment growth). That should mean that as long as the major host countries of OFDI are neighbouring countries with relatively similar factor costs, outward investors will not reduce employment in Estonia. The second major finding relates to the different behaviour of direct and indirect investors, in line with our second research proposition. Direct investors experienced in most cases more rapid growth of home employment than indirect investors. The third finding concerns the differences in employment growth in the two periods. In all sectors, domestic firms increased their number of employees on average more in the second period; thus any differences between the two periods may be linked at least partly to improved general macroeconomic performance in Estonia.

Within services, domestic firms are clearly outperformed in employment growth by all other categories of firms in wholesale and retail trade. In financial intermediation, the employment growth of outward investors changes from positive to negative between the two periods. In transport, storage and communications, indirect investors show negative employment growth. The negative employment growth for indirect investors may indicate the use of certain elements of vertical FDI, where optimisation occurs between different markets in the framework of the whole value chain of the multinationals.

Next, we will look at how employment has changed in firms with OFDI since they started to invest abroad. Although such calculations are not sufficient to make causal inferences (see discussions in the last section), they provide a useful first look at the data. Table 16.4 presents the results of the calculations. The last column shows the percentage change in the employment of the parent firms relative to their employment in the last year before making the investment.

As we can see, even in the first year of OFDI, employment in parent firms was 14.6% higher than before. Although in the second and third year extra jobs were added, we can see that most of the effect took place during the first year of investment. That may be because the auxiliary employment needed to service foreign investments has to be brought in right at the beginning of investment, and because manpower needs may be largely fixed, and little affected by subsequent growth in the scale of subsidiary operations. The positive home-country employment effect is quite broad-based — about 50–60% of all firms increase their employment after going abroad; thus the positive average employment growth is not due to a small number of outliers with exceptionally strong job creation. In the case of investments undertaken since 2000, the employment effect was clearly stronger than for earlier investments (for services, in the first year, 58% as compared to 18% for the earlier period). On the one hand, that can be explained by the growing share of service firms in total OFDI, as the effect of OFDI on parents' employment in the service sector seems to be stronger in both periods. The more vigorous growth of employment in services can be partly explained by the smaller size of service firms before the investment. At the time of investment (the last year a firm has no foreign affiliates), the average employment size in services was 25 in the case of direct investors, and 28 employees in that of indirect investors. In manufacturing, the respective figures were 99 and 178 (own calculations).

Table 16.4. Change in employment after implementing outward FDI, 1995–2002.

	Year of outward FDI	Number of firms used in calculations	Percentage of firms where employment after implementing outward FDI has... decreased	... not changed	... increased	Change in the number of employees relative to the initial level, %
Total sample	1	231	29.0	22.1	48.9	14.6
	2	114	28.1	16.7	55.3	19.5
	3	69	27.5	13.0	59.4	25.0
	4	38	31.6	7.9	60.5	9.9
	5	15	33.3	6.7	60.0	10.6
	6	4	50.0	0.0	50.0	195.5
Outward FDI made before 1999						
Manufacturing	1	17	47.1	11.8	41.2	8.5
	2	14	57.1	0	42.9	−11.1
	3	13	46.2	7.7	46.2	−14.3
Services	1	42	33.3	9.5	57.1	18.0
	2	37	32.4	13.5	54.1	28.7
	3	31	29	9.7	61.3	61.9
Outward FDI made since 2000						
Manufacturing	1	11	18.2	9.1	72.7	10.9
	2	9	22.2	11.1	66.7	22.3
	3	4	0	0	100	120.1
Services	1	67	16.4	26.9	56.7	57.9
	2	49	20.4	22.4	57.1	52.5
	3	17	17.6	29.4	52.9	39.8
Type of investors						
Direct investors	1	169	30.8	21.3	47.9	21.3
	2	75	30.7	18.7	50.7	28.4
	3	49	30.6	16.3	53.1	25.9
Indirect investors	1	62	24.2	24.2	51.6	0.4
	2	39	23.1	12.8	64.1	9.8
	3	20	20.0	5.0	75.0	23.3

Note: In our database, a significant proportion of observations lack data on the number of employees. In the calculations, we have used only those firms whose employment data were available for all the years of having OFDI and during the last year of undertaking OFDI.

Another striking result is the much stronger employment effect of direct OFDI than of indirect OFDI (see Table 16.4). In our opinion, that flows from the following three factors:

1) The subsidiaries of the direct investors are served from Estonia, so that the required ancillary employment is created over there. In the case of indirect investors, the subsidiaries are served from locations other than Estonia, so that no (or fewer) extra jobs are created in Estonia.

2) Our surveys among Estonian companies show that the subsidiaries of Estonian investors have a relatively low level of autonomy; functions that are not transferred to subsidiaries need to be fulfilled in Estonia, which means extra jobs (Männik et al., 2006).

3) The direct investors are relatively smaller at the time of investment than the indirect investors,[8] so they need to create more jobs to serve the investments, and to coordinate the use of distribution channels, sales promotion, advertising, logistics, while the indirect investors may have already built up the necessary capacity in the past. But we would also expect subsequent employment growth among direct investors to be more dependent on initial size than among indirect investors, as in the former case the investments are served from Estonia, in the latter, from other countries. Another reason why home job losses on account of OFDI are less likely in the case of direct investors is that, owing to their generally smaller size, direct investors are less able to divide and allocate different parts of the value chain among different countries.

5. Results of the Regression Analysis and Propensity Score Matching

We now move on to the results of the regression analysis. Table 16.5 shows the parameter estimates of the employment growth model. The interpretation is that a positive value of the outward FDI parameter indicates that Estonian firms with affiliates abroad have on average faster employment growth than firms without foreign affiliates.

The results from Table 16.5 indicate unambiguously that employment of small firms is growing more rapidly and that of old firms more slowly (because the estimated lagged firm size parameters are negative). That is a common finding in the literature on the determinants of firm-level employment growth. Labour cost (wages including payroll taxes) has a negative and statistically significant effect on employment growth, as expected, (since wage growth is expected to inhibit labour demand). Both labour productivity and capital intensity have a positive impact on employment growth. Such a result is not surprising, given the previous empirical evidence on the reallocation process in Estonia: more productive firms are able to increase their market share, and thus increase their employment at the expense of less productive firms. Being an exporter also means up to 4% faster employment growth. That

---

[8] At the time of investment (the last year a firm has no foreign affiliates), the average employment size was 40 employees in the case of direct investors, and 52 employees in the case of indirect. However, direct investors grow faster after the investment, and the overall average size of the direct investors in our sample was 113 employees *cf.* 83 employees for indirect investors. There were some differences between sectors: in the last year a firm has no foreign affiliates, the average size in services was 25 employees in the case of direct investors, and 28 employees in that of indirect investors; in manufacturing, the figures were respectively 99 and 178 (own calculations).

Table 16.5. Employment growth model parameter estimates: robust regressions.

Method	Robust regression (1)	Robust regression with selection correction (2)	Robust regression (X)[a] (3)	Robust regression with selection correction (X)[a] (4)
Log size (−2)	−0.0078 (4.10)***	−0.0144 (5.51)***	−0.0104 (3.92)***	−0.0093 (3.14)***
Log size squared (−2)	−0.0018 (5.18)***	−0.0011 (2.44)**	−0.0012 (2.70)***	−0.0013 (2.35)**
Log age (−2)	−0.0098 (2.52)**	−0.0171 (3.29)***	−0.0246 (4.68)***	−0.0242 (4.54)***
Log age squared (−2)	−0.0040 (2.42)**	−0.0032 (1.49)	0.0008 (0.38)	0.0008 (0.37)
Log size (−2) × Log age (−2)	0.0022 (2.29)**	0.0031 (2.38)**	0.0018 (1.34)	0.0014 (1.02)
Export dummy	0.0416 (20.90)***	0.0398 (16.09)***	0.0293 (11.44)***	0.0252 (9.78)***
Outward FDI	0.0303 (3.30)***	0.0417 (3.47)***	0.0303 (2.52)**	0.0331 (2.61)***
Foreign firm	0.0184 (6.47)***	0.0178 (4.96)***	0.0094 (2.54)**	0.0103 (2.73)***
Outward FDI × Foreign firm	0.0032 (0.23)	−0.0170 (0.91)	−0.0103 (0.55)	−0.0103 (0.54)
Outward FDI × post-2000	0.0412 (2.65)***	0.0293 (1.55)	0.0308 (1.62)	0.0214 (1.10)
State firm	−0.0323 (5.44)***	−0.0328 (4.45)***	−0.0271 (3.65)***	−0.0310 (4.08)***
Log wage cost per employee			−0.0079 (4.82)***	−0.0092 (5.27)***
Log capital intensity			0.0012 (1.81)*	0.0016 (2.14)**
Log labour productivity			0.0216 (16.26)***	0.0251 (17.53)***
Mills ratio		−0.0358 (12.85)***		−0.0318 (11.40)***
Constant	−0.0099 (1.77)*	0.0474 (5.85)***	−0.1183 (7.90)***	−0.1875 (12.04)***
Observations	50,644	36,458	36,498	35,347
R-squared	0.03	0.04	0.04	0.05

Notes: Absolute values of *t* statistics in parentheses; * Significant at 10%; ** Significant at 5%; *** Significant at 1%.

The comparison groups are domestic private firms, Northern Estonia (Tallinn, the capital, together with Harjumaa). Time, region and 1-digit industry dummies are included in all regressions. All the estimations are for the business sector (i.e., without public services).

The dummy for 'Foreign firms' indicates how much higher or lower employment growth is for firms with foreign owners but without foreign affiliates than that for domestic firms (our reference group). The dummy for outward FDI shows the impact on employment growth of foreign investment by direct investors. The effect of indirect OFDI can be viewed as the sum of the coefficients of OFDI and the interaction term 'Outward FDI × Foreign firm'.

'Post-2000' is the dummy variable for the period after 2000.

[a] Including three extra control variables — log of labour productivity, log of wage cost per employee, and log of capital intensity.

is reasonable, given that the growth prospects of domestic-market-oriented firms are limited, owing to the relatively small size of the Estonian market. The goodness-of-fit of the regressions (4%) is rather low; however, in earlier studies on firm-level growth the goodness-of-fit has been on similarly low levels. For instance, in Heshmati (2001) the adjusted R^2 was in the range of 8.5–19.8%, in Konings et al. (2002) 4.7%.

The estimation results support the hypothesis of a positive home country employment effect of OFDI from Estonia (the dummy for firms with foreign affiliates is always positive and significant). Holding the other determinants of firm growth constant, firms with outward investments experienced about 3% faster growth of employment in the period to 2000, and 7% faster growth in the period from 2000.[9] This re-confirms the differences between two periods detected by the descriptive tables. The effect is statistically significant and non-negligible.

However, no significant differences could be observed between direct and indirect investors (those owned by Estonian and foreign capital, respectively). The interaction effect (measured by the variable *Outward FDI × Foreign Firm*) has a negative sign, but is not significant. The reason why this difference appears in the descriptive tables but not in the regressions might be that in the regressions we control for factors like firm size: indirect investors are generally larger than direct investors, so at least some (or perhaps even most) of the faster growth of direct investors vis-à-vis indirect investors can be attributed to their smaller size. Another source of difference might be that foreign firms pay higher wages than domestic firms (we would expect the level of labour costs to affect net employment creation negatively). The effect of inward FDI on employment growth is positive and significant as well (as noted by Masso et al., 2006), i.e., foreign-owned firms create jobs faster than domestic firms. That effect is also highlighted in earlier studies on firm growth in transition economies (see Faggio and Konings, 2003). As we can see, the results from the two regressions with and without adjustment for selection owing to exit are qualitatively similar.

The results of the propensity score matching support the view that the effects of OFDI on employment in Estonia have not been negative. The results of probit estimation — used in calculating the conditional probability of investing abroad — are presented in Table 16.6, where the dependent variable (NEWOFDI) is the dummy variable indicating whether the firm has invested abroad for the first time. Note that this variable is thus different from the outward FDI dummy used in the regression analysis.[10] There, the outward FDI dummy indicated all firms that had outward FDI, including those that had been operating as multinationals during the whole period studied.

---

[9] The latter figure represents the sum of the values of the parameters for 'outward FDI' and 'Outward FDI × post-2000' in Table 16.5.
[10] Specifically, $NEWOFDI_{i,t} = 1$ if $OUTFDI_{i,t-1} = 0$ and $OUTFDI_{i,t} = 1$; otherwise $NEWOFDI_{i,t} = 0$.

Table 16.6. Probit model for making new outward FDI.

Variables	Services 1996–1999	Services 2000–2002	Manufacturing 1996–1999	Manufacturing 2000–2002
Size (−1)	0.388 (0.057)***	0.217 (0.043)***	0.476 (0.116)***	0.281 (0.088)**
Log age	0.068 (0.037)*	0.008 (0.018)	0.032 (0.074)	−0.014 (0.039)
Log labour productivity (−1)	0.643 (0.120)***	0.386 (0.096)***	1.016 (0.292)***	0.111 (0.193)
Foreign firm (−1)	−0.013 (0.186)	0.029 (0.121)	−0.196 (0.305)	−0.638 (0.311)**
Export dummy (−1)	0.154 (0.155)	0.258 (0.112)**		0.431 (0.332)
Log capital intensity (−1)	−0.041 (0.055)	0.054 (0.036)	−0.066 (0.115)	0.180 (0.094)*
Log labour cost per employee (−1)	−0.277 (0.105)***	0.064 (0.092)	−0.148 (0.333)	0.107 (0.231)
Equity/Assets (−1)	0.1 (0.25)	0.017 (0.143)	−0.215 (0.263)	−0.29 (0.216)
Profit/Sales (−1)	−0.906 (0.375)**	−0.668 (0.222)***	−1.476 (0.788)*	−0.056 (0.067)
Constant	−142.61 (73.756)*	−25.188 (36.914)	−77.438 (148.229)	20.461 (78.338)
Sector dummies	Yes	Yes	Yes	Yes
Regional dummies	Yes	Yes	Yes	Yes
Year dummies	Yes	Yes	Yes	Yes
Observations	11593	22072	1979	5516
Pseudo R-squared	0.228	0.21	0.3113	0.198
LR chi2	124.09	203.12	54.9	45.67

Note: Standard errors are in parentheses; * Significant at 10%; ** Significant at 5%; *** Significant at 1%. Exogenous variables are lagged by one period. The lagged export dummy for manufacturing in 1996–1999 was dropped in the probit model by the psmatch2.ado programme.

As OFDI at the beginning of the period is different from end-of-period OFDI,[11] we study these separately for the periods 1996–1999 and 2000–2002. We used the following pre-OFDI characteristics of firms to predict the probability of engaging in investment abroad: the size of the firm, labour productivity (value added per employee), age, foreign ownership, export dummy, capital intensity, wage per employee, profit-to-sales ratio (a proxy of the Lerner index), debt-to-equity ratio,

---

[11] For instance, macroeconomic conditions in Estonia changed in the course of time, as did the motives for undertaking foreign investment: in more recent years, moving production into locations with more favourable input costs might have become a more important reason for undertaking foreign investment, due to the high rate of wage growth at home.

sector dummies (at 2-digit NACE level), regional dummies, and year dummies. The choice of variables is quite similar to that used in other studies doing similar analysis based on other countries (see e.g. Barba Navaretti and Castellani, 2004).

The estimation results show quite plausible signs for the right-hand-side variables, although many of the variables are not significant in the case of manufacturing industry, and the results also show some differences between periods. As the aim of the probit models is to calculate the propensity score of doing outward FDI and not to study in detail the determinants of outward FDI, we will not spend time discussing the sign and significance of each exogenous variable. Note, however, that the probability of making FDI is generally larger for firms with higher labour productivity (*cf.* the implications of the model by Helpman *et al.*, 2004).[12]

Before calculating the ATT effect, we checked, using the standard t-test, whether the matching based on the estimated propensity score was successful, that is, whether the treatment and control group observations now had similar characteristics. We found that, after matching, the differences evident in the period before treatment were no longer significant (the test results for the services sector in 2000–2002 can be found in Table 16.A2; for the other sectors and periods they are available on request from the authors).

As the next step, the ATT of making outward FDI is found, with the change in the log of employment at the period of investment *t* as the outcome variable. We tried three different outcome variables — the employment growth rate over the first year, the first two years and the first three years of outward investment. Post-investment employment growth was compared between the treatment and control group, using the nearest neighbour matching with two or five neighbours, or kernel matching (with bandwidth of the size 0.06). The results are shown separately for the services sector in Table 16.7 and the manufacturing sector in Table 16.8. In services the estimated treatment effect is always positive, and in a number cases statistically significant. For the first year of investment, the effect is stronger in the second period (2000–2002); in that case the estimates lie within the range of 11–15 percentage points — that is undoubtedly an economically significant effect. The effect is larger than that found in the employment growth regressions. In manufacturing, ATT is positive and significant only in the second period (2000–2002), and for the second and third year of investment (in the second year after investment, the impact is significant for only one out of the three different matching algorithms used). In the first year of investment, the effect is stronger in services, while in the second year of investment it is stronger in manufacturing. A possible explanation is as follows. In manufacturing, in the short run, relocation abroad might decrease home employment

---

[12] In principle, in order to evaluate the significance of individual variables in the probit model, it would be preferable to use standard errors corrected for heteroscedasticity. However, that is not so important in the given context, since our interest is in calculating the propensity score.

Table 16.7. Effect of OFDI on employment growth at home (ATT): propensity score matching results for the service sector.

Period	Matching method	ATT 1-year Difference	ATT 1-year T-stat.	ATT 2-years Difference	ATT 2-years T-stat.	ATT 3-years Difference	ATT 3-years T-stat.
1996–1999	Unmatched	0.132	2.16**	0.012	1.940	0.231	2.11**
	NN 5	0.036	0.430	0.049	1.810	0.074	0.620
	NN 2	0.048	0.470	0.094	1.070	0.174	1.290
	Kernel	0.119	1.570	0.149	2.31**	0.218	2.00**
2000–2002	Unmatched	0.150	3.39***	1.670	1.070	0.109	1.460
	NN 5	0.110	1.67*	0.078	1.210	0.094	1.040
	NN 2	0.134	1.92*	0.121	1.590	0.089	0.880
	Kernel	0.148	2.37**	0.064	0.057	0.107	1.260

Note: * Significant at 10%; ** Significant at % ; *** Significant at 1%

NN 5: nearest neighbour matching with 5 matches; NN 2: nearest neighbour matching with 2 matches; ATT: Average Treatment Effect on the Treated, *t*-statistics in parentheses

For kernel matching, the Epanechnikov kernel was used, with the bandwidth set at 0.06 (the default value in psmatch2 programme).

Table 16.8. Effect of outward FDI on employment growth at home (ATT): propensity score matching results for the manufacturing sector.

Period	Matching method	ATT 1-year Difference	ATT 1-year T-stat.	ATT 2-years Difference	ATT 2-years T-stat.	ATT 3-years Difference	ATT 3-years T-stat.
1996–1999	Unmatched	−0.041	−0.360	−0.057	−0.390	−0.107	−0.620
	NN 5	0.060	0.630	−0.207	−1.400	−0.236	−1.310
	NN 2	0.092	0.690	−0.850	−0.850	−0.309	−1.320
	Kernel	−0.044	−0.570	−0.061	−0.540	−0.106	−0.690
2000–2002	Unmatched	0.101	1.000	0.144	1.020	0.448	2.63***
	NN 5	0.031	0.380	0.206	1.84*	0.447	2.54***
	NN 2	−0.058	−0.410	0.282	1.450	0.394	2.03**
	Kernel	0.101	1.79*	0.144	1.74*	0.447	2.67***

Note: As for Table 16.7.

if activities previously conducted at home are off-shored. In the long run, the positive effect on employment may show up due to the increased competitiveness of the investor, and complementarity between the foreign and home operations of the firm (see discussion in Section 1.2). The bigger number of treatment observations in the services sector enables more reliable detection of statistically significant results. Thus, although not all estimations have resulted in statistically significant results, at least in the services sector the difference between the treatment group and the control group (the ATT effect) was positive. We can certainly argue that in this sector, on average, OFDI does not cause job loss at home.

Table 16.9. Year-by-year matching for the service sector: the first year of OFDI.

Year	NN 5 matching	NN 2 matching	Kernel matching
1998	0.069	0.056	0.171
	(0.920)	(0.610)	(2.390**)
1999	0.140	0.158	0.088
	(0.730)	(0.790)	(0.470)
2000	0.182	0.179	0.179
	(1.250)	(1.210)	(1.290)
2001	0.253	0.168	0.219
	(1.750*)	(1.100)	(1.650)
2002	−0.008	0.069	−0.025
	(−0.140)	(1.520)	(−0.650)

Note: As for Table 16.7.

Table 16.10. Matching results for indirect and direct investors: the service sector, 2000–2002.

Type of investors	Method	ATT 1-year Difference	T-stat.	ATT 2-years Difference	T-stat.	ATT 3-years Difference	T-stat.
Indirect	Unmatched	0.111	1.44	0.108	0.98	0.071	0.53
	NN 5	0.030	0.52	0.034	0.36	0.004	0.02
	NN 2	0.111	0.77	0.021	0.19	0.045	0.21
	Kernel	0.105	2.14**	0.100	1.17	0.061	0.30
Direct	Unmatched	0.167	3.11***	0.045	0.61	0.121	1.32
	NN 5	0.184	1.95*	−0.036	−0.4	0.132	1.31
	NN 2	0.142	1.32	0.010	0.12	0.180	1.49
	Kernel	0.156	1.75*	0.045	0.61	0.118	1.37

Note: As for Table 16.7.

Although the probit model includes year dummies, the matches between the treatment group and the control group were sometimes from different years. This might not be a big problem, as we have divided the whole period into two parts which in terms of economic development are relatively homogeneous, but a robustness check might still be useful. In Table 16.9, year-by-year matching is performed on the basis of the services sector,[13] and the ATT effects are presented separately for each year. The years 1996 and 1997 were omitted because the number of new outward investors in these years was very low. The estimated ATTs were positive for all years (except 2002), although in most cases statistically not significant; the latter result was to be expected, given the rather small number of new investors in each separate year.

In addition, the ATT effect was calculated separately for indirect and direct investors in the services sector in the period 2000–2002 (Table 16.10). The effect was

---

[13] The number of treatment observations in each single year is too small in the manufacturing industry to enable year-by-year matching.

stronger for direct investors (e.g. in the case of kernel matching in the first year of investment by 4.5 percentage points). That is in accordance with our previous findings from the descriptive tables.

6. Conclusions and Implications

Traditional literature on relocation has exhaustively analysed the employment effect in the case of investments in the manufacturing sector from high-production-cost home countries to low-cost host countries. In the present chapter we analysed the home country employment effect of OFDI from Estonia as a low-cost transition economy. We used regression analyses and propensity score matching on firm-level panel data for the whole population of Estonian firms between 1995 and 2002.

The results of the employment growth regression analysis indicated that in general OFDI was positively related to home country employment growth. This supported our research proposition, and could be explained by the prevailing horizontal South–South type of OFDI from Estonia, in which the quest for new markets and economies of scale, and the need to follow customers played a dominant motivational role. Horizontal FDI in neighbouring catch-up economies helps to increase market share in the host country and facilitates the economies of scale effect, which supports home employment growth. Our results show that there is no firm ground for the fears about job-haemorraging often found among policymakers in the home countries of investors in the case of low-cost transition countries, and that OFDI in fact has a positive short-term effect on employment.

Our results also suggest differences between the home country employment effect for direct and indirect OFDI. For direct investors, employment growth is on average even higher than for indirect investors. This is explained by the following factors. First, subsidiaries of direct investors are served from other locations than Estonia, and no extra head office jobs are needed in Estonia. Second, due to the low level of autonomy of the subsidiaries of Estonian investors, more jobs are required in Estonia to fulfil the business functions not transferred to subsidiaries. Third, direct investors are much smaller at the time of investment than indirect investors, thus they need to create more jobs to serve the investments. However, the employment effect is also positive in the case of indirect investors. In the literature it has been found that low-wage countries could be employment substitutes for one another. This seems not to be the case with multinational investment in Estonia.

The effect was found to be stronger in the services sector than in manufacturing. We explain this in terms of the non-tradability of services, and the smaller size of the domestic service firms investing abroad, which means that outward investments could require additional jobs at home in order to manage the process of increasing the complexity of service provision. Both in manufacturing and services, the effect was found to be much stronger for investments started after 1999, which is connected to the improved macroeconomic performance of Estonia (particularly the faster rate of economic growth) since 2000.

Our results indicate a possible positive relationship between OFDI and employment growth at home in Estonia, and that the effects are likely to be significantly different in different time periods, types of investors and economic sectors. However, not all results are completely robust. One caveat in this analysis is that different matching algorithms sometimes gave somewhat different ATT effects (see discussion on p. 000)

The relevance of this topic is growing rapidly, as the stock of OFDI from new EU member states grows. Clearly, the employment effect of OFDI from new EU member states could be country-specific. It would be interesting to observe the difference between the employment effects in relatively high-income countries and in Estonia as a relatively low-income country.

The policy implications of our study are that there is no ground for fears about job losses at home when firms in low-cost countries establish affiliates in other countries. On the contrary, especially in the case of investments by domestically-owned firms, quite strong job creation can be expected at home after investment. Given that, government policy should rather concentrate on promoting OFDI, and facilitating the entry of domestic firms into new markets via direct investment, i.e. on reinforcing rather than seeking to change existing patterns of alignment.

References

Altzinger, W. and Bellak, C. (1999). 'Direct versus indirect FDI: Impact on domestic exports and employment', Vienna University of Economics and Business Administration Working Papers Series: *Growth and Employment in Europe: Sustainability and Competitiveness, Working Paper* No. 9.

Arnold, J.M. and Smarzynska Javorcik, B. (2005). 'Gifted kids or pushy parents? Foreign acquisitions and plant performance in Indonesia', *CEPR Discussion Paper* No. 5065.

Barba Navaretti, G. and Castellani, D. (2004). 'Investment abroad and performance at home: Evidence from Italian multinationals', *CEPR Discussion Paper* No. 4284.

Blomström, M., Fors, G. and Lipsey, R.E. (1997). 'Foreign direct investment and employment: Home country experience in the United States and Sweden', *Economic Journal* 107: 1987–1997.

Braconier, H. and Ekholm, K. (1999). 'Swedish multinationals and competition from high and low-wage countries', *CEPR Discussion Paper* No. 2323.

Braconier, H. and Ekholm, K. (2000). 'Swedish multinationals and competition from high and low-wage countries', *Review of International Economics* 8(3): 448–461.

Braconier, H. and Ekholm, K. (2001). 'Foreign direct investment in Central and Eastern Europe: Employment effects in the EU', *CEPR Working Paper* No. 3052.

Brainard, S.L. and Riker, D. (1997). 'Are U.S. multinationals exporting U.S. jobs?', *NBER Working Paper* No. 5958.

Braunerhjelm, P. and Oxelheim, L. (2000). 'Does foreign direct investment replace home country investment? The effect of European integration on the location of Swedish investment', *Journal of Common Market Studies* 38(2): 199–221.

Braunerhjelm, P., Oxelheim, L. and Thulin, P. (2005). 'The relationship between domestic and outward foreign investment revisited: The impact of industry-specific effects', Royal Institute of Technology, Stockholm, *CESIS Electronic Working Paper* No. 35.

Bruno, G. and Falzoni, A.M. (2000). 'Multinational corporations, wages and employment: Do adjustment costs matter?', *CEPR Working Paper* No. 2471.

Caliendo, M. and Kopeinig, S. (2005). 'Some practical guidance for the implementation of propensity score matching', *IZA Discussion Paper* No. 1588.

Cuyvers, L., Dumont, M., Rayp, G. and Stevens, K. (2005). 'Home employment effects of EU firms' activities in Central and Eastern European Countries', *Open Economies Review* 16(2): 153–174.

Dewit, G., Görg, H. and Montagna, C. (2004). 'Should I stay or should I go? A note on employment protection, domestic anchorage, and FDI', *IZA Discussion Paper* No. 845.

Ekholm, K. and Markusen, J. (2002). 'Foreign direct investment and EU — CEE integration', background paper for the conference *Danish and International Economic Policy*, Copenhagen, University of Copenhagen, 23–24 May.

Evans, D.S. (1987). 'The relationship between firm growth, size and age: Estimates for 100 manufacturing industries', *Journal of Industrial Economics* 35(4): 567–581.

Faggio, G. and Konings, J. (2003). 'Job creation, job destruction and employment growth in transition countries in the 90s', *Economic Systems* 27(2): 129–154.

Feenstra, R.C. and Hanson, G.H. (1996). 'Globalization, outsourcing, and wage inequality', *American Economic Review* 86(2): 240–245.

Hansson, P. (2005). 'Skill upgrading and production transfer within Swedish multinationals in the 1990s', *Scandinavian Journal of Economics* 107(4): 673–692.

Helpman, E., Melitz, M.J. and Yeaple, S.R. (2004). 'Export versus FDI with heterogeneous firms', *The American Economic Review* 94(1): 300–316.

Heshmati, A. (2001). 'On the growth of micro and small firms: Evidence from Sweden', *Small Business Economics* 17(3): 213–228.

Huttunen, K. (2005). 'The effect of foreign acquisition on employment and wages: Evidence from Finnish establishments', *HECER Discussion Paper* No. 62.

Jovanovic, B. (1982). 'Selection and the evolution of an industry', *Econometrica* 50(3): 649–670.

Kokko, A. (2006). 'The home country effects of FDI in developed economies', The European Institute of Japanese Studies, *EIJS Working Paper* No. 225.

Konings, J. and Murphy, A. (2001). 'Do multinational enterprises substitute parent jobs for foreign ones? Evidence from European firm-level panel data', *CEPR Discussion Paper* No. 2972.

Konings, J. and Murphy, A. (2003). 'Do multinational enterprises relocate employment to low wage regions? Evidence from European multinationals', *LICOS Centre for Transition Economics Discussion Paper* No. 131.

Konings, J., Kupets, O. and Lehmann, H. (2002). 'Gross job flows in Ukraine: Size, ownership and trade effects', *IZA Discussion Paper* No. 675.

Kravis, I. and Lipsey, R.E. (1988). 'The effect of multinational firms' foreign operations on their domestic employment', *NBER Working Paper* No. 2760.

Leuven, E. and Sianesi, B. (2003). 'PSMATCH2: Stata module to perform Mahalanobis and propensity score matching, common support graphing, and covariate testing', Statistical Software Components No. S432001, Boston College Department of Economics, http://ideas.repec.org/c/boc/bocode/s432001.html, Version 1.2.3.

Lipsey, R.E., Ramstetter, E. and Blomström, M. (2000). 'Outward FDI and parent exports and employment: Japan, the United States and Sweden', *Global Economy Quarterly* 1(4): 285–302.

Lopez-de-Silanes, F., Markusen, J.R. and Rutherford, T. (1996). 'Trade policy subtleties with multinational firms', *European Economic Review* 40(8): 1605–1627.

Männik, K., Hannula, H. and Varblane, U. (2006). 'Foreign subsidiary autonomy and performance in five Central and East European countries', in Hannula, H., Radosevic, S. and von Tunzelmann, N. (eds.). *Estonia, the New EU Economy: Building a Baltic Miracle?* London, Ashgate, pp. 258–284.

Mariotti, S., Mutinelli, M. and Piscitello, L. (2003). 'Home country employment and foreign direct investment: Evidence from the Italian case', *Cambridge Journal of Economics* 27(3): 419–431.

Markusen, J.R. (2002). *Multinational Firms and the Theory of International Trade*, Cambridge, MA, MIT Press.

Masso, J., Eamets, R. and Philips, K. (2006). 'Job creation and job destruction in Estonia: Labour reallocation and structural changes', in Hannula, H., Radosevic, S. and von Tunzelmann, N. (eds.), *Estonia, the New EU Economy: Building a Baltic Miracle?* London, Ashgate, pp. 105–142.

Masso, J., Varblane, U. and Vahter, P. (2007). 'The impact of outward FDI on home-country employment in a low-cost transition economy', *William Davidson Institute Working Paper* No. 873.

Pellenbarg, P.H., van Wissen, L.J.G. and van Dijk, J. (2002). 'Firm relocation: State of the art and research prospects', University of Groningen, *Research Institute SOM (Systems, Organisations and Management) Research Report* No. 02D31.

Pennings, E. and Sleuwaegen, L. (2000). 'International relocation: Firm and industry determinants', *Economics Letters* 67(2): 179–186.

Radosevic, S., Varblane, U. and Mickiewicz, T. (2003). 'Foreign direct investment and its effect on employment in Central Europe', *Transnational Corporations* 12(1): 53–90.

Rosenbaum, P. and Rubin, D. (1983). 'The central role of the propensity score in observational studies for causal effects', *Biometrika* 70(1): 41–50.

Sachs, J. and Shatz, H. (1994). 'Trade and jobs in U.S. manufacturing', *Brookings Papers on Economic Activity* 1994: 1: 1–69.

Slaughter, M.J. (1995). 'Multinational corporations, outsourcing, and American wage divergence', *NBER Working Paper* No. 5253.

Slaughter, M.J. (2000). 'Production transfer within multinational enterprises and American wages', *Journal of International Economics* 50(2): 449–472.

Smarzynska Javorcik, B. (2004). 'Does foreign direct investment increase the productivity of domestic firms? In search of spillovers through backward linkages,' *The American Economic Review* 94(3): 605–627.

StataCorp (2003). Stata Statistical Software: Release 8.0. College Station, TX: Stata Corporation.

Svetlicic, M. and Jaklic, A. (2003). 'Outward FDI by transition economies: basic features, trends and development implications', in Svetlicic, M. and Rojec, M. (eds.), *Facilitating Transition by Internationalization*, London, Ashgate, pp. 49–78.

Svetlicic, M., Jaklic, A. and Burger, A. (2003). 'Internationalization of small and medium-sized enterprises from selected Central European countries', *Eastern European Economics* 45(4): 36–64.

Vahter P. and Masso J. (2005). 'Home versus host country effects of FDI: Searching for new evidence of productivity spillovers', *Bank of Estonia Working Paper* No. 13.

Varblane, U., Reiljan, E. and Roolaht, T. (2003). 'The role of outward foreign direct investments in the internationalization of Estonian firms', in Svetlicic, M. and Rojec, M. (eds.), *Facilitating Transition by Internationalization*, London, Ashgate, pp. 133–154.

Varblane, U., Roolaht, T., Reiljan, E. and Jüriado, R. (2001). 'Estonian outward foreign direct investments', University of Tartu, *Faculty of Economics and Business Administration Working Paper* No. 9.

World Investment Report. Transnational Corporations and the Internationalization of R&D (2005). New York and Geneva, United Nations.

Appendix

Table 16.A1. Summary statistics of regressors used in the employment growth model and probit model for new outward investments.

Variable name	Variable definition	Mean	Std. Dev.	Coefficient of variation	Min	Max
Employment growth	The logarithmic employment growth rate	0.01	0.43	30.47	−8.19	8.19
Firm size	Number of employees at firm	14.06	94.84	6.75	0.00	20040.00
Firm age	The annual average growth rate of firm since entry	4.70	3.19	0.68	1.00	16.00
Wage cost per employee	Average wage costs divided by the total number of employees (€)	2321.68	4143.75	1.78	0.00	856452.70
Capital intensity	The ratio of fixed assets to the number of employees (€'000)	10.56	154.07	14.60	−8.23	28829.68
Labour productivity	The ratio of value added to number of employees (€'000)	8.90	36.33	4.08	0.00	6927.21
Export dummy	Dummy, 1 if firm has positive exports	0.15	0.35	2.40	0.00	1.00
Foreign firm	Dummy, 1 if foreign-owned firm	0.07	0.26	3.53	0.00	1.00
Outward FDI	Dummy, 1 if firm has OFDI	0.00	0.07	14.44	0.00	1.00
State firm	Dummy, 1 if state-owned firm	0.01	0.10	10.04	0.00	1.00
Equity/Assets	Shareholders' equity/ total assets	0.36	1.15	3.20	−24.36	1.00
Profit/Sales	The ratio of operating profit to sales	−0.06	0.82	−14.43	−14.09	3.87

Note: The number of observations in the dataset is 414 076, and the number of firms is 87310.
The Estonian kroon is fixed to the euro at the rate of 1 EEK = €5.6466. All monetary values are in 2001 prices.

Table 16.A2. Testing for balancing property by testing for differences in means: the service sector, 2000–2002.

Variable	Sample	Mean in the group of treated	Mean in the control group	Percent of bias	Percentage reduction in bias	Test for differences in means	P-value
Log size (−1)	Unmatched	2.64	1.72	86.30		7.64	0.00
	Matched	2.64	2.73	−8.90	89.70	−0.52	0.60
Log age	Unmatched	0.54	0.49	14.20		1.28	0.20
	Matched	0.54	0.54	−0.60	95.60	−0.04	0.97
Log labour productivity (−1)	Unmatched	12.43	11.30	117.10		9.56	0.00
	Matched	12.43	12.43	0.50	99.50	0.04	0.97
Foreign firm (−1)	Unmatched	0.29	0.08	55.50		7.03	0.00
	Matched	0.29	0.27	3.80	93.10	0.20	0.84
Export dummy (−1)	Unmatched	0.56	0.19	83.10		8.73	0.00
	Matched	0.56	0.57	−3.20	96.20	−0.19	0.85
Log capital intensity (−1)	Unmatched	11.26	9.99	77.50		7.12	0.00
	Matched	11.26	11.22	2.90	96.20	0.19	0.85
Log wage cost per employee (−1)	Unmatched	11.18	10.14	128.30		11.42	0.00
	Matched	11.18	11.16	3.30	97.50	0.23	0.82
Equity/Assets(−1)	Unmatched	0.35	0.33	3.20		0.23	0.82
	Matched	0.35	0.37	−4.30	−35.20	−0.41	0.68
Profit/Sales (−1)	Unmatched	0.03	−0.06	2.20		0.14	0.89
	Matched	0.03	0.08	−1.00	52.20	−1.45	0.15

CHAPTER 17

NETWORK ALIGNMENT IN THE AUTOMOTIVE
CLUSTERS OF TURKEY AND POLAND

GULDEM OZATAGAN

1. Introduction

In recent decades, many industries have seen significant internationalisation of their organisation beyond national boundaries. Traditionally, research tended to direct attention to international firms with a view of FDI as a means of extending the domain of internationalisation across international borders (Dunning, 1988). Over the last decade, however, research has shifted emphasis from investigating firms' FDI practices to analysing their interconnectedness with other firms in global networks of production. Internal and external linkages between companies have received growing recognition, and buyer/supplier relations have been predicated by many studies as the fundamentals for the working of the economy. While research on regional development has highlighted the importance of localised networks as vehicles for the exploitation of external economies of scale and as key instruments of technology transfer and hence innovation (Freeman and Soete, 1997; Piore and Sabel, 1984), studies of external linkages have identified globalised supply networks as key elements in the success of newly industrialising countries (Borrus et al., 2000; Ernst, 2004; Hobday, 1995). It has been a central argument in these studies that in the prevailing networked economy peripheral locations modernise through network integration and that catching-up by peripheral countries depends on the extent to which they have built linkages.

Following these arguments, the bulk of research has looked for an association between upgrading and exporting and/or upgrading and FDI, presupposing that supply relations and foreign ownership contribute to closing the technology gap. Over time, however, mounting doubts have emerged concerning the catch-up patterns of some peripheral countries. Research on buyer–supplier relations has revealed difficulties encountered by actors in peripheral countries in moving into higher value-added activities such as design, marketing and branding. Similarly, studies of FDI have shown that learning and the transfer of knowledge to subsidiaries and affiliates in peripheral production nodes takes place largely in the area of production, management and technology, and takes longer in areas going beyond production. Thus Narula (2005, 47) states that '...TNCs still tend to largely concentrate their more strategic and core activities close to home. In other words, they remain more deeply embedded in their home country than elsewhere'.

Since the 1990s the Turkish and Polish automotive industries have been increasingly integrated into global and European regional automotive production networks thanks to the combination of a number of forces: industry characteristics, global lead firms, international conditions, regional integration schemes and local contingencies. This chapter aims to analyse network alignment in the automotive clusters of Turkey and Poland and its impact on their ability to upgrade. The chapter first focuses on the dynamics behind their alignment. Such a focus should help us to understand differences in the ways in which they are aligned: Turkey, which began exporting to the car-producing countries in the 1980s, has been aligned since then to the European automotive system through the medium of exports by Turkish companies directly to the European market. In Poland, on the other hand, following the collapse of the socialist system, FDI emerged as the most active vehicle for its alignment to the European automotive system. The chapter further examines the association between networking and upgrading. Our analysis shows that there have been positive developments regarding the upgrading of peripheral actors, which conflict with some of the less optimistic arguments put forward in the literature. Despite their subordinate position in automotive production networks, component suppliers in Turkey and Poland have developed a capability to contribute to design and product development activities, and some component suppliers have shown themselves capable of undertaking marketing and branding activities. I argue, then, that their upgrading pattern is influenced by the ways in which their networks are aligned: such upgrading opportunities are available mainly for suppliers in export-oriented supply networks and also OEM networks, while barriers to learning and upgrading exist for suppliers aligned in TNC networks.

The chapter is structured as follows: the next part provides an overview of the existing literature, to highlight what insights it provides on learning from global networks. The rest of the chapter concentrates on the automotive clusters of Turkey and Poland, to back up these insights empirically. First, the dynamics behind the alignment of Bursa and Upper Silesia in automotive production networks are discussed. In the subsequent section I seek to understand the ways in which this alignment took place in the two clusters. Finally, the chapter provides an analysis of what upgrading opportunities are available in the different types of networks that characterise the alignment of the two production nodes. The chapter ends with the summary of key findings, and what they imply for the upgrading of Turkish and Polish firms.

2. Learning from Global Networks: An Overview

It is a commonplace in studies of upgrading and innovation that when countries start operating in global networks they become exposed to more competition and technological know-how and learn how to 'do things better', but face obstacles when it comes to 'making better things', and 'moving into higher value-added activities'. 'Doing things better' includes technological change to increase the efficiency of the production process by increasing flexibility, raising quality, speeding up the process, introducing superior technology, introducing new forms of organisational and managerial methods (such as team working, training, quality management, etc.) or reorganising existing methods (Yoruk, 2004). 'Making better things' is related to product upgrading and includes introducing new products or improving existing products. Finally, 'moving into higher value-added activities' is about functional upgrading, which means improving the ability of a firm to move to more profitable activities like design, marketing and branding.

Peripheral actors are usually considered to have capabilities inferior to those of the actors in the core. Moving into higher value-added activities by actors on the periphery has been viewed as encroaching on the core competence of lead firms, and has occurred in only a small number of high-performing newly industrialising countries — South Korea, Taiwan, Hong Kong and Singapore. Examples are cited by Gereffi (1999), who shows that East Asian garment producers underwent a shift from the assembly of imported goods, to local production and sourcing, to product design, and finally to branding. In a similar vein, Hobday (1995) showed how Taiwanese firms were able to overcome technology and market entry barriers and assimilate manufacturing and design technology as a result of their integration into global networks through subcontracting. Likewise, Kim and von Tunzelmann (1998) pointed to the role of various network dimensions (local, national and global) alongside the alignment of state, markets and firms in Taiwan's success in IT hardware. Lee and Chen (2000) similarly examine contract manufacturers in Taiwan to highlight a success story where the actors were able to acquire new capabilities by applying lessons from the past.

However, empirical evidence from the rest of the world has been far from uniform. Dyker *et al.* (2003) show that Hungarian and Slovenian firms in the automotive industry are dependent on networks as sources of information, learning and innovation. Eraydin and Armatli-Koroglu (2005), in their study of Turkish industrial clusters, found that firms with larger numbers of global linkages are more innovative than those with dense local and national linkages. Similarly, Tokatli (2007) showed that quite a number of suppliers to international networks from Turkey have successfully entered brand-name manufacturing in the blue-jeans industry since the 1990s. These pieces of evidence are reinforced by recent research by Tokatli and Kizilgun (2008), who mention a Turkish supplier who prepares his own fashion collections; and Tewari (2006), who provides evidence from India, where suppliers are capable of contributing to design and of introducing their own designs in consultation with their buyers.

A feature common to all these studies is that they consider external linkages as a starting point for moving to higher value-added activities. This view, however, contrasts with other studies which have been rather pessimistic about the scope for upgrading in peripheral economies. Sturgeon and Lester (2004) argue that the rise of global lead firms makes supplier-oriented industrial upgrading in the motor-vehicle industry increasingly difficult. Chiu and Wong's (2002, 11) evidence on the East Asian electronics industry show that 'most OEM suppliers remained locked in low-end production'. Radosevic and Yoruk (2004) demonstrate that the comparative strength of CEE firms lies in production activities, and that it is only for the domestic market that some firms showed functional upgrading towards non-production activities. Evidence on FDI also supports these assertions: Dyker (2007, 4) shows that despite a recent tendency for TNCs to establish R&D laboratories in transition countries, the seminal R&D work is kept at headquarters, and technology and knowledge dissemination by the multinationals in the transition region proceeds with the know-how coming for the most part from the laboratories of the parent company in the home country.

While these pieces of evidence challenge the perception of global linkages as a new source of competitive advantage, further evidence suggests that opportunities do exist for local producers in domestic networks to experience functional upgrading. Tewari (1999) shows that Indian knitwear firms have acquired design and quality capabilities by supplying the domestic market, which has in turn helped them to develop capabilities to produce for the international markets. Bazan and Navas-Aleman (2004) also show that, in the Brazilian case, shoe producers producing for the domestic market were able to build up capabilities in design and marketing, while those producing for European and North American supply networks were not.

One common assumption behind these studies is that suppliers operate in only one type of network. However, more often than not, suppliers operate in different networks simultaneously. Kishimoto's (2004) research on Taiwanese computer clusters shows that the firms which achieved functional upgrading were those that maintained contract manufacturing for their main buyers (OEMs) and simultaneously experimented with their own designs and brands in other markets. This evidence implies that new capabilities are acquired by applying lessons from one network to other networks. This idea prompted Lee and Chen (2000) to argue the importance of leveraging capabilities from different chains on the basis of the experience of some Taiwanese firms which take a design supplied by one customer and make adaptations to use the modified design to supply other customers in other markets. Similarly, a recent study by Tewari (2006) highlights the case of Indian contract manufacturers manufacturing garments to order for others, while simultaneously manufacturing own brands for the domestic market.

Our case-study uses the automotive clusters of Turkey and Poland — Bursa and Upper Silesia — to back up these arguments empirically. The two clusters are good examples of how a range of international, sectoral and local factors come together to make actors on the periphery producers for global lead firms, and press them to investigate the upgrading opportunities available in the networks to which they are aligned. In what follows I shall talk briefly about how these factors shed light on the dynamics behind the differences in the ways in which the two clusters are aligned. They represent two peripheral areas which are integrated into the European regional system of automotive production, and where the vehicle manufacturer Fiat has been the primary actor contributing to the development of a network of suppliers. Despite these similarities, however, the two clusters have different histories in automotive production, which have significantly shaped the ways in which they are aligned. Such a focus should help us to test the insights from existing research on innovation and upgrading in two different settings: one whose integration is mainly the result of export relations and one whose integration is the result of FDI.

3. Dynamics of Network Alignment in Bursa and Upper Silesia

During the 1990s Bursa and Upper Silesia found ways of aligning themselves to global networks by becoming manufacturers for the automotive lead firms. This transformation has gone on within the framework of the global restructuring of the automotive industry. In this context, CEE countries have become increasingly important for the internationalisation strategies of major vehicle assemblers and global supplier firms as core production sites, as trade partners, and as foreign investment locations.[1]

Three major forces had a significant role to play in this process. The first of these was the liberalisation policies associated with the changing policy regime in Turkey, away from import substitution towards export orientation; the second was the post-socialist transformation of Poland.

From the late 1960s to the 1980s the Turkish automotive industry developed through the supportive policies of the import substitution strategy adopted by the governments of the time. Under this regime, it progressed mainly on the basis of Western licenses; local content was encouraged, and local firms were protected from foreign competition, so that development proceeded without serious disruption.

---

[1] The industry-specific internationalisation strategies of vehicle assemblers are beyond the scope of this paper. For discussion of these see Dicken, 2003; Humphrey and Memedovic, 2003; Sturgeon and Florida, 2000.

Until the 1990s, the car industry in Poland developed under the strong division of labour imposed by the Council for Mutual Economic Assistance (CMEA) — the trading bloc of the Soviet sphere of influence — the main principle of which was to maintain a self-sufficient system based on natural resources and import substitution (Havas, 2000). The organisation of the industry was determined centrally by the CMEA, which defined the type and number of vehicles to be produced and traded within the CMEA, and with other countries and regions. Under such a regime the Polish car industry developed mainly on the basis of cooperation licenses with the Soviet Union and Italy, the latter forming the main vehicle for importing technology.

Both countries then entered a period of profound structural change, forcing the firms in these production nodes to face international competition. In Turkey this happened through a gradual process of deregulation and trade liberalisation. The supportive phase of the 1970s came to an end, following a period of political instability and an economic crisis in 1978. After that, export-oriented industrial development came to be defined as the main economic strategy by the governments of the time. In Poland, the process of deregulation and liberalisation was more rapid thanks to a set of radical economic reforms ('shock therapy') following the collapse of the socialist system in the 1990s, and the subsequent disintegration of the CMEA market and breakdown of established CMEA trade flows (Pavlinek, 2002). Both countries introduced far-reaching reforms phasing out local content requirements, relaxing regulations on foreign investment, and removing import restrictions for motor vehicles and parts.

At the regional level, a third force that shaped the transformation of the automotive industries of Turkey and Poland had to do with relations with the EU. In Turkey, the Customs Union agreement signed with the European Union in 1995 strengthened the long-standing relationship of Turkey with the EU. The agreement not only gave suppliers access to European countries, but also forced them to adopt the standardisation, measurement, accreditation, test, and certification legislation of the EU over a period of five years.[2] In Poland, the process of adjustment of the industry to EU rules, regulations and standards was achieved via full membership of the EU. By the 2000s Poland had already achieved full liberalisation of its economy and assimilation of EU rules and regulations, two criteria considered important for

---

[2] It should be noted that the restructuring efforts of suppliers in the years that followed continued in the face of a number of crises. First, the economic crisis in 1994 had serious impacts on the metropolitan areas of Turkey, causing a sharp decline in domestic demand. Second, the impact of the East Asian crisis in 1998 was followed by a major earthquake in a region of Turkey where a significant part of manufacturing industry, including the automotive, is located. Third, the IMF-backed stabilisation programme initiated in the aftermath of the 1998 crisis ended following further political instability and a financial crisis in 2001. As a result, demand volatility and market uncertainty have emerged as characteristic features of the industry (Duruiz, 2004).

car lead firms' decisions regarding which emerging economy to invest in, in the context of their globalisation strategies (Dunford, 2009). Hence, the establishment of the Customs Union in Turkey and EU membership in Poland initiated far-reaching transformation of the products, processes, management techniques and markets of the automotive industry in both countries, subsequently facilitating their regional integration into the European automotive system. From 1995 onwards the share of the value of Turkish automotive exports to EU countries increased gradually. By 2003, 70% of the automotive exports of Turkey were going to EU countries, with Germany accounting for 23%, followed by France (14%) and Italy (12%) (TAYSAD, 2007). In Poland, 80% of automotive trade was with EU countries in 1993, Germany taking 36% of total automotive exports and generating 41% of imports (Domanski *et al.*, 2005).

Thus the strategies of global lead firms, when coupled with the liberalisation trend and the pattern of evolution of relations with the EU, facilitated the integration of component suppliers in Bursa and Upper Silesia into global and European regional production networks. However, the ways in which the automotive clusters of Turkey and Poland were aligned was significantly influenced by specifically configured networks, which exhibited path-dependency, and helped shape the strategies of major automotive manufacturers and global lead firms in the two clusters.

Bursa has a long history of automotive production, the start of which dates back to the establishment of assembly plants in the 1960s. Three car manufacturing companies (Karsan under a Peugeot license in 1966, Tofas under a Fiat license in 1971 and Oyak-Renault under a Renault license in 1971) had an important role to play in the development of this niche of the components industry, thanks to their investments in component suppliers. From the late 1960s to the 1980s, the efforts of assemblers to develop their own supply base amidst a scarcity of local suppliers, together with the supportive policies of the import-substitution strategy adopted by the governments of the time, helped the development of the domestic components industry in Bursa. Thanks to these dynamics, there was already by the end of the 1970s an SME-dominated network of suppliers in Bursa working to the specifications of their customers to produce mainly for the domestic market. It was thanks to the existence of this network of domestic suppliers that Bursa was able to turn its face to the export market after the 1980s. Equally important in this sense was the fact that large and powerful domestic corporations, which had enjoyed oligopolistic profits and rents throughout the import-substitution period, controlled the automotive industry (also other industries like basic metals, petrochemicals, machinery and textiles) (Tokatli, 2003). Foreign investors entering the Turkish market after the 1990s took advantage of the existence of these strong domestic enterprises with high levels of industrial and managerial skill. Some of the foreign TNCs seeking to enter the Turkish market in pursuit of their internationalisation strategies did so by establishing equity linkages or JVs with such strong national leaders.[3]

Compared to Bursa, the development of the automotive industry in Upper Silesia is fairly recent. Despite this, however, links between Fiat and the Polish FSM, rooted in the 1970s, had an important role to play in the emergence of Upper Silesia from the 1990s onwards. In 1975 an FSM assembly plant was opened in Tychy, on the basis of Fiat technology, after a license agreement was signed between Fiat and FSM. Following this agreement, however, relations with Fiat were problematic up until 1992, when Fiat acquired FSM. After that time, in its pursuit of cost reduction, Fiat started to look for suppliers for the growing production runs of its Tychy plant, which had a significant impact on the selection by global component suppliers of Upper Silesia as a manufacturing location. The second factor contributing to the emergence of Upper Silesia as a production location for automotive components dates from the mid-1990s, with the investment of GM in a new integrated assembly plant at Gliwice. These two events later attracted other foreign component suppliers, and also led to the development of local Polish companies as suppliers to Fiat and Opel. Hence the development of the automotive components industry in Upper Silesia was boosted by the follow-the-source[4] strategies of two vehicle assemblers and the government policy of providing incentives to attract FDI. Also important for attracting lead firms to Upper Silesia were the incentives provided by the Polish government. Among these, a particularly important one was the establishment of special economic zones (where investors would be exempt from income tax for a period of ten years), introduced by the Polish government in 1995 as a regional policy measure, to attract new investors that would provide new jobs in areas of actual or potential unemployment (Domanski, 2003, 2005). This measure played a key role in attracting GM and its and Fiat's multinational suppliers to the Katowice special economic zone, which has facilitated the recent growth of Upper Silesia as a new node of automotive production in Poland, despite the fact that the node does not have a history of automotive production.

So the alignment of Bursa and Upper Silesia is the result of a complex process in which a variety of only partially aligned institutional factors played key roles. The focus here will be on the ways in which this alignment was fashioned in Bursa and Upper Silesia — two automotive clusters which were exposed to similar international, regional and industry-specific pressures but against a background of different histories of automotive production. The research is based on survey data collected in December 2005–December 2006 using structured face-to-face interviews in Bursa

---

[3] Figures provided by Balcet and Enrietti (2002, 86) indicate the extensive implementation of this strategy by Fiat: of its first ten suppliers in 1999, whose combined market share was equal to 38.6% of total purchases, six firms were JVs, accounting for 60% of that combined market share.

[4] Follow-the-source refers to the strategy of suppliers following their assemblers to the new markets in which the latter are investing (see Humphrey, 2003).

and telephone interviews in Upper Silesia. The list of firms operating in the auto components industry was provided by the Chamber of Industry and Commerce and the Undersecretariat of the Prime Ministry for Foreign Trade for Bursa (2005), and by the Central Statistical Office and Polish Information and Foreign Investment Agency (2006) for Upper Silesia. The original database included information on the name, location, telephone number and addresses of 406 firms in Bursa and 138 in Upper Silesia. Of these firms 38 were inaccessible in Bursa and 35 in Upper Silesia, either because of wrong contact information, or because the firm had moved to another sector. Out of the 368 accessible firms in Bursa, 103 provided consistent and usable information leading to a response rate of more than 25%. Of the 103 accessible firms in Upper Silesia, I managed to approach 31, but obtained only 19 usable interviews, resulting in an 18% response rate (Table 17.1). The survey was complemented by semi-structured interviews, with major vehicle manufacturers (with Tofas-Fiat and Karsan in Bursa and Fiat-Auto and GM in Upper Silesia) as well as suppliers in the two countries. The interviews aimed to unveil the corporate strategies of the vehicle manufacturers as the key actors in automotive production networks, and the ways in which these influence relations with suppliers.

4. Network Alignment in Bursa and Upper Silesia

In order to be able to identify the different types of networks to which suppliers in the two clusters might be aligned, firms were asked about their relationships with other firms and their external orientation. They were asked to indicate whether or not they were i) a subsidiary of a TNC, ii) a domestic supplier with equity links with a TNC, iii) a domestic supplier which supplies international markets, iv) a domestic supplier which supplies OEMs, or v) a domestic supplier which supplies other suppliers.

Table 17.2 provides information on our results, and is indicative of the different ways in which alignment into global auto-production networks was achieved in Bursa

Table 17.1. Survey results by country.

	Bursa, Turkey		Upper Silesia, Poland	
	Number of firms	%	Number of firms	%
Firms interviewed	103	28.0	19	18.1
Firms which provided inconsistent/ defective information	3	0.8	12	11.7
Firms which refused to be interviewed	24	6.5	72	69.9
Firms not contacted	238	64.7		
Total	368	100	103	100

*Includes firms which could not be accessed because of wrong telephone numbers or because they had changed sector.

Table 17.2. Network alignment in Bursa and Upper Silesia.

	Number of firms	Percent
Bursa		
TNC intra-firm network	18	17.5
Subsidiaries of foreign suppliers	8	7.8
Domestic suppliers with equity links with foreign suppliers	10	9.7
Export-oriented supply network	41	39.8
Domestic suppliers which supply international markets	18	**17.5**
Domestic suppliers which supply both international markets and OEMs	23	**22.3**
Domestic supply network	44	42.7
Domestic suppliers which supply OEMs	10	9.7
2nd and 3rd tier domestic suppliers	34	**33.0**
Total	103	100.0
Upper Silesia		
TNC intra-firm network	10	52.6
Subsidiaries of foreign suppliers	8	**42.1**
Domestic suppliers with equity links with foreign suppliers	2	10.5
Export-oriented supply network		26.3
Domestic suppliers which supply international markets	2	10.5
Domestic suppliers which supply both international markets and OEMs	3	15.8
Domestic supply network	4	21.1
Domestic suppliers which supply OEMs	1	5.3
2nd and 3rd tier domestic suppliers	3	15.8
Total	19	100.0

and Upper Silesia. The figures indicate that Polish networks are limited in scope, and are mainly intra-firm networks organised by TNCs (52.6%) and composed mainly of the parent firm and local subsidiaries (42.1%); the role of domestic suppliers with equity links with foreign TNCs is limited (10.5%). Compared to Upper Silesia, the scope of networks in Bursa is more diverse. There, it is domestically owned firms that drive network alignment in the automotive industry, and alignment focuses mainly around export-oriented supply networks (39.8%), with 17.5% around purely export-oriented supply networks and 22.3% around supply networks oriented to exports and OEM networks. On the other hand, the role of TNCs in network alignment remains limited (17.5%), relating to local firms with equity links with a foreign firm (9.7%), rather than to subsidiaries of TNCs (7.8%).

Country-specific contingencies go a long way towards explaining these differences in network alignment in Bursa and Upper Silesia. As mentioned earlier, when suppliers in Bursa opened up to the outside world during the late 1980s and 1990s, there was already a network of domestic suppliers working to the specifications of their customers, which gave these suppliers opportunities to learn. While some of them were forced to exit when faced with global competition during the adjustment process, others managed to adjust to the requirements of global competition and establish ties in global production networks. Likewise, it was the more competent suppliers which already had contractual links with Western lead firms that were acquired by, or sought a JV or equity relationship with, their partners from the 1990s onwards. The alignment dynamics were different in Upper Silesia. The state socialist regime of which Poland had been a part did not allow the development of a domestic production network of competent suppliers. In the absence of domestic production networks, the government strategy of promoting FDI in order to strengthen global ties after 1990, which coincided with the global strategies of foreign TNCs, made TNCs the focal points of alignment in the automotive industry in Upper Silesia.

5. Network Alignment and Upgrading

What upgrading opportunities are available in the different types of networks that characterise the alignment of these two production nodes operating on the periphery of automotive production? To address this question, three types of upgrading identified in the literature are taken into consideration: process, product and functional. In order to give a better insight into the characteristics of different types of upgrading, we disaggregated them into sub-categories of innovation activity: i) process improvements, ii) product and process development, iii) marketing and branding, iv) innovation in work systems, v) innovation in technology systems, and vi) innovation in organisational systems. Firms were asked about the extent to which they were engaged in innovation activities under these six headings. They were asked to formulate their answers at a range of levels.[5] A coefficient was then calculated for each of the six types of innovative behaviour (see Appendix for the variables used by type of innovative behaviour and for the calculation of the coefficients).

In order to test the significance of the type of networks in explaining the innovativeness of firms, an analysis of variance (ANOVA) approach is applied. A post-hoc test (least significant difference — LSD) is also carried out to detect the particular pairs of network types whose means are significantly different.

The Levene test is used to verify the assumption of homogeneity of variances between types of networks (see Table 17.3). For three variables — innovation in technology systems, innovation in work systems and process improvements — the Levene statistic is below the 0.05 significance level, which rejects the assumption of equal cell variances. Since this result implies that the variances of the different types of networks differ significantly, making the resulting F-test invalid, interpretations

---

[5] The research is based on a qualitative assessment of the firm's innovation activities. The main reason for this is that we were unable to collect quantitative data on innovation in the pilot survey. The firms were reluctant to share quantitative data for a variety of reasons, sometimes of secrecy and sometimes of lack of available data. At the same time, the qualitative nature of the questions helped unveil those innovation activities which are not reflected in R&D data, and also capture those innovation activities which firms hesitate to register or even report to their customers.

Table 17.3. Type of network and innovation: test of homogeneity of variances.

	Levene statistic	df1	df2	Sig.
Innovation in technology systems	4.243	5	116	0.001
Innovation in work systems	2.886	5	116	0.017
Innovation in organisational systems	0.176	5	116	0.971
Marketing and branding	0.659	5	116	0.655
Improvements in production process	2.531	5	116	0.033
Design, product and process development	0.646	5	116	0.665

Note: df = degrees of freedom.

Table 17.4. Type of network and innovation: robust tests of equality of means.*

	Brown–Forsythe statistic[a]	df1	df2	Sig.
Innovation in technology systems	6.071	5	92.918	0.000
Innovation in work systems	2.213	5	68.734	0.063
Innovation in organisational systems	2.796	5	82.992	0.022
Marketing and branding	5.318	5	86.158	0.000
Improvements in production process	0.856	5	82.125	0.515
Design, product and process development	1.351	5	91.164	0.250

Note: df = degrees of freedom.
[a] Asymptotically F distributed.
*Tests the equality of group means on the basis of the median, which is recommended to provide higher robustness than Levene's test when group variances are unequal.

were based on figures from the Brown–Forsythe test[6] as a substitute for the F-test. The Brown–Forsythe statistics do not provide significant results at the .05 level for innovation in technology systems (Table 17.4), implying that for this variable the variances of the different types of networks differ, hence casting some doubt on the significance of this variable as recorded in Table 17.3.

Table 17.5 provides results from ANOVA, which compares the amount of variation within the categories of networks to the amount of variation between the categories of networks. Overall, the results show that there is relatively little variation in the innovativeness of firms in work systems, process improvements, and design, product and process development across the different types of networks into which they are integrated. This finding implies that such innovation activities are widespread in auto-production networks of different types. What seems surprising in this regard is the pervasiveness of design and product development even in domestic supply networks comprised of lower-tier domestic suppliers.

---

[6] The Brown–Forsythe test is a statistical test for the equality of group variances based on performing an ANOVA on a modified F-test when cell variances are unequal.

Table 17.5. Results of ANOVA: variation in innovation within and between the different types of networks.

	Sum of squares	df	Mean square	F	Sig.
Innovation in technology systems					
Between Groups	1.247	5	0.249	5.037	0.000
Within Groups	5.744	116	0.050		
Total	6.991	121			
Innovation in work systems					
Between Groups	1.016	5	0.203	2.095	0.071
Within Groups	11.252	116	0.097		
Total	12.268	121			
Innovation in organisational systems					
Between Groups	1.929	5	0.386	2.871	0.018
Within Groups	15.584	116	0.134		
Total	17.513	121			
Marketing and branding					
Between Groups	3.499	5	0.700	5.273	0.000
Within Groups	15.395	116	0.133		
Total	18.893	121			
Improvements in production process					
Between Groups	0.094	5	0.019	0.757	0.583
Within Groups	2.881	116	0.025		
Total	2.975	121			
Design, product and process development					
Between Groups	0.827	5	0.165	1.313	0.263
Within Groups	14.606	116	0.126		
Total	15.433	121			

Note: df = degrees of freedom.

Published research asserts that lead firms are likely progressively to give up their production function, while they tend to retain design and marketing; the expectation is therefore that, for firms and production nodes on the periphery, moving into design and marketing activities is not so likely, especially when they supply global lead firms (Abernathy *et al.*, 1999; Hsing, 1999; Schmitz, 2006). At the same time, evidence from producer-driven chains shows a tendency towards increased supplier responsibility in design and product development, though this is mainly observed among global or first-tier suppliers (Ernst and Kim, 2002; Sturgeon, 2002; Sturgeon and Lee, 2001). Our research, however, shows that even lower-tier suppliers on the periphery of car production are capable of contributing to design. This finding is supported by Poon (2004, 134), who offers a similar observation in relation to the Taiwanese ICT industry:

> ... various types and levels of technological knowledge and skills absorbed from network flagships by the first tiers (...) were then diffused to smaller firms, resulting in the upgrading of all manufacturers operating within the ICT GPN.[7]

---

[7] GPN = Global Production Network.

Our evidence, together with Poon's, indicates that there is, indeed, room for manoeuvre for firms on the periphery to encroach on the so-called core competences of their customers.

On the other hand, our results indicate greater differences in firms' innovativeness in organisational systems, and in marketing and branding (Table 17.4), from one type of network to another relative to the differences within the different types. To clarify which differences are most important and contribute most to the significant F-ratios for these differences, Table 17.6 summarises results from a post-hoc test (LSD). This test compares the means of all possible pairs of types of networks, tests differences between all types of networks, and identifies those differences that are statistically significant. A synthesis of the results from the analysis regarding the innovative behaviour of firms in different types of networks is provided in Table 17.7.

Our initial finding that there is room for manoeuvre for firms on the periphery to encroach on the so-called core competences of their customers is complemented by the finding that one possibility to do so is to operate simultaneously in export-oriented supply networks and OEM networks. Our results show that these firms are significantly different from firms aligned in other types of networks, with their highest level of innovativeness in marketing and branding. This finding highlights the positive contribution of learning from different networks. As Bazan and Navas-Aleman (2004) and Tewari (1999) underline, it is important to leverage capabilities developed in one network over onto other networks. Similarly, our evidence is supportive of Pickles *et al.* (2006), who show in the case of apparel production that firms in CEECs are using their experience of original design manufacturing (ODM) and original brand manufacturing (OBM) for the domestic market to expand into export markets in the former Soviet Union.

The advantage of operating simultaneously in different networks is evident from our face-to-face interviews with both assemblers and suppliers. Vehicle manufacturers interviewed indicated that they motivate and provide incentives to their suppliers to adopt internationalisation strategies in terms of diversifying their customers and suppliers. They mentioned the importance of leveraging competencies from different customers, of reducing the risk of their suppliers being badly affected by falls in demand in times of crisis, and of reducing their suppliers' dependence on a small number of similar suppliers. The importance of diversifying customers was also stressed by the suppliers interviewed. One supplier stated that:

> working for a diversity of customers helps to improve our capabilities on different issues, and our ability to address the needs and requests of customers, which tend to vary. As we try to meet these requests, our firm develops in a positive way.

The importance of diversifying customers was also stressed by another supplier:

> It is important to develop diverse products for diverse customers. The best customers are suppliers which produce for OEMs. Because the demand is

Table 17.6. Post-hoc (LSD) test for differences in innovativeness by type of network

Type of innovation/ type of network*	I. TNC network as subsidiary	II. TNC network as equity owner	III. International supply network	IV. International supply network and national OEM network	V. National OEM network	VI. Domestic supply network	Anova test (Sig.)	Post-hoc test**
Innovation in technology systems	**0.8462**	**0.9167**	0.7346	**0.9260**	0.8392	0.6798	0.000	I, V > VI, II, IV > III, VI
Marketing and branding	0.1563	0.2500	**0.5250**	**0.5962**	0.5455	0.2568	0.000	III, IV > I, II, VI, V > I, VI
Design, product and process development	0.4375	0.4167	0.4375	**0.6442**	0.5227	0.4595	0.263	IV > VI
Innovation in work systems	1.0268	**1.1667**	0.9643	**1.1538**	1.0779	0.9421	0.071	II > VI, IV > III, VI
Innovation in organisational systems	0.8229	**1.0139**	0.6500	**0.8462**	0.7576	0.6261	0.018	II > III, VI, IV > VI
Improvements in production process	0.9063	0.9792	0.8875	0.9519	0.9545	0.9392	0.583	—

*Mean value per type of network.

**This test compares the means of all possible pairs of categories of 'type of network' and identifies the combinations of means which contribute most to a significant F-ratio. Information is provided on the pairs of means which are statistically different (for example the innovativeness of TNC network as subsidiary and national OEM networks are significantly higher than the innovativeness of domestic supply networks).

Table 17.7. Type of network and innovative behaviour: a synthesis.

	Innovative behaviour in:
International supply networks	
International supply network	**Marketing and branding**
	Design
	Process
	Work
International supply network and OEM network	**Organisational**
	Marketing and branding
	Design
	Process
	Work
Domestic supply networks	
OEM network	**Marketing and branding**
	Design
	Process
	Work
Domestic supply network	Design
	Process
	Work
TNC intra-firm networks	
Subsidiary	Design
	Process
	Work
Equity owner	**Organisational**
	Design
	Process
	Work

Boldness of type in column 2, **Innovative behaviour**, reflects significantly higher mean values relative to other types of networks. The bolder the type for a given type of innovation, the higher and more significant is its mean value in the given type of network relative to other types of networks.

guaranteed, the relationship is long-term, and they allow you to supply a diversity of products. Besides, they are more inclined to look for new suppliers in order to strengthen competitiveness among them to reduce costs.

For similar reasons of diversifying customers and expanding and diversifying its market, one other supplier actually chose to be a lower-tier supplier, rather than (as it had done previously) directly supplying OEMs.

Firms operating in *international supply networks* seem to be more innovative in marketing and branding than firms in TNC intra-firm networks and firms in domestic supply networks, providing supportive evidence to the main argument of existing studies, which underline the opportunities for upgrading in export networks. On the other hand, firms *supplying OEMs only* are more innovative than lower-tier suppliers in domestic supply networks. This is evident in their higher innovativeness regarding technology, as well as in marketing and branding. OEM networks are also more innovative in marketing and branding than firms in TNC networks as subsidiaries. One supplier stressed the advantage of working for OEMs in the following terms: 'working for OEMs gives us the opportunity to maintain our position in the market, because we see the project before it starts to be realised'. In contrast to these, firms in *domestic supply networks* seem to be associated with patterns of limited innovative activity: they are typically different from firms in other types of networks with their fairly low mean values for indicators of various types of innovation activity.

Firms in *TNC intra-firm networks as subsidiaries* are more innovative in technology than firms in domestic supply networks and those in international supply networks. Firms in *TNC intra-firm networks as equity partners* are relatively more innovative in organisational systems than firms in international supply networks and those in domestic supply networks. This finding is not unexpected. Previous research indicates that many TNC headquarters constantly exchange information on technologies and management techniques with their subsidiaries and equity partners, thus keeping relatively close to international best practices of production (Altenburg and Meyer-Stamer, 1999). However, as our research also shows, these innovations are limited to areas like human resource management, production and technology, and do not generally touch marketing and branding. The main weakness of such subsidiaries appears to be their failure to develop dynamic capabilities in knowledge-intensive areas (*ibid.*). As indicated by Dyker (2007), TNCs seem to play a key role in relation to knowledge transfer, but contribute little to the more fundamental process of knowledge accumulation such as might enable their subsidiaries in the periphery to move into higher-value-added activities.

6. Conclusions

Decades have passed since research first drew attention to the emergence of global production networks to coordinate internationally dispersed production activities, and to the fact that firms and production nodes on the periphery had become important actors in these networks. One of the assertions that emerged from this was that being part of such networks facilitated the flow of knowledge to the periphery and provided opportunities for learning which in turn increased the upgrading opportunities of the integrated periphery. Research that followed these early arguments, however, indicated that, although upgrading in production is easy, lead firms are unlikely to give the periphery space to encroach on activities like design, marketing and branding, which are part of lead firm core competencies.

Since then, the automotive clusters of Turkey and Poland have developed into major producers of automotive components for automotive lead firms. Our analysis shows, however, that the ways in which they are aligned is heavily influenced by the pattern of evolution of automotive production in the two countries. Thus network alignment in Bursa is driven by export-oriented supply networks, while in Poland alignment has developed around TNC production networks.

The focus of this chapter has been on whether the upgrading of the actors of the periphery is associated with the networks in which they are aligned. One of the main findings of our case study of suppliers in Bursa and Upper Silesia is that design capabilities have diffused even among lower-tier suppliers in the production nodes located on the periphery of automotive production. Design is no longer the preserve of either car manufacturers or global or first-tier suppliers. Our field study suggests that, as suppliers have learned that there are plenty of suppliers all around the world to replace them by manufacturing components much more cheaply, so they have started to realise the importance of moving into design and product development activities, which were previously defined as among the core activities of their lead firms. In this sense, our findings challenge the prevailing view in the literature, namely that design activities are likely to be controlled by lead firms in the core.

Furthermore, our evidence shows the importance of networks as sources of upgrading. Our research demonstrates that some firms move into marketing and branding activities, which are viewed in the literature as among the core competencies of lead firms. Our quantitative analysis shows that this opportunity has been open to suppliers which supply international markets and OEMs, but particularly to those which supply international markets *and* OEMs at the same time. This latter point brings out the importance of leveraging capabilities from alignment in different networks for moving into higher-value-added activities.

What are the main implications of our findings on networks as sources of learning and innovation regarding upgrading opportunities for Turkish and Polish firms? The predominance of firms operating in export markets, OEM networks and simultaneously in different networks in Turkey, indicates that for the time being Turkey's component suppliers have the advantage in that such networks have provided upgrading opportunities for Turkish firms to move into marketing and branding activities. That Polish firms are predominantly aligned in TNC intra-firm networks implies that the sustainability of their competitive edge is restricted by their failure to develop capabilities in these networks in knowledge-intensive areas. Obviously the fact that the two countries are aligned in specific networks does not guarantee a positive upgrading outcome in a particular case, but nor does it imply that barriers to learning and upgrading in particular networks cannot be broken. Strategic actions of individual firms are equally important, and future upgrading of firms in both countries depends not only on the ways in which the networks to which they are aligned will evolve, but also on the strategic efforts of individual firms to take steps to develop higher-value-added capabilities.

References

Abernathy, F. J.T., Dunlop, J. and Hammond, H. (1999). *A Stitch in Time: Lean Retailing and the Transformation of Manufacturing — Lessons from the Apparel and Textile Industries*, Oxford, Oxford University Press.

Altenburg, T. and Meyer-Stamer, J. (1999). 'How to promote clusters: Policy experiences from Latin America', *World Development* 27(9): 1693–1713.

Balcet, C. and Enrietti, A. (2002). *Partnership and Global Production: Fiat's Strategies in Turkey*, Actes du Gerpisa, No. 34.

Bazan, L. and Navas-Aleman, L. (2004). 'The underground revolution in the Sinos Valley — A comparison of upgrading in global and national value chains', in Schmitz, H. (ed.), *Local Enterprises in the Global Economy: Issues of Governance and Upgrading*, Cheltenham, Edward Elgar, pp. 110–139.

Borrus, M., Ernst, D. and Haggard, S. (eds.) (2000). *International Production Networks in Asia*, London and New York, Routledge.

Chiu, S.W.K. and Wong, K.-C. (2002). *The Hollowing Out of Hong Kong Electronics: Organisational Inertia and Industrial Restructuring in the 1990s*, mimeo, Hong Kong, Department of Sociology, The Chinese University of Hong Kong.

Dicken, P. (2003). 'Global production networks in Europe and East Asia: The automobile components industries', *GPN Working Paper* No. 7.

Domanski, B. (2003). 'Economic trajectory, path dependency and strategic intervention in an old industrial region: The case of Upper Silesia', in Domanski, R. (ed.), *Recent Advances in Urban and Regional Studies*, Warsaw, Polish Academy of Sciences, Committee for Space Economy and Regional Planning, pp. 133–153.

Domanski, B., Guzik, R. and Gwosdz, K. (2005). 'The new spatial organization of automotive industry in Poland in the context of its changing role in Europe', in Markowski, T. (ed.), *Regional Scientists' Tribute to Professor Ryszard Domanski*, Warsaw, Polish Academy of Sciences, Committee for Space Economy and Regional Planning, pp. 153–171.

Dunford, M. (2009). 'Globalization failures in a neo-liberal world: The case of Fiat Auto in the 1990s', *Geoforum* 40(2): 145–157.

Dunning, J.H. (1988). *Multinationals, Technology and Competitiveness*, London, Unwin Hyman.

Duruiz, L. (2004). 'Challenges for the Turkish car industry on its way to the integration with European Union', in Carillo, J. and van Tulder, R. (eds.), *Car: Carriers of Regionalism*, Basingstoke, Palgrave Macmillan, pp. 91–103.

Dyker, D. (2007). 'The governance and management of technical change in transition countries: Can the national innovation systems be improved?', *U-Know Project*, Deliverable No. 35c (2).

Dyker, D., Nagy, A., Spilek, H., Stanovnik, P., Turk, J. and Vince, P. (2003). '"East"–"West" networks and their alignment: Industrial networks in Hungary and Slovenia', *Technovation* 23: 603–616.

Eraydin, A. and Armatli-Koroglu, B. (2005). 'Innovation, networking and the new industrial clusters: the characteristics of networks and local innovation capabilities in the Turkish industrial clusters', *Entrepreneurship and Regional Development* 17: 237–266.

Ernst, D. (2004). 'Global production networks in East Asia's electronics industry and upgrading perspectives in Malaysia', in Yusuf, S., Altaf, M.A. and Nabeshima, K. (eds.), *Global Production Networking and Technological Change in East Asia*, Washington, DC, The World Bank, pp. 89–157.

Ernst, D. and Kim, L. (2002). 'Global production networks, knowledge diffusion, and local capability formation', *Research Policy* 31: 1417–1429.

Freeman, C. and Soete, L. (1997). *The Economics of Industrial Innovation* (3rd edn.), Pinter, London.

Gereffi, G. (1999). 'International trade and industrial upgrading in the apparel commodity chain', *Journal of International Economics* 48(1): 37–70.

Havas, A. (2000). 'Changing patterns of inter- and intra-regional division of labour: Central Europe's long and winding road', in Humphrey, J., Lecler, Y. and Salerno, M.S. (eds.), *Global Strategies and Local Realities: The Auto Industry in Emerging Markets*, London, Macmillan Press, pp. 234–262.

Hobday, M. (1995). *Innovation in East Asia: The Challenge to Japan*, Aldershot, Edward Elgar.

Hsing, Y.-T. (1999). 'Trading companies in Taiwan's fashion shoe networks', *Journal of International Economics* 48: 101–120.

Humphrey, J. (2003). 'Globalisation and supply chain networks: The auto industry in Brazil and India', *Global Networks* 3(2): 121–141.

Humphrey, J. and Memedovic, O. (2003). *The Global Automotive Industry Value Chain: What Prospects for Upgrading by Developing Countries*, UNIDO Sectoral Studies Series, Vienna.

Kim, S.-R. and von Tunzelmann, N. (1998). 'Aligning internal and external networks: Taiwan's specialization in IT', *SPRU Electronic working paper series* No. 17.

Kishimoto, C. (2004). 'Clustering and upgrading in global value chains: The Taiwanese personal computer industry', in Schmitz, H. (ed.), *Local Enterprises in the Global Economy: Issues of Governance and Upgrading*, Cheltenham, Edward Elgar, pp. 233–264.

Lee, J.-R. and Chen, J.-S. (2000). 'Dynamic synergy creation with multiple business activities: Toward a competence-based growth model for contract manufacturers,' in Sanchez R. and Heene, A. (eds.), *Theory Development for Competence-Based Management, Advances in Applied Business Strategy*, Stanford, CT, JAI Press, pp. 209–228.

Narula, R. (2005). 'Knowledge creation and why it matters for development: The role of TNCs', in UNCTAD, *Globalization of R&D and Developing Countries*, New York and Geneva, United Nations.

Pavlinek, P. (2002). 'Transformation of the Central and East European passenger car industry: Selective peripheral integration through foreign direct investment', *Environment and Planning A* 34: 1685–1709.

Pickles, J., Smith, A., Bucek, M., Roukova, P. and Begg, R. (2006). 'Upgrading, changing competitive pressures, and diverse practices in the East and Central European apparel industry', *Environment and Planning A* 38: 2305–2324.

Piore, M. and Sabel, C.F. (1984). *The Second Industrial Divide*, New York, Basic Books.

Poon, T. Shuk-Ching (2004). 'Beyond the global production networks: A case of further upgrading of Taiwan's information technology industry', *International Journal of Technology and Globalisation* 1(1): 130–144.

Radosevic, S. and Yoruk, D.E. (2004). 'Industrial networks in Central and Eastern Europe at the firm level: Summary and overview of ten case studies', in McGowan, F., Radosevic, S. and von Tunzelmann, G.N. (eds.), *The Emerging Industrial Structure of the Wider Europe*, London and New York, Routledge, pp. 57–76.

Schmitz, H. (2006). 'Learning and earning in global garment and footwear chains', *European Journal of Development Research* 18(4): 546–571.

Sturgeon, T.J. (2002). 'Modular production networks: A new American model of industrial organisation', *Industrial and Corporate Change* 11(3): 451–496.

Sturgeon, T.J. and Florida, R. (2000). *Globalisation and Jobs in the Automotive Industry*, IPC Working Paper 01-003, Cambridge, MA, MIT, Industrial Performance Center.

Sturgeon, T.J. and Lee, J. (2001). *Industry Co-Evolution and the Rise of a Shared Supply Base for Electronics Manufacturing*, IPC Working Paper 01-003, Cambridge, MA, MIT, Industrial Performance Center.

Sturgeon, T.J. and Lester, R.K. (2004). 'The new global supply-base: Challenges for local suppliers in East Asia', in Yusuf, S., Altaf, A. and Nabeshima, K. (eds.), *Global Production Networking and Technological Change in East Asia*, New York, Oxford University Press, pp. 35–87.

TAYSAD (2007). Turkish automotive suppliers, http://www.taysad.org.tr, June 2007.

Tewari, M. (1999). 'Successful adjustment in Indian industry: The case of Ludhiana's woollen knitwear cluster', *World Development* 27(9): 1651–1672.

Tewari, M. (2006). 'Adjustment in India's textile and apparel industry: Reworking historical legacies in a post-MFA world', *Environment and Planning A* 38: 2325–2344.

Tokatli, N. (2003). 'Globalization and the changing clothing industry in Turkey', *Environment and Planning A* 35: 1877–1894.

Tokatli, N. (2007). 'Networks, firms and upgrading within the blue-jeans industry: Evidence from Turkey', *Global Networks* 7(1): 51–68.

Tokatli, N. and Kizilgun, O. (2009). 'From manufacturing garments for ready-to-wear to designing collections for fast fashion: The changing role of suppliers in the clothing industry', *Environment and Planning A* 41(1): 146–162.

von Tunzelmann, G.N. (2003). 'Network alignment and innovation in transition economies', paper presented at the international conference on Innovation in Europe: Dynamics, Institutions and Values, Roskilde University, May.

Yoruk, D.E. (2004). 'Patterns of industrial upgrading in the clothing industry in Poland and Romania', in McGowan, F., Radosevic, S. and von Tunzelmann, G.N. (eds.), *The Emerging Industrial Structure of the Wider Europe*, London and New York, Routledge, pp. 95–110.

Appendix: Measuring Innovation

a. *Improvement of production process*

Firms were asked the extent to which they undertake the following activities on a Likert scale of 4-points: a) never b) sometimes c) usually d) always

Increasing production speed
Cost price reduction

Improving delivery speed
Improving product quality.

A coefficient was calculated as the sum of 'usually' and 'always' answers, divided by the number of variables (four).

b. *Product and process development*
Firms were asked the extent to which they undertake the following activities on a Likert scale of 4-points: a) never b) sometimes c) usually d) always

Development of new products
Development of new processes
Modification of existing products and processes
Development of new designs (moulds, equipment, etc.).

A coefficient was calculated as the sum of 'usually' and 'always' answers, divided by the number of variables (four).

c. *Marketing and branding*
Firms were asked the extent to which they undertake *marketing* and *branding* activities, on a Likert scale of 4-points: a) never b) sometimes c) usually d) always
A coefficient was calculated as the sum of 'usually' and 'always' answers, divided by the number of variables (two).

d. *Innovation in work systems*
Firms were asked the extent to which the following procedures are applied, on a Likert scale of 3-points: a) not applied b) to some extent c) to a great extent

Documentation of procedures
Use of batch trays
Use of statistical process cards
Use of travel cards
Collection and analysis of cell performance data
Stock control and traceability.

A coefficient was calculated as the sum of 'to a great extent' answers, divided by the number of variables (six).

e. *Innovation in HRM systems*
Firms were asked the extent to which the following activities are applied, on a Likert scale of 3-points: a) not applied b) to some extent c) to a great extent

Team working
Suggestion schemes
Workplace rotation

Delegation of responsibility
Performance award systems
Personal development schemes.

A coefficient was calculated as the sum of 'to a great extent' answers, divided by the number of variables (six).

f. *Innovation in technology systems*

Firms were asked whether or not they have invested in a number of *IT hardware and software measures.*

A coefficient was calculated as the sum of all 'yes' answers, divided by the number of these variables.

INDEX

Absorptive capacity   12, 13, 15, 227, 256, 281
Academy of Sciences   65, 69–73, 78, 79, 80, 115–117, 123, 124, 129, 137, 326
Academy-industry links   64
Additionality   38
Akrapovič exhaust system company   68
Alignment: see Network alignment
Alvey Programme   38
Armenia   70, 140, 235
Arrow, K.   64, 258
Atomic Energy Authority   28
Audi   66, 79, 118, 127, 148, 152, 155
Automotive industry   46, 47, 49, 52, 57, 58, 77, 107, 363, 365–368, 370, 371

Bank of Real Property (Turkey)   237
Banks   15, 16, 71, 102
BERD   27, 28, 32, 113
BERR   40
Biotechnology   6, 11, 48, 50, 57, 69, 79, 138, 218, 279, 280
BIS   40
Bologna Accords   179
Bosch   155
Boyer, R.   6
Brazil   380
Britain: see UK
British Academy   70, 73
Bulgaria   71, 73, 80, 81, 109, 163–165, 172, 174–177
Bursa   362, 365, 367–370, 378
Bush, V.   32

Campania   208, 217–227
Capabilities   3, 5, 11–13, 17–20, 40, 51, 57, 63, 67, 68, 75, 77, 78, 82, 148, 150, 154, 160, 210, 211, 217, 233, 283, 296, 304, 363, 364, 374, 377, 378
Car industry: see Automotive industry
Catching-up   3, 29, 112, 144, 303, 304, 361
Central planning   10, 77, 236
CEPREMAP   6
Certification: see Standards
Chandler, A.   35
Chemicals industry   47, 50, 89–91, 95, 97, 99, 101
Chesnais, F.   113
China   20, 70, 78, 95
Cisco   152
Clusters   9, 17, 36, 39, 94, 97, 98, 100, 107, 185, 235, 288, 361–365, 367–369, 377
Cobb–Douglas production function   263
Community Innovation Survey (CIS)   70, 78, 80, 140, 270, 284, 286, 287
Companies: see firms
Competencies   11–13, 112, 125, 126, 185, 190, 193, 181, 374, 377, 378
competition   11, 13, 17, 19, 26, 54, 56, 63, 77, 79, 93, 147, 152, 157, 161, 209, 283, 290, 297, 303, 363, 365, 366, 370
Competitiveness   7, 34, 37, 51, 58, 77, 90, 109, 110, 111, 120, 124, 127, 146, 156, 160, 161, 166, 175, 178, 181, 219, 281, 283, 303, 337, 353, 376

Complexity   4, 5, 7, 10–12, 15, 18, 46, 97, 103, 104, 235, 285, 335, 355
Consumption   6, 7, 15, 93
Credentialism   135, 139, 148, 186
Croatia   140, 165, 304, 308–311, 313–319, 321–325, 328, 329
Crowding out   17
Czech Republic   70, 71, 78, 79, 117, 137, 163, 164, 172, 174–177, 186
Czechoslovakia   71

Defence   29, 34
Deregulation   37, 109, 366
DIUS   40
DTI   40
Dyadic relationships   3

E.ON   153, 156
E-commerce   279, 280
Economies of scale and scope   19, 305
Edgerton, D.   25
Edquist, J.   108, 129
Education   6, 28, 48, 71, 92, 111, 133, 143, 160, 185, 207, 277, 333
    Higher education institutions: see universities
Electronics: see ICT
Employment protection legislation   162, 163, 177, 178
Endogenous growth theory   255, 262
Entrepreneurship   14, 46, 61, 114, 119, 120, 124, 125, 128, 161, 237
Ergas, H.   38
Ericsson   66, 153, 154, 156
ERM II   112
Ernst, D.   63, 67, 361, 373
Estonia   68–70, 72, 74, 78, 79–81, 137, 162–165, 172, 174–177, 186, 284, 288–290, 293, 297, 298, 308, 334–336, 340, 342–351, 355, 356
Ethiopia   22
EU   3, 15, 36, 46, 66, 68, 90, 92, 109, 110, 112, 117, 119, 121, 123, 125, 127, 133, 134, 140, 141, 151, 161–165, 167, 170–178, 208, 227, 277, 298, 308, 310, 329, 333–336, 356, 366, 367
    European Single Market   26
Euro   112, 208, 359
European Network of Centres of Excellence (ERA-NET)   118
European Research Area (ERA)   117, 118
European Working Conditions Survey   133, 134
Export   47, 50, 52, 77, 109, 119, 259, 265, 278, 349, 351, 359, 360, 362, 365–367, 370, 374, 376, 378

Fiat   365, 367–369
Finland   79, 80, 125, 144, 186, 288
Firms   4, 26, 50, 63, 90, 111, 135, 145, 165, 213, 255, 280, 303, 333, 361
    M-form   35
    Multinational companies (MNEs)   29, 51, 52, 89, 93, 106, 111, 113, 154, 156, 337
    U-form   35
Flexible production systems   75, 281
Food processing   89, 93, 107, 108
Fordism   75, 141
Fordist model   75
Foreign direct investment (FDI)   46, 65, 109–111, 119, 212, 257, 278, 303, 312, 314, 333, 361
    Outward foreign direct investment (OFDI)   333, 334, 336, 338–351, 353, 355, 356, 359
    South-South   333, 335, 338, 343, 355
Forestry: see wood industry
France   6, 28, 29, 38, 39, 49, 127, 144, 186, 367
Frascati Manual   26, 27
Freeman, C.   5–7, 25, 280, 361

Gazprom   76
GDR: see East Germany
GE (General Electric)   26, 66, 153

Gecekondu 235, 237, 239, 250
General Motors (GM) 51, 368, 369
General purpose technologies (GPTs) 279
Georgia 70, 140
GERD 27, 38, 72, 73, 113
Germany 5, 28, 29, 45–47, 49–55, 57, 58, 88, 89–92, 100, 102, 104, 106–108, 144, 186, 278, 304, 308–311, 313, 316, 317, 323–325, 328, 329, 367
    East Germany 45, 52–55, 58, 90–92, 102, 106, 108, 304, 308, 309, 310, 311, 313, 316, 317, 323–325, 328, 329
Global design networks 67
Governance 5, 8–10, 12, 15–17, 35, 36, 38, 64–68, 71, 72, 74–79, 82, 83, 112, 137, 175, 207, 215, 216, 310, 312
Government 6–9, 16, 17, 19, 26–30, 33, 34, 36–38, 40, 51, 54, 56, 59, 63, 68, 70–73, 81, 83, 91, 95, 97, 100, 102, 103, 106, 107, 111–113, 116, 119, 122–125, 128, 135, 138, 139, 141, 151, 156, 177, 182, 210, 212, 213, 215, 228, 233, 236–238, 241, 243, 246, 258, 259, 275, 356, 368, 371
Government Council for Science and Technology Policy (Slovakia) 112
Grabowska-Lusinska, I. 161
Grants: see Subsidies
Grey economy 140, 141, 173
Growth poles 5

Hanson, Lord 35, 337, 338
HERD 27, 28, 31, 33, 79
Hewlett Packard 154
Hierarchies 8, 9, 15, 66, 283
High-tech 10, 33, 34, 36, 37, 45, 66, 69, 73, 89, 104, 105, 108, 261, 265, 279
Homophily 3
Hong Kong 363
Household Labour Force Survey (AMIGO) (Romania) 168

Human capital 13, 46, 75, 80, 133, 143, 154, 157, 178, 207, 209–212, 214, 229, 258, 281, 303
Hungary 66, 68–70, 73, 79, 80, 111, 137, 139, 140, 141, 143–146, 148–157, 163–165, 172, 174–177, 308

IBM 63, 66, 149, 152, 154
ICT 11, 27, 33, 35, 38, 67, 138, 146, 166, 278, 279, 283, 373
    ARM semiconductors 33
    Software 27, 33, 57, 67, 79, 146, 148, 149, 151, 152, 154, 156, 157, 279, 285, 320, 383
Import 215, 284, 288, 290, 365, 366, 367
Incubators: see Technology incubators
India 70, 78, 95, 364
Industry 6, 27, 46, 64, 87, 114, 136, 146, 159, 185, 210, 277, 293, 337, 362
    Industry associations 17, 89, 299
Industrial policy 37
Informal economy: see Grey economy
Information 12, 20, 27, 48, 58, 67, 79, 88, 100, 106, 107, 114, 116, 119, 120, 124, 125, 127, 137, 141, 151, 160, 180, 182, 186–190, 192, 194–199, 210, 212, 218, 240, 242, 247–250, 280, 281–283, 288, 294, 296, 306, 308, 310, 314–320, 322, 325, 328, 339, 342, 343, 363, 369, 375, 377
Infrastructure 83, 95, 108, 119, 124, 125, 127, 129, 154, 155, 207, 210, 212, 214, 216, 228, 236, 238, 240, 242, 303, 305, 329
Innovation 3, 23, 45, 63, 87, 109, 149, 161, 185, 208, 255, 279, 303, 361
    Hidden innovation 30, 31, 36
    Innovation centres 81, 116, 122–125, 128
    Innovation management 13, 63, 114, 127
    Innovation surveys 18, 259

resource-based view (RBV) 13
strategic management view 13
Innovating Regions in Europe (IRE) 125
Innovation Fund (Slovakia) 116, 120
Innovation Strategy 2007–2013 (Slovakia) 122, 124, 129
Input-output 15, 16, 32, 33, 261
Intellectual property rights (IPRs) 53, 92, 93, 95, 98, 101, 102, 106, 120
International Labour Organization (ILO) 208, 244
Internationally interdependent laboratories 66
Ireland 144, 157
Iskra 77
ISKUR (Turkish Employment Centre) 247, 248
ISO: see Standards
Istanbul 233–239, 241, 242, 246, 248–250
IT: see ICT
Italy 17, 170, 171, 186, 207, 208, 210, 215, 217–228, 366, 367
IWH (Halle Institute of Economics) 90, 304, 308, 309, 311, 313, 315–319, 321, 322, 324–327

Japan 5, 6, 26, 29, 49, 243
Job matching 131, 133–139, 141, 145, 146, 147, 149, 152, 157

Katowice 368
Kazakhstan 68, 77, 79, 80, 136
Keating, J. 159
Kinship 8, 233
Knowledge 3, 4, 6, 8–10, 12, 17–19, 27, 34, 39, 45, 47, 52, 54, 56, 57, 63, 65–68, 74, 75, 77, 80–82, 88, 92, 95, 109, 110, 112, 114, 115–117, 120, 124, 126, 127, 134–137, 140, 141, 144, 146–151, 153, 154, 160, 185, 193, 208, 209, 211–214, 216, 219, 227–229, 255–258, 261, 262, 265, 270, 280–283, 285, 288, 294–296, 299, 303–308, 312–314, 321–323, 325, 327, 328, 333, 361, 364, 373, 377, 378
Tacit 77, 213, 282, 283, 296
Knowledge-intensive business services (KIBS) 279, 280
Kosovo 140
Kyrgyzstan 65

Labour 6, 36, 45, 65, 110, 131, 143, 159, 185, 207, 233, 256, 278, 303, 333, 366
Labour markets 6, 131, 134, 140, 160, 209, 233
Labour productivity 110, 159, 160, 174, 256, 262, 268–271, 340, 344, 348, 349, 351, 352
Lambert Report 208, 213
Latvia 70, 72, 111, 127, 162–165, 172, 174–177, 334, 335, 343
Lead-time 34
Learning 5, 6, 11, 13, 17–19, 27, 32, 36, 40, 56, 64, 110, 148, 151, 170, 180, 183, 185, 186, 209, 210, 214–216, 228, 255, 258, 264, 281, 284, 361–363, 374, 377, 378
Lisbon Agenda 134, 162, 163, 169, 182
List, F. 5
Lithuania 70, 74, 133, 141, 163–165, 172, 174–177, 334, 335, 343
Lundvall, B.-Å. 18, 32, 64, 110, 113

Macedonia 140
Mafia 215
Magnet employer 135, 150
Magyar Telekom 151
Malerba, F. 5, 6, 13, 33
Market failure 9, 37, 38, 40, 258
Market socialism 73
Marketing 14, 114, 119, 281, 316, 317, 319, 320, 336, 361–364, 371–378, 382

Markets   6, 8–10, 15, 16, 33–35, 39, 56, 77, 98, 109, 131, 134, 140, 159–161, 209, 233, 258, 280, 281, 283, 288, 305, 313, 314, 318, 323, 333–335, 346, 355, 356, 363, 364, 367–370, 374, 378
Mass Housing Fund (TOKI) (Turkey)   239
McKinsey & Co.   155
Mezzogiorno   217–227
Microsoft   152
Migration   112, 160, 161, 163, 170, 171, 174, 177, 182, 214, 233, 235, 244, 246
Military: see Defence
Ministry of Reconstruction and Resettlement (Turkey)   237
Misalignments: see Network misalignments
MITI   7
Mode 2 knowledge production   10
Mongolia   65
Monopoly   63

National Agency for Qualifications in Higher Education and Partnership with the Social and Economic Environment (Romania)   179
National Authority for Qualifications (NAQ) (Romania)   180
National Board for Technological and Industrial Development (Sweden)   125
National champions   26, 34, 37
National Development Plan Human Resource Development Operational Programme (Hungary)   151
National Health Service   33
National Housing Authority (Turkey)   239
National Office for Research and Technology (Hungary)   68, 154
National Qualifications Framework (NQF) (Romania)   179, 180

National Register of Qualifications for Higher Education (Romania)   179
National systems of innovation (NSIs)   5, 6, 11, 19, 46
Nelson, R.   5, 6, 258
Networks   3–5, 8–12, 15–20, 23, 32, 40, 50, 63, 66, 67, 69, 74–76, 78, 82, 87, 96, 98, 105, 111, 119, 123, 153, 156, 213, 215, 216, 227, 233, 234, 236–242, 246–251, 253, 281, 306, 307, 314, 324, 338, 361–365, 367, 369–378
   Network alignment   3–6, 9, 18, 19, 233, 361, 362, 365, 369, 370, 371, 378
   Network misalignment   10, 20, 242, 326
Network centrality   3
Nomenklatura   9
Norway   136, 186, 187, 191
Nuclear power   33, 37

OBM (original brand manufacturing)   374
ODM (original design manufacturing)   374
OECD   27, 33, 79, 110, 111, 113, 126, 140, 144, 150, 157, 242, 243, 316
OEM (original equipment manufacturer)   362, 364, 370, 374–378
Office of Science & Technology   30
Off-shoring   76, 336
Opel   51, 152, 368
Outsourcing   67

Padoa-Schioppa, F.   161
Paris   6, 140
Patents   18, 29, 30, 50, 57, 96, 101, 127, 217, 224–227, 284, 285, 294
   European Patent Office (EPO)   29, 49, 53, 217, 224, 226, 227
PHARE programme   149
PILOT programme   10

Plumbing   134
Poland   68, 71, 72, 79, 80, 111, 140, 161, 163, 164, 165, 172–177, 304, 308–311, 313, 316, 317, 324, 329, 361–363, 365–369, 371, 377, 378
Political economy   5
Political science   5, 19
Porter, M.   7, 32, 39
Post-industrial society   25
Post-Keynesian   6
PRACTING programme (Hungary)   149, 150
Privatisation   28, 37, 38, 71, 90, 109, 113, 291
Product lifecycles   11
Production function   63, 211, 256, 263, 373
Professor's privilege   53, 89
Putting-out system   32

Quality control: see Standards
Quantification   4

R&D   6, 27, 47, 63, 89, 110, 136, 154, 181, 208, 255, 278, 304, 364
    In services   352
    R&D vouchers   97
    Tax reliefs for R&D   59
Regional Development Agencies (RDAs)   39, 40
Regional/local development   39, 179, 229, 361
Regulation   6, 13, 33, 93, 235
Régulation school   6
Research Assessment Exercise (RAE)   19
Researcher Development Initiative (RDI) (Romania)   181
Romania   68, 109, 137, 138, 159, 161–178, 181–183, 304, 308–311, 313, 316–320, 323, 324, 329
Russia   65, 68, 70–72, 74, 76, 78, 80, 137, 288, 298, 334

SAP 'Learning Solution' system   151
SAPPHO   32
Schumpeter, J.   13, 212
Science and technology (S&T)   27, 72, 73, 79, 112, 113, 116, 118, 119, 125, 128, 217, 228, 303
Science and Technology Assistance Agency (Slovakia)   116, 118
Science and Technology Policy Council (Finland)   125
Science Citations Index   .30
Science parks   81, 122, 123
Second Industrial Revolution   26, 27
Second World War   26, 27, 32
Sectoral systems of innovation (SSIs)   5, 17, 33, 46
Sharp, M.   17, 38, 80, 160, 237, 243, 319, 366
Siemens   66, 150, 153, 155, 156
Singapore   363
Skills: see Training
Slovak Innovation and Energy Agency   116, 120
Slovakia   67, 109–120, 122, 124, 125, 128, 137, 163–165, 172–176, 308
Slovenia   68, 69, 73, 74, 111, 162–165, 172, 174–177, 255, 259–261, 263, 275, 304, 308–311, 313, 316, 317, 323, 324, 329
SMEs (small and medium-sized enterprises)   11, 34, 40, 54, 56, 59, 68, 69, 87, 95, 97, 98, 106, 116, 119, 123, 133, 134, 146, 147, 149–152, 154, 156, 157, 170, 171, 334
Social network analysis (SNA)   3, 9,
Social networks   4, 8, 248, 249
Social security contributions   140, 177
Sociology   8
South Korea   20, 26, 49, 363
Soviet bloc: see Soviet Union
Soviet Union   74, 77, 78, 79, 82, 109, 366, 374

Spillovers   13, 33, 52, 54, 214, 253, 255–258, 261, 262, 264, 265, 270, 305, 307
Spin-off companies   68, 123, 127
Squatters   236, 237
Standards   13, 39, 52, 58, 99, 109, 124, 164, 177, 179–181, 183, 191, 211, 212, 214, 236, 290, 325, 366
Start-ups   51, 119, 123
Structural Funds   119–121
Subsidies   38, 39, 56, 92, 93, 124, 212, 225, 256, 258–262, 264, 265, 270
Sun Microsystems   154
Suppliers   4, 12, 13, 16, 47, 52, 67, 68, 69, 76–78, 123, 159, 216, 238, 281–283, 304, 305, 323, 336, 362–374, 376, 378
    First-tier suppliers   67–69, 76–78, 378
    Supply chains   15, 32
    Supply networks: see supply chains
Suzuki   76, 152
Sweden   288
System integration   3, 12

Taiwan   138, 363, 364
Taxes   90, 177, 179, 212, 239, 348
    Tax wedge   177
Teach-First scheme (UK)   135
Technology   6, 26, 48, 65, 88, 111, 136, 152, 159, 188, 208, 255, 277, 303, 361
    Technical change   19, 26, 63, 143, 256, 263
    Technology foresight   73
    Technology incubators   120, 122, 128
    Technology transfer   72, 77, 88, 120, 121, 127, 154, 159, 208, 209, 212, 213, 255, 257, 258, 320, 323, 361
technological gatekeepers   281
Technological incongruence   75, 76, 83

Testing: see Standards
Thatcher, M.   36, 37
The National Agency for the Development of Small and Medium Enterprises (NADSME) (Slovakia)   119, 120
The Slovak Investment and Trade Development Agency (SARIO)   116, 119, 123
Third Industrial Revolution   11, 25, 27, 35
TNC: see MNC
Total factor productivity (TFP)   263–266, 270
Training   6, 7, 13, 46, 54, 65, 75, 123, 126, 127, 135–139, 145–148, 150–153, 155–157, 159, 160, 179, 180, 182, 183, 188, 189, 190, 194, 200, 208, 209, 210, 212, 213, 228, 283, 286, 294–299, 363
Transition   63–71, 73–83, 90, 99, 108, 136–138, 161, 164, 167, 168, 170, 175, 180, 183, 185, 186, 188, 203, 257, 280, 291, 292, 303, 309, 310, 312, 316, 329, 333–336, 343, 350, 355, 359, 364
Triple helix   87, 213, 216
Trust   51, 92–95, 100, 104, 106, 108, 111, 213, 216
Turkey   76, 140, 233, 234, 236–239, 242–246, 361–363, 365–367, 369, 377, 378
Turkmenistan   65, 70

UK   19, 25–41, 133–135, 139, 140, 144, 167, 186, 208, 213, 214
Ukraine   65, 70, 78, 80, 334
Unemployment   52, 81, 110, 112, 143, 160, 161, 164, 165, 167, 168, 169, 171–175, 177, 180, 182, 194–198, 200, 201, 203, 242–245, 248, 251, 368
Universities   4, 12, 16, 19, 28, 30, 31, 33, 51, 53–56, 59, 63–65, 68–73, 78, 80, 81, 88, 89, 92, 94–99, 101–103, 105, 118, 123, 124, 126, 127, 136–138,

147, 149, 152–157, 187, 191, 192, 207, 209, 210, 213, 214, 217 219, 220, 223, 228, 229, 282, 304
Upper Silesia   362, 365, 367–371, 378
Urban planning   235, 236, 237, 250
Urbanisation   233–236, 239, 246, 250
USA   5, 28, 29, 32, 38
Uzbekistan   65

Value chains   32, 52, 81
Vanichseni, S.   7

VEGA Grant Agency (Slovakia)   116, 118
Venture capital   46, 116, 124, 127, 216

Wage premium   144, 145
Wood industry   294, 297

Yesiltepe   234, 239–242, 247
Yugoslavia   140, 309

Ziman, J.   30